Special Edition Published for the University of Michigan

DIFFERENTIAL EQUATIONS
COMPUTING AND MODELING

Third Edition

C. Henry Edwards and David E. Penney
With Additional Material by Arthur G. Wasserman

Cover Photo: *"Boatbu1"* by Barry Cronin.

Content taken from:

Differential Equations: Computing and Modeling, Second Edition
by C. Henry Edwards and David E. Penney
Copyright © 2000, 1996 by Prentice-Hall, Inc.
A Pearson Education Company
Upper Saddle River, New Jersey 07458

Sections 1.5, 2.4, 3.1 (pp. 101-103), 3.2, 3.7, 5.4, and 6.4 by
Arthur G. Wasserman.

This special edition published in cooperation with Pearson Custom Publishing.

Printed in the United States of America

10 9 8 7 6 5 4 3 2 1

ISBN 0-536-74550-1

BA 997937

DG

Please visit our web site at *www.pearsoncustom.com*

PEARSON CUSTOM PUBLISHING
75 Arlington Street, Suite 300, Boston, MA 02116
A Pearson Education Company

CONTENTS

PREFACE

For the past half century, many introductory differential equations courses for science and engineering students have emphasized the formal solution of standard types of differential equations using a (seeming) grab-bag of systematic solution techniques. Students in such courses often have concentrated on learning to match memorized methods with memorized equations. The evolution of the present text is based on experience teaching a new course with a greater emphasis on conceptual ideas and the use of computer laboratory projects to involve students in more intense and sustained problem-solving experiences.

The availability of technical computing environments such as *Maple*, *Mathematica*, and MATLAB is now reshaping the role and applications of differential equations in science and engineering, and has shaped our approach in this text. New technology motivates a shift in emphasis from traditional manual methods to both qualitative and computer-based methods that:

- Render accessible a wider range of more realistic applications;
- Permit the use of both numerical computation and graphical visualization to develop greater conceptual understanding; and
- Encourage empirical investigations that involve deeper thought and analysis than standard textbook problems.

Major Features

The following features of this text are intended to support a contemporary differential equations course that augments traditional core skills with conceptual perspectives that students will need for the effective use of differential equations in their subsequent work and study:

- We have trimmed the coverage of seldom-used topics and added new topics in order to place throughout a greater emphasis on core techniques as well as qualitative aspects of the subject associated with direction fields, solution curves, phase plane portraits, and dynamical systems. To this end we combine symbolic, graphic, and numerical solution methods wherever it seems advantageous. A fresh new computational flavor should be evident in figures, examples, problems, and projects throughout the text. Almost a quarter of the examples in the text are new for this edition.
- The organization of the book places an increased emphasis on linear systems of differential equations, which are covered in Chapters 4 and 5 (together with the necessary linear algebra), followed by a substantial treatment in Chapter 6 of nonlinear systems and phenomena (including chaos in dynamical systems).
- This book begins and ends with discussions and examples of the mathematical modeling of real-world phenomena. The fact that differential equations have diverse and important applications is obvious enough—whole areas of the subject exist mainly because of their applications. Students learn through mathematical modeling and empirical investigation to balance the questions of what equation to formulate, how to solve it, and whether a solution will yield useful information.

- While according real-world applications their due, we also think the first course in differential equations should be a window on the world of mathematics. While it is neither feasible nor desirable to include proofs of the fundamental existence and uniqueness theorems along the way in an elementary course, students need to see precise and clear-cut statements of these theorems and to understand their role in the subject. We include appropriate existence and uniqueness proofs in the Appendix and occasionally refer to them in the main body of the text.

- While our approach reflects the widespread use of new computer methods for the solution of differential equations, we continue to believe that certain elementary analytical methods of solution (as in Chapters 1 and 3) are important for students to learn. One reason is that effective and reliable use of numerical methods often requires preliminary analysis using standard elementary techniques; the construction of a realistic numerical model often is based on the study of a simpler analytical model. We therefore continue to stress the mastery of traditional solution techniques (especially through the inclusion of extensive problem sets).

Computing Features

The following features highlight the flavor of computing technology that distinguishes much of our exposition.

- About 250 *computer-generated graphics*—over half of them new for this edition and most constructed using MATLAB—show students vivid pictures of direction fields, solution curves, and phase plane portraits that bring symbolic solutions of differential equations to life. For instance, the cover graphic shows an eigenfunction of the three-dimensional wave equation that illustrates surface waves on a spherical planet and was constructed using associated Legendre functions.

- A fresh *numerical emphasis* is afforded by the early introduction of numerical solution techniques in Chapter 2 (on mathematical models and numerical methods). Here and in Chapter 4, where numerical techniques for systems are treated, a concrete and tangible flavor is achieved by the inclusion of numerical algorithms presented in parallel fashion ranging from graphing calculators to MATLAB.

- A *conceptual perspective* is shaped by the availability of computational aids, which permits a leaner and more streamlined coverage of certain traditional manual topics (like exact equations and variation of parameters) in Chapters 1, 3, and 5.

Modeling Features

We take mathematical modeling as a goal and constant motivation for the study of differential equations. To sample the range of applications in this text, consider the following questions:

- What explains the commonly observed time lag between indoor and outdoor daily temperature oscillations? (Section 1.5)

- What makes the difference between doomsday and extinction in alligator populations? (Section 2.1)

- How do a unicycle and a two-axle car react differently to bumps in the road? (Section 5.3)

- How can you predict the time of next perihelion passage of a newly observed comet? (Section 4.3)

- Why might an earthquake demolish one building and leave standing the one next door? (Section 5.3)
- What determines whether two species will live harmoniously together, or whether competition will result in the extinction of one species and the survival of the other? (Section 6.3)

Organization and Content

We have reshaped the usual approach and sequence of topics to accommodate new technology and new perspectives. For instance:

- After a precis of first-order equations in Chapter 1 (with the coverage of certain traditional symbolic methods somewhat streamlined), Chapter 2 offers an unusually early introduction to mathematical modeling, stability and qualitative properties of differential equations and numerical methods—a combination of topics that usually are dispersed later in an introductory course.
- Chapters 4 and 5 provide a flexible treatment of linear systems. Motivated by current trends in science and engineering education and practice, Chapter 4 offers an early intuitive introduction to first-order systems, models, and numerical approximation techniques. Chapter 5 begins with a self-contained treatment of the linear algebra that is needed, then presents the eigenvalue approach to linear systems. It includes an unusual number of applications (ranging from railway cars to earthquakes) of all of the various cases of the eigenvalue method.
- Laplace transform methods (Chapter 7) follow the material on linear and nonlinear systems, but can be covered at any earlier point (after Chapter 3) the instructor prefers.

Problems and Projects

Probably no other mathematics course beyond calculus relies so much on the exercises and problem sets to promote adequate student learning. About 200 of the text's 1450 problems are new for this edition. Each section contains more computational problems ("solve the following equations," and so on) than any class will ordinarily use, plus an ample number of applied and conceptual problems.

The answer section includes the answers to most odd-numbered problems and to some of the even-numbered ones. The *Solutions Manual* accompanying this book provides worked-out solutions for over a quarter of the problems in the book; a majority of these solutions are for even-numbered problems. A brief hint or suggestion is provided for another quarter, and an answer alone for most of the remaining problems in the text that do not include answers in their statements.

Acknowledgments

In preparing this revision we profited greatly from the advice and assistance of the following very able reviewers:

George Dorner,
 William Rainey Harper College
Caroline N. Haddad,
 State University of New York at Geneseo
Da-Veig Ho,
 Georgia Institute of Technology
Robert R. Jensen,
 Loyola University Chicago

David A. Singer,
 Case Western Reserve University
Ram P. Srivastav,
 *State University of New York
  at Stony Brook*
Kenneth B. Stolarsky,
 *University of Illinois
  at Urbana-Champaign*

We thank also Bayani DeLeon for his efficient supervision of the process of book production and Patricia M. Daly, our copy editor, for her careful and diligent attention to the typescript. We owe special thanks to our editor, George Lobell, for his enthusiastic encouragement and advice concerning this revision and to Dennis Kletzing for his attractive design and composition of this book. Once again, we are unable to express adequately our debts to Alice F. Edwards and Carol W. Penney for their continued assistance, encouragement, support, and patience.

C. H. E.
hedwards@math.uga.edu
Athens, Georgia, U.S.A.

D. E. P.
dpenney@math.uga.edu
Athens, Georgia, U.S.A.

Further Acknowledgments

Parts of this text were derived from the 1998 Math 216 Lab Manual written by Prof. Charles R. Doering and Deborah A. Alterman under a FIPSE grant, specifically, Section 3.2–Review of complex numbers, Appendix B–An introduction to Matlab, and some of the computer labs. I would like to thank them for allowing that material to be incorporated here. I would also like to thank Chris Heath, Jesse Otero, Julia Gordon, Prof. Anton Dzhamay, Prof. Gavin LaRose and Prof. Ralf Wittenberg for their contributions and valuable suggestions. As part of a VIGRE project Dan Rogalski has gathered feedback from lab instructors and he and Jesse Otero have made very useful suggestions for further changes. However, any errors that occur are entirely my responsibility.

I would also like to thank Professor John C. Polking, Rice University, for making the **dfield6.m**, **ppn6out.m** and **pplane6.m** files freely available for educational use. We will use those files in Lab 1 and Lab 5.

Lab and Recitation

The recitation sessions allow you to ask questions about the lecture and text material and the homework problems in a smaller "discussion class" setting. Your GSI will go over problem areas, review materials, or work through homework exercises as appropriate.

The computer lab portion of the course consists of five lab projects to be completed on the schedule indicated in the course syllabus. These projects focus on numerical methods for differential equations. This area has become extremely important and necessary since the use of computers has become commonplace. The lab projects develop the computational techniques in the context of specific applications. In some of the early labs, the equations considered may also be solved by analytic methods developed in the course. The programs are then used to validate and explore the limitations of the computer solutions, as well as to illustrate some of the theoretical concepts discussed in the lectures and text. In the later lab projects, you will compute solutions that are either impractical or impossible to derive by hand. Then you will be using the computer to explore areas beyond those susceptible to purely analytic methods. Numerical simulations are directly analogous to laboratory experiments: they provide a mechanism to probe a model and extract its detailed predictions.

Labs 3 and 4 show you how to use Maple to solve differential equations analytically and/or numerically. In contrast to the Matlab programs we write and use which are mainly for educational purposes, the Maple techniques are "industrial strength".

Appendix B is a rapid introduction to Matlab, one of the computer program we shall be using in the lab portion of this course. It is included because you might also want to use Matlab to check your calculation of eigenvalues and eigenvectors, solve linear equations, etc.

The lab projects are divided into two parts. The *prelab* questions and exercises are to be completed individually, neatly written up, and turned in at the beginning of the lab session the week the project is being done (see syllabus). The prelab provides motivation and background for the computer programs that you will write in the lab session. The actual *lab projects* are done in the lab session. There you can enter and debug the programs in order to run them and complete the project. The lab projects throughout the semester will build on your programs from previous projects. Therefore, you should make sure you understand the Matlab programs you type. You should also make sure that you have a copy of all programs in your disk space. Your final write-up for each project should include responses to all the questions, all figures and plots as indicated, as well as relevant comments or observations about the systems under investigation. (Include extra plots, if those help to illustrate the points you're trying to make.) Each lab project should be completed, neatly written up, and turned in at the time indicated by your course instructor or GSI.

Differential equations play a central role in nearly every branch of science and engineering. It is the goal of this course to provide you with an introduction to the theoretical and computational methods that will be drawn upon in your future studies and your future work. Additionally, our focus on science and engineering applications of differential equations will help to indicate the scope of these techniques.

Arthur G. Wasserman
Department of Mathematics
University of Michigan
Ann Arbor, Michigan
May 2002

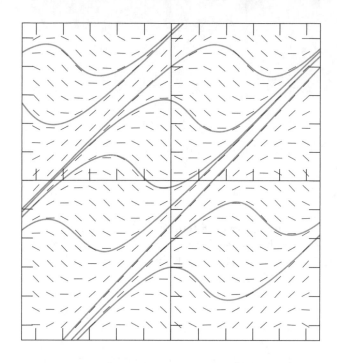

CHAPTER 1

First-Order Differential Equations

1.1 DIFFERENTIAL EQUATIONS AND MATHEMATICAL MODELS

The laws of the universe are written in the language of mathematics. Algebra is sufficient to solve many static problems, but the most interesting natural phenomena involve change and are described only by equations that relate changing quantities.

Because the derivative $dx/dt = f'(t)$ of the function f is the rate at which the quantity $x = f(t)$ is changing with respect to the independent variable t, it is natural that equations involving derivatives are frequently used to describe the changing universe. An equation relating an unknown function and one or more of its derivatives is called a **differential equation**.

EXAMPLE 1 The differential equation

$$\frac{dx}{dt} = x^2 + t^2$$

involves both the unknown function $x(t)$ and its first derivative $x'(t) = dx/dt$. The differential equation

$$\frac{d^2y}{dx^2} + 3\frac{dy}{dx} + 7y = 0$$

involves the unknown function y of the independent variable x and the first two derivatives y' and y'' of y. ■

The study of differential equations has three principal goals:

1. To discover the differential equation that describes a specified physical situation.
2. To find—either exactly or approximately—the appropriate solution of that equation.
3. To interpret the solution that is found.

In algebra, we typically seek the unknown *numbers* that satisfy an equation such as $x^3 + 7x^2 - 11x + 41 = 0$. By contrast, in solving a differential equation, we are challenged to find the unknown *functions* $y = y(x)$ for which an identity such as $y'(x) = 2xy(x)$—that is, the differential equation

$$\frac{dy}{dx} = 2xy$$

—holds on some interval of real numbers. Ordinarily, we will want to find *all* solutions of the differential equation, if possible.

EXAMPLE 2   If C is a constant and

$$y(x) = Ce^{x^2}, \tag{1}$$

then

$$\frac{dy}{dx} = C\left(2xe^{x^2}\right) = (2x)\left(Ce^{x^2}\right) = 2xy.$$

Thus every function $y(x)$ of the form in Eq. (1) *satisfies*—and thus is a solution of—the differential equation

$$\frac{dy}{dx} = 2xy \tag{2}$$

for all x. In particular, Eq. (1) defines an *infinite* family of different solutions of this differential equation, one for each choice of the arbitrary constant C. By the method of separation of variables (Section 1.4) it can be shown that every solution of the differential equation in (2) is of the form in Eq. (1). ∎

Differential Equations and Mathematical Models

The following three examples illustrate the process of translating scientific laws and principles into differential equations. In each of these examples the independent variable is time t, but we will see numerous examples in which some quantity other than time is the independent variable.

EXAMPLE 3   Newton's law of cooling may be stated in this way: The *time rate of change* (the rate of change with respect to time t) of the temperature $T(t)$ of a body is proportional to the difference between T and the temperature A of the surrounding medium (Fig. 1.1.1). That is,

$$\frac{dT}{dt} = -k(T - A), \tag{3}$$

where k is a positive constant. Observe that if $T > A$, then $dT/dt < 0$, so the temperature is a decreasing function of t and the body is cooling. But if $T < A$, then $dT/dt > 0$, so that T is increasing.

Thus the physical law is translated into a differential equation. If we are given the values of k and A, we should be able to find an explicit formula for $T(t)$, and then—with the aid of this formula—we can predict the future temperature of the body. ∎

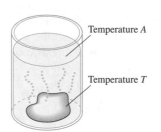

Temperature A

Temperature T

FIGURE 1.1.1. Newton's law of cooling, Eq. (3), describes the cooling of a hot rock in water.

EXAMPLE 4   Torricelli's law implies that the *time rate of change* of the volume V of water in a draining tank (Fig. 1.1.2) is proportional to the square root of the depth y of water in the tank:

$$\frac{dV}{dt} = -k\sqrt{y}, \tag{4}$$

where k is a constant. If the tank is a cylinder with vertical sides and cross-sectional area A, then $V = Ay$, so $dV/dt = A \cdot (dy/dt)$. In this case Eq. (4) takes the form

$$\frac{dy}{dt} = -h\sqrt{y}, \tag{5}$$

where $h = k/A$ is a constant. ∎

EXAMPLE 5   The *time rate of change* of a population $P(t)$ with constant birth and death rates is, in many simple cases, proportional to the size of the population. That is,

$$\frac{dP}{dt} = kP, \tag{6}$$

where k is the constant of proportionality. ∎

Let us discuss Example 5 further. Note first that each function of the form

$$P(t) = Ce^{kt} \tag{7}$$

is a solution of the differential equation

$$\frac{dP}{dt} = kP$$

FIGURE 1.1.2. Torricelli's law of draining, Eq. (4), describes the draining of a water tank.

in (6). We verify this assertion as follows:

$$P'(t) = Cke^{kt} = k\left(Ce^{kt}\right) = kP(t)$$

for all real numbers t. Because substitution of each function of the form given in (7) into Eq. (6) produces an identity, all such functions are solutions of Eq. (6).

Thus, even if the value of the constant k is known, the differential equation $dP/dt = kP$ has *infinitely many* different solutions of the form $P(t) = Ce^{kt}$, one for each choice of the "arbitrary" constant C. This is typical of differential equations. It is also fortunate, because it may allow us to use additional information to select from among all these solutions a particular one that fits the situation under study.

EXAMPLE 6 Suppose that $P(t) = Ce^{kt}$ is the population of a colony of bacteria at time t, that the population at time $t = 0$ (hours, h) was 1000, and that the population doubled after 1 h. This additional information about $P(t)$ yields the following equations:

$$1000 = P(0) = Ce^0 = C,$$
$$2000 = P(1) = Ce^k.$$

It follows that $C = 1000$ and that $e^k = 2$, so $k = \ln 2 \approx 0.693147$. With this value of k the differential equation in (6) is

$$\frac{dP}{dt} = (\ln 2)P \approx (0.693147)P.$$

Substitution of $k = \ln 2$ and $C = 1000$ in Eq. (7) yields the particular solution

$$P(t) = 1000e^{(\ln 2)t} = 1000(e^{\ln 2})^t = 1000 \cdot 2^t \qquad \text{(because } e^{\ln 2} = 2\text{)}$$

that satisfies the given conditions. We can use this particular solution to predict future populations of the bacteria colony. For instance, the predicted number of bacteria in the population after one and a half hours (when $t = 1.5$) is

$$P(1.5) = 1000 \cdot 2^{3/2} \approx 2828. \qquad \blacksquare$$

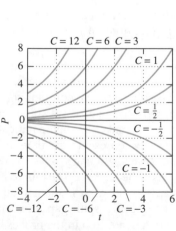

FIGURE 1.1.3. Graphs of $P(t) = Ce^{kt}$ with $k = \ln 2$.

The condition $P(0) = 1000$ in Example 6 is called an **initial condition** because we frequently write differential equations for which $t = 0$ is the "starting time." Figure 1.1.3 shows several different graphs of the form $P(t) = Ce^{kt}$ with $k = \ln 2$. The graphs of all the infinitely many solutions of $dP/dt = kP$ in fact fill the entire two-dimensional plane, and no two intersect. Moreover, the selection of any one point on the P-axis amounts to a determination of $P(0)$. Because exactly one solution passes through each such point, we see in this case that an initial condition $P(0) = P_0$ determines a unique solution agreeing with the given data.

Mathematical Models

Our brief discussion of population growth in Examples 5 and 6 illustrates the crucial process of *mathematical modeling* (Fig. 1.1.4), which involves the following:

1. The formulation of a real-world problem in mathematical terms; that is, the construction of a mathematical model.
2. The analysis or solution of the resulting mathematical problem.
3. The interpretation of the mathematical results in the context of the original real-world situation; for example, answering the question originally posed.

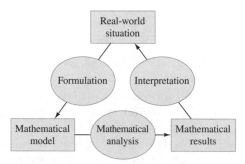

FIGURE 1.1.4. The process of mathematical modeling.

In the population example, the real-world problem is that of determining the population at some future time. A **mathematical model** consists of a list of variables (P and t) that describe the given situation, together with one or more equations relating these variables ($dP/dt = kP$, $P(0) = P_0$) that are known or are assumed to hold. The mathematical analysis consists of solving these equations (here, for P as a function of t). Finally, we apply these mathematical results to attempt to answer the original real-world question.

Nevertheless, it is quite possible that no one solution of the differential equation fits *all* the known information. In such a case we must suspect that the differential equation may not adequately describe the real world. For instance, the solutions of Eq. (6) are of the form $P(t) = Ce^{kt}$, where C is a positive constant, but for *no* choice of the constants k and C does $P(t)$ accurately describe the actual growth of the human population of the world over the past few centuries. We must therefore write a perhaps more complicated differential equation, one that takes into account the effects of population pressure on the birth rate, the declining food supply, and other factors. This should not be regarded as a failure of the model in Example 5, but as an insight into what additional factors must be considered in studying the growth of populations. Indeed, Eq. (6) is quite accurate under certain circumstances—for example, the growth of a bacterial population under conditions of unlimited food and space.

But in our population example we ignored the effects of such factors as varying birth and death rates. This made the mathematical analysis quite simple, perhaps unrealistically so. A satisfactory mathematical model is subject to two contradictory requirements: It must be sufficiently detailed to represent the real-world situation with relative accuracy, yet it must be sufficiently simple to make the mathematical analysis practical. If the model is so detailed that it fully represents the physical situation, then the mathematical analysis may be too difficult to carry out. If the model is too simple, the results may be so inaccurate as to be useless. Thus there is an inevitable tradeoff between what is physically realistic and what is mathematically possible. The construction of a model that adequately bridges this gap between realism and feasibility is therefore the most crucial and delicate step in the process. Ways must be found to simplify the model mathematically without sacrificing essential features of the real-world situation.

Mathematical models are discussed throughout this book. The remainder of this introductory section is devoted to simple examples and to standard terminology used in discussing differential equations and their solutions.

Examples and Terminology

EXAMPLE 7 If C is a constant and $y(x) = 1/(C - x)$, then

$$\frac{dy}{dx} = \frac{1}{(C-x)^2} = y^2$$

if $x \neq C$. Thus

$$y(x) = \frac{1}{C - x} \qquad (8)$$

defines a solution of the differential equation

$$\frac{dy}{dx} = y^2 \qquad (9)$$

on any interval of real numbers not containing the point $x = C$. Actually, Eq. (8) defines a *one-parameter family* of solutions of $dy/dx = y^2$, one for each value of the arbitrary constant or "parameter" C. With $C = 1$ we get the particular solution

$$y(x) = \frac{1}{1 - x}$$

that satisfies the initial condition $y(0) = 1$. As indicated in Fig. 1.1.5, this solution is continuous on the interval $(-\infty, 1)$ but has a vertical asymptote at $x = 1$. ∎

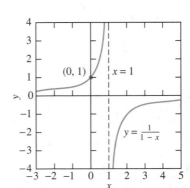

FIGURE 1.1.5. The solution of $y' = y^2$ defined by $y(x) = 1/(1 - x)$.

EXAMPLE 8 Verify that the function $y(x) = 2x^{1/2} - x^{1/2} \ln x$ satisfies the differential equation

$$4x^2 y'' + y = 0 \qquad (10)$$

for all $x > 0$.

Solution First we compute the derivatives

$$y'(x) = -\tfrac{1}{2}x^{-1/2} \ln x \quad \text{and} \quad y''(x) = \tfrac{1}{4}x^{-3/2} \ln x - \tfrac{1}{2}x^{-3/2}.$$

Then substitution into Eq. (10) yields

$$4x^2 y'' + y = 4x^2 \left(\tfrac{1}{4}x^{-3/2} \ln x - \tfrac{1}{2}x^{-3/2}\right) + 2x^{1/2} - x^{1/2} \ln x = 0$$

if x is positive, so the differential equation is satisfied for all $x > 0$. ∎

The fact that we can write a differential equation is not enough to guarantee that it has a solution. For example, it is clear that the differential equation

$$(y')^2 + y^2 = -1 \qquad (11)$$

has *no* (real-valued) solution because the sum of nonnegative numbers cannot be negative. For a variation on this theme, note that the equation

$$(y')^2 + y^2 = 0 \qquad (12)$$

obviously has only the (real-valued) solution $y(x) \equiv 0$. In our previous examples any differential equation having at least one solution indeed had infinitely many.

The **order** of a differential equation is the order of the highest derivative that appears in it. The differential equation of Example 8 is of second order, those in Examples 2 through 7 are first-order equations, and

$$y^{(4)} + x^2 y^{(3)} + x^5 y = \sin x$$

is a fourth-order equation. The most general form of an **n th-order** differential equation with independent variable x and unknown function or dependent variable $y = y(x)$ is

$$F\left(x, y, y', y'', \ldots, y^{(n)}\right) = 0, \tag{13}$$

where F is a specific real-valued function of $n + 2$ variables.

Our use of the word *solution* has been until now somewhat informal. To be precise, we say that the function $u = u(x)$ is a **solution** of the differential equation in (13) **on the interval** I provided that the derivatives $u', u'', \ldots, u^{(n)}$ exist on I and

$$F\left(x, u, u', u'', \ldots, u^{(n)}\right) = 0$$

for all x in I. When brevity is important, we say that $u = u(x)$ **satisfies** the differential equation in (13) on I.

EXAMPLE 9   If A and B are constants and

$$y(x) = A\cos 3x + B\sin 3x, \tag{14}$$

then two successive differentiations yield

$$y'(x) = -3A\sin 3x + 3B\cos 3x,$$
$$y''(x) = -9A\cos 3x - 9B\sin 3x = -9y(x)$$

for all x. Consequently, Eq. (14) defines what it is natural to call a *two-parameter family* of solutions of the second-order differential equation

$$y'' + 9y = 0 \tag{15}$$

on the whole real number line.   ∎

Although the differential equations in (11) and (12) are exceptions to the general rule, we will see that an nth-order differential equation ordinarily has an n-parameter family of solutions—one involving n different arbitrary constants or parameters.

In both Eqs. (11) and (12), the appearance of y' as an implicitly defined function causes complications. For this reason, we will ordinarily assume that any differential equation under study can be solved explicitly for the highest derivative that appears; that is, that the equation can be written in the so-called *normal form*

$$y^{(n)} = G\left(x, y, y', y'', \ldots, y^{(n-1)}\right), \tag{16}$$

where G is a real-valued function of $n + 1$ variables. In addition, we will always seek only real-valued solutions unless we warn the reader otherwise.

All the differential equations we have mentioned so far are **ordinary** differential equations, meaning that the unknown function (dependent variable) depends on only a *single* independent variable. If the dependent variable is a function of two or more independent variables, then partial derivatives are likely to be involved; if they are, the equation is called a **partial** differential equation. For example, the temperature $u = u(x, t)$ of a long thin uniform rod at the point x at time t satisfies (under appropriate simple conditions) the partial differential equation

$$\frac{\partial u}{\partial t} = k\frac{\partial^2 u}{\partial x^2},$$

where k is a constant (called the *thermal diffusivity* of the rod). In Chapters 1 through 8 we will be concerned only with *ordinary* differential equations and will refer to them simply as differential equations.

In this chapter we concentrate on *first-order* differential equations of the form

$$\frac{dy}{dx} = f(x, y). \tag{17}$$

We also will sample the wide range of applications of such equations. A typical mathematical model of an applied situation will be an **initial value problem**, consisting of a differential equation of the form in (17) together with an **initial condition** $y(x_0) = y_0$. Note that we call $y(x_0) = y_0$ an initial condition whether or not $x_0 = 0$. To **solve** the initial value problem

$$\frac{dy}{dx} = f(x, y), \quad y(x_0) = y_0 \tag{18}$$

means to find a differentiable function $y = y(x)$ that satisfies both conditions in Eq. (18) on some interval containing x_0.

EXAMPLE 10 Given the solution $y(x) = 1/(C - x)$ of the differential equation $dy/dx = y^2$ discussed in Example 7, solve the initial value problem

$$\frac{dy}{dx} = y^2, \quad y(1) = 2.$$

Solution We need only find a value of C so that the solution $y(x) = 1/(C - x)$ satisfies the initial condition $y(1) = 2$. Substitution of the values $x = 1$ and $y = 2$ in the given solution yields

$$2 = y(1) = \frac{1}{C - 1},$$

so $2C - 2 = 1$, and hence $C = \frac{3}{2}$. With this value of C we obtain the desired solution

$$y(x) = \frac{1}{\frac{3}{2} - x} = \frac{2}{3 - 2x}. \qquad \blacksquare$$

The central question of greatest immediate interest to us is this: If we are given a differential equation known to have a solution satisfying a given initial condition, how do we actually *find* or *compute* that solution? And, once found, what can we do with it? We will see that a relatively few simple techniques—separation of variables (Section 1.4), solution of linear equations (Section 1.5), elementary substitution methods (Section 1.6)—are enough to enable us to solve a variety of first-order equations having impressive applications.

1.1 *Problems*

In Problems 1 through 12, verify by substitution that each given function is a solution of the given differential equation. Throughout these problems, primes denote derivatives with respect to x.

1. $y' = 3x^2$; $y = x^3 + 7$

2. $y' + 2y = 0$; $y = 3e^{-2x}$

3. $y'' + 4y = 0$; $y_1 = \cos 2x$, $y_2 = \sin 2x$

4. $y'' = 9y$; $y_1 = e^{3x}$, $y_2 = e^{-3x}$

5. $y' = y + 2e^{-x}$; $y = e^x - e^{-x}$

6. $y'' + 4y' + 4y = 0$; $y_1 = e^{-2x}$, $y_2 = xe^{-2x}$

7. $y'' - 2y' + 2y = 0$; $y_1 = e^x \cos x$, $y_2 = e^x \sin x$

8. $y'' + y = 3\cos 2x$, $y_1 = \cos x - \cos 2x$, $y_2 = \sin x - \cos 2x$

9. $y' + 2xy^2 = 0$; $y = \dfrac{1}{1 + x^2}$

10. $x^2 y'' + xy' - y = \ln x$; $y_1 = x - \ln x$, $y_2 = \dfrac{1}{x} - \ln x$

11. $x^2 y'' + 5xy' + 4y = 0$; $y_1 = \dfrac{1}{x^2}$, $y_2 = \dfrac{\ln x}{x^2}$

12. $x^2 y'' - xy' + 2y = 0$; $y_1 = x \cos(\ln x)$, $y_2 = x \sin(\ln x)$

In Problems 13 through 16, substitute $y = e^{rx}$ into the given differential equation to determine all values of the constant r for which $y = e^{rx}$ is a solution of the equation.

13. $3y' = 2y$

14. $4y'' = y$

15. $y'' + y' - 2y = 0$

16. $3y'' + 3y' - 4y = 0$

In Problems 17 through 26, first verify that $y(x)$ satisfies the given differential equation. Then determine a value of the constant C so that $y(x)$ satisfies the given initial condition.

17. $y' + y = 0$; $y(x) = Ce^{-x}$, $y(0) = 2$

18. $y' = 2y$; $y(x) = Ce^{2x}$, $y(0) = 3$

19. $y' = y + 1$; $y(x) = Ce^{x} - 1$, $y(0) = 5$

20. $y' = x - y$; $y(x) = Ce^{-x} + x - 1$, $y(0) = 10$

21. $y' + 3x^2 y = 0$; $y(x) = Ce^{-x^3}$, $y(0) = 7$

22. $e^y y' = 1$; $y(x) = \ln(x + C)$, $y(0) = 0$

23. $x\dfrac{dy}{dx} + 3y = 2x^5$; $y(x) = \frac{1}{4}x^5 + Cx^{-3}$, $y(2) = 1$

24. $xy' - 3y = x^3$; $y(x) = x^3(C + \ln x)$, $y(1) = 17$

25. $y' = 3x^2(y^2 + 1)$; $y(x) = \tan(x^3 + C)$, $y(0) = 1$

26. $y' + y \tan x = \cos x$; $y(x) = (x + C)\cos x$, $y(\pi) = 0$

In Problems 27 through 31, a function $y = g(x)$ is described by some geometric property of its graph. Write a differential equation of the form $dy/dx = f(x, y)$ having the function g as its solution (or as one of its solutions).

27. The slope of the graph of g at the point (x, y) is the sum of x and y.

28. The line tangent to the graph of g at the point (x, y) intersects the x-axis at the point $(x/2, 0)$.

29. Every straight line normal to the graph of g passes through the point $(0, 1)$.

30. The graph of g is normal to every curve of the form $y = x^2 + k$ (k is a constant) where they meet.

31. The line tangent to the graph of g at (x, y) passes through the point $(-y, x)$.

In Problems 32 through 36, write—in the manner of Eqs. (3) through (6) of this section—a differential equation that is a mathematical model of the situation described.

32. The time rate of change of a population P is proportional to the square root of P.

33. The time rate of change of the velocity v of a coasting motorboat is proportional to the square of v.

34. The acceleration dv/dt of a Lamborghini is proportional to the difference between 250 km/h and the velocity of the car.

35. In a city having a fixed population of P persons, the time rate of change of the number N of those persons who have heard a certain rumor is proportional to the number of those who have not yet heard the rumor.

36. In a city with a fixed population of P persons, the time rate of change of the number N of those persons infected with a certain contagious disease is proportional to the product of the number who have the disease and the number who do not.

In Problems 37 through 42, determine by inspection at least one solution of the given differential equation. That is, use your knowledge of derivatives to make an intelligent guess. Then test your hypothesis.

37. $y'' = 0$ **38.** $y' = y$

39. $xy' + y = 3x^2$ **40.** $(y')^2 + y^2 = 1$

41. $y' + y = e^x$ **42.** $y'' + y = 0$

43. In Example 7 we saw that $y(x) = 1/(C - x)$ defines a one-parameter family of solutions of the differential equation $dy/dx = y^2$. (a) Determine a value of C so that $y(10) = 10$. (b) Is there a value of C such that $y(0) = 0$? Can you nevertheless find by inspection a solution of $dy/dx = y^2$ such that $y(0) = 0$? (c) Figure 1.1.6 shows typical graphs of solutions of the form $y(x) = 1/(C - x)$. Does it appear that these solution curves fill the entire xy-plane? Can you conclude that, given any point (a, b) in the plane, the differential equation $dy/dx = y^2$ has exactly one solution $y(x)$ satisfying the condition $y(a) = b$?

44. (a) Show that $y(x) = Cx^4$ defines a one-parameter family of differentiable solutions of the differential equation $xy' = 4y$ (Fig. 1.1.7). (b) Show that

$$y(x) = \begin{cases} -x^4 & \text{if } x < 0, \\ x^4 & \text{if } x \geq 0 \end{cases}$$

defines a differentiable solution of $xy' = 4y$ for all x, but is not of the form $y(x) = Cx^4$. (c) Given any two real numbers a and b, explain why—in contrast to the situation in part (c) of Problem 43—there exist infinitely many differentiable solutions of $xy' = 4y$ that all satisfy the condition $y(a) = b$.

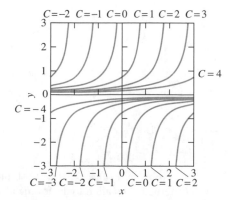

FIGURE 1.1.6. Graphs of solutions of the equation $dy/dx = y^2$.

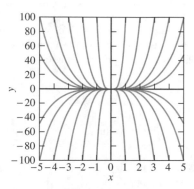

FIGURE 1.1.7. The graph $y = Cx^4$ for various values of C.

1.2 INTEGRALS AS GENERAL AND PARTICULAR SOLUTIONS

The first-order equation $dy/dx = f(x, y)$ takes an especially simple form if the function f is independent of the dependent variable y:

$$\frac{dy}{dx} = f(x). \tag{1}$$

In this special case we need only integrate both sides of Eq. (1) to obtain

$$y = y(x) = \int f(x)\, dx + C. \tag{2}$$

This is a **general solution** of Eq. (1), meaning that it involves an arbitrary constant C, and for every choice of C it is a solution of the differential equation in (1). If $G(x)$ is a particular antiderivative of f—that is, if $G'(x) \equiv f(x)$—then

$$y(x) = G(x) + C. \tag{3}$$

The graphs of any two such solutions $y_1(x) = G(x) + C_1$ and $y_2(x) = G(x) + C_2$ on the same interval I are "parallel" in the sense illustrated by Figs. 1.2.1 and 1.2.2. There we see that the constant C is geometrically the vertical distance between the two curves $y(x) = G(x)$ and $y(x) = G(x) + C$.

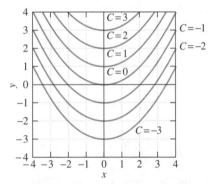

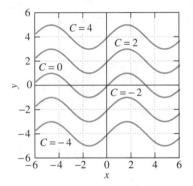

FIGURE 1.2.1. Graphs of $y = x^2 + C$ for various values of C.

FIGURE 1.2.2. Graphs of $y = \sin x + C$ for various values of C.

To satisfy an initial condition $y(x_0) = y_0$, we need only substitute $x = x_0$ and $y = y_0$ into Eq. (3) to obtain $y_0 = G(x_0) + C$, so that $C = y_0 - G(x_0)$. With this choice of C, we obtain the **particular solution** of Eq. (1) satisfying the initial value problem

$$\frac{dy}{dx} = f(x), \quad y(x_0) = y_0.$$

We will see that this is the typical pattern for solutions of first-order differential equations. Ordinarily, we will first find a *general solution* involving an arbitrary constant C. We can then attempt to obtain, by appropriate choice of C, a *particular solution* satisfying a given initial condition $y(x_0) = y_0$.

Remark: As the term is used in the previous paragraph, a *general solution* of a first-order differential equation is simply a one-parameter family of solutions. A natural question is whether a given general solution contains *every* particular solution of the differential equation. When this is known to be true, we call it **the** general solution of the differential equation. For example, because any two antiderivatives of the same function $f(x)$ can differ only by a constant, it follows that every solution of Eq. (1) is of the form in (2). Thus Eq. (2) serves to define **the** general solution of (1). ∎

EXAMPLE 1   Solve the initial value problem

$$\frac{dy}{dx} = 2x + 3, \quad y(1) = 2.$$

Solution   Integration of both sides of the differential equation as in Eq. (2) immediately yields the general solution

$$y = y(x) = \int (2x + 3)\,dx = x^2 + 3x + C.$$

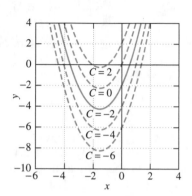

FIGURE 1.2.3. Solution curves for the differential equation in Example 1.

Figure 1.2.3 shows the graph $y = x^2 + 3x + C$ for various values of C. The particular solution we seek corresponds to the curve that passes through the point $(1, 2)$, thereby satisfying the initial condition

$$y(1) = (1)^2 + 3 \cdot (1) + C = 2.$$

It follows that $C = -2$, so the desired particular solution is

$$y(x) = x^2 + 3x - 2. \qquad \blacksquare$$

The observation that the special first-order equation $dy/dx = f(x)$ is readily solvable (provided that an antiderivative of f can be found) extends to second-order differential equations of the special form

$$\frac{d^2y}{dx^2} = g(x), \tag{4}$$

in which the function g on the right-hand side involves neither the dependent variable y nor its derivative dy/dx. We simply integrate once to obtain

$$\frac{dy}{dx} = \int y''(x)\,dx = \int g(x)\,dx = G(x) + C_1,$$

where G is an antiderivative of g and C_1 is an arbitrary constant. Then another integration yields

$$y(x) = \int y'(x)\,dx = \int [G(x) + C_1]\,dx = \int G(x)\,dx + C_1 x + C_2.$$

where C_2 is a second arbitrary constant. In effect, the second-order differential equation in (4) is one that can be solved by solving successively the *first-order* equations

$$\frac{dv}{dx} = g(x) \quad \text{and} \quad \frac{dy}{dx} = v(x).$$

Velocity and Acceleration

Direct integration is sufficient to allow us to solve a number of important problems concerning the motion of a particle (or *mass point*) in terms of the forces acting on it. The motion of a particle along a straight line (the x-axis) is described by its **position function**

$$x = f(t) \tag{5}$$

giving its x-coordinate at time t. The **velocity** of the particle is defined to be

$$v(t) = f'(t); \quad \text{that is,} \quad v = \frac{dx}{dt}. \tag{6}$$

Its **acceleration** $a(t)$ is $a(t) = v'(t) = x''(t)$; in Leibniz notation,

$$a = \frac{dv}{dt} = \frac{d^2x}{dt^2}. \qquad (7)$$

Newton's *second law of motion* implies that if a force $F(t)$ acts on the particle and is directed along its line of motion, then

$$ma(t) = F(t); \quad \text{that is,} \quad F = ma, \qquad (8)$$

where m is the mass of the particle. If the force F is known, then the equation $x''(t) = F(t)/m$ can be integrated twice to find the position function $x(t)$ in terms of two constants of integration. These two arbitrary constants are frequently determined by the **initial position** $x_0 = x(0)$ and the **initial velocity** $v_0 = v(0)$ of the particle.

For instance, suppose that the force F, and therefore the acceleration $a = F/m$, are *constant*. Then we begin with the equation

$$\frac{dv}{dt} = a \quad (a \text{ is a constant}) \qquad (9)$$

and integrate both sides to obtain

$$v = v(t) = \int a \, dt = at + C_1.$$

We know that $v = v_0$ when $t = 0$, and substitution of this information into the preceding equation yields the fact that $C_1 = v_0$. So

$$v = v(t) = \frac{dx}{dt} = at + v_0. \qquad (10)$$

A second integration gives

$$x(t) = \int v(t) \, dt = \int (at + v_0) \, dt = \tfrac{1}{2}at^2 + v_0 t + C_2,$$

and the substitution $t = 0$, $x = x_0$ gives $C_2 = x_0$. Therefore

$$x(t) = \tfrac{1}{2}at^2 + v_0 t + x_0. \qquad (11)$$

Thus, with Eq. (10) we can find the velocity, and with Eq. (11) the position, of the particle at any time t in terms of its *constant* acceleration a, its initial velocity v_0, and its initial position x_0.

EXAMPLE 2 A lunar lander is falling freely toward the surface of the moon at a speed of 1000 miles per hour (mi/h). Its retrorockets, when fired, provide a constant deceleration of 20000 miles per hour per hour (mi/h^2) (the gravitational acceleration produced by the moon is assumed to be included in the given deceleration). At what height above the lunar surface should the retrorockets be activated to ensure a "soft touchdown" ($v = 0$ at impact)?

Solution We denote by $x(t)$ the height of the lunar lander above the surface, as indicated in Fig. 1.2.4. We let $t = 0$ denote the time at which the retrorockets should be fired. Then $v_0 = -1000$ (mi/h, negative because the height $x(t)$ is decreasing), and $a = +20000$ because an upward thrust increases the velocity v (although it decreases the *speed* $|v|$). Then Eqs. (10) and (11) become

$$v(t) = 20000t - 1000 \qquad (12)$$

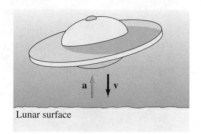

FIGURE 1.2.4. The lunar lander of Example 2.

and

$$x(t) = 10000t^2 - 1000t + x_0, \tag{13}$$

where x_0 is the height of the lander above the lunar surface at the time $t = 0$ when the retrorockets should be activated.

From Eq. (12) we see that $v = 0$ (soft touchdown) occurs when $t = \frac{1}{20}$ (h; thus 3 min); then substitution of $t = \frac{1}{20}$, $x = 0$ into Eq. (13) yields

$$x_0 = -10000 \left(\frac{1}{20}\right)^2 + 1000 \left(\frac{1}{20}\right) = 25$$

(mi). Thus the retrorockets should be activated when the lunar lander is 25 mi above the surface, and it will reach the surface 3 min later. ∎

Physical Units

Numerical work requires units for the measurement of physical quantities such as distance and time. We sometimes use ad hoc units—such as distance in miles or kilometers and time in hours—in special situations (such as the lunar lander of Example 2). Nevertheless, the foot-pound-second (fps) and meter-kilogram-second (mks) unit systems summarized in the following table are used more generally. In fact, fps units are commonly used only in the United States (and a few other countries), while mks units constitute the standard international system of scientific units.

	fps units	mks units
Force	pound (lb)	newton (N)
Mass	slug	kilogram (kg)
Distance	foot (ft)	meter (m)
Time	second (s)	second (s)
g	32 ft/s^2	9.8 m/s^2

The last line of this table gives values for the gravitational acceleration g at the surface of the earth. Although these approximate values will suffice for most examples and problems, more precise values are 9.7805 m/s^2 and 32.088 ft/s^2 (at sea level at the equator).

Both systems are compatible with Newton's second law $F = ma$. Thus 1 N is (by definition) the force required to impart an acceleration of 1 m/s^2 to a mass of 1 kg. Similarly, 1 slug is (by definition) the mass that experiences an acceleration of 1 ft/s^2 under a force of 1 lb. (We will use mks units in all problems requiring mass units, and thus will rarely need slugs to measure mass.)

Inches and centimeters (as well as miles and kilometers) also are commonly used in describing distances. For conversions between fps and mks units it helps to remember that

$$1 \text{ in.} = 2.54 \text{ cm (exactly)} \quad \text{and} \quad 1 \text{ lb} \approx 4.448 \text{ N}.$$

For instance,

$$1 \text{ ft} = 12 \text{ in.} \times 2.54 \frac{\text{cm}}{\text{in.}} = 30.48 \text{ cm},$$

and it follows that

$$1 \text{ mi} = 5280 \text{ ft} \times 30.48 \frac{\text{cm}}{\text{ft}} = 160934.4 \text{ cm} \approx 1.609 \text{ km}.$$

Thus a posted U.S. speed limit of 50 mi/h means that—in international terms—the legal speed limit is about $50 \times 1.609 \approx 80.45$ km/h.

Vertical Motion with Gravitational Acceleration

The **weight** W of a body is the force exerted on the body by gravity. Substitution of $a = g$ and $F = W$ in Newton's second law $F = ma$ gives

$$W = mg \tag{14}$$

for the weight W of the mass m at the surface of the earth (where $g \approx 32$ ft/s$^2 \approx 9.8$ m/s^2). For instance, a mass of $m = 20$ kg has a weight of $W = (20$ kg$)(9.8$ m/s$^2) = 196$ N. Similarly, a mass m weighing 100 pounds has mks weight

$$W = (100 \text{ lb})(4.448 \text{ N/lb}) = 444.8 \text{ N},$$

so its mass is

$$m = \frac{W}{g} = \frac{444.8 \text{ N}}{9.8 \text{ m/s}^2} \approx 45.4 \text{ kg}.$$

To discuss vertical motion it is natural to choose the y-axis as the coordinate system for position, frequently with $y = 0$ corresponding to "ground level." If we choose the *upward* direction as the positive direction, then the effect of gravity on a vertically moving body is to decrease its height and also to decrease its velocity $v = dy/dt$. Consequently, if we ignore air resistance, then the acceleration $a = dv/dt$ of the body is given by

$$\frac{dv}{dt} = -g. \tag{15}$$

This acceleration equation provides a starting point in many problems involving vertical motion. Successive integrations (as in Eqs. (10) and (11)) yield the velocity and height formulas

$$v(t) = -gt + v_0 \tag{16}$$

and

$$y(t) = -\tfrac{1}{2}gt^2 + v_0 t + y_0. \tag{17}$$

Here, y_0 denotes the initial ($t = 0$) height of the body and v_0 its initial velocity.

EXAMPLE 3   (a) Suppose that a ball is thrown straight upward from the ground ($y_0 = 0$) with initial velocity $v_0 = 96$ (ft/s, so we use $g = 32$ ft/s^2 in fps units). Then it reaches its maximum height when its velocity (Eq. (16)) is zero,

$$v(t) = -32t + 96 = 0,$$

and thus when $t = 3$ s. Hence the maximum height that the ball attains is

$$y(3) = -\tfrac{1}{2} \cdot 32 \cdot 3^2 + 96 \cdot 3 + 0 = 144 \text{ (ft)}$$

(with the aid of Eq. (17)).

(b) If an arrow is shot straight upward from the ground with initial velocity $v_0 = 49$ (m/s, so we use $g = 9.8$ m/s^2 in mks units), then it returns to the ground when

$$y(t) = -\tfrac{1}{2} \cdot (9.8)t^2 + 49t = (4.9)t(-t + 10) = 0,$$

and thus after 10 s in the air.   ∎

A Swimmer's Problem

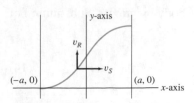

FIGURE 1.2.5. A swimmer's problem (Example 4).

Figure 1.2.5 shows a northward-flowing river of width $w = 2a$. The lines $x = \pm a$ represent the banks of the river and the y-axis its center. Suppose that the velocity v_R at which the water flows increases as one approaches the center of the river, and indeed is given in terms of distance x from the center by

$$v_R = v_0 \left(1 - \frac{x^2}{a^2}\right). \tag{18}$$

You can use Eq. (18) to verify that the water does flow the fastest at the center, where $v_R = v_0$, and that $v_R = 0$ at each riverbank.

Suppose that a swimmer starts at the point $(-a, 0)$ on the west bank and swims due east (relative to the water) with constant speed v_S. As indicated in Fig. 1.2.5, his velocity vector (relative to the ground) has horizontal component v_S and vertical component v_R. Hence the swimmer's direction angle α is given by

$$\tan \alpha = \frac{v_R}{v_S}.$$

Because $\tan \alpha = dy/dx$, substitution using (18) gives the differential equation

$$\frac{dy}{dx} = \frac{v_0}{v_S} \left(1 - \frac{x^2}{a^2}\right) \tag{19}$$

for the swimmer's trajectory $y = y(x)$ as he crosses the river.

EXAMPLE 4   Suppose that the river is 1 mile wide and that its midstream velocity is $v_0 = 9$ mi/h. If the swimmer's velocity is $v_S = 3$ mi/h, then Eq. (19) takes the form

$$\frac{dy}{dx} = 3(1 - 4x^2).$$

Integration yields

$$y = y(x) = \int (3 - 12x^2)\, dx = 3x - 4x^3 + C$$

for the swimmer's trajectory. The initial condition $y\left(-\frac{1}{2}\right) = 0$ yields $C = 1$, so

$$y(x) = 3x - 4x^3 + 1.$$

Then

$$y\left(\tfrac{1}{2}\right) = 3\left(\tfrac{1}{2}\right) - 4\left(\tfrac{1}{2}\right)^3 + 1 = 2,$$

so the swimmer drifts 2 miles downstream while he swims 1 mile across the river. ∎

1.2 Problems

In Problems 1 through 10, find a function $y = f(x)$ satisfying the given differential equation and the prescribed initial condition.

1. $\dfrac{dy}{dx} = 2x + 1$; $y(0) = 3$

2. $\dfrac{dy}{dx} = (x - 2)^2$; $y(2) = 1$

3. $\dfrac{dy}{dx} = \sqrt{x}$; $y(4) = 0$

4. $\dfrac{dy}{dx} = \dfrac{1}{x^2}$; $y(1) = 5$

5. $\dfrac{dy}{dx} = \dfrac{1}{\sqrt{x + 2}}$; $y(2) = -1$

6. $\dfrac{dy}{dx} = x\sqrt{x^2 + 9}$; $y(-4) = 0$

7. $\dfrac{dy}{dx} = \dfrac{10}{x^2 + 1}$; $y(0) = 0$

8. $\dfrac{dy}{dx} = \cos 2x$; $y(0) = 1$

9. $\dfrac{dy}{dx} = \dfrac{1}{\sqrt{1 - x^2}}$; $y(0) = 0$

10. $\dfrac{dy}{dx} = xe^{-x}$; $y(0) = 1$

In Problems 11 through 18, find the position function $x(t)$ of a moving particle with the given acceleration $a(t)$, initial position $x_0 = x(0)$, and initial velocity $v_0 = v(0)$.

11. $a(t) = 50$, $v_0 = 10$, $x_0, = 20$

12. $a(t) = -20$, $v_0 = -15$, $x_0 = 5$

13. $a(t) = 3t$, $v_0 = 5$, $x_0 = 0$

14. $a(t) = 2t + 1$, $v_0 = -7$, $x_0 = 4$

15. $a(t) = 4(t + 3)^2$, $v_0 = -1$, $x_0 = 1$

16. $a(t) = \dfrac{1}{\sqrt{t + 4}}$, $v_0 = -1$, $x_0 = 1$

17. $a(t) = \dfrac{1}{(t + 1)^3}$, $v_0 = 0$, $x_0 = 0$

18. $a(t) = 50 \sin 5t$, $v_0 = -10$, $x_0 = 8$

19. What is the maximum height attained by the arrow of part (b) of Example 3?

20. A ball is dropped from the top of a building 400 ft high. How long does it take to reach the ground? With what speed does the ball strike the ground?

21. The brakes of a car are applied when it is moving at 100 km/h and provide a constant deceleration of 10 meters per second per second (m/s^2). How far does the car travel before coming to a stop?

22. A projectile is fired straight upward with an initial velocity of 100 m/s from the top of a building 20 m high and falls to the ground at the base of the building. Find (a) its maximum height above the ground; (b) when it passes the top of the building; (c) its total time in the air.

23. A ball is thrown straight downward from the top of a tall building. The initial speed of the ball is 10 m/s. It strikes the ground with a speed of 60 m/s. How tall is the building?

24. A baseball is thrown straight downward with an initial speed of 40 ft/s from the top of the Washington Monument (555 ft high). How long does it take to reach the ground, and with what speed does the baseball strike the ground?

25. A diesel car gradually speeds up so that for the first 10 s its acceleration is given by

$$\frac{dy}{dx} = (0.12)t^2 + (0.6)t \quad (\text{ft/s}^2).$$

If the car starts from rest ($x_0 = 0$, $v_0 = 0$), find the distance it has traveled at the end of the first 10 s and its velocity at that time.

26. A car traveling at 60 mi/h (88 ft/s) skids 176 ft after its brakes are suddenly applied. Under the assumption that the braking system provides constant deceleration, what is that deceleration? For how long does the skid continue?

27. The skid marks made by an automobile indicated that its brakes were fully applied for a distance of 75 m before it came to a stop. The car in question is known to have a constant deceleration of 20 m/s^2 under these conditions. How fast—in km/h—was the car traveling when the brakes were first applied?

28. Suppose that a car skids 15 m if it is moving at 50 km/h when the brakes are applied. Assuming that the car has the same constant deceleration, how far will it skid if it is moving at 100 km/h when the brakes are applied?

29. On the planet Gzyx, a ball dropped from a height of 20 ft hits the ground in 2 s. If a ball is dropped from the top of a 200-ft-tall building on Gzyx, how long will it take to hit the ground? With what speed will it hit?

30. A person can throw a ball straight upward from the surface of the earth to a maximum height of 144 ft. How high could this person throw the ball on the planet Gzyx of Problem 29?

31. A stone is dropped from rest at an initial height h above the surface of the earth. Show that the speed with which it strikes the ground is $v = \sqrt{2gh}$.

32. If a woman has enough "spring" in her legs to jump vertically to a height of 2.25 ft on the earth, how high could she jump on the moon, where the surface gravitational acceleration is (approximately) 5.3 ft/s^2?

33. At noon a car starts from rest at point A and proceeds at constant acceleration along a straight road toward point B. If the car reaches B at 12:50 P.M. with a velocity of 60 mi/h, what is the distance from A to B?

34. At noon a car starts from rest at point A and proceeds with constant acceleration along a straight road toward point C, 35 miles away. If the constantly accelerated car arrives at C with a velocity of 60 mi/h, at what time does it arrive at C?

35. If $a = 0.5$ mi and $v_0 = 9$ mi/h as in Example 4, what must the swimmer's speed v_S be in order that he drifts only 1 mile downstream as he crosses the river?

36. Suppose that $a = 0.5$ mi, $v_0 = 9$ mi/h, and $v_S = 3$ mi/h as in Example 4, but that the velocity of the river is given by the fourth-degree function

$$v_R = v_0 \left(1 - \frac{x^4}{a^4}\right)$$

rather than the quadratic function in Eq. (18). Now find how far downstream the swimmer drifts as he crosses the river.

1.3 DIRECTION FIELDS AND SOLUTION CURVES

In the case of a general first-order differential equation of the form

$$\frac{dy}{dx} = f(x, y), \tag{1}$$

we cannot simply integrate each side as in Section 1.2, because now the right-hand side involves the unknown function $y(x)$. Before one spends much time trying to solve a differential equation, it is wise to know that solutions actually *exist*. We may also want to know whether there is only one solution of the equation satisfying a given initial condition—that is, whether solutions are *unique*. For instance, you can verify readily (by direct substitution) that such a simple-looking initial value problem as

$$\frac{dy}{dx} = 2\sqrt{y}, \quad y(0) = 0 \tag{2}$$

has the two *different* solutions $y_1(x) = x^2$ and $y_2(x) \equiv 0$.

The questions of existence and uniqueness also bear on the process of mathematical modeling. Suppose that we are studying a physical system whose behavior is determined completely by certain initial conditions, but that our proposed mathematical model involves a differential equation *not* having a unique solution. This raises an immediate question as to whether the mathematical model adequately represents the physical system.

Direction Fields

To investigate the possible behavior of solutions of a differential equation of the form $dy/dx = f(x, y)$, we may think of it in a very geometric way: At various points (x, y) of the two-dimensional coordinate plane, the value of $f(x, y)$ determines a slope $m = y'(x) = f(x, y)$. A *solution* of this differential equation is a differentiable function with graph having slope $y'(x)$ at each point (x, y) through which the graph passes. The graph of a solution of a differential equation is sometimes called a **solution curve** of the equation. From this geometric viewpoint, a solution curve of a differential equation is then a curve in the plane whose tangent at each point (x, y) has slope $m = f(x, y)$.

This idea of a solution curve suggests the following *graphical method* for constructing approximate solutions of the differential equation $dy/dx = f(x, y)$. Through each of a representative collection of points (x, y) we draw a short line segment having slope $m = f(x, y)$. The set of all these line segments is called a **direction field** (or *slope field*) for the equation $dy/dx = f(x, y)$. We can attempt to sketch a solution curve that threads its way through the direction field in such a way that the curve is tangent to each of the short line segments that it intersects.

EXAMPLE 1   Figures 1.3.1 (a)–(d) show direction fields and solution curves for the differential equation

$$\frac{dy}{dx} = ky \tag{3}$$

with the values $k = 2, 0.5, -1$, and -3 of the parameter k in Eq. (3). Note that each direction field yields important qualitative information about the set of all solutions of the differential equation. For instance, Figs. 1.3.1 (a) and (b) suggest that each solution $y(x)$ approaches $\pm\infty$ as $x \to +\infty$ if $k > 0$, whereas Figs. 1.3.1 (c) and (d) suggest that $y(x) \to 0$ as $x \to +\infty$ if $k < 0$. Moreover, although the sign of k determines the *direction* of increase or decrease of $y(x)$, its absolute value $|k|$ appears to determine the rate of change of $y(x)$. All this is apparent from direction fields like those in Fig. 1.3.1 even without knowing that the general solution of Eq. (3) is given explicitly by $y(x) = Ce^{kx}$.   ∎

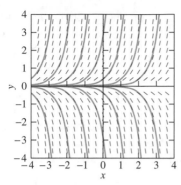

FIGURE 1.3.1(a) Direction field and solution curves for $y' = 2y$.

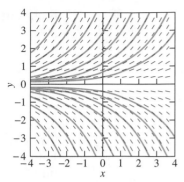

FIGURE 1.3.1(b) Direction field and solution curves for $y' = (0.5)y$.

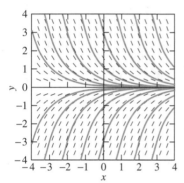

FIGURE 1.3.1(c) Direction field and solution curves for $y' = -y$.

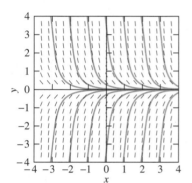

FIGURE 1.3.1(d) Direction field and solution curves for $y' = -3y$.

Isoclines

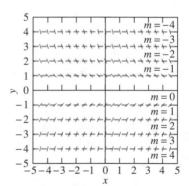

FIGURE 1.3.2. Isolines and direction field for $y' = -y$.

It is easy to instruct a computer to draw a direction field for a given differential equation $dy/dx = f(x, y)$, and programs for doing so are readily available. There is also an older manual method still useful on occasion: An **isocline** of the differential equation $dy/dx = f(x, y)$ is a curve of the form

$$f(x, y) = c \quad (c \text{ is a constant}) \tag{4}$$

on which the slope $y'(x)$ is *constant*. If these isoclines are simple and familiar curves, we first sketch several of them, then draw short line segments with the same slope c at representative points of each isocline $f(x, y) = c$.

For example, $f(x, y) = -y$ for the equation $dy/dx = -y$ of Fig. 1.3.1(c), so the isoclines are horizontal straight lines of the form $y = -c$. Several of these isoclines, each embellished with short line segments of slope $m = c$, are shown in Fig. 1.3.2. Observe that the resulting direction field is consistent with the more detailed one shown in Fig. 1.3.1(c).

EXAMPLE 2   The typical isocline of the differential equation

$$\frac{dy}{dx} = x^2 + y^2 \tag{5}$$

has the equation $x^2 + y^2 = c > 0$, and thus is a circle centered at the origin and having radius $r = \sqrt{c}$. Several of these circles are shown in Fig. 1.3.3, each marked with its direction lines of slope $m = r^2$, together with some typical solution curves of the differential equation in (5). It happens that the equation

$$\frac{dy}{dx} = x^2 + y^2$$

is quite difficult to solve explicitly; its general solution involves the Bessel functions of Section 8.5. But even without an explicit knowledge of the solutions, it seems apparent from Fig. 1.3.3 that on each solution curve, $y(x) \to +\infty$ as x increases. This observation is quite correct and illustrates the qualitative information about solutions of a differential equation that frequently is revealed by an easily constructed direction field.   ∎

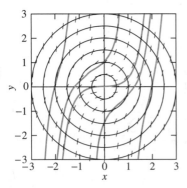

FIGURE 1.3.3. Isolines, direction field, and solution curves for $y' = x^2 + y^2$.

EXAMPLE 3   The isoclines of the differential equation

$$\frac{dy}{dx} = \sin(x - y) \tag{6}$$

are of the form

$$\sin(x - y) = c;$$

that is, $x - y = \sin^{-1} c$, and thus of the form $y = x - \sin^{-1} c$. Therefore, the isoclines of Eq. (6) are all straight lines of slope 1 in the xy-plane. The direction field and some typical solution curves are shown in Fig. 1.3.4. Most of the solution curves one sees in this figure appear to exhibit the oscillatory behavior suggested by the presence of the sine function in Eq. (6). Yet there is one solution curve that appears to be a straight line! This observation prompts us to inspect Eq. (6) more closely. When we do, we spot the particular solution

$$y = x - \frac{\pi}{2}$$

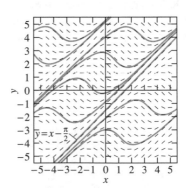

FIGURE 1.3.4. Direction field and solution curves for $y' = \sin(x - y)$ in Example 3.

for which $y'(x) \equiv 1$ and $x - y = \pi/2$, so that $\sin(x - y) \equiv 1$ as well. Do you see in Fig. 1.3.4 any indication of *another* straight line solution curve for Eq. (6)?   ∎

EXAMPLE 4   Consider the differential equation

$$y^2 + x^2 \frac{dy}{dx} = 0. \tag{7}$$

If we write this equation in the form

$$\frac{dy}{dx} = -\frac{y^2}{x^2}, \tag{8}$$

we see that the isoclines are of the form $-y^2/x^2 = c$—that is, $y = kx$—and thus are straight lines through the origin. We show a direction field and a typical solution curve for this equation in Fig. 1.3.5. Indeed, because $dy/dx = -(y/x)^2$, we see that each differentiable solution must be decreasing except on the coordinate axes (where x or y is zero). Much additional qualitative information can be read from the direction field of Eq. (7).

In Section 1.4 we will solve equations like this one—known as **separable** differential equations—by separating the variables. Here's how: First we rewrite Eq. (8) in the "separated form"

$$-\frac{dy}{y^2} = \frac{dx}{x^2}.$$

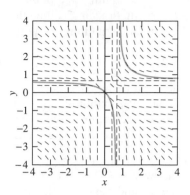

FIGURE 1.3.5. Direction field for $y^2 + x^2 y' = 0$ and the graph of one solution of this equation.

Next we integrate each side,

$$-\int \frac{dy}{y^2} = \int \frac{dx}{x^2} + C,$$

to obtain

$$\frac{1}{y} = -\frac{1}{x} + C.$$

Finally, we solve for y to obtain

$$y = y(x) = \frac{x}{Cx - 1}. \tag{9}$$

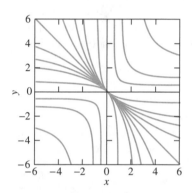

FIGURE 1.3.6. Solution curves for $y^2 + x^2 y' = 0$.

Figure 1.3.6 shows a number of solution curves calculated with different values of C. Each solution curve of the form in Eq. (9) with $C \neq 0$ has a pair of vertical and horizontal asymptotes $x = 1/C$ and $y = 1/C$ (like the ones shown in Fig. 1.3.5). In fact, each of these solution curves consists of the two branches of a rectangular hyperbola, one branch of which passes through the origin. When $C = 0$ we obtain the "different" solution $y = -x$. Moreover, the solution process displayed here excludes the function $y(x) \equiv 0$, which (by substitution in Eq. (7)) is yet another solution. ◼

The remarkable feature of the differential equation in (7) and its solutions is this: First, there are *infinitely many* different solutions satisfying the initial condition $y(0) = 0$. But it follows from Eq. (7) that $y(0) = 0$, so if $b \neq 0$, then there is *no* solution satisfying the initial condition $y(0) = b$. Finally, if $a \neq 0$ and b is arbitrary, there is exactly one solution with $y(a) = b$. All these observations are evident from inspection of Fig. 1.3.6.

Existence and Uniqueness of Solutions

Example 4 shows that an initial value problem may have either no solution, a unique (that is, one and only one) solution, or many—even infinitely many—solutions. The following theorem provides sufficient conditions to ensure existence and uniqueness of solutions, so that neither extreme case (no solution or nonunique solutions) can occur. Methods of proving existence and uniqueness theorems are discussed in the Appendix.

THEOREM 1: Existence and Uniqueness of Solutions

Suppose that the real-valued function $f(x, y)$ is continuous on some rectangle in the xy-plane containing the point (a, b) in its interior. Then the initial value problem

$$\frac{dy}{dx} = f(x, y), \quad y(a) = b \tag{10}$$

has at least one solution defined on some open interval J containing the point a. If, in addition, the partial derivative $\partial f / \partial y$ is continuous on that rectangle, then the solution is unique on some (perhaps smaller) open interval J_0 containing the point $x = a$.

Remark 1: In the case of the differential equation $dy/dx = -y$ of Example 1, both the function $f(x, y) = -y$ and the partial derivative $\partial f / \partial y = -1$ are continuous everywhere, so Theorem 1 implies the existence of a unique solution for any initial data (a, b). Although the theorem ensures existence only on some open interval containing $x = a$, each solution $y(x) = Ce^{-x}$ actually is defined for all x.

Remark 2: In the case of the differential equation $dy/dx = 2\sqrt{y}$ in Eq. (2), the function $f(x, y) = 2\sqrt{y}$ is continuous wherever $y > 0$, but the partial derivative $\partial f / \partial y = 1/\sqrt{y}$ is discontinuous when $y = 0$, and hence at the point $(0, 0)$. This is why it is possible for there to exist two different solutions $y_1(x) = x^2$ and $y_2(x) \equiv 0$, each of which satisfies the initial condition $y(0) = 0$.

Remark 3: In Example 4 we analyzed the differential equation $y^2 + x^2 y' = 0$ and found that there was no solution passing through $(0, 1)$. If we take $f(x, y) = -(y/x)^2$, we see that Theorem 1 cannot guarantee existence of a solution through $(0, 1)$ because f is not continuous there. (Note that f is also not continuous at $(0, 0)$, but some solutions *do* pass through this point. Thus the continuity of f is a sufficient condition, but not a necessary condition, for the existence of solutions.)

Remark 4: Finally, in Example 7 of Section 1.1 we examined the especially simple differential equation $dy/dx = y^2$. Here we have $f(x, y) = y^2$ and $\partial f / \partial y = 2y$. Both of these functions are continuous everywhere in the xy-plane, and in particular on the rectangle $-2 < x < 2, 0 < y < 2$. Because the point $(0, 1)$ lies in the interior of this rectangle, Theorem 1 guarantees a unique solution—necessarily a continuous function—of the initial value problem

$$\frac{dy}{dx} = y^2, \quad y(0) = 1$$

on some open interval containing $x_0 = 0$. This is the solution

$$y(x) = \frac{1}{1 - x}$$

that we discussed in Example 7. But $1/(1 - x)$ is discontinuous at $x = 1$, so we do *not* have *existence* of a solution on the entire interval $-2 < x < 2$. This means that the interval J of Theorem 1 may not be as wide as the rectangle. Thus, even though the hypotheses of the theorem are satisfied for all x in an interval I (and all y in an appropriate interval), the solution may, as in Example 7, exist only on a smaller interval J. Similarly, the interval J_0 of uniqueness may be even smaller than J. ∎

EXAMPLE 5 Consider the first-order differential equation

$$x\frac{dy}{dx} = 2y. \tag{11}$$

Applying Theorem 1 with $f(x, y) = 2y/x$, we see that Eq. (11) has a unique solution near any point where $x \neq 0$. Indeed, we see readily that

$$y(x) = Cx^2 \tag{12}$$

satisfies Eq. (11) for any value of the constant C and for all values of x.

With these preliminary observations in mind, let us consider the initial value problem

$$x\frac{dy}{dx} = 2y, \quad y(-1) = 1. \tag{13}$$

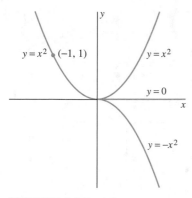

FIGURE 1.3.7. Three solutions of the initial value problem in Eq. (13).

The initial condition $y(-1) = 1$ implies that $C = 1$ in Eq. (12), so on some open interval containing $x = -1$ we have the unique solution $y(x) = x^2$ which passes through the origin $(0, 0)$. But to the right of the origin we may choose any value we please for C in Eq. (12). That is, for any fixed C, a solution of the initial value problem in Eq. (13) is given by

$$y(x) = \begin{cases} x^2 & \text{if } x \leq 0, \\ Cx^2 & \text{if } x > 0. \end{cases}$$

Thus this initial value problem has infinitely many different solutions, despite the fact that (in accord with Theorem 1) there is a unique solution on *some* open interval containing the point $x = -1$. Figure 1.3.7 shows three of these different solutions of Eq. (13).   ■

The point is that Theorem 1 guarantees uniqueness *near* the point (a, b), but the solution curve may branch elsewhere and uniqueness will be lost. Similarly, Theorem 1 can guarantee existence of a solution *near* the point (a, b), but the differential equation may have no solution for some other values of x.

1.3 *Problems*

In Problems 1 through 10, we have provided the direction field of the indicated differential equation, together with one or more solution curves. Sketch likely solution curves through the additional points marked in each direction field. (One method: Photocopy the direction field and draw your solution curves in a second color. Another method: Use tracing paper.)

1. $\dfrac{dy}{dx} = -y - \sin x$

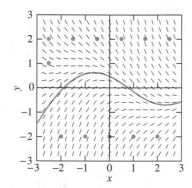

FIGURE 1.3.8.

2. $\dfrac{dy}{dx} = x + y$

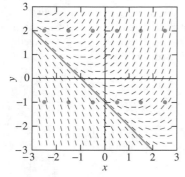

FIGURE 1.3.9.

3. $\dfrac{dy}{dx} = y - \sin x$

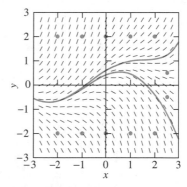

FIGURE 1.3.10.

4. $\dfrac{dy}{dx} = x - y$

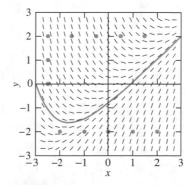

FIGURE 1.3.11.

5. $\dfrac{dy}{dx} = y - x + 1$

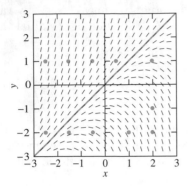

FIGURE 1.3.12.

6. $\dfrac{dy}{dx} = x - y + 1$

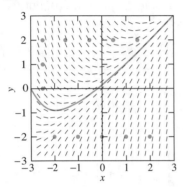

FIGURE 1.3.13.

7. $\dfrac{dy}{dx} = \sin x + \sin y$

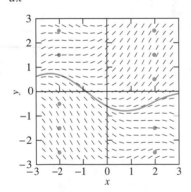

FIGURE 1.3.14.

8. $\dfrac{dy}{dx} = x^2 - y$

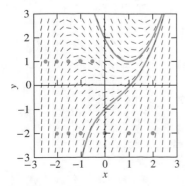

FIGURE 1.3.15.

9. $\dfrac{dy}{dx} = x^2 - y - 2$

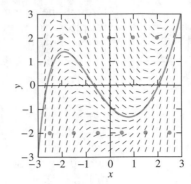

FIGURE 1.3.16.

10. $\dfrac{dy}{dx} = -x^2 + \sin y$

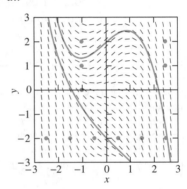

FIGURE 1.3.17.

In Problems 11 through 20, identify the isoclines of the given differential equation. Draw a sketch showing several of these isoclines, each marked with short line segments having the appropriate slope.

11. $\dfrac{dy}{dx} = x - 1$ **12.** $\dfrac{dy}{dx} = x + y$

13. $\dfrac{dy}{dx} = y^2$ **14.** $\dfrac{dy}{dx} = \sqrt[3]{y}$

15. $\dfrac{dy}{dx} = \dfrac{y}{x}$ **16.** $\dfrac{dy}{dx} = x^2 - y^2$

17. $\dfrac{dy}{dx} = xy$ **18.** $\dfrac{dy}{dx} = x - y^2$

19. $\dfrac{dy}{dx} = y - x^2$ **20.** $\dfrac{dy}{dx} = ye^{-x}$

In Problems 21 through 30, determine whether Theorem 1 does or does not guarantee existence of a solution of the given initial value problem. If existence is guaranteed, determine whether Theorem 1 does or does not guarantee uniqueness of that solution.

21. $\dfrac{dy}{dx} = 2x^2 y^2; \quad y(1) = -1$

22. $\dfrac{dy}{dx} = x \ln y; \quad y(1) = 1$

23. $\dfrac{dy}{dx} = \sqrt[3]{y}; \quad y(0) = 1$

24. $\dfrac{dy}{dx} = \sqrt[3]{y}; \quad y(0) = 0$

25. $\dfrac{dy}{dx} = \sqrt{x - y}; \quad y(2) = 2$

26. $\dfrac{dy}{dx} = \sqrt{x - y}; \quad y(2) = 1$

27. $y\dfrac{dy}{dx} = x - 1; \quad y(0) = 1$

28. $y\dfrac{dy}{dx} = x - 1; \quad y(1) = 0$

29. $\dfrac{dy}{dx} = \ln(1 + y^2); \quad y(0) = 0$

30. $\dfrac{dy}{dx} = x^2 - y^2; \quad y(0) = 1$

The next six problems illustrate that if the hypotheses of Theorem 1 fail at a point (a, b), then there may be no solutions, finitely many solutions, or infinitely many solutions passing through (a, b).

31. Show that on the interval $[0, \pi]$, the functions $y_1(x) \equiv 1$ and $y_2(x) = \cos x$ both satisfy the initial value problem

$$\frac{dy}{dx} + \sqrt{1 - y^2} = 0, \quad y(0) = 1.$$

Why does this fact not contradict Theorem 1? Explain your answer carefully.

32. Find by inspection two different solutions of the initial value problem

$$\frac{dy}{dx} = 3y^{2/3}, \quad y(0) = 0.$$

Why does the existence of different solutions not contradict Theorem 1?

33. Use Fig. 1.3.18 as a suggestion for showing that the initial value problem

$$\frac{dy}{dx} = 3y^{2/3}, \quad y(-1) = -1$$

has infinitely many solutions. Why does this not contradict Theorem 1?

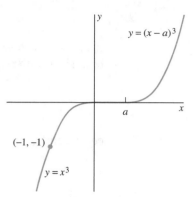

FIGURE 1.3.18.   A suggestion for Problem 33.

34. Verify that if k is a constant, then $y = kx$ satisfies the differential equation $xy' = y$. Hence conclude that the initial value problem

$$x\frac{dy}{dx} = y, \quad y(0) = 0$$

has infinitely many solutions on any open interval containing $x = 0$.

35. Use isoclines to construct a direction field for the differential equation $xy' = y$. Explain why this direction field suggests that the initial value problem

$$x\frac{dy}{dx} = y, \quad y(a) = b$$

has   (a) a unique solution if $a \neq 0$,   (b) no solution if $a = 0$ and $b \neq 0$,   (c) infinitely many solutions if $a = b = 0$. Are these results consistent with Theorem 1?

36. Consider the differential equation $dy/dx = 4x\sqrt{y}$ for $y \geqq 0$. Apply Theorem 1 to find those points (a, b) such that a solution of the differential equation *must* exist on an open interval J containing a. Next, find those points (a, b) such that a unique solution exists on an open interval J_0 containing a. Then find how many solutions pass through $(0, 0)$. (*Suggestion*: Note that $y_1(x) \equiv 0$ is a solution, as is $y_2(x) = (x^2 + C)^2$ if $x^2 + C \geqq 0$.)

1.4 SEPARABLE EQUATIONS AND APPLICATIONS

The first-order differential equation

$$\frac{dy}{dx} = H(x, y) \tag{1}$$

is called **separable** provided that $H(x, y)$ can be written as the product of a function of x and a function of y:

$$\frac{dy}{dx} = g(x)\phi(y) = \frac{g(x)}{f(y)},$$

where $\phi(y) = 1/f(y)$. In this case the variables x and y can be *separated*—isolated on opposite sides of an equation—by writing informally the equation

$$f(y)\,dy = g(x)\,dx,$$

which we understand to be concise notation for the differential equation

$$f(y)\frac{dy}{dx} = g(x). \tag{2}$$

It is easy to solve this special type of differential equation simply by integrating both sides with respect to x:

$$\int f(y(x))\frac{dy}{dx}\, dx = \int g(x)\, dx + C;$$

equivalently,

$$\int f(y)\, dy = \int g(x)\, dx + C. \tag{3}$$

All that is required is that the antiderivatives

$$F(y) = \int f(y)\, dy \quad \text{and} \quad G(x) = \int g(x)\, dx$$

can be found. To see that Eqs. (2) and (3) are equivalent, note the following consequence of the chain rule:

$$D_x[F(y(x))] = F'(y(x))y'(x) = f(y)\frac{dy}{dx} = g(x) = D_x[G(x)],$$

which in turn is equivalent to

$$F(y(x)) = G(x) + C, \tag{4}$$

because two functions have the same derivative on an interval if and only if they differ by a constant on that interval.

EXAMPLE 1   Solve the initial value problem

$$\frac{dy}{dx} = -6xy, \quad y(0) = 7.$$

Solution   Informally, we divide both sides of the differential equation by y and multiply each side by dx to get

$$\frac{dy}{y} = -6x\, dx.$$

Hence

$$\int \frac{dy}{y} = \int (-6x)\, dx;$$

$$\ln|y| = -3x^2 + C.$$

We see from the initial condition $y(0) = 7$ that $y(x)$ is positive near $x = 0$, so we may delete the absolute value symbols:

$$\ln y = -3x^2 + C,$$

and hence

$$y(x) = e^{-3x^2+C} = e^{-3x^2}e^C = Ae^{-3x^2},$$

where $A = e^C$. The condition $y(0) = 7$ yields $A = 7$, so the desired solution is

$$y(x) = 7e^{-3x^2}.$$

This is the top solution curve shown in Fig. 1.4.1.

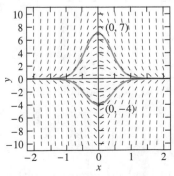

FIGURE 1.4.1. Direction field and solution curves for $y' = -6xy$ in Example 1.

Remark: Suppose, instead, that the initial condition in Example 1 had been $y(0) = -4$. Then it would follow that $y(x)$ is *negative* near $x = 0$. We should therefore replace $|y|$ with $-y$ in the integrated equation $\ln|y| = -3x^2 + C$ to obtain

$$\ln(-y) = -3x^2 + C.$$

The initial condition then yields $C = \ln 4$, so $\ln(-y) = -3x^2 + \ln 4$, and hence

$$y(x) = -4e^{-3x^2}.$$

This is the bottom solution curve in Fig. 1.4.1. ∎

EXAMPLE 2   Solve the differential equation

$$\frac{dy}{dx} = \frac{4 - 2x}{3y^2 - 5}. \tag{5}$$

Solution   When we separate the variables and integrate both sides, we get

$$\int (3y^2 - 5)\,dy = \int (4 - 2x)\,dx;$$

$$y^3 - 5y = 4x - x^2 + C. \tag{6}$$

This equation is not readily solved for y as an explicit function of x. ∎

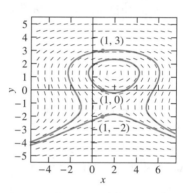

FIGURE 1.4.2. Direction field and solution curves for $y' = (4 - 2x)/(3y^2 - 5)$ in Example 2.

As Example 2 illustrates, it may or may not be possible or practical to solve Eq. (4) explicitly for y in terms of x. If not, then we call (4) an *implicit solution* of the differential equation in (2). Thus Eq. (6) gives an implicit solution of the differential equation in (5). Although it is not convenient to solve Eq. (6) explicitly in terms of x, we see that each solution curve $y = y(x)$ lies on a contour (or level) curve where the function

$$H(x, y) = x^2 - 4x + y^3 - 5y$$

is constant. Figure 1.4.2 shows several of these contour curves.

EXAMPLE 3   To solve the initial value problem

$$\frac{dy}{dx} = \frac{4 - 2x}{3y^2 - 5}, \quad y(1) = 3, \tag{7}$$

we substitute $x = 1$ and $y = 3$ in Eq. (6) and get $C = 9$. Thus the desired particular solution $y(x)$ is defined implicitly by the equation

$$y^3 - 5y = 4x - x^2 + 9. \tag{8}$$

The corresponding solution curve $y = y(x)$ lies on the upper contour curve in Fig. 1.4.2—the one passing through $(1, 3)$. Because the graph of a differentiable solution cannot have a vertical tangent line anywhere, it appears from the figure that this particular solution is defined on the interval $(-2, 6)$ but not on the interval $(-3, 7)$. ∎

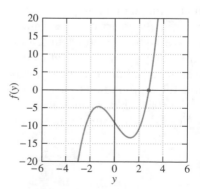

FIGURE 1.4.3. Graph of $f(y) = y^3 - 5y - 9$.

Remark 1: When a specific value of x is substituted in Eq. (8), we can attempt to solve numerically for y. For instance, $x = 4$ yields the equation

$$f(y) = y^3 - 5y - 9 = 0.$$

Figure 1.4.3 shows the graph of f. With a graphing calculator we can solve for the single real root $y \approx 2.8552$. This yields the value $y(4) \approx 2.8552$ of the particular solution in Example 3.

Remark 2: If the initial condition in (7) is replaced with the condition $y(1) = 0$, then the resulting particular solution of the differential equation in (5) lies on the lower "half" of the oval contour curve in Fig. 1.4.2. It appears that this particular solution through $(1, 0)$ is defined on the interval $(0, 4)$ but not on the interval $(-1, 5)$. On the other hand, with the initial condition $y(1) = -2$ we get the lower contour curve in Fig. 1.4.2. This particular solution is defined for all x. Thus the initial condition can determine whether a particular solution is defined on the whole real line or only on some bounded interval.   ■

Implicit Solutions and Singular Solutions

In general, the equation $K(x, y) = 0$ is called an **implicit solution** of a differential equation if it is satisfied (on some interval) by some solution $y = y(x)$ of the differential equation. But note that a particular solution $y = y(x)$ of $K(x, y) = 0$ may or may not satisfy a given initial condition. For example, differentiation of $x^2 + y^2 = 4$ yields

$$x + y\frac{dy}{dx} = 0,$$

so $x^2 + y^2 = 4$ is an implicit solution of the differential equation $x + yy' = 0$. But only the first of the two explicit solutions

$$y(x) = +\sqrt{4 - x^2} \quad \text{and} \quad y(x) = -\sqrt{4 - x^2}$$

satisfies the initial condition $y(0) = 2$ (Fig. 1.4.4).

The argument preceding Example 1 shows that every particular solution of Eq. (2) satisfies Eq. (4) for some choice of C; *this* is why it is appropriate to call (4) the **general solution** of Eq. (2).

Warning: Suppose, however, that we begin with the differential equation

$$\frac{dy}{dx} = g(x)h(y) \tag{9}$$

and divide by $h(y)$ to obtain the separated equation

$$\frac{1}{h(y)}\frac{dy}{dx} = g(x). \tag{10}$$

If y_0 is a root of the equation $h(y) = 0$—that is, if $h(y_0) = 0$—then the constant function $y(x) \equiv y_0$ is clearly a solution of Eq. (9), but may *not* be contained in the general solution of Eq. (10). Thus solutions of a differential equation may be lost upon division by a vanishing factor. (Indeed, false solutions may be gained upon multiplication by a vanishing factor. This phenomenon is similar to the introduction of extraneous roots in solving algebraic equations.)

In Section 1.5 we shall see that every particular solution of a *linear* first-order differential equation is contained in its general solution. By contrast, it is common for a nonlinear first-order differential equation to have both a general solution involving an arbitrary constant C and one or several particular solutions that cannot be obtained by selecting a value for C. These exceptional solutions are frequently called **singular solutions**. In Example 4 of Section 1.3 we found that the solution $y(x) \equiv 0$ was a singular solution of the equation $y^2 + x^2 y' = 0$; this solution cannot be obtained from the general solution $y(x) = x/(Cx - 1)$ by any choice of the constant C.

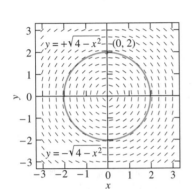

FIGURE 1.4.4. Direction field and solution curves for $y' = -x/y$.

EXAMPLE 4   Find all solutions of the differential equation

$$\frac{dy}{dx} = 6x(y - 1)^{2/3}.$$

Solution   Separation of variables gives

$$\int \frac{1}{3(y-1)^{2/3}}\, dy = \int 2x\, dx;$$

$$(y-1)^{1/3} = x^2 + C;$$

$$y(x) = 1 + (x^2 + C)^3.$$

Positive values of the arbitrary constant C give the solution curves in Fig. 1.4.5 that lie above the line $y = 1$, whereas negative values yield those that dip below it. The value $C = 0$ gives the solution $y(x) = 1 + x^6$, but *no* value of C gives the singular solution $y(x) \equiv 1$ that was lost when the variables were separated. Note that the two different solutions $y(x) \equiv 1$ and $y(x) = 1 + (x^2 - 1)^3$ both satisfy the initial condition $y(1) = 1$. Indeed, the whole singular solution curve $y = 1$ consists of points where the solution is not unique and where the function $f(x, y) = 6x(y - 1)^{2/3}$ is not differentiable. ∎

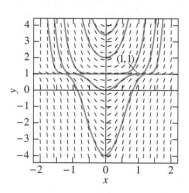

FIGURE 1.4.5. Direction field and solution curves for $y' = 6x(y - 1)^{2/3}$.

Natural Growth and Decay

The differential equation

➤
$$\frac{dy}{dx} = ky \quad (k \text{ a constant}) \tag{11}$$

serves as a mathematical model for a remarkably wide range of natural phenomena—any involving a quantity whose time rate of change is proportional to its current size. Here are some examples.

POPULATION GROWTH: Suppose that $P(t)$ is the number of individuals in a population (of humans, or insects, or bacteria) having *constant* birth and death rates β and δ (in births or deaths per individual per unit of time). Then, during a short time interval Δt, approximately $\beta P(t)\Delta t$ births and $\delta P(t)\Delta t$ deaths occur, so the change in $P(t)$ is given approximately by

$$\Delta P \approx (\beta - \delta)P(t)\Delta t,$$

and therefore

$$\frac{dP}{dt} = \lim_{\Delta t \to 0} \frac{\Delta P}{\Delta t} = kP, \tag{12}$$

where $k = \beta - \delta$.

COMPOUND INTEREST: Let $A(t)$ be the number of dollars in a savings account at time t (in years), and suppose that the interest is *compounded continuously* at an annual interest rate r. (Note that 10% annual interest means that $r = 0.10$.) Continuous compounding means that during a short time interval Δt, the amount of interest added to the account is approximately $\Delta A = rA(t)\Delta t$, so that

$$\frac{dA}{dt} = \lim_{\Delta t \to 0} \frac{\Delta A}{\Delta t} = rA. \tag{13}$$

RADIOACTIVE DECAY: Consider a sample of material that contains $N(t)$ atoms of a certain radioactive isotope at time t. It has been observed that a constant fraction of those radioactive atoms will spontaneously decay (into atoms of another element or into another isotope of the same element) during each unit of time. Consequently, the sample behaves exactly like a population with a constant death rate and no births. To write a model for $N(t)$, we use Eq. (12) with N in place of P, with $k > 0$ in place of δ, and with $\beta = 0$. We thus get the differential equation

$$\frac{dN}{dt} = -kN. \tag{14}$$

The value of k depends on the particular radioactive isotope.

The key to the method of *radiocarbon dating* is that a constant proportion of the carbon atoms in any living creature is made up of the radioactive isotope ^{14}C of carbon. This proportion remains constant because the fraction of ^{14}C in the atmosphere remains almost constant, and living matter is continuously taking up carbon from the air or is consuming other living matter containing the same constant ratio of ^{14}C atoms to ordinary ^{12}C atoms. This same ratio permeates all life, because organic processes seem to make no distinction between the two isotopes.

The ratio of ^{14}C to normal carbon remains constant in the atmosphere because, although ^{14}C is radioactive and slowly decays, the amount is continuously replenished through the conversion of ^{14}N (ordinary nitrogen) to ^{14}C by cosmic rays bombarding the upper atmosphere. Over the long history of the planet, this decay and replenishment process has come into nearly steady state.

Of course, when a living organism dies, it ceases its metabolism of carbon and the process of radioactive decay begins to deplete its ^{14}C content. There is no replenishment of this ^{14}C, and consequently the ratio of ^{14}C to normal carbon begins to drop. By measuring this ratio, the amount of time elapsed since the death of the organism can be estimated. For such purposes it is necessary to measure the decay constant k. For ^{14}C, it is known that $k \approx 0.0001216$ if t is measured in years.

(Matters are not as simple as we have made them appear. In applying the technique of radiocarbon dating, extreme care must be taken to avoid contaminating the sample with organic matter or even with ordinary fresh air. In addition, the cosmic ray levels apparently have not been constant, so the ratio of ^{14}C in the atmosphere has varied over the past centuries. By using independent methods of dating samples, researchers in this area have compiled tables of correction factors to enhance the accuracy of this process.)

DRUG ELIMINATION: In many cases the amount $A(t)$ of a certain drug in the bloodstream, measured by the excess over the natural level of the drug, will decline at a rate proportional to the current excess amount. That is,

$$\frac{dA}{dt} = -\lambda A, \tag{15}$$

where $\lambda > 0$. The parameter λ is called the **elimination constant** of the drug.

The Natural Growth Equation

The prototype differential equation $dx/dt = kx$ with $x(t) > 0$ and k a constant (either negative or positive) is readily solved by separating the variables and integrating:

$$\int \frac{1}{x}\, dx = \int k\, dt;$$

$$\ln x = kt + C.$$

Then we solve for x:

$$e^{\ln x} = e^{kt+C}; \quad x = x(t) = e^C e^{kt} = Ae^{kt}.$$

Because C is a constant, so is $A = e^C$. It is also clear that $A = x(0) = x_0$, so the particular solution of Eq. (11) with the initial condition $x(0) = x_0$ is simply

$$x(t) = x_0 e^{kt}. \tag{16}$$

Because of the presence of the natural exponential function in its solution, the differential equation

$$\frac{dx}{dt} = kx \tag{17}$$

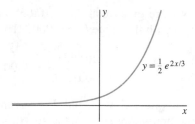

FIGURE 1.4.6.   Natural growth.   **FIGURE 1.4.7.**   Natural decay.

is often called the **exponential** or **natural growth equation.** Figure 1.4.6 shows a typical graph of $x(t)$ in the case $k > 0$; the case $k < 0$ is illustrated in Fig. 1.4.7.

EXAMPLE 5   In May 1993 the world population had reached 5.5 billion and was increasing then at the rate of 250 thousand persons each day. Assuming constant birth and death rates, when should a world population of 11 billion be expected?

Solution   From Eq. (16), with P in place of x, we know that $P(t) = P_0 e^{kt}$. We measure the world population $P(t)$ in billions and measure time t in years. We take $t = 0$ to correspond to 1993, so that $P_0 = 5.5$. The fact that P was increasing by 250 thousand, or 0.00025 billion, persons per day at time $t = 0$ means that

$$P'(0) = (0.00025)(365.25) \approx 0.0913$$

billion per year. From Eq. (12) we now obtain

$$k = \left[\frac{1}{P} \cdot \frac{dP}{dt} \right]_{t=0} = \frac{P'(0)}{P(0)} \approx \frac{0.0913}{5.5} = 0.0166.$$

Thus the population was growing at the rate of about 1.66% in 1993.

To find the time T when the population will be 11 billion, we need only solve the equation

$$11 = P(T) = (5.5)e^{(0.0166)T}$$

for

$$T = \frac{\ln(11/5.5)}{0.0166} \approx 42 \text{ (years)},$$

which corresponds to the year 2035. Assuming that birth and death rates held constant, the world population thereafter would continue to double every 42 years. ■

The decay constant of a radioactive isotope is often specified in terms of another empirical constant, the *half-life* of the isotope, because this parameter is more convenient. The **half-life** τ of a radioactive isotope is the time required for *half* of it to decay. To find the relationship between k and τ, we set $t = \tau$ and $N = \frac{1}{2}N_0$ in the equation $N(t) = N_0 e^{kt}$, so that $\frac{1}{2}N_0 = N_0 e^{k\tau}$. When we solve for τ, we find that

$$\tau = \frac{\ln 2}{k}. \tag{18}$$

For example, the half-life of ^{14}C is $\tau \approx (\ln 2)/(0.0001216)$, approximately 5700 years.

EXAMPLE 6   A specimen of charcoal found at Stonehenge turns out to contain 63% as much ^{14}C as a sample of present-day charcoal of equal mass. What is the age of the sample?

Solution   We take $t = 0$ as the time of the death of the tree from which the Stonehenge charcoal was made and N_0 as the number of ^{14}C atoms that the Stonehenge sample contained then. We are given that $N = (0.63)N_0$ now, so we solve the equation $(0.63)N_0 = N_0 e^{-kt}$ with the value $k = 0.0001216$. Thus we find that

$$t = -\frac{\ln(0.63)}{0.0001216} \approx 3800 \text{ (years)}.$$

Thus the sample is about 3800 years old. If it has any connection with the builders of Stonehenge, our computations suggest that this observatory, monument, or temple—whichever it may be—dates from 1800 B.C. or earlier. ∎

Cooling and Heating

According to Newton's law of cooling (Eq. (3) of Section 1.1), the time rate of change of the temperature $T(t)$ of a body immersed in a medium of constant temperature A is proportional to the difference $A - T$. That is,

$$\frac{dT}{dt} = k(A - T), \tag{19}$$

where k is a positive constant. This is an instance of the linear first-order differential equation with constant coefficients:

$$\frac{dx}{dt} = ax + b. \tag{20}$$

It includes the exponential equation as a special case ($b = 0$) and is also easy to solve by separation of variables.

EXAMPLE 7   A 4-lb roast, initially at $50°F$, is placed in a $375°F$ oven at 5:00 P.M. After 75 minutes it is found that the temperature $T(t)$ of the roast is $125°F$. When will the roast be $150°F$ (medium rare)?

Solution   We take time t in minutes, with $t = 0$ corresponding to 5:00 P.M. We also assume (somewhat unrealistically) that at any instant the temperature $T(t)$ of the roast is uniform throughout. We have $T(t) < A = 375$, $T(0) = 50$, and $T(75) = 125$. Hence

$$\frac{dT}{dt} = k(375 - T);$$

$$\int \frac{1}{375 - T} \, dT = \int k \, dt;$$

$$-\ln(375 - T) = kt + C;$$

$$375 - T = Be^{-kt}.$$

Now $T(0) = 50$ implies that $B = 325$, so $T(t) = 375 - 325e^{-kt}$. We also know that $T = 125$ when $t = 75$. Substitution of these values in the preceding equation yields

$$k = -\tfrac{1}{75} \ln \left(\tfrac{250}{375}\right) \approx 0.0035.$$

Hence we finally solve the equation

$$150 = 375 - 215e^{(-0.0035)t}$$

for $t = -[\ln(225/375)]/(0.0035) \approx 105$ (min), the total cooking time required. Because the roast was placed in the oven at 5:00 P.M., it should be removed at about 6:45 P.M. ∎

Torricelli's Law

Suppose that a water tank has a hole with area a at its bottom, from which water is leaking. Denote by $y(t)$ the depth of water in the tank at time t, and by $V(t)$ the volume of water in the tank then. It is plausible—and true, under ideal conditions—that the velocity of water exiting through the hole is

$$v = \sqrt{2gy}, \tag{21}$$

which is the velocity a drop of water would acquire in falling freely from the surface of the water to the hole (see Problem 31 of Section 1.2). One can derive this formula beginning with the assumption that the sum of the kinetic and potential energy of the system remains constant. Under real conditions, taking into account the constriction of a water jet from an orifice, $v = c\sqrt{2gy}$, where c is an empirical constant between 0 and 1 (usually about 0.6 for a small continuous stream of water). For simplicity we take $c = 1$ in the following discussion.

As a consequence of Eq. (21), we have

$$\frac{dV}{dt} = -av = -a\sqrt{2gy}; \tag{22a}$$

equivalently,

$$\frac{dV}{dt} = -k\sqrt{y} \quad \text{where} \quad k = a\sqrt{2g}. \tag{22b}$$

This is a statement of Torricelli's law for a draining tank. If $A(y)$ denotes the horizontal cross-sectional area of the tank at height y above the hole, the method of volume by cross sections gives

$$V = \int_0^y A(y)\, dy,$$

so the fundamental theorem of calculus implies that $dV/dy = A(y)$ and therefore that

$$\frac{dV}{dt} = \frac{dV}{dy} \cdot \frac{dy}{dt} = A(y)\frac{dy}{dt}. \tag{23}$$

From Eqs. (22) and (23) we finally obtain

$$A(y)\frac{dy}{dt} = -a\sqrt{2gy} = -k\sqrt{y}, \tag{24}$$

an alternative form of Torricelli's law.   ∎

EXAMPLE 8   A hemispherical bowl has top radius 4 ft and at time $t = 0$ is full of water. At that moment a circular hole with diameter 1 in. is opened in the bottom of the tank. How long will it take for all the water to drain from the tank?

Solution   From the right triangle in Fig. 1.4.8, we see that

$$A(y) = \pi r^2 = \pi\left[16 - (4 - y)^2\right] = \pi(8y - y^2).$$

With $g = 32$ ft/s^2, Eq. (24) becomes

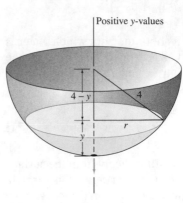

Positive y-values

$4 - y$

4

r

y

FIGURE 1.4.8. Draining a hemispherical tank.

$$\pi(8y - y^2)\frac{dy}{dt} = -\pi \left(\tfrac{1}{24}\right)^2 \sqrt{2 \cdot 32y};$$

$$\int (8y^{1/2} - y^{3/2})\, dy = -\int \tfrac{1}{72}\, dt;$$

$$\tfrac{16}{3}y^{3/2} - \tfrac{2}{5}y^{5/2} = -\tfrac{1}{72}t + C.$$

Now $y(0) = 4$, so

$$C = \tfrac{16}{3} \cdot 4^{3/2} - \tfrac{2}{5} \cdot 4^{5/2} = \tfrac{448}{15}.$$

The tank is empty when $y = 0$, thus when

$$t = 72 \cdot \tfrac{448}{15} \approx 2150 \text{ (s)};$$

that is, about 35 min 50 s. So it takes slightly less than 36 min for the tank to drain. ∎

1.4 Problems

Find general solutions (implicit if necessary, explicit if convenient) of the differential equations in Problems 1 through 18. Primes denote derivatives with respect to x.

1. $\dfrac{dy}{dx} + 2xy = 0$

2. $\dfrac{dy}{dx} + 2xy^2 = 0$

3. $\dfrac{dy}{dx} = y \sin x$

4. $(1 + x)\dfrac{dy}{dx} = 4y$

5. $2\sqrt{x}\dfrac{dy}{dx} = \sqrt{1 - y^2}$

6. $\dfrac{dy}{dx} = 3\sqrt{xy}$

7. $\dfrac{dy}{dx} = (64xy)^{1/3}$

8. $\dfrac{dy}{dx} = 2x \sec y$

9. $(1 - x^2)\dfrac{dy}{dx} = 2y$

10. $(1 + x)^2\dfrac{dy}{dx} = (1 + y)^2$

11. $y' = xy^3$

12. $yy' = x(y^2 + 1)$

13. $y^3\dfrac{dy}{dx} = (y^4 + 1)\cos x$

14. $\dfrac{dy}{dx} = \dfrac{1 + \sqrt{x}}{1 + \sqrt{y}}$

15. $\dfrac{dy}{dx} = \dfrac{(x - 1)y^5}{x^2(2y^3 - y)}$

16. $(x^2 + 1)(\tan y)y' = x$

17. $y' = 1 + x + y + xy$ (*Suggestion*: Factor the right-hand side.)

18. $x^2y' = 1 - x^2 + y^2 - x^2y^2$

Find explicit particular solutions of the initial value problems in Problems 19 through 28.

19. $\dfrac{dy}{dx} = ye^x$, $y(0) = 2e$

20. $\dfrac{dy}{dx} = 3x^2(y^2 + 1)$, $y(0) = 1$

21. $2y\dfrac{dy}{dx} = \dfrac{x}{\sqrt{x^2 - 16}}$, $y(5) = 2$

22. $\dfrac{dy}{dx} = 4x^3y - y$, $y(1) = -3$

23. $\dfrac{dy}{dx} + 1 = 2y$, $y(1) = 1$

24. $(\tan x)\dfrac{dy}{dx} = y$, $y\left(\tfrac{1}{2}\pi\right) = \tfrac{1}{2}\pi$

25. $x\dfrac{dy}{dx} - y = 2x^2y$, $y(1) = 1$

26. $\dfrac{dy}{dx} = 2xy^2 + 3x^2y^2$, $y(1) = -1$

27. $\dfrac{dy}{dx} = 6e^{2x-y}$, $y(0) = 0$

28. $2\sqrt{x}\dfrac{dy}{dx} = \cos^2 y$, $y(4) = \pi/4$

29. (Population growth) A certain city had a population of 25000 in 1960 and a population of 30000 in 1970. Assume that its population will continue to grow exponentially at a constant rate. What population can its city planners expect in the year 2000?

30. (Population growth) In a certain culture of bacteria, the number of bacteria increased sixfold in 10 h. How long did it take for the population to double?

31. (Radiocarbon dating) Carbon extracted from an ancient skull contained only one-sixth as much ^{14}C as carbon extracted from present-day bone. How old is the skull?

32. (Radiocarbon dating) Carbon taken from a purported relic of the time of Christ contained 4.6×10^{10} atoms of ^{14}C per gram. Carbon extracted from a present-day specimen of the same substance contained 5.0×10^{10} atoms of ^{14}C per gram. Compute the approximate age of the relic. What is your opinion as to its authenticity?

33. (Continuously compounded interest) Upon the birth of their first child, a couple deposited $5000 in an account that pays 8% interest compounded continuously. The interest payments are allowed to accumulate. How much will the account contain on the child's eighteenth birthday?

34. (Continuously compounded interest) Suppose that you discover in your attic an overdue library book on which your grandfather owed a fine of 30 cents 100 years ago. If an overdue fine grows exponentially at a 5% annual rate compounded continuously, how much would you have to pay if you returned the book today?

35. (Drug elimination) Suppose that sodium pentobarbitol is used to anesthetize a dog. The dog is anesthetized when its bloodstream contains at least 45 milligrams (mg) of sodium pentobarbitol per kilogram of the dog's body weight. Suppose also that sodium pentobarbitol is eliminated exponentially from the dog's bloodstream, with a

half-life of 5 h. What single dose should be administered in order to anesthetize a 50-kg dog for 1 h?

36. The half-life of radioactive cobalt is 5.27 years. Suppose that a nuclear accident has left the level of cobalt radiation in a certain region at 100 times the level acceptable for human habitation. How long will it be until the region is again habitable? (Ignore the probable presence of other radioactive isotopes.)

37. Suppose that a mineral body formed in an ancient cataclysm—perhaps the formation of the earth itself—originally contained the uranium isotope ^{238}U (which has a half-life of 4.51×10^9 years) but no lead, the end product of the radioactive decay of ^{238}U. If today the ratio of ^{238}U atoms to lead atoms in the mineral body is 0.9, when did the cataclysm occur?

38. A certain moon rock was found to contain equal numbers of potassium and argon atoms. Assume that all the argon is the result of radioactive decay of potassium (its half-life is about 1.28×10^9 years) and that one of every nine potassium atom disintegrations yields an argon atom. What is the age of the rock, measured from the time it contained only potassium?

39. A pitcher of buttermilk initially at $25°C$ is to be cooled by setting it on the front porch, where the temperature if $0°C$. Suppose that the temperature of the buttermilk has dropped to $15°C$ after 20 min. When will it be at $5°C$?

40. When sugar is dissolved in water, the amount A that remains undissolved after t minutes satisfies the differential equation $dA/dt = -kA$ ($k > 0$). If 25% of the sugar dissolves after 1 min, how long does it take for half of the sugar to dissolve?

41. The intensity I of light at a depth of x meters below the surface of a lake satisfies the differential equation $dI/dx = (-1.4)I$. (a) At what depth is the intensity half the intensity I_0 at the surface (where $x = 0$)? (b) What is the intensity at a depth of 10 m (as a fraction of I_0)? (c) At what depth will the intensity be 1% of that at the surface?

42. The barometric pressure p (in inches of mercury) at an altitude x miles above sea level satisfies the initial value problem $dp/dx = (-0.2)p$, $p(0) = 29.92$. (a) Calculate the barometric pressure at 10000 ft and again at 30000 ft. (b) Without prior conditioning, few people can survive when the pressure drops to less than 15 in. of mercury. How high is that?

43. Consider a savings account that contains A_0 dollars initially and earns interest at the annual rate r compounded continuously. Suppose that the interest is allowed to accrue and that additional deposits are added to this account at the rate of Q dollars per year. To simplify the mathematical model, assume that these deposits are made continuously rather than (for instance) monthly. (a) Derive the differential equation for the amount $A(t)$ in the account at time t years. (b) Suppose that you wish to arrange, at the time of her birth, for your daughter to have $40000 available for college expenses on her eighteenth birthday. You plan to do so by making small—essentially continuous—deposits in a savings account, at the rate of Q thousand dollars per year. This account accumulates interest at an annual rate of 11%, compounded continuously. What should Q be so that you may achieve your goal?

44. According to one cosmological theory, there were equal amounts of the two uranium isotopes ^{235}U and ^{238}U at the creation of the universe in the "big bang." At present there are 137.7 atoms of ^{238}U for each atom of ^{235}U. Using the half-lives 4.51×10^9 years for ^{238}U and 7.10×10^8 years for ^{235}U, calculate the age of the universe.

45. A cake is removed from an oven at $210°F$ and left to cool at room temperature, which is $70°F$. After 30 min the temperature of the cake is $140°F$. When will it be $100°F$?

46. (a) Payments are made continuously on a mortgage of P_0 dollars at the constant rate of c dollars per month. Let $P(t)$ denote the principal (amount still owed to the lender) after t months, and let r denote the monthly interest rate paid by the borrower (for instance, $r = (0.12)/12 = 0.01$ if the annual interest rate is 12%). Derive the differential equation

$$\frac{dP}{dt} = rP - c, \quad P(0) = P_0.$$

(b) An automobile loan of $10800 is to be paid off continuously over a period of 60 months. Determine the monthly payment required if the annual interest rate is 12%. (c) Repeat part (b) with annual interest rate 18%.

47. A certain piece of dubious information about phenylethylamine in the drinking water began to spread one day in a city with a population of 100,000. Within a week, 10000 people had heard this rumor. Assume that the rate of increase of the number who have heard the rumor is proportional to the number who have not yet heard it. How long will it be until half the population of the city has heard the rumor?

48. A tank is shaped like a vertical cylinder; it initially contains water to a depth of 9 ft, and a bottom plug is removed at time $t = 0$ (hours). After 1 h the depth of the water has dropped to 4 ft. How long does it take for all the water to drain from the tank?

49. Suppose that the tank of Problem 48 has a radius of 3 ft and that its bottom hole is circular with radius 1 in. How long will it take the water (initially 9 ft deep) to drain completely?

50. At time $t = 0$ the bottom plug (at the vertex) of a full conical water tank 16 ft high is removed. After 1 h the water in the tank is 9 ft deep. When will the tank be empty?

51. Suppose that a cylindrical tank initially containing V_0 gallons of water drains (through a bottom hole) in T minutes. Use Torricelli's law to show that the volume of water in the tank after $t \leq T$ minutes is $V = V_0 \left[1 - (t/T)^2\right]$.

52. A water tank has the shape obtained by revolving the curve $y = x^{4/3}$ around the y-axis. A plug at the bottom is removed at 12 noon, when the depth of water in the tank is 12 ft. At 1 P.M. the depth of the water is 6 ft. When will the tank be empty?

53. A water tank has the shape obtained by revolving the parabola $x^2 = by$ around the y-axis. The water depth is 4 ft at 12 noon, when a circular plug in the bottom of the tank is removed. At 1 P.M. the depth of the water is 1 ft. (a) Find the depth $y(t)$ of water remaining after t hours. (b) When will the tank be empty? (c) If the initial radius of the top surface of the water is 2 ft, what is the radius of the circular hole in the bottom?

54. A cylindrical tank with length 5 ft and radius 3 ft is situated with its axis horizontal. If a circular bottom hole with a radius of 1 in. is opened and the tank is initially half full of xylene, how long will it take for the liquid to drain completely?

55. A spherical tank of radius 4 ft is full of gasoline when a circular bottom hole with radius 1 in. is opened. How long will be required for all the gasoline to drain from the tank?

56. Suppose that an initially full hemispherical water tank of radius 1 m has its flat side as its bottom. It has a bottom hole of radius 1 cm. If this bottom hole is opened at 1 P.M., when will the tank be empty?

57. Consider the initially full hemispherical water tank of Example 8, except that the radius r of its circular bottom hole is now unknown. At 1 P.M. the bottom hole is opened and at 1:30 P.M. the depth of water in the tank is 2 ft. (a) Use Torricelli's law in the form $dV/dt = -(0.6)\pi r^2\sqrt{2gy}$ (taking constriction into account) to determine when the tank will be empty. (b) What is the radius of the bottom hole?

58. (The *clepsydra*, or water clock) A 12-h water clock is to be designed with the dimensions shown in Fig. 1.4.9, shaped like the surface obtained by revolving the curve $y = f(x)$ around the y-axis. What should be this curve, and what should be the radius of the circular bottom hole, in order that the water level will fall at the *constant* rate of 4 inches per hour (in./h)?

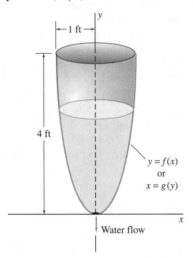

FIGURE 1.4.9. The clepsydra.

59. Just before midday the body of an apparent homicide victim is found in a room that is kept at a constant temperature of 70°F. At 12 noon the temperature of the body is 80°F and at 1 P.M. it is 25°F. Assume that the temperature of the body at the time of death was 98.6°F and that it has cooled in accord with Newton's law. What was the time of death?

60. Early one morning it began to snow at a constant rate. At 7 A.M. a snowplow set off to clear a road. By 8 A.M. it had traveled 2 miles, but it took two more hours (until 10 A.M.) for the snowplow to go an additional 2 miles. (a) Let $t = 0$ when it began to snow and let x denote the distance traveled by the snowplow at time t. Assuming that the snowplow clears snow from the road at a constant rate (in cubic feet per hour, say), show that

$$k\frac{dx}{dt} = \frac{1}{t}$$

where k is a constant. (b) What time did it start snowing? (*Answer*: 6 A.M.)

61. A snowplow sets off at 7 A.M. as in Problem 60. Suppose now that by 8 A.M. it had traveled 4 miles and that by 9 A.M. it had moved an additional 3 miles. What time did it start snowing? This is a more difficult snowplow problem because now a transcendental equation must be solved numerically to find the value of k. (*Answer*: 4:27 A.M.)

1.5 LINEAR FIRST-ORDER EQUATIONS

In Section 1.4 we saw how to solve a separable differential equation by integrating *after* multiplying both sides by an appropriate factor. For instance, to solve the equation

$$\frac{dy}{dx} = 2xy \quad (y > 0), \tag{1}$$

we multiply both sides by the factor $1/y$ to get

$$\frac{1}{y} \cdot \frac{dy}{dx} = 2x; \quad \text{that is,} \quad D_x(\ln y) = D_x\left(x^2\right). \tag{2}$$

Because each side of the equation in (2) is recognizable as a *derivative* (with respect to the independent variable x), all that remains are two simple integrations, which yield $\ln y = x^2 + C$. For this reason, the function $\rho(y) = 1/y$ is called an *integrating factor* for the original equation in (1). An **integrating factor** for a differential equation is a function $\rho(x, y)$ such that the multiplication of each side of the differential equation by $\rho(x, y)$ yields an equation in which each side is recognizable as a derivative.

With the aid of the appropriate integrating factor, there is a standard technique for solving the *linear* **first-order equation**

$$\frac{dy}{dx} + P(x)y = Q(x) \tag{3}$$

on an interval on which the coefficient functions $P(x)$ and $Q(x)$ are continuous. We multiply each side in Eq. (3) by the integrating factor

$$\rho(x) = e^{\int P(x)\,dx}. \tag{4}$$

The result is

$$e^{\int P(x)\,dx} \frac{dy}{dx} + P(x)e^{\int P(x)\,dx} y = Q(x)e^{\int P(x)\,dx}. \tag{5}$$

Because

$$D_x \left[\int P(x)\,dx \right] = P(x),$$

the left-hand side is the derivative of the *product* $y(x) \cdot e^{\int P(x)\,dx}$, so Eq. (5) is equivalent to

$$D_x \left[y(x) \cdot e^{\int P(x)\,dx} \right] = Q(x)e^{\int P(x)\,dx}.$$

Integration of both sides of this equation gives

$$y(x)e^{\int P(x)\,dx} = \int \left(Q(x)e^{\int P(x)\,dx} \right) dx + C.$$

Finally solving for y, we obtain the general solution of the linear first-order equation in (3):

$$y(x) = e^{-\int P(x)\,dx} \left[\int \left(Q(x)e^{\int P(x)\,dx} \right) dx + C \right]. \tag{6}$$

This formula should **not** be memorized. In a specific problem it generally is simpler to use the *method* by which we developed the formula. That is, in order to solve an equation written in the form in Eq. (3) with the coefficient functions $P(x)$ and $Q(x)$ displayed explicitly, you should carry out the following steps.

METHOD: SOLUTION OF FIRST-ORDER EQUATIONS

1. Begin by calculating the integrating factor $\rho(x) = e^{\int P(x)\,dx}$.
2. Then multiply both sides of the differential equation by $\rho(x)$.
3. Next, recognize the left-hand side of the resulting equation as the derivative of a product:
$$D_x\left[\rho(x)y(x)\right] = \rho(x)Q(x).$$
4. Finally, integrate this equation,

$$\rho(x)y(x) = \int \rho(x)Q(x)\,dx + C,$$

then solve for y to obtain the general solution of the original differential equation.

Remark 1: Given an initial condition $y(x_0) = y_0$, you can (as usual) substitute $x = x_0$ and $y = y_0$ into the general solution and solve for the value of C yielding the particular solution that satisfies this initial condition.

Remark 2:   The integrating factor $\rho(x)$ is determined only to within a multiplicative constant. If we replace

$$\int P(x)\,dx \quad \text{with} \quad \int P(x)\,dx + K$$

in Eq. (4), the result is

$$\rho(x) = e^{K + \int P(x)\,dx} = e^{K} e^{\int P(x)\,dx}.$$

But the constant factor e^{K} does not affect the result of multiplying both sides of the differential equation in (3) by $\rho(x)$. Hence we may choose for $\int P(x)\,dx$ any convenient antiderivative of $P(x)$. ∎

EXAMPLE 1   Solve the initial value problem

$$\frac{dy}{dx} - y = \tfrac{11}{8} e^{-x/3}, \quad y(0) = -1.$$

Solution   Here we have $P(x) \equiv -1$ and $Q(x) = \tfrac{11}{8} e^{-x/3}$, so the integrating factor is

$$\rho(x) = e^{\int (-1)\,dx} = e^{-x}.$$

Multiplication of both sides of the given equation by e^{-x} yields

$$e^{-x} \frac{dy}{dx} - e^{-x} y = \tfrac{11}{8} e^{-4x/3}, \tag{7}$$

which we recognize as

$$\frac{d}{dx}\left(e^{-x} y \right) = \tfrac{11}{8} e^{-4x/3}.$$

Hence integration with respect to x gives

$$e^{-x} y = \int \tfrac{11}{8} e^{-4x/3}\,dx = -\tfrac{33}{32} e^{-4x/3} + C,$$

and multiplication by e^{x} gives the general solution

$$y(x) = C e^{x} - \tfrac{33}{32} e^{-x/3}. \tag{8}$$

Substitution of $x = 0$ and $y = -1$ now gives $C = \tfrac{1}{32}$, so the desired particular solution is

$$y(x) = \tfrac{1}{32} e^{x} - \tfrac{33}{32} e^{-x/3} = \tfrac{1}{32}\left(e^{x} - 33 e^{-x/3} \right). \quad ∎$$

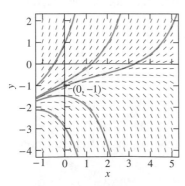

FIGURE 1.5.1.   Direction field and solution curves for $y' = y + \tfrac{11}{8} e^{-x/3}$.

Remark: Figure 1.5.1 shows a direction field and typical solution curves for Eq. (7), including the one passing through the point $(0, -1)$. Note that some solutions grow rapidly in the positive direction as x increases, while others grow rapidly in the negative direction. The behavior of a given solution curve is determined by its initial condition $y(0) = y_0$. The two types of behavior are separated by the particular solution $y(x) = -\tfrac{33}{32} e^{-x/3}$ for which $C = 0$ in Eq. (8), so $y_0 = -\tfrac{33}{32}$. If $y_0 > -\tfrac{33}{32}$ then $C > 0$ in Eq. (8), so the term e^{x} eventually dominates the behavior of $y(x)$, and hence $y(x) \to +\infty$ as $x \to +\infty$. But if $y_0 < -\tfrac{33}{32}$ then $C < 0$, so both terms in $y(x)$ are negative and therefore $y(x) \to -\infty$ as $x \to +\infty$. Thus the initial condition $y_0 = -\tfrac{33}{32}$ is *critical* in the sense that solutions that start above $-\tfrac{33}{32}$ on the y-axis grow in the positive direction, while solutions that start lower than $-\tfrac{33}{32}$ grow in the negative direction as $x \to +\infty$. The interpretation of a mathematical model often hinges on finding such a critical condition that separates one kind of behavior of a solution from a different kind of behavior. ∎

EXAMPLE 2 Find a general solution of

$$(x^2 + 1)\frac{dy}{dx} + 3xy = 6x. \tag{9}$$

Solution After division of both sides of the equation by $x^2 + 1$, we recognize the result

$$\frac{dy}{dx} + \frac{3x}{x^2 + 1}y = \frac{6x}{x^2 + 1}$$

as a first-order linear equation with $P(x) = 3x/(x^2 + 1)$ and $Q(x) = 6x/(x^2 + 1)$. Multiplication by

$$\rho(x) = \exp\left(\int \frac{3x}{x^2+1}\, dx\right) = \exp\left(\tfrac{3}{2}\ln(x^2 + 1)\right) = (x^2 + 1)^{3/2}$$

yields

$$(x^2 + 1)^{3/2}\frac{dy}{dx} + 3x(x^2 + 1)^{1/2}y = 6x(x^2 + 1)^{1/2},$$

and thus

$$D_x\left[(x^2 + 1)^{3/2}y\right] = 6x(x^2 + 1)^{1/2}.$$

Integration then yields

$$(x^2 + 1)^{3/2}y = \int 6x(x^2 + 1)^{1/2}\, dx = 2(x^2 + 1)^{3/2} + C.$$

Multiplication of both sides by $(x^2 + 1)^{-3/2}$ gives the general solution

$$y(x) = 2 + C(x^2 + 1)^{-3/2}. \tag{10}$$

■

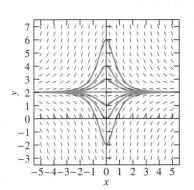

FIGURE 1.5.2. Direction field and solution curves for the differential equation in Eq. (9).

Remark: Figure 1.5.2 shows a direction field and typical solution curves for Eq. (9). Note that, as $x \to +\infty$, all other solution curves approach the constant solution curve $y(x) \equiv 2$ that corresponds to $C = 0$ in Eq. (10). This constant solution can be described as an *equilibrium solution* of the differential equation, because $y(0) = 2$ implies that $y(x) = 2$ for all x (and thus the value of the solution remains forever where it starts). ■

A Closer Look at the Method

The preceding derivation of the solution in Eq. (6) of the linear first-order equation $y' + Py = Q$ bears closer examination. Suppose that the coefficient functions $P(x)$ and $Q(x)$ are continuous on the (possibly unbounded) open interval I. Then the antiderivatives

$$\int P(x)\, dx \quad \text{and} \quad \int \left(Q(x)e^{\int P(x)\, dx}\right) dx$$

exist on I. Our derivative of Eq. (6) shows that *if* $y = y(x)$ is a solution of Eq. (3) on I, *then* $y(x)$ is given by the formula in Eq. (6) for some choice of the constant C. Conversely, you may verify by direct substitution (Problem 31) that the function $y(x)$ given in Eq. (6) satisfies Eq. (3). Finally, given a point x_0 of I and any number y_0, there is—as previously noted—a unique value of C such that $y(x_0) = y_0$. Consequently, we have proved the following existence-uniqueness theorem.

THEOREM 1: The Linear First-Order Equation

If the functions $P(x)$ and $Q(x)$ are continuous on the open interval I containing the point x_0, then the initial value problem

$$\frac{dy}{dx} + P(x)y = Q(x), \quad y(x_0) = y_0 \tag{11}$$

has a unique solution $y(x)$ on I, given by the formula in Eq. (6) with an appropriate value of C.   ∎

Remark 1: Theorem 1 gives a solution on the *entire* interval I for a *linear* differential equation, in contrast with Theorem 1 of Section 1.3, which guarantees only a solution on a possibly smaller interval J.

Remark 2: Theorem 1 tells us that every solution of Eq. (3) is included in the general solution given in Eq. (6). Thus a *linear* first-order differential equation has *no* singular solutions.

Remark 3: The appropriate value of the constant C in Eq. (6)—as needed to solve the initial value problem in Eq. (11)—can be selected "automatically" by writing

$$\rho(x) = \exp\left(\int_{x_0}^{x} P(t)\, dt\right),$$

$$y(x) = \frac{1}{\rho(x)}\left[y_0 + \int_{x_0}^{x} \rho(t) Q(t)\, dt\right]. \tag{12}$$

The indicated limits x_0 and x effect a choice of indefinite integrals in Eq. (6) that guarantees in advance that $\rho(x_0) = 1$ and that $y(x_0) = y_0$ (as you can verify directly by substituting $x = x_0$ in Eq. (12)).   ∎

EXAMPLE 3   Solve the initial value problem

$$x^2 \frac{dy}{dx} + xy = \sin x, \quad y(1) = y_0. \tag{13}$$

Solution   Division by x^2 gives the linear first-order equation

$$\frac{dy}{dx} + \frac{1}{x} y = \frac{\sin x}{x^2}$$

with $P(x) = 1/x$ and $Q(x) = (\sin x)/x^2$. With $x_0 = 1$ the integrating factor in (12) is

$$\rho(x) = \exp\left(\int_{1}^{x} \frac{1}{t}\, dt\right) = \exp(\ln x) = x,$$

so the desired particular solution is given by

$$y(x) = \frac{1}{x}\left[y_0 + \int_{1}^{x} \frac{\sin t}{t}\, dt\right]. \tag{14}$$

In accord with Theorem 1, this solution is defined on the whole positive x-axis.   ∎

Comment: In general, an integral such as the one in Eq. (14) would (for given x) need to be approximated numerically—using Simpson's rule, for instance—to find the value $y(x)$ of the solution at x. In this case, however, we have the sine integral function

$$\mathrm{Si}(x) = \int_{0}^{x} \frac{\sin t}{t}\, dt,$$

which appears with sufficient frequency in applications that its values have been tabulated. A good set of tables of special functions is Abramowitz and Stegun, *Handbook of Mathematical Functions* (New York: Dover, 1965). Then the particular solution in Eq. (14) reduces to

$$y(x) = \frac{1}{x}\left[y_0 + \int_{0}^{x} \frac{\sin t}{t}\, dt - \int_{0}^{1} \frac{\sin t}{t}\, dt\right] = \frac{1}{x}[y_0 + \mathrm{Si}(x) - \mathrm{Si}(1)]. \tag{15}$$

The sine integral function is available in most technical computing systems and can be used to plot typical solution curves defined by Eq. (15). Figure 1.5.3 shows a selection of solution curves with initial values $y(1) = y_0$ ranging from $y_0 = -3$ to $y_0 = 3$. It appears that on each solution curve, $y(x) \to 0$ as $x \to +\infty$, and this is in fact true because the sine integral function is bounded.

In the sequel we will see that it is the exception—rather than the rule—when a solution of a differential equation can be expressed in terms of elementary functions. We will study various devices for obtaining good approximations to the values of the nonelementary functions we encounter. In Chapter 2 we will discuss numerical integration of differential equations in some detail.

Mixture Problems

As a first application of linear first-order equations, we consider a tank containing a solution—a mixture of solute and solvent—such as salt dissolved in water. There is both inflow and outflow, and we want to compute the *amount* $x(t)$ of solute in the tank at time t, given the amount $x(0) = x_0$ at time $t = 0$. Suppose that solution with a concentration of c_i grams of solute per liter of solution flows into the tank at the constant rate of r_i liters per second, and that the solution in the tank—kept thoroughly mixed by stirring—flows out at the constant rate of r_o liters per second.

To set up a differential equation for $x(t)$, we estimate the change Δx in x during the brief time interval $[t, t + \Delta t]$. The amount of solute that flows into the tank during Δt seconds is $r_i c_i \Delta t$ grams. To check this, note how the cancellation of dimensions checks our computations:

$$\left(r_i \frac{\text{liters}}{\text{second}}\right) \left(c_i \frac{\text{grams}}{\text{liter}}\right) (\Delta t \text{ seconds})$$

yields a quantity measured in grams.

The amount of solute that flows out of the tank during the same time interval depends on the concentration $c_o(t)$ of solute in the solution at time t. But as noted in Fig. 1.5.4, $c_o(t) = x(t)/V(t)$, where $V(t)$ denotes the volume (not constant unless $r_i = r_o$) of solution in the tank at time t. Then

$$\Delta x = \{\text{grams input}\} - \{\text{grams output}\} \approx r_i c_i \Delta t - r_o c_o \Delta t.$$

We now divide by Δt:

$$\frac{\Delta x}{\Delta t} \approx r_i c_i - r_o c_o.$$

Finally, we take the limit as $\Delta t \to 0$; if all the functions involved are continuous and $x(t)$ is differentiable, then the error in this approximation also approaches zero, and we obtain the differential equation

$$\frac{dx}{dt} = r_i c_i - r_o c_o, \tag{16}$$

in which r_i, c_i, and r_o are constants, but c_o denotes the variable concentration

$$c_o(t) = \frac{x(t)}{V(t)} \tag{17}$$

of solute in the tank at time t. Thus the amount $x(t)$ of solute in the tank satisfies the differential equation

$$\frac{dx}{dt} = r_i c_i - \frac{r_o}{V} x. \tag{18}$$

If $V_0 = V(0)$, then $V(t) = V_0 + (r_i - r_o)t$, so Eq. (18) is a linear first-order differential equation for the amount $x(t)$ of solute in the tank at time t.

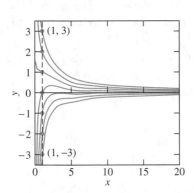

FIGURE 1.5.3. Typical solution curves defined by Eq. (15).

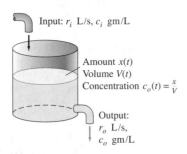

Input: r_i L/s, c_i gm/L

Amount $x(t)$
Volume $V(t)$
Concentration $c_o(t) = \frac{x}{V}$

Output:
r_o L/s,
c_o gm/L

FIGURE 1.5.4. The single-tank mixture problem.

Important: Equation (18) is *not* one you should commit to memory. It is the process we used to obtain that equation—examination of the behavior of the system over a short time interval $[t, t + \Delta t]$—that you should strive to understand, because it is a very useful tool for obtaining all sorts of differential equations.

Remark: In deriving Eq. (18) we used g/L mass/volume units for convenience. Any other consistent system of units can be used to measure amounts of solute and volumes of solution. In the following example we measure both in cubic kilometers.   ∎

EXAMPLE 4   Assume that Lake Erie has a volume of 480 km³ and that its rate of inflow (from Lake Huron) and outflow (to Lake Ontario) are both 350 km³ per year. Suppose that at the time $t = 0$ (years), the pollutant concentration of Lake Erie—caused by past industrial pollution that has now been ordered to cease—is five times that of Lake Huron. If the outflow henceforth is perfectly mixed lake water, how long will it take to reduce the pollution concentration in Lake Erie to twice that of Lake Huron?

Solution   Here we have

$$V = 480 \quad (\text{km}^3),$$

$$r_i = r_o = r = 350 \ (\text{km}^3/\text{yr}),$$

$$c_i = c \ (\text{the pollutant concentration of Lake Huron), and}$$

$$x_0 = x(0) = 5cV,$$

and the question is this: When is $x(t) = 2cV$? With this notation, Eq. (18) is the separable equation

$$\frac{dx}{dt} = rc - \frac{r}{V}x, \tag{19}$$

which we rewrite in the linear first-order form

$$\frac{dx}{dt} + px = q \tag{20}$$

with constant coefficients $p = r/V$, $q = rc$, and integrating factor $\rho = e^{pt}$. You can either solve this equation directly or apply the formula in (12). The latter gives

$$x(t) = e^{-pt}\left[x_0 + \int_0^t qe^{pt}\,dt\right] = e^{-pt}\left[x_0 + \frac{q}{p}\left(e^{pt} - 1\right)\right]$$

$$= e^{-rt/V}\left[5cV + \frac{rc}{r/V}\left(e^{rt/V} - 1\right)\right];$$

$$x(t) = cV + 4cVe^{-rt/V}. \tag{21}$$

To find when $x(t) = 2cV$, we therefore need only solve the equation $cV + 4cVe^{-rt/V} = 2cV$ for

$$t = \frac{V}{r}\ln 4 = \frac{480}{350}\ln 4 \approx 1.901 \ (\text{years}). \qquad ∎$$

EXAMPLE 5   A 120-gallon (gal) tank initially contains 90 lb of salt dissolved in 90 gal of water. Brine containing 2 lb/gal of salt flows into the tank at the rate of 4 gal/min, and the well-stirred mixture flows out of the tank at the rate of 3 gal/min. How much salt does the tank contain when it is full?

Solution   The interesting feature of this example is that, due to the differing rates of inflow and outflow, the volume of brine in the tank increases steadily with $V(t) = 90 + t$ gallons. The change Δx in the amount x of salt in the tank from time t to time $t + \Delta t$ (minutes) is given by

$$\Delta x \approx (4)(2)\Delta t - 3\left(\frac{x}{90+t}\right)\Delta t,$$

so our differential equation is

$$\frac{dx}{dt} + \frac{3}{90 + t}x = 8.$$

An integrating factor is

$$\rho(x) = \exp\left(\int \frac{3}{90 + t}\, dt\right) = e^{3\ln(90+t)} = (90 + t)^3,$$

which gives

$$D_t\left[(90 + t)^3 x\right] = 8(90 + t)^3;$$
$$(90 + t)^3 x = 2(90 + t)^4 + C.$$

Substitution of $x(0) = 90$ gives $C = -(90)^4$, so the amount of salt in the tank at time t is

$$x(t) = 2(90 + t) - \frac{90^4}{(90 + t)^3}.$$

The tank is full after 30 min, and when $t = 30$, we have

$$x(30) = 2(90 + 30) - \frac{90^4}{120^3} \approx 202 \text{ (lb)}$$

of salt in the tank. ∎

1.5 *Problems*

Find general solutions of the differential equations in Problems 1 through 25. If an initial condition is given, find the corresponding particular solution. Throughout, primes denote derivatives with respect to x.

1. $y' + y = 2$, $y(0) = 0$

2. $y' - 2y = 3e^{2x}$, $y(0) = 0$

3. $y' + 3y = 2xe^{-3x}$

4. $y' - 2xy = e^{x^2}$

5. $xy' + 2y = 3x$, $y(1) = 5$

6. $xy' + 5y = 7x^2$, $y(2) = 5$

7. $2xy' + y = 10\sqrt{x}$

8. $3xy' + y = 12x$

9. $xy' - y = x$, $y(1) = 7$

10. $2xy' - 3y = 9x^3$

11. $xy' + y = 3xy$, $y(1) = 0$

12. $xy' + 3y = 2x^5$, $y(2) = 1$

13. $y' + y = e^x$, $y(0) = 1$

14. $xy' - 3y = x^3$, $y(1) = 10$

15. $y' + 2xy = x$, $y(0) = -2$

16. $y' = (1 - y)\cos x$, $y(\pi) = 2$

17. $(1 + x)y' + y = \cos x$, $y(0) = 1$

18. $xy' = 2y + x^3 \cos x$

19. $y' + y \cos x = \cos x$

20. $y' = 1 + x + y + xy$, $y(0) = 0$

21. $xy' = 3y + x^4 \cos x$, $y(2\pi) = 0$

22. $y' = 2xy + 3x^2 \exp(x^2)$, $y(0) = 5$

23. $xy' + (2x - 3)y = 4x^4$

24. $(x^2 + 4)y' + 3xy = x$, $y(0) = 1$

25. $(x^2 + 1)\frac{dy}{dx} + 3x^3 y = 6x \exp\left(-\frac{3}{2}x^2\right)$, $y(0) = 1$

Solve the differential equations in Problems 26 through 28 by regarding y as the independent variable rather than x.

26. $(1 - 4xy^2)\frac{dy}{dx} = y^3$

27. $(x + ye^y)\frac{dy}{dx} = 1$

28. $(1 + 2xy)\frac{dy}{dx} = 1 + y^2$

29. Express the general solution of $dy/dx = 1 + 2xy$ in terms of the **error function**

$$\text{erf}(x) = \frac{2}{\sqrt{\pi}} \int_0^x e^{-t^2}\, dt.$$

30. Express the solution of the initial value problem

$$2x\frac{dy}{dx} = y + 2x\cos x, \quad y(1) = 0$$

as an integral as in Example 3 of this section.

31. (a) Show that

$$y_c(x) = Ce^{-\int P(x)\,dx}$$

is a general solution of $dy/dx + P(x)y = 0$. (b) Show that

$$y_p(x) = e^{-\int P(x)\,dx}\left[\int \left(Q(x)e^{\int P(x)\,dx}\right)dx\right]$$

is a particular solution of $dy/dx + P(x)y = Q(x)$. (c) Suppose that $y_c(x)$ is any general solution of $dy/dx + P(x)y = 0$ and that $y_p(x)$ is any particular solution of $dy/dx + P(x)y = Q(x)$. Show that $y(x) = y_c(x) + y_p(x)$ is a general solution of $dy/dx + P(x)y = Q(x)$.

32. (a) Find constants A and B such that $y_p(x) = A\sin x + B\cos x$ is a solution of $dy/dx + y = 2\sin x$. (b) Use the result of part (a) and the method of Problem 31 to find the general solution of $dy/dx + y = 2\sin x$. (c) Solve the initial value problem $dy/dx + y = 2\sin x$, $y(0) = 1$.

33. A tank contains 1000 liters (L) of a solution consisting of 100 kg of salt dissolved in water. Pure water is pumped into the tank at the rate of 5 L/s, and the mixture—kept uniform by stirring—is pumped out at the same rate. How long will it be until only 10 kg of salt remains in the tank?

34. Consider a reservoir with a volume of 8 billion cubic feet (ft^3) and an initial pollutant concentration of 0.25%. There is a daily inflow of 500 million ft^3 of water with a pollutant concentration of 0.05% and an equal daily outflow of the well-mixed water in the reservoir. How long will it take to reduce the pollutant concentration in the reservoir to 0.10%?

35. Rework Example 4 for the case of Lake Ontario. The only differences are that this lake has a volume of 1640 km^3 and an inflow-outflow rate of 410 km^3/year.

36. A tank initially contains 60 gal of pure water. Brine containing 1 lb of salt per gallon enters the tank at 2 gal/min, and the (perfectly mixed) solution leaves the tank at 3 gal/min; thus the tank is empty after exactly 1 h. (a) Find the amount of salt in the tank after t minutes. (b) What is the maximum amount of salt ever in the tank?

37. A 400-gal tank initially contains 100 gal of brine containing 50 lb of salt. Brine containing 1 lb of salt per gallon enters the tank at the rate of 5 gal/s, and the well-mixed brine in the tank flows out at the rate of 3 gal/s. How much salt will the tank contain when it is full of brine?

38. Consider the *cascade* of two tanks shown in Fig. 1.5.5, with $V_1 = 100$ (gal) and $V_2 = 200$ (gal) the volumes of brine in the two tanks. Each tank also initially contains 50 lb of salt. The three flow rates indicated in the figure are each 5 gal/min, with pure water flowing into tank 1. (a) Find the amount $x(t)$ of salt in tank 1 at time t. (b) Suppose that $y(t)$ is the amount of salt in tank 2 at time t. Show first that

$$\frac{dy}{dt} = \frac{5x}{100} - \frac{5y}{200},$$

and then solve for $y(t)$, using the function $x(t)$ found in part (a). (c) Finally, find the maximum amount of salt ever in tank 2.

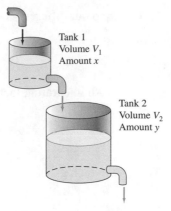

FIGURE 1.5.5. A cascade of two tanks.

39. Suppose that in the cascade shown in Fig. 1.5.5, tank 1 initially contains 100 gal of pure ethanol and tank 2 initially contains 100 gal of pure water. Pure water flows into tank 1 at 10 gal/min, and the other two flow rates are also 10 gal/min. (a) Find the amounts $x(t)$ and $y(t)$ of ethanol in the two tanks at time $t \geq 0$. (b) Find the maximum amount of ethanol ever in tank 2.

40. A multiple cascade is shown in Fig. 1.5.6. At time $t = 0$, tank 0 contains 1 gal of ethanol and 1 gal of water; all the remaining tanks contain 2 gal of pure water each. Pure water is pumped into tank 0 at 1 gal/min, and the varying mixture in each tank is pumped into the one below it at the same rate. Assume, as usual, that the mixtures are kept perfectly uniform by stirring. Let $x_n(t)$ denote the amount of ethanol in tank n at time t. (a) Show that $x_0(t) = e^{-t/2}$. (b) Show by induction on n that

$$x_n(t) = \frac{t^n e^{-t/2}}{n!\,2^n} \quad \text{for } n > 0.$$

(c) Show that the maximum value of $x_n(t)$ for $n > 0$ is $M_n = n^n e^{-n}/n!$. (d) Conclude from **Stirling's approximation** $n! \approx n^n e^{-n}\sqrt{2\pi n}$ that $M_n \approx (2\pi n)^{-1/2}$.

FIGURE 1.5.6. A multiple cascade.

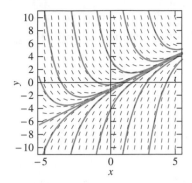

FIGURE 1.5.7. Direction field and solution curves for $y' = x - y$.

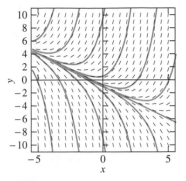

FIGURE 1.5.8. Direction field and solution curves for $y' = x + y$.

41. A 30-year-old woman accepts an engineering position with a starting salary of \$30000 per year. Her salary $S(t)$ increases exponentially, with $S(t) = 30e^{t/20}$ thousand dollars after t years. Meanwhile, 12% of her salary is deposited continuously in a retirement account, which accumulates interest at a continuous annual rate of 6%. (a) Estimate ΔA in terms of Δt to derive the differential equation satisfied by the amount $A(t)$ in her retirement account after t years. (b) Compute $A(40)$, the amount available for her retirement at age 70.

42. Suppose that a falling hailstone with density $\delta = 1$ starts from rest with negligible radius $r = 0$. Thereafter its radius is $r = kt$ (k is a constant) as it grows by accretion during its fall. Set up and solve the initial value problem

$$\frac{d}{dt}(mv) = mg, \quad v(0) = 0,$$

where m is the variable mass of the hailstone, $v = dy/dt$

is its velocity, and the positive y-axis points downward. Then show that $dv/dt = g/4$. Thus the hailstone falls as though it were under *one-fourth* the influence of gravity.

43. Figure 1.5.7 shows a direction field and typical solution curves for the equation $y' = x - y$. (a) Show that every solution curve approaches the straight line $y = x - 1$ as $x \to +\infty$. (b) For each of the five values $y_1 = 3.998$, 3.999, 4.000, 4.001, and 4.002, determine the initial value y_0 (accurate to four decimal places) such that $y(5) = y_1$ for the solution satisfying the initial condition $y(-5) = y_0$.

44. Figure 1.5.8 shows a direction field and typical solution curves for the equation $y' = x + y$. (a) Show that every solution curve approaches the straight line $y = -x - 1$ as $x \to -\infty$. (b) For each of the five values $y_1 = -10$, $-5, 0, 5$, and 10, determine the initial value y_0 (accurate to five decimal places) such that $y(5) = y_1$ for the solution satisfying the initial condition $y(-5) = y_0$.

1.5 Lab 1: Graphical Solutions to 1st Order ODEs

Log on! Next, type **matlab** and hit enter. The gears will start cranking, a logo and 3D graph will show up and eventually a window will open with the Matlab prompt. (It is **>>**). Now you are ready to go!

Type **dfield6** in the Command window and hit return.

A dialog box opens with lots of little boxes all filled in; ignore them and click on the **Proceed** button. You will see a graph with a direction field entitled $x' = x^2 - t$.

Now put the cursor on the point $(2, 1)$ and click. Now you know what the solution to the ODE $x' = x^2 - t$ with initial condition $x(2) = 1$ looks like.

Click somewhere else on the graph (that is, try another initial condition). Fool around a bit. Convince yourself that **solution curves do not cross**. (Why not?) If the picture gets crowed you can erase the picture by going to the **edit** menu.

Problems

1. Let $y(t)$ be the solution curve to ODE $y' = \sin(y + t)$ with initial condition $y(0) = 0$. What is $y(5)$? A ballpark estimate is good enough.

Answer: _____

To do this problem you will have to click on the dialog box and change the equation!

2. Let $y(t)$ be the solution to the ODE $y' = \sin(y + t)$ with initial condition $y(20) = 0$. What is $y(25)$? A ballpark estimate is good enough.

   Answer: _____

   To do this problem you will have to click on the dialog box and change the minimum and maximum value of t.

3. Let $y(x)$ be the solution to the ODE $y' = \sin(xy)$ with initial condition $y(0) = 0.1$. What is $y(2)$? A ballpark estimate is good enough.

   Answer: _____

   To do this problem you will have to click on the dialog box and change the equation and also change the name of the independent variable. Speaking of ballpark: I threw you a curve ball. Did you get an error message? Well, xy is written x*y in Matlab. Try again!

4. Let $x(t)$ be the solution curve to the ODE $x' = (x^2 - 1) \sin(xt)$.
   (a) If the initial condition is $x(0) = 1.01$ what is $x(2)$? $x(-2)$? By the way, x^2 is typed x^2 so you would enter `x'=(x^2-1)*sin(x*t)`.

   Answer: _____
   (b) Repeat part (a) but with $x(0) = 1.001$.

   Answer: _____
   (c) Repeat part (a) but with $x(0) = 1.00001$.

   Answer: _____
   (d) Repeat part (a) but with $x(0) = 1$.

   Answer: _____
   (e) Repeat part (a) but with $x(0) = 0.99$.

   Answer: _____

How do you do these problems? You really cannot position the cursor on the graph to 5 decimal place accuracy even if you are steady handed. However, if you go to the **Options** menu and choose **Keyboard input** you can enter the initial condition accurately. Of course, you must also choose appropriate ranges for your variables.

In some problems it doesn't make too much difference in the final answer if your hand shakes a bit. In others it does. Can you look at the direction field and tell—in advance—which questions you can answer confidently and which are iffy?

5. Let $y(x)$ be the solution to the ODE $y' = y^2 \cos(xy)$ with initial condition $y(0) = 1.217$. To 3 decimal place accuracy what is $y(1)$?

   Answer: _____

   To do this problem you will have to left click on the **Edit** menu and choose **Zoom in**; then use the mouse with the left button depressed to draw a rectangle you want to enlarge. You can repeat the procedure on the new graph if you need to.

If you have time, you can experiment with some of the other buttons and settings. For example, you can write some text on the graph or plot the direction field with arrows or remove the lines. You can also change the numerical method used; we will study different numerical methods in class, and in Lab 2.

You are done with this lab. If you need to solve a first order ODE quickly you can do it! What about higher order ODEs? Systems? Stay tuned!

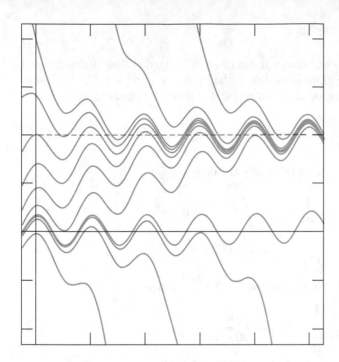

CHAPTER 2

Mathematical Models and Numerical Methods

2.1 POPULATION MODELS

In Section 1.4 we introduced the exponential differential equation $dP/dt = kP$, with solution $P(t) = P_0 e^{kt}$, as a mathematical model for natural population growth that occurs as a result of constant birth and death rates. Here we present a more general population model that accommodates birth and death rates that are not necessarily constant. As before, however, our population function $P(t)$ will be a *continuous* approximation to the actual population, which of course grows by integral increments.

Suppose that the population changes only by the occurrence of births and deaths—there is no immigration or emigration from outside the country or environment under consideration. It is customary to track the growth or decline of a population in terms of its *birth rate* and *death rate* functions defined as follows:

- $\beta(t)$ is the number of births per unit of population per unit of time at time t;
- $\delta(t)$ is the number of deaths per unit of population per unit of time at time t.

Then the numbers of births and deaths that occur during the time interval $[t, t + \Delta t]$ is given (approximately) by

$$\text{births:} \quad \beta(t) \cdot P(t) \cdot \Delta t, \qquad \text{deaths:} \quad \delta(t) \cdot P(t) \cdot \Delta t.$$

Hence the change ΔP in the population during the time interval $[t, t + \Delta t]$ of length Δt is

$$\Delta P = \{\text{births}\} - \{\text{deaths}\} \approx \beta(t) \cdot P(t) \cdot \Delta t - \delta(t) \cdot P(t) \cdot \Delta t,$$

so

$$\frac{\Delta P}{\Delta t} \approx [\beta(t) - \delta(t)] \, P(t).$$

The error in this approximation should approach zero as $\Delta t \to 0$, so—taking the limit—we get the differential equation

$$\frac{dP}{dt} = (\beta - \delta)P, \tag{1}$$

in which we write $\beta = \beta(t)$, $\delta = \delta(t)$, and $P = P(t)$ for brevity. Equation (1) is the **general population equation.** If β and δ are constant, Eq. (1) reduces to the natural growth equation with $k = \beta - \delta$. But it also includes the possibility that β and δ are variable functions of t. The birth and death rates need not be known in advance; they may well depend on the unknown function $P(t)$.

EXAMPLE 1 Suppose that an alligator population numbers 100 initially, and that its death rate is $\beta = 0$ (so none of the alligators is dying). If the birth rate is $\beta = (0.0005)P$—and thus increases as the population does—then Eq. (1) gives the initial value problem

$$\frac{dP}{dt} = (0.0005)P^2, \quad P(0) = 100$$

(with t in years). Then upon separating the variables we get

$$\int \frac{1}{P^2}\, dP = \int (0.0005)\, dt;$$

$$\frac{1}{P} = (0.0005)t + C.$$

Substitution of $t = 0$, $P = 100$ gives $C = -1/100$, and then we readily solve for

$$P(t) = \frac{2000}{20 - t}.$$

For instance, $P(10) = 2000/10 = 200$, so after 10 years the alligator population has doubled. But we see that $P \to +\infty$ as $t \to 20$, so a real "population explosion" occurs in 20 years. Indeed, the direction field and solution curves shown in Fig. 2.1.1 indicate that a population explosion always occurs, whatever the size of the (positive) initial population $P(0) = P_0$. In particular, it appears that the population always becomes unbounded in a *finite* period of time. ∎

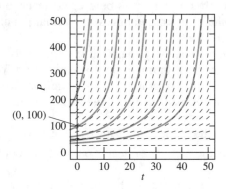

FIGURE 2.1.1. Direction field and solution curves for the equation $dP/dt = (0.0005)P^2$ in Example 1.

Bounded Populations and the Logistic Equation

In situations as diverse as the human population of a nation and a fruit fly population in a closed container, it is often observed that the birth rate decreases as the population itself increases. The reasons may range from increased scientific or cultural sophistication to a limited food supply. Suppose, for example, that the birth rate β is a *linear* decreasing function of the population size P, so that $\beta = \beta_0 - \beta_1 P$, where β_0 and β_1 are positive constants. If the death rate $\delta = \delta_0$ remains constant, then Eq. (2) takes the form

$$\frac{dP}{dt} = (\beta_0 - \beta_1 P - \delta_0)P;$$

that is,

$$\frac{dP}{dt} = aP - bP^2 \tag{2}$$

where $a = \beta_0 - \delta_0$ and $b = \beta_1$.

If the coefficients a and b are both positive, then Eq. (2) is called the **logistic equation.** For the purpose of relating the behavior of the population $P(t)$ to the values of the parameters in the equation, it is useful to rewrite the logistic equation in the form

$$\frac{dP}{dt} = kP(M - P) \qquad (3)$$

where $k = b$ and $M = a/b$ are constants. If we assume that $0 < M < P$, then Eq. (3) can be solved by separation of variables as follows:

$$\int \frac{dP}{P(M - P)} = \int k \, dt;$$

$$\frac{1}{M} \int \left(\frac{1}{P} + \frac{1}{M - P} \right) dP = \int k \, dt;$$

$$\ln \left(\frac{P}{M - P} \right) = kMt + C.$$

Exponentiation gives

$$\frac{P}{M - P} = Ae^{kMt},$$

where $A = e^C$. We substitute $t = 0$ into both sides of this equation to find that $A = P_0/(M - P_0)$. So

$$\frac{P}{M - P} = \frac{P_0 e^{kMt}}{M - P_0}.$$

This equation is easy to solve for

$$P(t) = \frac{M P_0}{P_0 + (M - P_0)e^{-kMt}}. \qquad (4)$$

While we made the assumption that $0 < P < M$ in order to derive Eq. (4), this restriction is unnecessary, because we can verify by direct substitution into Eq. (3) that $P(t)$ as given in (4) satisfies the logistic equation whether $0 < P < M$ or $P \geqq M$.

Limiting Populations and Carrying Capacity

If the initial population satisfies $0 < P_0 < M$, then Eq. (4) shows that $P(t) < M$ for all $t \geqq 0$, and also that

$$\lim_{t \to \infty} P(t) = M. \qquad (5)$$

Thus a population that satisfies the logistic equation is *not* like a naturally growing population; it does not grow without bound, but instead approaches the finite **limiting population** M as $t \to +\infty$. Figure 2.1.2 (in which $M = k = 1$) shows typical solution curves corresponding to different initial populations and illustrates the fact that, whatever the (positive) initial population P_0 may be, $P(t) \to M$ as $t \to +\infty$. Because

$$P'(t) = kP(M - P) > 0$$

if $0 < P < M$, we see in this case that the population is steadily increasing while approaching the limiting population M. Sometimes M is called the **carrying capacity** of the environment, considering it to be the maximum population that the environment can support on a long-term basis.

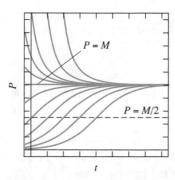

FIGURE 2.1.2. Typical solution curves for the logistic equation $dP/dt = kP(M - P)$.

To investigate the shape of the solution curves illustrated in Fig. 2.1.2, let us differentiate each side of the logistic equation $dP/dt = kP(M - P)$ with respect to t. This gives

$$\frac{d^2P}{dt^2} = \left[\frac{d}{dP}\left(\frac{dP}{dt}\right)\right]\left(\frac{dP}{dt}\right) = (kM - 2kP)[kP(M - P)]$$

$$= 2k^2P\left(P - \frac{M}{2}\right)(P - M).$$

Thus

- $P'' > 0$ if $0 < P < \dfrac{M}{2}$;

- $P'' = 0$ if $P = \dfrac{M}{2}$;

- $P'' < 0$ if $\dfrac{M}{2} < P < M$.

Hence any solution curve that crosses the line $P = M/2$ has an inflection point where it crosses that line, and therefore looks like one of the lower S-shaped curves in Fig. 2.1.2. In this case the population increases at an increasing rate until $P = M/2$ and thereafter increases at a decreasing rate.

If $P_0 > M$, so that the initial population exceeds the limiting population, then a similar analysis (Problem 17 in this section) shows that $P(t)$ is a steadily decreasing function with a graph resembling one of the upper curves in Fig. 2.1.1.

Can you see—both from Eq. (3) and in Fig. 2.1.2—that if $P_0 = M$, then $P(t) = M$ for all $t \geq 0$? In this case the population remains constant.

Historical Note

The logistic equation was introduced (around 1840) by the Belgian mathematician and demographer P. F. Verhulst as a possible model for human population growth. In the next two examples we compare natural growth and logistic model fits to the 19th-century U.S. population census data, then compare projections for the 20th century.

EXAMPLE 2   The U.S. population in 1800 was 5.308 million and in 1900 was 76.212 million. If we take $P_0 = 5.308$ (with $t = 0$ in 1800) in the natural growth model $P(t) = P_0e^{rt}$ and substitute $t = 100$, $P = 76.212$, we find that

$$76.212 = 5.308e^{100r}, \quad \text{so} \quad r = \frac{1}{100}\ln\frac{76.212}{5.308} \approx 0.026643.$$

Thus our natural growth model for the U.S. population during the 19th century is

$$P(t) = (5.308)e^{(0.026643)t} \tag{6}$$

(with t in years and P in millions). Because $e^{0.026643} \approx 1.02700$, the average population growth between 1800 and 1900 was about 2.7% per year.   ∎

EXAMPLE 3   The U.S. population in 1850 was 23.192 million. If we take $P_0 = 5.308$ and substitute the data pairs $t = 50$, $P = 23.192$ (for 1850) and $t = 100$, $P = 76.212$ (for 1900) in the logistic model formula in Eq. (4), we get the two equations

$$\frac{(5.308)M}{5.308 + (M - 5.308)e^{-50kM}} = 23.192,$$

$$\frac{(5.308)M}{5.308 + (M - 5.308)e^{-100kM}} = 76.212 \tag{7}$$

in the two unknowns k and M. Nonlinear systems like this ordinarily are solved numerically using an appropriate computer system. But with the right algebraic trick (Problem 28 in this section) the equations in (7) can be solved manually for $k = 0.000167716$, $M = 188.121$. Substitution of these values in Eq. (4) yields the logistic model

$$P(t) = \frac{998.546}{5.308 + (182.813)e^{-(0.031551)t}}. \tag{8}$$

The table in Fig. 2.1.3 compares the actual 1800–1990 U.S. census population figures with those predicted by the exponential growth model in (6) and the logistic model in (8). Both agree well with the 19th-century figures. But the exponential model diverges appreciably from the census data in the early decades of the 20th century, whereas the logistic model remains accurate until 1940. By the end of the 20th century the exponential model vastly overestimates the actual U.S. population—predicting over a billion in the year 2000—whereas the logistic model somewhat underestimates it.

Year	Actual U.S. Pop.	Exponential Model	Exponential Error	Logistic Model	Logistic Error
1800	5.308	5.308	0.000	5.308	0.000
1810	7.240	6.929	0.311	7.202	0.038
1820	9.638	9.044	0.594	9.735	-0.097
1830	12.861	11.805	1.056	13.095	-0.234
1840	17.064	15.409	1.655	17.501	-0.437
1850	23.192	20.113	3.079	23.192	0.000
1860	31.443	26.253	5.190	30.405	1.038
1870	38.558	34.268	4.290	39.326	-0.768
1880	50.189	44.730	5.459	50.034	0.155
1890	62.980	58.387	4.593	62.435	0.545
1900	76.212	76.212	0.000	76.213	-0.001
1910	92.228	99.479	-7.251	90.834	1.394
1920	106.022	129.849	-23.827	105.612	0.410
1930	123.203	169.492	-46.289	119.834	3.369
1940	132.165	221.237	-89.072	132.886	-0.721
1950	151.326	288.780	-137.454	144.354	6.972
1960	179.323	376.943	-197.620	154.052	25.271
1970	203.302	492.023	-288.721	161.990	41.312
1980	226.542	642.236	-415.694	168.316	58.226
1990	248.710	838.308	-589.598	173.252	76.458
2000	?	1094.240	?	177.038	?

FIGURE 2.1.3. Comparison of exponential growth and logistic models with U.S. census populations (in millions).

In order to measure the extent to which a given model fits actual data, it is customary to define the **average error** (in the model) as *the square root of the average of the squares of the individual errors* (the latter appearing in the fourth and sixth columns of the table in Fig. 2.1.3). Using only the 1800–1900 data, this definition gives 3.162 for the average error in the exponential model, while the average error in the logistic model is only 0.452. Consequently, even in 1900 we might well have anticipated that the logistic model would predict the U.S. population growth during the 20th century more accurately than the exponential model. ∎

EXAMPLE 4   Suppose that in 1885 the population of a certain country was 50 million and was growing at the rate of 750,000 people per year at that time. Suppose also that in

1940 its population was 100 million and was then growing at the rate of 1 million per year. Assume that this population satisfies the logistic equation. Determine both the limiting population M and the predicted population for the year 2000.

Solution   We substitute the two given pairs of data in Eq. (3) and find that

$$0.75 = 50k(M - 50), \quad 1.00 = 100k(M - 100).$$

We solve simultaneously for $M = 200$ and $k = 0.0001$. Thus the limiting population of the country in question is 200 million. With these values of M and k, and with $t = 0$ corresponding to the year 1940 (in which $P_0 = 100$), we find that—according to Eq. (4)—the population in the year 2000 will be

$$P(60) = \frac{100 \cdot 200}{100 + (200 - 100)e^{-(0.0001)(200)(60)}},$$

about 153.7 million people.   ■

More Applications of the Logistic Equation

We next describe some situations that illustrate the varied circumstances in which the logistic equation is a satisfactory mathematical model.

1. *Limited environment situation.* A certain environment can support a population of at most M individuals. It is then reasonable to expect the growth rate $\beta - \delta$ (the combined birth and death rates) to be proportional to $M - P$, because we may think of $M - P$ as the potential for further expansion. Then $\beta - \delta = k(M - P)$, so that

$$\frac{dP}{dt} = (\beta - \delta)P = kP(M - P).$$

The classic example of a limited environment situation is a fruit fly population in a closed container.

2. *Competition situation.* If the birth rate β is constant but the death rate δ is proportional to P, so that $\delta = \alpha P$, then

$$\frac{dP}{dt} = (\beta - \alpha P)P = kP(M - P).$$

This might be a reasonable working hypothesis in a study of a cannibalistic population, in which all deaths result from chance encounters between individuals. Of course, competition between individuals is not usually so deadly, nor its effects so immediate and decisive.

3. *Joint proportion situation.* Let $P(t)$ denote the number of individuals in a constant-size susceptible population M who are infected with a certain contagious and incurable disease. The disease is spread by chance encounters. Then $P'(t)$ should be proportional to the product of the number P of individuals having the disease and the number $M - P$ of those not having it, and therefore $dP/dt = kP(M - P)$. Again we discover that the mathematical model is the logistic equation. The mathematical description of the spread of a rumor in a population of M individuals is identical.

EXAMPLE 5   Suppose that at time $t = 0$, 10 thousand people in a city with population $M = 100$ thousand people have heard a certain rumor. After 1 week the number $P(t)$ of those who have heard it has increased to $P(1) = 20$ thousand. Assuming that $P(t)$ satisfies a logistic equation, when will 80% of the city's population have heard the rumor?

Solution Substituting $P_0 = 10$ and $M = 100$ (thousand) in Eq. (4), we get

$$P(t) = \frac{1000}{10 + 90e^{-100kt}}. \tag{9}$$

Then substitution of $t = 1$, $P = 20$ gives the equation

$$20 = \frac{1000}{10 + 90e^{-100k}}$$

that is readily solved for

$$e^{-100k} = \tfrac{4}{9}, \quad \text{so} \quad k = \tfrac{1}{100}\ln\tfrac{9}{4} \approx 0.008109.$$

With $P(t) = 80$, Eq. (9) takes the form

$$80 = \frac{1000}{10 + 90e^{-100kt}},$$

which we solve for $e^{-100kt} = \tfrac{1}{36}$. It follows that 80% of the population has heard the rumor when

$$t = \frac{\ln 36}{100k} = \frac{\ln 36}{\ln\tfrac{9}{4}} \approx 4.42,$$

thus after about 4 weeks and 3 days. ∎

Doomsday versus Extinction

Consider a population $P(t)$ of unsophisticated animals in which females rely solely on chance encounters to meet males for reproductive purposes. It is reasonable to expect such encounters to occur at a rate that is proportional to the product of the number $P/2$ of males and the number $P/2$ of females, hence at a rate proportional to P^2. We therefore assume that births occur at the rate kP^2 (per unit time, with k constant). The birth rate (births/time/population) is then given by $\beta = kP$. If the death rate δ is constant, then the general population equation in (2) yields the differential equation

$$\frac{dP}{dt} = kP^2 - \delta P = kP(P - M) \tag{10}$$

(where $M = \delta/k > 0$) as a mathematical model of the population.

Note that the right-hand side in Eq. (10) is the *negative* of the right-hand side in the logistic equation in (4). We will see that the constant M is now a **threshold population**, with the way the population behaves in the future depending critically on whether the initial population P_0 is less than or greater than M.

CASE 1: $P_0 > M$. From Eq. (10) we see that $P'(0) = kP_0(P_0 - M) > 0$, so $P(t)$ starts out increasing. Hence $P'(t)$ remains positive, so $P(t)$ continues to increase, and therefore $P(t) > M$ for all $t \geq 0$. We note that

$$\frac{1}{P(P - M)} = -\frac{1}{M}\left(\frac{1}{P} - \frac{1}{P - M}\right).$$

We separate the variables in Eq. (10) and integrate as follows:

$$\int \frac{dP}{P(P - M)} = \int k\,dt;$$

$$\int \left(\frac{1}{P} - \frac{1}{P - M}\right)dP = -\int kM\,dt;$$

$$\ln\frac{P}{P - M} = -kMt + C_1.$$

Substitution of P_0 for P and 0 for t then gives

$$C_1 = \ln \frac{P_0}{P_0 - M} = \ln C$$

where $C = P_0/(P_0 - M) > 1$. Exponentiation then yields $P/(P - M) = Ce^{-kMt}$, which we solve for

$$P(t) = \frac{CMe^{-kMt}}{Ce^{-kMt} - 1}. \tag{11}$$

Note that the denominator in Eq. (11) approaches zero as

$$t \to T = \frac{\ln C}{kM} = \frac{1}{kM} \ln \frac{P_0}{P_0 - M} > 0.$$

Thus $P(t) \to +\infty$ as $t \to T$. This is a *doomsday* situation.

CASE 2: $0 < P_0 < M$. In this case $P'(0) < 0$, and it follows that $P(t) < M$ for all $t \geq 0$. A similar separation of variables (Problem 24 in this section) now leads to

$$P(t) = \frac{CMe^{-kMt}}{Ce^{-kMt} + 1}, \tag{12}$$

where $C = P_0/(M - P_0) > 0$. The difference between this case and the doomsday situation of case 1 is that the denominator in Eq. (12) remains greater than 1. It follows that $P(t) \to 0$ as $t \to +\infty$. This is an *extinction* situation.

Thus the population either explodes or is an endangered species threatened with extinction, depending on its initial size. An approximation to this phenomenon is sometimes observed with animal populations, such as the alligator population in certain areas of the southern United States.

Figure 2.1.4 shows typical solution curves that illustrate cases 1 and 2 for a population $P(t)$ satisfying Eq. (10). If $P_0 = M$ then the population remains constant. But if P_0 exceeds M (even slightly), then $P(t)$ rapidly increases without bound, whereas if the initial (positive) population is less than M then it decreases (more gradually) toward zero as $t \to +\infty$.

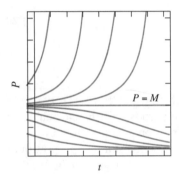

FIGURE 2.1.4. Typical solution curves for the explosion/extinction equation $dP/dt = kP(P - M)$.

2.1 Problems

Separate variables and use partial fractions to solve the initial value problems in Problems 1 through 4.

1. $\dfrac{dx}{dt} = 3x(5 - x)$, $x(0) = 8$

2. $\dfrac{dx}{dt} = 3x(x - 5)$, $x(0) = 2$

3. $\dfrac{dx}{dt} = 4x(7 - x)$, $x(0) = 11$

4. $\dfrac{dx}{dt} = 7x(x - 13)$, $x(0) = 17$

5. The time rate of change of a rabbit population P is proportional to the square root of P. At time $t = 0$ (months) the population numbers 100 rabbits and is increasing at the rate of 20 rabbits per month. How many rabbits will there be one year later?

6. Suppose that the fish population $P(t)$ in a lake is attacked by a disease at time $t = 0$, with the result that the fish cease to reproduce (so that the birth rate is $\beta = 0$) and the

death rate δ (deaths per week per fish) is thereafter proportional to $1/\sqrt{P}$. If there were initially 900 fish in the lake and 441 were left after 6 weeks, how long did it take all the fish in the lake to die?

7. Suppose that when a certain lake is stocked with fish, the birth and death rates β and δ are both inversely proportional to $\sqrt{P}$. (a) Show that

$$P(t) = \left(\tfrac{1}{2}kt + \sqrt{P}\right)^2,$$

where k is a constant. (b) If $P_0 = 100$ and after 6 months there are 169 fish in the lake, how many will there be after 1 year?

8. The time rate of change of an alligator population P in a swamp is proportional to the square of P. The swamp contained a dozen alligators in 1988, two dozen in 1998. When will there be four dozen alligators in the swamp? What happens thereafter?

9. Consider a prolific breed of rabbits whose birth and death rates, β and δ, are each proportional to the rabbit population $P = P(t)$, with $\beta > \delta$. (a) Show that

$$P(t) = \frac{P_0}{1 - kP_0 t}, \quad k \text{ constant.}$$

Note that $P(t) \to +\infty$ as $t \to 1/(kP_0)$. This is doomsday. (b) Suppose that $P_0 = 6$ and that there are nine rabbits after ten months. When does doomsday occur?

10. Repeat part (a) of Problem 9 in the case $\beta < \delta$. What now happens to the rabbit population in the long run?

11. Consider a population $P(t)$ satisfying the logistic equation $dP/dt = aP - bP^2$, where $B = aP$ is the time rate at which births occur and $D = bP^2$ is the rate at which deaths occur. If the initial population is $P(0) = P_0$, and B_0 births per month and D_0 deaths per month are occurring at time $t = 0$, show that the limiting population is $M = B_0 P_0/D_0$.

12. Consider a rabbit population $P(t)$ satisfying the logistic equation as in Problem 11. If the initial population is 120 rabbits and there are 8 births per month and 6 deaths per month occurring at time $t = 0$, how many months does it take for $P(t)$ to reach 95% of the limiting population M?

13. Consider a rabbit population $P(t)$ satisfying the logistic equation as in Problem 11. If the initial population is 240 rabbits and there are 9 births per month and 12 deaths per month occurring at time $t = 0$, how many months does it take for $P(t)$ to reach 105% of the limiting population M?

14. Consider a population $P(t)$ satisfying the extinction/explosion equation $dP/dt = aP^2 - bP$, where $B = aP^2$ is the time rate at which births occur and $D = bP$ is the rate at which deaths occur. If the initial population is $P(0) = P_0$ and B_0 births per month and D_0 deaths per month are occurring at time $t = 0$, show that the threshold population is $M = D_0 P_0/B_0$.

15. Consider an alligator population $P(t)$ satisfying the extinction/explosion equation as in Problem 14. If the initial population is 100 alligators and there are 10 births per month and 9 deaths per months occurring at time $t = 0$, how many months does it take for $P(t)$ to reach 10 times the threshold population M?

16. Consider an alligator population $P(t)$ satisfying the extinction/explosion equation as in Problem 14. If the initial population is 110 alligators and there are 11 births per month and 12 deaths per month occurring at time $t = 0$, how many months does it take for $P(t)$ to reach 10% of the threshold population M?

17. Derive the solution in Eq. (4) of the logistic equation in (3) under the assumption that $P > M$, and show in this case that the graph of $P(t)$ resembles the upper curves in Fig. 2.1.2.

18. Suppose that at time $t = 0$, half of a "logistic" population of 100,000 persons have heard a certain rumor, and that the number of those who have heard it is then increasing at the rate of 1000 persons per day. How long will it take for this rumor to spread to 80% of the population? (*Suggestion*: Find the value of k by substituting $P(0)$ and $P'(0)$ in the logistic equation, Eq. (3).)

19. Suppose that as a certain salt dissolves in a solvent, the number $x(t)$ of grams of the salt in solution after t seconds satisfies the logistic equation $dx/dt = (0.8)x - (0.004)x^2$.

(a) What is the maximum amount of the salt that will dissolve in this solvent? (b) If $x = 50$ when $t = 0$, how long will it take for an additional 50 g of the salt to dissolve?

20. Suppose that a community contains 15000 people who are susceptible to a spreading contagious disease. At time $t = 0$ the number $N(t)$ of people who have the disease is 5000 and is increasing by 500 per day. How long will it take for another 5000 people to contract the disease? Assume that $N'(t)$ is proportional to the product of the numbers of those who have the disease and those who do not.

21. The data in the table in Fig. 2.1.5 are given for a certain population $P(t)$ that satisfies the logistic equation in (3). (a) What is the limiting population M? (*Suggestion*: Use the approximation

$$P'(t) \approx \frac{P(t+h) - P(t-h)}{2h}$$

with $h = 1$ to estimate the values of $P'(t)$ when $P = 25.00$ and when $P = 47.54$. Then substitute these values in the logistic equation and solve for k and M.) (b) Use the values of k and M found in part (a) to determine when $P = 75$. (*Suggestion*: Take $t = 0$ to correspond to the year 1925.)

Year	P (millions)
1924	24.63
1925	25.00
1926	25.38
$\vdots$	$\vdots$
1974	47.04
1975	47.54
1976	48.04

FIGURE 2.1.5. Population data for Problem 21.

22. A population $P(t)$ of small rodents has birth rate $\beta = (0.001)P$ (births per month per rodent) and *constant* death rate δ. If $P(0) = 100$ and $P'(0) = 8$, how long (in months) will it take this population to double to 200 rodents? (*Suggestion*: First find the value of δ.)

23. Consider an animal population $P(t)$ with constant death rate $\delta = 0.01$ and with birth rate β proportional to P. Suppose that $P(0) = 200$ and $P'(0) = 2$. (a) When is $P = 1000$? (b) When does doomsday occur?

24. Derive the solution in Eq. (12) of Eq. (10) in the case $0 < P(0) < M$.

25. A tumor may be regarded as a population of multiplying cells. It is found empirically that the "birth rate" of the cells in a tumor decreases exponentially with time, so that $\beta(t) = \beta_0 e^{-\alpha t}$ (where α and β_0 are positive constants), and hence

$$\frac{dP}{dt} = \beta_0 e^{-\alpha t} P, \quad P(0) = P_0.$$

Solve this initial value problem for

$$P(t) = P_0 \exp\left(\frac{\beta_0}{\alpha}(1 - e^{-\alpha t})\right).$$

Observe that $P(t)$ approaches the finite limiting population $P_0 \exp(\beta_0/\alpha)$ as $t \to +\infty$.

26. For the tumor of Problem 25, suppose that at time $t = 0$ there are $P_0 = 10^6$ cells and that $P(t)$ is then increasing at the rate of 3×10^5 cells per month. After 6 months the tumor has doubled (in size and in number of cells). Solve numerically for α, and then find the limiting population of the tumor.

27. Consider two population functions $P_1(t)$ and $P_2(t)$, both of which satisfy the logistic equation with the same limiting population M, but with different values k_1 and k_2 of the constant k in Eq. (3). Assume that $k_1 < k_2$. Which population approaches M the most rapidly? You can reason *geometrically* by examining slope fields (especially if appropriate software is available), *symbolically* by analyzing the solution given in Eq. (4), or *numerically* by substituting successive values of t.

28. To solve the two equations in (7) for the values of k and M, begin by solving the first equation for the quantity $x = e^{-50kM}$ and the second equation for $x^2 = e^{-100kM}$. Upon equating the two resulting expressions for x^2 in terms of M, you get an equation that is readily solved for M. With M now known, either of the original equations is readily solved for k. This technique can be used to "fit" the logistic equation to any three population values P_0, P_1, and P_2 corresponding to *equally spaced* times $t_0 = 0$, t_1, and $t_2 = 2t_1$.

29. Use the method of Problem 28 to fit the logistic equation to the actual U.S. population data (Fig. 2.1.3) for the years 1850, 1900, and 1950. Solve the resulting logistic equation and compare the predicted and actual populations for the years 1990 and 2000 (consult an almanac or check **www.census.gov** to find the year 2000 population).

30. Fit the logistic equation to the actual U.S. population data (Fig. 2.1.3) for the years 1900, 1930, and 1960. Solve the resulting logistic equation, then compare the predicted and actual populations for the years 1980, 1990, and 2000.

2.1 Computing Project: Logistic Modeling of Population Data

This project deals with the problem of fitting a logistic model to given population data. Thus we want to determine the numerical constants a and b so that the solution $P(t)$ of the initial value problem

$$\frac{dP}{dt} = aP + bP^2, \quad P(0) = P_0 \tag{1}$$

approximates the given values $P_0, P_1, \ldots, P_n$ of the population at the times $t_0 = 0$, $t_1, \ldots, t_n$. If we rewrite Eq. (1) (the logistic equation with $kM = a$ and $k = -b$) in the form

$$\frac{1}{P}\frac{dP}{dt} = a + bP, \tag{2}$$

then we see that the points

$$\left(P(t_i), \frac{P'(t_i)}{P(t_i)} \right), \quad i = 0, 1, 2, \ldots, n,$$

should all lie on the straight line with y-intercept a and slope b (as determined by the function of P on the right-hand side in Eq. (2)).

This observation provides a way to find a and b. If we can determine the approximate values of the derivatives $P_1', P_2', \ldots$ corresponding to the given population data, then we can proceed with the following agenda:

- First plot the points $(P_1, P_1'/P_1)$, $(P_2, P_2'/P_2)$, $\ldots$ on a sheet of graph paper with horizontal P-axis.
- Then use a ruler to draw a straight line that appears to approximate these points well.
- Finally, measure this straight line's y-intercept a and slope b.

But where are we to find the needed values of the derivative $P'(t)$ of the (as yet) unknown function P? It is easiest to use the approximation

$$P_i' = \frac{P_{i+1} - P_{i-1}}{t_{i+1} - t_{i-1}} \tag{3}$$

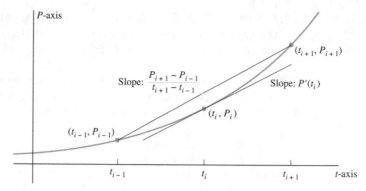

FIGURE 2.1.6. The symmetric difference approximation
$$\frac{P_{i+1} - P_{i-1}}{t_{i+1} - t_{i-1}}$$ to the derivative $P'(t_i)$.

suggested by Fig. 2.1.6. For instance, if we take $i = 0$ corresponding to the year 1790, then the U.S. population data in Fig. 2.1.7 give

$$P_1' = \frac{P_2 - P_0}{t_2 - t_0} = \frac{7.240 - 3.929}{20} \approx 0.166$$

for the slope at (t_1, P_1) corresponding to the year 1800.

Year	i	t_i	Population P_i	Slope P_i'
1790	0	−10	3.929	
1800	1	0	5.308	0.166
1810	2	10	7.240	0.217
1820	3	20	9.638	0.281
1830	4	30	12.861	0.371
1840	5	40	17.064	0.517
1850	6	50	23.192	0.719
1860	7	60	31.443	0.768
1870	8	70	38.558	0.937
1880	9	80	50.189	1.221
1890	10	90	62.980	1.301
1900	11	100	76.212	1.462
1910	12	110	92.228	

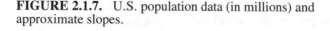

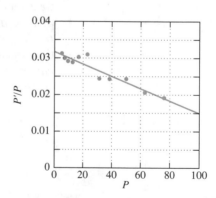

FIGURE 2.1.7. U.S. population data (in millions) and approximate slopes.

FIGURE 2.1.8. Points and approximating straight line for U.S. population data from 1800 to 1900.

INVESTIGATION A: Use Eq. (3) to verify the slope figures shown in the final column of the table in Fig. 2.1.7, then plot the points $(P_1, P_1'/P_1), \ldots, (P_{11}, P_{11}'/P_{11})$ indicated by the asterisks in Fig. 2.1.8. If an appropriate graphing calculator, spreadsheet, or computer program is available, use it to find the straight line $y = a + bP$ as in (2) that best fits these points. If not, draw your own straight line approximating these points, and then measure its intercept a and slope b as accurately as you can. Next, solve the logistic equation in (1) with these numerical parameters, taking $t = 0$ corresponding to the year 1800. Finally, compare the predicted 20th-century U.S. population figures with the actual data listed in Fig. 2.1.3.

INVESTIGATION B: Repeat Investigation A, but take $t = 0$ in 1900 and use only 20th-century population data. Do you get a better approximation for the U.S. population during the final decades of the 20th century?

INVESTIGATION C: Model similarly the world population data shown in Fig. 2.1.9. The Population Division of the United Nations predicts a world population of 8.177 billion in the year 2025. What do you predict?

Year	World Population (billions)
1960	3.049
1965	3.358
1970	3.721
1975	4.103
1980	4.473
1985	4.882
1990	5.249
1995	5.679
2000	6.127

FIGURE 2.1.9. World population data.

2.2 EQUILIBRIUM SOLUTIONS AND STABILITY

In previous sections we have often used explicit solutions of differential equations to answer specific numerical questions. But even when a given differential equation is difficult or impossible to solve explicitly, it still may be possible to extract *qualitative* information about general properties of its solutions. For example, we may be able to establish that every solution $x(t)$ grows without bound as $t \to +\infty$, or approaches a finite limit, or is a periodic function of t. In this section we introduce—mainly by consideration of simple differential equations that *can* be solved explicitly—some of the more important qualitative questions that can sometimes be answered for less tractable equations.

EXAMPLE 1   Let $x(t)$ denote the temperature of a body with initial temperature $x(0) = x_0$. At time $t = 0$ this body is immersed in a medium with constant temperature A. Assuming Newton's law of cooling,

$$\frac{dx}{dt} = -k(x - A) \qquad (k > 0 \quad \text{constant}), \tag{1}$$

we readily solve (by separation of variables) for the explicit solution

$$x(t) = A + (x_0 - A)e^{-kt}.$$

It follows immediately that

$$\lim_{t \to \infty} x(t) = A, \tag{2}$$

so the temperature of the body approaches that of the surrounding medium (as is evident to one's intuition). Note that the constant function $x(t) \equiv A$ is a solution of Eq. (1); it corresponds to the temperature of the body when it is in thermal equilibrium with the surrounding medium. In Fig. 2.2.1 the limit in (2) means that every other solution curve approaches the equilibrium solution curve $x = A$ asymptotically as $t \to +\infty$. ∎

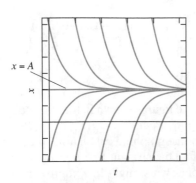

$x = A$

FIGURE 2.2.1. Typical solution curves for the equation of Newton's law of cooling, $dx/dt = -k(x - A)$.

Remark: The behavior of solutions of Eq. (1) is summarized briefly by the **phase diagram** in Fig. 2.2.2. The right-hand side $f(x) = -k(x - A) = k(A - x)$ is positive if $x < A$, negative if $x > A$. This observation corresponds to the fact that solutions starting above the line $x = A$ and those starting below it both approach the limiting solution $x(t) \equiv A$ as t increases (as indicated by the arrows). ∎

FIGURE 2.2.2. Phase diagram for the equation $dx/dt = f(x) = k(A - x)$.

In Section 2.1 we introduced the general population equation

$$\frac{dx}{dt} = (\beta - \delta)x, \tag{3}$$

where β and δ are the birth and death rates, respectively, in births or deaths per individual per unit of time. The question of whether a population $x(t)$ is bounded or unbounded as $t \to +\infty$ is of evident interest. In many situations—like the logistic and explosion/extinction populations of Section 2.1—the birth and death rates are known functions of x. Then Eq. (3) takes the form

$$\frac{dx}{dt} = f(x). \tag{4}$$

This is an **autonomous** first-order differential equation—one in which the independent variable t does not appear explicitly. As in Example 1, the solutions of the equation $f(x) = 0$ play an important role, and are called **critical points** of the autonomous differential equation $dx/dt = f(x)$.

If $x = c$ is a critical point of Eq. (4), then the differential equation has the constant solution $x(t) \equiv c$. A constant solution of a differential equation is sometimes called an **equilibrium solution** (one may think of a population that remains constant because it is in "equilibrium" with its environment). Thus the critical point $x = c$, a number, corresponds to the equilibrium solution $x(t) \equiv c$, a constant-valued function.

Example 2 illustrates the fact that the qualitative behavior (as t increases) of the solutions of an autonomous first-order equation can be described in terms of its critical points.

EXAMPLE 2   Consider the logistic differential equation

$$\frac{dx}{dt} = kx(M - x) \tag{5}$$

(with $k > 0$ and $M > 0$). It has two critical points—the solutions $x = 0$ and $x = M$ of the equation

$$f(x) = kx(M - x) = 0.$$

In Section 2.1 we found the solution

$$x(t) = \frac{Mx_0}{x_0 + (M - x_0)e^{-kMt}} \tag{6}$$

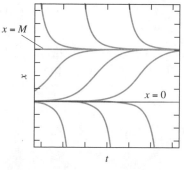

FIGURE 2.2.3. Typical solution curves for the logistic equation $dx/dt = kx(M - x)$.

satisfying the initial condition $x(0) = x_0$. Note that the initial values $x_0 = 0$ and $x_0 = M$ yield the equilibrium solutions $x(t) \equiv 0$ and $x(t) \equiv M$ of Eq. (5).

We observed in Section 2.1 that if $x_0 > 0$ then $x(t) \to M$ as $t \to +\infty$. But if $x_0 < 0$, then the denominator in Eq. (6) initially is positive, but vanishes when

$$t = t_1 = \frac{1}{kM} \ln \frac{M - x_0}{-x_0} > 0.$$

Because the numerator in (6) is negative in this case, it follows that

$$\lim_{t \to t_1^-} x(t) = -\infty \quad \text{if} \quad x_0 < 0.$$

It follows that the solution curves of the logistic equation in (6) look as illustrated in Fig. 2.2.3.

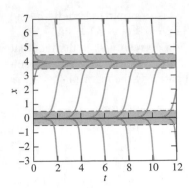

FIGURE 2.2.4. Solution curves, funnel, and spout for $dx/dt = 4x - x^2$.

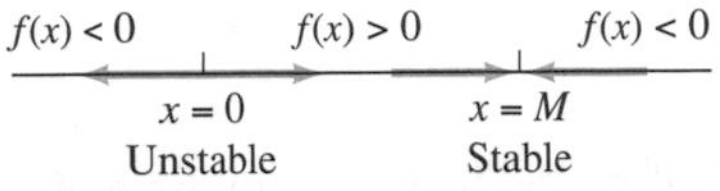

$f(x) < 0$ $f(x) > 0$ $f(x) < 0$

$x = 0$ $x = M$
Unstable   Stable

FIGURE 2.2.5. Phase diagram for the logistic equation $dx/dt = f(x) = kx(M - x)$.

Figure 2.2.3 illustrates the concept of *stability*. A critical point $x = c$ of an autonomous first-order equation is said to be *stable* provided that, if the initial value x_0 is sufficiently close to c, then $x(t)$ remains close to c for all $t > 0$. More precisely, the critical point c is **stable** if, for each $\epsilon > 0$, there exists $\delta > 0$ such that

$$|x_0 - c| < \delta \quad \text{implies that} \quad |x(t) - c| < \epsilon \tag{7}$$

for all $t > 0$. The critical point $x = c$ is **unstable** if it is not stable.

Figure 2.2.4 shows a "wider view" of the solution curves of a logistic equation with $k = 1$ and $M = 4$. Note that the strip $3.5 < x < 4.5$ enclosing the stable equilibrium curve $x = 4$ acts like a *funnel*—solution curves (moving from left to right) enter this strip and thereafter remain within it. By contrast, the strip $-0.5 < x < 0.5$ enclosing the unstable solution curve $x = 0$ acts like a *spout*—solution curves leave this strip and thereafter remain outside it. Thus the critical point $x = M$ is stable, whereas the critical point $x = 0$ is unstable.

We can summarize the behavior of solutions of the logistic equation in (5)—in terms of their initial values—by means of the phase diagram shown in Fig. 2.2.5. It indicates that $x(t) \to M$ as $t \to +\infty$ if either $x_0 > M$ or $0 < x_0 < M$, whereas $x(t) \to -\infty$ as t increases if $x_0 < 0$. The fact that M is a stable critical point would be important, for instance, if we wished to conduct an experiment with a population of M bacteria. It is impossible to count precisely M bacteria for M large, but any initially positive population will approach M as t increases.

An important consequence of the stability of the limiting solution $M = a/b$ of the logistic equation

$$\frac{dx}{dt} = ax - bx^2 \tag{8}$$

is the "predictability" of M for an actual population. The coefficients a and b are unlikely to be known precisely for an actual population. But if they are replaced with close approximations $a^\star$ and $b^\star$, then the approximate limiting population $M^\star = a^\star/b^\star$ will be close to the actual limiting population $M = a/b$. Thus the limiting population that Eq. (8) predicts is stable with respect to small perturbations of its constant coefficients.

EXAMPLE 3   Consider now the explosion/extinction equation

$$\frac{dx}{dt} = kx(x - M) \tag{9}$$

of Eq. (10) in Section 2.1. Like the logistic equation, it has the two critical points $x = 0$ and $x = M$ corresponding to the equilibrium solutions $x(t) \equiv 0$ and $x(t) \equiv M$. In Problem 15 we ask you to show that its solution with $x(0) = x_0$ is given by

$$x(t) = \frac{Mx_0}{x_0 + (M - x_0)e^{kMt}} \tag{10}$$

(with only a single difference in sign from the logistic solution in (6)). If $x_0 < M$, then (because the coefficient of the exponential in the denominator is positive) it follows immediately from Eq. (10) that $x(t) \to 0$ as $t \to +\infty$. But if $x_0 > M$, then the denominator in (10) initially is positive, but vanishes when

$$t = t_1 = \frac{1}{kM} \ln \frac{x_0 - M}{x_0} > 0.$$

Because the numerator in (10) is positive in this case, it follows that

$$\lim_{t \to t_1^-} x(t) = +\infty \quad \text{if} \quad x_0 > M.$$

Therefore, the solution curves of the explosion/extinction equation in (9) look as illustrated in Fig. 2.2.6. A narrow band along the equilibrium curve $x = 0$ (as in Fig. 2.2.4) would serve as a funnel, while a band along the solution curve $x = M$ would serve as a spout for solutions. The behavior of the solutions of Eq. (9) is summarized by the phase diagram in Fig. 2.2.7, where we see that the critical point $x = 0$ is stable and the critical point $x = M$ is unstable.   ■

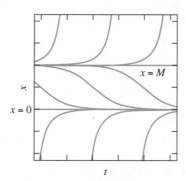

FIGURE 2.2.6. Typical solution curves for the explosion/extinction equation $dx/dt = kx(x - M)$.

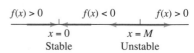

FIGURE 2.2.7. Phase diagram for the explosion/extinction equation $dx/dt = f(x) = kx(x - M)$.

Harvesting a Logistic Population

The autonomous differential equation

$$\frac{dx}{dt} = ax - bx^2 - h \tag{11}$$

(with a, b, and h all positive) may be considered to describe a logistic population *with harvesting*. For instance, we might think of the population of fish in a lake from which h fish per year are removed by fishing.

EXAMPLE 4   Let us rewrite Eq. (11) in the form

$$\frac{dx}{dt} = kx(M - x) - h, \tag{12}$$

which exhibits the limiting population M in the case $h = 0$ of no harvesting. Assuming hereafter that $h > 0$, we can solve the quadratic equation $-kx^2 + kMx - h = 0$ for the two critical points

$$H, N = \frac{kM \pm \sqrt{(kM)^2 - 4hk}}{2k} = \frac{1}{2}\left(M \pm \sqrt{M^2 - 4h/k}\right), \tag{13}$$

assuming that the harvesting rate h is sufficiently small that $4h < kM^2$, so both roots H and N are real with $0 < H < N < M$. Then we can rewrite Eq. (12) in the form

$$\frac{dx}{dt} = k(N - x)(x - H). \tag{14}$$

In Problem 16 we ask you to solve this equation for the solution

$$x(t) = \frac{N(x_0 - H) - H(x_0 - N)e^{-k(N-H)t}}{(x_0 - H) - (x_0 - N)e^{-k(N-H)t}} \tag{15}$$

in terms of the initial value $x(0) = x_0$.

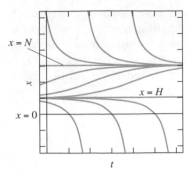

FIGURE 2.2.8. Typical solution curves for the logistic harvesting equation $dx/dt = k(N - x)(x - H)$.

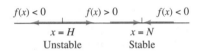

FIGURE 2.2.9. Phase diagram for the logistic harvesting equation $dx/dt = f(x) = k(N - x)(x - H)$.

Note that the exponent $-k(N - H)t$ is negative for $t > 0$. If $x_0 > N$ then each of the coefficients within parentheses in Eq. (15) is positive; it follows that

$$\text{If} \quad x_0 > N \quad \text{then} \quad x(t) \to N \quad \text{as} \quad t \to +\infty. \qquad (16)$$

In Problem 17 we ask you to deduce also from Eq. (15) that

$$\text{If} \quad H < x_0 < N \quad \text{then} \quad x(t) \to N \quad \text{as} \quad t \to +\infty, \quad \text{whereas} \qquad (17)$$

$$\text{if} \quad x_0 < H \quad \text{then} \quad x(t) \to -\infty \quad \text{as} \quad t \to t_1 \qquad (18)$$

for a positive value t_1 that depends on x_0. It follows that the solution curves of Eq. (12)—still assuming that $4h < kM^2$—look as illustrated in Fig. 2.2.8. (Can you visualize a funnel along the line $x = N$ and a spout along the line $x = H$?) Thus the constant solution $x(t) \equiv N$ is an equilibrium *limiting solution*, whereas $x(t) \equiv H$ is a *threshold solution* that separates different behaviors—the population approaches N if $x_0 > H$, while it becomes extinct because of harvesting if $x_0 < H$. Finally, the stable critical point $x = N$ and the unstable critical point $x = H$ are illustrated in the phase diagram in Fig. 2.2.9. ■

For a concrete application of our stability conclusions in Example 4, suppose that $k = 1$ and $M = 4$ for a logistic population $x(t)$ of fish in a lake, measured in hundreds after t years. Without any fishing at all, the lake would eventually contain nearly 400 fish, whatever the initial population. Now suppose that $h = 3$, so that 300 fish are "harvested" annually (at a constant rate throughout the year). Equation (12) is then $dx/dt = x(4 - x) - 4$, and the quadratic equation

$$-x^2 + 4x - 3 = (3 - x)(x - 1) = 0$$

has solutions $H = 1$ and $N = 3$. Thus the threshold population is 100 fish and the (new) limiting population is 300 fish. In short, if the lake is stocked initially with more than 100 fish, then as t increases the fish population will approach a limiting value of 300 fish. But if the lake is stocked initially with fewer than 100 fish, then the lake will be "fished out" and the fish will disappear entirely within a finite period of time.

2.2 Problems

In Problems 1 through 12 first solve the equation $f(x) = 0$ to find the critical points of the given autonomous differential equation $dx/dt = f(x)$. Then analyze the sign of $f(x)$ to determine whether each critical point is stable or unstable, and construct the corresponding phase diagram for the differential equation. Next sketch typical solution curves of the equation (as in several figures in this section). Finally, solve the differential equation explicitly for $x(t)$ in terms of t and the initial value $x(0) = x_0$, and use your solution to verify the forms of the various solution curves.

1. $\dfrac{dx}{dt} = x - 4$

2. $\dfrac{dx}{dt} = 3 - x$

3. $\dfrac{dx}{dt} = x^2 - 4x$

4. $\dfrac{dx}{dt} = 3x - x^2$

5. $\dfrac{dx}{dt} = x^2 - 4$

6. $\dfrac{dx}{dt} = 9 - x^2$

7. $\dfrac{dx}{dt} = (x - 2)^2$

8. $\dfrac{dx}{dt} = -(3 - x)^2$

9. $\dfrac{dx}{dt} = x^2 - 5x + 4$

10. $\dfrac{dx}{dt} = 7x - x^2 - 10$

11. $\dfrac{dx}{dt} = (x - 1)^3$

12. $\dfrac{dx}{dt} = (2 - x)^3$

13. Consider the differential equation $dx/dt = kx - x^3$. (a) If $k \leq 0$, show that the only critical value $c = 0$ of x is stable. (b) If $k > 0$, show that the critical value $c = 0$ is now unstable, but that the critical values $c = \pm\sqrt{k}$ are stable. *Note:* Figure 2.2.10 shows a plot of all points of the form (k, c) where c is a critical point of the equation $dx/dt = kx - x^3$. The value $k = 0$ of the parameter, for which the qualitative nature of the solutions changes as k increases, is called a **bifurcation point** for the differential equation.

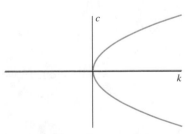

FIGURE 2.2.10. Bifurcation diagram for $dx/dt = kx - x^3$.

14. Suppose that the logistic equation $dx/dt = kx(M - x)$ models a population $x(t)$ of fish in a lake after t months during which no fishing occurs. Now suppose that, because of fishing, fish are removed from the lake at the rate of hx fish per month (with h a positive constant). Thus fish are "harvested" at a rate proportional to the existing fish population, rather than at the constant rate of Example 4. (a) If $0 < h < kM$, show that the population is still logistic. What is the new limiting population? (b) If $h \geq kM$, show that $x(t) \to 0$ are $t \to +\infty$, so the lake is eventually fished out.

15. Separate variables in the explosion/extinction equation $dx/dt = kx(x - M)$ and then use partial fractions to derive the solution given in Eq. (10).

16. Separate variables in the logistic harvesting equation $dx/dt = k(N - x)(x - H)$ and then use partial fractions to derive the solution given in Eq. (15).

17. Use the alternative forms

$$x(t) = \frac{N(x_0 - H) + H(N - x_0)e^{-k(N-H)t}}{(x_0 - H) + (N - x_0)e^{-k(N-H)t}}$$

$$= \frac{H(N - x_0)e^{-k(N-H)t} - N(H - x_0)}{(N - x_0)e^{-k(N-H)t} - (H - x_0)}$$

of the solution in (15) to establish the conclusions stated in (17) and (18).

Example 4 dealt with the case $4h > kM^2$ in the equation $dx/dt = kx(M - x) - h$ that describes constant-rate harvesting of a logistic population. Problems 18 and 19 deal with the other cases.

18. If $4h = kM^2$, show that typical solution curves look as illustrated in Fig. 2.2.11. Thus if $x_0 \geq M/2$, then $x(t) \to M/2$ as $t \to +\infty$. But if $x_0 < M/2$, then $x(t) = 0$ after a finite period of time, so the lake is fished out. The critical point $x = M/2$ might be called *semistable,* because it looks stable from one side, unstable from the other.

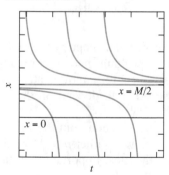

FIGURE 2.2.11. Solution curves for harvesting a logistic population with $4h = kM^2$.

19. If $4h > kM^2$, show that $x(t) = 0$ after a finite period of time, so the lake is fished out (whatever the initial population). *Suggestion:* Complete the square to rewrite the differential equation in the form $dx/dt = -k[(x-a)^2 + b^2]$. Then solve explicitly by separation of variables. The results of this and the previous problem (together with Example 4) show that $h = \frac{1}{4}kM^2$ is a critical harvesting rate for a logistic population. At any lesser harvesting rate the population approaches a limiting population N that is less than M (why?), whereas at any greater harvesting rate the population reaches extinction.

20. This problem deals with the differential equation $dx/dt = kx(x - M) - h$ that models the harvesting of an unsophisticated population (such as alligators). Show that this equation can be rewritten in the form $dx/dt = k(x - H)(x - K)$, where

$$H = \tfrac{1}{2}\left(M + \sqrt{M^2 + 4h/k}\right) > 0,$$

$$K = \tfrac{1}{2}\left(M - \sqrt{M^2 + 4h/k}\right) < 0.$$

Show that typical solution curves look as illustrated in Fig. 2.2.12.

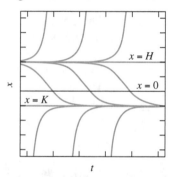

FIGURE 2.2.12. Solution curves for harvesting a population of alligators.

21. Consider the two differential equations

$$\frac{dx}{dt} = (x - a)(x - b)(x - c) \tag{19}$$

and $$\frac{dx}{dt} = (a - x)(b - x)(c - x), \tag{20}$$

each having the critical points a, b, and c; suppose that $a < b < c$. For one of these equations, only the critical point b is stable; for the other equation, b is the only unstable critical point. Construct phase diagrams for the two equations to determine which is which. Without attempting to solve either equation explicitly, make rough sketches of typical solution curves for each. You should see two funnels and a spout in one case, two spouts and a funnel in the other.

2.3 ACCELERATION-VELOCITY MODELS

In Section 1.2 we discussed vertical motion of a mass m near the surface of the earth under the influence of constant gravitational acceleration. If we neglect any effects of air resistance, then Newton's second law ($F = ma$) implies that the velocity v of the mass m satisfies the equation

$$m\frac{dv}{dt} = F_G \tag{1}$$

where $F_G = -mg$ is the (downward-directed) force of gravity, where the gravitational acceleration is $g \approx 9.8$ m/s^2 (in mks units; $g \approx 32$ ft/s^2 in fps units).

EXAMPLE 1   Suppose that a crossbow bolt is shot straight upward from the ground ($y_0 = 0$) with initial velocity $v_0 = 49$ (m/s). Then Eq. (1) with $g = 9.8$ gives

$$\frac{dv}{dt} = -9.8, \quad \text{so} \quad v(t) = -(9.8)t + v_0 = -(9.8)t + 49.$$

Hence the bolt's height function $y(t)$ is given by

$$y(t) = \int [-(9.8)t + 49]\, dt = -(4.9)t^2 + 49t + y_0 = -(4.9)t^2 + 49t.$$

The bolt reaches its maximum height when $v = -(9.8)t + 49 = 0$, hence when $t = 5$ (s). Thus its maximum height is

$$y_{max} = y(5) = -(4.9)(5^2) + (49)(5) = 122.5 \text{ (m)}.$$

The bolt returns to the ground when $y = -(4.9)t(t - 10) = 0$, and thus after 10 seconds aloft.   ∎

Now we want to take account of air resistance in a problem like Example 1. The force F_R exerted by air resistance on the moving mass m must be added in Eq. (1), so now

$$m\frac{dv}{dt} = F_G + F_R. \tag{2}$$

Newton showed in his *Principia Mathematica* that certain simple physical assumptions imply that F_R is proportional to the *square* of the velocity: $F_R = kv^2$. But empirical investigations indicate that the actual dependence of air resistance on velocity can be quite complicated. For many purposes it suffices to assume that

$$F_R = kv^p,$$

where $1 \leqq p \leqq 2$ and the value of k depends on the size and shape of the body, as well as the density and viscosity of the air. Generally speaking, $p = 1$ for relatively low speeds and $p = 2$ for high speeds, whereas $1 < p < 2$ for intermediate speeds. But how slow "low speed," and how fast "high speed" are, depend on the same factors that determine the value of the coefficient k.

Thus air resistance is a complicated physical phenomenon. But the simplifying assumption that F_R is exactly of the form given here, with either $p = 1$ or $p = 2$, yields a tractable mathematical model that exhibits the most important qualitative features of motion with resistance.

Resistance Proportional to Velocity

Let us first consider the vertical motion of a body with mass m near the surface of the earth, subject to two forces: a downward gravitational force F_G and a force F_R of air resistance that is proportional to velocity (so that $p = 1$) and of course directed opposite the direction of motion of the body. If we set up a coordinate system with the positive y-direction upward and with $y = 0$ at ground level, then $F_G = -mg$ and

$$F_R = -kv, \tag{3}$$

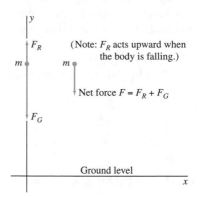

FIGURE 2.3.1. Vertical motion with air resistance.

where k is a positive constant and $v = dy/dt$ is the velocity of the body. Note that the minus sign in Eq. (3) makes F_R positive (an upward force) if the body is falling (v is negative) and makes F_R negative (a downward force) if the body is rising (v is positive). As indicated in Fig. 2.3.1, the net force acting on the body is then

$$F = F_R + F_G = -kv - mg,$$

and Newton's law of motion $F = m(dv/dt)$ yields the equation

$$m\frac{dv}{dt} = -kv - mg.$$

Thus

$$\frac{dv}{dt} = -\rho v - g \tag{4}$$

where $\rho = k/m > 0$. You should verify for yourself that, if the positive y-axis were directed downward, then Eq. (4) would take the form $dv/dt = -\rho v + g$.

Equation (4) is a separable first-order differential equation, and its solution is

$$v(t) = \left(v_0 + \frac{g}{\rho}\right)e^{-\rho t} - \frac{g}{\rho}. \tag{5}$$

Here, $v_0 = v(0)$ is the initial velocity of the body. Note that

$$v_\tau = \lim_{t \to \infty} v(t) = -\frac{g}{\rho}. \tag{6}$$

Thus the speed of a body falling with air resistance does *not* increase indefinitely; instead, it approaches a *finite* limiting speed, or **terminal speed,**

$$|v_\tau| = \frac{g}{\rho} = \frac{mg}{k}. \tag{7}$$

This fact is what makes a parachute a practical invention; it even helps explain the occasional survival of people who fall without parachutes from high-flying airplanes.

We now rewrite Eq. (5) in the form

$$\frac{dy}{dt} = (v_0 - v_\tau)e^{-\rho t} + v_\tau. \tag{8}$$

Integration gives

$$y(t) = -\frac{1}{\rho}(v_0 - v_\tau)e^{-\rho t} + v_\tau t + C.$$

We substitute 0 for t and let $y_0 = y(0)$ denote the initial height of the body. Thus we find that $C = y_0 + (v_0 - v_\tau)/\rho$, and so

$$y(t) = y_0 + v_\tau t + \frac{1}{\rho}(v_0 - v_\tau)(1 - e^{-\rho t}). \tag{9}$$

Equations (8) and (9) give the velocity v and height y of a body moving vertically under the influence of gravity and air resistance. The formulas depend on the initial height y_0 of the body, its initial velocity v_0, and the *drag coefficient* ρ, the constant such that the acceleration due to air resistance is $a_R = -\rho v$. The two equations also involve the terminal velocity v_τ defined in Eq. (6).

For a person descending with the aid of a parachute, a typical value of ρ is 1.5, which corresponds to a terminal speed of $|v_\tau| \approx 21.3$ ft/s, or about 14.5 mi/h. With an unbuttoned overcoat flapping in the wind in place of a parachute, an unlucky skydiver might increase ρ to perhaps as much as 0.5, which gives a terminal speed of $|v_\tau| \approx 65$ ft/s, about 44 mi/h. See Problems 10 and 11 for some parachute-jump computations.

EXAMPLE 2   We again consider a bolt shot straight upward with initial velocity $v_0 = 49$ m/s from a crossbow at ground level. But now we take air resistance into account, with $\rho = 0.04$ in Eq. (4). We ask how the resulting maximum height and time aloft compare with the values found in Example 1.

Solution   We substitute $y_0 = 0$, $v_0 = 49$, and $v_\tau = -g/\rho = -245$ in Eqs. (5) and (9), and obtain

$$v(t) = 294e^{-t/25} - 245,$$

$$y(t) = 7350 - 245t - 7350e^{-t/25}.$$

To find the time required for the bolt to reach its maximum height (when $v = 0$), we solve the equation

$$v(t) = 294e^{-t/25} - 245 = 0$$

for $t_m = 25 \ln(294/245) \approx 4.558$ (s). Its maximum height is then $y_{max} = v(t_m) \approx 108.280$ meters (as opposed to 122.5 meters without air resistance). To find when the bolt strikes the ground, we must solve the equation

$$y(t) = 7350 - 245t - 7350e^{-t/25} = 0.$$

Using Newton's method, we can begin with the initial guess $t_0 = 10$ and carry out the iteration $t_{n+1} = t_n - y(t_n)/y'(t_n)$ to generate successive approximations to the root. Or we can simply use the **Solve** command on a calculator or computer. We find that the bolt is in the air for $t_f \approx 9.411$ seconds (as opposed to 10 seconds without air resistance). It hits the ground with a reduced speed of $|v(t_f)| \approx 43.227$ m/s (as opposed to its initial velocity of 49 m/s).

Thus the effect of air resistance is to decrease the bolt's maximum height, the total time spent aloft, and its final impact speed. Note also that the bolt now spends more time in descent ($t_f - t_m \approx 4.853$ s) than in ascent ($t_m \approx 4.558$ s).   ■

Resistance Proportional to Square of Velocity

Now we assume that the force of air resistance is proportional to the *square* of the velocity:

$$F_R = \pm kv^2, \tag{10}$$

with $k > 0$. The choice of signs here depends on the direction of motion, which the force of resistance always opposes. Taking the positive y-direction as upward, $F_R < 0$ for upward motion (when $v > 0$) while $F_R > 0$ for downward motion (when $v < 0$). Thus the sign of F_R is always opposite that of v, so we can rewrite Eq. (10) as

$$F_R = -kv|v|. \tag{10'}$$

Then Newton's second law gives

$$m\frac{dv}{dt} = F_G + F_R = -mg - kv|v|;$$

that is,

$$\frac{dv}{dt} = -g - \rho v|v| \tag{11}$$

where $\rho = k/m > 0$. We must discuss the cases of upward and downward motion separately.

UPWARD MOTION: Suppose that a projectile is launched straight upward from the initial position y_0 with initial velocity $v_0 > 0$. Then Eq. (11) with $v > 0$ gives the differential equation

$$\frac{dv}{dt} = -g - \rho v^2 = -g\left(1 + \frac{\rho}{g}v^2\right).\tag{12}$$

In Problem 13 we ask you to make the substitution $u = v\sqrt{\rho/g}$ and apply the familiar integral

$$\int \frac{1}{1+u^2}\,du = \tan^{-1} u + C$$

to derive the projectile's velocity function

$$v(t) = \sqrt{\frac{g}{\rho}}\tan\left(C_1 - t\sqrt{\rho g}\right) \quad\text{with}\quad C_1 = \tan^{-1}\left(v_0\sqrt{\frac{\rho}{g}}\right).\tag{13}$$

Because $\int \tan u\,du = -\ln|\cos u| + C$, a second integration (see Problem 14) yields the position function

$$y(t) = y_0 + \frac{1}{\rho}\ln\left|\frac{\cos\left(C_1 - t\sqrt{\rho g}\right)}{\cos C_1}\right|.\tag{14}$$

DOWNWARD MOTION: Suppose that a projectile is launched (or dropped) straight downward from the initial position y_0 with initial velocity $v_0 \leqq 0$. Then Eq. (11) with $v < 0$ gives the differential equation

$$\frac{dv}{dt} = -g + \rho v^2 = -g\left(1 - \frac{\rho}{g}v^2\right).\tag{15}$$

In Problem 15 we ask you to make the substitution $u = v\sqrt{\rho/g}$ and apply the integral

$$\int \frac{1}{1-u^2}\,du = \tanh^{-1} u + C$$

to derive the projectile's velocity function

$$v(t) = \sqrt{\frac{g}{\rho}}\tanh\left(C_2 - t\sqrt{\rho g}\right) \quad\text{with}\quad C_2 = \tanh^{-1}\left(v_0\sqrt{\frac{\rho}{g}}\right).\tag{16}$$

Because $\int \tanh u\,du = \ln|\cosh u| + C$, another integration (Problem 16) yields the position function

$$y(t) = y_0 - \frac{1}{\rho}\ln\left|\frac{\cosh\left(C_2 - t\sqrt{\rho g}\right)}{\cosh C_2}\right|.\tag{17}$$

(Note the analogy between Eqs. (16) and (17) and Eqs. (13) and (14) for upward motion.)

If $v_0 = 0$, then $C_2 = 0$, so $v(t) = -\sqrt{g/\rho}\tanh\left(t\sqrt{\rho g}\right)$. Because

$$\lim_{x\to\infty}\tanh x = \lim_{x\to\infty}\frac{\sinh x}{\cosh x} = \lim_{x\to\infty}\frac{\frac{1}{2}(e^x - e^{-x})}{\frac{1}{2}(e^x + e^{-x})} = 1,$$

it follows that in the case of downward motion the body approaches the terminal speed

$$|v_\tau| = \sqrt{\frac{g}{\rho}}\tag{18}$$

(as compared with $|v_\tau| = g/\rho$ in the case of downward motion with linear resistance described by Eq. (4)).

EXAMPLE 3 We consider once more a bolt shot straight upward with initial velocity $v_0 = 49$ m/s from a crossbow at ground level, as in Example 2. But now we assume air resistance proportional to the square of the velocity, with $\rho = 0.0011$ in Eqs. (12) and (15). In Problems 17 and 18 we ask you to verify the entries in the last line of the following table.

Air Resistance	Maximum Height (ft)	Time Aloft	Ascent Time (s)	Descent Time (s)	Impact Speed (ft/s)
0.0	122.5	10	5	5	49
$(0.04)v$	108.28	9.41	4.56	4.85	43.23
$(0.0011)v^2$	108.47	9.41	4.61	4.80	43.49

Although scientists and engineers have occasionally debated the differences between motion with linear air resistance and motion with air resistance proportional to the square of the velocity, comparison of the last two lines of data here suggests a close similarity in the case of our crossbow bolt. In Fig. 2.3.2—where the height functions are graphed—the difference is hardly visible. ■

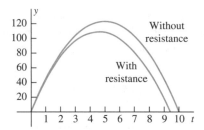

FIGURE 2.3.2. The height function in Example 1 (without air resistance), Example 2 (with linear air resistance), and Example 3 (with air resistance proportional to the square of the velocity) are all plotted. The graphs of the latter two are visually indistinguishable.

Variable Gravitational Acceleration

Unless a projectile in vertical motion remains in the immediate vicinity of the earth's surface, the gravitational acceleration acting on it is not constant. According to Newton's law of gravitation, the gravitational force of attraction between two point masses M and m located at a distance r apart is given by

$$F = \frac{GMm}{r^2}, \tag{19}$$

where G is a certain empirical constant ($G \approx 6.6726 \times 10^{-11}$ N·(m/kg)^2 in mks units). The formula is also valid if either or both of the two masses are homogeneous spheres; in this case, the distance r is measured between the centers of the spheres.

The following example is similar to Example 2 in Section 1.2, but now we take account of lunar gravity.

EXAMPLE 4 A lunar lander is free-falling toward the moon's surface at a speed of $v_0 = 450$ m/s (that is, 1620 km/h). Its retrorockets, when fired in free space, provide a deceleration of $T = 4$ m/s^2. At what height above the lunar surface should the retrorockets be activated to ensure a "soft touchdown" ($v = 0$ at impact)?

Solution Let $r(t)$ denote the lander's distance from the center of the moon at time t (Fig 2.3.3). When we combine the (positive) thrust acceleration T and the (negative) lunar acceleration $F/m = GM/r^2$ of Eq. (19), we get the (acceleration) differential equation

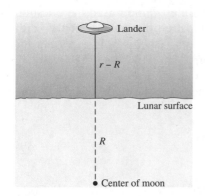

Lander

$r - R$

Lunar surface

R

Center of moon

FIGURE 2.3.3. The lunar lander descending to the surface of the moon.

$$\frac{d^2r}{dt^2} = T - \frac{GM}{r^2},$$ (20)

where $M = 7.35 \times 10^{22}$ (kg) is the mass of the moon, which has a radius of $R = 1.74 \times 10^6$ (m) (or 1740 km, a little over a quarter of the earth's radius). In terms of the lander's velocity $v = dr/dt$, Eq. (20) is

$$\frac{dv}{dt} = T - \frac{GM}{r^2}.$$

Substitution using the chain rule formula

$$\frac{dv}{dt} = \frac{dv}{dr} \cdot \frac{dr}{dt} = v\frac{dv}{dr}$$

gives the first-order equation

$$v\frac{dv}{dr} = T - \frac{GM}{r^2}$$

with r as new independent variable. Because the left-hand side is the derivative of $\frac{1}{2}v^2$ with respect to r, integration of both sides yields the implicit solution

$$\frac{1}{2}v^2 = Tr + \frac{GM}{r} + C.$$

The desired condition that $v = 0$ when $r = R$ gives $C = -TR - GM/R$, so

$$\frac{1}{2}v^2 = Tr + \frac{GM}{r} - TR - \frac{GM}{R};$$

that is,

$$Tr^2 - \left(TR + \frac{GM}{R} + \tfrac{1}{2}v^2\right)r + GM = 0$$ (21)

(upon multiplication by r). Finally, we need to know the value of r when $v = -450$ (m/s). Substitution of this given initial velocity of the lander, the thrust $T = 4$ (m/s^2), and the known values of G, M, and R yields the quadratic equation

$$4r^2 - (9.87985 \times 10^6)r + 4.90436 \times 10^{12} = 0$$

with approximate roots $r = 0.68809 \times 10^6$ and $r = 1.78187 \times 10^6$. The latter is the one we seek (why?), so the lander's desired initial height *above the lunar surface* is $r - R = 1781870 - 1740000 = 41870$ meters; that is, 41.87 kilometers (just over 26 miles). ∎

Escape Velocity

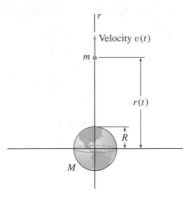

FIGURE 2.3.4. A mass m at a great distance from the earth.

In his novel *From the Earth to the Moon* (1865), Jules Verne raised the question of the initial velocity necesary for a projectile fired from the surface of the earth to reach the moon. Similarly, we can ask what initial velocity v_0 is necessary for the projectile to escape from the earth altogether. This will be so if its velocity $v = dr/dt$ remains *positive* for all $t > 0$, so it continues forever to move away from the earth. With $r(t)$ denoting the projectile's distance from the earth's center at time t (Fig. 2.3.4), we have the equation

$$\frac{dv}{dt} = \frac{d^2r}{dt^2} = -\frac{GM}{r^2}, \tag{22}$$

similar to Eq. (21), but with $T = 0$ (no thrust) and with $M = 5.975 \times 10^{24}$ (kg) denoting the mass of the earth, which has an equatorial radius of $R = 6.378 \times 10^6$ (m). Substitution of the chain rule expression $dv/dt = v(dr/dr)$ as in Example 4 gives

$$v\frac{dv}{dr} = -\frac{GM}{r^2}.$$

Then integration of both sides with respect to r yields

$$\frac{1}{2}v^2 = \frac{GM}{r} + C.$$

Now $v = v_0$ and $r = R$ when $t = 0$, so $C = \frac{1}{2}v_0^2 - GM/R$, and hence solution for v^2 gives

$$v^2 = v_0^2 + 2GM\left(\frac{1}{r} - \frac{1}{R}\right). \tag{23}$$

This implicit solution of Eq. (22) determines the projectile's velocity v as a function of its distance r from the earth's center. In particular,

$$v^2 > v_0^2 - \frac{2GM}{R},$$

so v will remain positive provided that $v_0^2 \geqq 2GM/R$. Therefore, the **escape velocity** from the earth is given by

$$v_0 = \sqrt{\frac{2GM}{R}}. \tag{24}$$

With the given values of G and the earth's mass M and radius R, this gives $v_0 \approx$ 11180 (m/s) (about 36680 ft/s, about 6.95 mi/s, about 25000 mi/h).

Remark: Equation (24) gives the escape velocity for any other (spherical) planetary body when we use *its* mass and radius. For instance, when we use the mass M and radius R for the moon given in Example 4, we find that escape velocity from the lunar surface is $v_0 \approx 2375$ m/s. This is just over one-fifth of the escape velocity from the earth's surface, a fact that greatly facilitates the return trip ("From the Moon to the Earth"). ■

2.3 Problems

1. The acceleration of a Maserati is proportional to the difference between 250 km/h and the velocity of this sports car. If this machine can accelerate from rest to 100 km/h in 10 s, how long will it take for the car to accelerate from rest to 200 km/h?

2. Suppose that a body moves through a resisting medium with resistance proportional to its velocity v, so that $dv/dt = -kv$. (a) Show that its velocity and position at time t are given by

$$v(t) = v_0 e^{-kt}$$

and

$$x(t) = x_0 + \left(\frac{v_0}{k}\right)(1 - e^{-kt}).$$

(b) Conclude that the body travels only a finite distance, and find that distance.

3. Suppose that a motorboat is moving at 40 ft/s when its motor suddenly quits, and that 10 s later the boat has slowed to 20 ft/s. Assume, as in Problem 2, that the resistance it encounters while coasting is proportional to its velocity. How far will the boat coast in all?

4. Consider a body that moves horizontally through a medium whose resistance is proportional to the *square* of the velocity v, so that $dv/dt = -kv^2$. Show that

$$v(t) = \frac{v_0}{1 + v_0 kt}$$

and that

$$x(t) = x_0 + \frac{1}{k}\ln(1 + v_0 kt).$$

Note that, in contrast with the result of Problem 2, $x(t) \to +\infty$ as $t \to +\infty$.

5. Assuming resistance proportional to the square of the velocity (as in Problem 4), how far does the motorboat of Problem 3 coast in the first minute after its motor quits?

6. Assume that a body moving with velocity v encounters resistance of the form $dv/dt = -kv^{3/2}$. Show that

$$v(t) = \frac{4v_0}{\left(kt\sqrt{v_0} + 2\right)^2}$$

and that

$$x(t) = x_0 + \frac{2}{k}\sqrt{v_0}\left(1 - \frac{2}{kt\sqrt{v_0} + 2}\right).$$

Conclude that under a $\frac{3}{2}$-power resistance a body coasts only a finite distance before coming to a stop.

7. Suppose that a car starts from rest, its engine providing an acceleration of 10 ft/s², while air resistance provides 0.1 ft/s² of deceleration for each foot per second of the car's velocity. (a) Find the car's maximum possible (limiting) velocity. (b) Find how long it takes the car to attain 90% of its limiting velocity, and how far it travels while doing so.

8. Rework both parts of Problem 7, with the sole difference that the deceleration due to air resistance now is $(0.001)v^2$ ft/s² when the car's velocity is v feet per second.

9. A motorboat weighs 32000 lb and its motor provides a thrust of 5000 lb. Assume that the water resistance is 100 pounds for each foot per second of the speed v of the boat. Then

$$1000\frac{dv}{dt} = 5000 - 100v.$$

If the boat starts from rest, what is the maximum velocity that it can attain?

10. A woman bails out of an airplane at an altitude of 10000 ft, falls freely for 20 s, then opens her parachute. How long will it take her to reach the ground? Assume linear air resistance ρv ft/s², taking $\rho = 0.15$ without the parachute and $\rho = 1.5$ with the parachute. (*Suggestion*: First determine her height and velocity when the parachute opens.)

11. According to a newspaper account, a paratrooper survived a training jump from 1200 ft when his parachute failed to open but provided some resistance by flapping unopened in the wind. Allegedly he hit the ground at 100 mi/h after falling for 8 s. Test the accuracy of this account. (*Suggestion*: Find ρ in Eq. (4) by assuming a terminal velocity of 100 mi/h. Then calculate the time required to fall 1200 ft.)

12. It is proposed to dispose of nuclear wastes—in drums with weight $W = 640$ lb and volume 8 ft³—by dropping them into the ocean ($v_0 = 0$). The force equation for a drum falling through water is

$$m\frac{dv}{dt} = -W + B + F_R,$$

where the buoyant force B is equal to the weight (at 62.5 lb/ft³) of the volume of water displaced by the drum (Archimedes' principle) and F_R is the force of water resistance, found empirically to be 1 lb for each foot per second of the velocity of a drum. If the drums are likely to burst upon an impact of more than 75 ft/s, what is the maximum depth to which they can be dropped in the ocean without likelihood of bursting?

13. Separate variables in Eq. (12) and substitute $u = v\sqrt{\rho/g}$ to obtain the upward-motion velocity function given in Eq. (13) with initial condition $v(0) = v_0$.

14. Integrate the velocity function in Eq. (13) to obtain the upward-motion position function given in Eq. (14) with initial condition $y(0) = y_0$.

15. Separate variables in Eq. (15) and substitute $u = v\sqrt{\rho/g}$ to obtain the downward-motion velocity function given in Eq. (16) with initial condition $v(0) = v_0$.

16. Integrate the velocity function in Eq. (16) to obtain the downward-motion position function given in Eq. (17) with initial condition $y(0) = y_0$.

17. Consider the crossbow bolt of Example 3, shot straight upward from the ground ($y = 0$) at time $t = 0$ with initial velocity $v_0 = 49$ m/s. Take $g = 9.8$ m/s² and $\rho = 0.0011$ in Eq. (12). Then use Eqs. (13) and (14) to show that the bolt reaches its maximum height of about 108.47 m in about 4.61 s.

18. Continuing Problem 17, suppose that the bolt is now dropped ($v_0 = 0$) from a height of $y_0 = 108.47$ m. Then use Eqs. (16) and (17) to show that it hits the ground about 4.80 s later with an impact speed of about 43.49 m/s.

19. A motorboat starts from rest (initial velocity $v(0) = v_0 = 0$). Its motor provides a constant acceleration of 4 ft/s², but water resistance causes a deceleration of $v^2/400$ ft/s². Find v when $t = 10$ s, and also find the *limiting velocity* as $t \to +\infty$ (that is, the maximum possible speed of the boat).

20. An arrow is shot straight upward from the ground with an initial velocity of 160 ft/s. It experiences both the deceleration of gravity and deceleration $v^2/800$ due to air resistance. How high in the air does it go?

21. If a ball is projected upward from the ground with initial velocity v_0, deduce from Eq. (17) that the maximum height it attains is

$$y_{max} = \frac{1}{2\rho}\ln\left(1 + \frac{\rho v_0^2}{g}\right).$$

22. Suppose that $\rho = 0.075$ (in fps units, with $g = 32 \text{ ft/s}^2$) in Eq. (15) for a paratrooper falling with parachute open. If he jumps from an altitude of 10000 ft and opens his parachute immediately, what will be his terminal speed? How long will it take him to reach the ground?

23. Suppose that the paratrooper of Problem 22 falls freely for 30 s with $\rho = 0.00075$ before opening his parachute. How long will it now take him to reach the ground?

24. The mass of the sun is 329,320 times that of the earth and its radius is 109 times the radius of the earth. (a) To what radius (in meters) would the earth have to be compressed in order for it to become a *black hole*—the escape velocity from its surface equal to the velocity $c = 3 \times 10^8$ m/s of light? (b) Repeat part (a) with the sun in place of the earth.

25. (a) Show that if a projectile is launched straight upward from the surface of the earth with initial velocity v_0 less than escape velocity, then the maximum distance from the center of the earth attained by the projectile is

$$r_{\max} = \frac{2GMR}{2GM - Rv_0^2},$$

where M and R are the mass and radius of the earth, respectively. (b) With what initial velocity v_0 (in miles per hour) must such a projectile be launched to yield a maximum height of 100 mi above the surface of the earth? (Take the radius of the earth to be 3960 mi.) (c) Find the maximum distance from the center of the earth, expressed in terms of earth radii, attained by a projectile launched from the surface of the earth with 90% of escape velocity.

26. (a) Suppose that a body is dropped ($v_0 = 0$) from a distance r_0 from the earth's center, so its acceleration is $dv/dt = -GM/r^2$. Ignoring air resistance, show that it reaches the height r at time

$$t = \sqrt{\frac{r_0}{2GM}} \left(\sqrt{rr_0 - r^2} + r_0 \cos^{-1} \sqrt{\frac{r}{r_0}} \right).$$

(*Suggestion:* Substitute $r = r_0 \cos^2 \theta$ to evaluate $\int \sqrt{r/(r_0 - r)} \, dr$.) (b) If a body is dropped from a height of 1000 km above the earth's surface and air resistance is neglected, how long does it take to fall and with what speed will it strike the earth's surface?

27. Suppose that a projectile is fired straight upward from the surface of the earth with initial velocity v_0. Then its height $y(t)$ above the surface satisfies the initial value problem

$$\frac{d^2y}{dt^2} = -\frac{GM}{(y+R)^2}; \quad y(0) = 0, \quad y'(0) = v_0.$$

Substitute $dv/dt = v(dv/dy)$ and then integrate to obtain

$$v^2 = \frac{R(R+y)v_0^2 - 2GMy}{R(R+y)}$$

for the velocity v of the projectile at height y. What maximum height does it reach if its initial velocity is 1 km/s?

28. In Jules Verne's original problem, the projectile launched from the surface of the earth is attracted by both the earth and the moon, so its distance $r(t)$ from the center of the earth satisfies the initial value problem

$$\frac{d^2r}{dt^2} = -\frac{GM_e}{r^2} + \frac{GM_m}{(S-r)^2}; \quad r(0) = R, \quad r'(0) = v_0$$

where M_e and M_m denote the masses of the earth and the moon, respectively; R is the radius of the earth and $S = 384,400$ km is the distance between the centers of the earth and the moon. To reach the moon, the projectile must only just pass the point between the moon and earth where its net acceleration vanishes. Thereafter it is "under the control" of the moon, and falls from there to the lunar surface. Find the *minimal* launch velocity v_0 that suffices for the projectile to make it "From the Earth to the Moon."

2.4 NUMERICAL APPROXIMATION: EULER'S METHOD

It is the exception rather than the rule when a differential equation of the general form

$$\frac{dy}{dx} = f(x, y)$$

can be solved exactly and explicitly by elementary methods like those discussed in Chapter 1. For example, consider the simple equation

$$\frac{dy}{dx} = e^{-x^2}. \tag{1}$$

A solution of Eq. (1) is simply an antiderivative of e^{-x^2}. But it is known that every antiderivative of $f(x) = e^{-x^2}$ is a **nonelementary** function—one that cannot be expressed as a finite combination of the familiar functions of elementary calculus. Hence no particular solution of Eq. (1) is finitely expressible in terms of elementary functions.

Finding a particular solution of a differential equation is, in most applications, merely a means to an end. The goal is to be able to predict—with a reasonable degree of accuracy—the shape of a support column, the trajectory of a particle, or the modes of vibration of a mechanical system. Suppose that the system under investigation is modeled by the initial value problem

$$\frac{dy}{dx} = f(x, y), \quad y(a) = y_0. \tag{2}$$

For purposes such as those mentioned previously, it might be quite adequate to have a table of values of the unknown solution $y(x)$ at selected points of some interval $[a, b]$. In this section we discuss **Euler's method** for computing a table of numerical approximations to the solution of the initial value problem in (2).

To describe Euler's method, we first choose a fixed **step size** $h > 0$ and consider the points

$$x_0 = a, x_1, x_2, \ldots, x_n, \ldots$$

where $x_n = a + nh$, so that

$$x_{n+1} = x_n + h$$

for $n = 0, 1, 2, \ldots$. Our goal is to find suitable *approximations*

$$y_1, y_2, y_3, \ldots, y_n, \ldots$$

to the true values

$$y(x_1), y(x_2), y(x_3), \ldots, y(x_n), \ldots$$

of the solution $y(x)$ of Eq. (2) at the points $x_1, x_2, x_3, \ldots$. Thus we seek reasonably accurate approximations

$$y_n \approx y(x_n) \tag{3}$$

for $n = 1, 2, 3, \ldots$. The question is this: How do we "step" from the approximate value y_n at x_n to the approximate value y_{n+1} at x_{n+1}?

When $x = x_0$, the rate of change of y with respect to x is $y' = f(x_0, y_0)$. If y continued to change at this same rate from $x = x_0$ to $x = x_1 = x_0 + h$, then the change in y would be exactly $h \cdot f(x_0, y_0)$. We therefore take

$$y_1 = y_0 + h \cdot f(x_0, y_0) \tag{4}$$

as our approximation to the true value $y(x_1)$ of the solution at $x = x_1$. Similarly, we take

$$y_2 = y_1 + h \cdot f(x_1, y_1) \tag{5}$$

as our approximation to $y(x_2)$. In general, having reached the nth approximate value $y_n \approx y(x_n)$, we take

$$y_{n+1} = y_n + h \cdot f(x_n, y_n) \tag{6}$$

as our approximation to the true value $y(x_{n+1})$.

Equation (6) tells us how to make the typical step from y_n to y_{n+1} and is the heart of Euler's method. Note that the formulas in Eqs. (4) and (5) are the first two cases, $n = 0$ and $n = 1$, of the general iterative formula in Eq. (6).

ALGORITHM: The Euler Method

Given the initial value problem

$$\frac{dy}{dx} = f(x, y), \quad y(a) = y_0, \tag{2}$$

Euler's method with step size h consists in applying the iterative formula

➤
$$y_{n+1} = y_n + h \cdot f(x_n, y_n) \quad (n \geq 0) \tag{6}$$

(with $x_0 = a$) to compute successive approximations $y_1, y_2, y_3, \ldots$ to the [true] values $y(x_1), y(x_2), y(x_3), \ldots$ of the [exact] solution $y = y(x)$ at the points $x_1, x_2, x_3, \ldots$, respectively. ∎

Although the most important practical applications of Euler's method are to nonlinear differential equations, we will first illustrate the method with the initial value problem

$$\frac{dy}{dx} = x + y, \quad y(0) = 1, \tag{7}$$

in order that we may compare our approximate solution with the exact solution

$$y(x) = 2e^x - x - 1. \tag{8}$$

(This solution is readily found using the methods of Section 1.5.)

EXAMPLE 1   Apply Euler's method with step size $h = 0.1$ to approximate the solution of the initial value problem in (7) on the interval $0 \leq x \leq 1$.

Solution   Here $f(x, y) = x + y$, so the iterative formula in (6) takes the form

$$y_{n+1} = y_n + h \cdot (x_n + y_n). \tag{9}$$

Beginning with $x_0 = 0$, $y_0 = 1$, and rounding values to four decimal places, the first three approximate values given by (9) are

$$y_1 = 1.0000 + (0.1) \cdot (0.0 + 1.0000) = 1.1000,$$
$$y_2 = 1.1000 + (0.1) \cdot (0.1 + 1.1000) = 1.2200,$$
$$y_3 = 1.2200 + (0.1) \cdot (0.2 + 1.2200) = 1.3620.$$

The table in Fig. 2.4.1 shows the approximate values obtained in all ten steps, together with the actual values $y(x_n)$ given in Eq. (8) and the error

$$y_{\text{actual}} - y_{\text{approx}} = y(x_n) - y_n$$

at each step. Observe that the error in y_n increases as n increases—that is, as x_n gets farther and farther from the starting point x_0. The final column of the table shows the percentage error $100 \cdot (y_{\text{actual}} - y_{\text{approx}})/y_{\text{actual}}$ in each approximate value; these percentage errors increase from 0.93% at $x_1 = 0.1$ to 7.25% at $x_{10} = 1.0$. ∎

n	x_n	**Approximate** y_n	**Actual** $y(x_n)$	**Error** $y(x_n) - y_n$	**Percent Error**
0	0.0	1.0000	1.0000	0.0000	0.00%
1	0.1	1.1000	1.1103	0.0103	0.93%
2	0.2	1.2200	1.2428	0.0228	1.84%
3	0.3	1.3620	1.3997	0.0377	2.69%
4	0.4	1.5282	1.5836	0.0554	3.50%
5	0.5	1.7210	1.7974	0.0764	4.25%
6	0.6	1.9431	2.0442	0.1011	4.95%
7	0.7	2.1974	2.3275	0.1301	5.59%
8	0.8	2.4872	2.6511	0.1639	6.18%
9	0.9	2.8159	3.0192	0.2033	6.73%
10	1.0	3.1875	3.4366	0.2491	7.25%

FIGURE 2.4.1.   Using Euler's method to approximate the solution of Eq. (7).

Local and Cumulative Errors

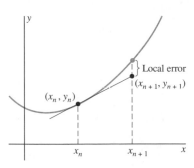

FIGURE 2.4.2. The local error in Euler's method.

There are several sources of error in Euler's method that may make the approximation y_n to $y(x_n)$ unreliable for large values of n, those for which x_n is not sufficiently close to x_0. The error in the linear approximation formula

$$y(x_{n+1}) \approx y_n + h \cdot f(x_n, y_n) = y_{n+1} \tag{10}$$

is the amount by which the tangent line at (x_n, y_n) departs from the solution curve through (x_n, y_n), as illustrated in Fig. 2.4.2. This error, introduced at each step in the process, is called the **local error** in Euler's method.

The local error indicated in Fig. 2.4.2 *would be* the total error in y_{n+1} *if* the starting point y_n in (10) were an exact value, rather than merely an approximation to the actual value $y(x_n)$. But y_n itself suffers from the accumulated effects of all the local errors introduced at the previous steps. Thus the tangent line in Fig. 2.4.2 is tangent to the "wrong" solution curve—the one through (x_n, y_n) rather than the actual solution curve through the initial point (x_0, y_0). Figure 2.4.3 illustrates this **cumulative error** in Euler's method; it is the amount by which the polygonal step-wise path from (x_0, y_0) departs from the actual solution curve through (x_0, y_0).

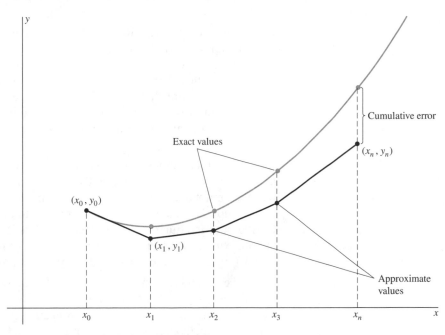

FIGURE 2.4.3. The cummulative error in Euler's method.

The usual way of attempting to reduce the cumulative error in Euler's method is to decrease the step size h. The table in Fig. 2.4.4 shows the results obtained in approximating the solution of the initial value problem

$$\frac{dy}{dx} = x + y, \quad y(0) = 1,$$

of Example 1, using the successively smaller step sizes $h = 0.1$, $h = 0.02$, $h = 0.005$, and $h = 0.001$. We show computed values only at intervals of $\Delta x = 0.1$. For instance, with $h = 0.001$, the computation required 1000 Euler steps, but the value y_n is shown only when n is a multiple of 100, so that x_n is an integral multiple of 0.1.

By scanning the column in Fig. 2.4.4 we observe that, for each fixed step size h, the error $y_{\text{actual}} - y_{\text{approx}}$ increases as x gets farther from the starting point $x_0 = 0$. But by scanning the rows of the table we see that for each fixed x, the error decreases as the step size h is reduced. The percentage errors at the final point $x = 1$ range from 7.25% with $h = 0.1$ down to only 0.08% with $h = 0.001$. Thus the smaller

x	y with $h = 0.1$	y with $h = 0.02$	y with $h = 0.005$	y with $h = 0.001$	Actual y
0.1	1.1000	1.1082	1.1098	1.1102	1.1103
0.2	1.2200	1.2380	1.2416	1.2426	1.2428
0.3	1.3620	1.3917	1.3977	1.3993	1.3997
0.4	1.5282	1.5719	1.5807	1.5831	1.5836
0.5	1.7210	1.7812	1.7933	1.7966	1.7974
0.6	1.9461	2.0227	2.0388	2.0431	2.0442
0.7	2.1974	2.2998	2.3205	2.3261	2.3275
0.8	2.4872	2.6161	2.6422	2.6493	2.6511
0.9	2.8159	2.9757	3.0082	3.0170	3.0192
1.0	3.1875	3.3832	3.4230	3.4238	3.4266

FIGURE 2.4.4. Approximating the solution of $dy/dx = x + y$, $y(0) = 1$ with successively smaller step sizes.

the step size, the more slowly does the error grow with increasing distance from the starting point.

The column of data for $h = 0.1$ in Fig. 2.4.4 requires only 10 steps, so Euler's method can be carried out (as in Example 1) with a hand-held calculator. But 50 steps are required to reach $x = 1$ with $h = 0.02$, 200 steps with $h = 0.005$, and 1000 steps with $h = 0.001$. A computer is almost always used to implement Euler's method when more than 10 or 20 steps are required. Once an appropriate computer program has been written, one step size is—in principle—just as convenient as another; after all, the computer hardly cares how many steps it is asked to carry out.

Why, then, do we not simply choose an exceedingly small step size (such as $h = 10^{-12}$), with the expectation that very great accuracy will result? There are two reasons for not doing so. The first is obvious: the time required for the computation. For example, the data in Fig. 2.4.4 were obtained using a hand-held calculator that carried out nine Euler steps per second. Thus it required slightly over one second to approximate $y(1)$ with $h = 0.1$ and about 1 min 50 s with $h = 0.001$. But with $h = 10^{-12}$ it would require over 3000 years!

The second reason is more subtle. In addition to the local and cumulative errors discussed previously, the computer itself will contribute **roundoff error** at each stage because only finitely many significant digits can be used in each calculation. An Euler's method computation with $h = 0.0001$ will introduce roundoff errors 1000 times as often as one with $h = 0.1$. Hence with certain differential equations, $h = 0.1$ might actually produce more accurate results than those obtained with $h = 0.0001$, because the cumulative effect of roundoff error in the latter case might exceed combined cumulative and roundoff error in the case $h = 0.1$.

The "best" choice of h is difficult to determine in practice as well as in theory. It depends on the nature of the function $f(x, y)$ in the initial value problem in (2), on the exact code in which the program is written, and on the specific computer used. With a step size that is too large, the approximations inherent in Euler's method may not be sufficiently accurate, whereas if h is too small, then roundoff errors may accumulate to an unacceptable degree or the program may require too much time to be practical. The subject of *error propagation* in numerical algorithms is treated in numerical analysis courses and textbooks.

The computations in Fig. 2.4.4 illustrate the common strategy of applying a numerical algorithm, such as Euler's method, several times in succession, beginning with a selected number n of subintervals for the first application, then doubling n for each succeeding application of the method. Visual comparison of successive results often can provide an "intuitive feel" for their accuracy. In the next two examples we present graphically the results of successive applications of Euler's method.

EXAMPLE 2   The exact solution of the logistic initial value problem

$$\frac{dy}{dx} = \tfrac{1}{3}y(8 - y), \quad y(0) = 1$$

is $y(x) = 8/(1 + 7e^{-8x/3})$. Figure 2.4.5 shows both the exact solution curve and approximate solution curves obtained by applying Euler's method on the interval $0 \le x \le 5$ with $n = 5$, $n = 10$, and $n = 20$ subintervals. Each of these "curves" actually consists of line segments joining successive points (x_n, y_n) and (x_{n+1}, y_{n+1}). The Euler approximation with 5 subintervals is poor, and the approximation with 10 subintervals also overshoots the limiting value $y = 8$ of the solution before leveling off, but with 20 subintervals we obtain fairly good qualitative agreement with the actual behavior of the solution. ∎

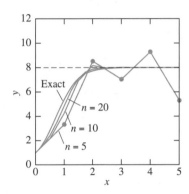

FIGURE 2.4.5. Approximating a logistic solution using Euler's method with $n = 5$, $n = 10$, and $n = 20$ subintervals.

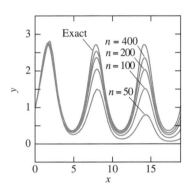

FIGURE 2.4.6. Approximating the exact solution $y = e^{\sin x}$ using Euler's method with 50, 100, 200, and 400 subintervals.

EXAMPLE 3   The exact solution of the initial value problem

$$\frac{dy}{dx} = y \cos x, \quad y(0) = 1$$

is the periodic function $y(x) = e^{\sin x}$. Figure 2.4.6 shows both the exact solution curve and approximate solution curves obtained by applying Euler's method on the interval $0 \le x \le 6\pi$ with $n = 50$, $n = 100$, $n = 200$, and $n = 400$ subintervals. Even with this many subintervals, Euler's method evidently has considerable difficulty keeping up with the oscillations in the actual solution. Consequently, the more accurate methods discussed in succeeding sections are needed for serious numerical investigations. ∎

A Word of Caution

The data shown in Fig. 2.4.4 indicate that Euler's method works well in approximating the solution of $dy/dx = x + y$, $y(0) = 1$ on the interval $[0, 1]$. That is, for each fixed x it appears that the approximate values approach the actual value of $y(x)$ as the step size h is decreased. For instance, the approximate values in the rows corresponding to $x = 0.3$ and $x = 0.5$ suggest that $y(0.3) \approx 1.40$ and $y(0.5) \approx 1.80$, in accord with the actual values shown in the final column of the table.

Example 4, in contrast, shows that some initial value problems are not so well behaved.

EXAMPLE 4   Use Euler's method to approximate the solution of the initial value problem

$$\frac{dy}{dx} = x^2 + y^2, \quad y(0) = 1 \tag{11}$$

on the interval [0, 1].

Solution   Here $f(x, y) = x^2 + y^2$, so the iterative formula of Euler's method is

$$y_{n+1} = y_n + h \cdot (x_n^2 + y_n^2). \tag{12}$$

With step size $h = 0.1$ we obtain

$$y_1 = (0.1) \cdot [(0)^2 + (1)^2] = 1.1,$$
$$y_2 = 1.1 + (0.1) \cdot [(0.1)^2 + (1.1)^2] = 1.222,$$
$$y_3 = 1.222 + (0.1) \cdot [(0.2)^2 + (1.222)^2] \approx 1.3753,$$

and so forth. Rounded to four decimal places, the first ten values obtained in this manner are

$$
\begin{array}{ll}
y_1 = 1.1000 & y_6 = 2.1995 \\
y_2 = 1.2220 & y_7 = 2.7193 \\
y_3 = 1.3753 & y_8 = 3.5078 \\
y_4 = 1.5735 & y_9 = 4.8023 \\
y_5 = 1.8371 & y_{10} = 7.1895
\end{array}
$$

But instead of naively accepting these results as accurate approximations, we decided to use a computer to repeat the computations with smaller values of h. The table in Fig. 2.4.7 shows the results obtained with step sizes $h = 0.1$, $h = 0.02$, and $h = 0.005$. Observe that now the "stability" of the procedure in Example 1 is missing. Indeed, it seems obvious that something is going wrong near $x = 1$.

x	y with $h = 0.1$	y with $h = 0.02$	y with $h = 0.005$
0.1	1.1000	1.1088	1.1108
0.2	1.2220	1.2458	1.2512
0.3	1.3753	1.4243	1.4357
0.4	1.5735	1.6658	1.6882
0.5	1.8371	2.0074	2.0512
0.6	2.1995	2.5201	2.6104
0.7	2.7193	3.3612	3.5706
0.8	3.5078	4.9601	5.5763
0.9	4.8023	9.0000	12.2061
1.0	7.1895	30.9167	1502.2090

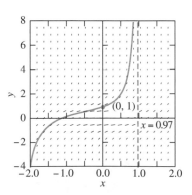

FIGURE 2.4.7.   Attempting to approximate the solution of $dy/dx = x^2 + y^2$, $y(0) = 1$.

FIGURE 2.4.8.   Solution of $dy/dx = x^2 + y^2$, $y(0) = 1$.

Figure 2.4.8 provides a graphical clue to the difficulty. It shows a slope field for $dy/dx = x^2 + y^2$, together with a solution curve through (0, 1) plotted using one of the more accurate approximation methods of the following two sections. It appears that this solution curve may have a vertical asymptote near $x = 0.97$. Indeed, an exact solution using Bessel functions (see Problem 16 in Section 8.6) can be used to show that $y(x) \to +\infty$ as $x \to 0.969811$ (approximately). Although Euler's method gives values (albeit spurious ones) at $x = 1$, the actual solution does not exist on the entire interval [0, 1]. Moreover, Euler's method is unable to "keep up" with the rapid changes in $y(x)$ that occur as x approaches the infinite discontinuity near 0.969811. ∎

The moral of Example 4 is that there are pitfalls in the numerical solution of certain initial value problems. Certainly it's pointless to attempt to approximate a solution on an interval where it doesn't even exist (or where it is not unique, in which case there's no general way to predict which way the numerical approximations will branch at a point of nonuniqueness). One should never accept as accurate the results of applying Euler's method with a single fixed step size h. A second "run" with smaller step size ($h/2$, say, or $h/5$, or $h/10$) may give seemingly consistent results, thereby suggesting their accuracy, or it may—as in Example 4—reveal the presence of some hidden difficulty in the problem. Many problems simply require the more accurate and powerful methods that are discussed in the final two sections of this chapter.

2.4 *Problems*

A hand-held calculator will suffice for Problems 1 through 10. In each problem, find the exact solution of the given initial value problem. Then apply Euler's method twice to approximate (to four decimal places) this solution on the interval $[0.0, 0.5]$, first with step size $h = 0.1$, then with $h = 0.05$. Make a table showing the approximate values with $h = 0.1$, the approximate values with $h = 0.05$, and the actual values of the solution at the points $x = 0.1, 0.2, 0.3, 0.4$, and 0.5.

1. $\dfrac{dy}{dx} = -y, \, y(0) = 2$

2. $\dfrac{dy}{dx} = 2y, \, y(0) = \frac{1}{2}$

3. $\dfrac{dy}{dx} = y + 1, \, y(0) = 1$

4. $\dfrac{dy}{dx} = x - y, \, y(0) = 1$

5. $\dfrac{dy}{dx} = y - x - 1, \, y(0) = 1$

6. $\dfrac{dy}{dx} = -2xy, \, y(0) = 2$

7. $\dfrac{dy}{dx} = -3x^2 y, \, y(0) = 3$

8. $\dfrac{dy}{dx} = e^{-y}, \, y(0) = 0$

9. $\dfrac{dy}{dx} = \frac{1}{4}(1 + y^2), \, y(0) = 1$

10. $\dfrac{dy}{dx} = 2xy^2, \, y(0) = 1$

Note: The project following this problem set lists illustrative calculator/computer programs that can be used in the remaining problems.

A programmable calculator or a computer will be useful for Problems 11 through 16. In each problem find the exact solution of the given initial value problem. Then apply Euler's method twice to approximate (to four decimal places) this solution on the given interval, first with step size $h = 0.01$, then with step size $h = 0.005$. Make a table showing the approximate values and the actual value, together with the percentage error in the more accurate approximation, for x an integral multiple of 0.2. Throughout, primes denote derivatives with respect to x.

11. $y' = y - 2, \, y(0) = 1; \, 0 \le x \le 1$

12. $y' = \frac{1}{2}(y - 1)^2, \, y(0) = 2; \, 0 \le x \le 1$

13. $yy' = 2x^3, \, y(1) = 3; \, 1 \le x \le 2$

14. $xy' = y^2, \, y(1) = 1; \, 1 \le x \le 2$

15. $xy' = 3x - 2y, \, y(2) = 3; \, 2 \le x \le 3$

16. $y^2 y' = 2x^5, \, y(2) = 3; \, 2 \le x \le 3$

A computer with a printer is required for Problems 17 through 24. In these initial value problems, use Euler's method with step sizes $h = 0.1, 0.02, 0.004$, and 0.0008 to approximate to four decimal places the values of the solution at ten equally spaced points of the given interval. Print the results in tabular form with appropriate headings to make it easy to gauge the effect of varying the step size h. Throughout, primes denote derivatives with respect to x.

17. $y' = x^2 + y^2, \, y(0) = 0; \, 0 \le x \le 1$

18. $y' = x^2 - y^2, \, y(0) = 1; \, 0 \le x \le 2$

19. $y' = x + \sqrt{y}, \, y(0) = 1; \, 0 \le x \le 2$

20. $y' = x + \sqrt[3]{y}, \, y(0) = -1; \, 0 \le x \le 2$

21. $y' = \ln y, \, y(1) = 2; \, 1 \le x \le 2$

22. $y' = x^{2/3} + y^{2/3}, \, y(0) = 1; \, 0 \le x \le 2$

23. $y' = \sin x + \cos y, \, y(0) = 0; \, 0 \le x \le 1$

24. $y' = \dfrac{x}{1 + y^2}, \, y(-1) = 1; \, -1 \le x \le 1$

25. Consider the initial value problem

$$7x \frac{dy}{dx} + y = 0, \quad y(-1) = 1.$$

(a) Solve this problem for the exact solution

$$y(x) = -\frac{1}{x^{1/7}},$$

which has an infinite discontinuity at $x = 0$. (b) Apply Euler's method with step size $h = 0.15$ to approximate this solution on the interval $-1 \le x \le 0.5$. Note that, from these data alone, you might not suspect any difficulty near $x = 0$. The reason is that the numerical approximation "jumps across the discontinuity" to another solution of $7xy' + y = 0$ for $x > 0$. (c) Finally, apply Euler's method with step sizes $h = 0.03$ and $h = 0.006$, but still printing results only at the original points $x = -1.00$, $-0.85, -0.70, \ldots, 1.20, 1.35$. and 1.50. Would you now suspect a discontinuity in the exact solution?

26. Apply Euler's method with successively smaller step sizes on the interval $[0, 2]$ to verify empirically that the solution of the initial value problem

$$\frac{dy}{dx} = x^2 + y^2, \quad y(0) = 0$$

has a vertical asymptote near $x = 2.003147$. (Contrast this with Example 2, in which $y(0) = 1$.)

27. The general solution of the equation

$$\frac{dy}{dx} = (1 + y^2)\cos x$$

is $y(x) = \tan(C + \sin x)$. With the initial condition $y(0) = 0$ the solution $y(x) = \tan(\sin x)$ is well behaved. But with $y(0) = 1$ the solution $y(x) = \tan\left(\frac{1}{4}\pi + \sin x\right)$ has a vertical asymptote at $x = \sin^{-1}(\pi/4) \approx 0.90334$. Use Euler's method to verify this fact empirically.

2.4 Lab 2: Euler's Method and RC Circuits

Goals

In this lab you will implement Euler's method to approximate measurements of the charge on a capacitor in a basic RC circuit. You will learn how to write .m files for Matlab, how to program Euler's method; then you will investigate some of the limitations of the method.

Application: A Basic RC Circuit

The state of electrical circuits consisting of resistors, capacitors, and an applied voltage can be described by differential equations.

Consider the following circuit

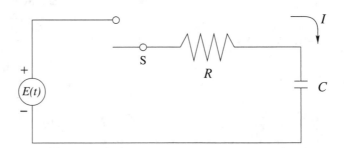

with resistance R ohms, capacitance C farads, and applied voltage $E(t)$ volts. The charge on the top plate of the capacitor at time t is $Q(t)$ coulombs, and the current through the resistor is $I(t)$ amperes. The resistor has a voltage drop of RI, and the capacitor has a voltage drop of $\frac{1}{C}Q$. When switch S is closed at time $t = 0$, the sum of the voltage across the resistor and the capacitor must equal the applied voltage. This gives us the equation

$$RI + \frac{1}{C}Q = E(t)$$

The current in the circuit is the rate of change of the amount of charge on the capacitor. So using the relationship $\frac{dQ}{dt} = I$, this becomes a first order differential equation for $Q(t)$:

$$R\frac{dQ}{dt} + \frac{1}{C}Q = E(t)$$

The initial condition for this equation is $Q_0 = Q(0)$, the initial amount of charge on the capacitor. (Q_0 could be set by imposing a voltage $V_0 = Q_0/C$ across the capacitor before inserting it into the circuit.)

In this lab, we will use Euler's method to numerically solve this differential equation for two different applied voltages: a constant voltage E_0, and then an AC voltage $E(t) = 117 \sin(120\pi t)$ which corresponds to the voltage out of a standard wall socket.

Prelab Assignment

Before arriving in lab, answer the following questions. Your answers should be neatly presented and handed in at the beginning of lab session.

1. (a) Verify that the function

$$Q_1(t) = E_0 C \left(1 - e^{-t/RC}\right)$$

is a solution to the **Initial Value Problem (IVP)**

$$\frac{dQ_1}{dt} = -\frac{1}{RC} Q_1 + \frac{1}{R} E_0 \qquad Q_1(0) = 0 \tag{1}$$

where R, C and E_0 are constants. That is, check that the function satisfies the differential equation and the initial condition. (That means plug and chug–do NOT solve.) Use this analytic solution (with $R = 20000$, $C = .00001$, $E_0 = 117$) to complete column one on Table 2 on the last page of the lab, for use in Lab problem 1.

   (b) Verify that the function

$$Q_2(t) = \frac{E_0}{R(\gamma^2 + (120\pi)^2)} \left[120\pi \left(e^{-t\gamma} - \cos(120\pi t)\right) + \gamma \sin(120\pi t)\right]$$

satisfies the IVP

$$\frac{dQ_2}{dt} = -\frac{1}{RC} Q_2 + \frac{1}{R} E_0 \sin(120\pi t) \qquad Q_2(0) = 0 \tag{2}$$

where $\gamma = \frac{1}{RC}$. What do these initial conditions represent for the system at the time the switch is closed?

2. Suppose you implement Euler's method using Matlab, using step size h, and create a vector t of time steps from $t = 0$ to $t = 1$. Often we refer to the first entry as $t_0 = 0$, the next as t_1 and the final entry will be $t_N = 1$ where $Nh = 1$. Matlab does not enumerate these entries in the same way. The first element of the vector is always $t(1)$. In this case, we will have $t(1) = 0$, and $t(N+1) = 1$. Find the Matlab indices n so that $t(n) = 0, .5, .86$, and 1 if you used
   (a) $N = 10$ (Note: you cannot get $t(n) = .86$ in this case.)
   (b) $N = 100$
   (c) $N = 500$
   (d) $N = 1000$
   Record these values of n in Table 1 below.

N	$t(n) = 0$	$t(n) = .5$	$t(n) = .86$	$t(n) = 1$
10			X	
100				
500				
1000				

Table 1: Matlab Indices for Time Vector

Creating a (new) file

Launch **Matlab**. Go to the **File** menu and use the left button to select **New** then **M-file**; a new window called **untitled** will open. Choose **Save** from the **File** menu on that window and a dialog box will open. In the box labelled **Enter file name** there is a default entry **untitled.m**. Replace that with **EULER.m** and left click OK. The window should now be titled **EULER.m**. You have created an (empty) file called `EULER.m`. (Matlab file names all end in `.m`). It is important here that `EULER` is capitalized.

The contents of the `EULER.m` file

This program will implement Euler's method to solve the differential equation

$$\frac{dy}{dt} = f(t, y) \qquad y(a) = y_0 \tag{3}$$

In this application, $y(t)$ is the charge on the capacitor $Q(t)$.

In this program, everything following a `%` is a **comment**. Comments give you information about the program, but are not evaluated by the computer. You may choose whether or not to type these comments into your program, but if you include the comments in your file you must include the `%`, or the computer will try to read them. Type in the following program up to the line:

```
clear t                         % Clears old time steps and
clear y                         % y values from previous runs
a=0;                            % Initial time
b=1;                            % Final time
N=100;                          % Number of time steps
y0=0;                           % Initial value y(a)
h=(b-a)/N;                      % Time step
t(1)=a;
y(1)=y0;
for n=1:N                       % For loop, sets next t, y values
  t(n+1)=t(n)+h;
  y(n+1)=y(n)+h*f(t(n),y(n));   % Calls the function f(t,y)=dy/dt
end
plot(t,y)
title(['Euler Method using N=',num2str(N),' steps, by MYNAME'])
                                % Include your own name
```

The contents of the files `f.m` and `yE.m`

Since this program calls the function `f(t,y)`, we must create a second `.m` file called `f.m`. Go to the **File** menu and select **New** then **M-file**. A new window called **untitled** will open. Choose **Save** from the **File** menu on that window and a dialog box will open. In the box labelled **Enter file name** there is a default entry **untitled.m** Replace that with `f.m` and left click OK as you did before. (You now know how to create `.m` files; you have done it twice already.) You should then type in the following commands up to the line:

```
function f=f(t,y)
R=20000;                 % Resistance
C=.00001;                % Capacitance
E0=117;                  % Constant Voltage
f=-y/(R*C)+E0/R;         % Defines the function f
```

The file **f.m** contains the function $f(t, y)$ for the general differential equation (3) above; the particular form of $f(t, y)$ corresponds to equation (1). To solve a different differential equation with **EULER.m** or another solver, you need only change this file. These constants correspond to using $R = 20\text{k}\Omega$, $C = 10\mu\text{F}$ and $E_0 = 117\text{V}$.

Lastly, you should create another new file called **yE.m**. The file **yE.m** contains the exact solution $Q_1(t)$ of equation (1), corresponding to the above function $f(t, y)$ defined in the file **f.m**. If you solve a different differential equation with **EULER.m** or one of the other numerical methods described below, and you wish to compare with an analytical expression for the exact solution, you should modify the file **yE.m** as well as **f.m**. Type the following commands up to the line:

```
function yE=yE(t)
R=20000;                                  % Resistance
C=.00001;                                 % Capacitance
E0=117;                                   % Constant Voltage
gam=1/(R*C);
yE=E0*C*(ones(size(t))-exp(-gam*t));      % Exact solution yE
% Note the ones() command, creating a vector of ones.
```

Running your program

So far you have written a program and saved it. Now you want to use the program.

In the Matlab command window (see introduction to Matlab) type **EULER**. The plot of the solution curve should appear.

Note: To solve an ODE you need a solver—in this case, **EULER** is your solver. Then you must tell your solver what it is suppose to solve—that is your **f.m** file. The solver must also know where to start—initial conditions. In this case the initial conditions are entered directly into the solver—those are the lines **a=0** and **y0=0**. You 'fine tune' your solver by changing N. The stopping time is also entered in the solver as **b=1**.

Lab Problems

1. Solve equation (1) using **EULER.m** with $N = 10$.
   (a) Print your results as follows:
      After the plot has appeared, go to the **File** menu on the **Figure** window and choose **Print**; a dialog box will appear. If you click **OK** in the dialog box the plot will print on the printer in your lab.
      By the way, you can use the dialog box to change the size of your plot, add text, labels, legends, titles, etc.
   (b) Using your indices from Prelab problem 2 and your approximate solution vector y, complete columns 2 through 4 of the first part of Table 2, at the final page of this lab. To view the value of $y(n)$, type **y(n)** in the Matlab window and press return. Make sure you have enough significant digits to compare to the exact answer. You can see more significant digits in Matlab by typing **format long** in the Matlab command window and then hitting return.

2. Repeat Problem 1 again using $N = 100$ and $N = 1000$. Use this data to complete the rest of Table 2.

3. What guesses can you make about the error at a given time as N increases?

4. Graphically investigate the error in solving equation (2). To solve this equation using **EULER.m**, you will have to change your file **f.m**, replacing the line

   ```
   f=-y/(R*C)+E0/R;
   ```

   with the line

   ```
   f=-y/(R*C)+(E0/R)*sin(120*pi*t);
   ```

To compute the exact solution $Q_2(t)$ for equation (2), you will need to modify the file **yE.m**, replacing the line

```
yE=E0*C*(ones(size(t))-exp(-gam*t);
```

with

```
omg=120*pi;
A=E0*omg/(R*(gam^2+omg^2));
B=E0*gam/(R*(gam^2+omg^2));
yE=A*(exp(-gam*t)-cos(omg*t))+B*sin(omg*t);
```

(A suggestion: Save your original files **f.m** and **yE.m**, for instance by renaming them as **f1.m** and **yE1.m**; also, save copies of these modified files as **f2.m** and **yE2.m**, as you will be able to reuse them in Lab 3.)

To plot the approximate solution and the exact one on the same set of axes, replace the line **plot(t,y)** near the end of the file **EULER.m** with

```
yexact=yE(t);
plot(t,y,':',t,yexact,'-')
legend('approximate','exact')
```

This defines a vector corresponding to the exact solution. Sample values of the exact solution are plotted connected by a solid line, and the Euler's method approximation is plotted on the same axes as a dotted line. The **legend** command puts a helpful box in the corner of the plot to help you identify which graph corresponds to which function. You can move the legend around the graph by clicking on it with your mouse, then dragging it to the new location and releasing.

5. Run EULER using $N = 50$, $N = 100$, $N = 200$, $N = 500$, $N = 1000$ and $N = 2000$. Why does the exact solution look different on the first few plots? How large must N be for the approximate solution to qualitatively match the exact one? We say that two graphs agree qualitatively if they have roughly the same shape, for example, they might both be increasing or have two maximums or be periodic with approximately the same period. Print out a plot where the exact solution appears to have a lower frequency than 60 Hz, one where the approximate solution appears qualitatively correct, and one where the approximate solution appears quantitatively correct. (See if you can print out clearer plots with fewer oscillations by using an **axis** command, or by changing the final time **b**.)

6. Many different situations can give rise to error in numerical approximations. One such situation, **undersampling** comes in to play in this last problem. **Undersampling** occurs when the data points are spaced too far apart to capture all the behavior of the equation. You may know this phenomenon as "aliasing",

Time	Exact y	Approximate y	Error	Percent Error
t	$y_{exact}(t)$	$y_n = y_{approx}(t)$	$\lvert y_{approx}(t) - y_{exact}(t) \rvert$	$\left\lvert \frac{y_{approx}(t) - y_{exact}(t)}{y_{exact}(t)} \right\rvert \times 100$
$N = 10$				
.5				
1				
$N = 100$				
.5				
.86				
1				
$N = 1000$				
.5				
.86				
1				

Table 2: Approximate Solutions to Equation (1)

when an insufficiently sampled high frequency signal appears to be a lower frequency signal. Even if you have calculated the exact solution correctly its graph may not be accurate; imagine plotting a sine wave with frequency 120 cycles per second by sampling the function 120 times a second—it will appear to be the constant function.

Did you see this problem when you used $h = 0.01$? What about $h = 0.001$? (Lab 3 will develop more numerical methods which are potentially more accurate.)

2.5 A CLOSER LOOK AT THE EULER METHOD

The Euler method as presented in Section 2.4 is not often used in practice, mainly because more accurate methods are available. But Euler's method has the advantage of simplicity, and a careful study of this method yields insights into the workings of more accurate methods, because many of the latter are extensions or refinements of the Euler method. To compare two different methods of numerical approximation, we need some way to measure the accuracy of each. Theorem 1 tells what degree of accuracy we can expect when we use Euler's method.

> **THEOREM 1: The Error in the Euler Method**

Suppose that the initial value problem

$$\frac{dy}{dx} = f(x, y), \quad y(a) = y_0 \tag{1}$$

has a unique solution $y(x)$ on the closed interval $[a, b]$, and assume that $y(x)$ has a continuous second derivative on $[a, b]$. (This would follow from the assumption that f, f_x, and f_y are all continuous for $a \leq x \leq b$ and $c \leq y \leq d$, where $c \leq y(x) \leq d$ for all x in $[a, b]$.) Then there exists a constant C such that the following is true: If the approximations $y_1, y_2, y_3, \ldots, y_k$ to the actual values $y(x_1), y(x_2), y(x_3), \ldots, y(x_k)$ at points of $[a, b]$ are computed using Euler's method with step size $h > 0$, then

$$|y_n - y(x_n)| \leq Ch \tag{2}$$

for each $n = 1, 2, 3, \ldots, k$. ∎

Remark: The **error**

$$y_{\text{actual}} - y_{\text{approx}} = y(x_n) - y_n$$

in (2) denotes the [cumulative] error in Euler's method after n steps in the approximation, *exclusive* of roundoff error (as though we were using a perfect machine that made no roundoff errors). The theorem can be summarized by saying that *the error in Euler's method is of order* h; that is, the error is bounded by a [predetermined] constant C multiplied by the step size h. It follows, for instance, that (on a given closed interval) halving the step size cuts the maximum error in half; similarly, with step size $h/10$ we get 10 times the accuracy (that is, $1/10$ the maximum error) as with step size h. Consequently, we can—in principle—get any degree of accuracy we want by choosing h sufficiently small. ∎

We will omit the proof of this theorem, but one can be found in Chapter 7 of G. Birkhoff and G.-C. Rota, *Ordinary Differential Equations*, 4th ed. (New York: John Wiley, 1989). The constant C deserves some comment. Because C tends to increase as the maximum value of $|y''(x)|$ on $[a, b]$ increases, it follows that C must depend in a fairly complicated way on y, and actual computation of a value of C such that the inequality in (2) holds is usually impractical. In practice, the following type of procedure is commonly employed.

1. Apply Euler's method to the initial value problem in (1) with a reasonable value of h.
2. Repeat with $h/2$, $h/4$, and so forth, at each stage halving the step size for the next application of Euler's method.
3. Continue until the results obtained at one stage agree—to an appropriate number of significant digits—with those obtained at the previous stage. Then the approximate values obtained at this stage are considered likely to be accurate to the indicated number of significant digits.

EXAMPLE 1 Carry out this procedure with the initial value problem

$$\frac{dy}{dx} = -\frac{2xy}{1 + x^2}, \quad y(0) = 1 \tag{3}$$

to approximate accurately the value $y(1)$ of the solution at $x = 1$.

Solution Using an Euler method program, perhaps one of those listed in Figs. 2.4.7 and 2.4.8, we begin with a step size $h = 0.04$ requiring $n = 25$ steps to reach $x = 1$. The table in Fig. 2.5.1 shows the approximate values of $y(1)$ obtained with successively smaller values of h. The data suggest that the true value of $y(1)$ is exactly 0.5. Indeed, the exact solution of the initial value problem in (3) is $y(x) = 1/(1 + x^2)$, so the true value of $y(1)$ is exactly $\frac{1}{2}$. ■

h	Approximate $y(1)$	Actual $y(1)$	$|\text{Error}|/h$
0.04	0.50451	0.50000	0.11
0.02	0.50220	0.50000	0.11
0.01	0.50109	0.50000	0.11
0.005	0.50054	0.50000	0.11
0.0025	0.50027	0.50000	0.11
0.00125	0.50013	0.50000	0.10
0.000625	0.50007	0.50000	0.11
0.0003125	0.50003	0.50000	0.10

FIGURE 2.5.1. Table of values in Example 1.

The final column of the table in Fig. 2.5.1 displays the ratio of the magnitude of the error to h; that is, $|y_{\text{actual}} - y_{\text{approx}}|/h$. Observe how the data in this column substantiate Theorem 1—in this computation, the error bound in (2) appears to hold with a value of C slightly larger than 0.1.

An Improvement in Euler's Method

As Fig. 2.5.2 shows, Euler's method is rather unsymmetrical. It uses the predicted slope $k = f(x_n, y_n)$ of the graph of the solution at the left-hand endpoint of the interval $[x_n, x_n + h]$ as if it were the actual slope of the solution over that entire interval. We now turn our attention to a way in which increased accuracy can easily be obtained; it is known as the *improved Euler method*.

Given the initial value problem

$$\frac{dy}{dx} = f(x, y), \quad y(x_0) = y_0, \tag{4}$$

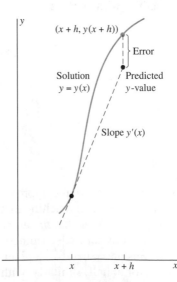

FIGURE 2.5.2. True and predicted values in Euler's method.

suppose that after carrying out n steps with step size h we have computed the approximation y_n to the actual value $y(x_n)$ of the solution at $x_n = x_0 + nh$. We can use the Euler method to obtain a first estimate—which we now call u_{n+1} rather than y_{n+1}—of the value of the solution at $x_{n+1} = x_n + h$. Thus

➤
$$u_{n+1} = y_n + h \cdot f(x_n, y_n) = y_n + h \cdot k_1.$$

Now that $u_{n+1} \approx y(x_{n+1})$ has been computed, we can take

➤
$$k_2 = f(x_{n+1}, u_{n+1})$$

as a second estimate of the slope of the solution curve $y = y(x)$ at $x = x_{n+1}$.

Of course, the approximate slope $k_1 = f(x_n, y_n)$ at $x = x_n$ has already been calculated. Why not *average* these two slopes to obtain a more accurate estimate of the average slope of the solution curve over the entire subinterval $[x_n, x_{n+1}]$? This idea is the essence of the *improved* Euler method. Figure 2.5.3 shows the geometry behind this method.

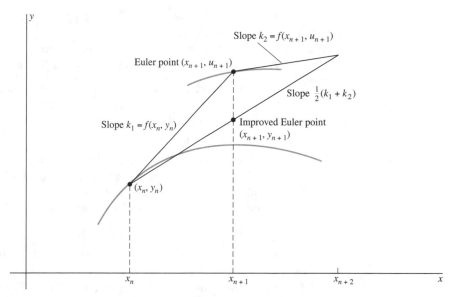

FIGURE 2.5.3. The improved Euler method: Average the slopes of the tangent lines at (x_n, y_n) and (x_{n+1}, u_{n+1}).

ALGORITHM: The Improved Euler Method

Given the initial value problem

$$\frac{dy}{dx} = f(x, y), \quad y(x_0) = y_0,$$

the **improved Euler method with step size** h consists in applying the iterative formulas

$$
\begin{aligned}
k_1 &= f(x_n, y_n), \\
u_{n+1} &= y_n + h \cdot k_1, \\
k_2 &= f(x_{n+1}, u_{n+1}), \\
y_{n+1} &= y_n + h \cdot \tfrac{1}{2}(k_1 + k_2)
\end{aligned}
\tag{5}
$$

to compute successive approximations $y_1, y_2, y_3, \ldots$ to the [true] values $y(x_1)$, $y(x_2)$, $y(x_3)$, $\ldots$ of the [exact] solution $y = y(x)$ at the points $x_1, x_2, x_3, \ldots$, respectively.

Remark: Note that the final formula in (5) takes the "Euler form"

$$y_{n+1} = y_n + h \cdot k$$

if we write

$$k = \frac{k_1 + k_2}{2}$$

for the approximate *average slope* on the interval $[x_n, x_{n+1}]$. ◼

The improved Euler method is one of a class of numerical techniques known as **predictor-corrector** methods. First a predictor u_{n+1} of the next y-value is computed; then it is used to correct itself. Thus the **improved Euler method** with step size h consists in using the **predictor**

$$u_{n+1} = y_n + h \cdot f(x_n, y_n) \tag{6}$$

and the **corrector**

$$y_{n+1} = y_n + h \cdot \tfrac{1}{2} \left[f(x_n, y_n) + f(x_{n+1}, u_{n+1}) \right] \tag{7}$$

iteratively to compute successive approximations $y_1, y_2, y_2, \ldots$ to the values $y(x_1)$, $y(x_2), y(x_3), \ldots$ of the actual solution of the initial value problem in (4).

Remark: Note that each improved Euler step requires two evaluations of the function $f(x, y)$, as compared with the single function evaluation required for an ordinary Euler step. We naturally wonder whether this doubled computational labor is worth the trouble.

Answer: Under the assumption that the exact solution $y = y(x)$ of the initial value problem in (4) has a continuous third derivative, it can be proved—see Chapter 7 of Birkhoff and Rota—that the error in the improved Euler method is of order h^2. This means that on a given bounded interval $[a, b]$, each approximate value y_n satisfies the inequality

$$|y(x_n) - y_n| \leqq Ch^2 \tag{8}$$

where the constant C does not depend on h. Because h^2 is much smaller than h if h itself is small, this means that the improved Euler method is more accurate than Euler's method itself. This advantage is offset by the fact that about twice as many computations are required. But the factor h^2 in (8) means that halving the step size results in 1/4 the maximum error, and with step size $h/10$ we get 100 times the accuracy (that is, 1/100 the maximum error) as with step size h. ◼

EXAMPLE 2 In Example 1 of Section 2.4 we applied Euler's method to the initial value problem

$$\frac{dy}{dx} = x + y, \quad y(0) = 1 \tag{9}$$

with exact solution $y(x) = 2e^x - x - 1$. With $f(x, y) = x + y$ in Eqs. (6) and (7), the predictor-corrector formulas for the improved Euler method are

$$u_{n+1} = y_n + h \cdot (x_n + y_n),$$
$$y_{n+1} = y_n + h \cdot \tfrac{1}{2} \left[(x_n + y_n) + (x_{n+1} + u_{n+1}) \right].$$

With step size $h = 0.1$ we calculate

$$u_1 = 1 + (0.1) \cdot (0 + 1) = 1.1,$$
$$y_1 = 1 + (0.05) \cdot [(0 + 1) + (0.1 + 1.1)] = 1.11,$$
$$u_2 = 1.11 + (0.1) \cdot (0.1 + 1.11) = 1.231,$$
$$y_2 = 1.11 + (0.05) \cdot [(0.1 + 1.11) + (0.2 + 1.231)] = 1.24205,$$

x	Euler method, h = 0.1 Values of y	Euler method, h = 0.005 Values of y	Improved Euler, h = 0.1 Values of y	Actual y
0.1	1.1000	1.1098	1.1100	1.1103
0.2	1.2200	1.2416	1.2421	1.2428
0.3	1.3620	1.3977	1.3985	1.3997
0.4	1.5282	1.5807	1.5818	1.5836
0.5	1.7210	1.7933	1.7949	1.7974
0.6	1.9431	2.0388	2.0409	2.0442
0.7	2.1974	2.3205	2.3231	2.3275
0.8	2.4872	2.6422	2.6456	2.6511
0.9	2.8159	3.0082	3.0124	3.0192
1.0	3.1875	3.4230	3.4282	3.4366

FIGURE 2.5.4. Euler and improved Euler approximations to the solution of $dy/dx = x + y$, $y(0) = 1$.

x	Improved Euler, Approximate y	Actual y
0.0	1.00000	1.00000
0.1	1.11034	1.11034
0.2	1.24280	1.24281
0.3	1.39971	1.39972
0.4	1.58364	1.58365
0.5	1.79744	1.79744
0.6	2.04423	2.04424
0.7	2.32749	2.32751
0.8	2.65107	2.65108
0.9	3.01919	3.01921
1.0	3.43654	3.43656

FIGURE 2.5.5. Improved Euler approximations to the solution of Eq. (9) with step size $h = 0.005$.

and so forth. The table in Fig. 2.5.4 compares the results obtained using the improved Euler method with those obtained previously using the "unimproved" Euler method. When the same step size $h = 0.1$ is used, the error in the Euler approximation to $y(1)$ is 7.25%, but the error in the improved Euler approximation is only 0.24%.

Indeed, the improved Euler method with $h = 0.1$ is more accurate (in this example) than the original Euler method with $h = 0.005$. The latter requires 200 evaluations of the function $f(x, y)$, but the former requires only 20 such evaluations, so in this case the improved Euler method yields greater accuracy with only about one-tenth the work.

Figure 2.5.5 shows the results obtained when the improved Euler method is applied to the initial value problem in (9) using step size $h = 0.005$. Accuracy of five significant figures is apparent in the table. This suggests that, in contrast with the original Euler method, the improved Euler method is sufficiently accurate for certain practical applications—such as plotting solution curves. ∎

An improved Euler program (similar to the ones listed in the project material for this section) was used to compute approximations to the exact value $y(1) = 0.5$ of the solution $y(x) = 1/(1 + x^2)$ of the initial value problem

$$\frac{dy}{dx} = -\frac{2xy}{1 + x^2}, \quad y(0) = 1 \tag{3}$$

of Example 1. The results obtained by successively halving the step size appear in the table in Fig. 2.5.6. Note that the final column of this table impressively corroborates the form of the error bound in (8), and that each halving of the step size reduces the error by a factor of almost exactly 4, as should happen if the error is proportional to h^2.

In the following two examples we exhibit graphical results obtained by employing this strategy of successively halving the step size, and thus doubling the number of subintervals of a fixed interval on which we are approximating a solution.

EXAMPLE 3 In Example 2 of Section 2.4 we applied Euler's method to the logistic initial value problem

$$\frac{dy}{dx} = \tfrac{1}{3}y(8 - y), \quad y(0) = 1.$$

Figure 2.4.5 shows an obvious difference between the exact solution $y(x) = 8/(1 + 7e^{-8x/3})$ and the Euler approximation on $0 \leq x \leq 5$ using $n = 20$ subintervals.

h	Improved Euler Approximation to $y(1)$	Error	$\|$Error$\|/h^2$
0.04	0.500195903	−0.000195903	0.12
0.02	0.500049494	−0.000049494	0.12
0.01	0.500012437	−0.000012437	0.12
0.005	0.500003117	−0.000003117	0.12
0.0025	0.500000780	−0.000000780	0.12
0.00125	0.500000195	−0.000000195	0.12
0.000625	0.500000049	−0.000000049	0.12
0.0003125	0.500000012	−0.000000012	0.12

FIGURE 2.5.6. Improved Euler approximation to $y(1)$ for $dy/dx = -2xy/(1+x^2)$, $y(0) = 1$.

Figure 2.5.7 shows approximate solution curves plotted using the improved Euler's method.

The approximation with five subintervals is still bad—perhaps worse! It appears to level off considerably short of the actual limiting population $M = 8$. You should carry out at least the first two improved Euler steps manually to see for yourself how it happens that, after increasing appropriately during the first step, the approximate solution *decreases* in the second step rather than continuing to increase (as it should). In the project for this section we ask you to show empirically that the improved Euler approximate solution with step size $h = 1$ levels off at $y \approx 4.3542$.

In contrast, the approximate solution curve with $n = 20$ subintervals tracks the exact solution curve rather closely, and with $n = 40$ subintervals the exact and approximate solution curves are indistinguishable in Fig. 2.5.7. The table in Fig. 2.5.8 indicates that the improved Euler approximation with $n = 200$ subintervals is accurate rounded to three decimal places (that is, four significant digits) on the interval $0 \leq x \leq 5$. Because discrepancies in the fourth significant digit are not visually apparent at the resolution of an ordinary computer screen, the improved Euler method (using several hundred subintervals) is considered adequate for many graphical purposes. ∎

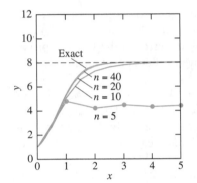

FIGURE 2.5.7. Approximating a logistic solution using the improved Euler method with $n = 5$, $n = 10$, and $n = 40$ subintervals.

x	Actual $y(x)$	Improved Euler with $n = 200$
0	1.0000	1.0000
1	5.3822	5.3809
2	7.7385	7.7379
3	7.9813	7.9812
4	7.9987	7.9987
5	7.9999	7.9999

FIGURE 2.5.8. Using the improved Euler method to approximate the actual solution of the initial value problem in Example 3.

EXAMPLE 4 In Example 3 of Section 2.4 we applied Euler's method to the initial value problem

$$\frac{dy}{dx} = y \cos x, \quad y(0) = 1.$$

Figure 2.4.6 shows obvious visual differences between the periodic exact solution

$y(x) = e^{\sin x}$ and the Euler approximations on $0 \le x \le 6\pi$ with as many as $n = 400$ subintervals.

Figure 2.5.9 shows the exact solution curve and approximate solution curves plotted using the improved Euler method with $n = 50$, $n = 100$, and $n = 200$ subintervals. The approximation obtained with $n = 200$ is indistinguishable from the exact solution curve, and the approximation with $n = 100$ is only barely distinguishable from it. ∎

Although Figs. 2.5.7 and 2.5.9 indicate that the improved Euler method can provide accuracy that suffices for many graphical purposes, it does not provide the higher-precision numerical accuracy that sometimes is needed for more careful investigations. For instance, consider again the initial value problem

$$\frac{dy}{dx} = -\frac{2xy}{1 + x^2}, \quad y(0) = 1$$

of Example 1. The final column of the table in Fig. 2.5.6 suggests that, if the improved Euler method is used on the interval $0 \le x \le 1$ with n subintervals and step size $h = 1/n$, then the resulting error E in the final approximation $y_n \approx y(1)$ is given by

$$E = |y(1) - y_n| \approx (0.12)h^2 = \frac{0.12}{n^2}.$$

If so, then 12-place accuracy (for instance) in the value $y(1)$ would require that $(0.12)n^{-2} < 5 \times 10^{-13}$, which means that $n \ge 489{,}898$. Thus, roughly half a million steps of length $h \approx 0.000002$ would be required. Aside from the possible impracticality of this many steps (using available computational resources), the roundoff error resulting from so many successive steps might well overwhelm the cumulative error predicted by theory (which assumes exact computations in each separate step). Consequently, still more accurate methods than the improved Euler method are needed for such high-precision computations.

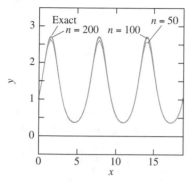

FIGURE 2.5.9. Approximating the exact solution $y = e^{\sin x}$ using the improved Euler method with $n = 50$, 100, and 200 subintervals.

2.5 _Problems_

A hand-held calculator will suffice for Problems 1 through 10. In each problem, find the exact solution of the given initial value problem. Then apply the improved Euler method to approximate to four decimal places this solution on the interval [0, 0.5] with step size $h = 0.1$. Make a table showing the approximate values and the actual values of the solution at the points $x = 0.1, 0.2, 0.3, 0.4,$ and 0.5.

1. $\dfrac{dy}{dx} = -y$, $y(0) = 2$

2. $\dfrac{dy}{dx} = 2y$, $y(0) = \frac{1}{2}$

3. $\dfrac{dy}{dx} = y + 1$, $y(0) = 1$

4. $\dfrac{dy}{dx} = x - y$, $y(0) = 1$

5. $\dfrac{dy}{dx} = y - x - 1$, $y(0) = 1$

6. $\dfrac{dy}{dx} = -2xy$, $y(0) = 2$

7. $\dfrac{dy}{dx} = -3x^2y$, $y(0) = 3$

8. $\dfrac{dy}{dx} = e^{-y}$, $y(0) = 0$

9. $\dfrac{dy}{dx} = \frac{1}{4}(1 + y^2)$, $y(0) = 1$

10. $\dfrac{dy}{dx} = 2xy^2$, $y(0) = 1$

Note: The project following this problem set lists illustrative calculator/computer programs that can be used in Problems 11 through 24.

A programmable calculator or a computer will be useful for Problems 11 through 16. In each problem find the exact solution of the given initial value problem. Then apply the improved Euler method twice to approximate (to five decimal places) this solution on the given interval, first with step size $h = 0.01$, then with step size $h = 0.005$. Make a table showing the approximate values and the actual value, together with the percentage error in the more accurate approximations, for x an integral multiple of 0.2. Throughout, primes denote derivatives with respect to x.

11. $y' = y - 2$, $y(0) = 1$; $0 \le x \le 1$

12. $y' = \frac{1}{2}(y - 1)^2$, $y(0) = 2$; $0 \le x \le 1$

13. $yy' = 2x^3$, $y(1) = 3$; $1 \le x \le 2$

14. $xy' = y^2$, $y(1) = 1$; $1 \le x \le 2$

15. $xy' = 3x - 2y$, $y(2) = 3$; $2 \le x \le 3$

16. $y^2y' = 2x^5$, $y(2) = 3$; $2 \le x \le 3$

A computer with a printer is required for Problems 17 through 24. In these initial value problems, use the improved Euler method with step sizes $h = 0.1, 0.02, 0.004$, and 0.0008 to approximate to five decimal places the values of the solution at ten equally spaced points of the given interval. Print the results in tabular form with appropriate headings to make it easy to gauge the effect of varying the step size h. Throughout, primes denote derivatives with respect to x.

17. $y' = x^2 + y^2$, $y(0) = 0$; $0 \leq x \leq 1$

18. $y' = x^2 - y^2$, $y(0) = 1$; $0 \leq x \leq 2$

19. $y' = x + \sqrt{y}$, $y(0) = 1$; $0 \leq x \leq 2$

20. $y' = x + \sqrt[3]{y}$, $y(0) = -1$; $0 \leq x \leq 2$

21. $y' = \ln y$, $y(1) = 2$; $1 \leq x \leq 2$

22. $y' = x^{2/3} + y^{2/3}$, $y(0) = 1$; $0 \leq x \leq 2$

23. $y' = \sin x + \cos y$, $y(0) = 0$; $0 \leq x \leq 1$

24. $y' = \dfrac{x}{1 + y^2}$, $y(-1) = 1$; $-1 \leq x \leq 1$

25. Consider the crossbow bolt of Example 2 in Section 2.3, shot straight upward from the ground with an initial velocity of 49 m/s. Because of linear air resistance, its velocity function $v(t)$ satisfies the initial value problem

$$\frac{dv}{dt} = -(0.04)v - 9.8, \quad v(0) = 49$$

with exact solution $v(t) = 294e^{-t/25} - 245$. Use a calculator or computer implementation of the improved Euler method to approximate $v(t)$ for $0 \leq t \leq 10$ using both $n = 50$ and $n = 100$ subintervals. Display the results

at intervals of 1 second. Do the two approximations—each rounded to two decimal places—agree both with each other and with the exact solution? If the exact solution were unavailable, explain how you could use the improved Euler method to approximate closely (a) the bolt's time of ascent to its apex (given in Section 2.3 as 4.56 s) and (b) its impact velocity after 9.41 s in the air.

26. Consider now the crossbow bolt of Example 3 in Section 2.3. It still is shot straight upward from the ground with an initial velocity of 49 m/s, but because of air resistance proportional to the square of its velocity, its velocity function $v(t)$ satisfies the initial value problem

$$\frac{dv}{dt} = -(0.0011)v|v| - 9.8, \quad v(0) = 49.$$

The symbolic solution discussed in Section 2.3 required separate investigations of the bolt's ascent and its descent, with $v(t)$ given by a tangent function during ascent and by a hyperbolic tangent function during descent. But the improved Euler method requires no such distinction. Use a calculator or computer implementation of the improved Euler method to approximate $v(t)$ for $0 \leq t \leq 10$ using both $n = 100$ and $n = 200$ subintervals. Display the results at intervals of 1 second. Do the two approximations—each rounded to two decimal places—agree with each other? If an exact solution were unavailable, explain how you could use the improved Euler method to approximate closely (a) the bolt's time of ascent to its apex (given in Section 2.3 as 4.61 s) and (b) its impact velocity after 9.41 s in the air.

2.6 THE RUNGE-KUTTA METHOD

We now discuss a method for approximating the solution $y = y(x)$ of the initial value problem

$$\frac{dy}{dx} = f(x, y), \quad y(x_0) = y_0 \tag{1}$$

that is considerably more accurate than the improved Euler method and is more widely used in practice than any of the numerical methods discussed in Sections 2.4 and 2.5. It is called the *Runge-Kutta method*, after the German mathematicians who developed it, Carl Runge (1856–1927) and Wilhelm Kutta (1867–1944).

With the usual notation, suppose that we have computed the approximations $y_1, y_2, y_3, \ldots, y_n$ to the actual values $y(x_1), y(x_2), y(x_3), \ldots, y(x_n)$ and now want to compute $y_{n+1} \approx y(x_{n+1})$. Then

$$y(x_{n+1}) - y(x_n) = \int_{x_n}^{x_{n+1}} y'(x)\,dx = \int_{x_n}^{x_n+h} y'(x)\,dx \tag{2}$$

by the fundamental theorem of calculus. Next, Simpson's rule for numerical integration yields

$$y(x_{n+1}) - y(x_n) \approx \frac{h}{6}\left[y'(x_n) + 4y'\left(x_n + \frac{h}{2}\right) + y'(x_{n+1})\right]. \tag{3}$$

Hence we want to define y_{n+1} so that

$$y_{n+1} \approx y_n + \frac{h}{6}\left[y'(x_n) + 2y'\left(x_n + \frac{h}{2}\right) + 2y'\left(x_n + \frac{h}{2}\right) + y'(x_{n+1})\right]; \tag{4}$$

we have split $4y'\left(x_n + \frac{1}{2}h\right)$ into a sum of two terms because we intend to approximate the slope $y'\left(x_n + \frac{1}{2}h\right)$ at the midpoint $x_n + \frac{1}{2}h$ of the interval $[x_n, x_{n+1}]$ in two different ways.

On the right-hand side in (4), we replace the [true] slope values $y'(x_n)$, $y'\left(x_n + \frac{1}{2}h\right)$, $y'\left(x_n + \frac{1}{2}h\right)$, and $y'(x_{n+1})$, respectively, with the following estimates.

➤
$$k_1 = f(x_n, y_n). \tag{5a}$$

- This is the Euler method slope at x_n.

➤
$$k_2 = f\left(x_n + \tfrac{1}{2}h, y_n + \tfrac{1}{2}hk_1\right). \tag{5b}$$

- This is an estimate of the slope at the midpoint of the interval $[x_n, x_{n+1}]$ using the Euler method to predict the ordinate there.

➤
$$k_3 = f\left(x_n + \tfrac{1}{2}h, y_n + \tfrac{1}{2}hk_2\right). \tag{5c}$$

- This is an improved Euler value for the slope at the midpoint.

➤
$$k_4 = f(x_{n+1}, y_n + hk_3). \tag{5d}$$

- This is the Euler method slope at x_{n+1}, using the improved slope k_3 at the midpoint to step to x_{n+1}.

When these substitutions are made in (4), the result is the iterative formula

➤
$$y_{n+1} = y_n + \frac{h}{6}(k_1 + 2k_2 + 2k_3 + k_4). \tag{6}$$

The use of this formula to compute the approximations $y_1, y_2, y_3, \ldots$ successively constitutes the **Runge-Kutta method.** Note that Eq. (6) takes the "Euler form"

$$y_{n+1} = y_n + h \cdot k$$

if we write

$$k = \frac{1}{6}(k_1 + 2k_2 + 2k_3 + k_4) \tag{7}$$

for the approximate *average slope* on the interval $[x_n, x_{n+1}]$.

The Runge-Kutta method is a *fourth-order* method—it can be proved that the cumulative error on a bounded interval $[a, b]$ with $a = x_0$ is of order h^4. (Thus the iteration in (6) is sometimes called the *fourth-order* Runge-Kutta method because it is possible to develop Runge-Kutta methods of other orders.) That is,

➤
$$|y(x_n) - y_n| \leqq Ch^4, \tag{8}$$

where the constant C depends on the function $f(x, y)$ and the interval $[a, b]$, but does not depend on the step size h. The following example illustrates this high accuracy in comparison with the lower-order accuracy of our previous numerical methods.

EXAMPLE 1   We first apply the Runge-Kutta method to the illustrative initial value problem

$$\frac{dy}{dx} = x + y, \quad y(0) = 1 \tag{9}$$

that we considered in Example 1 of Section 2.4 and again in Example 2 of Section 2.5. The exact solution of this problem is $y(x) = 2e^x - x - 1$. To make a point we use $h = 0.5$, a larger step size than in any previous example, so only two steps are required to go from $x = 0$ to $x = 1$.

In the first step we use the formulas in (5) and (6) to calculate

$$k_1 = 0 + 1 = 1,$$
$$k_2 = (0 + 0.25) + (1 + (0.25) \cdot (1)) = 1.5,$$
$$k_3 = (0 + 0.25) + (1 + (0.25) \cdot (1.5)) = 1.625,$$
$$k_4 = (0.5) + (1 + (0.5) \cdot (1.625)) = 2.3125,$$

and thence

$$y_1 = 1 + \frac{0.5}{6}[1 + 2 \cdot (1.5) + 2 \cdot (1.625) + 2.3125] \approx 1.7969.$$

Similarly, the second step yields $y_2 \approx 3.4347$.

Figure 2.6.1 presents these results together with the results (from Fig. 2.5.4) of applying the improved Euler method with step size $h = 0.1$. We see that even with the larger step size, the Runge-Kutta method gives (for this problem) four to five times the accuracy (in terms of relative percentage errors) of the improved Euler method. ∎

	Improved Euler		Runge-Kutta		
x	y with $h = 0.1$	Percent Error	y with $h = 0.5$	Percent Error	Actual y
0.0	1.0000	0.00%	1.0000	0.00%	1.0000
0.5	1.7949	0.14%	1.7969	0.03%	1.7974
1.0	3.4282	0.24%	3.4347	0.05%	3.4366

FIGURE 2.6.1. Runge-Kutta and improved Euler results for the initial value problem $dy/dx = x + y$, $y(0) = 1$.

It is customary to measure the computational labor involved in solving $dy/dx = f(x, y)$ numerically by counting the number of evaluations of the function $f(x, y)$ that are required. In Example 1, the Runge-Kutta method required eight evaluations of $f(x, y) = x + y$ (four at each step), whereas the improved Euler method required 20 such evaluations (two for each of 10 steps). Thus the Runge-Kutta method gave over four times the accuracy with only 40% of the labor.

Computer programs implementing the Runge-Kutta method are listed in the project material for this section. Figure 2.6.2 shows the results obtained by applying the improved Euler and Runge-Kutta methods to the problem $dy/dx = x + y$, $y(0) = 1$ with the same step size $h = 0.1$. The relative error in the improved Euler value at $x = 1$ is about 0.24%, but for the Runge-Kutta value it is 0.00012%. In this comparison the Runge-Kutta method is about 2000 times as accurate, but requires only twice as many function evaluations, as the improved Euler method.

The error bound

$$|y(x_n) - y_n| \leq Ch^4 \tag{8}$$

for the Runge-Kutta method results in a rapid decrease in the magnitude of errors when the step size h is reduced (except for the possibility that very small step sizes may result in unacceptable roundoff errors). It follows from the inequality in (8) that (on a fixed bounded interval) halving the step size decreases the absolute error by a factor of $\left(\frac{1}{2}\right)^4 = \frac{1}{16}$. Consequently, the common practice of successively halving the step size until the computed results "stabilize" is particularly effective with the Runge-Kutta method.

x	Improved Euler y	Runge-Kutta y	Actual y
0.1	1.1100	1.110342	1.110342
0.2	1.2421	1.242805	1.242806
0.3	1.3985	1.399717	1.399718
0.4	1.5818	1.583648	1.583649
0.5	1.7949	1.797441	1.797443
0.6	2.0409	2.044236	2.044238
0.7	2.3231	2.327503	2.327505
0.8	2.6456	2.651079	2.651082
0.9	3.0124	3.019203	3.019206
1.0	3.4282	3.436559	3.436564

FIGURE 2.6.2. Runge-Kutta and improved Euler results for the initial value problem $dy/dx = x + y$, $y(0) = 1$, with the same step size $h = 0.1$.

EXAMPLE 2   In Example 2 of Section 2.4 we saw that Euler's method is not adequate to approximate the solution $y(x)$ of the initial value problem

$$\frac{dy}{dx} = x^2 + y^2, \quad y(0) = 1 \tag{10}$$

as x approaches the infinite discontinuity near $x = 0.969811$ (see Fig. 2.6.3). Now we apply the Runge-Kutta method to this initial value problem.

Figure 2.6.4 shows Runge-Kutta results on the interval [0.0, 0.9], computed with step sizes $h = 0.1$, $h = 0.05$, and $h = 0.025$. There is still some difficulty near $x = 0.9$, but it seems safe to conclude from these data that $y(0.5) \approx 2.0670$.

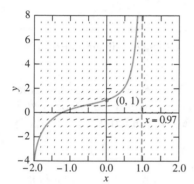

FIGURE 2.6.3. Solutions of $dy/dx = x^2 + y^2$, $y(0) = 1$.

x	y with h = 0.1	y with h = 0.05	y with h = 0.025
0.1	1.1115	1.1115	1.1115
0.3	1.4397	1.4397	1.4397
0.5	2.0670	2.0670	2.0670
0.7	3.6522	3.6529	3.6529
0.9	14.0218	14.2712	14.3021

FIGURE 2.6.4. Approximating the solution of the initial value problem in Eq. (10).

We therefore begin anew and apply the Runge-Kutta method to the initial value problem

$$\frac{dy}{dx} = x^2 + y^2, \quad y(0.5) = 2.0670. \tag{11}$$

Figure 2.6.5 shows results on the interval [0.5, 0.9], obtained with step sizes $h = 0.01$, $h = 0.005$, and $h = 0.0025$. We now conclude that $y(0.9) \approx 14.3049$.

Finally, Fig. 2.6.6 shows results on the interval [0.90, 0.95] for the initial value problem

$$\frac{dy}{dx} = x^2 + y^2, \quad y(0.9) = 14.3049, \tag{12}$$

obtained using step sizes $h = 0.002$, $h = 0.001$, and $h = 0.0005$. Our final approximate result is $y(0.95) \approx 50.4723$. The actual value of the solution at $x = 0.95$ is $y(0.95) \approx 50.471867$. Our slight overestimate results mainly from the fact that the four-place initial value in (12) is (in effect) the result of rounding *up* the actual value $y(0.9) \approx 14.304864$; such errors are magnified considerably as we approach the vertical asymptote. ∎

x	y with $h = 0.01$	y with $h = 0.005$	y with $h = 0.0025$
0.5	2.0670	2.0670	2.0670
0.6	2.6440	2.6440	2.6440
0.7	3.6529	3.6529	3.6529
0.8	5.8486	5.8486	5.8486
0.9	14.3048	14.3049	14.3049

FIGURE 2.6.5. Approximating the solution of the initial value problem in Eq. (11).

x	y with $h = 0.002$	y with $h = 0.001$	y with $h = 0.0005$
0.90	14.3049	14.3049	14.3049
0.91	16.7024	16.7024	16.7024
0.92	20.0617	20.0617	20.0617
0.93	25.1073	25.1073	25.1073
0.94	33.5363	33.5363	33.5363
0.95	50.4722	50.4723	50.4723

FIGURE 2.6.6. Approximating the solution of the initial value problem in Eq. (12).

EXAMPLE 3 A skydiver with a mass of 60 kg jumps from a helicopter hovering at an initial altitude of 5 kilometers. Assume that she falls vertically with initial velocity zero and experiences an upward force F_R of air resistance given in terms of her velocity v (in meters per second) by

$$F_R = (0.0096)(100v + 10v^2 + v^3)$$

(in newtons, and with the coordinate axis directed downward so that $v > 0$ during her descent to the ground). If she does not open her parachute, what will be her terminal velocity? How fast will she be falling after 5 s have elapsed? After 10 s? After 20 s?

Solution Newton's law $F = ma$ gives

$$m\frac{dv}{dt} = mg - F_R;$$

that is,

$$60\frac{dv}{dt} = (60)(9.8) - (0.0096)(100v + 10v^2 + v^3) \tag{13}$$

because $m = 60$ and $g = 9.8$. Thus the velocity function $v(t)$ satisfies the initial value problem

$$\frac{dv}{dt} = f(v), \quad v(0) = 0, \tag{14}$$

where

$$f(v) = 9.8 - (0.00016)(100v + 10v^2 + v^3). \tag{15}$$

The skydiver reaches her terminal velocity when the forces of gravity and air resistance balance, so $f(v) = 0$. We can therefore calculate her terminal velocity immediately by solving the equation

$$f(v) = 9.8 - (0.00016)(100v + 10v^2 + v^3) = 0. \tag{16}$$

Figure 2.6.7 shows the graph of the function $f(v)$ and exhibits the single real solution $v \approx 35.5780$ (found graphically or by using a calculator or computer `Solve` procedure). Thus the skydiver's terminal speed is approximately 35.578 m/s, about 128 km/h (almost 80 mi/h).

Figure 2.6.8 shows the results of Runge-Kutta approximations to the solution of the initial value problem in (14); the step sizes $h = 0.2$ and $h = 0.1$ yield the same results (to three decimal places). Observe that the terminal velocity is effectively attained in only 15 s. But the skydiver's velocity is 91.85% of her terminal velocity after only 5 s, and 99.78% after 10 s. ∎

t (s)	v (m/s)	t (s)	v (m/s)
0	0	11	35.541
1	9.636	12	35.560
2	18.386	13	35.569
3	25.299	14	35.574
4	29.949	15	35.576
5	32.678	16	35.577
6	34.137	17	35.578
7	34.875	18	35.578
8	35.239	19	35.578
9	35.415	20	35.578
10	35.500		

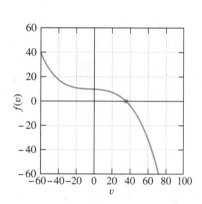

FIGURE 2.6.7. Graph of $f(v) = 9.8 - (0.00016)(100v + 10v^2 + v^3)$.

FIGURE 2.6.8. The skydiver's velocity data.

The final example of this section contains a *warning*: For certain types of initial value problems, the numerical methods we have discussed are not nearly so successful as in the previous examples.

EXAMPLE 4 Consider the seemingly innocuous initial value problem

$$\frac{dy}{dx} = 5y - 6e^{-x}, \quad y(0) = 1 \tag{17}$$

whose exact solution is $y(x) = e^{-x}$. The table in Fig. 2.6.9 shows the results obtained by applying the Runge-Kutta method on the interval $[0, 4]$ with step sizes

x	Runge-Kutta y with $h = 0.2$	Runge-Kutta y with $h = 0.1$	Runge-Kutta y with $h = 0.05$	Actual y
0.4	0.66880	0.67020	0.67031	0.67032
0.8	0.43713	0.44833	0.44926	0.44933
1.2	0.21099	0.29376	0.30067	0.30199
1.6	−0.46019	0.14697	0.19802	0.20190
2.0	−4.72142	−0.27026	0.10668	0.13534
2.4	−35.53415	−2.90419	−0.12102	0.09072
2.8	−261.25023	−22.05352	−1.50367	0.06081
3.2	−1,916.69395	−163.25077	−11.51868	0.04076
3.6	−14059.35494	−1205.71249	−85.38156	0.02732
4.0	−103,126.5270	−8903.12866	−631.03934	0.01832

FIGURE 2.6.9. Runge-Kutta attempts to solve numerically the initial value problem in Eq. (17).

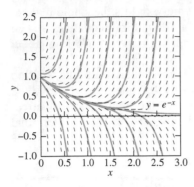

FIGURE 2.6.10. Direction field and solution curves for $dy/dx = 5y - 6e^{-x}$.

$h = 0.2$, $h = 0.1$, and $h = 0.05$. Obviously these attempts are spectacularly unsuccessful. Although $y(x) = e^{-x} \to 0$ as $x \to +\infty$, it appears that our numerical approximations are headed toward $-\infty$ rather than zero.

The explanation lies in the fact that the general solution of the equation $dy/dx = 5y - 6e^{-x}$ is

$$y(x) = e^{-x} + Ce^{5x}. \tag{18}$$

The particular solution of (17) satisfying the initial condition $y(0) = 1$ is obtained with $C = 0$. But any departure, however small, from the exact solution $y(x) = e^{-x}$—even if due only to roundoff error—introduces [in effect] a nonzero value of C in Eq. (18). And as indicated in Fig. 2.6.10, all solution curves of the form in (18) with $C \neq 0$ diverge rapidly away from the one with $C = 0$, even if their initial values are close to 1. ∎

Difficulties of the sort illustrated by Example 4 sometimes are unavoidable, but one can at least hope to recognize such a problem when it appears. Approximate values whose order of magnitude varies with changing step size are a common indicator of such instability. These difficulties are discussed in numerical analysis textbooks and are the subject of current research in the field.

2.6 _Problems_

A hand-held calculator will suffice for Problems 1 through 10. In each problem, find the exact solution of the given initial value problem. Then apply the Runge-Kutta method with step size $h = 0.25$ to approximate to five decimal places this solution on the interval $[0.0, 0.5]$. Make a table showing the approximate values and the actual values of the solution at the points $x = 0.25$ and $x = 0.50$.

1. $\dfrac{dy}{dx} = -y$, $y(0) = 2$

2. $\dfrac{dy}{dx} = 2y$, $y(0) = \frac{1}{2}$

3. $\dfrac{dy}{dx} = y + 1$, $y(0) = 1$

4. $\dfrac{dy}{dx} = x - y$, $y(0) = 1$

5. $\dfrac{dy}{dx} = y - x - 1$, $y(0) = 1$

6. $\dfrac{dy}{dx} = -2xy$, $y(0) = 2$

7. $\dfrac{dy}{dx} = -3x^2 y$, $y(0) = 3$

8. $\dfrac{dy}{dx} = e^{-y}$, $y(0) = 0$

9. $\dfrac{dy}{dx} = \frac{1}{4}(1 + y^2)$, $y(0) = 1$

10. $\dfrac{dy}{dx} = 2xy^2$, $y(0) = 1$

Note: The project following this problem set lists illustrative calculator/computer programs that can be used in the remaining problems.

A programmable calculator or a computer will be useful for Problems 11 through 16. In each problem find the exact solution of the given initial value problem. Then apply the Runge-Kutta method twice to approximate (to five decimal places) this solution on the given interval, first with step size

$h = 0.2$, then with step size $h = 0.1$. Make a table showing the approximate values and the actual value, together with the percentage error in the more accurate approximation, for x an integral multiple of 0.2. Throughout, primes denote derivatives with respect to x.

11. $y' = y - 2$, $y(0) = 1$; $0 \leq x \leq 1$

12. $y' = \frac{1}{2}(y - 1)^2$, $y(0) = 2$; $0 \leq x \leq 1$

13. $yy' = 2x^3$, $y(1) = 3$; $1 \leq x \leq 2$

14. $xy' = y^2$, $y(1) = 1$; $1 \leq x \leq 2$

15. $xy' = 3x - 2y$, $y(2) = 3$; $2 \leq x \leq 3$

16. $y^2 y' = 2x^5$, $y(2) = 3$; $2 \leq x \leq 3$

A computer with a printer is required for Problems 17 through 24. In these initial value problems, use the Runge-Kutta method with step sizes $h = 0.2, 0.1, 0.05,$ and 0.025 to approximate to six decimal places the values of the solution at five equally spaced points of the given interval. Print the results in tabular form with appropriate headings to make it easy to gauge the effect of varying the step size h. Throughout, primes denote derivatives with respect to x.

17. $y' = x^2 + y^2$, $y(0) = 0$; $0 \leq x \leq 1$

18. $y' = x^2 - y^2$, $y(0) = 1$; $0 \leq x \leq 2$

19. $y' = x + \sqrt{y}$, $y(0) = 1$; $0 \leq x \leq 2$

20. $y' = x + \sqrt[3]{y}$, $y(0) = -1$; $0 \leq x \leq 2$

21. $y' = \ln y$, $y(1) = 2$; $1 \leq x \leq 2$

22. $y' = x^{2/3} + y^{2/3}$, $y(0) = 1$; $0 \leq x \leq 2$

23. $y' = \sin x + \cos y$, $y(0) = 0$; $0 \leq x \leq 1$

24. $y' = \dfrac{x}{1 + y^2}$, $y(-1) = 1$; $-1 \leq x \leq 1$

Velocity-Acceleration Problems

In Problems 25 and 26, the linear acceleration $a = dv/dt$ of a moving particle is given by a formula $dv/dt = f(t, v)$, where the velocity $v = dy/dt$ is the derivative of the function $y = y(t)$ giving the position of the particle at time t. Suppose that the velocity $v(t)$ is approximated using the Runge-Kutta method to solve numerically the initial value problem

$$\frac{dv}{dt} = f(t, v), \quad v(0) = v_0. \qquad (19)$$

That is, starting with $t_0 = 0$ and v_0, the formulas in Eqs. (5) and (6) are applied—with t and v in place of x and y—to calculate the successive approximate velocity values $v_1, v_2, v_3, \ldots, v_m$ at the successive times $t_1, t_2, t_3, \ldots, t_m$ (with $t_{n+1} = t_n + h$). Now suppose that we also want to approximate the *distance* $y(t)$ traveled by the particle. We can do this by beginning with the initial position $y(0) = y_0$ and calculating

$$y_{n+1} = y_n + v_n h + \tfrac{1}{2} a_n h^2 \qquad (20)$$

($n = 1, 2, 3, \ldots$), where $a_n = f(t_n, v_n) \approx v'(t_n)$ is the particle's approximate acceleration at time t_n. The formula in (20) would give the correct increment (from y_n to y_{n+1}) if the acceleration a_n remained constant during the time interval $[t_n, t_{n+1}]$.

Thus, once a table of approximate velocities has been calculated, Eq. (20) provides a simple way to calculate a table of corresponding successive positions. This process is illustrated in the project for this section, by beginning with the velocity data in Fig. 2.6.8 (Example 3) and proceeding to follow the skydiver's position during her descent to the ground.

25. Consider again the crossbow bolt of Example 2 in Section 2.3, shot straight upward from the ground with an initial velocity of 49 m/s. Because of linear air resistance, its velocity function $v = dy/dt$ satisfies the initial value problem

$$\frac{dv}{dt} = -(0.04)v - 9.8, \quad v(0) = 49$$

with exact solution $v(t) = 294e^{-t/25} - 245$. (a) Use a calculator or computer implementation of the Runge-Kutta method to approximate $v(t)$ for $0 \leq t \leq 10$ using both $n = 100$ and $n = 200$ subintervals. Display the results at intervals of 1 second. Do the two approximations—each rounded to four decimal places—agree both with each other and with the exact solution? (b) Now use the velocity data from part (a) to approximate $y(t)$ for $0 \leq t \leq 10$ using $n = 200$ subintervals. Display the results at intervals of 1 second. Do these approximate position values—each rounded to two decimal places—agree with the exact solution

$$y(t) = 7350 \left(1 - e^{-t/25}\right) - 245t?$$

(c) If the exact solution were unavailable, explain how you could use the Runge-Kutta method to approximate closely the bolt's times of ascent and descent and the maximum height it attains.

26. Now consider again the crossbow bolt of Example 3 in Section 2.3. It still is shot straight upward from the ground with an initial velocity of 49 m/s, but because of air resistance proportional to the square of its velocity, its velocity function $v(t)$ satisfies the initial value problem

$$\frac{dv}{dt} = -(0.0011)v|v| - 9.8, \quad v(0) = 49.$$

Beginning with this initial value problem, repeat parts (a) through (c) of Problem 25 (except that you may need $n = 200$ subintervals to get four-place accuracy in part (a) and $n = 400$ subintervals for two-place accuracy in part (b)). According to the results of Problem 17 and 18 in Section 2.3, the bolt's velocity and position functions during ascent and descent are given by the following formulas.

Ascent:
$v(t) = (94.388) \tan(0.478837 - [0.103827]t),$
$y(t) = 108.465$
$\qquad + (909.091) \ln (\cos(0.478837 - [0.103827]t));$

Descent:
$v(t) = -(94.388) \tanh(0.103827[t - 4.6119]),$
$y(t) = 108.465$
$\qquad - (909.091) \ln (\cosh(0.103827[t - 4.6119])).$

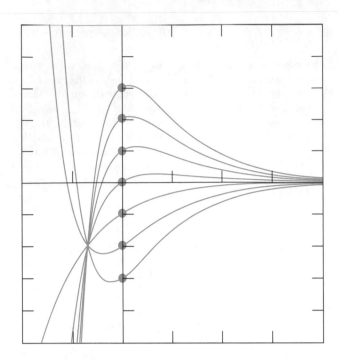

CHAPTER 3

Linear Equations of Higher Order

3.1 INTRODUCTION: SECOND-ORDER LINEAR EQUATIONS

In Chapters 1 and 2 we confined our attention to first-order differential equations. We now turn to equations of higher order $n \geq 2$, beginning in this chapter with equations that are linear. The general theory of linear differential equations parallels the case of second-order linear equations (the case $n = 2$), which we outline in this initial section.

Recall that a second-order differential equation in the (unknown) function $y(x)$ is one of the form

$$G(x, y, y', y'') = 0. \tag{1}$$

This differential equation is said to be **linear** provided that G is linear in the dependent variable y and its derivatives y' and y''. Thus a linear second-order equation takes the form

➤ $$A(x)y'' + B(x)y' + C(x)y = F(x). \tag{2}$$

Unless otherwise noted, we will always assume that the (known) coefficient functions $A(x)$, $B(x)$, $C(x)$, and $F(x)$ are continuous on some open interval I (perhaps unbounded) on which we wish to solve this differential equation, but we do *not* require that they be linear functions. Thus the differential equation

$$e^x y'' + (\cos x)y' + (1 + \sqrt{x})y = \tan^{-1} x$$

is linear because the dependent variable and its derivatives appear linearly. By contrast, the equations

$$y'' = yy' \quad \text{and} \quad y'' + 3(y')^2 + 4y^3 = 0$$

are not linear because products and powers of y or its derivatives appear.

If the function $F(x)$ on the right-hand side of Eq. (2) vanishes identically on I, then we call Eq. (2) a **homogeneous** linear equation; otherwise, it is **nonhomogeneous**. For example, the second-order equation

$$x^2 y'' + 2xy' + 3y = \cos x$$

is nonhomogeneous; its *associated* homogeneous equation is

$$x^2 y'' + 2xy' + 3y = 0.$$

In general, the homogeneous linear equation **associated** with Eq. (2) is

$$A(x)y'' + B(x)y' + C(x)y = 0. \tag{3}$$

In case the differential equation in (2) models a physical system, the nonhomogeneous term $F(x)$ frequently corresponds to some *external* influence on the system.

A Typical Application

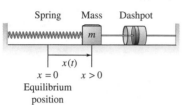

Linear differential equations frequently appear as mathematical models of mechanical systems and electrical circuits. For example, suppose that a mass m is attached both to a spring that exerts on it a force F_S and to a dashpot (shock absorber) that exerts a force F_R on the mass (Fig. 3.1.1). Assume that the restoring force F_S of the spring is proportional to the displacement x (positive to the right, negative to the left) of the mass from equilibrium, and that the dashpot force F_R is proportional to the velocity $v = dx/dt$ of the mass. With the aid of Fig. 3.1.2 we also get the appropriate directions of action of these two forces:

$$F_S = -kx \quad \text{and} \quad F_R = -cv \quad (k, c > 0).$$

FIGURE 3.1.1. A mass-spring-dashpot system.

The minus signs are correct—F_S is negative when x is positive, F_R is negative when v is positive. Newton's law $F = ma$ now gives

$$mx'' = F_S + F_R; \tag{4}$$

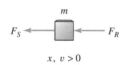

that is,

FIGURE 3.1.2. Directions of the forces acting on m.

$$m\frac{d^2x}{dt^2} + c\frac{dx}{dt} + kx = 0. \tag{5}$$

Thus we have a differential equation satisfied by the position function $x(t)$ of the mass m. This homogeneous second-order linear equation governs the *free vibrations* of the mass; we will return to this problem in detail in Section 3.4.

If, in addition to F_S and F_R, the mass m is acted on by an external force $F(t)$—which must then be added to the right-hand side in Eq. (4)—the resulting equation is

$$m\frac{d^2x}{dt^2} + c\frac{dx}{dt} + kx = F(t). \tag{6}$$

This nonhomogeneous linear differential equation governs the *forced vibrations* of the mass under the influence of the external force $F(t)$.

Homogeneous Second-Order Linear Equations

Consider the general second-order linear equation

$$A(x)y'' + B(x)y' + C(x)y = F(x), \tag{7}$$

where the coefficient functions A, B, C, and F are continuous on the open interval I. Here we assume in addition that $A(x) \neq 0$ at each point of I, so we can divide each term in Eq. (7) by $A(x)$ and write it in the form

$$y'' + p(x)y' + q(x)y = f(x). \tag{8}$$

We will discuss first the associated homogeneous equation

$$y'' + p(x)y' + q(x)y = 0. \tag{9}$$

A particularly useful property of this *homogeneous* linear equation is the fact that the sum of any two solutions of Eq. (9) is again a solution, as is any constant multiple of a solution. This is the central idea of the following theorem.

THEOREM 1: Principle of Superposition

Let y_1 and y_2 be two solutions of the homogeneous linear equation in (9) on the interval I. If c_1 and c_2 are constants, then the linear combination

$$y = c_1 y_1 + c_2 y_2 \tag{10}$$

is also a solution of Eq. (9) on I.

Proof :   The conclusion follows almost immediately from the linearity of the operation of differentiation, which gives

$$y' = c_1 y_1' + c_2 y_2' \quad \text{and} \quad y'' = c_1 y_1'' + c_2 y_2''.$$

Then

$$\begin{aligned}
y'' + py' + qy &= (c_1 y_1 + c_2 y_2)'' + p(c_1 y_1 + c_2 y_2)' + q(c_1 y_1 + c_2 y_2) \\
&= (c_1 y_1'' + c_2 y_2'') + p(c_1 y_1' + c_2 y_2') + q(c_1 y_1 + c_2 y_2) \\
&= c_1(y_1'' + py_1' + qy_1) + c_2(y_2'' + py_2' + qy_2) \\
&= c_1 \cdot 0 + c_2 \cdot 0 = 0
\end{aligned}$$

because y_1 and y_2 are solutions. Thus $y = c_1 y_1 + c_2 y_2$ is also a solution. ∎

EXAMPLE 1   We can see by inspection that

$$y_1 = \cos x \quad \text{and} \quad y_2(x) = \sin x$$

are two solutions of the equation

$$y'' + y = 0.$$

Theorem 1 tells us that any linear combination of these solutions, such as

$$y(x) = 3y_1(x) - 2y_2(x) = 3\cos x - 2\sin x,$$

is also a solution. We will see later that, conversely, *every* solution of $y'' + y = 0$ is a linear combination of these two particular solutions y_1 and y_2. Thus a general solution of $y'' + y = 0$ is

$$y(x) = c_1 \cos x + c_2 \sin x.$$

It is important to understand that this single formula for the general solution encompasses a "twofold infinity" of particular solutions, because the two coefficients c_1 and c_2 can be selected independently. Figures 3.1.3 through 3.1.5 illustrate some of the possibilities, with either c_1 or c_2 set equal to zero, or with both nonzero. ∎

Earlier in this section we gave the linear equation $mx'' + cx' + kx = F(t)$ as a mathematical model of the motion of the mass shown in Fig. 3.1.1. Physical considerations suggest that the motion of the mass should be determined by its initial position and initial velocity. Hence, given any preassigned values of $x(0)$ and $x'(0)$, Eq. (6) ought to have a *unique* solution satisfying these initial conditions. More generally, in order to be a "good" mathematical model of a deterministic physical situation, a differential equation must have unique solutions satisfying any appropriate initial conditions. The following existence and uniqueness theorem (proved in the Appendix) gives us this assurance for the general second-order equation.

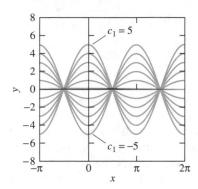

FIGURE 3.1.3. Solutions $y(x) = c_1 \cos x$ of $y'' + y = 0$.

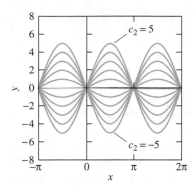

FIGURE 3.1.4. Solutions $y(x) = c_2 \sin x$ of $y'' + y = 0$.

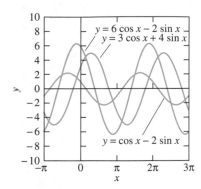

FIGURE 3.1.5. Solutions of $y'' + y = 0$ with c_1 and c_2 nonzero.

THEOREM 2: Existence and Uniqueness

Suppose that the functions p, q, and f are continuous on the open interval I containing the point a. Then, given any two numbers b_0 and b_1, the equation

$$y'' + p(x)y' + q(x)y = f(x) \tag{8}$$

has a unique (that is, one and only one) solution on the entire interval I that satisfies the initial conditions

$$y(a) = b_0, \quad y'(a) = b_1. \tag{11}$$

∎

Remark 1: Equation (8) and the conditions in (11) constitute a second-order linear **initial value problem.** Theorem 2 tells us that any such initial value problem has a unique solution on the *whole* interval I where the coefficient functions in (8) are continuous. Recall from Section 1.3 that a *nonlinear* differential equation generally has a unique solution on only a smaller interval. ∎

Theorem 2 tells us that there is exactly one solution to the initial value problem given by the equation (8) and initial conditions (11) but does not tell us how to find it. The rest of this chapter explains a three step strategy for finding solutions to the initial value problem for second order linear equations.

To illustrate how this strategy works, let's consider a simple example we can solve easily: $y'' = x^3 + e^{5x}$, $y(0) = -1$, $y'(0) = 7$. Integrating once gives

$$y' = \frac{x^4}{4} + \frac{e^{5x}}{5} + c_1$$

and another integration gives

$$y = \frac{x^5}{20} + \frac{e^{5x}}{25} + c_1 x + c_2.$$

Plugging in the initial conditions $y() = -1$, $y'(0) = 7$ gives us the two equations

$$-1 = \frac{1}{25} + c_2, \quad 7 = \frac{1}{5} + c_1$$

which we can solve for the constants; the result is $c_1 = \frac{34}{5}$, $c_2 = -\frac{26}{25}$. Our final answer is therefore

$$y = \left(\frac{x^5}{20} + \frac{e^{5x}}{25}\right) + \left(\frac{34}{5}x - \frac{26}{25}\right).$$

Let's look at the answer more closely. The function

$$y_p = \frac{x^5}{20} + \frac{e^{5x}}{25}$$

is called a *particular* solution; it satisfies the differential equation $y'' = x^3 + e^{5x}$ but does *not* satisfy the initial conditions $y(0) = -1$, $y'(0) = 7$. We modify y_p by adding on the function $y_c = \left(\frac{34}{5}x - \frac{26}{25}\right) = c_1 x + c_2$ called a *complementary* solution which satisfies the *associated homogeneous* equation $y'' = 0$. We then choose the constants in the complementary solution so as to satisfy the initial conditions.

This is the strategy: 1) find a particular solution y_p, 2) find the complementary solution y_c and 3) choose the constants in the general solution of the equation $y = y_p + y_c$ to satisfy the initial conditions. It works because we have a *linear* equation; we can add on any complementary solution to y_p and the sum will also be a particular solution because $(y_p + y_c)'' = y_p'' + y_c'' = y_p'' + 0 = y_p''$. In other words, if y_p satisfies the differential equation $y'' = x^3 + e^{5x}$ then so does $y_p + y_c$ and we then have a couple of arbitrary constants to play with in $y_p + y_c$ which allows us to satisfy the initial conditions.

Here is another example: $y'' + y = x^3 + e^x$, $y(0) = 7$, $y'(0) = -1$. We use the 3 step strategy.

Step 1. Find some particular solution. How we do that is the content of section 3.5. For now we will just pull the function $x^3 - 6x + \dfrac{e^x}{2}$ out of the air, plug it into the equation to verify that it does satisfy the equation. We set $y_p = x^3 - 6x + \dfrac{e^x}{2}$. Note that y_p does not satisfy the initial conditions.

Step 2. Find the complementary solution. How we do that is the content of sections 3.1 and 3.3. For this problem (example 1) we know the function $y_c = c_1 \sin x + c_2 \cos x$ satisfies the associated homogeneous equation $y'' + y = 0$.

Step 3. Choose the constants so that $y_p + y_c$ satisfies **both** the equation and the initial conditions. To do that we put $y = y_p + y_c$, $y' = y_p' + y_c'$ and use the initial conditions. We get

$$y = y_p + y_c = \left(x^3 - 6x + \frac{e^x}{2}\right) + (c_1 \sin x + c_2 \cos x)$$

$$y' = y_p' + y_c' = \left(3x^2 - 6 + \frac{e^x}{2}\right) + (c_1 \cos x - c_2 \sin x).$$

Inserting the values $x = 0$, $y(0) = 7$ and $y'(0) = -1$ we get two equations, $7 = \frac{1}{2} + c_2$ and $-1 = -6 + \frac{1}{2} + c_1$, in two unknowns, c_1 and c_2. We can solve these to get $c_1 = \frac{9}{2}$ and $c_2 = \frac{13}{2}$. The answer to our problem is thus

$$y = \left(x^3 - 6x + \frac{e^x}{2}\right) + \left(\frac{9}{2}\sin x + \frac{13}{2}\cos x\right).$$

Remark 2: The function $y = y_p + y_c$ is called the *general solution* of the equation. There are two constants in the general solution that we adjust in step 3 to satisfy the initial conditions.

Remark 3: The three step strategy we have outlined for finding solutions to the initial value problem for second order linear equations also works for third order linear equations, twenty first order linear equations and even first order linear equations (we used a different method for this case in section 1.5 but the strategy also works). For example, in the general solution of a third order linear equation there are three constants that we adjust in step 3 to satisfy the three initial conditions.

Remark 4: Equation (8) is sometimes written in the simple form $Ly = f(x)$, where $Ly = y'' + p(x)y' + q(x)y$, to emphasize the fact that the only thing we

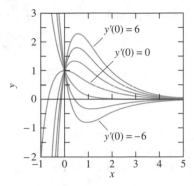

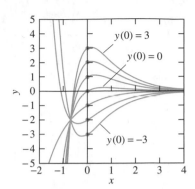

FIGURE 3.1.6. Solutions of $y'' + 3y' + 2y = 0$ with the same initial value $y(0) = 1$ but different initial slopes.

FIGURE 3.1.7. Solutions of $y'' + 3y' + 2y = 0$ with the same initial slope $y'(0) = 1$ but different initial values.

need to know about the left hand side of equation (8), to implement our three step strategy is that it is *linear* in y, that is, $L(cy) = cL(y)$ and $L(y_1 + y_2) = Ly_1 + Ly_2$. We used linearity to show (quickly) that the function $y_p + y_c$ is a solution of the equation $Ly = f(x)$; using the second property $L(y_p + y_c) = Ly_p + Ly_c = f(x) + 0 = f(x)$. We do not need to know what $p(x)$ is or what $q(x)$ is—those details are irrelevant to the argument. ∎

L is called a linear differential operator; L operates on functions to give a new function. Given any function y, Ly is the function $y'' + p(x)y' + q(x)y$.

Step 3 is simple algebra. Step 2 is more subtle and we will consider only homogeneous equations for the rest of section 3.1 and section 3.3. Step 3 will be studied in section 3.5.

Example 1 suggests how, given a *homogeneous* second-order linear equation, we might actually find the solution whose existence is assured by Theorem 2. First, we find two "essentially different" solutions y_1 and y_2; second, we attempt to impose on the general solution

$$y = c_1 y_1 + c_2 y_2 \tag{12}$$

the initial conditions $y(a) = b_0$, $y'(a) = b_1$. That is, we attempt to solve the simultaneous equations

$$c_1 y_1(a) + c_2 y_2(a) = b_0, \quad c_1 y_1'(a) + c_2 y_2'(a) = b_1 \tag{13}$$

for the coefficients c_1 and c_2.

EXAMPLE 2   Verify that the functions

$$y_1(x) = e^x \quad \text{and} \quad y_2(x) = xe^x$$

are solutions of the differential equation

$$y'' - 2y' + y = 0,$$

and then find a solution satisfying the initial conditions $y(0) = 3$, $y'(0) = 1$.

Solution   The verification is routine; we omit it. We impose the given initial conditions on the general solution

$$y(x) = c_1 e^x + c_2 x e^x,$$

for which

$$y'(x) = (c_1 + c_2)e^x + c_2 x e^x,$$

to obtain the simultaneous equations

$$y(0) = c_1 \qquad = 3,$$
$$y'(0) = c_1 + c_2 = 1.$$

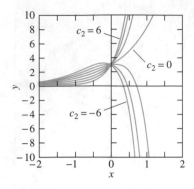

FIGURE 3.1.8. Different solutions $y(x) = 3e^x + c_2 xe^x$ of $y'' - 2y' + y = 0$ with the same initial value $y(0) = 3$.

The resulting solution is $c_1 = 3$, $c_2 = -2$. Hence the solution of the original initial value problem is

$$y(x) = 3e^x - 2xe^x.$$

Figure 3.1.8 shows several additional solutions of $y'' - 2y' + y = 0$, all having the same initial value $y(0) = 3$. ∎

In order for the procedure of Example 2 to succeed, the two solutions y_1 and y_2 must have the elusive property that the equations in (13) can always be solved for c_1 and c_2, no matter what the initial conditions b_0 and b_1 might be. The following definition tells precisely how different the two functions y_1 and y_2 must be.

DEFINITION: Linear Independence of Two Functions

Two functions defined on an open interval I are said to be **linearly independent** on I provided that neither is a constant multiple of the other. ∎

Two functions are said to be **linearly dependent** on an open interval provided that they are not linearly independent there; that is, one of them is a constant multiple of the other. We can always determine whether two given functions f and g are linearly dependent on an interval I by noting at a glance whether either of the two quotients f/g or g/f is a constant on I.

EXAMPLE 3 Thus it is clear that the following pairs of functions are linearly independent on the entire real line:

$$\sin x \quad \text{and} \quad \cos x;$$
$$e^x \quad \text{and} \quad e^{-2x};$$
$$e^x \quad \text{and} \quad xe^x;$$
$$x + 1 \quad \text{and} \quad x^2;$$
$$x \quad \text{and} \quad |x|.$$

But the identically zero function and any other function g are linearly dependent on every interval because $0 \cdot g(x) = 0$. Also, the functions

$$f(x) = \sin 2x \quad \text{and} \quad g(x) = \sin x \cos x$$

are linearly dependent on any interval because $f(x) = 2g(x)$ (a familiar trigonometric identity). ∎

General Solutions

But does the homogeneous equation $y'' + py' + qy = 0$ always have two linearly independent solutions? Theorem 2 says yes! We need only choose y_1 and y_2 so that

$$y_1(a) = 1, \ y_1'(a) = 0 \quad \text{and} \quad y_2(a) = 0, \ y_2'(a) = 1.$$

It is then impossible that either $y_1 = ky_2$ or $y_2 = ky_1$ because $k \cdot 0 \neq 1$ for any constant k. Theorem 2 tells us that two such linearly independent solutions *exist*; actually finding them is a crucial matter that we will discuss briefly at the end of this section, and in greater detail beginning in Section 3.3.

We want to show, finally, that given *any* two linearly independent solutions y_1 and y_2 of the homogeneous equation

$$y''(x) + p(x)y'(x) + q(x)y(x) = 0, \tag{9}$$

every solution y of Eq. (9) can be expressed as a linear combination

$$y = c_1 y_1 + c_2 y_2 \qquad (12)$$

of y_1 and y_2. This means that the function in (12) is the *general solution* of Eq. (9).

As suggested by the equations in (13), the determination of the constants c_1 and c_2 in (12) depends on a certain 2×2 determinant of values of y_1, y_2, and their derivatives. Given two functions f and g, the **Wronskian** of f and g is the determinant

$$W = \begin{vmatrix} f & g \\ f' & g' \end{vmatrix} = fg' - f'g.$$

We write either $W(f, g)$ or $W(x)$, depending on whether we wish to emphasize the two functions or the point x at which the Wronskian is to be evaluated. For example,

$$W(\cos x, \sin x) = \begin{vmatrix} \cos x & \sin x \\ -\sin x & \cos x \end{vmatrix} = \cos^2 x + \sin^2 x = 1$$

and

$$W(e^x, xe^x) = \begin{vmatrix} e^x & xe^x \\ e^x & e^x + xe^x \end{vmatrix} = e^{2x}.$$

These are examples of linearly *independent* pairs of solutions of differential equations (see Examples 1 and 2). Note that in both cases the Wronskian is everywhere *nonzero*.

On the other hand, if the functions f and g are linearly dependent, with $f = kg$ (for example), then

$$W(f, g) = \begin{vmatrix} kg & g \\ kg' & g' \end{vmatrix} = kgg' - kg'g \equiv 0.$$

Thus the Wronskian of two linearly *dependent* functions is identically zero. In Section 3.2 we will prove that, if the two functions y_1 and y_2 are solutions of a homogeneous second-order linear equation, then the strong converse stated in part (b) of Theorem 3 holds.

THEOREM 3: Wronskians of Solutions

Suppose that y_1 and y_2 are two solutions of the homogeneous second-order linear equation (Eq. (9))

$$y'' + p(x)y' + q(x)y = 0$$

on an open interval I on which p and q are continuous.

(a) If y_1 and y_2 are linearly dependent, then $W(y_1, y_2) \equiv 0$ on I.

(b) If y_1 and y_2 are linearly independent, then $W(y_1, y_2) \neq 0$ at each point of I. ∎

Thus, given two solutions of Eq. (9), there are just two possibilities: The Wronskian W is identically zero if the solutions are linearly dependent; the Wronskian is never zero if the solutions are linearly independent. The latter fact is what we need to show that $y = c_1 y_1 + c_2 y_2$ is the general solution of Eq. (9) if y_1 and y_2 are linearly independent solutions.

THEOREM 4: General Solutions

Let y_1 and y_2 be two linearly independent solutions of the homogeneous equation (Eq. (9))

$$y'' + p(x)y' + q(x)y = 0$$

with p and q continuous on the open interval I. If Y is any solution whatsoever of Eq. (9) on I, then there exist numbers c_1 and c_2 such that

$$Y(x) = c_1 y_1(x) + c_2 y_2(x)$$

for all x in I.   ∎

In essence, Theorem 4 tells us that when we have found *two* linearly independent solutions of the homogeneous equation in (9), then we have found *all* of its solutions.

Proof of Theorem 4: Choose a point a of I, and consider the simultaneous equations

$$\begin{aligned}
c_1 y_1(a) + c_2 y_2(a) &= Y(a), \\
c_1 y_1'(a) + c_2 y_2'(a) &= Y'(a).
\end{aligned} \tag{14}$$

The determinant of the coefficients in this system of linear equations in the unknowns c_1 and c_2 is simply the Wronskian $W(y_1, y_2)$ evaluated at $x = a$. By Theorem 3, this determinant is nonzero, so by elementary algebra it follows that the equations in (14) can be solved for c_1 and c_2. With these values of c_1 and c_2, we define the solution

$$G(x) = c_1 y_1(x) + c_2 y_2(x)$$

of Eq. (9); then

$$G(a) = c_1 y_1(a) + c_2 y_2(a) = Y(a)$$

and

$$G'(a) = c_1 y_1'(a) + c_2 y_2'(a) = Y'(a).$$

Thus the two solutions Y and G have the same initial values at a, as do Y' and G'. By the uniqueness of a solution determined by such initial values (Theorem 2), it follows that Y and G agree on I. Thus we see that

$$Y(x) \equiv G(x) = c_1 y_1(x) + c_2 y_2(x),$$

as desired.   ∎

EXAMPLE 4   It is evident that

$$y_1(x) = e^{2x} \quad \text{and} \quad y_2(x) = e^{-2x}$$

are linearly independent solutions of

$$y'' - 4y = 0. \tag{15}$$

But $y_3(x) = \cosh 2x$ and $y_4(x) = \sinh 2x$ are also solutions of Eq. (15), because

$$\frac{d^2}{dx^2}(\cosh 2x) = \frac{d}{dx}(2 \sinh 2x) = 4 \cosh 2x$$

and, similarly, $(\sinh 2x)'' = 4 \sinh 2x$. It therefore follows from Theorem 4 that the functions $\cosh 2x$ and $\sinh 2x$ can be expressed as linear combinations of $y_1(x) = e^{2x}$ and $y_2(x) = e^{-2x}$. Of course, this is no surprise, because

$$\cosh 2x = \tfrac{1}{2}e^{2x} + \tfrac{1}{2}e^{-2x} \quad \text{and} \quad \sinh 2x = \tfrac{1}{2}e^{2x} - \tfrac{1}{2}e^{-2x}$$

by the definitions of the hyperbolic cosine and hyperbolic sine.   ∎

Linear Second-Order Equations with Constant Coefficients

As an illustration of the general theory introduced in this section, we discuss the homogeneous second-order linear differential equation

$$ay'' + by' + cy = 0 \tag{16}$$

with constant coefficients a, b, and c. We first look for a *single* solution of Eq. (16) and begin with the observation that

$$(e^{rx})' = re^{rx} \quad \text{and} \quad (e^{rx})'' = r^2 e^{rx}, \tag{17}$$

so any derivative of e^{rx} is a constant multiple of e^{rx}. Hence, if we substituted $y = e^{rx}$ in Eq. (16), then each term would be a constant multiple of e^{rx}, with the constant coefficients dependent on r and the coefficients a, b, and c. This suggests that we try to find a value of r so that these multiples of e^{rx} will have sum zero. If we succeed, then $y = e^{rx}$ will be a solution of Eq. (16).

For example, if we substitute $y = e^{rx}$ in the equation

$$y'' - 5y' + 6y = 0,$$

we obtain

$$r^2 e^{rx} - 5re^{rx} + 6e^{rx} = 0.$$

Thus

$$(r^2 - 5r + 6)e^{rx} = 0; \quad (r - 2)(r - 3)e^{rx} = 0.$$

Hence $y = e^{rx}$ will be a solution if either $r = 2$ or $r = 3$. So, in searching for a single solution, we actually have found two solutions: $y_1(x) = e^{2x}$ and $y_2(x) = e^{3x}$.

To carry out this procedure in the general case, we substitute $y = e^{rx}$ in Eq. (16). With the aid of the equations in (17), we find the result to be

$$ar^2 e^{rx} + bre^{rx} + ce^{rx} = 0.$$

Because e^{rx} is never zero, we conclude that $y(x) = e^{rx}$ will satisfy the differential equation in (16) precisely when r is a root of the *algebraic* equation

$$\blacktriangleright \qquad ar^2 + br + c = 0. \tag{18}$$

This quadratic equation is called the **characteristic equation** of the homogeneous linear differential equation

$$ay'' + by' + cy = 0. \tag{16}$$

If Eq. (18) has two *distinct* (unequal) roots r_1 and r_2, then the corresponding solutions $y_1(x) = e^{r_1 x}$ and $y_2(x) = e^{r_2 x}$ of (16) are linearly independent. (Why?) This gives the following result.

THEOREM 5: Distinct Real Roots

If the roots r_1 and r_2 of the characteristic equation in (18) are real and distinct, then

$$y_1(x) = c_1 e^{r_1 x} + c_2 e^{r_2 x} \tag{19}$$

is the general solution of Eq. (16). ∎

EXAMPLE 5   Find the general solution of

$$2y'' - 7y' + 3y = 0.$$

Solution   We can solve the characteristic equation

$$2r^2 - 7r + 3 = 0$$

by factoring:

$$(2r - 1)(r - 3) = 0.$$

The roots $r_1 = \frac{1}{2}$ and $r_2 = 3$ are real and distinct, so Theorem 5 yields the general solution

$$y(x) = c_1 e^{x/2} + c_2 e^{3x}. \qquad \blacksquare$$

EXAMPLE 6   The differential equation $y'' + 2y' = 0$ has characteristic equation

$$r^2 + 2r = r(r + 2) = 0$$

with distinct real roots $r_1 = 0$ and $r_2 = -2$. Because $e^{0 \cdot x} \equiv 1$, we get the general solution

$$y(x) = c_1 + c_2 e^{-2x}.$$

Figure 3.1.9 shows several different solution curves with $c_1 = 1$, all appearing to approach the solution curve $y(x) \equiv 1$ (with $c_2 = 0$) as $x \to +\infty$. $\qquad \blacksquare$

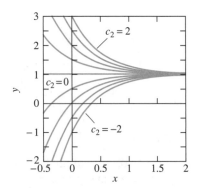

FIGURE 3.1.9. Solutions $y(x) = 1 + c_2 e^{-2x}$ of $y'' + 2y' = 0$ with different values of c_2.

Remark: Note that Theorem 5 changes a problem involving a differential equation into one involving only the solution of an *algebraic* equation. $\qquad \blacksquare$

If the characteristic equation in (18) has equal roots $r_1 = r_2$, we get (at first) only the single solution $y_1(x) = e^{r_1 x}$ of Eq. (16). The problem in this case is to produce the "missing" second solution of the differential equation.

A double root $r = r_1$ will occur precisely when the characteristic equation is a constant multiple of the equation

$$(r - r_1)^2 = r^2 - 2r_1 r + r_1^2 = 0.$$

Any differential equation with this characteristic equation is equivalent to

$$y'' - 2r_1 y' + r_1^2 y = 0. \qquad (20)$$

But it is easy to verify by direct substitution that $y = x e^{r_1 x}$ is a second solution of Eq. (20). It is clear (but you should verify) that

$$y_1(x) = e^{r_1 x} \quad \text{and} \quad y_2(x) = x e^{r_1 x}$$

are linearly independent functions, so the general solution of the differential equation in (20) is

$$y(x) = c_1 e^{r_1 x} + c_2 x e^{r_1 x}.$$

THEOREM 6: Repeated Roots

If the characteristic equation in (18) has equal (necessarily real) roots $r_1 = r_2$, then

$$y(x) = (c_1 + c_2 x) e^{r_1 x} \qquad (21)$$

is the general solution of Eq. (16). $\qquad \blacksquare$

EXAMPLE 7   To solve the initial value problem

$$y'' + 2y' + y = 0;$$
$$y(0) = 5, \quad y'(0) = -3,$$

we note first that the characteristic equation

$$r^2 + 2r + 1 = (r + 1)^2 = 0$$

has equal roots $r_1 = r_2 = -1$. Hence the general solution provided by Theorem 6 is

$$y(x) = c_1 e^{-x} + c_2 x e^{-x}.$$

Differentiation yields

$$y'(x) = -c_1 e^{-x} + c_2 e^{-x} - c_2 x e^{-x},$$

so the initial conditions yield the equations

$$y(0) = c_1 = 5,$$
$$y'(0) = -c_1 + c_2 = -3,$$

which imply that $c_1 = 5$ and $c_2 = 2$. Thus the desired particular solution of the initial value problem is

$$y(x) = 5e^{-x} + 2xe^{-x}.$$

This particular solution, together with several others of the form $y(x) = c_1 e^{-x} + 2xe^{-x}$, is illustrated in Fig. 3.1.10. ∎

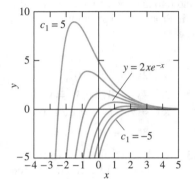

FIGURE 3.1.10. Solutions $y(x) = c_1 e^{-x} + 2xe^{-x}$ of $y'' + 2y' + y = 0$ with different values of c_1.

The characteristic equation in (18) may have either real or complex roots. The case of complex roots will be discussed in Section 3.3.

3.1 *Problems*

In Problems 1 through 16, a homogeneous second-order linear differential equation, two functions y_1 and y_2, and a pair of initial conditions are given. First verify that y_1 and y_2 are solutions of the differential equation. Then find a particular solution of the form $y = c_1 y_1 + c_2 y_2$ that satisfies the given initial conditions. Primes denote derivatives with respect to x.

1. $y'' - y = 0$; $y_1 = e^x$, $y_2 = e^{-x}$; $y(0) = 0$, $y'(0) = 5$
2. $y'' - 9y = 0$; $y_1 = e^{3x}$, $y_2 = e^{-3x}$; $y(0) = -1$, $y'(0) = 15$
3. $y'' + 4y = 0$; $y_1 = \cos 2x$, $y_2 = \sin 2x$; $y(0) = 3$, $y'(0) = 8$
4. $y'' + 25y = 0$; $y_1 = \cos 5x$, $y_2 = \sin 5x$; $y(0) = 10$, $y'(0) = -10$
5. $y'' - 3y' + 2y = 0$; $y_1 = e^x$, $y_2 = e^{2x}$; $y(0) = 1$, $y'(0) = 0$
6. $y'' + y' - 6y = 0$; $y_1 = e^{2x}$, $y_2 = e^{-3x}$; $y(0) = 7$, $y'(0) = -1$
7. $y'' + y' = 0$; $y_1 = 1$, $y_2 = e^{-x}$; $y(0) = -2$, $y'(0) = 8$
8. $y'' - 3y' = 0$; $y_1 = 1$, $y_2 = e^{3x}$; $y(0) = 4$, $y'(0) = -2$
9. $y'' + 2y' + y = 0$; $y_1 = e^{-x}$, $y_2 = xe^{-x}$; $y(0) = 2$, $y(0) = -1$
10. $y'' - 10y' + 25y = 0$; $y_1 = e^{5x}$, $y_2 = xe^{5x}$; $y(0) = 3$, $y'(0) = 13$
11. $y'' - 2y' + 2y = 0$; $y_1 = e^x \cos x$, $y_2 = e^x \sin x$; $y(0) = 0$, $y'(0) = 5$

12. $y'' + 6y' + 13y = 0$; $y_1 = e^{-3x} \cos 2x$, $y_2 = e^{-3x} \sin 2x$; $y(0) = 2$, $y'(0) = 0$
13. $x^2 y'' - 2xy' + 2y = 0$; $y_1 = x$, $y_2 = x^2$; $y(1) = 3$, $y'(1) = 1$
14. $x^2 y'' + 2xy' - 6y = 0$; $y_1 = x^2$, $y_2 = x^{-3}$; $y(2) = 10$, $y'(2) = 15$
15. $x^2 y'' - xy' + y = 0$; $y_1 = x$, $y_2 = x \ln x$; $y(1) = 7$, $y'(1) = 2$
16. $x^2 y'' + xy' + y = 0$; $y_1 = \cos(\ln x)$, $y_2 = \sin(\ln x)$; $y(1) = 2$, $y'(1) = 3$

The following three problems illustrate the fact that the superposition principle does not generally hold for nonlinear equations.

17. Show that $y = 1/x$ is a solution of $y' + y^2 = 0$, but that if $c \neq 0$ and $c \neq 1$, then $y = c/x$ is not a solution.
18. Show that $y = x^3$ is a solution of $yy'' = 6x^4$, but that if $c^2 \neq 1$, then $y = cx^3$ is not a solution.
19. Show that $y_1 \equiv 1$ and $y_2 = \sqrt{x}$ are solutions of $yy'' + (y')^2 = 0$, but that their sum $y = y_1 + y_2$ is not a solution.

Determine whether the pairs of functions in Problems 20 through 26 are linearly independent or linearly dependent on the real line.

20. $f(x) = \pi, g(x) = \cos^2 x + \sin^2 x$

21. $f(x) = x^3, g(x) = x^2|x|$

22. $f(x) = 1 + x, g(x) = 1 + |x|$

23. $f(x) = xe^x, g(x) = |x|e^x$

24. $f(x) = \sin^2 x, g(x) = 1 - \cos 2x$

25. $f(x) = e^x \sin x, g(x) = e^x \cos x$

26. $f(x) = 2\cos x + 3\sin x, g(x) = 3\cos x - 2\sin x$

27. Let y_p be a particular solution of the nonhomogeneous equation $y'' + py' + qy = f(x)$ and let y_c be a solution of its associated homogeneous equation. Show that $y = y_c + y_p$ is a solution of the given nonhomogeneous equation.

28. With $y_p = 1$ and $y_c = c_1 \cos x + c_2 \sin x$ in the notation of Problem 27, find a solution of $y'' + y = 1$ satisfying the initial conditions $y(0) = -1 = y'(0)$.

29. Show that $y_1 = x^2$ and $y_2 = x^3$ are two different solutions of $x^2 y'' - 4xy' + 6y = 0$, both satisfying the initial conditions $y(0) = 0 = y'(0)$. Explain why these facts do not contradict Theorem 2 (with respect to the guaranteed uniqueness).

30. (a) Show that $y_1 = x^3$ and $y_2 = |x^3|$ are linearly independent solutions on the real line of the equation $x^2 y'' - 3xy' + 3y = 0$. (b) Verify that $W(y_1, y_2)$ is identically zero. Why do these facts not contradict Theorem 3?

31. Show that $y_1 = \sin x^2$ and $y_2 = \cos x^2$ are linearly independent functions, but that their Wronskian vanishes at $x = 0$. Why does this imply that there is *no* differential equation of the form $y'' + p(x)y' + q(x)y = 0$, with both p and q continuous everywhere, having both y_1 and y_2 as solutions?

32. Let y_1 and y_2 be two solutions of $A(x)y'' + B(x)y' + C(x)y = 0$ on an open interval I where A, B, and C are continuous and $A(x)$ is never zero. (a) Let $W = W(y_1, y_2)$. Show that

$$A(x)\frac{dW}{dx} = (y_1)(Ay_2'') - (y_2)(Ay_1'').$$

Then substitute for Ay_2'' and Ay_1'' from the original differential equation to show that

$$A(x)\frac{dW}{dx} = -B(x)W(x).$$

(b) Solve this first-order equation to deduce **Abel's formula**

$$W(x) = K\exp\left(-\int \frac{B(x)}{A(x)}\,dx\right),$$

where K is a constant. (c) Why does Abel's formula imply that the Wronskian $W(y_1, y_2)$ is either zero everywhere or nonzero everywhere (as stated in Theorem 3)?

Apply Theorems 5 and 6 to find general solutions of the differential equations given in Problems 33 through 42. Primes denote derivatives with respect to x.

33. $y'' - 3y' + 2y = 0$ **34.** $y'' + 2y' - 15y = 0$

35. $y'' + 5y' = 0$ **36.** $2y'' + 3y' = 0$

37. $2y'' - y' - y = 0$ **38.** $4y'' + 8y' + 3y = 0$

39. $4y'' + 4y' + y = 0$ **40.** $9y'' - 12y' + 4y = 0$

41. $6y'' - 7y' - 20y = 0$ **42.** $35y'' - y' - 12y = 0$

Each of Problems 43 through 48 gives the general solution $y(x)$ of a homogeneous second-order differential equation $ay'' + by' + cy = 0$ with constant coefficients. Find this equation.

43. $y(x) = c_1 + c_2 e^{-10x}$

44. $y(x) = c_1 e^{10x} + c_2 e^{-10x}$

45. $y(x) = c_1 e^{-10x} + c_2 x e^{-10x}$

46. $y(x) = c_1 e^{10x} + c_2 e^{100x}$

47. $y(x) = c_1 + c_2 x$

48. $y(x) = e^x\left(c_1 e^{x\sqrt{2}} + c_2 e^{-x\sqrt{2}}\right)$

Problems 49 and 50 deal with the solution curves of $y'' + 3y' + 2y = 0$ shown in Figs. 3.1.6 and 3.1.7.

49. Find the highest point on the solution curve with $y(0) = 1$ and $y'(0) = 6$ in Fig. 3.1.6.

50. Find the third-quadrant point of intersection of the solution curves shown in Fig. 3.1.7.

3.2 REVIEW OF COMPLEX NUMBERS

Introduction

This is a short review of the main concepts about *complex numbers*. Complex numbers are used throughout mathematics and its applications. In particular, when we try to solve differential equations it is often convenient and natural to use complex numbers to express the solutions. Here we only review ideas and results that will be used later on in the course and in the labs.

A complex number z may be expressed as an <u>ordered</u> pair of *real* numbers:

$$z = (x, y) = x + iy$$

where $i := \sqrt{-1}$ (so $i^2 = -1$) and x and y are real numbers.

The following notations are often used:

$$x = Re(z) \text{ is the real part of } z$$
$$y = Im(z) \text{ is the imaginary part of } z$$

Recall that two complex numbers are equal if and only if both the real and the imaginary parts are equal. In other words, $z_1 := (x_1, y_1)$ equals $z_2 := (x_2, y_2)$ if and only if $x_1 = x_2$ and $y_1 = y_2$.

A convenient way of thinking about complex numbers is to imagine them as points in the x-y plane (called the "complex plane").

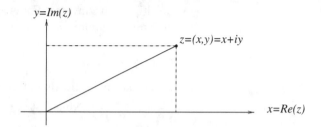

Operations with complex numbers

Addition: $z_1 + z_2 := (x_1 + x_2, y_1 + y_2)$.
(Note that this is just like the usual vector addition in the plane.)

Multiplication: $z_1 z_2 := (x_1, y_1)(x_2, y_2) = (x_1 x_2 - y_1 y_2, x_1 y_2 + x_2 y_1)$.

It is very important to keep in mind that the complex numbers generalize the notion of the real numbers. Indeed, we can think of the real number x as the complex number x or $(x, 0)$ or $x + i0$.

One way to think of $(0, 1)$ is as the *new* number i which is 'purely imaginary' and so $(x, y) = x + iy$ is the sum of the real number x and the purely imaginary number iy.

Note that the multiplication of two complex numbers is different than what you would probably expected it to be, but if we are only multiplying real numbers $(x, 0)$ then it is just like the usual multiplication. In fact all the new operations defined for complex numbers when applied to real numbers give the usual familiar corresponding operations.

EXAMPLES

$$(x, 0) + (0, y) = (x, y)$$
$$(0, 1)(y, 0) = (0, y)$$

Therefore,

$$(x, y) = (x, 0) + (0, 1)(y, 0)$$

Note that $zz = z^2$, $zzz = z^3$, so $i^2 = (0, 1)(0, 1) = (-1, 0) = -1$ as expected.

With the $x + iy$ notation, addition and multiplication are expressed as

$$z_1 + z_2 = (x_1 + iy_1) + (x_2 + iy_2) = x_1 + iy_1 + x_2 + iy_2$$
$$= (x_1 + x_2) + i(y_1 + y_2)$$
$$z_1 z_2 = (x_1 + iy_1)(x_2 + iy_2) = x_1 x_2 + ix_1 y_2 + iy_1 x_2 + i^2 y_1 y_2$$
$$= (x_1 x_2 - y_1 y_2) + i(x_1 y_2 + x_2 y_1),$$

because $i^2 = -1$.

These operations on complex numbers enjoy all the usual algebraic properties that we are familiar with:

- Commutative Law of Addition: $z_1 + z_2 = z_2 + z_1$
- Associative Law of Addition: $(z_1 + z_2) + z_3 = z_1 + (z_2 + z_3)$
- Commutative Law of Multiplication: $z_1 z_2 = z_2 z_1$
- Distributive Law: $z_1(z_2 + z_3) = z_1 z_2 + z_1 z_3$
- Unique Additive Identity $0 = (0, 0)$: $z + 0 = 0 + z = z$
- Unique Multiplicative Identity $1 = (1, 0)$: $z \cdot 1 = 1 \cdot z = z$
- Additive inverse: $-z = (-x, -y) = -x - iy : z + (-z) = 0$
- Multiplicative inverse: For every complex number $z = (x, y) \neq 0$ there exists a complex number $w = (u, v)$ such that $(x, y)(u, v) = (u, v)(x, y) = (1, 0)$

Exercise

Check that the multiplicative inverse of a nonzero complex number $z = (x, y)$ is $\frac{1}{z} = \left(\frac{x}{x^2 + y^2}, \frac{-y}{x^2 + y^2} \right)$. Note that if $z = 0$ then it has no multiplicative inverse.

Now we can define the division of two complex numbers:

$$\frac{z_1}{z_2} = z_1 \cdot \frac{1}{z_2} = \frac{1}{z_2} \cdot z_1.$$

For example,

$$\frac{2}{i} = 2 \cdot \frac{1}{i} = -2i.$$

Why bother with all these? Complex numbers were introduced as an extension of real numbers because we need a number system in which (all) polynomials have roots.

For example, the equation $x^2 - 3x + 2 = 0$ has two real solutions, $x = 1$ or $x = 2$.

But $x^2 - 3x + 3 = 0$ does not have any real roots, but only complex roots $\frac{3}{2} + i \frac{\sqrt{3}}{2}$ and $\frac{3}{2} - i \frac{\sqrt{3}}{2}$.

That is, for $a_0, a_1, \ldots, a_n$ real, $a_n x^n + \cdots + a_1 x_1 + a_0 = 0$ does not always have real solutions. But complex numbers enjoy the property that if $a_0, a_1, \ldots, a_n$ are complex, then $a_n z^n + \cdots + a_1 z_1 + a_0 = 0$ always has n solutions (for $a_n \neq 0$, and not all roots are necessarily distinct). This fact is known as the "Fundamental Theorem of Algebra".

Let us introduce now some useful notions related to complex numbers.

We define the <u>absolute value</u> or the <u>modulus</u> of z as $|z| = \sqrt{x^2 + y^2}$

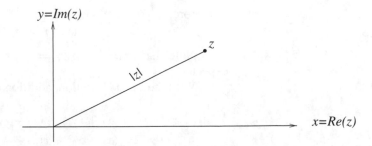

Note: Unless z_1 and z_2 are real "$z_1 < z_2$" has no meaning. But $|z_1| < |z_2|$ means that z_1 is closer to $(0, 0)$ than z_2.

EXAMPLE $|(1, 2)| = \sqrt{1^2 + 2^2} = \sqrt{5}$

Exercises

Show that for a nonzero complex number $z = (x, y)$, $\left|\frac{1}{z}\right| = \frac{1}{|z|} = \frac{1}{\sqrt{x^2+y^2}}$.

Show that the equation $|z| = 1$ describes the set of points on the unit circle.

We define the <u>complex conjugate</u> of a complex number $z = (x, y) = x + iy$ as $\overline{(x, -y) = x - iy}$ and denote it by $\overline{z}$ or z^*.

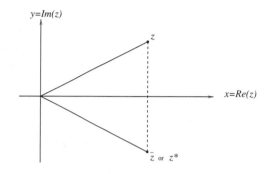

EXAMPLES

$$\overline{1} = 1$$
$$\overline{i} = -i$$

Note that (prove!)

$$\overline{z_1 \pm z_2} = \overline{z_1} \pm \overline{z_2}$$

$$\overline{z_1 \cdot z_2} = \overline{z_1} \cdot \overline{z_2}$$

$$\overline{\left(\frac{z_1}{z_2}\right)} = \frac{\overline{z_1}}{\overline{z_2}}$$

$$\overline{\overline{z}} = z$$

EXAMPLES

$$z + \overline{z} = (x, y) + (x, -y) = (2x, 0) = 2 \cdot Re(z)$$
$$z - \overline{z} = (x, y) - (x, -y) = (0, 2y) = 2i \cdot Im(z)$$

That is, we have that

$$Re(z) = \frac{1}{2}(z + \overline{z}) \quad \text{and} \quad Im(z) = \frac{1}{2i}(z - \overline{z}).$$

Another important result is

$$z\overline{z} = (x + iy)(x - iy) = x^2 - ixy + ixy + y^2 = x^2 + y^2 = |z|^2,$$

from which it follows that

$$z^{-1} = \frac{1}{z} = \frac{\overline{z}}{|z|^2}.$$

Polar form for complex numbers

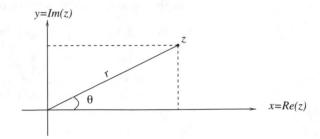

As we can see in the picture, we can identify z by its rectangular coordinates (x, y) or by its polar coordinates (r, θ).

Note that $x = r \cos \theta$ and $y = r \sin \theta$, so

$$z = x + iy = r \cos \theta + ir \sin \theta = r(\cos \theta + i \sin \theta).$$

Also, $|z| = \sqrt{r^2 \cos^2 \theta + r^2 \sin^2 \theta} = r\sqrt{\cos^2 \theta + \sin^2 \theta} = r$.

EXAMPLE   For $z = 1 - i$ we have $r = \sqrt{2}$ and $\theta = -\frac{\pi}{4}$, therefore

$$1 - i = \sqrt{2}\left[\cos\left(-\frac{\pi}{4}\right) + i \sin\left(-\frac{\pi}{4}\right)\right].$$

The angle θ is ambiguous modulo factors of 2π. For example, $\theta = 2\pi n - \frac{\pi}{4}$ works too, for any $n = 0, \pm 1, \pm 2, \ldots$.

The angle θ is called the argument of z:

$$\theta = arg(z).$$

Note:

$$z = r[\cos(\theta + 2\pi n) + i \sin(\theta + 2\pi n)]$$

$$\tan \theta = \frac{y}{x} = \frac{Im(z)}{Re(z)}$$

$z = 0$ has no argument.

We define the principal value of $arg(z)$ as the unique value of $arg(z)$ between $-\pi$ and π. We denote the principal value by $Arg(z)$: $-\pi < Arg(z) \leq \pi$.

Complex multiplication has a simple geometric interpretation in the polar representation:

If

$$z_1 = r_1(\cos \theta_1 + i \sin \theta_1)$$
$$z_2 = r_2(\cos \theta_2 + i \sin \theta_2)$$

then

$$z_1 z_2 = r_1 r_2 (\cos \theta_1 + i \sin \theta_1)(\cos \theta_2 + i \sin \theta_2)$$
$$= r_1 r_2 [(\cos \theta_1 \cos \theta_2 - \sin \theta_1 \sin \theta_2) + i (\sin \theta_1 \cos \theta_2 + \cos \theta_1 \sin \theta_2)]$$
$$= r_1 r_2 [\cos(\theta_1 + \theta_2) + i \sin(\theta_1 + \theta_2)].$$

We used trigonometric identities in the last step above. In particular, this means that

$$|z_1 z_2| = |z_1| |z_2|$$
$$arg(z_1 z_2) = arg(z_1) + arg(z_2).$$

That is, when we multiply two complex numbers we multiply their moduli and add their arguments.

Exercises

Show that $|i^2| = 1$ and $arg(i^2) = \pi$.

Note that if $r \neq 0$, then

$$\frac{1}{z} = \frac{1}{r(\cos\theta + i\sin\theta)} \cdot \frac{r(\cos\theta - i\sin\theta)}{r(\cos\theta - i\sin\theta)}$$

$$= \frac{1}{r}(\cos\theta - i\sin\theta)$$

$$= \frac{1}{r}[\cos(-\theta) + i\sin(-\theta)]$$

so $\left|\frac{1}{z}\right| = \frac{1}{|z|}$ and $arg\left(\frac{1}{z}\right) = -arg(z)$. Note also $arg(\bar{z}) = -arg(z)$.

Exponential form of a complex number: Euler's formula

Using the power series expansion defining e^z it is easy to see that the following (known as Euler's formula) is true:

$$e^{i\theta} = \cos\theta + i\sin\theta.$$

Keeping this in mind, we see that the polar form of a complex number can be rewritten

$$z = r(\cos\theta + i\sin\theta) = re^{i\theta}$$

where $r = |z|$ is the absolute value of z and $\theta = arg(z)$ is the argument.

It follows from the rules for multiplying exponentials that

$$z_1 z_2 = r_1 e^{i\theta_1} r_2 e^{i\theta_2} = r_1 r_2 e^{i(\theta_1 + \theta_2)}$$

$$\frac{1}{z} = \frac{1}{re^{i\theta}} = \left(\frac{1}{r}\right) e^{-i\theta}$$

$$\frac{z_1}{z_2} = \frac{r_1}{r_2} e^{i(\theta_1 - \theta_2)}.$$

Note that for any $n = 0, \pm 1, \pm 2, \ldots$ we have $z = re^{i(\theta + 2\pi n)}$; also $\bar{z} = re^{-i\theta}$.

Using the exponential form of a complex number we can compute easily its powers. Indeed, $z^n = (re^{i\theta})^n = r^n e^{in\theta}$.

Combining this with Euler's formula we have DeMoivre's Theorem:

$$(\cos\theta + i\sin\theta)^n = \cos(n\theta) + i\sin(n\theta)$$

Proof: $(\cos\theta + i\sin\theta)^n = (e^{i\theta})^n = e^{in\theta} = \cos(n\theta) + i\sin(n\theta)$.

EXAMPLE

$$\cos(2\theta) + i\sin(2\theta) = (\cos\theta + i\sin\theta)^2 = \cos^2\theta - \sin^2\theta + i2\sin\theta\cos\theta.$$

Hence, $\cos(2\theta) = \cos^2\theta - \sin^2\theta$ and $\sin(2\theta) = 2\sin\theta\cos\theta$. DeMoivre's Theorem provides an easy way to remember the multiple angle trigonometry formulae.

What about the roots?

$$z^{\frac{1}{2}} = (re^{i\theta})^{\frac{1}{2}} = r^{\frac{1}{2}} e^{i\frac{\theta}{2}}$$

but it also is

$$\left(re^{i(\theta+2\pi k)}\right)^{\frac{1}{2}} = r^{\frac{1}{2}}e^{i\left(\frac{\theta}{2}+\pi k\right)}$$

so

$$arg\left(z^{\frac{1}{2}}\right) = \frac{1}{2}\theta \quad \text{or} \quad \frac{1}{2}\theta + \pi k$$

for $k = 0, \pm 1, \pm 2, \ldots$.

Similarly, we have for the n-th root of z that

$$z^{\frac{1}{n}} = r^{\frac{1}{n}}e^{i(\theta+2\pi k)/n}$$
$$= r^{\frac{1}{n}}e^{i(\theta/n+2\pi k/n)},$$

for all $k = 0, \pm 1, \pm 2, \ldots$.

Exercise

Find the distinct cube roots of 1.

Answer: $a^{\frac{1}{3}} = 1$ or $1^{\frac{1}{3}} = e^{\frac{2\pi i}{3}}$ or $1^{\frac{1}{3}} = e^{\frac{4\pi i}{3}}$.

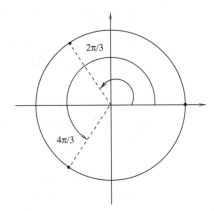

Complex Numbers Homework Problems

1. Compute the following (express in the form $x + iy$):
   (a) $(2 + 3i)(5 + 7i)$
   (b) $(2 + 3i)^2$
   (c) $(2 + 3i) + (-5 - 7i)$
   (d) $(2i)^3 - (2i)^2 + 2i - 1$
   (e) $(5e^{i7\pi/6})^3$
   (f) $\sqrt{e^{i\pi/3}}$ (Give two answers)

2. Solve the following for z, expressed as $x + iy$:
   (a) $z^2 - 2z + 2 = 0$
   (b) $z^2 + z + 1 = 0$

3. Compute the following if $z = x + iy$ (express in terms of x and/or y):
   (a) $Im(iz)$
   (b) $Re(z)$
   (c) $Re(iz)$
   (d) $-Im(z)$

4. Locate the numbers $z_1 + z_2$ and $z_1 - z_2$ vectorially (sketch the plot):
   (a) $z_1 = 2i$ and $z_2 = \frac{2}{3} - i$

(b) $z_1 = -\sqrt{3} + i$ and $z_2 = \sqrt{3}$

(c) $z_1 = -3 + i$ and $z_2 = 1 + 4i$

5. Simplify the following:

   (a) $\overline{z} + 3i =$

   (b) $\overline{iz} =$

   (c) $\overline{(2+i)^2} =$

6. Sketch the set of points determined by the following:

   (a) $|z - (1 - i)| = 1$

   (b) $Re(\overline{z} - i) = 2$

7. Solve the following simultaneous equations for z_1 and z_2:

   (a) $z_1 + z_2 = 2$
   $(i - 1)z_1 + (1 + i)z_2 = 3$

   (b) $z_1 + z_2 = 2$
   $(i - 1)z_1 + (1 + i)z_2 = 0$

8. Determine $Arg(z)$ for each of the following:

   (a) $z = \frac{-2}{1 + \sqrt{3}i}$

   (b) $z = \frac{i}{-2 - 2i}$

   (c) $z = (\sqrt{3} - i)^6$

9. Use the exponential form to compute the following:

   (a) $i(1 - \sqrt{3}i)(\sqrt{3} + i) =$

   (b) $\frac{5i}{1 + i} =$

   (c) $(-1 + i)^7 =$

10. Use DeMoivre's Theorem to show the following:

    (a) $\cos(3\theta) = \cos(\theta)^3 - 3\cos(\theta)\sin(\theta)^2$

    (b) $\sin(3\theta) = 3\cos(\theta)^2 \sin(\theta) - \sin(\theta)^3$

    Hint: Expand $(\cos\theta + i\sin\theta)^3$ and use DeMoivre's Theorem.

11. Find all the roots for the following and exhibit them geometrically:

    (a) $(2i)^{\frac{1}{2}} =$

    (b) $(1 - \sqrt{3}i)^{\frac{1}{2}} =$

    (c) $(-1)^{\frac{1}{3}} =$

    (d) $(-16)^{\frac{1}{4}} =$

    Hint: Use $z^{\frac{1}{n}} = r^{\frac{1}{n}} e^{i(\theta + 2\pi k)/n}$ for all $k = 0, \pm 1, \pm 2, \ldots$.

12. If the roots of the equation $x^2 + 2bx + c = 0$ are the complex numbers $p \pm iq$ (p and q are real), find expressions for b and c in terms of p and q.

3.3 HOMOGENEOUS EQUATIONS WITH CONSTANT COEFFICIENTS

In Section 3.2 we saw that a general solution of an nth-order homogeneous linear equation is a linear combination of n linearly independent particular solutions, but we said little about how actually to find even a single solution. The solution of a linear differential equation with *variable* coefficients ordinarily requires numerical methods (Chapter 2) or infinite series methods (Chapter 8). But we can now show how to find, explicitly and in a rather straightforward way, n linearly independent solutions of a given nth-order linear equation if it has *constant* coefficients. The general such equation may be written in the form

$$a_n y^{(n)} + a_{n-1} y^{(n-1)} + \cdots + a_2 y'' + a_1 y' + a_0 y = 0, \tag{1}$$

where the coefficients $a_0, a_1, a_2, \ldots, a_n$ are real constants with $a_n \neq 0$.

The Characteristic Equation

We first look for a *single* solution of Eq. (1), and begin with the observation that

$$\frac{d^k}{dx^k}(e^{rx}) = r^k e^{rx}, \tag{2}$$

so any derivative of e^{rx} is a constant multiple of e^{rx}. Hence, if we substituted $y = e^{rx}$ in Eq. (1), each term would be a constant multiple of e^{rx}, with the constant coefficients depending on r and the coefficients a_i. This suggests that we try to find r so that all these multiples of e^{rx} will have sum zero, in which case $y = e^{rx}$ will be a solution of Eq. (1).

For example, in Section 3.1 we substituted $y = e^{rx}$ in the second-order equation

$$ay'' + by' + cy = 0$$

to derive the characteristic equation

$$ar^2 + br + c = 0$$

that r must satisfy.

To carry out this technique in the general case, we substitute $y = e^{rx}$ in Eq. (1), and with the aid of Eq. (2) we find the result to be

$$a_n r^n e^{rx} + a_{n-1} r^{n-1} e^{rx} + \cdots + a_2 r^2 e^{rx} + a_1 r e^{rx} + a_0 e^{rx} = 0;$$

that is,

$$e^{rx} \left(a_n r^n + a_{n-1} r^{n-1} + \cdots + a_2 r^2 + a_1 r + a_0 \right) = 0.$$

Because e^{rx} is never zero, we see that $y = e^{rx}$ will be a solution of Eq. (1) precisely when r is a root of the equation

$$a_n r^n + a_{n-1} r^{n-1} + \cdots + a_2 r^2 + a_1 r + a_0 = 0. \tag{3}$$

This equation is called the **characteristic equation** or **auxiliary equation** of the differential equation in (1). Our problem, then, is reduced to the solution of this purely algebraic equation.

According to the fundamental theorem of algebra, every nth-degree polynomial—such as the one in Eq. (3)—has n zeros, though not necessarily distinct and not necessarily real. Finding the exact values of these zeros may be difficult or even impossible; the quadratic formula is sufficient for second-degree equations, but for equations of higher degree we may need either to spot a fortuitous factorization or to apply a numerical technique such as Newton's method (or use a calculator/computer `solve` command).

Distinct Real Roots

Whatever the method we use, let us suppose that we have solved the characteristic equation. Then we can always write a general solution of the differential equation. The situation is slightly more complicated in the case of repeated roots or complex roots of Eq. (3), so let us first examine the simplest case—in which the characteristic equation has n distinct (no two equal) *real* roots $r_1, r_2, \ldots, r_n$. Then the functions

$$e^{r_1 x}, e^{r_2 x} \ldots , e^{r_n x}$$

are all solutions of Eq. (1), and (by Problem 34 of Section 3.2) these n solutions are linearly independent on the entire real line. In summary, we have proved Theorem 1.

THEOREM 1: Distinct Real Roots

If the roots $r_1, r_2, \ldots, r_n$ of the characteristic equation in (3) are real and distinct, then

$$y(x) = c_1 e^{r_1 x} + c_2 e^{r_2 x} + \cdots + c_n e^{r_n x} \tag{4}$$

is the general solution of Eq. (1). ∎

EXAMPLE 1 Solve the initial value problem

$$y^{(3)} + 3y'' - 10y' = 0;$$
$$y(0) = 7, \quad y'(0) = 0, \quad y''(0) = 70.$$

Solution The characteristic equation of the given differential equation is

$$r^3 + 3r^2 - 10r = 0.$$

We solve by factoring:

$$r(r^2 + 3r - 10) = r(r + 5)(r - 2) = 0,$$

and so the characteristic equation has the three distinct real roots $r = 0$, $r = -5$, and $r = 2$. Because $e^0 = 1$, Theorem 1 gives the general solution

$$y(x) = c_1 + c_2 e^{-5x} + c_3 e^{2x}.$$

Then the given initial conditions yield the linear equations

$$
\begin{aligned}
y(0) &= c_1 + c_2 + c_3 = 7, \\
y'(0) &= \quad\;\; - 5c_2 + 2c_3 = 0, \\
y''(0) &= \quad\;\; 25c_2 + 4c_3 = 70
\end{aligned}
$$

in the coefficients c_1, c_2, and c_3. The last two equations give $y''(0) - 2y'(0) = 35c_2 = 70$, so $c_2 = 2$. Then the second equation gives $c_3 = 5$, and finally the first equation gives $c_1 = 0$. Thus the desired particular solution is

$$y(x) = 2e^{-5x} + 5e^{2x}.$$ ∎

Polynomial Operators

If the roots of the characteristic equation in (3) are *not* distinct—there are repeated roots—then we cannot produce n linearly independent solutions of Eq. (1) by the method of Theorem 1. For example, if the roots are 1, 2, 2, and 2, we obtain only the *two* functions e^x and e^{2x}. The problem, then, is to produce the missing linearly independent solutions. For this purpose it is convenient to adopt the operator notation introduced in Section 3.1. Equation (1) corresponds to the operator equation $Ly = 0$, where L is the operator

$$L = a_n \frac{d^n}{dx^n} + a_{n-1} \frac{d^{n-1}}{dx^{n-1}} + \cdots + a_2 \frac{d^2}{dx^2} + a_1 \frac{d}{dx} + a_0. \tag{5}$$

We also denote by $D = d/dx$ the operation of differentiation with respect to x, so that

$$Dy = y', \quad D^2 y = y'', \quad D^3 y = y^{(3)},$$

and so on. In terms of D, the operator L in (5) may be written

$$L = a_n D^n + a_{n-1} D^{n-1} + \cdots + a_2 D^2 + a_1 D + a_0, \tag{6}$$

and we will find it useful to think of the right-hand side in Eq. (6) as a (formal) nth-degree polynomial in the "variable" D; it is a **polynomial operator.**

A first-degree polynomial operator has the form $D - a$ where a is a real number. It operates on the function $y = y(x)$ to produce

$$(D - a)y = Dy - ay = y' - ay.$$

The important fact about such operators is that any two of them *commute*:

$$(D - a)(D - b)y = (D - b)(D - a)y \tag{7}$$

for any twice differentiable function $y = y(x)$. The proof of the formula in (7) is the following computation:

$$
\begin{aligned}
(D - a)(D - b)y &= (D - a)(y' - by) \\
&= D(y' - by) - a(y' - by) \\
&= y'' - (b + a)y' + aby = y'' - (a + b)y' + bay \\
&= D(y' - ay) - b(y' - ay) \\
&= (D - b)(y' - ay) = (D - b)(D - a)y.
\end{aligned}
$$

Repeated Roots

Let us now consider the possibility that the characteristic equation

$$a_n r^n + a_{n-1} r^{n-1} + \cdots + a_2 r^2 + a_1 r + a_0 = 0 \tag{3}$$

has *repeated* roots. For example, suppose that Eq. (3) has only two distinct roots, r_0 of multiplicity 1 and r_1 of multiplicity $k > 1$. Then (after dividing by a_n) Eq. (3) can be rewritten in the form

$$(r - r_1)^k (r - r_0) = (r - r_0)(r - r_1)^k = 0. \tag{8}$$

Similarly, the corresponding operator L in (6) can be written as

$$L = (D - r_1)^k (D - r_0) = (D - r_0)(D - r_1)^k, \tag{9}$$

the order of the factors making no difference because of the formula in (7).

Two solutions of the differential equation $Ly = 0$ are certainly $y_0 = e^{r_0 x}$ and $y_1 = e^{r_1 x}$. This is, however, not sufficient; we need $k + 1$ linearly independent solutions in order to construct a general solution, because the equation is of order $k + 1$. To find the missing $k - 1$ solutions, we note that

$$Ly = (D - r_0)[(D - r_1)^k y] = 0.$$

Consequently, *every* solution of the kth-order equation

$$(D - r_1)^k y = 0 \tag{10}$$

will also be a solution of the original equation $Ly = 0$. Hence our problem is reduced to that of finding the general solution of the differential equation in (10).

The fact that $y_1 = e^{r_1 x}$ is one solution of Eq. (10) suggests that we try the substitution

$$y(x) = u(x)y_1(x) = u(x)e^{r_1 x}, \tag{11}$$

where $u(x)$ is a function yet to be determined. Observe that

$$(D - r_1)\left[u e^{r_1 x}\right] = (Du)e^{r_1 x} + r_1 u e^{r_1 x} - r_1 u e^{r_1 x}, \tag{12}$$

so

$$(D - r_1)^k \left[u e^{r_1 x}\right] = (D^k u)e^{r_1 x} \tag{13}$$

for any function $u(x)$. Hence $y = u e^{r_1 x}$ will be a solution of Eq. (10) if and only if $D^k u = u^{(k)} = 0$. But this is so if and only if

$$u(x) = c_1 + c_2 x + c_3 x^2 + \cdots + c_k x^{k-1},$$

a polynomial of degree at most $k - 1$. Hence our desired solution of Eq. (10) is

$$y(x) = u e^{r_1 x} = (c_1 + c_2 x + c_3 x^2 + \cdots + c_k x^{k-1})e^{r_1 x}.$$

In particular, we see here the additional solutions $x e^{r_1 x}, x^2 e^{r_1 x}, \ldots, x^{k-1} e^{r_1 x}$ of the original differential equation $Ly = 0$.

The preceding analysis can be carried out with the operator $D - r_0$ replaced with an arbitrary polynomial operator. When this is done, the result is a proof of the following theorem.

THEOREM 2: Repeated Roots

If the characteristic equation in (3) has a repeated root r of multiplicity k, then the part of the general solution of the differential equation in (1) corresponding to r is of the form

$$\blacktriangleright \qquad (c_1 + c_2 x + c_3 x^2 + \cdots + c_k x^{k-1})e^{rx}. \tag{14}$$

∎

We may observe that according to Problem 29 of Section 3.2, the k functions $e^{rx}, x e^{rx}, x^2 e^{rx}, \ldots$, and $x^{k-1} e^{rx}$ involved in (14) are linearly independent on the real line. Thus a root of multiplicity k corresponds to k linearly independent solutions of the differential equation.

EXAMPLE 2   Find a general solution of the fifth-order differential equation

$$9y^{(5)} - 6y^{(4)} + y^{(3)} = 0.$$

Solution The characteristic equation is

$$9r^5 - 6r^4 + r^3 = r^3(9r^2 - 6r + 1) = r^3(3r - 1)^2 = 0.$$

It has the triple root $r = 0$ and the double root $r = \frac{1}{3}$. The triple root $r = 0$ contributes

$$c_1 e^{0 \cdot x} + c_2 x e^{0 \cdot x} + c_3 x^2 e^{0 \cdot x} = c_1 + c_2 x + c_3 x^2$$

to the solution, while the double root $r = \frac{1}{3}$ contributes $c_4 e^{x/3} + c_5 x e^{x/3}$. Hence the general solution of the given differential equation is

$$y(x) = c_1 + c_2 x + c_3 x^2 + c_4 e^{x/3} + c_5 x e^{x/3}.$$ ∎

Complex-Valued Functions and Euler's Formula

Because we have assumed that the coefficients of the differential equation and its characteristic equation are real, any complex (nonreal) roots will occur in complex conjugate pairs $a \pm bi$ where a and b are real and $i = \sqrt{-1}$. This raises the question as to what might be meant by an exponential such as $\exp([a + bi]x)$.

To answer this question, we recall from elementary calculus the Taylor series for the exponential function

$$e^t = \sum_{n=0}^{\infty} \frac{t^n}{n!} = 1 + t + \frac{t^2}{2!} + \frac{t^3}{3!} + \frac{t^4}{4!} + \cdots .$$

If we substitute $t = ix$ in this series, we get

$$e^{ix} = \sum_{n=0}^{\infty} \frac{(ix)^n}{n!}$$

$$= 1 + ix - \frac{x^2}{2!} - \frac{ix^3}{3!} + \frac{x^4}{4!} + \frac{ix^5}{5!} - \cdots$$

$$= \left(1 - \frac{x^2}{2!} + \frac{x^4}{4!} - \cdots \right) + i \left(x - \frac{x^3}{3!} + \frac{x^5}{5!} - \cdots \right).$$

Because the two real series in the last line are the Taylor series for $\cos x$ and $\sin x$, respectively, this implies that

$$e^{ix} = \cos x + i \sin x. \tag{15}$$

This result is known as **Euler's formula**. Because of it we *define* the exponential function e^z, for $z = x + iy$ an arbitrary complex number, to be

$$e^z = e^{x+iy} = e^x e^{iy} = e^x (\cos y + i \sin y). \tag{16}$$

Thus it appears that complex roots of the characteristic equation will lead to complex-valued solutions of the differential equation. A **complex-valued function** F of the real variable x associates with each real number x (in its domain of definition) the complex number

$$z = F(x) = f(x) + ig(x). \tag{17}$$

The real-valued functions f and g are called the **real** and **imaginary** parts, respectively, of F. If they are differentiable, we define the **derivative** F' to be

$$F'(x) = f'(x) + ig'(x). \tag{18}$$

Thus we simply differentiate the real and imaginary parts of F separately. Similarly, we say that the complex-valued function $y = F(x)$ **satisfies** the differential equation in (1) provided that its real and imaginary parts separately satisfy that differential equation.

The particular complex-valued functions of interest here are of the form $F(x) = e^{rx}$ where $r = a \pm bi$. We note from Euler's formula that

$$e^{(a+bi)x} = e^{ax}(\cos bx + i \sin bx) \tag{19a}$$

and

$$e^{(a-bi)x} = e^{ax}(\cos bx - i \sin bx). \tag{19b}$$

The most important property of e^{rx} is that

$$D_x(e^{rx}) = re^{rx}, \tag{20}$$

even if r should be a complex number. The proof of this assertion is a straightforward computation based on the definitions and formulas given earlier:

$$\begin{aligned}
D_x(e^{rx}) &= D_x(e^{ax}\cos bx) + i D_x(e^{ax}\sin bx) \\
&= \left(ae^{ax}\cos bx - be^{ax}\sin bx\right) + i \left(ae^{ax}\sin bx + be^{ax}\cos bx\right) \\
&= (a + bi)(e^{ax}\cos bx + ie^{ax}\sin bx) = re^{rx}.
\end{aligned}$$

Complex Roots

It follows from Eq. (20) that when r is complex (just as when r is real), e^{rx} will be a solution of the differential equation in (1) if and only if r is a root of its characteristic equation. If the complex conjugate pair of roots $r_1 = a + bi$ and $r_2 = a - bi$ are simple (nonrepeated), then the corresponding part of a general solution of Eq. (1) is

$$\begin{aligned}
C_1 e^{(a+bi)x} + C_2 e^{(a-bi)x} &= C_1 e^{ax}(\cos bx + i \sin bx) + C_2 e^{ax}(\cos bx - i \sin bx) \\
&= e^{ax}(c_1 \cos bx + c_2 \sin bx),
\end{aligned}$$

where $c_1 = C_1 + C_2$ and $c_2 = (C_1 - C_2)i$. Thus the conjugate pair of roots $a \pm bi$ leads to the linearly independent *real-valued* solutions $e^{ax}\cos bx$ and $e^{ax}\sin bx$. This yields the following result.

THEOREM 3:   Complex Roots

If the characteristic equation in (3) has an unrepeated pair of complex conjugate roots $a \pm bi$ (with $b \neq 0$), then the corresponding part of a general solution of Eq. (1) has the form

➤
$$e^{ax}(c_1 \cos bx + c_2 \sin bx). \tag{21}$$

∎

EXAMPLE 3   The characteristic equation of

$$y'' + b^2 y = 0 \quad (b > 0)$$

is $r^2 + b^2 = 0$, with roots $r = \pm bi$. So Theorem 3 (with $a = 0$) gives the general solution

$$y(x) = c_1 \cos bx + c_2 \sin bx.$$

∎

EXAMPLE 4   Find the particular solution of

$$y'' - 4y' + 5y = 0$$

for which $y(0) = 1$ and $y'(0) = 5$.

Solution   The characteristic equation is

$$r^2 - 4r + 5 = (r - 2)^2 + 1 = 0,$$

with roots $2 + i$ and $2 - i$. Hence a general solution is

$$y(x) = e^{2x}(c_1 \cos x + c_2 \sin x).$$

Then

$$y'(x) = 2e^{2x}(c_1 \cos x + c_2 \sin x) + e^{2x}(-c_1 \sin x + c_2 \cos x),$$

so the initial conditions give

$$y(0) = c_1 = 1 \quad \text{and} \quad y'(0) = 2c_1 + c_2 = 5.$$

It follows that $c_2 = 3$, and so the desired particular solution is

$$y(x) = e^{2x}(\cos x + 3 \sin x). \qquad \blacksquare$$

EXAMPLE 5   Find a general solution of $y^{(4)} + 4y = 0$.

Solution   The characteristic equation is

$$r^4 + 4 = (r^2 + 2i)(r^2 - 2i) = 0,$$

and its four roots are $\pm\sqrt{\pm 2i}$. Now $i = e^{i\pi/2}$ and $-i = e^{3\pi/2}$, so

$$\sqrt{i} = \left(e^{i\pi/2}\right)^{1/2} = e^{i\pi/4} = \frac{1+i}{\sqrt{2}}$$

and

$$\sqrt{-i} = \left(e^{3i\pi/2}\right)^{1/2} = e^{3i\pi/4} = \frac{-1+i}{\sqrt{2}}.$$

Thus the four (distinct) roots of the characteristic equation are $r = \pm(1 \pm i)$. These two pairs of complex conjugate roots, $1 \pm i$ and $-1 \pm i$, give a general solution

$$y(x) = e^x(c_1 \cos x + c_2 \sin x) + e^{-x}(c_3 \cos x + c_4 \sin x)$$

of the differential equation $y^{(4)} + 4y = 0$. $\qquad \blacksquare$

In Example 5 we employed the polar form

$$x + iy = re^{i\theta} \qquad (22)$$

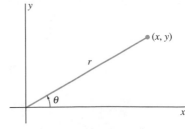

FIGURE 3.3.1. Modulus and argument of the complex number $x + iy$.

of a complex number. The relations between the real and imaginary parts x and y and the **modulus** r and **argument** θ are indicated in Fig. 3.3.1. One consequence of Eq. (22) is that the nonzero complex number $x + iy$ has the two square roots

$$\pm(x + iy)^{1/2} = \pm(re^{i\theta})^{1/2} = \pm r^{1/2}e^{i\theta/2}. \qquad (23)$$

Repeated Complex Roots

Theorem 2 holds for repeated complex roots. If the conjugate pair $a + bi$ has multiplicity k, then the corresponding part of the general solution has the form

$$(A_1 + A_2 x + \cdots + A_k x^{k-1})e^{(a+bi)x} + (B_1 + B_2 x + \cdots + B_k x^{k-1})e^{(a-bi)x}$$

$$= \sum_{p=0}^{k-1} x^p e^{ax}(c_i \cos bx + d_i \sin bx). \qquad (24)$$

It can be shown that the $2k$ functions

$$x^p e^{ax} \cos bx, \quad x^p e^{ax} \sin bx, \quad 0 \leq p \leq k - 1$$

that appear in Eq. (24) are linearly independent.

EXAMPLE 6   Find a general solution of $(D^2 + 6D + 13)^2 y = 0$.

Solution   By completing the square, we see that the characteristic equation

$$(r^2 + 6r + 13)^2 = [(r + 3)^2 + 4]^2 = 0$$

has as its roots the conjugate pair $-3 \pm 2i$ of multiplicity $k = 2$. Hence Eq. (24) gives the general solution

$$y(x) = e^{-3x}(c_1 \cos 2x + d_1 \sin 2x) + xe^{-3x}(c_2 \cos 2x + d_2 \sin 2x). \qquad ■$$

In applications we are seldom presented in advance with a factorization as convenient as the one in Example 6. Often the most difficult part of solving a homogeneous linear equation is finding the roots of its characteristic equation. Example 7 illustrates an approach that may succeed when a root of the characteristic equation can be found by inspection. The project material for this section illustrates other possibilities.

EXAMPLE 7   The characteristic equation of the differential equation

$$y^{(3)} + y' - 10y = 0$$

is the cubic equation

$$r^3 + r - 10 = 0.$$

By a standard theorem of elementary algebra, the only possible rational roots are the factors ± 1, ± 2, ± 5, and ± 10 of the constant term 10. By trial and error (if not by inspection) we discover the root 2. The factor theorem of elementary algebra implies that $r - 2$ is a factor of $r^3 + r - 10$, and division of the former into the latter produces as quotient the quadratic polynomial

$$r^2 + 2r + 5 = (r + 1)^2 + 4.$$

The roots of this quotient are the complex conjugates $-1 \pm 2i$. The three roots we have found now yield the general solution

$$y(x) = c_1 e^{2x} + e^{-x}(c_2 \cos 2x + c_3 \sin 2x). \qquad ■$$

EXAMPLE 8   The roots of the characteristic equation of a certain differential equation are 3, -5, 0, 0, 0, 0, -5, $2 \pm 3i$, and $2 \pm 3i$. Write the general solution of this homogeneous differential equation.

Solution   The solution can be read directly from the list of roots. It is

$$y(x) = c_1 + c_2 x + c_3 x^2 + c_4 x^3 + c_5 e^{3x} + c_6 e^{-5x} + c_7 xe^{-5x}$$

$$+ e^{2x}(c_8 \cos 3x + c_9 \sin 3x) + xe^{2x}(c_{10} \cos 3x + c_{11} \sin 3x). \qquad ■$$

3.3 *Problems*

Find the general solutions of the differential equations in Problems 1 through 30.

1. $y'' - 4y = 0$
2. $2y'' - 3y' = 0$
3. $y'' + 3y' - 10y = 0$
4. $2y'' - 7y' + 3y = 0$
5. $y'' + 6y' + 9y = 0$
6. $y'' + 5y' + 5y = 0$
7. $4y'' - 12y' + 9y = 0$
8. $y'' - 6y' + 13y = 0$
9. $y'' + 8y' + 25y = 0$
10. $5y^{(4)} + 3y^{(3)} = 0$
11. $y^{(4)} - 8y^{(3)} + 16y'' = 0$
12. $y^{(4)} - 3y^{(3)} + 3y'' - y' = 0$
13. $9y^{(3)} + 12y'' + 4y' = 0$
14. $y^{(4)} + 3y'' - 4y = 0$
15. $y^{(4)} - 8y'' + 16y = 0$
16. $y^{(4)} + 18y'' + 81y = 0$
17. $6y^{(4)} + 11y'' + 4y = 0$
18. $y^{(4)} = 16y$
19. $y^{(3)} + y'' - y' = 0$
20. $y^{(4)} + 2y^{(3)} + 3y'' + 2y' + y = 0$ (*Suggestion*: Expand $(r^2 + r + 1)^2$.)

Solve the initial value problems given in Problems 21 through 26.

21. $y'' - 4y' + 3y = 0$; $y(0) = 7$, $y'(0) = 11$
22. $9y'' + 6y' + 4y = 0$; $y(0) = 3$, $y'(0) = 4$
23. $y'' - 6y' + 25y = 0$; $y(0) = 3$, $y'(0) = 1$
24. $2y^{(3)} - 3y'' - 2y' = 0$; $y(0) = 1$, $y'(0) = -1$, $y''(0) = 3$
25. $3y^{(3)} + 2y'' = 0$; $y(0) = -1$, $y'(0) = 0$, $y''(0) = 1$
26. $y^{(3)} + 10y'' + 25y' = 0$; $y(0) = 3$, $y'(0) = 4$, $y''(0) = 5$

Find general solutions of the equations in Problems 27 through 32. First find a small integral root of the characteristic equation by inspection; then factor by division.

27. $y^{(3)} + 3y'' - 4y = 0$
28. $2y^{(3)} - y'' - 5y' - 2y = 0$
29. $y^{(3)} + 27y = 0$
30. $y^{(4)} - y^{(3)} + y'' - 3y' - 6y = 0$
31. $y^{(3)} + 3y'' + 4y' - 8y = 0$
32. $y^{(4)} + y^{(3)} - 3y'' - 5y' - 2y = 0$

In Problems 33 through 36, one solution of the differential equation is given. Find the general solution.

33. $y^{(3)} + 3y'' - 54y = 0$; $y = e^{3x}$
34. $3y^{(3)} - 2y'' + 12y' - 8y = 0$; $y = e^{2x/3}$
35. $6y^{(4)} + 5y^{(3)} + 25y'' + 20y' + 4y = 0$; $y = \cos 2x$
36. $9y^{(3)} + 11y'' + 4y' - 14y = 0$; $y = e^{-x} \sin x$
37. Find a function $y(x)$ such that $y^{(4)}(x) = y^{(3)}(x)$ for all x and $y(0) = 18$, $y'(0) = 12$, $y''(0) = 13$, and $y^{(3)}(0) = 7$.
38. Solve the initial value problem

$$y^{(3)} - 5y'' + 100y' - 500y = 0;$$
$$y(0) = 0, \quad y'(0) = 10, \quad y''(0) = 250$$

given that $y_1(x) = e^{5x}$ is one particular solution of the differential equation.

In Problems 39 through 42, find a linear homogeneous constant-coefficient equation with the given general solution.

39. $y(x) = (A + Bx + Cx^2)e^{2x}$
40. $y(x) = Ae^{2x} + B \cos 2x + C \sin 2x$
41. $y(x) = A \cos 2x + B \sin 2x + C \cosh 2x + D \sinh 2x$
42. $y(x) = (A + Bx + Cx^2) \cos 2x + (D + Ex + Fx^2) \sin 2x$

Problems 43 through 47 pertain to the solution of differential equations with complex coefficients.

43. (a) Use Euler's formula to show that every complex number can be written in the form $re^{i\theta}$, where $r \geq 0$ and $-\pi < \theta \leq \pi$. (b) Express the numbers 4, -2, $3i$, $1 + i$, and $-1 + i\sqrt{3}$ in the form $re^{i\theta}$. (c) The two square roots of $re^{i\theta}$ are $\pm e^{i\theta/2} \sqrt{r}$. Find the square roots of the numbers $2 - 2i\sqrt{3}$ and $-2 + 2i\sqrt{3}$.

44. Use the quadratic formula to solve the following equations. Note in each case that the roots are not complex conjugates.

    (a) $x^2 + ix + 2 = 0$ (b) $x^2 - 2ix + 3 = 0$

45. Find a general solution of $y'' - 2iy' + 3y = 0$.
46. Find a general solution of $y'' - iy' + 6y = 0$
47. Find a general solution of $y'' = \left(-2 + 2i\sqrt{3}\right)y$.
48. Solve the initial value problem

$$y^{(3)} = y; \quad y(0) = 1, \quad y'(0) = y''(0) = 0.$$

(*Suggestion*: Impose the given initial conditions on the general solution

$$y(x) = Ae^x + Be^{\alpha x} + Ce^{\beta x},$$

where α and β are the complex conjugate roots of $r^3 - 1 = 0$, to discover that

$$y(x) = \frac{1}{3}\left(e^x + 2e^{-x/2} \cos \frac{x\sqrt{3}}{2}\right)$$

is a solution.)

49. Solve the initial value problem

$$y^{(4)} = y^{(3)} + y'' + y' + 2y;$$
$$y(0) = y'(0) = y''(0) = 0, \ y^{(3)}(0) = 30.$$

50. The differential equation

$$y'' + (\operatorname{sgn} x)y = 0 \tag{25}$$

has the discontinuous coefficient function

$$\operatorname{sgn} x = \begin{cases} +1 & \text{if } x > 0, \\ -1 & \text{if } x < 0. \end{cases}$$

Show that Eq. (25) nevertheless has two linearly independent solutions $y_1(x)$ and $y_2(x)$ defined for all x such that

- Each satisfies Eq. (25) at each point $x \neq 0$;
- Each has a continuous derivative at $x = 0$;
- $y_1(0) = y_2'(0) = 1$ and $y_2(0) = y_1'(0) = 0$.

(*Suggestion*: Each $y_i(x)$ will be defined by one formula for $x < 0$ and by another for $x \geq 0$.)

3.4 MECHANICAL VIBRATIONS

The motion of a mass attached to a spring serves as a relatively simple example of the vibrations that occur in more complex mechanical systems. For many such systems, the analysis of these vibrations is a problem in the solution of linear differential equations with constant coefficients.

We consider a body of mass m attached to one end of an ordinary spring that resists compression as well as stretching; the other end of the spring is attached to a fixed wall, as shown in Fig. 3.4.1. Assume that the body rests on a frictionless horizontal plane, so that it can move only back and forth as the spring compresses and stretches. Denote by x the distance of the body from its **equilibrium position**— its position when the spring is unstretched. We take $x > 0$ when the spring is stretched, and thus $x < 0$ when it is compressed.

According to Hooke's law, the restorative force F_S that the spring exerts on the mass is proportional to the distance x that the spring has been stretched or compressed. Because this is the same as the displacement x of the mass m from its equilibrium position, it follows that

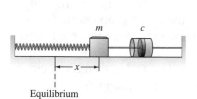

FIGURE 3.4.1. A mass-spring-dashpot system.

$$F_S = -kx. \tag{1}$$

The positive constant of proportionality k is called the **spring constant.** Note that F_S and x have opposite signs: $F_S < 0$ when $x > 0$, $F_S > 0$ when $x < 0$.

Figure 3.4.1 shows the mass attached to a dashpot—a device, like a shock absorber, that provides a force directed opposite to the instantaneous direction of motion of the mass m. We assume the dashpot is so designed that this force F_R is proportional to the velocity $v = dx/dt$ of the mass; that is,

$$F_R = -cv = -c\frac{dx}{dt}. \tag{2}$$

The positive constant c is the **damping constant** of the dashpot. More generally, we may regard Eq. (2) as specifying frictional forces in our system (including air resistance to the motion of m).

If, in addition to the forces F_S and F_R, the mass is subjected to a given **external force** $F_E = F(t)$, then the total force acting on the mass is $F = F_S + F_R + F_E$. Using Newton's law

$$F = ma = m\frac{d^2x}{dt^2} = mx'',$$

we obtain the second-order linear differential equation

$$mx'' + cx' + kx = F(t) \tag{3}$$

that governs the motion of the mass.

If there is no dashpot (and we ignore all frictional forces), then we set $c = 0$ in Eq. (3) and call the motion **undamped**; it is **damped** motion if $c > 0$. If there is no external force we replace $F(t)$ with 0 in Eq. (3). We refer to the motion as **free** in this case and **forced** in the case $F(t) \neq 0$. Thus the homogeneous equation

$$mx'' + cx' + kx = 0 \tag{4}$$

describes free motion of a mass on a spring with dashpot but with no external forces applied. We will defer discussion of forced motion until Section 3.6.

For an alternative example, we might attach the mass to the lower end of a spring that is suspended vertically from a fixed support, as in Fig. 3.4.2. In this case the weight $W = mg$ of the mass would stretch the spring a distance s_0 determined by Eq. (1) with $F_S = -W$ and $x = s_0$. That is, $mg = ks_0$, so that $s_0 = mg/k$. This gives the **static** equilibrium position of the mass. If y denotes the displacement of the mass in motion, measured downward from its static equilibrium position, then we ask you to show in Problem 9 that y satisfies Eq. (3); specifically, that

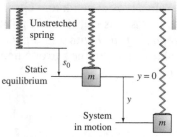

FIGURE 3.4.2. A mass suspended vertically from a spring.

$$my'' + cy' + ky = F(t) \tag{5}$$

if we include damping and external forces.

The Simple Pendulum

The importance of the differential equation that appears in Eqs. (3) and (5) stems from the fact that it describes the motion of many other simple mechanical systems. For example, a **simple pendulum** consists of a mass m swinging back and forth on the end of a string (or better, a *massless rod*) of length L, as shown in Fig. 3.4.3. We may specify the position of the mass at time t by giving the counterclockwise angle $\theta = \theta(t)$ that the string or rod makes with the vertical at time t. To analyze the motion of the mass m, we will apply the law of the conservation of mechanical energy, according to which the sum of the kinetic energy and the potential energy of m remains constant.

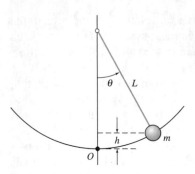

FIGURE 3.4.3. The simple pendulum.

The distance along the circular arc from 0 to m is $s = L\theta$, so the velocity of the mass is $v = ds/dt = L(d\theta/dt)$, and therefore its kinetic energy is

$$T = \frac{1}{2}mv^2 = \frac{1}{2}m\left(\frac{ds}{dt}\right)^2 = \frac{1}{2}mL^2\left(\frac{d\theta}{dt}\right)^2.$$

We next choose as reference point the lowest point O reached by the mass (see Fig. 3.4.3). Then its potential energy V is the product of its weight mg and its vertical height $h = L(1 - \cos\theta)$ above O, so

$$V = mgL(1 - \cos\theta).$$

The fact that the sum of T and V is a constant C therefore gives

$$\frac{1}{2}mL^2\left(\frac{d\theta}{dt}\right)^2 + mgL(1 - \cos\theta) = C.$$

We differentiate both sides of this identity with respect to t to obtain

$$mL^2\left(\frac{d\theta}{dt}\right)\left(\frac{d^2\theta}{dt^2}\right) + mgL(\sin\theta)\frac{d\theta}{dt} = 0,$$

so

$$\frac{d^2\theta}{dt^2} + \frac{g}{L}\sin\theta = 0 \tag{6}$$

after removal of the common factor $mL^2(d\theta/dt)$.

Now recall that $\sin\theta \approx \theta$ when θ is small; in fact, $\sin\theta$ and θ agree to two decimal places when $|\theta|$ is at most $\pi/12$ (that is, $15°$). In a typical pendulum clock, for example, θ would never exceed $15°$. It therefore seems reasonable to simplify our mathematical model of the simple pendulum by replacing $\sin\theta$ with θ in Eq. (6). If we also insert a term $c\theta'$ to account for the frictional resistance of the surrounding medium, the result is an equation in the form of Eq. (4):

$$\theta'' + c\theta' + k\theta = 0, \tag{7}$$

where $k = g/L$. Note that this equation is independent of the mass m on the end of the rod. We might, however, expect the effects of the discrepancy between θ and $\sin\theta$ to accumulate over a period of time, so that Eq. (7) will probably not describe accurately the actual motion of the pendulum over a long period of time.

In the remainder of this section, we first analyze free undamped motion and then free damped motion.

Free Undamped Motion

If we have only a mass on a spring, with neither damping nor external force, then Eq. (3) takes the simpler form

$$mx'' + kx = 0. \tag{8}$$

It is convenient to define

$$\omega_0 = \sqrt{\frac{k}{m}}, \tag{9}$$

and rewrite Eq. (8) as

$$x'' + \omega_0^2 x = 0. \tag{8'}$$

The general solution of Eq. (8') is

$$x(t) = A \cos \omega_0 t + B \sin \omega_0 t. \tag{10}$$

To analyze the motion described by this solution, we choose constants C and α so that

$$C = \sqrt{A^2 + B^2}, \quad \cos \alpha = \frac{A}{C}, \quad \text{and} \quad \sin \alpha = \frac{B}{C}, \tag{11}$$

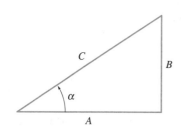

FIGURE 3.4.4. The angle α.

as indicated in Fig. 3.4.4. Note that, although $\tan \alpha = B/A$, the angle α is *not* given by the principal branch of the inverse tangent function (which gives values only in the interval $-\pi/2 < x < \pi/2$). Instead, α is the angle between 0 and 2π whose cosine and sine have the signs given in (11), where either A or B or both may be negative. Thus

$$\alpha = \begin{cases} \tan^{-1}(B/A) & \text{if } A > 0, B > 0 \text{ (first quadrant)}, \\ \pi + \tan^{-1}(B/A) & \text{if } A < 0 \text{ (second or third quadrant)}, \\ 2\pi + \tan^{-1}(B/A) & \text{if } A > 0, B < 0 \text{ (fourth quadrant)}, \end{cases}$$

where $\tan^{-1}(B/A)$ is the angle in $(-\pi/2, \pi/2)$ given by a calculator or computer. In any event, from (10) and (11) we get

$$x(t) = C \left(\frac{A}{C} \cos \omega_0 t + \frac{B}{C} \sin \omega_0 t \right) = C(\cos \alpha \cos \omega_0 t + \sin \alpha \sin \omega_0 t).$$

With the aid of the cosine addition formula, we find that

$$x(t) = C \cos(\omega_0 t - \alpha). \tag{12}$$

Thus the mass oscillates to and fro about its equilibrium position with

Amplitude	C,
Circular frequency	ω_0, and
Phase angle	α.

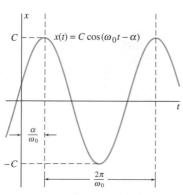

FIGURE 3.4.5. Simple harmonic motion.

Such motion is called **simple harmonic motion**. A typical graph of $x(t)$ is shown in Fig. 3.4.5. If time t is measured in seconds, the circular frequency ω_0 has dimensions of radians per second (rad/s). The **period** of the motion is the time required for the system to complete one full oscillation, so is given by

$$T = \frac{2\pi}{\omega_0} \tag{13}$$

seconds; its **frequency** is

$$\nu = \frac{1}{T} = \frac{\omega_0}{2\pi} \qquad (14)$$

in hertz (Hz), which measures the number of complete cycles per second. Note that frequency is measured in cycles per second, whereas circular frequency has the dimensions of radians per second.

If the initial position $x(0) = x_0$ and initial velocity $x'(0) = v_0$ of the mass are given, we first determine the values of the coefficients A and B in Eq. (10), then find the amplitude C and phase angle α by carrying out the transformation of $x(t)$ to the form in Eq. (12), as indicated previously.

EXAMPLE 1   A body with mass $m = \frac{1}{2}$ kilogram (kg) is attached to the end of a spring that is stretched 2 meters (m) by a force of 100 newtons (N). It is set in motion with initial position $x_0 = 0.5$ (m) and initial velocity $v_0 = -10$ (m/s). (Note that these data indicate that the body is displaced to the right and moving to the left at time $t = 0$.) Find the position function of the body as well as the amplitude, frequency, period of oscillation, and phase angle of its motion.

Solution   The spring constant is $k = (100\ \text{N})/(2\ \text{m}) = 50$ (N/m), so Eq. (8) yields $\frac{1}{2}x'' + 50x = 0$; that is,

$$x'' + 100x = 0.$$

Consequently, the circular frequency will be $\omega_0 = 10$ (rad/s). So the body will oscillate with

$$\text{frequency:}\quad \frac{10}{2\pi} \approx 1.59\ \text{Hz}$$

and

$$\text{period:}\quad \frac{2\pi}{10} \approx 0.63\ \text{s}.$$

We now impose the initial conditions $x(0) = 0.5$ and $x'(0) = -10$ on the general solution $x(t) = A\cos 10t + B\sin 10t$, and it follows that $A = 0.5$ and $B = -1$. So the position function of the body is

$$x(t) = \tfrac{1}{2}\cos 10t - \sin 10t.$$

Hence its amplitude of motion is

$$C = \sqrt{\left(\tfrac{1}{2}\right)^2 + 1^2} = \tfrac{1}{2}\sqrt{5} \approx 1.12\ \text{(m)}.$$

To find the phase angle, we write

$$x(t) = \frac{\sqrt{5}}{2}\left(\frac{1}{\sqrt{5}}\cos 10t - \frac{2}{\sqrt{5}}\sin 10t\right) = \frac{5}{2}\cos(10t - \alpha).$$

Thus we require

$$\cos\alpha = \frac{1}{\sqrt{5}} > 0 \quad \text{and} \quad \sin\alpha = -\frac{2}{\sqrt{5}} < 0.$$

Hence α is the fourth-quadrant angle

$$\alpha = 2\pi - \tan^{-1}\left(\frac{\frac{2}{5}\sqrt{5}}{\frac{1}{5}\sqrt{5}}\right) \approx 5.1760\ \text{(rad)}.$$

In the form in which the amplitude and phase angle are made explicit, the position function is

$$x(t) \approx \frac{\sqrt{5}}{2}\cos(10t - 5.1760). \qquad \blacksquare$$

Free Damped Motion

With damping but no external force, the differential equation we have been studying takes the form $mx'' + cx' + kx = 0$; alternatively,

$$x'' + 2px' + \omega_0^2 x = 0, \tag{15}$$

where $\omega_0 = \sqrt{k/m}$ is the corresponding *undamped* circular frequency and

$$p = \frac{c}{2m} > 0. \tag{16}$$

The characteristic equation $r^2 + 2pr + \omega_0^2 = 0$ of Eq. (15) has roots

$$r_1, \ r_2 = -p \pm (p^2 - \omega_0^2)^{1/2} \tag{17}$$

that depend on the sign of

$$p^2 - \omega_0^2 = \frac{c^2}{4m^2} - \frac{k}{m} = \frac{c^2 - 4km}{4m^2}.$$

The **critical damping** c_{cr} is given by $c_{cr} = \sqrt{4km}$, and we distinguish three cases, according as $c > c_{cr}$, $c = c_{cr}$, or $c < c_{cr}$.

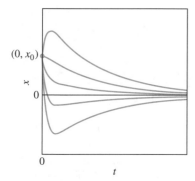

FIGURE 3.4.6. Overdamped motion:
$x(t) = c_1 \exp(r_1 t) + c_2 \exp(r_2 t)$ with $r_1 < 0$ and $r_2 < 0$. Solution curves are graphed with the same initial position x_0 and different initial velocities.

OVERDAMPED CASE: $c > c_{cr}$ ($c^2 > 4km$). Because c is relatively large in this case, we are dealing with a strong resistance in comparison with a relatively weak spring or a small mass. Then (17) gives distinct real roots r_1 and r_2, both of which are negative. The position function has the form

$$x(t) = c_1 e^{r_1 t} + c_2 e^{r_2 t}. \tag{18}$$

It is easy to see that $x(t) \to 0$ as $t \to +\infty$ and that the body settles to its equilibrium position without any oscillations (Problem 27). Figure 3.4.6 shows some typical graphs of the position function for the overdamped case; we chose x_0 a fixed positive number and illustrated the effects of changing the initial velocity v_0. In every case the would-be oscillations are damped out.

CRITICALLY DAMPED CASE: $c = c_{cr}$ ($c^2 = 4km$). In this case, (17) gives equal roots $r_1 = r_2 = -p$ of the characteristic equation, so the general solution is

$$x(t) = e^{-pt}(c_1 + c_2 t). \tag{19}$$

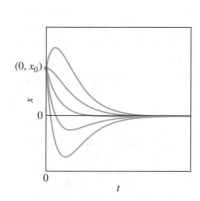

FIGURE 3.4.7. Critically damped motion:
$x(t) = (c_1 + c_2 t)e^{-pt}$ with $p > 0$. Solution curves are graphed with the same initial position x_0 and different initial velocities.

Because $e^{-pt} > 0$ and $c_1 + c_2 t$ has at most one positive zero, the body passes through its equilibrium position at most once, and it is clear that $x(t) \to 0$ as $t \to +\infty$. Some graphs of the motion in the critically damped case appear in Fig. 3.4.7, and they resemble those of the overdamped case (Fig. 3.4.6). In the critically damped case, the resistance of the dashpot is just large enough to damp out any oscillations, but even a slight decrease in resistance will bring us to the remaining case, the one that shows the most dramatic behavior.

UNDERDAMPED CASE: $c < c_{cr}$ ($c^2 < 4km$). The characteristic equation now has two complex conjugate roots $-p \pm i\sqrt{\omega_0^2 - p^2}$, and the general solution is

$$x(t) = e^{-pt}(A\cos\omega_1 t + B\sin\omega_1 t), \qquad (20)$$

where

$$\omega_1 = \sqrt{\omega_0^2 - p^2} = \frac{\sqrt{4km - c^2}}{2m}. \qquad (21)$$

Using the cosine addition formula as in the derivation of Eq. (12), we may rewrite Eq. (20) as

$$x(t) = Ce^{-pt}\left(\frac{A}{C}\cos\omega_1 t + \frac{B}{C}\sin\omega_1 t\right),$$

so

$$x(t) = Ce^{-pt}\cos(\omega_1 t - \alpha) \qquad (22)$$

where

$$C = \sqrt{A^2 + B^2}, \quad \cos\alpha = \frac{A}{C}, \quad \text{and} \quad \sin\alpha = \frac{B}{C}.$$

The solution in (22) represents exponentially damped oscillations of the body around its equilibrium position. The graph of $x(t)$ lies between the curves $x = -Ce^{-pt}$ and $x = Ce^{-pt}$ and touches them when $\omega_1 t - \alpha$ is an integral multiple of π. The motion is not actually periodic, but it is nevertheless useful to call ω_1 its **circular frequency,** $T_1 = 2\pi/\omega_1$ its **pseudoperiod** of oscillation, and Ce^{-pt} its **time-varying amplitude.** Most of these quantities are shown in the typical graph of underdamped motion shown in Fig. 3.4.8. Note from Eq. (21) that in this case ω_1 is less than the undamped circular frequency ω_0, so T_1 is larger than the period T of oscillation of the same mass without damping on the same spring. Thus the action of the dashpot has at least three effects:

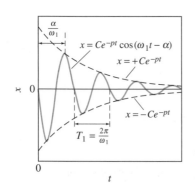

FIGURE 3.4.8. Underdamped oscillations:
$x(t) = Ce^{-pt}\cos(\omega_1 t - \alpha)$.

1. It exponentially damps the oscillations, in accord with the time-varying amplitude.
2. It slows the motion; that is, the dashpot decreases the frequency of the motion.
3. It delays the motion—this is the effect of the phase angle in Eq. (22).

EXAMPLE 2 The mass and spring of Example 1 are now attached also to a dashpot that provides 6 N of resistance for each meter per second of velocity. The mass is set in motion with the same initial position $x(0) = 0.5$ (m) and the same initial velocity $x'(0) = -10$ (m/s). Find the position function of the mass, its new frequency and pseudoperiod, its phase angle, and the amplitudes of its first four (local) maxima and minima.

Solution Rather than memorizing the various formulas given in the preceding discussion, it is better practice in a particular case to set up the differential equation and then solve it directly. Recall that $m = \frac{1}{2}$ and $k = 50$; we are now given $c = 6$ in mks units. Hence Eq. (3) is $\frac{1}{2}x'' + 6x' + 50x = 0$; that is,

$$x'' + 12x' + 100 = 0.$$

The roots of the characteristic equation $r^2 + 12r + 100 = 0$ are

$$r_1, r_2 = \frac{-12 \pm \sqrt{144 - 400}}{2} = -6 \pm 8i,$$

so the general solution is

$$x(t) = e^{-6t}(A \cos 8t + B \sin 8t). \tag{23}$$

The new circular frequency is $\omega_1 = 8$ (rad/s) and the pseudoperiod and new frequency are

$$T_1 = \frac{2\pi}{8} \approx 0.79 \text{ (s)}$$

and

$$\frac{1}{T_1} = \frac{8}{2\pi} \approx 1.27 \text{ (Hz)}$$

(in contrast with 0.63 s and 1.59 Hz, respectively, in the undamped case).
 From Eq. (23) we compute

$$x'(t) = e^{-6t}(-8A \sin 8t + 8B \cos 8t) - 6e^{-6t}(A \cos 8t + B \sin 8t).$$

The initial conditions therefore produce the equations

$$x(0) = A = \tfrac{1}{2} \quad \text{and} \quad x'(0) = -6A + 8B = -10,$$

so $A = \frac{1}{2}$ and $B = -\frac{7}{8}$. Thus

$$x(t) = e^{-6t}\left(\tfrac{1}{2} \cos 8t - \tfrac{7}{8} \sin 8t\right),$$

and so with

$$C = \sqrt{\left(\tfrac{1}{2}\right)^2 + \left(\tfrac{7}{8}\right)^2} = \tfrac{1}{8}\sqrt{65}$$

we have

$$x(t) = \frac{\sqrt{65}}{8} e^{-6t} \left(\frac{4}{\sqrt{65}} \cos 8t - \frac{7}{\sqrt{65}} \sin 8t\right).$$

We require

$$\cos\alpha = \frac{4}{\sqrt{65}} > 0 \quad \text{and} \quad \sin\alpha = -\frac{7}{\sqrt{65}} < 0,$$

so α is the fourth-quadrant angle

$$\alpha = 2\pi - \tan^{-1}\left(\frac{7}{4}\right) \approx 5.2315 \text{ (rad)}.$$

Finally,

$$x(t) \approx \frac{\sqrt{65}}{8} e^{-6t} \cos(8t - 5.2315). \tag{24}$$

The local maxima and minima of $x(t)$ occur when

$$0 = x'(t) \approx \frac{\sqrt{65}}{8}\left[-6e^{-6t} \cos(8t - 5.2315) - 8e^{-6t} \sin(8t - 5.2315)\right],$$

and thus when

$$\tan(8t - 5.2315) \approx -0.75.$$

Because $\tan^{-1}(-0.75) \approx -0.6435$, we want to find the first four positive values of t such that $8t - 5.2315$ is the sum of -0.6435 and an integral multiple of π. These values of t and the corresponding values of x computed with the aid of (24) are as follows:

t (s)	0.1808	0.5735	0.9662	1.3589
x (m)	−0.2725	0.0258	−0.0024	0.0002

We see that the oscillations are damped out very rapidly, with their amplitude decreasing by a factor of about 10 every half-cycle. See Problems 30 and 31 for a more general discussion of this phenomenon. ∎

3.4 *Problems*

1. Determine the period and frequency of the simple harmonic motion of a 4-kg mass on the end of a spring with spring constant 16 N/m.

2. Determine the period and frequency of the simple harmonic motion of a body of mass 0.75 kg on the end of a spring with spring constant 48 N/m.

3. A mass of 3 kg is attached to the end of a spring that is stretched 20 cm by a force of 15 N. It is set in motion with initial position $x_0 = 0$ and initial velocity $v_0 = -10$ m/s. Find the amplitude, period, and frequency of the resulting motion.

4. A body with mass 250 g is attached to the end of a spring that is stretched 25 cm by a force of 9 N. At time $t = 0$ the body is pulled 1 m to the right, stretching the spring, and set in motion with an initial velocity of 5 m/s to the left. (a) Find $x(t)$ in the form $C \cos(\omega_0 t + \alpha)$. (b) Find the amplitude and period of motion of the body.

   In Problems 5 through 8, assume that the differential equation of a simple pendulum of length L is $L\theta'' + g\theta = 0$, where $g = GM/R^2$ is the gravitational acceleration at the location of the pendulum (at distance R from the center of the earth; M denotes the mass of the earth).

5. Two pendulums are of lengths L_1 and L_2 and—when located at the respective distances R_1 and R_2 from the center of the earth—have periods p_1 and p_2. Show that

$$\frac{p_1}{p_2} = \frac{R_1\sqrt{L_1}}{R_2\sqrt{L_2}}.$$

6. A certain pendulum keeps perfect time in Paris, where the radius of the earth is $R = 3956$ (mi). But this clock loses 2 min 40 s per day at a location on the equator. Use the result of Problem 5 to find the amount of the equatorial bulge of the earth.

7. A pendulum of length 100.10 in., located at a point at sea level where the radius of the earth is $R = 3960$ (mi), has the same period as does a pendulum of length 100.00 in. atop a nearby mountain. Use the result of Problem 5 to find the height of the mountain.

8. Most grandfather clocks have pendulums with adjustable lengths. One such clock loses 10 min per day when the length of its pendulum is 30 in. With what length pendulum will this clock keep perfect time?

9. Derive Eq. (5) describing the motion of a mass attached to the bottom of a vertically suspended spring. (*Suggestion*: First denote by $x(t)$ the displacement of the mass below the unstretched position of the spring; set up the differential equation for x. Then substitute $y = x - x_0$ in this differential equation.)

10. Consider a floating cylindrical buoy with radius r, height h, and uniform density $\rho \le 0.5$ (recall that the density of water is 1 g/cm³). The buoy is initially suspended at rest with its bottom at the top surface of the water and is released at time $t = 0$. Thereafter it is acted on by two forces: a downward gravitational force equal to its weight $mg = \rho\pi r^2 hg$ and an upward force of buoyancy equal to the weight $\pi r^2 xg$ of water displaced, where $x = x(t)$ is the depth of the bottom of the buoy beneath the surface

at time t (Fig. 3.4.9). Conclude that the buoy undergoes simple harmonic motion around its equilibrium position $x_e = \rho h$ with period $p = 2\pi\sqrt{\rho h/g}$. Compute p and the amplitude of the motion if $\rho = 0.5$ g/cm³, $h = 200$ cm, and $g = 980$ cm/s².

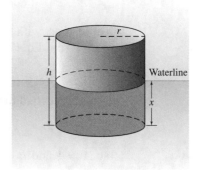

FIGURE 3.4.9.   The buoy of Problem 10.

11. A cylindrical buoy weighing 100 lb (thus of mass $m = 3.125$ slugs in ft-lb-s (fps) units) floats in water with its axis vertical (as in Problem 10). When depressed slightly and released, it oscillates up and down four times every 10 s. Assume that friction is negligible. Find the radius of the buoy.

12. Assume that the earth is a solid sphere of uniform density, with mass M and radius $R = 3960$ (mi). For a particle of mass m *within* the earth at distance r from the center of the earth, the gravitational force attracting m toward the center is $F_r = -GM_r m/r^2$, where M_r is the mass of the part of the earth within a sphere of radius r. (a) Show that $F_r = -GMmr/R^3$. (b) Now suppose that a small hole is drilled straight through the center of the earth, thus connecting two antipodal points on its surface. Let a particle of mass m be dropped at time $t = 0$ into this hole with initial speed zero, and let $r(t)$ be its distance from the center of the earth at time t (Fig. 3.4.10). Conclude from Newton's second law and part (a) that $r''(t) = -k^2 r(t)$, where $k^2 = GM/R^3 = g/R$. (c) Take $g = 32.2$ ft/s², and conclude from part (b) that the particle undergoes simple harmonic motion back and forth between the ends of the hole, with a period of about 84 min. (d) Look up (or derive) the period of a satellite that just skims the surface of the earth; compare with the result in part (c). How do you explain the coincidence. Or *is* it a coincidence? (e) With what speed (in miles per hour) does the particle pass through the center of the earth? (f) Look up (or derive) the orbital velocity of a satellite that just skims the surface of the earth; compare with the result in part (e). How do you explain the coincidence? Or *is* it a coincidence?

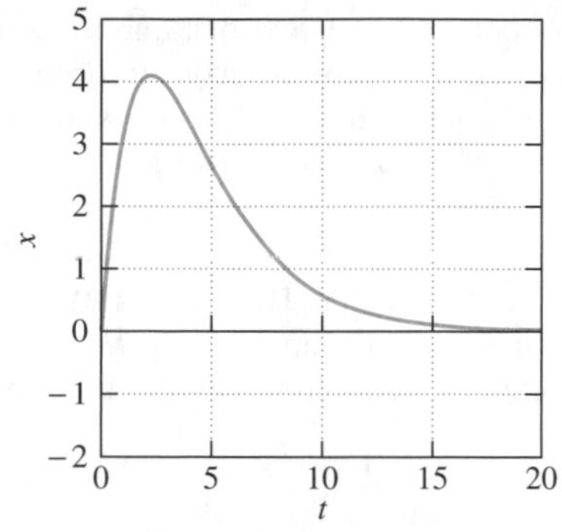

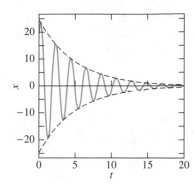

FIGURE 3.4.11. The position
function $x(t)$ of Problem 13.

FIGURE 3.4.12. The position
function $x(t)$ of Problem 14.

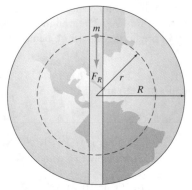

FIGURE 3.4.10. A mass m
falling down a hole through the
center of the earth (Problem 12).

13. Suppose that the mass in a mass-spring-dashpot system
with $m = 10$, $c = 9$, and $k = 2$ is set in motion with
$x(0) = 0$ and $x'(0) = 5$.   (a) Find the position function $x(t)$ and show that its graph looks as indicated in
Fig. 3.4.11.   (b) Find how far the mass moves to the right
before starting back toward the origin.

14. Suppose that the mass in a mass-spring-dashpot system
with $m = 25$, $c = 10$, and $k = 226$ is set in motion
with $x(0) = 20$ and $x'(0) = 41$.   (a) Find the position
function $x(t)$ and show that its graph looks as indicated in
Fig. 3.4.12.   (b) Find the pseudoperiod of the oscillations
and the equations of the "envelope curves" that are dashed
in the figure.

The remaining problems in this section deal with free
damped motion. In Problems 15 through 21, a mass m is attached to both a spring (with given spring constant k) and a
dashpot (with given damping constant c). The mass is set in
motion with initial position x_0 and initial velocity v_0. Find
the position function $x(t)$ and determine whether the motion
is overdamped, critically damped, or underdamped. If it is underdamped, write $x(t)$ in the form $Ce^{-pt}\cos(\omega_1 t - \alpha)$.

15. $m = \frac{1}{2}$, $c = 3$, $k = 4$; $x_0 = 2$, $v_0 = 0$

16. $m = 3$, $c = 30$, $k = 63$; $x_0 = 2$, $v_0 = 2$

17. $m = 1$, $c = 8$, $k = 16$; $x_0 = 5$, $v_0 = -10$

18. $m = 2$, $c = 12$, $k = 50$; $x_0 = 0$, $v_0 = -8$

19. $m = 4$, $c = 20$, $k = 169$; $x_0 = 4$, $v_0 = 16$

20. $m = 2$, $c = 16$, $k = 40$; $x_0 = 5$, $v_0 = 4$

21. $m = 1$, $c = 10$, $k = 125$; $x_0 = 6$, $v_0 = 50$

22. A 12-lb weight (mass $m = 0.375$ slugs in fps units)
is attached both to a vertically suspended spring that it
stretches 6 in. and to a dashpot that provides 3 lb of resistance for every foot per second of velocity.   (a) If the
weight is pulled down 1 ft below its static equilibrium position and then released from rest at time $t = 0$, find its position function $x(t)$.   (b) Find the frequency, time-varying
amplitude, and phase angle of the motion.

23. This problem deals with a highly simplified model of a car
of weight 3200 lb (mass $m = 100$ slugs in fps units). Assume that the suspension system acts like a single spring
and its shock absorbers like a single dashpot, so that its
vertical vibrations satisfy Eq. (4) with appropriate values
of the coefficients.   (a) Find the stiffness coefficient k of
the spring if the car undergoes free vibrations at 80 cycles per minute (cycles/min) when its shock absorbers are
disconnected.   (b) With the shock absorbers connected
the car is set into vibration by driving it over a bump, and
the resulting damped vibrations have a frequency of 78
cycles/min. After how long will the time-varying amplitude be 1% of its initial value?

Problems 24 through 34 deal with a mass-spring-
dashpot system having position function $x(t)$ satisfying
Eq. (4). We write $x_0 = x(0)$ and $v_0 = x'(0)$ and recall that
$p = c/(2m)$, $\omega_0^2 = k/m$, and $\omega_1^2 = \omega_0^2 - p^2$. The system is
critically damped, overdamped, or underdamped, as specified
in each problem.

24. (Critically damped) Show in this case that

$$x(t) = (x_0 + v_0 t + px_0 t)e^{-pt}.$$

25. (Critically damped) Deduce from Problem 24 that the
mass passes through $x = 0$ at some instant $t > 0$ if and
only if x_0 and $v_0 + px_0$ have opposite signs.

26. (Critically damped) Deduce from Problem 24 that $x(t)$ has
a local maximum or minimum at some instant $t > 0$ if and
only if v_0 and $v_0 + px_0$ have the same sign.

27. (Overdamped) Show in this case that

$$x(t) = \frac{1}{2\gamma}\left[(v_0 - r_2 x_0)e^{r_1 t} - (v_0 - r_1 x_0)e^{r_2 t}\right],$$

where $r_1, r_2 = -p \pm \sqrt{p^2 - \omega_0^2}$ and $\gamma = (r_1 - r_2)/2 > 0$.

28. (Overdamped) If $x_0 = 0$, deduce from Problem 27 that

$$x(t) = \frac{v_0}{\gamma}e^{-pt}\sinh \gamma t.$$

29. (Overdamped) Prove that in this case the mass can pass through its equilibrium position $x = 0$ at most once.

30. (Underdamped) Show that in this case

$$x(t) = e^{-pt}\left(x_0 \cos \omega_1 t + \frac{v_0 + px_0}{\omega_1}\sin \omega_1 t\right).$$

31. (Underdamped) If the damping constant c is small in comparison with $\sqrt{8mk}$, apply the binomial series to show that

$$\omega_1 \approx \omega_0\left(1 - \frac{c^2}{8mk}\right).$$

32. (Underdamped) Show that the local maximum and minima of

$$x(t) = Ce^{-pt}\cos(\omega_1 t - \alpha)$$

occur where

$$\tan(\omega_1 t - \alpha) = -\frac{p}{\omega_1}.$$

Conclude that $t_2 - t_1 = 2\pi/\omega_1$ if two consecutive maxima occur at times t_1 and t_2.

33. (Underdamped) Let x_1 and x_2 be two consecutive local maximum values of $x(t)$. Deduce from the result of Problem 32 that

$$\ln \frac{x_1}{x_2} = \frac{2\pi p}{\omega_1}.$$

The constant $\Delta = 2\pi p/\omega_1$ is called the **logarithmic decrement** of the oscillation. Note also that $c = m\omega_1 \Delta/\pi$ because $p = c/(2m)$.

Note: The result of Problem 33 provides an accurate method for measuring the *viscosity* of a fluid, which is an important parameter in fluid dynamics, but which is not easy to measure directly. According to Stokes' drag law, a spherical body of radius a moving at a (relatively slow) speed through a fluid of viscosity μ experiences a resistive force $F_R = 6\pi\mu av$. Thus if a spherical mass on a spring is immersed in the fluid and set in motion, this drag resistance damps its oscillations with damping constant $c = 6\pi a\mu$. The frequency ω_1 and logarithmic decrement Δ of the oscillations can be measured by direct observation. The final formula in Problem 33 then gives c and hence the viscosity of the fluid.

34. (Underdamped) A body weighing 100 lb (mass $m = 3.125$ slugs in fps units) is oscillating attached to a spring

and a dashpot. Its first two maximum displacements of 6.73 in. and 1.46 in. are observed to occur at times 0.34 s and 1.17 s, respectively. Compute the damping constant (in pound-seconds per foot) and spring constant (in pounds per foot).

Differential Equations and Determinism

Given a mass m, a dashpot constant c, and a spring constant k, Theorem 2 of Section 3.1 implies that the equation

$$mx'' + cx' + kx = 0 \qquad (25)$$

has a *unique* solution for $t \geq 0$ satisfying given initial conditions $x(0) = x_0$, $x'(0) = v_0$. Thus the future motion of an ideal mass-spring-dashpot system is completely determined by the differential equation and the initial conditions. Of course in a real physical system it is impossible to measure the parameters m, c, and k *precisely*. Problems 35 through 38 explore the resulting uncertainty in predicting the future behavior of a physical system.

35. Suppose that $m = 1$, $c = 2$, and $k = 1$ in Eq. (25). Show that the solution with $x(0) = 0$ and $x'(0) = 1$ is

$$x_1(t) = te^{-t}.$$

36. Suppose that $m = 1$ and $c = 2$ but $k = 1 - 10^{-2n}$. Show that the solution of Eq. (25) with $x(0) = 0$ and $x'(0) = 1$ is

$$x_2(t) = 10^n e^{-t}\sinh 10^{-n}t.$$

37. Suppose that $m = 1$ and $c = 2$ but that $k = 1 + 10^{-2n}$. Show that the solution of Eq. (25) with $x(0) = 0$ and $x'(0) = 1$ is

$$x_3(t) = 10^n e^{-t}\sin 10^{-n}t.$$

38. Whereas the graphs of $x_1(t)$ and $x_2(t)$ resemble those shown in Figs. 3.4.6 and 3.4.7, the graph of $x_3(t)$ exhibits damped oscillations like those illustrated in Fig. 3.4.8, but with a very long pseudoperiod. Nevertheless, show that for each fixed $t > 0$ it is true that

$$\lim_{n\to\infty} x_2(t) = \lim_{n\to\infty} x_3(t) = x_1(t).$$

Conclude that *on a given finite time interval* the three solutions are in "practical" agreement if n is sufficiently large.

3.5 NONHOMOGENEOUS EQUATIONS AND THE METHOD OF UNDETERMINED COEFFICIENTS

We learned in Section 3.3 how to solve homogeneous linear equations with constant coefficients, but we saw in Section 3.4 that an external force in a simple mechanical system contributes a nonhomogeneous term to its differential equation. The general nonhomogeneous nth-order linear equation with constant coefficients has the form

$$a_n y^{(n)} + a_{n-1}y^{(n-1)} + \cdots + a_1 y' + a_0 y = f(x). \qquad (1)$$

By Theorem 5 of Section 3.2, a general solution of Eq. (1) has the form

$$y = y_c + y_p \qquad (2)$$

where the complementary function $y_c(x)$ is a general solution of the associated homogeneous equation

$$a_n y^{(n)} + a_{n-1} y^{(n-1)} + \cdots + a_1 y' + a_0 y = 0, \qquad (3)$$

and $y_p(x)$ is a particular solution of Eq. (1). Thus our remaining task is to find y_p.

The **method of undetermined coefficients** is a straightforward way of doing this when the given function $f(x)$ in Eq. (1) is sufficiently simple that we can make an intelligent guess as to the general form of y_p. For example, suppose that $f(x)$ is a polynomial of degree m. Then, because the derivatives of a polynomial are themselves polynomials of lower degree, it is reasonable to suspect a particular solution

$$y_p(x) = A_m x^m + A_{m-1} x^{m-1} + \cdots + A_1 x + A_0$$

that is also a polynomial of degree m, but with as yet undetermined coefficients. We may, therefore, substitute this expression for y_p into Eq. (1), and then—by equating coefficients of like powers of x on the two sides of the resulting equation—attempt to determine the coefficients $A_0, A_1, \ldots, A_m$ so that y_p will, indeed, be a particular solution of Eq. (1).

Similarly, suppose that

$$f(x) = a \cos kx + b \sin kx.$$

Then it is reasonable to expect a particular solution of the same form:

$$y_p(x) = A \cos kx + B \sin kx,$$

a linear combination with undetermined coefficients A and B. The reason is that any derivative of such a linear combination of $\cos kx$ and $\sin kx$ has the same form. We may therefore substitute this form of y_p in Eq. (1), and then—by equating coefficients of $\cos kx$ and $\sin kx$ on both sides of the resulting equation—attempt to determine the coefficients A and B so that y_p will, indeed, be a particular solution.

It turns out that this approach does succeed whenever all the derivatives of $f(x)$ have the same form as $f(x)$ itself. Before describing the method in full generality, we illustrate it with several preliminary examples.

EXAMPLE 1 Find a particular solution of $y'' + 3y' + 4y = 3x + 2$.

Solution Here $f(x) = 3x + 2$ is a polynomial of degree 1, so our guess is that

$$y_p(x) = Ax + B.$$

Then $y_p' = A$ and $y_p'' = 0$, so y_p will satisfy the differential equation provided that

$$(0) + 3(A) + 4(Ax + B) = 3x + 2.$$

This is so if and only if $4A = 3$ and $3A + 4B = 2$. These two equations yield $A = \frac{3}{4}$ and $B = -\frac{1}{16}$, so we have found the particular solution

$$y_p(x) = \tfrac{3}{4}x - \tfrac{1}{16}. \qquad \blacksquare$$

EXAMPLE 2 Find a particular solution of $y'' - 4y = 2e^{3x}$.

Solution Any derivative of e^{3x} is a constant multiple of e^{3x}, so it is reasonable to try

$$y_p(x) = Ae^{3x}.$$

Then $y_p'' = 9Ae^{3x}$, so the given differential equation will be satisfied provided that

$$9Ae^{3x} - 4(Ae^{3x}) = 2e^{3x};$$

that is, $5A = 2$, so that $A = \frac{2}{5}$. Thus our particular solution is $y_p(x) = \frac{2}{5}e^{3x}$. $\blacksquare$

EXAMPLE 3   Find a particular solution of $3y'' + y' - 2y = 2\cos x$.

Solution   A first guess might be $y_p(x) = A\cos x$, but the presence of y' on the left-hand side signals that we probably need a term involving $\sin x$ as well. So we try

$$
\begin{aligned}
y_p(x) &= A\cos x + B\sin x; \\
y'_p(x) &= -A\sin x + B\cos x, \\
y''_p(x) &= -A\cos x - B\sin x.
\end{aligned}
$$

Then substitution of y_p and its derivatives into the given differential equation yields

$$3(-A\cos x - B\sin x) + (-A\sin x + B\cos x) - 2(A\cos x + B\sin x) = 2\cos x.$$

We equate the coefficient of $\cos x$ on the left-hand side with that of $\cos x$ on the right and do the same with $\sin x$ to get the equations

$$
\begin{aligned}
-5A + B &= 2, \\
-A - 5B &= 0,
\end{aligned}
$$

with solution $A = -\frac{5}{13}$, $B = \frac{1}{13}$. Hence a particular solution is

$$y_p(x) = -\tfrac{5}{13}\cos x + \tfrac{1}{13}\sin x.$$ ■

The following example, which superficially resembles Example 2, indicates that the method of undetermined coefficients is not always quite so simple as we have made it appear.

EXAMPLE 4   Find a particular solution of $y'' - 4y = 2e^{2x}$.

Solution   If we try $y_p(x) = Ae^{2x}$, we find that

$$y''_p - 4y_p = 4Ae^{2x} - 4Ae^{2x} = 0 \neq 2e^{2x}.$$

Thus, no matter how A is chosen, Ae^{2x} cannot satisfy the given nonhomogeneous equation. In fact, the preceding computation shows that Ae^{2x} satisfies instead the associated *homogeneous* equation. Therefore, we should begin with a trial function $y_p(x)$ whose derivative involves both e^{2x} *and something else* that can cancel upon substitution into the differential equation to leave the e^{2x} term that we need. A reasonable guess is

$$y_p(x) = Axe^{2x},$$

for which

$$y'_p(x) = Ae^{2x} + 2Axe^{2x} \quad \text{and} \quad y''_p(x) = 4Ae^{2x} + 4Axe^{2x}.$$

Substitution into the original differential equation yields

$$(4Ae^{2x} + 4Axe^{2x}) - 4(Axe^{2x}) = 2e^{2x}.$$

The terms involving xe^{2x} obligingly cancel, leaving only $4Ae^{2x} = 2e^{2x}$, so that $A = \frac{1}{2}$. Consequently, a particular solution is

$$y_p(x) = \tfrac{1}{2}xe^{2x}.$$ ■

The General Approach

Our initial difficulty in Example 4 resulted from the fact that $f(x) = 2e^{2x}$ satisfies the associated homogeneous equation. Rule 1, given shortly, tells what to do when we do not have this difficulty, and Rule 2 tells what to do when we do have it.

The method of undetermined coefficients applies whenever the function $f(x)$ in Eq. (1) is a linear combination of (finite) products of functions of the following three types:

1. A polynomial in x;
2. An exponential function e^{rx};   (4)
3. $\cos kx$ or $\sin kx$.

Any such function, for example

$$f(x) = (3 - 4x^2)e^{5x} - 4x^3 \cos 10x,$$

has the crucial property that only *finitely* many linearly independent functions appear as terms (summands) in $f(x)$ and its derivatives of all orders. In Rules 1 and 2 we assume that $Ly = f(x)$ is a nonhomogeneous linear equation with constant coefficients and that $f(x)$ is a function of this kind.

RULE 1: Method of Undetermined Coefficients

Suppose that no term appearing either in $f(x)$ or in any of its derivatives satisfies the associated homogeneous equation $Ly = 0$. Then take as a trial solution for y_p a linear combination of all linearly independent such terms and their derivatives. Then determine the coefficients by substitution of this trial solution into the nonhomogeneous equation $Ly = f(x)$.   ■

Note that this rule is not a theorem requiring proof; it is merely a procedure to be followed in searching for a particular solution y_p. If we succeed in finding y_p, then nothing more need be said. It can be proved, however, that this procedure will always succeed under the conditions specified here.

In practice we check the supposition made in Rule 1 by first using the characteristic equation to find the complementary function y_c, and then write a list of all the terms appearing in $f(x)$ and its successive derivatives. If none of the terms in this list duplicates a term in y_c, then we proceed with Rule 1.

EXAMPLE 5   Find a particular solution of

$$y'' + 4y = 3x^3.$$ (5)

Solution   The (familiar) complementary solution of Eq. (5) is

$$y_c(x) = c_1 \cos 2x + c_2 \sin 2x.$$

The function $f(x) = 3x^3$ and its derivatives are constant multiples of the linearly independent functions x^3, x^2, x, and 1. Because none of these appears in y_c, we try

$$y_p = Ax^3 + Bx^2 + Cx + D,$$
$$y_p' = 3Ax^2 + 2Bx + C,$$
$$y_p'' = 6Ax + 2B.$$

Substitution in Eq. (5) gives

$$y_p'' + 4y_p = (6Ax + 2B) + 4(Ax^3 + Bx^2 + Cx + D)$$
$$= 4Ax^3 + 4Bx^2 + (6A + 4C)x + (2B + D) = 3x^3.$$

We equate coefficients of like powers of x in the last equation to get

$$4A = 3, \qquad 4B = 0,$$
$$6A + 4C = 0, \qquad 2B + D = 0$$

with solution $A = \frac{3}{4}$, $B = 0$, $C = -\frac{9}{8}$, and $D = 0$. Hence a particular solution of Eq. (5) is

$$y_p(x) = \tfrac{3}{4}x^3 - \tfrac{9}{8}x.$$ ∎

EXAMPLE 6   Solve the initial value problem

$$y'' - 3y' + 2y = 3e^{-x} - 10\cos 3x;$$
$$y(0) = 1, \quad y'(2) = 2. \tag{6}$$

Solution   The characteristic equation $r^2 - 3r + 2 = 0$ has roots $r = 1$ and $r = 2$, so the complementary function is

$$y_c(x) = c_1 e^x + c_2 e^{2x}.$$

The terms involved in $f(x) = 3e^{-x} - 10\cos 3x$ and its derivatives are e^{-x}, $\cos 3x$, and $\sin 3x$. Because none of these appears in y_c, we try

$$y_p = \quad Ae^{-x} + \quad B\cos 3x + \quad C\sin 3x,$$
$$y'_p = -Ae^{-x} - \quad 3B\sin 3x + 3C\cos 3x,$$
$$y''_p = \quad Ae^{-x} - \quad 9B\cos 3x - \quad 9C\sin 3x.$$

After we substitute these expressions into the differential equation in (6) and collect coefficients, we get

$$y''_p - 3y'_p + 2y_p = 6Ae^{-x} + (-7B - 9C)\cos 3x + (9B - 7C)\sin 3x$$
$$= 3e^{-x} - 10\cos 3x.$$

We equate the coefficients of the terms involving e^{-x}, those involving $\cos 3x$, and those involving $\sin 3x$. The result is the system

$$6A = \quad 3,$$
$$-7B - 9C = -10,$$
$$9B - 7C = \quad 0$$

with solution $A = \frac{1}{2}$, $B = \frac{7}{13}$, and $C = \frac{9}{13}$. This gives the particular solution

$$y_p(x) = \tfrac{1}{2}e^{-x} + \tfrac{7}{13}\cos 3x + \tfrac{9}{13}\sin 3x,$$

which, however, does not have the required initial values in (6).

To satisfy those initial conditions, we begin with the *general* solution

$$y(x) = y_c(x) + y_p(x)$$

$$= c_1 e^x + c_2 e^{2x} + \tfrac{1}{2}e^{-x} + \tfrac{7}{13}\cos 3x + \tfrac{9}{13}\sin 3x,$$

with derivative

$$y'(x) = c_1 e^x + 2c_2 e^{2x} - \tfrac{1}{2}e^{-x} - \tfrac{21}{13}\sin 3x + \tfrac{27}{13}\cos 3x.$$

The initial conditions in (6) lead to the equations

$$y(0) = c_1 + c_2 + \tfrac{1}{2} + \tfrac{7}{13} = 1,$$

$$y'(0) = c_1 + 2c_2 - \tfrac{1}{2} + \tfrac{27}{13} = 2$$

with solution $c_1 = -\tfrac{1}{2}$, $c_2 = \tfrac{6}{13}$. The desired particular solution is therefore

$$y(x) = -\tfrac{1}{2}e^x + \tfrac{6}{13}e^{2x} + \tfrac{1}{2}e^{-x} + \tfrac{7}{13}\cos 3x + \tfrac{9}{13}\sin 3x. \qquad \blacksquare$$

EXAMPLE 7 Find the general form of a particular solution of

$$y^{(3)} + 9y' = x\sin x + x^2 e^{2x}. \tag{7}$$

Solution The characteristic equation $r^3 + 9r = 0$ has roots $r = 0$, $r = -3i$, and $r = 3i$. So the complementary function is

$$y_c(x) = c_1 + c_2\cos 3x + c_3\sin 3x.$$

The derivatives of the right-hand side in Eq. (7) involve the terms

$$\cos x, \quad \sin x, \quad x\cos x, \quad x\sin x,$$
$$e^{2x}, \quad xe^{2x}, \quad \text{and} \quad x^2 e^{2x}.$$

Because there is no duplication with the terms of the complementary function, the trial solution takes the form

$$y_p(x) = A\cos x + B\sin x + Cx\cos x + Dx\sin x + Ee^{2x} + Fxe^{2x} + Gx^2 e^{2x}.$$

Upon substituting y_p in Eq. (7) and equating coefficients of like terms, we get seven equations determining the seven coefficients A, B, C, D, E, F, and G. $\qquad \blacksquare$

The Case of Duplication

Now we turn our attention to the situation in which Rule 1 does not apply: Some of the terms involved in $f(x)$ and its derivatives satisfy the associated homogeneous equation. For instance, suppose that we want to find a particular solution of the differential equation

$$(D - r)^3 y = (2x - 3)e^{rx}. \tag{8}$$

Proceeding as in Rule 1, out first guess would be

$$y_p(x) = Ae^{rx} + Bxe^{rx}. \tag{9}$$

This form of $y_p(x)$ will not be adequate because the complementary function of Eq. (8) is

$$y_c(x) = c_1 e^{rx} + c_2 xe^{rx} + c_3 x^2 e^{rx}, \tag{10}$$

so substitution of (9) in the left-hand side of (8) would yield zero rather than $(2x - 3)e^{rx}$.

To see how to amend our first guess, we observe that

$$(D - r)^2[(2x - 3)e^{rx}] = [D^2(2x - 3)]e^{rx} = 0$$

by Eq. (13) of Section 3.3. If $y(x)$ is *any* solution of Eq. (8) and we apply the operator $(D - r)^2$ to both sides, we see that $y(x)$ is also a solution of the equation $(D - r)^5 y = 0$. The general solution of this *homogeneous* equation can be written as

$$y(x) = \underbrace{c_1 e^{rx} + c_2 x e^{rx} + c_3 x^2 e^{rx}}_{y_c} + \underbrace{A x^3 e^{rx} + B x^4 e^{rx}}_{y_p}.$$

Thus *every* solution of our original equation in (8) is the sum of a complementary function and a *particular solution* of the form

$$y_p(x) = A x^3 e^{rx} + B x^4 e^{rx}. \tag{11}$$

Note that the right-hand side in Eq. (11) can be obtained by multiplying each term of our first guess in (9) by the least positive integral power of x (in this case, x^3) that suffices to eliminate duplication between the terms of the resulting trial solution $y_p(x)$ and the complementary function $y_c(x)$ given in (10). This procedure succeeds in the general case.

To simplify the general statement of Rule 2, we observe that to find a particular solution of the nonhomogeneous linear differential equation

$$L y = f_1(x) + f_2(x), \tag{12}$$

it suffices to find *separately* particular solutions $Y_1(x)$ and $Y_2(x)$ of the two equations

$$L y = f_1(x) \quad \text{and} \quad L y = f_2(x), \tag{13}$$

respectively. For linearity then gives

$$L[Y_1 + Y_2] = L Y_1 + L Y_2 = f_1(x) + f_2(x),$$

and therefore $y_p = Y_1 + Y_2$ is a particular solution of Eq. (12). This is the **principle of superposition** for nonhomogeneous linear equations.

Now our problem is to find a particular solution of the equation $L y = f(x)$, where $f(x)$ is a linear combination of products of the elementary functions listed in (4). Thus $f(x)$ can be written as a sum of terms each of the form

$$P_m(x) e^{rx} \cos kx \quad \text{or} \quad P_m(x) e^{rx} \sin kx, \tag{14}$$

where $P_m(x)$ is a polynomial in x of degree m. Note that any derivative of such a term is of the same form but with *both* sines and cosines appearing. The procedure by which we arrived earlier at the particular solution in (11) of Eq. (8) can be generalized to show that the following procedure is always successful.

RULE 2: Method of Undetermined Coefficients

If the function $f(x)$ is of either form in (14), take as the trial solution

$$\begin{aligned} y_p(x) = x^s [& (A_0 + A_1 x + A_2 x^2 + \cdots + A_m x^m) e^{rx} \cos kx \\ & + (B_0 + B_1 x + B_2 x^2 + \cdots + B_m x^m) e^{rx} \sin kx], \end{aligned} \tag{15}$$

where s is the smallest nonnegative integer such that such that no term in y_p duplicates a term in the complementary function y_c. Then determine the coefficients in Eq. (15) by substituting y_p into the nonhomogeneous equation. ∎

In practice we seldom need to deal with a function $f(x)$ exhibiting the full generality in (14). The table in Fig. 3.5.1 lists the form of y_p in various common cases, corresponding to the possibilities $m = 0, r = 0$, and $k = 0$.

On the other hand, it is not uncommon to have

$$f(x) = f_1(x) + f_2(x),$$

where $f_1(x)$ and $f_2(x)$ are different functions of the sort listed in the table in Fig. 3.5.1. In this event we take as y_p the sum of the indicated particular functions, choosing s *separately* for each part to eliminate duplication with the complementary function. This procedure is illustrated in Examples 8 through 10.

$f(x)$	y_p
$P_m = b_0 + b_1 x + b_2 x^2 + \cdots + b_m x^m$	$x^s(A_0 + A_1 x + A_2 x^2 + \cdots + A_m x^m)$
$a \cos kx + b \sin kx$	$x^s(A \cos kx + B \sin kx)$
$e^{rx}(a \cos kx + b \sin kx)$	$x^s e^{rx}(A \cos kx + B \sin kx)$
$P_m(x)e^{rx}$	$x^s(A_0 + A_1 x + A_2 x^2 + \cdots + A_m x^m)e^{rx}$
$P_m(x)(a \cos kx + b \sin kx)$	$x^s[(A_0 + A_1 x + \cdots + A_m x^m) \cos kx$ $+ (B_0 + B_1 x + \cdots + B_m x^m) \sin kx]$

FIGURE 3.5.1. Substitutions in the method of undetermined coefficients.

EXAMPLE 8   Find a particular solution of

$$y^{(3)} + y'' = 3e^x + 4x^2. \tag{16}$$

Solution   The characteristic equation $r^3 + r^2 = 0$ has roots $r_1 = r_2 = 0$ and $r_3 = -1$, so the complementary function is

$$y_c(x) = c_1 + c_2 x + c_3 e^{-x}.$$

As a first step toward our particular solution, we form the sum

$$(Ae^x) + (B + Cx + Dx^2).$$

The part Ae^x corresponding to $3e^x$ does not duplicate any part of the complementary function, but the part $B + Cx + Dx^2$ must be multiplied by x^2 to eliminate duplication. Hence we take

$$y_p = Ae^x + Bx^2 + Cx^3 + Dx^4,$$

$$y_p' = Ae^x + 2Bx + 3Cx^2 + 4Dx^3,$$

$$y_p'' = Ae^x + 2B + 6Cx + 12Dx^2, \quad \text{and}$$

$$y_p^{(3)} = Ae^x + 6C + 24Dx.$$

Substitution of these derivatives in Eq. (16) yields

$$2Ae^x + (2B + 6C) + (6C + 24D)x + 12Dx^2 = 3e^x + 4x^2.$$

The system of equations

$$2A = 3, \quad 2B + 6C = 0,$$
$$6C + 24D = 0, \quad 12D = 4$$

has the solution $A = \frac{3}{2}$, $B = 4$, $C = -\frac{4}{3}$, and $D = \frac{1}{3}$. Hence the desired particular solution is

$$y_p(x) = \tfrac{3}{2}e^x + 4x^2 - \tfrac{4}{3}x^3 + \tfrac{1}{3}x^4.$$ ∎

EXAMPLE 9   Determine the appropriate form for a particular solution of

$$y'' + 6y' + 13y = e^{-3x} \cos 2x.$$

Solution   The characteristic equation $r^2 + 6r + 13 = 0$ has roots $-3 \pm 2i$, so the complementary function is

$$y_c(x) = e^{-3x}(c_1 \cos 2x + c_2 \sin 2x).$$

This is the same form as a first attempt $e^{-3x}(A \cos 2x + B \sin 2x)$ at a particular solution, so we must multiply by x to eliminate duplication. Hence we would take

$$y_p(x) = e^{-3x}(Ax \cos 2x + Bx \sin 2x).$$ ■

EXAMPLE 10   Determine the appropriate form for a particular solution of the fifth-order equation

$$(D - 2)^3(D^2 + 9)y = x^2 e^{2x} + x \sin 3x.$$

Solution   The characteristic equation $(r - 2)^3(r^2 + 9) = 0$ has roots $r = 2, 2, 2, 3i$, and $-3i$, so the complementary function is

$$y_c(x) = c_1 e^{2x} + c_2 x e^{2x} + c_3 x^2 e^{2x} + c_4 \cos 3x + c_5 \sin 3x.$$

As a first step toward the form of a particular solution, we examine the sum

$$[(A + Bx + Cx^2)e^{2x}] + [(D + Ex) \cos 3x + (F + Gx) \sin 3x].$$

To eliminate duplication with terms of $y_c(x)$, the first part—corresponding to $x^2 e^{2x}$—must be multiplied by x^3, and the second part—corresponding to $x \sin 3x$—must be multiplied by x. Hence we would take

$$y_p(x) = (Ax^3 + Bx^4 + Cx^5)e^{2x} + (Dx + Ex^2) \cos 3x + (Fx + Gx^2) \sin 3x.$$ ■

Variation of Parameters

Finally, let us point out the kind of situation in which the method of undetermined coefficients cannot be used. Consider, for example, the equation

$$y'' + y = \tan x, \tag{17}$$

which at first glance may appear similar to those considered in the preceding examples. Not so; the function $f(x) = \tan x$ has *infinitely many* linearly independent derivatives

$$\sec^2 x, \quad 2 \sec^2 x \tan x, \quad 4 \sec^2 x \tan^2 x + 2 \sec^4 x, \quad \dots .$$

Therefore we do not have available a *finite* linear combination to use as a trial solution.

We discuss here the method of **variation of parameters**, which—in principle (that is, if the integrals that appear can be evaluated)—can always be used to find a particular solution of the nonhomogeneous linear differential equation

$$y^{(n)} + p_{n-1}(x)y^{(n-1)} + \cdots + p_1(x)y' + p_0(x)y = f(x), \tag{18}$$

provided that we already know the general solution

$$y_c = c_1 y_1 + c_2 y_2 + \cdots + c_n y_n \tag{19}$$

of the associated homogeneous equation

$$y^{(n)} + p_{n-1}(x)y^{(n-1)} + \cdots + p_1(x)y' + p_0(x)y = 0. \tag{20}$$

Here, in brief, is the basic idea of the method of variation of parameters. Suppose that we replace the constants, or *parameters*, $c_1, c_2, \ldots, c_n$ in the complementary function in Eq. (19) with *variables*: functions $u_1, u_2, \ldots, u_n$ of x. We ask whether it is possible to choose these functions in such a way that the combination

$$y_p(x) = u_1(x)y_1(x) + u_2(x)y_2(x) + \cdots + u_n(x)y_n(x) \tag{21}$$

is a particular solution of the nonhomogeneous equation in (18). It turns out that this *is* always possible.

The method is essentially the same for all orders $n \geq 2$, but we will describe it in detail only for the case $n = 2$. So we begin with the second-order nonhomogeneous equation

$$\blacktriangleright \qquad L[y] = y'' + P(x)y' + Q(x)y = f(x) \tag{22}$$

with complementary function

$$y_c(x) = c_1 y_1(x) + c_2 y_2(x) \tag{23}$$

on some open interval I where the functions P and Q are continuous. We want to find functions u_1 and u_2 such that

$$\blacktriangleright \qquad y_p(x) = u_1(x)y_1(x) + u_2(x)y_2(x) \tag{24}$$

is a particular solution of Eq. (22).

One condition on the two functions u_1 and u_2 is that $L[y_p] = f(x)$. Because two conditions are required to determine two functions, we are free to impose an additional condition of our choice. We will do so in a way that simplifies the computations as much as possible. But first, to impose the condition $L[y_p] = f(x)$, we must compute the derivatives y_p' and y_p''. The product rule gives

$$y_p' = (u_1 y_1' + u_2 y_2') + (u_1' y_1 + u_2' y_2).$$

To avoid the appearance of the second derivatives u_1'' and u_2'', the additional condition that we now impose is that the second sum here must vanish:

$$u_1' y_1 + u_2' y_2 = 0. \tag{25}$$

Then

$$y_p' = u_1 y_1' + u_2 y_2', \tag{26}$$

and the product rule gives

$$y_p'' = (u_1 y_1'' + u_2 y_2'') + (u_1' y_1' + u_2' y_2'). \tag{27}$$

But both y_1 and y_2 satisfy the homogeneous equation

$$y'' + Py' + Qy = 0$$

associated with the nonhomogeneous equation in (22), so

$$y_i'' = -Py_i' - Qy_i \tag{28}$$

for $i = 1, 2$. It therefore follows from Eq. (27) that

$$y_p'' = (u_1' y_1' + u_2' y_2') - P \cdot (u_1 y_1' + u_2 y_2') - Q \cdot (u_1 y_1 + u_2 y_2).$$

In view of Eqs. (24) and (26), this means that

$$y_p'' = (u_1' y_1' + u_2' y_2') - P y_p' - Q y_p;$$

that is, that

$$L[y_p] = u_1' y_1' + u_2' y_2'. \qquad (29)$$

The requirement that y_p satisfy the nonhomogeneous equation in (22)—that is, that $L[y_p] = f(x)$—therefore implies that

$$u_1' y_1' + u_2' y_2' = f(x). \qquad (30)$$

Finally, Eqs. (25) and (30) determine the functions u_1 and u_2 that we need. Collecting these equations, we obtain a system

$$\begin{aligned} u_1' y_1 + u_2' y_2 &= 0, \\ u_1' y_1' + u_2' y_2' &= f(x) \end{aligned} \qquad (31)$$

of two linear equations in the two *derivatives* u_1' and u_2'. Note that the determinant of coefficients in (31) is simply the Wronskian $W(y_1, y_2)$. Once we have solved the equations in (31) for the derivatives u_1' and u_2', we integrate each to obtain the functions u_1 and u_2 such that

$$y_p = u_1 y_1 + u_2 y_2 \qquad (32)$$

is the desired particular solution of Eq. (22). In Problem 63 we ask you to carry out this process explicitly and thereby verify the formula for $y_p(x)$ in the following theorem.

THEOREM: Variation of Parameters

If the nonhomogeneous equation $y'' + P(x)y' + Q(x)y = f(x)$ has complementary function $y_c(x) = c_1 y_1(x) + c_2 y_2(x)$, then a particular solution is given by

$$y_p(x) = -y_1(x) \int \frac{y_2(x) f(x)}{W(x)} \, dx + y_2(x) \int \frac{y_1(x) f(x)}{W(x)} \, dx \qquad (33)$$

where $W = W(y_1, y_2)$ is the Wronskian of the two independent solutions y_1 and y_2 of the associated homogeneous equation. ∎

EXAMPLE 11   Find a particular solution of the equation $y'' + y = \tan x$.

Solution   The complementary function is $y_c(x) = c_1 \cos x + c_2 \sin x$, and we could simply substitute directly in Eq. (33). But it is more instructive to set up the equations in (31) and solve for u_1' and u_2', so we begin with

$$y_1 = \cos x, \qquad y_2 = \sin x,$$
$$y_1' = -\sin x, \qquad y_2' = \cos x.$$

Hence the equations in (31) are

$$(u_1')(\cos x) + (u_2')(\sin x) = 0,$$
$$(u_1')(-\sin x) + (u_2')(\cos x) = \tan x.$$

We easily solve these equations for

$$u_1' = -\sin x \tan x = -\frac{\sin^2 x}{\cos x} = \cos x - \sec x,$$

$$u_2' = \cos x \tan x = \sin x.$$

Hence we take

$$u_1 = \int (\cos x - \sec x)\, dx = \sin x - \ln|\sec x + \tan x|$$

and

$$u_2 = \int \sin x \, dx = -\cos x.$$

(Do you see why we choose the constants of integration to be zero?) Thus our particular solution is

$$y_p(x) = u_1(x)y_1(x) + u_2(x)y_2(x)$$
$$= (\sin x - \ln|\sec x + \tan x|)\cos x + (-\cos x)(\sin x);$$

that is,

$$y_p(x) = -(\cos x)\ln|\sec x + \tan x|. \qquad \blacksquare$$

3.5 Problems

In Problems 1 through 20, find a particular solution y_p of the given equation. In all these problems, primes denote derivatives with respect to x.

1. $y'' + 16y = e^{3x}$

2. $y'' - y' - 2y = 3x + 4$

3. $y'' - y' - 6y = 2\sin 3x$

4. $4y'' + 4y' + y = 3xe^x$

5. $y'' + y' + y = \sin^2 x$

6. $2y'' + 4y' + 7y = x^2$

7. $y'' - 4y = \sinh x$

8. $y'' - 4y = \cosh 2x$

9. $y'' + 2y' - 3y = 1 + xe^x$

10. $y'' + 9y = 2\cos 3x + 3\sin 3x$

11. $y^{(3)} + 4y' = 3x - 1$

12. $y^{(3)} + y' = 2 - \sin x$

13. $y'' + 2y' + 5y = e^x \sin x$

14. $y^{(4)} - 2y'' + y = xe^x$

15. $y^{(5)} + 5y^{(4)} - y = 17$

16. $y'' + 9y = 2x^2 e^{3x} + 5$

17. $y'' + y = \sin x + x\cos x$

18. $y^{(4)} - 5y'' + 4y = e^x - xe^{2x}$

19. $y^{(5)} + 2y^{(3)} + 2y'' = 3x^2 - 1$

20. $y^{(3)} - y = e^x + 7$

In Problems 21 through 30, set up the appropriate form of a particular solution y_p, but do not determine the values of the coefficients.

21. $y'' - 2y' + 2y = e^x \sin x$

22. $y^{(5)} - y^{(3)} = e^x + 2x^2 - 5$

23. $y'' + 4y = 3x\cos 2x$

24. $y^{(3)} - y'' - 12y' = x - 2xe^{-3x}$

25. $y'' + 3y' + 2y = x(e^{-x} - e^{-2x})$

26. $y'' - 6y' + 13y = xe^{3x}\sin 2x$

27. $y^{(4)} + 5y'' + 4y = \sin x + \cos 2x$

28. $y^{(4)} + 9y'' = (x^2 + 1) \sin 3x$

29. $(D - 1)^3(D^2 - 4)y = xe^x + e^{2x} + e^{-2x}$

30. $y^{(4)} - 2y'' + y = x^2 \cos x$

Solve the initial value problems in Problems 31 through 40.

31. $y'' + 4y = 2x$; $y(0) = 1$, $y'(0) = 2$

32. $y'' + 3y' + 2y = e^x$; $y(0) = 0$, $y'(0) = 3$

33. $y'' + 9y = \sin 2x$; $y(0) = 1$, $y'(0) = 0$

34. $y'' + y = \cos x$; $y(0) = 1$, $y'(0) = -1$

35. $y'' - 2y' + 2y = x + 1$; $y(0) = 3$, $y'(0) = 0$

36. $y^{(4)} - 4y'' = x^2$; $y(0) = y'(0) = 1$, $y''(0) = y^{(3)}(0) = -1$

37. $y^{(3)} - 2y'' + y' = 1 + xe^x$; $y(0) = y'(0) = 0$, $y''(0) = 1$

38. $y'' + 2y' + 2y = \sin 3x$; $y(0) = 2$, $y'(0) = 0$

39. $y^{(3)} + y'' = x + e^{-x}$; $y(0) = 1$, $y'(0) = 0$, $y''(0) = 1$

40. $y^{(4)} - y = 5$; $y(0) = y'(0) = y''(0) = y^{(3)}(0) = 0$

41. Find a particular solution of the equation

$$y^{(4)} - y^{(3)} - y'' - y' - 2y = 8x^5.$$

42. Find the solution of the initial value problem consisting of the differential equation of Problem 41 and the initial conditions

$$y(0) = y'(0) = y''(0) = y^{(3)}(0) = 0.$$

43. (a) Write

$$\cos 3x + i \sin 3x = e^{3ix} = (\cos x + i \sin x)^3$$

by Euler's formula, expand, and equate real and imaginary parts to derive the identities

$$\cos^3 x = \tfrac{3}{4} \cos x + \tfrac{1}{4} \cos 3x,$$
$$\sin^3 x = \tfrac{3}{4} \sin x - \tfrac{1}{4} \sin 3x.$$

(b) Use the result of part (a) to find a general solution of

$$y'' + 4y = \cos^3 x.$$

Use trigonometric identities to find general solutions of the equations in Problems 44 through 46.

44. $y'' + y' + y = \sin x \sin 3x$

45. $y'' + 9y = \sin^4 x$

46. $y'' + y = x \cos^3 x$

In Problems 47 through 56, use the method of variation of parameters to find a particular solution of the given differential equation.

47. $y'' + 3y' + 2y = 4e^x$

48. $y'' - 2y' - 8y = 3e^{-2x}$

49. $y'' - 4y' + 4y = 2e^{2x}$

50. $y'' - 4y = \sinh 2x$

51. $y'' + 4y = \cos 3x$

52. $y'' + 9y = \sin 3x$

53. $y'' + 9y = 2 \sec 3x$

54. $y'' + y = \csc^2 x$

55. $y'' + 4y = \sin^2 x$

56. $y'' - 4y = xe^x$

57. You can verify by substitution that $y_c = c_1 x + c_2 x^{-1}$ is a complementary function for the nonhomogeneous second-order equation

$$x^2 y'' + xy' - y = 72x^5.$$

But before applying the method of variation of parameters, you must first divide this equation by its leading coefficient x^2 to rewrite it in the standard form

$$y'' + \frac{1}{x}y' - \frac{1}{x^2}y = 72x^3.$$

Thus $f(x) = 72x^3$ in Eq. (22). Now proceed to solve the equations in (31) and thereby derive the particular solution $y_p = 3x^5$.

In Problems 58 through 62 a nonhomogeneous second-order linear equation and a complementary function y_c are given. Apply the method of Problem 57 to find a particular solution of the equation.

58. $x^2 y'' - 4xy' + 6y = x^3$; $y_c = c_1 x^2 + c_2 x^3$

59. $x^2 y'' - 3xy' + 4y = x^4$; $y_c = x^2(c_1 + c_2 \ln x)$

60. $4x^2 y'' - 4xy' + 3y = 8x^{4/3}$; $y_c = c_1 x + c_2 x^{3/4}$

61. $x^2 y'' + xy' + y = \ln x$; $y_c = c_1 \cos(\ln x) + c_2 \sin(\ln x)$

62. $(x^2 - 1)y'' - 2xy' + 2y = x^2 - 1$; $y_c = c_1 x + c_2(1 + x^2)$

63. Carry out the solution process indicated in the text to derive the variation of parameters formula in (33) from Eqs. (31) and (32).

64. Apply the variation of parameters formula in (33) to find the particular solution $y_p(x) = -x \cos x$ of the nonhomogeneous equation $y'' + y = 2 \sin x$.

3.6 FORCED OSCILLATIONS AND RESONANCE

In Section 3.4 we derived the differential equation

$$mx'' + cx' + kx = F(t) \tag{1}$$

that governs the one-dimensional motion of a mass m that is attached to a spring (with constant k) and a dashpot (with constant c) and is also acted on by an external force $F(t)$. Machines with rotating components commonly involve mass-spring systems (or their equivalents) in which the external force is simple harmonic:

$$F(t) = F_0 \cos \omega t \quad \text{or} \quad F(t) = F_0 \sin \omega t, \tag{2}$$

where the constant F_0 is the amplitude of the periodic force and ω is its circular frequency.

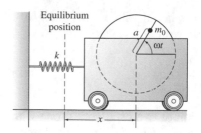

FIGURE 3.6.1. The cart-with-flywheel system.

For an example of how a rotating machine component can provide a simple harmonic force, consider the cart with a rotating vertical flywheel shown in Fig. 3.6.1. The cart has mass $m - m_0$, not including the flywheel of mass m_0. The centroid of the flywheel is off center at a distance a from its center, and its angular speed is ω radians per second. The cart is attached to a spring (with constant k) as shown. Assume that the centroid of the cart itself is directly beneath the center of the flywheel, and denote by $x(t)$ its displacement from its equilibrium position (where the spring is unstretched). Figure 3.6.1 helps us to see that the displacement $\overline{x}$ of the centroid of the combined cart plus flywheel is given by

$$\overline{x} = \frac{(m - m_0)x + m_0(x + a\cos\omega t)}{m} = x + \frac{m_0 a}{m}\cos\omega t.$$

Let us ignore friction and apply Newton's second law $m\overline{x}'' = -kx$, because the force exerted by the spring is $-kx$. We substitute for $\overline{x}$ in the last equation to obtain

$$mx'' - m_0 a\omega^2 \cos\omega t = -kx;$$

that is,

$$mx'' + kx = m_0 a\omega^2 \cos\omega t. \tag{3}$$

Thus the cart with its rotating flywheel acts like a mass on a spring under the influence of a simple harmonic external force with amplitude $F_0 = m_0 a\omega^2$. Such a system is a reasonable model of a front-loading washing machine with the clothes being washed loaded off center. This illustrates the practical importance of analyzing solutions of Eq. (1) with external forces as in (2).

Undamped Forced Oscillations

To study undamped oscillations under the influence of the external force $F(t) = F_0\cos\omega t$, we set $c = 0$ in Eq. (1), and thereby begin with the equation

$$mx'' + kx = F_0\cos\omega t \tag{4}$$

whose complementary function is $x_c = c_1\cos\omega_0 t + c_2\sin\omega_0 t$. Here,

$$\omega_0 = \sqrt{\frac{k}{m}}$$

is the (circular) **natural frequency** of the mass-spring system. Let us assume initially that the external and natural frequencies are *unequal*: $\omega \neq \omega_0$. We substitute $x_p = A\cos\omega t$ in Eq. (4) to find a particular solution. (No sine term is needed in x_p because there is no term involving x' on the left-hand side in Eq. (4).) This gives

$$-m\omega^2 A\cos\omega t + kA\cos\omega t = F_0\cos\omega t,$$

so

$$A = \frac{F_0}{k - m\omega^2} = \frac{F_0/m}{\omega_0^2 - \omega^2}, \tag{5}$$

and thus

$$x_p(t) = \frac{F_0/m}{\omega_0^2 - \omega^2}\cos\omega t. \tag{6}$$

Therefore the general solution $x = x_c + x_p$ is given by

$$x(t) = c_1\cos\omega_0 t + c_2\sin\omega_0 t + \frac{F_0/m}{\omega_0^2 - \omega^2}\cos\omega t, \tag{7}$$

where the constants c_1 and c_2 are determined by the initial values $x(0)$ and $x'(0)$. Equivalently, as in Eq. (12) of Section 3.4, we can rewrite Eq. (7) as

$$x(t) = C \cos(\omega_0 t - \alpha) + \frac{F_0/m}{\omega_0^2 - \omega^2} \cos \omega t, \qquad (8)$$

so we see that the resulting motion is a superposition of two oscillations, one with natural circular frequency ω_0, the other with the frequency ω of the external force.

EXAMPLE 1   Suppose that $m = 1$, $k = 9$, $F_0 = 80$, and $\omega = 5$, so the differential equation in (4) is

$$x'' + 9x = 80 \cos 5t.$$

Find $x(t)$ if $x(0) = x'(0) = 0$.

Solution   Here the natural frequency $\omega_0 = 3$ and the frequency $\omega = 5$ of the external force are unequal, as in the preceding discussion. First we substitute $x_p = A \cos 5t$ in the differential equation and find that $-25A + 9A = 80$, so that $A = -5$. Thus a particular solution is

$$x_p(t) = -5 \cos 5t.$$

The complementary function is $x_c = c_1 \cos 3t + c_2 \sin 3t$, so the general solution of the given nonhomogeneous equation is

$$x(t) = c_1 \cos 3t + c_2 \sin 3t - 5 \cos 5t,$$

with derivative

$$x'(t) = -3c_1 \sin 3t + 3c_2 \cos 3t + 25 \sin 5t.$$

The initial conditions $x(0) = 0$ and $x'(0) = 0$ now yield $c_1 = 5$ and $c_2 = 0$, so the desired particular solution is

$$x(t) = 5 \cos 3t - 5 \cos 5t.$$

As indicated in Fig. 3.6.2, the period of $x(t)$ is the least common multiple 2π of the periods $2\pi/3$ and $2\pi/5$ of the two cosine terms. ∎

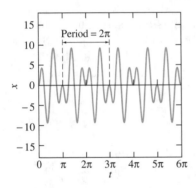

FIGURE 3.6.2. The response $x(t) = 5 \cos 3t - 5 \cos 5t$ in Example 1.

Beats

If we impose the initial conditions $x(0) = x'(0) = 0$ on the solution in (7), we find that

$$c_1 = -\frac{F_0}{m(\omega_0^2 - \omega^2)} \quad \text{and} \quad c_2 = 0,$$

so the particular solution is

$$x(t) = \frac{F_0}{m(\omega_0^2 - \omega^2)} (\cos \omega t - \cos \omega_0 t). \qquad (9)$$

The trigonometric identity $2 \sin A \sin B = \cos(A - B) - \cos(A + B)$, applied with $A = \frac{1}{2}(\omega_0 + \omega)t$ and $B = \frac{1}{2}(\omega_0 - \omega)t$, enables us to rewrite Eq. (9) in the form

$$x(t) = \frac{2F_0}{m(\omega_0^2 - \omega^2)} \sin \tfrac{1}{2}(\omega_0 - \omega)t \sin \tfrac{1}{2}(\omega_0 + \omega)t. \qquad (10)$$

Suppose now that $\omega \approx \omega_0$, so that $\omega_0 + \omega$ is very large in comparison with $|\omega_0 - \omega|$. Then $\sin \frac{1}{2}(\omega_0 + \omega)t$ is a *rapidly* varying function, whereas $\sin \frac{1}{2}(\omega_0 - \omega)t$ is a *slowly* varying function. We may therefore interpret Eq. (10) as a rapid oscillation with circular frequency $\frac{1}{2}(\omega_0 + \omega)$,

$$x(t) = A(t) \sin \tfrac{1}{2}(\omega_0 + \omega)t,$$

but with a slowly varying amplitude

$$A(t) = \frac{2F_0}{m(\omega_0^2 - \omega^2)} \sin \tfrac{1}{2}(\omega_0 - \omega)t.$$

EXAMPLE 2   With $m = 0.1$, $F_0 = 50$, $\omega_0 = 55$, and $\omega = 45$, Eq. (10) gives

$$x(t) = \sin 5t \sin 50t.$$

Figure 3.6.3 shows the corresponding oscillation of frequency $\frac{1}{2}(\omega_0 + \omega) = 50$ that is "modulated" by the amplitude function $A(t) = \sin 5t$ of frequency $\frac{1}{2}(\omega_0 - \omega) = 5$.   ∎

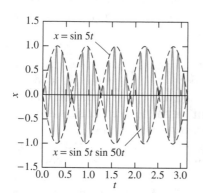

FIGURE 3.6.3. The phenomenon of beats.

A rapid oscillation with a (comparatively) slowly varying periodic amplitude exhibits the phenomenon of *beats*. For example, if two horns not exactly attuned to one another simultaneously play their middle C, one at $\omega_0/(2\pi) = 258$ Hz and the other at $\omega/(2\pi) = 254$ Hz, then one hears a beat—an audible variation in the *amplitude* of the combined sound—with a frequency of

$$\frac{(\omega_0 - \omega)/2}{2\pi} = \frac{258 - 254}{2} = 2 \text{ (Hz)}.$$

Resonance

Looking at Eq. (6), we see that the amplitude A of x_p is large when the natural and external frequencies ω_0 and ω are approximately equal. It is sometimes useful to rewrite Eq. (5) in the form

$$A = \frac{F_0}{k - m\omega^2} = \frac{F_0/k}{1 - (\omega/\omega_0)^2} = \pm\frac{\rho F_0}{k}, \qquad (11)$$

where F_0/k is the **static displacement** of a spring with constant k due to a *constant* force F_0, and the **amplification factor** ρ is defined to be

$$\rho = \frac{1}{|1 - (\omega/\omega_0)^2|}. \qquad (12)$$

It is clear that $\rho \to +\infty$ as $\omega \to \omega_0$. This is the phenomenon of **resonance**— the increase without bound (as $\omega \to \omega_0$) in the amplitude of oscillations of an undamped system with natural frequency ω_0 in response to an external force with frequency $\omega \approx \omega_0$.

We have been assuming that $\omega \neq \omega_0$. What sort of catastrophe should one expect if ω and ω_0 are precisely equal? Then Eq. (4), upon division of each term by m, becomes

$$x'' + \omega_0^2 x = \frac{F_0}{m} \cos \omega_0 t. \qquad (13)$$

Because $\cos \omega_0 t$ is a term of the complementary function, the method of undetermined coefficients calls for us to try

$$x_p(t) = t(A \cos \omega_0 t + B \sin \omega_0 t).$$

We substitute this in Eq. (13), and thereby find that $A = 0$ and $B = F_0/(2m\omega_0)$. Hence the particular solution is

$$x_p(t) = \frac{F_0}{2m\omega_0} t \sin \omega_0 t. \tag{14}$$

The graph of $x_p(t)$ in Fig. 3.6.4 (in which $m = 1$, $F_0 = 100$, and $\omega_0 = 50$) shows vividly how the amplitude of the oscillation theoretically would increase without bound in this case of *pure resonance*, $\omega = \omega_0$. We may interpret this phenomenon as reinforcement of the natural vibrations of the system by externally impressed vibrations at the same frequency.

EXAMPLE 3   Suppose that $m = 5$ kg and that $k = 500$ N/m in the cart with the flywheel of Fig. 3.6.1. Then the natural frequency is $\omega_0 = \sqrt{k/m} = 10$ rad/s; that is, $10/(2\pi) \approx 1.59$ Hz. We would therefore expect oscillations of very large amplitude to occur if the flywheel revolves at about $(1.59)(60) \approx 95$ revolutions per minute (rpm). ■

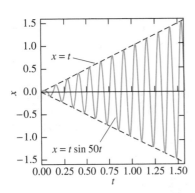

FIGURE 3.6.4. The phenomenon of resonance.

In practice, a mechanical system with very little damping can be destroyed by resonance vibrations. A spectacular example can occur when a column of soldiers marches in step over a bridge. Any complicated structure such as a bridge has many natural frequencies of vibration. If the frequency of the soldiers' cadence is approximately equal to one of the natural frequencies of the structure, then—just as in our simple example of a mass on a spring—resonance will occur. Indeed, the resulting resonance vibrations can be of such large amplitude that the bridge will collapse. This has actually happened—for example, the collapse of Broughton Bridge near Manchester, England, in 1831—and it is the reason for the now-standard practice of breaking cadence when crossing a bridge. Resonance may have been involved in the 1981 Kansas City disaster in which a hotel balcony (called a *skywalk*) collapsed with dancers on it. The collapse of a building in an earthquake is sometimes due to resonance vibrations caused by the ground oscillating at one of the natural frequencies of the structure; this happened to many buildings in the Mexico City earthquake of September 19, 1985. On occasion an airplane has crashed because of resonant wing oscillations caused by vibrations of the engines. It is reported that for some of the first commercial jet aircraft, the natural frequency of the vertical vibrations of the airplane during turbulence was almost exactly that of the mass-spring system consisting of the pilot's head (mass) and spine (spring). Resonance occurred, causing pilots to have difficulty in reading the instruments. Large modern commercial jets have different natural frequencies, so that this resonance problem no longer occurs.

Modeling Mechanical Systems

The avoidance of destructive resonance vibrations is an ever-present consideration in the design of mechanical structures and systems of all types. Often the most important step in determining the natural frequency of vibration of a system is the formulation of its differential equation. In addition to Newton's law $F = ma$, the principle of conservation of energy is sometimes useful for this purpose (as in the derivation of the pendulum equation in Section 3.4). The following kinetic and potential energy formulas are often useful.

1. *Kinetic energy*: $T = \frac{1}{2}mv^2$ for translation of a mass m with velocity v;
2. *Kinetic energy*: $T = \frac{1}{2}I\omega^2$ for rotation of a body of a moment of inertia I with angular velocity ω;
3. *Potential energy*: $V = \frac{1}{2}kx^2$ for a spring with constant k stretched or compressed a distance x;
4. *Potential energy*: $V = mgh$ for the gravitational potential energy of a mass m at height h above the reference level (the level at which $V = 0$), provided that g may be regarded as essentially constant.

EXAMPLE 4 Find the natural frequency of a mass m on a spring with constant k if, instead of sliding without friction, it is a uniform disk of radius a that rolls without slipping, as shown in Fig 3.6.5.

Solution With the preceding notation, the principle of conservation of energy gives

$$\tfrac{1}{2}mv^2 + \tfrac{1}{2}I\omega^2 + \tfrac{1}{2}kx^2 = E$$

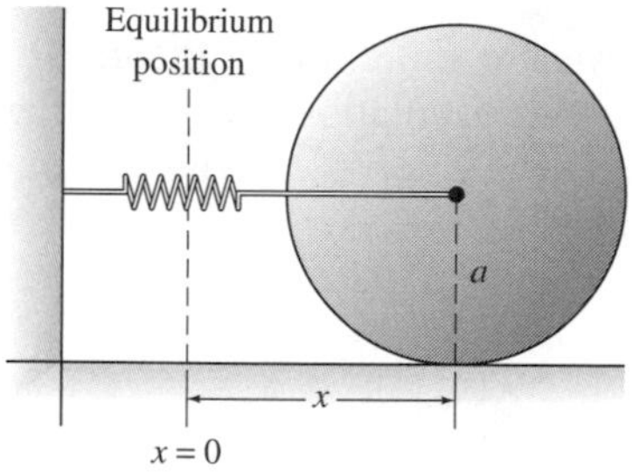

where E is a constant (the total mechanical energy of the system). We note that $v = a\omega$ and recall that $I = ma^2/2$ for a uniform circular disk. Then we may simplify the last equation to

$$\tfrac{3}{4}mv^2 + \tfrac{1}{2}kx^2 = E.$$

Differentiation ($v = x'$, $v' = x''$) now gives

$$\tfrac{3}{2}mx'x'' + kxx' = 0.$$

We divide each term by $\tfrac{3}{2}mx'$ to obtain

$$x'' + \frac{2k}{3m}x = 0.$$

Thus the natural circular frequency is $\omega_0 = \sqrt{2k/(3m)}$, which is $\sqrt{2/3} \approx 0.8165$ times the frequency in the previous situation of sliding without friction. ∎

FIGURE 3.6.5. The rolling disk.

(to the left:)
Equilibrium position

$x = 0$

a

x

EXAMPLE 5 Suppose that a car oscillates vertically as if it were a mass $m = 800$ kg on a single spring (with constant $k = 7 \times 10^4$ N/m), attached to a single dashpot (with constant $c = 2000$ N-s/m). Suppose that this car with the dashpot *disconnected* is driven along a washboard road surface with an amplitude of 5 cm and a wavelength of $L = 10$ m (Fig. 3.6.6). At what car speed will resonance vibrations occur?

Solution We think of the car as a unicycle, as pictured in Fig. 3.6.7. Let $x(t)$ denote the upward displacement of the mass m from its equilibrium position; we ignore the force of gravity, because it merely displaces the equilibrium position as in Problem 9 of Section 3.4. We write the equation of the road surface as

$$y = a\cos\frac{2\pi s}{L} \quad (a = 0.05 \text{ m}, L = 10 \text{ m}). \tag{15}$$

When the car is in motion, the spring is stretched by the amount $x - y$, so Newton's second law, $F = ma$, gives

$$mx'' = -k(x - y);$$

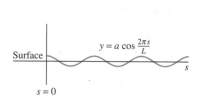

FIGURE 3.6.6. The washboard road surface of Example 5.

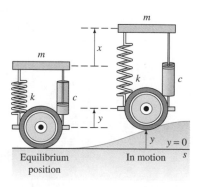

FIGURE 3.6.7. The "unicycle model" of a car.

that is,

$$mx'' + kx = ky \tag{16}$$

If the velocity of the car is v, then $s = vt$ in Eq. (15), so Eq. (16) takes the form

$$mx'' + kx = ka \cos \frac{2\pi vt}{L}. \tag{16'}$$

This is the differential equation that governs the vertical oscillations of the car. In comparing it with Eq. (4), we see that we have forced oscillations with circular frequency $\omega = 2\pi v/L$. Resonance will occur when $\omega = \omega_0 = \sqrt{k/m}$. We use our numerical data to find the speed of the car at resonance:

$$v = \frac{L}{2\pi}\sqrt{\frac{k}{m}} = \frac{10}{2\pi}\sqrt{\frac{7 \times 10^4}{800}} \approx 14.89 \text{ (m/s)};$$

that is, about 33.3 mi/h (using the conversion factor of 2.237 mi/h per m/s).   ■

Damped Forced Oscillations

In real physical systems there is always some damping, from frictional effects if nothing else. The complementary function x_c of the equation

$$mx'' + cx' + kx = F_0 \cos \omega t \tag{17}$$

is given by Eq. (18), (19), or (20) of Section 3.4, depending on whether $c > c_{cr} = \sqrt{4km}$, $c = c_{cr}$, or $c < c_{cr}$. The specific form is not important here. What is important is that, in any case, these formulas show that $x_c(t) \to 0$ as $t \to +\infty$. Thus x_c is a **transient solution** of Eq. (17)—one that dies out with the passage of time, leaving only the particular solution x_p.

The method of undetermined coefficients indicates that we should substitute

$$x(t) = A \cos \omega t + B \sin \omega t$$

in Eq. (17). When we do, collect terms, and equate coefficients of $\cos \omega t$ and $\sin \omega t$, we obtain the two equations

$$(k - m\omega^2)A + c\omega B = F_0, \qquad -c\omega A + (k - m\omega^2)B = 0 \tag{18}$$

that we solve without difficulty for

$$A = \frac{(k - m\omega^2)F_0}{(k - m\omega^2)^2 + (c\omega)^2}, \qquad B = \frac{c\omega F_0}{(k - m\omega^2)^2 + (c\omega)^2}. \tag{19}$$

If we write

$$A \cos \omega t + B \sin \omega t = C(\cos \omega t \cos \alpha + \sin \omega t \sin \alpha) = C \cos(\omega t - \alpha)$$

as usual, we see that the resulting steady periodic oscillation

$$x_p(t) = C \cos(\omega t - \alpha) \tag{20}$$

has amplitude

$$C = \sqrt{A^2 + B^2} = \frac{F_0}{\sqrt{(k - m\omega^2)^2 + (c\omega)^2}}. \tag{21}$$

Now (19) implies that $\sin \alpha = B/C > 0$, so it follows that the phase angle α lies in the first or second quadrant. Thus

$$\tan \alpha = \frac{B}{A} = \frac{c\omega}{k - m\omega^2} \quad \text{with} \quad 0 < \alpha < \pi, \tag{22}$$

so

$$\alpha = \begin{cases} \tan^{-1} \dfrac{c\omega}{k - m\omega^2} & \text{if } k > m\omega^2, \\[2mm] \pi + \tan^{-1} \dfrac{c\omega}{k - m\omega^2} & \text{if } k < m\omega^2 \end{cases}$$

(whereas $\alpha = \pi/2$ if $k = m\omega^2$).

Note that if $c > 0$, then the "forced amplitude"—defined as a function $C(\omega)$ by (21)—always remains finite, in contrast with the case of resonance in the undamped case when the forcing frequency ω equals the critical frequency $\omega_0 = \sqrt{k/m}$. But the forced amplitude may attain a maximum for some value of ω, in which case we speak of *practical resonance*. To see if and when practical resonance occurs, we need only graph C as a function of ω and look for a global maximum. It can be shown (Problem 27) that C is a steadily decreasing function of ω if $c \geq \sqrt{2km}$. But if $c < \sqrt{2km}$, then the amplitude of C attains a maximum value—and so practical resonance occurs—at some value of ω less than ω_0, and then approaches zero as $\omega \to +\infty$. It follows that an underdamped system typically will undergo forced oscillations whose amplitude is:

- Large if ω is close to the critical resonance frequency;
- Close to F_0/k if ω is very small;
- Very small if ω is very large.

EXAMPLE 6 Find the transient motion and steady periodic oscillations of a damped mass-and-spring system with $m = 1$, $c = 2$, and $k = 26$ under the influence of an external force $F(t) = 82 \cos 4t$ with $x(0) = 6$ and $x'(0) = 0$. Also investigate the possibility of practical resonance for this system.

Solution The resulting motion $x(t) = x_{tr}(t) + x_{sp}(t)$ of the mass satisfies the initial value problem

$$x'' + 2x' + 26x = 82 \cos 4t; \quad x(0) = 6, \, x'(0) = 0. \tag{23}$$

Instead of applying the general formulas derived earlier in this section, it is better in a concrete problem to work it directly. The roots of the characteristic equation

$$r^2 + 2r + 26 = (r + 1)^2 + 25 = 0$$

are $r = -1 \pm 5i$, so the complementary function is

$$x_c(t) = e^{-t}(c_1 \cos 5t + c_2 \sin 5t).$$

When we substitute the trial solution

$$x(t) = A \cos 4t + B \sin 4t$$

in the given equation, collect like terms, and equate coefficients of $\cos 4t$ and $\sin 4t$, we get the equations

$$\begin{aligned} 10A + 8B &= 82, \\ -8A + 10B &= 0 \end{aligned}$$

with solution $A = 5$, $B = 4$. Hence the general solution of the equation in (23) is

$$x(t) = e^{-t}(c_1 \cos 5t + c_2 \sin 5t) + 5 \cos 4t + 4 \sin 4t.$$

At this point we impose the initial conditions $x(0) = 6$, $x'(0) = 0$ and find that $c_1 = 1$ and $c_2 = -3$. Therefore, the transient motion and the steady periodic oscillation of the mass are given by

$$x_{tr}(t) = e^{-t}(\cos 5t - 3\sin 5t)$$

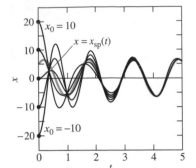

FIGURE 3.6.8. Solutions of the initial value problem in (24) with $x_0 = -20, -10, 0, 10,$ and 20.

and

$$x_{sp}(t) = 5\cos 4t + 4\sin 4t = \sqrt{41}\left(\frac{5}{\sqrt{41}}\cos 4t + \frac{4}{\sqrt{41}}\sin 4t\right)$$
$$= \sqrt{41}\cos(4t - \alpha)$$

where $\alpha = \tan^{-1}\left(\frac{4}{5}\right) \approx 0.6747$.

Figure 3.6.8 shows graphs of the solution $x(t) = x_{tr}(t) + x_{sp}(t)$ of the initial value problem

$$x'' + 2x' + 26x = 82\cos 4t, \quad x(0) = x_0, x'(0) = 0 \tag{24}$$

for the different values $x_0 = -20, -10, 0, 10,$ and 20 of the initial position. Here we see clearly what it means for the transient solution $x_{tr}(t)$ to "die out with the passage of time," leaving only the steady periodic motion $x_{sp}(t)$. Indeed, because $x_{tr}(t) \to 0$ exponentially, within a very few cycles the full solution $x(t)$ and the steady periodic solution $x_{sp}(t)$ are virtually indistinguishable.

To investigate the possibility of practical resonance in the given system, we substitute the values $m = 1$, $c = 2$, and $k = 26$ in (21) and find that the forced amplitude at frequency ω is

$$C(\omega) = \frac{82}{\sqrt{676 - 48\omega^2 + \omega^4}}.$$

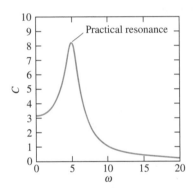

FIGURE 3.6.9. Plot of amplitude C versus external frequency ω.

The graph of $C(\omega)$ is shown in Fig. 3.6.9. The maximum amplitude occurs when

$$C'(\omega) = \frac{-41(4\omega^3 - 96\omega)}{(676 - 48\omega^2 + \omega^4)^{3/2}} = \frac{-164\omega(\omega^2 - 24)}{(676 - 48\omega^2 + \omega^4)^{3/2}} = 0.$$

Thus practical resonance occurs when the external frequency is $\omega = \sqrt{24}$ (a bit less than the mass-and-spring's undamped critical frequency of $\omega_0 = \sqrt{k/m} = \sqrt{26}$).

3.6 Problems

In Problems 1 through 6, express the solution of the given initial value problem as a sum of two oscillations as in Eq. (8). Throughout, primes denote derivatives with respect to time t.

1. $x'' + 9x = 10\cos 2t$; $x(0) = x'(0) = 0$

2. $x'' + 4x = 5\sin 3t$; $x(0) = x'(0) = 0$

3. $x'' + 100x = 15\cos 5t + 20\sin 5t$; $x(0) = 25, x'(0) = 0$

4. $x'' + 25x = 10\cos 4t$; $x(0) = 25, x'(0) = 10$

5. $mx'' + kx = F_0\cos\omega t$ with $\omega \neq \omega_0$; $x(0) = x_0, x'(0) = 0$

6. $mx'' + kx = F_0\cos\omega t$ with $\omega = \omega_0$; $x(0) = 0, x'(0) = v_0$

In Problems 7 through 14, find the steady periodic solution in the form $x_{sp}(t) = C\cos(\omega t - \alpha)$ with $C > 0$. If initial conditions are given, also find the transient solution.

7. $x'' + 4x' + 4x = 10\cos 3t$

8. $x'' + 3x' + 5x = -4\cos 5t$

9. $2x'' + 2x' + x = 3\sin 10t$

10. $x'' + 3x' + 3x = 8\cos 10t + 6\sin 10t$

11. $x'' + 4x' + 5x = 10\cos 3t$; $x(0) = x'(0) = 0$

12. $x'' + 6x' + 13x = 10\sin 5t$; $x(0) = x'(0) = 0$

13. $x'' + 2x' + 6x = 3\cos 10t$; $x(0) = 10, x'(0) = 0$

14. $x'' + 8x' + 25x = 5\cos t + 13\sin t$; $x(0) = 5, x'(0) = 0$

Each of Problems 15 through 18 gives the parameters for a forced mass-spring-dashpot system with equation $mx'' + cx' + kx = F_0\cos\omega t$. Investigate the possibility of practical resonance of this system. In particular, find the amplitude $C(\omega)$ of steady periodic forced oscillations with frequency ω. Sketch the graph of $C(\omega)$ and find the practical resonance frequency ω (if any).

15. $m = 1, c = 2, k = 2, F_0 = 2$

16. $m = 1, c = 4, k = 5, F_0 = 10$

17. $m = 1, c = 6, k = 45, F_0 = 50$

18. $m = 1, c = 10, k = 650, F_0 = 100$

19. A mass weighing 100 lb (mass $m = 3.125$ slugs in fps units) is attached to the end of a spring that is stretched 1 in. by a force of 100 lb. A force $F_0 \cos \omega t$ acts on the mass. At what frequency (in hertz) will resonance oscillations occur? Neglect damping.

20. A front-loading washing machine is mounted on a thick rubber pad that acts like a spring; the weight $W = mg$ (with $g = 9.8$ m/s^2) of the machine depresses the pad exactly 0.5 cm. When its rotor spins at ω radians per second, the rotor exerts a vertical force $F_0 \cos \omega t$ newtons on the machine. At what speed (in revolutions per minute) will resonance vibrations occur? Neglect friction.

21. Figure 3.6.10 shows a mass m on the end of a pendulum (of length L) also attached to a horizontal spring (with constant k). Assume small oscillations of m so that the spring remains essentially horizontal and neglect damping. Find the natural circular frequency ω_0 of motion of the mass in terms of L, k, m, and the gravitational constant g.

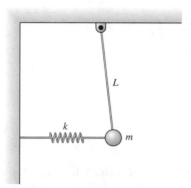

FIGURE 3.6.10. The pendulum-and-spring system of Problem 21.

22. A mass m hangs on the end of a cord around a pulley of radius a and moment of inertia I, as shown in Fig. 3.6.11. The rim of the pulley is attached to a spring (with constant k). Assume small oscillations so that the spring remains essentially horizontal and neglect friction. Find the natural circular frequency of the system in terms of m, a, k, I, and g.

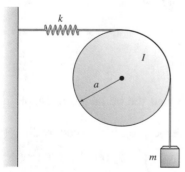

FIGURE 3.6.11. The mass-spring-pulley system of Problem 22.

23. A building consists of two floors. The first floor is attached rigidly to the ground, and the second floor is of mass $m = 1000$ slugs (fps units) and weighs 16 tons

(32000 lb). The elastic frame of the building behaves as a spring that resists horizontal displacements of the second floor; it requires a horizontal force of 5 tons to displace the second floor a distance of 1 ft. Assume that in an earthquake the ground oscillates horizontally with amplitude A_0 and circular frequency ω, resulting in an external horizontal force $F(t) = mA_0\omega^2 \sin \omega t$ on the second floor. (a) What is the natural frequency (in hertz) of oscillations of the second floor? (b) If the ground undergoes one oscillation every 2.25 s with an amplitude of 3 in., what is the amplitude of the resulting forced oscillations of the second floor?

24. A mass on a spring without damping is acted on by the external force $F(t) = F_0 \cos^2 \omega t$. Show that there are *two* values of ω for which resonance occurs, and find both.

25. Derive the steady periodic solution of

$$mx'' + cx' + kx = F_0 \sin \omega t.$$

In particular, show that it is what one would expect—the same as the formula in (20) with the same values of C and ω, except with $\sin(\omega t - \alpha)$ in place of $\cos(\omega t - \alpha)$.

26. Given the differential equation

$$mx'' + cx' + kx = E_0 \cos \omega t + F_0 \sin \omega t$$

—with both cosine and sine forcing terms—derive the steady periodic solution

$$x_{sp}(t) = \frac{\sqrt{E_0^2 + F_0^2}}{\sqrt{(k - m\omega^2)^2 + (c\omega)^2}} \cos(\omega t - \alpha - \beta),$$

where α is defined in Eq. (22) and $\beta = \tan^{-1}(F_0/E_0)$. (*Suggestion*: Add the steady periodic solutions separately corresponding to $E_0 \cos \omega t$ and $F_0 \sin \omega t$ (see Problem 25).)

27. According to Eq. (21), the amplitude of forced steady periodic oscillations for the system $mx'' + cx' + kx = F_0 \cos \omega t$ is given by

$$C(\omega) = \frac{F_0}{\sqrt{(k - m\omega^2)^2 + (c\omega)^2}}.$$

(a) If $c \geq c_{cr}/\sqrt{2}$, where $c_{cr} = \sqrt{4km}$, show that C steadily decreases as ω increases. (b) If $c < c_{cr}/\sqrt{2}$, show that C attains a maximum value (practical resonance) when

$$\omega = \omega_m = \sqrt{\frac{k}{m} - \frac{c^2}{2m^2}} < \omega_0 = \sqrt{\frac{k}{m}}.$$

28. As indicated by the cart-with-flywheel example discussed in this section, an unbalanced rotating machine part typically results in a force having amplitude proportional to the *square* of the frequency ω. (a) Show that the amplitude of the steady periodic solution of the differential equation

$$mx'' + cx' + kx = mA\omega^2 \cos \omega t$$

(with a forcing term similar to that in Eq. (17)) is given by

$$C(\omega) = \frac{mA\omega^2}{\sqrt{(k - m\omega^2)^2 + (c\omega)^2}}.$$

(b) Suppose that $c^2 < 2mk$. Show that the maximum amplitude occurs at the frequency ω_m given by

$$\omega_m = \sqrt{\frac{k}{m}\left(\frac{2mk}{2mk - c^2}\right)}.$$

Thus the resonance frequency in this case is *larger* (in contrast with the result of Problem 27) than the natural frequency $\omega_0 = \sqrt{k/m}$. (*Suggestion*: Maximize the *square* of C.)

Automobile Vibrations

Problems 29 and 30 deal further with the car of Example 5. Its upward displacement function satisfies the equation $mx'' + cx' + kx = cy' + ky$ when the shock absorber is connected (so that $c > 0$). With $y = a \sin \omega t$ for the road surface, this differential equation becomes

$$mx'' + cx' + kx = E_0 \cos \omega t + F_0 \sin \omega t$$

where $E_0 = c\omega a$ and $F_0 = ka$.

29. Apply the result of Problem 26 to show that the amplitude C of the resulting steady periodic oscillation for the car is given by

$$C = \frac{a\sqrt{k^2 + (c\omega)^2}}{\sqrt{(k - m\omega^2)^2 + (c\omega)^2}}.$$

Because $\omega = 2\pi v/L$ when the car is moving with velocity v, this gives C as a function of v.

30. Figure 3.6.12 shows the graph of the amplitude function $C(\omega)$ using the numerical data given in Example 5 (including $c = 3000$ N·s/m). It indicates that, as the car accelerates gradually from rest, it initially oscillates with amplitude slightly over 5 cm. Maximum resonance vibrations with amplitude about 14 cm occur around 32 mi/h, but then subside to more tolerable levels at high speeds. Verify these graphically based conclusions by analyzing the function $C(\omega)$. In particular, find the practical resonance frequency and the corresponding amplitude.

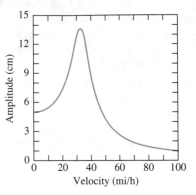

FIGURE 3.6.12. Amplitude of vibrations of the car on a washboard surface.

3.7 Lab 3: Solving ODEs Using Maple

In this tutorial you will learn how to use Maple to solve differential equations analytically (when that is possible) or numerically; then you will learn how to plot solutions.

In the prelab you first learn how to write differential equations in Maple notation.

At the end of the tutorial you are expected to be able to use Maple to do and/or check homework problems.

We start with a quick review of Maple syntax as we need it to solve ODEs. If you are already comfortable with Maple you can skip the material below between the lines of stars and go directly to the prelab.

After the stars are some examples that you should understand **before** you go to lab and some problems you should complete **before** lab.

* *

Writing Differential Equations in Maple Notation

The input to Maple is typed after the prompt > and the output from Maple is **indented**.

The derivative of an expression $y(t)$ with respect to t is denoted by diff(y(t),t).

To enter the ODE $ty' + 5y = \ln t$, that is, $t\left(\dfrac{\partial}{\partial t}y(t)\right) + 5y(t) = \ln(t)$, into Maple we type the line below and hit the ENTER key.

```
> t*diff(y(t),t)+5*y(t)=ln(t);
```

$$t\left(\frac{\partial}{\partial t}y(t)\right) + 5y(t) = \ln(t)$$

The output is a "pretty print" of the equation.

Notice that we refer to y consistently as $y(t)$.

It is useful to give the equation a name and add some spaces for readibility.

When you give something a name in Maple you use the assignment operator :=, that is, a colon : followed by an equal sign = (no spaces in between). In an equation you use just the equal sign =.

Let's go back and change the entry to

```
> ex1 := t*diff(y(t),t) + 5*y(t) = ln(t);
```

$$ex1 := t\left(\frac{\partial}{\partial t}y(t)\right) + 5y(t) = \ln(t)$$

Note that you must end every entry with a semicolon or colon if you want Maple to pay attention. (Use a colon only if you do **not** want to see the result.)

Hit the Enter key after each command that you want Maple to execute.

The second derivative of an expression $y(t)$ with respect to t is denoted by diff(y(t),t,t). Here is how you enter the equation $y'' + 4y = t$.

```
> ex2 := diff(y(t),t,t) + 4*y(t) = t;
```

$$ex2 := \left(\frac{\partial^2}{\partial t^2}y(t)\right) + 4y(t) = t$$

You can guess how to write the third derivative.

Again, when you give something a name in Maple you use the assignment operator :=

```
> b := x^2 + 3*sin(x) - 7;
```

$$b := x^2 + 3\sin(x) - 7$$

Since **b** is the name of an expression we can differentiate it or plot it or evaluate it as $x = 3$, etc.

```
> diff(b,x);
```

$$2x + 3\cos(x)$$

```
> plot(b, x=-Pi..2);
```
This is the command for plotting an expression.

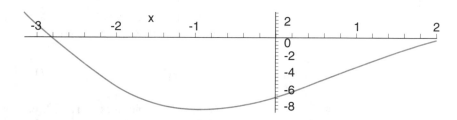

```
> plot({b,diff(b,x)}, x=-Pi..2);
```
this is how you plot two functions on the same graph.

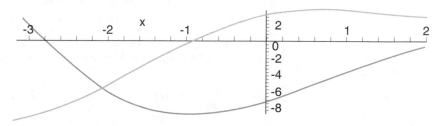

```
> eval(b,x = 3);
```
This is how you evaluate the expression at a point.

$$2 + 3\sin(3)$$

> `evalf(%);`   This is how you approximate your answer by a decimal. The ditto operator, `%`, means the last result.

$$2.423360024$$

Now you should be able to write down equations and have Maple understand them. Some standard functions: abs(x) for $|x|$, sin(x), arcsin(x), arctan(x), sec(x), exp(x) for e^x, cot(x), ln(x), csc(x), etc.

HELP Type **?cotangent** and hit enter if you are not sure how to write that. (Sad fact: Maple says it does not know anything about cotangent. Keep trying other things **?tan** hits the jackpot for trig functions.)

Summary

- end commands with a `;` or `:`
- always use `*` for multiplication
- use `:=` for assignment and `=` for equations
- use y(t) or y(x) not y in your equations
- use diff(y(x),x) not y'(x)

* *

Solving Differential Equations Analytically

Now that you know how to enter equations into Maple we look at some examples using Maple to solve ODEs analytically, that is, expressing the answer in terms of known functions.

Pay attention to the syntax—your turn is coming soon.

We will first ask for the general solution of the ODE $y'' + y = t^5 + \cos(3t)$

> `ex3 := diff(y(t),t,t) + y(t) = t^5 + cos(3*t);`   This names the equation **ex3**.

$$ex3 := \left(\frac{\partial^2}{\partial t^2} y(t) \right) + y(t) = t^5 + \cos(3t)$$

This output is a "pretty print" of the equation.

> `dsolve(ex3,y(t));`   This command tells Maple to solve the equation for the unknown function $y(t)$.

$$y(t) = \sin(t)\_C2 + \cos(t)\_C1 + t^5 - 20t^3 + 120t - \frac{1}{8}\cos(3t)$$

Note that Maple uses _C1, _C2, etc. as constants of integration. It would be nicer if Maple wrote _C2 sin(t) rather than sin(t)_C2 but it doesn't.

Notice that the command syntax isn't very complicated: **dsolve(equation, function)** means "solve the (differential) **equation** for the unknown **function**".

We will now ask for the solution of the ODE $y'' + y = t^5 + \cos(3t)$ satisfying the initial conditions, $y(0) = 1/3$, $y'(0) = 2/5$.

> `dsolve({ex3, y(0) = 1/3, D(y)(0) = 2/5},y(t));`   This command tells Maple to solve the equation for the unknown function $y(t)$.

$$y(t) = -\frac{598}{5} \sin(t) + \frac{11}{24} \cos(t) + t^5 - 20t^3 + 120t - \frac{1}{8} \cos(3t)$$

Important: D stands for derivative so you enter $y'(0) = 2/5$ by saying the derivative of y, D(y), evaluated at 0, D(y)(0)=2/5.

This form of the command is **dsolve({equation, initial conditions}, unknown function);**

Beware: Wiggly brackets are not the same as parentheses!

The solution is free of constants so we can plot it. The answer to dsolve was an equation so...

> `Y1:=rhs(%);` This names the **R**ight **H**and **S**ide of the equation we got as an answer. `%` (the ditto operator) means the previous result.

$$Y1 := -\frac{598}{5}\sin(t) + \frac{11}{24}\cos(t) + t^5 - 20t^3 + 120t - \frac{1}{8}\cos(3t)$$

Now that we have named the solution we can evaluate it. If we want the value of the solution at $t = .32$ we enter

> `eval(Y1,t = .32);`

$$.4892110217$$

Plots of solutions are often useful. To plot the solution we enter

> `plot(Y1,t = -1..1);` This plots the solution for $-1 \le t \le 1$; the notation `t=-1..1` indicates the range of t-values.

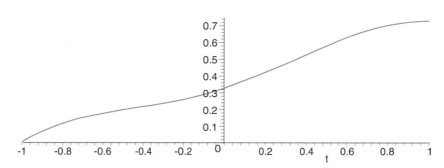

Now it is your turn to write some equations in Maple notation.

Prelab Problems

1. In each part of the problem write down the Maple commands to solve the equation.

(a) $x^2\left(\dfrac{\partial}{\partial x}y(x)\right) + xy(x) - y(x)^2 = 0$

(b) $y' = \dfrac{xy + y^2}{x^2}$

(c) $y'' + y' + y = te^{(-t)}$ Here y' means $\dfrac{\partial}{\partial t}y$

(d) $y'' + 25y = \cos^2 t$ Here y' means $\dfrac{\partial}{\partial t}y$

The answer to 1(a) is given below; you must do the others.

By the way, it is okay to put two commands on the same line; you only have to hit ENTER once.

Answer 1(a) `eq1a:=x^2*diff(y(x),x)+x*y(x)-y(x)^2=0;`
`dsolve(eq1a,y(x));`

2. In each part of the problem write down the Maple commands to solve the equation.

(a) $x^2\left(\dfrac{\partial}{\partial x}y(x)\right) + xy(x) - y(x)^2 = 0,\ y(1) = \dfrac{1}{3}$

(b) $y' = \dfrac{xy + y^2}{x^2},\ y(1) = 2/3$

(c) $y'' + y' + y = te^{(-t)},\ y(0) = 0,\ y'(0) = -1$

(d) $y'' + 25y = \cos^2 t$, $y(0) = 0$, $y'(0) = 0$.

The answer to 2(a) is given below; you must do the others.

Answer 2(a) `dsolve({eq1a,y(1)=1/3},y(x));`

Bring the answers to the prelab problems with you to the lab; you will need them.

Using Maple to Solve Differential Equations

There are 3 problems to be solved in this tutorial, one with several parts. Enter and execute the examples to learn the techniques required.

Open Maple. Before you start typing clear out all previous definitions.

> `restart;`   This is a very important command; it erases Maple's memory.

3. In each part of the problem use your prelab prelab answers to find the answer.
   (a) Find $y(2)$ and plot $y(x)$ for $1 \le x \le 2$ if

$$x^2 \left(\frac{\partial}{\partial x} y(x) \right) + xy(x) - y(x)^2 = 0, \quad y(1) = \frac{1}{3}$$

The answer to 3(a) is given below; you must do the others.

> `eq1a := x^2*diff(y(x), x)+x*y(x)-y(x)^2 = 0;`
This is part of the prelab answer.

`ans3a:=dsolve({eq1a, y(1) = 1/3 }, y(x));`   Also a part of the prelab answer but we have now named the solution so that we can evaluate it and plot it.

`Y3a:=rhs(ans3a); eval(Y3a,x=2); plot(Y3a,x=1..2);`

That is all there is to finding solutions analytically.

$$eq1a := x^2 \left(\frac{\partial}{\partial x} y(x) \right) + xy(x) - y(x)^2 = 0$$

$$ans3a := y(x) = 2\frac{x}{1 + 5x^2}$$

$$Y3a := 2\frac{x}{1 + 5x^2}$$

$$\frac{4}{21}$$

Open a new Maple worksheet by selecting **New** in the **File** menu, Save the file as **initials.mws**, that is, replace the ***.mws** by **fs.mws** if your name is Francis Smith. Use **initials.mws** to record your answers (cut and paste) and then print it out at the end of the lab. (Choose **Print** from the **File** menu on **initials.mws**.)

(b) Find $y(2)$ and plot $y(x)$ for $1 \le x \le 2$ if $y' = \dfrac{xy + y^2}{x^2}$, $y(1) = 2/3$.

(c) Find $y(2)$ and plot $y(t)$ for $0 \le t \le 10$ if $y'' + y' + y = te^{(-t)}$, $y(0) = 0$, $y'(0) = -1$.

(d) Find $y(2)$ and plot $y(t)$ for $0 \le t \le 20$ if $y'' + 25y = \cos^2 t$, $y(0) = 0$, $y'(0) = 0$.

Solving Differential Equations Numerically

Solutions to ODEs are hard to find! Maple does not always succeed. Here is a simple second order linear homogeneous ode: $y'' + y' + x^3 y = 0$.

Look at what happens when we enter the equation into Maple and try to solve it.

> **ex4:= diff(y(x),x,x) + diff(y(x),x) + x^3*y(x)=0;** We enter the equation into Maple and name it.

$$ex4 := \left(\frac{\partial^2}{\partial x^2} y(x)\right) + \left(\frac{\partial}{\partial x} y(x)\right) + x^3 y(x) = 0$$

> **dsolve(ex4,y(x));** Now we ask for the solution.

$$y(x) = \text{DESol}\left(\left\{x^3\_Y(x) + \left(\frac{\partial}{\partial x}\_Y(x)\right) + \left(\frac{\partial^2}{\partial x^2}\_Y(x)\right)\right\}, \{\_Y(x)\}\right)$$

Maple can not solve this and just recopies the problem.

Most differential equations do not have explicit solutions in terms of known functions; the best you can do is to find numerical solutions. Here is how you do that.

We must have initial conditions that are numbers, not symbolic constants. $y(0) = 3$, $y'(0) = -2$ is okay but $y(0) = c$, $y'(0) = n$ is not.

> **ans4:=dsolve({ex4,y(0)=3,D(y)(0)=-2},y(x),numeric);**
The word **numeric** tells Maple to calculate numerically rather than analytically.

$$ans4 := \textbf{proc}(rkf45\_x) \quad \ldots \quad \textbf{end proc}$$

Maple returns a procedure (a type of function) as its answer. To get values from that procedure we enter:

> **ans4(.3);**

$$\left[x = .3, y(x) = 2.48133135015252337, \frac{\partial}{\partial x} y(x) = -1.48654581883813397\right]$$

Now we know the values of y and y' at $x = .3$.

In addition to getting the value of the solution at a point we will want to plot the solution.

Here is the easiest way to do that. We first load a package called **plots**. We only have to do this once a session. (Of course, if we ever restart we will have to reload the package.)

> **with(plots):** That is how packages are loaded.

Use a **colon** after the command rather than a **semicolon** or the screen will fill up with a list of all the new commands available in **plots**.

Warning, the name changecoords has been redefined

(You can ignore the warning that appears.)
Now we can use the **odeplot** command. Here is the syntax for that.

> **odeplot(ans4,[x, y(x)], 0..1);**

This command plots x on the horizontal axis and y on the vertical axis, that is, y versus x.

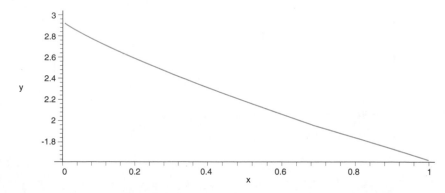

> `odeplot(ans4,[x, diff(y(x),x)], 0..1);` This command plots x on the horizontal axis and y' on the vertical axis, that is, y' versus x.

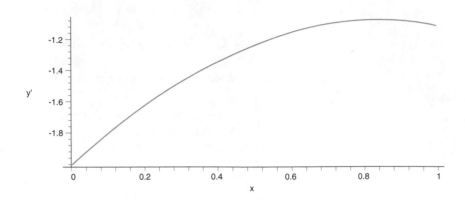

> `odeplot(ans4,[[x, y(x)], [x, diff(y(x),x)]], 0..1);`
This command plots both y and y' versus x. Note that you have an extra set of brackets [ ] in this case.

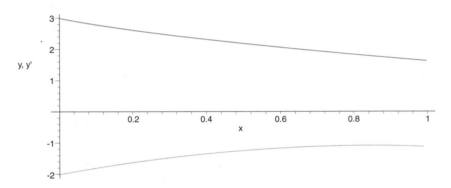

4. Find $y(1)$ and $y'(1)$ if $y'' + \sin(xy) = 0$, $y(0) = 1$, $y'(0) = 2$. Plot $y(t)$ and $y'(t)$ on the same graph over the range $0 \le t \le 1$.

5. A mass m is suspended from an undamped "hard" spring moves according to the equation $mx'' + kx(1 + sx^2) = 0$. (A hard spring is a nonlinear spring; the "stiffness" increases with displacement.) The mass is 2 kilograms and the spring constant k is 3 N/m. The position at time $t = 0$ is 0 and the initial velocity is $+2$ m/sec.

   (a) Assume $s = 0$; find (exactly) the third time that $x(t) = 0$. The first time is $t = 0$.

   (b) Assume $s = 0.4$; find (to three decimal places) the third time that $x(t) = 0$. The first time is $t = 0$.

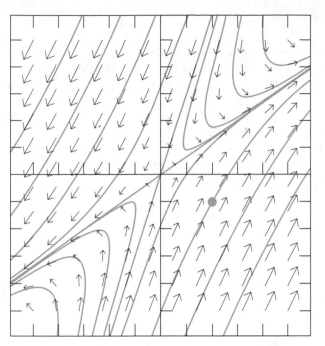

CHAPTER 4

Introduction to Systems of Differential Equations

4.1 FIRST-ORDER SYSTEMS AND APPLICATIONS

In the preceding chapters we have discussed methods for solving an ordinary differential equation that involves only one dependent variable. Many applications, however, require the use of two or more dependent variables, each a function of a single independent variable (typically time). Such a problem leads naturally to a *system* of simultaneous ordinary differential equations. We will usually denote the independent variable by t and the dependent variables (the unknown functions of t) by $x_1, x_2, x_3, \ldots$, or by $x, y, z, \ldots$. Primes will indicate derivatives with respect to t.

We will restrict our attention to systems in which the number of equations is the same as the number of dependent variables (unknown functions). For instance, a system of two first-order equations in the dependent variables x and y has the general form

$$\begin{aligned} f(t, x, y, x', y') &= 0, \\ g(t, x, y, x', y') &= 0, \end{aligned} \tag{1}$$

where the functions f and g are given. A **solution** of this system is a pair $x(t)$, $y(t)$ of functions of t that satisfy both equations identically over some interval of values of t.

For an example of a second-order system, consider a particle of mass m that moves in space under the influence of a force field $\mathbf{F}$ that depends on time t, the position $(x(t), y(t), z(t))$ of the particle, and its velocity $(x'(t), y'(t), z'(t))$. Applying Newton's law $m\mathbf{a} = \mathbf{F}$ componentwise, we get the system

$$\begin{aligned} mx'' &= F_1(t, x, y, z, x', y', z'), \\ my'' &= F_2(t, x, y, z, x', y', z'), \\ mz'' &= F_3(t, x, y, z, x', y', z'), \end{aligned} \tag{2}$$

where F_1, F_2, and F_3 are the three components of the vector function $\mathbf{F}$.

Initial Applications

Examples 1 through 3 further illustrate how systems of differential equations arise naturally in scientific problems.

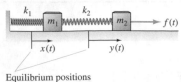

FIGURE 4.1.1. The mass-and-spring system of Example 1.

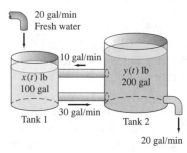

FIGURE 4.1.2. The "free body diagrams" for the system of Example 1.

EXAMPLE 1 Consider the system of two masses and two springs shown in Fig. 4.1.1, with a given external force $f(t)$ acting on the right-hand mass m_2. We denote by $x(t)$ the displacement (to the right) of the mass m_1 from its static equilibrium position (when the system is motionless and in equilibrium and $f(t) = 0$), and by $y(t)$ the displacement of the mass m_2 from its static position. Thus the two springs are neither stretched nor compressed when x and y are zero.

In the configuration in Fig. 4.1.1, the first spring is stretched x units and the second by $y - x$ units. We apply Newton's law of motion to the two "free body diagrams" shown in Fig. 4.1.2; we thereby obtain the system

$$m_1 x'' = -k_1 x + k_2(y - x),$$
$$m_2 y'' = -k_2(y - x) + f(t) \tag{3}$$

of differential equations that the position functions $x(t)$ and $y(t)$ must satisfy. For instance, if $m_1 = 2$, $m_2 = 1$, $k_1 = 4$, $k_2 = 2$, and $f(t) = 40 \sin 3t$ in appropriate physical units, then the system in (3) reduces to

$$2x'' = -6x + 2y,$$
$$y'' = 2x - 2y + 40 \sin 3t. \tag{4}$$

■

EXAMPLE 2 Consider two brine tanks connected as shown in Fig. 4.1.3. Tank 1 contains $x(t)$ pounds of salt in 100 gal of brine and tank 2 contains $y(t)$ pounds of salt in 200 gal of brine. The brine in each tank is kept uniform by stirring, and brine is pumped from each tank to the other at the rates indicated in Fig. 4.1.3. In addition, fresh water flows into tank 1 at 20 gal/min, and the brine in tank 2 flows out at 20 gal/min (so the total volume of brine in the two tanks remains constant). The salt concentrations in the two tanks are $x/100$ pounds per gallon and $y/200$ pounds per gallon, respectively. When we compute the rates of change of the amount of salt in the two tanks, we therefore get the system of differential equations that $x(t)$ and $y(t)$ must satisfy:

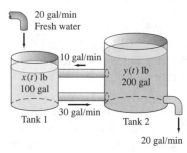

FIGURE 4.1.3. The two brine tanks of Example 2.

$$x' = -30 \cdot \frac{x}{100} + 10 \cdot \frac{y}{200} = -\frac{3}{10}x + \frac{1}{20}y,$$
$$y' = 30 \cdot \frac{x}{100} - 10 \cdot \frac{y}{200} - 20 \cdot \frac{y}{200} = \frac{3}{10}x - \frac{3}{20}y;$$

that is,

$$20x' = -6x + y,$$
$$20y' = 6x - 3y. \tag{5}$$

■

EXAMPLE 3 Consider the electrical network shown in Fig. 4.1.4, where $I_1(t)$ denotes the current in the indicated direction through the inductor L and $I_2(t)$ denotes the current

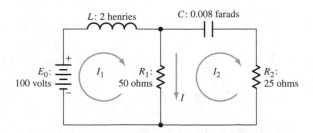

FIGURE 4.1.4. The electrical network of Example 3.

Circuit Element	Voltage Drop
Inductor	$L\dfrac{dI}{dt}$
Resistor	RI
Capacitor	$\dfrac{1}{C}Q$

FIGURE 4.1.5. Voltage drops across common circuit elements.

through the resistor R_2. The current through the resistor R_1 is $I = I_1 - I_2$ in the direction indicated. We recall Kirchhoff's voltage law to the effect that the (algebraic) sum of the voltage drops around any closed loop of such a network is zero. As in Section 3.7, the voltage drops across the three types of circuit elements are those shown in Fig. 4.1.5. We apply Kirchhoff's law to the left-hand loop of the network to obtain

$$2\frac{dI_1}{dt} + 50(I_1 - I_2) - 100 = 0, \tag{6}$$

because the voltage drop from the negative to the positive pole of the battery is -100. The right-hand loop yields the equation

$$125Q_2 + 25I_2 + 50(I_2 - I_1) = 0, \tag{7}$$

where $Q_2(t)$ is the charge on the capacitor. Because $dQ_2/dt = I_2$, differentiation of each side of Eq. (7) yields

$$-50\frac{dI_1}{dt} + 75\frac{dI_2}{dt} + 125I_2 = 0. \tag{8}$$

After dividing Eqs. (6) and (8) by the factors 2 and -25, respectively, we get the system

$$\frac{dI_1}{dt} + 25I_1 - 25I_2 = 50,$$

$$2\frac{dI_1}{dt} - 3\frac{dI_2}{dt} - 5I_2 = 0 \tag{9}$$

of differential equations that the currents $I_1(t)$ and $I_2(t)$ must satisfy. ∎

First-Order Systems

Consider a system of differential equations that can be solved for the highest-order derivatives of the dependent variables that appear, as explicit functions of t and lower-order derivatives of the dependent variables. For instance, in the case of a system of two second-order equations, our assumption is that it can be written in the form

$$\begin{aligned} x_1'' &= f_1(t, x_1, x_2, x_1', x_2'), \\ x_2'' &= f_2(t, x_1, x_2, x_1', x_2'). \end{aligned} \tag{10}$$

It is of both practical and theoretical importance that any such higher-order system can be transformed into a equivalent system of *first-order* equations.

To describe how such a transformation is accomplished, we consider first the "system" consisting of the single nth-order equation

$$x^{(n)} = f(t, x, x', \dots, x^{(n-1)}). \tag{11}$$

We introduce the dependent variables $x_1, x_2, \dots, x_n$ defined as follows:

$$x_1 = x, \quad x_2 = x', \quad x_3 = x'', \quad \dots, \quad x_n = x^{(n-1)}. \tag{12}$$

Note that $x_1' = x' = x_2$, $x_2' = x'' = x_3$, and so on. Hence the substitution of (12) in Eq. (11) yields the system

$$\begin{aligned} x_1' &= x_2, \\ x_2' &= x_3, \\ &\ \ \vdots \\ x_{n-1}' &= x_n, \\ x_n' &= f(t, x_1, x_2, \dots, x_n) \end{aligned} \tag{13}$$

of *n first-order* equations. Evidently, this system is equivalent to the original *n*th-order equation in (11), in the sense that $x(t)$ is a solution of Eq. (11) if and only if the functions $x_1(t), x_2(t), \ldots, x_n(t)$ defined in (12) satisfy the system of equations in (13).

EXAMPLE 4   The third-order equation

$$x^{(3)} + 3x'' + 2x' - 5x = \sin 2t$$

is of the form in (11) with

$$f(t, x, x', x'') = 5x - 2x' - 3x'' + \sin 2t.$$

Hence the substitutions

$$x_1 = x, \quad x_2 = x' = x_1', \quad x_3 = x'' = x_2'$$

yield the system

$$x_1' = x_2,$$
$$x_2' = x_3,$$
$$x_3' = 5x_1 - 2x_2 - 3x_3 + \sin 2t$$

of three first-order equations.   ■

It may appear that the first-order system obtained in Example 4 offers little advantage because we could use the methods of Chapter 3 to solve the original (linear) third-order equation. But suppose that we were confronted with the nonlinear equation

$$x'' = x^3 + (x')^3,$$

to which none of our earlier methods can be applied. The corresponding first-order system is

$$x_1' = x_2,$$
$$x_2' = (x_1)^3 + (x_2)^3, \tag{14}$$

and we will see in Section 4.3 that there exist effective numerical techniques for approximating the solution of essentially any first-order system. So in this case the transformation to a first-order system *is* advantageous. From a practical viewpoint, large systems of higher-order differential equations typically are solved numerically with the aid of the computer, and the first step is to transform such a system into a first-order system for which a standard computer program is available.

EXAMPLE 5   The system

$$2x'' = -6x + 2y,$$
$$y'' = 2x - 2y + 40 \sin 3t \tag{4}$$

of second-order equations was derived in Example 1. Transform this system into an equivalent first-order system.

Solution   Motivated by the equations in (12), we define

$$x_1 = x, \quad x_2 = x' = x_1', \quad y_1 = y, \quad y_2 = y' = y_1'.$$

Then the system in (4) yields the system

$$x_1' = x_2,$$
$$2x_2' = -6x_1 + 2y_1,$$
$$y_1' = y_2,$$
$$y_2' = 2x_1 - 2y_1 + 40 \sin 3t \tag{15}$$

of four first-order equations in the dependent variables x_1, x_2, y_1, and y_2.   ■

Simple Two-Dimensional Systems

The linear second-order differential equation

$$x'' + px' + qx = 0 \tag{16}$$

(with constant coefficients and independent variable t) transforms via the substitutions $x' = y$, $x'' = y'$ into the two-dimensional linear system

$$x' = y,$$
$$y' = -qx - py. \tag{17}$$

Conversely, we can solve this system in (17) by solving the familiar single equation in (16).

EXAMPLE 6 To solve the two-dimensional system

$$x' = -2y,$$
$$y' = \tfrac{1}{2}x, \tag{18}$$

we begin with the observation that

$$x'' = -2y' = -2\left(\tfrac{1}{2}x\right) = -x.$$

This gives the single second-order equation $x'' + x = 0$ with general solution

$$x(t) = A\cos t + B\sin t = C\cos(t - \alpha)$$

where $A = C\cos\alpha$ and $B = C\sin\alpha$. Then

$$y(t) = -\tfrac{1}{2}x'(t) = -\tfrac{1}{2}(-A\sin t + B\cos t)$$
$$= \tfrac{1}{2}C\sin(t - \alpha).$$

The identity $\cos^2\theta + \sin^2\theta = 1$ therefore implies that, for each value of t, the point $(x(t), y(t))$ lies on the ellipse

$$\frac{x^2}{C^2} + \frac{y^2}{(C/2)^2} = 1$$

with semiaxes C and $C/2$. Figure 4.1.6 shows several such ellipses in the xy-plane. ∎

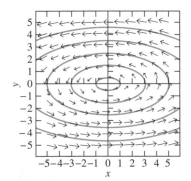

FIGURE 4.1.6. Direction field and solution curves for the system $x' = -2y$, $y' = \tfrac{1}{2}x$ of Example 6.

A solution $(x(t), y(t))$ of a two-dimensional system

$$x' = f(t, x, y),$$
$$y' = g(t, x, y)$$

may be regarded as a parametrization of a **solution curve** or **trajectory** of the system in the xy-plane. Thus the trajectories of the system in (18) are the ellipses of Fig. 4.1.6. The choice of an initial point $(x(0), y(0))$ determines which one of these trajectories a particular solution parametrizes.

The picture showing a system's trajectories in the xy-plane—its so-called *phase plane portrait*—fails to reveal precisely how the point $(x(t), y(t))$ moves along its trajectory. If the functions f and g do not involve the independent variable t, then a direction field—showing typical arrows representing vectors with components (proportional to) the derivatives $x' = f(x, y)$ and $y' = g(x, y)$—can be plotted. Because the moving point $(x(t), y(t))$ has velocity vector $(x'(t), y'(t))$, this direction field indicates the point's direction of motion along its trajectory. For instance, the direction field plotted in Fig. 4.1.6 indicates that each such point moves counterclockwise around its elliptical trajectory. Additional information can be shown in the separate graphs of $x(t)$ and $y(t)$ as functions of t.

EXAMPLE 6
CONTINUED

With initial values $x(0) = 2$, $y(0) = 0$, the general solution in Example 6 yields

$$x(0) = A = 2, \quad y(0) = -\tfrac{1}{2}B = 0.$$

The resulting particular solution is given by

$$x(t) = 2\cos t, \quad y(t) = \sin t.$$

The graphs of the two functions are shown in Fig. 4.1.7. We see that $x(t)$ initially decreases while $y(t)$ increases. It follows that, as t increases, the solution point $(x(t), y(t))$ traverses the trajectory $\tfrac{1}{4}x^2 + y^2 = 1$ in the counterclockwise direction, as indicated by the direction field vectors in Fig. 4.1.6. ∎

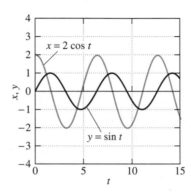

FIGURE 4.1.7. x- and y-solution curves for the initial value problem $x' = -2y$, $y' = \tfrac{1}{2}x$, $x(0) = 2$, $y(0) = 0$.

EXAMPLE 7

To find a general solution of the system

$$\begin{aligned} x' &= y, \\ y' &= 2x + y, \end{aligned} \tag{19}$$

we begin with the observation that

$$x'' = y' = 2x + y = x' + 2x.$$

This gives the single linear second-order equation

$$x'' - x' - 2x = 0$$

with characteristic equation

$$r^2 - r - 2 = (r + 1)(r - 2) = 0$$

and general solution

$$x(t) = Ae^{-t} + Be^{2t}. \tag{20}$$

Then

$$y(t) = x'(t) = -Ae^{-t} + 2Be^{2t}. \tag{21}$$

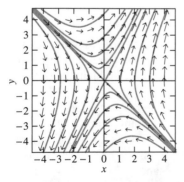

FIGURE 4.1.8. Direction field and solution curves for the system $x' = y$, $y' = 2x + y$ of Example 7.

Typical phase plane trajectories of the system in (19) parametrized by Eqs. (20) and (21) are shown in Fig. 4.1.8. See Problem 23 for further discussion of these trajectories. ∎

EXAMPLE 8   To solve the initial value problem

$$x' = -y,$$
$$y' = (1.01)x - (0.2)y, \tag{22}$$
$$x(0) = 0, \quad y(0) = -1,$$

we begin with the observation that

$$x'' = -y' = -[(1.01)x - (0.2)y] = (-1.01)x - (0.2)x'.$$

This gives the single linear second-order equation

$$x'' + (0.2)x' + (1.01)x = 0$$

with characteristic equation

$$r^2 + (0.2)r + 1.01 = (r + 0.1)^2 + 1 = 0,$$

characteristic roots $-0.1 \pm i$, and general solution

$$x(t) = e^{-t/10}(A \cos t + B \sin t).$$

Then $x(0) = A = 0$, so

$$x(t) = Be^{-t/10} \sin t,$$
$$y(t) = -x'(t) = \tfrac{1}{10}Be^{-t/10} \sin t - Be^{-t/10} \cos t.$$

Finally, $y(0) = -B = -1$, so the desired solution of the system in (22) is

$$x(t) = e^{-t/10} \sin t,$$
$$y(t) = \tfrac{1}{10}e^{-t/10}(\sin t - 10 \cos t). \tag{23}$$

These equations parametrize the spiral trajectory in Fig. 4.1.9; the trajectory approaches the origin as $t \to +\infty$. Figure 4.1.10 shows the x- and y-solution curves given in (23). ∎

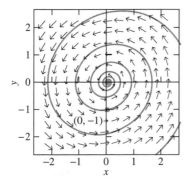

FIGURE 4.1.9. Direction field and solution curve for the system
$x' = -y,$
$y' = (1.01)x - (0.2)y$ of Example 8.

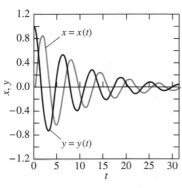

FIGURE 4.1.10. x- and y-solution curves for the initial value problem of Example 8.

When we study linear systems in Chapter 5, we will learn why the superficially similar systems in Examples 6 through 8 have the markedly different trajectories shown in Figs. 4.1.6, 4.1.8, and 4.1.9.

Linear Systems

In addition to practical advantages for numerical computation, the general theory of systems and systematic solution techniques are more easily and more concisely described for first-order systems than for higher-order systems. For instance, consider a *linear* first-order system of the form

$$
\begin{aligned}
x_1' &= p_{11}(t)x_1 + p_{12}(t)x_2 + \cdots + p_{1n}x_n + f_1(t), \\
x_2' &= p_{21}(t)x_1 + p_{22}(t)x_2 + \cdots + p_{2n}x_n + f_2(t), \\
&\vdots \\
x_n' &= p_{n1}(t)x_1 + p_{n2}(t)x_2 + \cdots + p_{nn}x_n + f_n(t).
\end{aligned}
\tag{24}
$$

We say that this system is **homogeneous** if the functions $f_1, f_2, \ldots, f_n$ are all identically zero; otherwise, it is **nonhomogeneous.** Thus the linear system in (5) is homogeneous, whereas the linear system in (15) is nonhomogeneous. The system in (14) is nonlinear because the right-hand side of the second equation is not a linear function of the dependent variables x_1 and x_2.

A **solution** of the system in (24) is an n-tuple of functions $x_1(t)$, $x_2(t)$, ..., $x_n(t)$ that (on some interval) identically satisfy each of the equations in (24). We will see that the general theory of a system of n linear first-order equations shares many similarities with the general theory of a single nth-order linear differential equation. Theorem 1 (proved in the Appendix) is analogous to Theorem 2 of Section 3.2. It tells us that if the coefficient functions p_{ij} and f_j in (24) are continuous, then the system has a unique solution satisfying given initial conditions.

THEOREM 1: Existence and Uniqueness for Linear Systems

Suppose that the functions p_{11}, p_{12}, ..., p_{nn} and the functions f_1, f_2, ..., f_n are continuous on the open interval I containing the point a. Then, given the n numbers $b_1, b_2, \ldots, b_n$, the system in (24) has a unique solution on the entire interval I that satisfies the n initial conditions

$$x_1(a) = b_1, \quad x_2(a) = b_2, \quad \ldots, \quad x_n(a) = b_n. \tag{25}$$

∎

Thus n initial conditions are needed to determine a solution of a system of n linear first-order equations, and we therefore expect a general solution of such a system to involve n arbitrary constants. For instance, we saw in Example 5 that the second-order linear system

$$\begin{aligned} 2x'' &= -6x + 2y, \\ y'' &= 2x - 2y + 40\sin 3t, \end{aligned}$$

which describes the position functions $x(t)$ and $y(t)$ of Example 1, is equivalent to the system of *four* first-order linear equations in (15). Hence four initial conditions would be needed to determine the subsequent motions of the two masses in Example 1. Typical initial values would be the initial positions $x(0)$ and $y(0)$ and the initial velocities $x'(0)$ and $y'(0)$. On the other hand, we found that the amounts $x(t)$ and $y(t)$ of salt in the two tanks of Example 2 are described by the system

$$\begin{aligned} 20x' &= -6x + y, \\ 20y' &= 6x - 3y \end{aligned}$$

of *two* first-order linear equations. Hence the two initial values $x(0)$ and $y(0)$ should suffice to determine the solution. Given a higher-order system, we often must transform it into an equivalent first-order system to discover how many initial conditions are needed to determine a unique solution. Theorem 1 tells us that the number of such conditions is precisely the same as the number of equations in the equivalent first-order system.

4.1 *Problems*

In Problems 1 through 10, transform the given differential equation or system into an equivalent system of first-order differential equations.

1. $x'' + 3x' + 7x = t^2$

2. $x^{(4)} + 6x'' - 3x' + x = \cos 3t$

3. $t^2 x'' + tx' + (t^2 - 1)x = 0$

4. $t^3 x^{(3)} - 2t^2 x'' + 3tx' + 5x = \ln t$

5. $x^{(3)} = (x')^2 + \cos x$

6. $x'' - 5x + 4y = 0$, $y'' + 4x - 5y = 0$

7. $x'' = -\dfrac{kx}{(x^2 + y^2)^{3/2}}$, $y'' = -\dfrac{ky}{(x^2 + y^2)^{3/2}}$

8. $x'' + 3x' + 4x - 2y = 0$, $y'' + 2y' - 3x + y = \cos t$

9. $x'' = 3x - y + 2z$, $y'' = x + y - 4z$, $z'' = 5x - y - z$

10. $x'' = (1 - y)x$, $y'' = (1 - x)y$

Use the method of Examples 6, 7, and 8 to find general solutions of the systems in Problems 11 through 20. If initial conditions are given, find the corresponding particular solutions.

11. $x' = y, y' = -x$

12. $x' = y, y' = x$

13. $x' = -2y, y' = 2x; x(0) = 1, y(0) = 0$

14. $x' = 10y, y' = -10x; x(0) = 3, y(0) = 4$

15. $x' = \frac{1}{2}y, y' = -8x$

16. $x' = 8y, y' = -2x$

17. $x' = y, y' = 6x - y; x(0) = 1, y(0) = 2$

18. $x' = -y, y' = 10x - 7y; x(0) = 2, y(0) = -7$

19. $x' = -y, y' = 13x + 4y; x(0) = 0, y(0) = 3$

20. $x' = y, y' = -9x + 6y$

21. (a) Calculate $[x(t)]^2 + [y(t)]^2$ to show that the trajectories of the system $x' = y, y' = -x$ of Problem 11 are circles. (b) Calculate $[x(t)]^2 - [y(t)]^2$ to show that the trajectories of the system $x' = y, y' = x$ of Problem 12 are hyperbolas.

22. (a) Beginning with the general solution of the system $x' = -2y, y' = 2x$ of Problem 13, calculate $x^2 + y^2$ to show that the trajectories are circles. (b) Show similarly that the trajectories of the system $x' = \frac{1}{2}y, y' = -8x$ of Problem 15 are ellipses with equations of the form $16x^2 + y^2 = C^2$.

23. First solve Eqs. (20) and (21) for e^{-t} and e^{2t} in terms of $x(t), y(t)$, and the constants A and B. Then substitute the results in $(e^{2t})(e^{-t})^2 = 1$ to show that the trajectories of the system $x' = y, y' = 2x + y$ in Example 7 satisfy an equation of the form

$$4x^3 - 3xy^2 + y^3 = C \quad \text{(constant)}.$$

Then show that $C = 0$ yields the straight lines $y = -x$ and $y = 2x$ that are visible in Fig. 4.1.8.

24. Derive the equations

$$m_1 x_1'' = -(k_1 + k_2)x_1 + k_2 x_2,$$
$$m_2 x_2'' = k_2 x_1 - (k_2 + k_3)x_2$$

for the displacements (from equilibrium) of the two masses shown in Fig. 4.1.11.

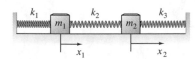

FIGURE 4.1.11. The system of Problem 24.

25. Two particles each of mass m are attached to a string under (constant) tension T, as indicated in Fig. 4.1.12. Assume that the particles oscillate vertically (that is, parallel to the y-axis) with amplitudes so small that the sines of the angles shown are accurately approximated by their tangents. Show that the displacements y_1 and y_2 satisfy the equations

$$ky_1'' = -2y_1 + y_2, \quad ky_2'' = y_1 - 2y_2$$

where $k = mL/T$.

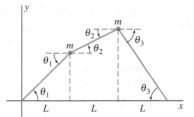

FIGURE 4.1.12. The mechanical system of Problem 25.

26. Three 100-gal fermentation vats are connected as indicated in Fig. 4.1.13, and the mixtures in each tank are kept uniform by stirring. Denote by $x_i(t)$ the amount (in pounds) of alcohol in tank T_i at time t ($i = 1, 2, 3$). Suppose that the mixture circulates between the tanks at the rate of 10 gal/min. Derive the equations

$$10x_1' = -x_1 \qquad + x_3$$
$$10x_2' = \quad x_1 - x_2$$
$$10x_3' = \qquad x_2 - x_3.$$

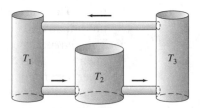

FIGURE 4.1.13. The fermentation tanks of Problem 26.

27. Set up a system of first-order differential equations for the currents in the electrical circuit shown in Fig. 4.1.14.

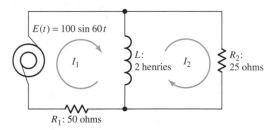

FIGURE 4.1.14. The electrical circuit of Problem 27.

28. Repeat Problem 27, except with the generator replaced with a battery supplying an emf of 100 V and with the inductor replaced with a 1-millifarad (mF) capacitor.

29. A particle of mass m moves in the plane with coordinates $(x(t), y(t))$ under the influence of a force that is directed toward the origin and has magnitude $k/(x^2 + y^2)$—an inverse-square central force field. Show that

$$mx'' = -\frac{kx}{r^3} \quad \text{and} \quad my'' = -\frac{ky}{r^3},$$

where $r = \sqrt{x^2 + y^2}$.

30. Suppose that a projectile of mass m moves in a vertical plane in the atmosphere near the surface of the earth under the influence of two forces: a downward gravitational force of magnitude mg, and a resistive force $\mathbf{F}_R$ that is directed opposite to the velocity vector $\mathbf{v}$ and has magnitude kv^2 (where $v = |\mathbf{v}|$ is the speed of the projectile; see Fig. 4.1.15). Show that the equations of motion of the projectile are

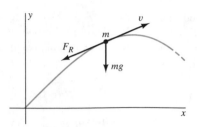

FIGURE 4.1.15. The trajectory of the projectile of Problem 30.

$$mx'' = -kvx', \quad my'' = -kvy' - mg,$$

where $v = \sqrt{(x')^2 + (y')^2}$.

31. Suppose that a particle with mass m and electrical charge q moves in the xy-plane under the influence of the magnetic field $\mathbf{B} = B\mathbf{k}$ (thus a uniform field parallel to the z-axis), so the force on the particle is $\mathbf{F} = q\mathbf{v} \times \mathbf{B}$ if its velocity is $\mathbf{v}$. Show that the equations of motion of the particle are

$$mx'' = +qBy', \quad my'' = -qBx'.$$

4.2 THE METHOD OF ELIMINATION

The most elementary approach to linear systems of differential equations involves the elimination of dependent variables by appropriately combining pairs of equations. The object of this procedure is to eliminate dependent variables in succession until there remains only a single equation containing only one dependent variable. This remaining equation will usually be a linear equation of high order and can frequently be solved by the methods of Chapter 3. After its solution has been found, the other dependent variables can be found in turn, using either the original differential equations or those that have appeared in the elimination process.

The *method of elimination* for linear differential systems is quite similar to the solution of linear algebraic equations by elimination of the variables until only one remains. It is most convenient in the case of manageably small systems: those containing no more than two or three equations. For such systems the method of elimination provides a simple and concrete approach that requires little preliminary theory or formal machinery. But for larger systems of differential equations, as well as for theoretical discussion, the matrix methods of Chapter 5 are preferable.

EXAMPLE 1   Find the particular solution of the system

$$x' = 4x - 3y, \quad y' = 6x - 7y \tag{1}$$

that satisfies the initial conditions $x(0) = 2$, $y(0) = -1$.

Solution   If we solve the second equation in (1) for x, we get

$$x = \tfrac{1}{6}y' + \tfrac{7}{6}y, \tag{2}$$

so that

$$x' = \tfrac{1}{6}y'' + \tfrac{7}{6}y'. \tag{3}$$

We then substitute these expressions for x and x' in the first equation of the system in (1); this yields

$$\tfrac{1}{6}y'' + \tfrac{7}{6}y' = 4\left(\tfrac{1}{6}y' + \tfrac{7}{6}y\right) - 3y,$$

which we simplify to

$$y'' + 3y' - 10y = 0.$$

This second-order linear equation has characteristic equation

$$r^2 + 3r - 10 = (r - 2)(r + 5) = 0,$$

so its general solution is

$$y(t) = c_1 e^{2t} + c_2 e^{-5t}. \qquad (4)$$

Next, substitution of (4) in (2) gives

$$x(t) = \tfrac{1}{6}\left(2c_1 e^{2t} - 5c_2 e^{-5t}\right) + \tfrac{7}{6}\left(c_1 e^{2t} + c_2 e^{-5t}\right);$$

that is,

$$x(t) = \tfrac{3}{2}c_1 e^{2t} + \tfrac{1}{3}c_2 e^{-5t}. \qquad (5)$$

Thus Eqs. (4) and (5) constitute the general solution of the system in (1). The given initial conditions imply that

$$x(0) = \tfrac{3}{2}c_1 + \tfrac{1}{3}c_2 = 2$$

and that

$$y(0) = c_1 + c_2 = -1;$$

these equations are readily solved for $c_1 = 2$ and $c_2 = -3$. Hence the desired solution is

$$x(t) = 3e^{2t} - e^{-5t}, \qquad y(t) = 2e^{2t} - 3e^{-5t}.$$

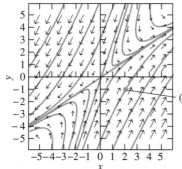

FIGURE 4.2.1. Direction field and solution curves for the system $x' = 4x - 3y$, $y' = 6x - 7y$ of Example 1.

Figure 4.2.1 shows this and other typical solution curves parametrized by the equations $x(t) = \tfrac{3}{2}c_1 e^{2t} + \tfrac{1}{3}c_2 e^{-5t}$, $y(t) = c_1 e^{2t} + c_2 e^{-5t}$ with different values of the arbitrary constants c_1 and c_2. We see two families of curves resembling hyperbolas sharing the same pair of (oblique) asymptotes. ∎

Remark: The general solution defined by Eqs. (4) and (5) may be regarded as the pair or vector $(x(t), y(t))$. Recalling the componentwise addition of vectors (and multiplication of vectors by scalars), we can write the general solution in (4) and (5) in the form

$$(x(t), y(t)) = \left(\tfrac{3}{2}c_1 e^{2t} + \tfrac{1}{3}c_2 e^{-5t}, c_1 e^{2t} + c_2 e^{-5t}\right)$$

$$= c_1\left(\tfrac{3}{2}e^{2t}, e^{2t}\right) + c_2\left(\tfrac{1}{3}e^{-5t}, e^{-5t}\right).$$

This expression presents the general solution of the system in (1) as a linear combination of the two particular solutions

$$(x_1, y_1) = \left(\tfrac{3}{2}e^{2t}, e^{2t}\right) \quad \text{and} \quad (x_2, y_2) = \left(\tfrac{1}{3}e^{-5t}, e^{-5t}\right). \qquad ∎$$

4.2 Problems

Find general solutions of the linear systems in Problems 1 through 20. If initial conditions are given, find the particular solution that satisfies them.

1. $x' = -x + 3y$, $y' = 2y$
2. $x' = x - 2y$, $y' = 2x - 3y$
3. $x' = -3x + 2y$, $y' = -3x + 4y$; $x(0) = 0$, $y(0) = 2$
4. $x' = 3x - y$, $y' = 5x - 3y$; $x(0) = 1$, $y(0) = -1$
5. $x' = -3x - 4y$, $y' = 2x + y$
6. $x' = x + 9y$, $y' = -2x - 5y$; $x(0) = 3$, $y(0) = 2$
7. $x' = 4x + y + 2t$, $y' = -2x + y$
8. $x' = 2x + y$, $y' = x + 2y - e^{2t}$
9. $x' = 2x - 3y + 2\sin 2t$, $y' = x - 2y - \cos 2t$
10. $x' + 2y' = 4x + 5y$, $2x' - y' = 3x$; $x(0) = 1$, $y(0) = -1$
11. $2y' - x' = x + 3y + e^t$, $3x' - 4y' = x - 15y + e^{-t}$
12. $x'' = 6x + 2y$, $y'' = 3x + 7y$
13. $x'' = -5x + 2y$, $y'' = 2x - 8y$

14. $x'' = -4x + \sin t, \ y'' = 4x - 8y$

15. $x'' - 3y' - 2x = 0, \ y'' + 3x' - 2y = 0$

16. $x'' + 13y' - 4x = 6\sin t, \ y'' - 2x' - 9y = 0$

17. $x'' + y'' - 3x' - y' - 2x + 2y = 0,$
$2x'' + 3y'' - 9x' - 2y' - 4x + 6y = 0$

18. $x' = x + 2y + z, \ y' = 6x - y, \ z' = -x - 2y - z$

19. $x' = 4x - 2y, \ y' = -4x + 4y - 2z, \ z' = -4y + 4z$

20. $x' = y + z + e^{-t}, \ y' = x + z, \ z' = x + y$ (*Suggestion:* Solve the characteristic equation by inspection.)

21. Suppose that $L_1 = a_1 D^2 + b_1 D + C_1$ and $L_2 = a_2 D^2 + b_2 D + c_2$, where the coefficients are all constants, and that $x(t)$ is a twice differentiable function. Verify that $L_1 L_2 x = L_2 L_1 x$.

22. Suppose that $L_1 x = t D x + x$ and that $L_2 x = Dx + tx$. Show that $L_1 L_2 x \neq L_2 L_1 x$. Thus linear operators with *variable* coefficients generally do not commute.

Show that the systems in Problems 23 through 25 are degenerate. In each problem determine—by attempting to solve the system—whether it has infinitely many solutions or no solutions.

23. $(D + 2)x + (D + 2)y = e^{-3t}$
$(D + 3)x + (D + 3)y = e^{-2t}$

24. $(D + 2)x + (D + 2)y = t$
$(D + 3)x + (D + 3)y = t^2$

25. $(D^2 + 5D + 6)x + D(D + 2)y = 0$
$(D + 3)x + Dy = 0$

In Problems 26 through 29, first calculate the operational determinant, then attempt to solve the given system in order to determine the number of arbitrary constants that appear in its general solution.

26. $(D^2 + 1)x + D^2 y = 2e^{-t}$
$(D^2 - 1)x + D^2 y = 0$

27. $(D^2 + 1)x + (D^2 + 2)y = 2e^{-t}$
$(D^2 - 1)x + D^2 y = 0$

28. $(D^2 + D)x + D^2 y = 2e^{-t}$
$(D^2 - 1)x + (D^2 - D)y = 0$

29. $(D^2 + 1)x - D^2 y = 2e^{-t}$
$(D^2 - 1)x + D^2 y = 0$

30. Suppose that the salt concentration in each of the two brine tanks of Example 2 of Section 4.1 initially ($t = 0$) is 0.5 lb/gal. Then solve the system in Eq. (5) there to find the amounts $x(t)$ and $y(t)$ of salt in the two tanks at time t.

31. Suppose that the electrical network of Example 3 of Section 4.1 is initially open—no currents are flowing. Assume that it is closed at time $t = 0$; solve the system in Eq. (9) there to find $I_1(t)$ and $I_2(t)$.

32. Repeat Problem 31, except use the electrical network of Problem 27 of Section 4.1.

33. Repeat Problem 31, except use the electrical network of Problem 28 of Section 4.1. Assume that $I_1(0) = 2$ and $Q(0) = 0$, so that at time $t = 0$ there is no charge on the capacitor.

34. Three 100-gal brine tanks are connected as indicated in Fig. 4.1.13 of Section 4.1. Assume that the first tank initially contains 100 lb of salt, whereas the other two are filled with fresh water. Find the amounts of salt in each of the three tanks at time t. (*Suggestion:* Examine the equations to be derived in Problem 26 of Section 4.1.)

35. From Problem 31 of Section 4.1, recall the equations of motion

$$mx'' = qBy', \quad my'' = -qBx'$$

for a particle of mass m and electrical charge q under the influence of the uniform magnetic field $\mathbf{B} = B\mathbf{k}$. Suppose that the initial conditions are $x(0) = r_0$, $y(0) = 0$, $x'(0) = 0$, and $y'(0) = -\omega r_0$ where $\omega = qB/m$. Show that the trajectory of the particle is a circle of radius r_0.

36. If, in addition to the magnetic field $\mathbf{B} = B\mathbf{k}$, the charged particle of Problem 35 moves with velocity $\mathbf{v}$ under the influence of a uniform electric field $\mathbf{E} = E\mathbf{i}$, then the force acting on it is $\mathbf{F} = q(\mathbf{E} + \mathbf{v} \times \mathbf{B})$. Assume that the particle starts from rest at the origin. Show that its trajectory is the cycloid

$$x = a(1 - \cos \omega t), \quad y = -a(\omega t - \sin \omega t)$$

where $a = E/(\omega B)$ and $\omega = qB/m$. The graph of such a cycloid is shown in Fig. 4.2.2.

FIGURE 4.2.2. The cycloidal path of the particle of Problem 36.

37. In the mass-and-spring system of Example 3, suppose instead that $m_1 = 2$, $m_2 = 0.5$, $k_1 = 75$, and $k_2 = 25$. (a) Find the general solution of the equations of motion of the system. In particular, show that its natural frequencies are $\omega_1 = 5$ and $\omega_2 = 5\sqrt{3}$. (b) Describe the natural modes of oscillation of the system.

38. Consider the system of two masses and three springs shown in Fig. 4.2.3. Derive the equations of motion

$$m_1 x'' = -(k_1 + k_2)x + k_2 y$$
$$m_2 y'' = \qquad k_2 x - (k_2 + k_3)y.$$

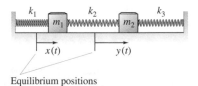

Equilibrium positions

FIGURE 4.2.3. The mechanical system of Problem 38.

In Problems 39 through 43, find the general solution of the system in Problem 38 with the given masses and spring constants. Find the natural frequencies of the mass-and-spring system and describe its natural mode of oscillation.

39. $m_1 = 4, m_2 = 2, k_1 = 8, k_2 = 4, k_3 = 0$

40. $m_1 = 2, m_2 = 1, k_1 = 100, k_2 = 50, k_3 = 0$

41. $m_1 = 1, m_2 = 1, k_1 = 1, k_2 = 4, k_3 = 1$

42. $m_1 = 1, m_2 = 2, k_1 = 1, k_2 = 2, k_3 = 2$

43. $m_1 = 1, m_2 = 1, k_1 = 1, k_2 = 2, k_3 = 1$

44. $m_1 = 1, m_2 = 1, k_1 = 2, k_2 = 1, k_3 = 2$

45. $m_1 = 1, m_2 = 2, k_1 = 2, k_2 = 4, k_3 = 4$

46. $m_1 = 1, m_2 = 1, k_1 = 4, k_2 = 6, k_3 = 4$

47. (a) For the system shown in Fig. 4.2.4, derive the equations of motion

$$mx'' = -2kx + ky$$
$$my'' = kx - 2ky + kz$$
$$mz'' = ky - 2kz.$$

(b) Assume that $m = k = 1$. Show that the natural frequencies of oscillation of the system are

$$\omega_1 = \sqrt{2}, \ \omega_2 = \sqrt{2 - \sqrt{2}}, \text{ and } \omega_3 = \sqrt{2 + \sqrt{2}}.$$

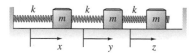

FIGURE 4.2.4. The mechanical system of Problem 47.

48. Suppose that the trajectory $(x(t), y(t))$ of a particle moving in the plane satisfies the initial value problem

$$x'' - 2y' + 3x = 0,$$
$$y'' + 2x' + 3y = 0;$$
$$x(0) = 4, \quad y(0) = x'(0) = y'(0) = 0.$$

Solve this problem. You should obtain

$$x(t) = 3\cos t + \cos 3t,$$
$$y(t) = 3\sin t - \sin 3t.$$

Verify that these equations describe the *hypocycloid* traced by a point $P(x, y)$ fixed on the circumference of a circle of radius $b = 1$ that rolls around inside a circle of radius $a = 4$. If P begins at $A(a, 0)$ when $t = 0$, then the parameter t represents the angle AOC shown in Fig. 4.2.5.

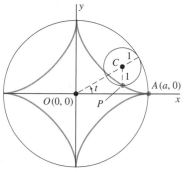

FIGURE 4.2.5. The hypocycloid of Problem 48.

4.3 NUMERICAL METHODS FOR SYSTEMS

We now discuss the numerical approximation of solutions of systems of differential equations. Our goal is to apply the methods of Sections 2.4 through 2.6 to the initial value problem

$$\mathbf{x}' = \mathbf{f}(t, \mathbf{x}), \quad \mathbf{x}(t_0) = \mathbf{x}_0 \tag{1}$$

for a system of m first-order differential equations. In (1) the independent variable is the scalar t, and

$$\mathbf{x} = (x_1, x_2, \ldots, x_m) \quad \text{and} \quad \mathbf{f} = (f_1, f_2, \ldots, f_m)$$

are vector-valued functions. If the component functions of $\mathbf{f}$ and their first-order partial derivatives are all continuous in a neighborhood of the point $(t_0, \mathbf{x}_0)$, then Theorems 3 and 4 of the Appendix guarantee the existence and uniqueness of a solution $\mathbf{x} = \mathbf{x}(t)$ of (1) on some subinterval [of the t-axis] containing t_0. With this assurance we can proceed to discuss the numerical approximation of this solution.

Beginning with step size h, we want to approximate the values of $\mathbf{x}(t)$ at the points $t_1, t_2, t_3, \ldots$, where $t_{n+1} = t_n + h$ for $n \geq 0$. Suppose that we have already computed the *approximations*

$$\mathbf{x}_1, \quad \mathbf{x}_2, \quad \mathbf{x}_3, \quad \ldots, \quad \mathbf{x}_n$$

to the *actual values*

$$\mathbf{x}(t_1), \quad \mathbf{x}(t_2), \quad \mathbf{x}(t_3), \quad \ldots, \quad \mathbf{x}(t_n)$$

of the exact solution of the system in (1). We can then make the step from $\mathbf{x}_n$ to the next approximation $\mathbf{x}_{n+1} \approx \mathbf{x}(t_{n+1})$ by any one of the methods of Sections 2.4 through 2.6. Essentially all that is required is to write the iterative formula of the selected method in the vector notation of the present discussion.

Euler Methods for Systems

For example, the iterative formula of Euler's method for systems is

$$\mathbf{x}_{n+1} = \mathbf{x}_n + h\mathbf{f}(t, \mathbf{x}_n). \tag{2}$$

To examine the case $m = 2$ of a pair of first-order differential equations, let us write

$$\mathbf{x} = \begin{bmatrix} x \\ y \end{bmatrix} \quad \text{and} \quad \mathbf{f} = \begin{bmatrix} f \\ g \end{bmatrix}.$$

Then the initial value problem in (1) is

$$
\begin{aligned}
x' &= f(t, x, y), & x(t_0) &= x_0, \\
y' &= g(t, x, y), & y(t_0) &= y_0,
\end{aligned}
\tag{3}
$$

and the scalar components of the vector formula in (2) are

$$
\begin{aligned}
x_{n+1} &= x_n + hf(t_n, x_n, y_n), \\
y_{n+1} &= y_n + hg(t_n, x_n, y_n).
\end{aligned}
\tag{4}
$$

Note that each iterative formula in (4) has the form of a single Euler iteration, but with y_n inserted like a parameter in the first formula (for x_{n+1}) and with x_n inserted like a parameter in the second formula (for y_{n+1}). The generalization to the system in (3) of each of the other methods in Sections 2.4 through 2.6 follows a similar pattern.

The improved Euler method for systems consists at each step of calculating first the predictor

$$\mathbf{u}_{n+1} = \mathbf{x}_n + h\mathbf{f}(t_n, \mathbf{x}_n) \tag{5}$$

and then the corrector

$$\mathbf{x}_{n+1} = \mathbf{x}_n + \frac{h}{2}[\mathbf{f}(t_n, \mathbf{x}_n) + \mathbf{f}(t_{n+1}, \mathbf{u}_{n+1})]. \tag{6}$$

For the case of the two-dimensional initial value problem in (3), the scalar components of the formulas in (5) and (6) are

$$
\begin{aligned}
u_{n+1} &= x_n + hf(t_n, x_n, y_n), \\
v_{n+1} &= y_n + hg(t_n, x_n, y_n)
\end{aligned}
\tag{7}
$$

and

$$x_{n+1} = x_n + \frac{h}{2}[f(t_n, x_n, y_n) + f(t_{n+1}, u_{n+1}, v_{n+1})],$$

$$y_{n+1} = y_n + \frac{h}{2}[g(t_n, x_n, y_n) + g(t_{n+1}, u_{n+1}, v_{n+1})]. \tag{8}$$

EXAMPLE 1   Consider the initial value problem

$$
\begin{aligned}
x' &= 3x - 2y, & x(0) &= 3; \\
y' &= 5x - 4y, & y(0) &= 6.
\end{aligned}
\tag{9}
$$

The exact solution of the system in (9) is

$$x(t) = 2e^{-2t} + e^t, \qquad y(t) = 5e^{-2t} + e^t. \tag{10}$$

Here we have $f(x, y) = 3x - 2y$ and $g(x, y) = 5x - 4y$ in (3), so the Euler iterative formulas in (4) are

$$x_{n+1} = x_n + h \cdot (3x_n - 2y_n), \quad y_{n+1} = y_n + h \cdot (5x_n - 4y_n).$$

With step size $h = 0.1$ we calculate

$$x_1 = 3 + (0.1) \cdot [3 \cdot 3 - 2 \cdot 6] = 2.7,$$
$$y_1 = 6 + (0.1) \cdot [5 \cdot 3 - 4 \cdot 6] = 5.1$$

and

$$x_2 = 2.7 + (0.1) \cdot [3 \cdot (2.7) - 2 \cdot (5.1)] = 2.49,$$
$$y_2 = 5.1 + (0.1) \cdot [5 \cdot (2.7) - 4 \cdot (5.1)] = 4.41.$$

The actual values at $t_2 = 0.2$ given by (10) are $x(0.2) \approx 2.562$ and $y(0.2) \approx 4.573$.

To compute the improved Euler approximations to $x(0.2)$ and $y(0.2)$ with a single step of size $h = 0.2$, we first calculate the predictors

$$u_1 = 3 + (0.2) \cdot [3 \cdot 3 - 2 \cdot 6] = 2.4,$$
$$v_1 = 6 + (0.2) \cdot [5 \cdot 3 - 4 \cdot 6] = 4.2.$$

Then the corrector formulas in (8) yield

$$x_1 = 3 + (0.1) \cdot ([3 \cdot 3 - 2 \cdot 6] + [3 \cdot (2.4) - 2 \cdot (4.2)]) = 2.58,$$
$$y_1 = 6 + (0.1) \cdot ([5 \cdot 3 - 4 \cdot 6] + [5 \cdot (2.4) - 4 \cdot (4.2)]) = 4.62.$$

As we would expect, a single improved Euler step gives better accuracy than two ordinary Euler steps. ∎

The Runge-Kutta Method and Second-Order Equations

The vector version of the iterative formula for the Runge-Kutta method is

$$\mathbf{x}_{n+1} = \mathbf{x}_n + \frac{h}{6}(\mathbf{k}_1 + 2\mathbf{k}_2 + 2\mathbf{k}_3 + \mathbf{k}_4) \tag{11}$$

where the vectors $\mathbf{k}_1, \mathbf{k}_2, \mathbf{k}_3$, and $\mathbf{k}_4$ are defined (in analogy with Eqs. (5a)–(5d) of Section 2.6) as follows:

$$\begin{aligned}
\mathbf{k}_1 &= \mathbf{f}(t_n, \mathbf{x}_n), \\
\mathbf{k}_2 &= \mathbf{f}\left(t_n + \tfrac{1}{2}h, \mathbf{x}_n + \tfrac{1}{2}h\mathbf{k}_1\right), \\
\mathbf{k}_3 &= \mathbf{f}\left(t_n + \tfrac{1}{2}h, \mathbf{x}_n + \tfrac{1}{2}h\mathbf{k}_2\right), \\
\mathbf{k}_4 &= \mathbf{f}(t_n + h, \mathbf{x}_n + h\mathbf{k}_3).
\end{aligned} \tag{12}$$

To describe in scalar notation the Runge-Kutta method for the two-dimensional initial value problem

$$\begin{aligned}
x' &= f(t, x, y), & x(t_0) &= x_0, \\
y' &= g(t, x, y), & y(t_0) &= y_0,
\end{aligned} \tag{3}$$

let us write

$$\mathbf{x} = \begin{bmatrix} x \\ y \end{bmatrix}, \quad \mathbf{f} = \begin{bmatrix} f \\ g \end{bmatrix}, \quad \text{and} \quad \mathbf{k}_i = \begin{bmatrix} F_i \\ G_i \end{bmatrix}.$$

Then the Runge-Kutta iterative formulas for the step from (x_n, y_n) to the next approximation $(x_{n+1}, y_{n+1}) \approx (x(t_{n+1}), y(t_{n+1}))$ are

$$x_{n+1} = x_n + \frac{h}{6}(F_1 + 2F_2 + 2F_3 + F_4),$$

$$y_{n+1} = y_n + \frac{h}{6}(G_1 + 2G_2 + 2G_3 + G_4),$$

$$(13)$$

where the values F_1, F_2, F_3, and F_4 of the function f are

$$
\begin{aligned}
F_1 &= f(t_n, x_n, y_n), \\
F_2 &= f\left(t_n + \tfrac{1}{2}h, x_n + \tfrac{1}{2}hF_1, y_n + \tfrac{1}{2}hG_1\right), \\
F_3 &= f\left(t_n + \tfrac{1}{2}h, x_n + \tfrac{1}{2}hF_2, y_n + \tfrac{1}{2}hG_2\right), \\
F_4 &= f(t_n + h, x_n + hF_3, y_n + hG_3);
\end{aligned}
$$

$$(14)$$

G_1, G_2, G_3, and G_4 are the similarly defined values of the function g.

Perhaps the most common application of the two-dimensional Runge-Kutta method is to the numerical solution of second-order initial value problems of the form

$$
\begin{aligned}
x'' &= g(t, x, x'), \\
x(t_0) &= x_0, \quad x'(t_0) = y_0.
\end{aligned}
$$

$$(15)$$

If we introduce the auxiliary variable $y = x'$, then the problem in (15) translates into the two-dimensional first-order problem

$$
\begin{aligned}
x' &= y, & x(t_0) &= x_0, \\
y' &= g(t, x, y), & y(t_0) &= y_0.
\end{aligned}
$$

$$(16)$$

This is a problem of the form in (3) with $f(t, x, y) = y$.

If the functions f and g are not too complicated, then it is feasible to carry out manually a reasonable number of steps of the two-dimensional Runge-Kutta method described here. But the first operating electronic computers were constructed (during World War II) specifically to implement methods similar to the Runge-Kutta method for the numerical computation of trajectories of artillery projectiles. The project material for this section lists TI-85 and BASIC versions of Program RK2DIM that can be used with two-dimensional systems.

EXAMPLE 2   The exact solution of the initial value problem

$$x'' = -x; \quad x(0) = 0, \quad x'(0) = 1 \tag{17}$$

is $x(t) = \sin t$. The substitution $y = x'$ translates (17) into the two-dimensional problem

$$
\begin{aligned}
x' &= y, & x(0) &= 0; \\
y' &= -x, & y(0) &= 1,
\end{aligned}
$$

$$(18)$$

which has the form in (3) with $f(t, x, y) = y$ and $g(t, x, y) = -x$. The table in Fig. 4.3.1 shows the results produced for $0 \leq t \leq 5$ (radians) using Program RK2DIM with step size $h = 0.05$. The values shown for $x = \sin t$ and $y = \cos t$ are all accurate to five decimal places. ∎

EXAMPLE 3

t	$x = \sin t$	$y = \cos t$
0.5	+0.47943	+0.87758
1.0	+0.84147	+0.54030
1.5	+0.99749	+0.07074
2.0	+0.90930	−0.41615
2.5	+0.59847	−0.80114
3.0	+0.14112	−0.98999
3.5	−0.35078	−0.93646
4.0	−0.75680	−0.65364
4.5	−0.97753	−0.21080
5.0	−0.95892	+0.28366

FIGURE 4.3.1. Runge-Kutta values (with $h = 0.05$) for the problem in Eq. (18).

In Example 4 of Section 2.3 we considered a lunar lander that initially is falling freely toward the surface of the moon at a speed of 450 m/s (that is, 1620 km/h). Its retrorockets, when fired in free space, provide a deceleration of $T = 450$ m/s^2. In addition, the lander is subject to the gravitational attraction of the moon. We found that a soft touchdown ($v = 0$ at impact) is achieved by firing the rockets beginning at time $t = 0$ at a height of 41870 meters (just over 26 mi) above the lunar surface.

Now we want to compute the *descent time* of the lunar lander. Let the distance $x(t)$ of the lander from the center of the moon be measured in meters and measure time t in seconds. According to the analysis in Section 2.3 (where we used $r(t)$ instead of $x(t)$), $x(t)$ satisfies the initial value problem

$$\frac{d^2x}{dt^2} = T - \frac{GM}{x^2} = 4 - \frac{4.9044 \times 10^{12}}{x^2},$$

$$x(0) = R + 41870 = 1781870, \quad x'(0) = -450$$

(19)

where $G \approx 6.6726 \times 10^{-11}$ N·(m/kg)^2 is the universal gravitational constant and $M = 7.35 \times 10^{22}$ kg and $R = 1.74 \times 10^6$ m are the mass and radius of the moon. We seek the value of t when $x(t) = R = 1740000$.

The problem in (19) is equivalent to the first-order system

$$\frac{dx}{dt} = y, \quad x(0) = 1781870;$$

$$\frac{dy}{dx} = 4 - \frac{4.9044 \times 10^{12}}{x^2}, \quad y(0) = -450.$$

(20)

The table in Fig. 4.3.2 shows the result of a Runge-Kutta approximation with step size $h = 1$ (the indicated data agreeing with those obtained with step size $h = 2$). Evidently, touchdown on the lunar surface ($x = 1740000$) occurs at some time between $t = 180$ and $t = 190$ seconds. The table in Fig. 4.3.3 shows a second Runge-Kutta approximation with $t(0) = 180$, $x(0) = 1740059$, $y(0) = -16.83$, and $h = 0.1$. Now it is apparent that the lander's time of descent to the lunar surface is very close to 187 seconds; that is, 3 min 7 s. ■

t (s)	x (m)	v (m/s)
0	1781870	−450.00
20	1773360	−401.04
40	1765826	−352.37
60	1759264	−303.95
80	1753667	−255.74
100	1749033	−207.73
120	1745357	−159.86
140	1742637	−112.11
160	1740872	−64.45
180	1740059	−16.83
200	1740199	30.77

FIGURE 4.3.2. The lander's descent to the lunar surface.

t (s)	x (m)	v (m/s)
180	1740059	−16.83
181	1740044	−14.45
182	1740030	−12.07
183	1740019	−9.69
184	1740011	−7.31
185	1740005	−4.93
186	1740001	−2.55
187	1740000	−0.17
188	1740001	2.21
189	1740004	4.59
190	1740010	6.97

FIGURE 4.3.3. Focusing on the lunar lander's soft touchdown.

Higher-Order Systems

As we saw in Section 4.1, any system of higher-order differential equations can be replaced with an equivalent system of first-order differential equations. For example, consider the system

$$x'' = F(t, x, y, x', y'),$$
$$y'' = G(t, x, y, x', y') \tag{21}$$

of second-order equations. If we substitute

$$x = x_1, \quad y = x_2, \quad x' = x_3 = x_1', \quad y' = x_4 = x_2',$$

then we get the equivalent system

$$x_1' = x_3,$$
$$x_2' = x_4,$$
$$x_3' = F(t, x_1, x_2, x_3, x_4), \tag{22}$$
$$x_4' = G(t, x_1, x_2, x_3, x_4)$$

of four first-order equations in the unknown functions $x_1(t) = x(t)$, $x_2(t) = y(t)$, $x_3(t)$, and $x_4(t)$. It would be a routine (if slightly tedious) matter to write a four-dimensional version of program RK2DIM for the purpose of solving such a system. But in a programming language that accommodates vectors, an n-dimensional Runge-Kutta program is scarcely more complicated than a one-dimensional program. For instance, the project material for this section lists the n-dimensional MATLAB program **rkn** that closely resembles the one-dimensional program **rk** of Fig. 2.6.11.

EXAMPLE 4 Suppose that a batted ball starts at $x_0 = 0$, $y_0 = 0$ with initial velocity $v_0 = 160$ ft/s and with initial angle of inclination $\theta = 30°$. If air resistance is ignored, we find by the elementary methods of Section 1.2 that the baseball travels a [horizontal] distance of $400\sqrt{3}$ ft (approximately 693 ft) in 5 s before striking the ground. Now suppose that in addition to a downward gravitational acceleration ($g = 32$ ft/s^2), the baseball experiences an acceleration due to air resistance of $(0.0025)v^2$ feet per second per second, directed opposite to its instantaneous direction of motion. Determine how far the baseball will travel horizontally under these conditions.

Solution According to Problem 30 of Section 4.1, the equations of motion of the baseball are

$$\frac{d^2x}{dt^2} = -cv\frac{dx}{dt}, \quad \frac{d^2y}{dt^2} = -cv\frac{dy}{dt} - g \tag{23}$$

where $v = \sqrt{(x')^2 + (y')^2}$ is the speed of the ball, and where $c = 0.0025$ and $g = 32$ in fps units. We convert to a first-order system as in (22) and thereby obtain the system

$$x_1' = x_3,$$
$$x_2' = x_4,$$
$$x_3' = -cx_3\sqrt{x_3^2 + x_4^2}, \tag{24}$$
$$x_4' = -cx_4\sqrt{x_3^2 + x_4^2} - g$$

of four first-order differential equations with

$$x_1(0) = x_2(0) = 0,$$
$$x_3(0) = 80\sqrt{3}, \quad x_4(0) = 80. \tag{25}$$

Note that $x_3(t)$ and $x_4(t)$ are simply the x- and y-components of the baseball's velocity vector, so $v = \sqrt{x_3^2 + x_4^2}$.

WITHOUT AIR RESISTANCE: Figure 4.3.4 shows the numerical results obtained when a Runge-Kutta program such as `rkn` is applied with step size $k = 0.1$ and with $c = 0$ (no air resistance). For convenience in interpreting the results, the printed output at each selected step consists of the horizontal and vertical coordinates x and y of the baseball, its velocity v, and the angle of inclination α of its velocity vector (in degrees measured from the horizontal). These results agree with the exact solution when $c = 0$. The ball travels a horizontal distance of $400\sqrt{3} \approx 692.82$ ft in exactly 5 s, having reached a maximum height of 100 ft after 2.5 s. Note also that the ball strikes the ground at the same angle and with the same speed as its initial angle and speed.

WITH AIR RESISTANCE: Figure 4.3.5 shows the results obtained with the fairly realistic value of $c = 0.0025$ for the air resistance for a batted baseball. To within a hundredth of a foot in either direction, the same results are obtained with step sizes $h = 0.05$ and $h = 0.025$. We now see that with air resistance the ball travels a distance well under 400 ft in just over 4 s. The more refined data in Fig. 4.3.6 show that the ball travels horizontally only about 340 ft and that its maximum height is only about 66 ft. As illustrated in Fig. 4.3.7, air resistance has converted a massive home run into a routine fly ball (if hit straightaway to center field). Note also that

t	x	y	v	α
0.0	0.00	0.00	160.00	+30
0.5	69.28	36.00	152.63	+25
1.0	138.56	64.00	146.64	+19
1.5	207.85	84.00	142.21	+13
2.0	277.13	96.00	139.48	+7
2.5	346.41	100.00	138.56	+0
3.0	415.69	96.00	139.48	−7
3.5	484.97	84.00	142.21	−13
4.0	554.26	64.00	146.64	−19
4.5	623.54	36.00	152.63	−25
5.0	692.82	0.00	160.00	−30

FIGURE 4.3.4. The batted baseball with no air resistance ($c = 0$).

t	x	y	v	α
0.0	0.00	0.00	160.00	+30
0.5	63.25	32.74	127.18	+24
1.0	117.11	53.20	104.86	+17
1.5	164.32	63.60	89.72	+8
2.0	206.48	65.30	80.17	−3
2.5	244.61	59.22	75.22	−15
3.0	279.29	46.05	73.99	−27
3.5	310.91	26.41	75.47	−37
4.0	339.67	0.91	78.66	−46

FIGURE 4.3.5. The batted baseball with air resistance ($c = 0.0025$).

t	x	y	v	α	
1.5	164.32	63.60	89.72	+8	
1.6	173.11	64.60	87.40	+5	
1.7	181.72	65.26	85.29	+3	
1.8	190.15	65.60	83.39	+1	
1.9	198.40	65.61	81.68	−1	← Apex
2.0	206.48	65.30	80.17	−3	
⋮	⋮	⋮	⋮	⋮	
3.8	328.50	11.77	77.24	−42	
3.9	334.14	6.45	77.93	−44	
4.0	339.67	0.91	78.66	−46	← Impact
4.1	345.10	−4.84	79.43	−47	
4.2	350.41	−10.79	80.22	−49	

FIGURE 4.3.6. The batted ball's apex and its impact with the ground.

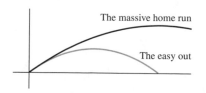

FIGURE 4.3.7. An "easy out" or a home run?

when the ball strikes the ground, it has slightly under *half* its initial speed (only about 79 ft/s) and is falling at a steeper angle (about 46°). Every baseball fan has observed empirically these aspects of the trajectory of a fly ball.

Variable Step Size Methods

The Runge-Kutta method for a large system requires an appreciable amount of computational labor, even when a computer is employed. Therefore, just as the step size h should not be so large that the resulting error in the solution is unacceptable, h ought not to be so small that too many steps are needed, hence requiring an unacceptable amount of computation. Thus the practical numerical solution of differential equations involves a tradeoff between accuracy and efficiency.

To facilitate this tradeoff, modern *variable step size methods* vary the step size h as the solution process proceeds. Large steps are taken in regions where the dependent variables are changing slowly; smaller steps are taken when these variables are changing rapidly, in order to prevent large errors.

An *adaptable* or *variable step size* Runge-Kutta method employs both a preassigned minimum error tolerance *MinTol* and a maximum error tolerance *MaxTol* to attempt to ensure that the error made in the typical step from $\mathbf{x}_n$ to $\mathbf{x}_{n+1}$ is neither too large (and hence inaccurate) nor too small (and hence inefficient). A fairly simple scheme for doing this may be outlined as follows:

- Having reached $\mathbf{x}_n$ with a Runge-Kutta step of length $t_n - t_{n-1} = h$, let $\mathbf{x}^{(1)}$ denote the result of a further Runge-Kutta step of length h and let $\mathbf{x}^{(2)}$ denote the result of *two* successive Runge-Kutta steps each of length $h/2$.
- On the grounds that $\mathbf{x}^{(2)}$ should be a more accurate approximation to $\mathbf{x}(t_n + h)$ than is $\mathbf{x}^{(1)}$, take

$$Err = |\mathbf{x}^{(1)} - \mathbf{x}^{(2)}|$$

  as an estimate of the error in $\mathbf{x}^{(1)}$.
- If *MinTol* $\leq$ *Err* $\leq$ *MaxTol*, then let $\mathbf{x}_{n+1} = \mathbf{x}^{(1)}$, $t_{n+1} = t_n + h$, and proceed to the next step.
- If *Err* < *MinTol*, then the error is too small! Hence let $\mathbf{x}_{n+1} = \mathbf{x}^{(1)}$, $t_{n+1} = t_n + h$, but *double* the step size to $2h$ before making the next step.
- If *Err* > *MaxTol*, then the error is too large. Hence reject $\mathbf{x}^{(1)}$ and start afresh at $\mathbf{x}_n$ with the *halved* step size $h/2$.

The detailed implementation of such a scheme can be complicated. For a much more complete but readable discussion of adaptive Runge-Kutta methods, see Section 15.2 of William H. Press et al., *Numerical Recipes: The Art of Scientific Computing* (Cambridge University Press, 1986).

Several widely available scientific computing packages (such as *Maple*, *Mathematica*, and MATLAB) include sophisticated variable step size programs that will accommodate an essentially arbitrary number of simultaneous differential equations. Such a general-purpose program might be used, for example, to model numerically the major components of the solar system: the sun and the nine (known) major planets. If m_i denotes the mass and $\mathbf{r}_i = (x_i, y_i, z_i)$ denotes the position vector of the ith one of these 10 bodies, then—by Newton's laws—the equation of motion of m_i is

$$m_i \mathbf{r}_i'' = \sum_{j \neq i} \frac{Gm_i m_j}{(r_{ij})^3}(\mathbf{r}_j - \mathbf{r}_i), \tag{26}$$

where $r_{ij} = |\mathbf{r}_j - \mathbf{r}_i|$ denotes the distance between m_i and m_j. For each $i = 1$, 2, ..., 10, the summation in Eq. (26) is over all values of $j \neq i$ from 1 to 10. The 10 vector equations in (26) constitute a system of 30 second-order scalar equations, and the equivalent first-order system consists of 60 differential equations in the coordinates and velocity components of the 10 major bodies in the solar system.

Mathematical models that involve this many (or more) differential equations—and that require sophisticated software and hardware for their numerical analysis—are quite common in science, engineering, and applied technology.

Earth-Moon Satellite Orbits

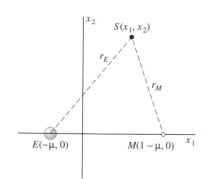

FIGURE 4.3.8. The earth-moon center-of-mass coordinate system.

For an example of a program whose efficient solution requires adaptive step size methods, we consider an Apollo satellite in orbit about the Earth E and Moon M. Figure 4.3.8 shows an x_1x_2-coordinate system whose origin lies at the center of mass of the Earth and the Moon, and which rotates at the rate of one revolution per "moon month" of approximately $\tau = 27.32$ days, so the Earth and Moon remain fixed in their positions on the x_1-axis. If we take as unit distance the distance (about 239,000 miles, assumed constant) between the Earth and Moon centers, then their coordinates are $E(-\mu, 0)$ and $M(1 - \mu, 0)$, where $\mu = m_M/(m_E + m_M)$ in terms of the Earth mass m_E and Moon mass m_M. If we take the total mass $m_E + m_M$ as the unit of mass and $\tau/(2\pi) \approx 4.35$ days as the unit of time, then the gravitational constant is $G = 1$ in Eq. (26), and the equations of motion of the satellite position $S(x_1, x_2)$ are

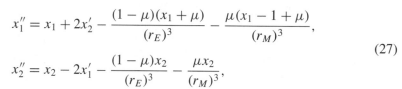

$$x_1'' = x_1 + 2x_2' - \frac{(1 - \mu)(x_1 + \mu)}{(r_E)^3} - \frac{\mu(x_1 - 1 + \mu)}{(r_M)^3},$$

$$x_2'' = x_2 - 2x_1' - \frac{(1 - \mu)x_2}{(r_E)^3} - \frac{\mu x_2}{(r_M)^3},$$

$$(27)$$

where r_E and r_M denote the satellite's distance to the Earth and Moon (indicated in Fig. 4.3.8). The initial two terms on the right-hand side of each equation result from the rotation of the coordinate system. In the system of units described here, the lunar mass is approximately $m_M = 0.012277471$. The second-order system in (27) can be converted to an equivalent first-order system (of four differential equations) by substituting

$$x_1' = x_3, \quad x_2' = x_4, \quad \text{so that} \quad x_1'' = x_3', \quad x_2'' = x_4'.$$

Suppose that the satellite initially is in a clockwise circular orbit of radius about 1500 miles about the Moon. At its farthest point from the Earth ($x_1 = 0.994$) it is "launched" into Earth-Moon orbit with initial velocity v_0. The corresponding initial conditions are

$$x_1(0) = 0.994, \quad x_2(0) = 0, \quad x_3(0) = 0, \quad x_4(0) = -v_0.$$

An adaptive step size method (**ode45**) in the MATLAB software system was used to solve numerically the system in (27). The orbits in Figs. 4.3.9 and 4.3.10 were obtained with

$$v_0 = 2.031732629557 \quad \text{and} \quad v_0 = 2.001585106379,$$

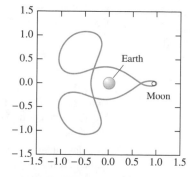

FIGURE 4.3.9. Apollo moon-earth bus orbit with insertion velocity $v_0 = 4653$ mi/h.

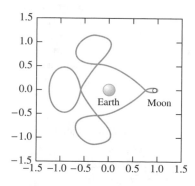

FIGURE 4.3.10. Apollo moon-earth bus orbit with insertion velocity $v_0 = 4582$ mi/h.

respectively. [In the system of units used here, the unit of velocity is approximately 2290 mi/h.] In each case a closed but multilooped periodic trajectory about the Earth and the Moon—a so-called bus orbit—is obtained, but a relatively small change in the initial velocity changes the number of loops! For more information, see NASA Contractor Report CR-61139, "Study of the Methods for the Numerical Solution of Ordinary Differential Equations," prepared by O. B. Francis, Jr. et al. for the NASA–George C. Marshall Space Flight Center, June 7, 1966.

4.3 Problems

A hand-held calculator will suffice for Problems 1 through 8. In each problem an initial value problem and its exact solution are given. Approximate the values of $x(0.2)$ and $y(0.2)$ in three ways: (a) by the Euler method with two steps of size $h = 0.1$; (b) by the improved Euler method with a single step of size $h = 0.2$; and (c) by the Runge-Kutta method with a single step of size $h = 0.2$. Compare the approximate values with the actual values $x(0.2)$ and $y(0.2)$.

1. $x' = x + 2y$, $x(0) = 0$,
   $y' = 2x + y$, $y(0) = 2$;
   $x(t) = e^{3t} - e^{-t}$, $y(t) = e^{3t} + e^{-t}$

2. $x' = 2x + 3y$, $x(0) = 1$,
   $y' = 2x + y$, $y(0) = -1$;
   $x(t) = e^{-t}$, $y(t) = -e^{-t}$

3. $x' = 3x + 4y$, $x(0) = 1$,
   $y' = 3x + 2y$, $y(0) = 1$;
   $x(t) = \frac{1}{7}(8e^{6t} - e^{-t})$, $y(t) = \frac{1}{7}(6e^{6t} + e^{-t})$

4. $x' = 9x + 5y$, $x(0) = 1$,
   $y' = -6x - 2y$, $y(0) = 0$;
   $x(t) = -5e^{3t} + 6e^{4t}$, $y(t) = 6e^{3t} - 6e^{4t}$

5. $x' = 2x - 5y$, $x(0) = 2$,
   $y' = 4x - 2y$, $y(0) = 3$;
   $x(t) = 2\cos 4t - \frac{11}{4}\sin 4t$, $y(t) = 3\cos 4t + \frac{1}{2}\sin 4t$

6. $x' = x - 2y$, $x(0) = 0$,
   $y' = 2x + y$, $y(0) = 4$;
   $x(t) = -4e^t \sin 2t$, $y(t) = 4e^t \cos 2t$

7. $x' = 3x - y$, $x(0) = 2$,
   $y' = x + y$, $y(0) = 1$;
   $x(t) = (t + 2)e^{2t}$, $y(t) = (t + 1)e^{2t}$

8. $x' = 5x - 9y$, $x(0) = 0$,
   $y' = 2x - y$, $y(0) = -1$;
   $x(t) = 3e^{2t} \sin 3t$, $y(t) = e^{2t}(\sin 3t - \cos 3t)$

A computer will be required for the remaining problems in this section. In Problems 9 through 12, an initial value problem and its exact solution are given. In each of these four problems, use the Runge-Kutta method with step sizes $h = 0.1$ and $h = 0.05$ to approximate to five decimal places the values $x(1)$ and $y(1)$. Compare the approximations with the actual values.

9. $x' = 2x - y$, $x(0) = 1$,
   $y' = x + 2y$, $y(0) = 0$;
   $x(t) = e^{2t} \cos t$, $y(t) = e^{2t} \sin t$

10. $x' = x + 2y$, $x(0) = 0$,
    $y' = x + e^{-t}$, $y(0) = 0$;
    $x(t) = \frac{1}{9}(2e^{2t} - 2e^{-t} + 6te^{-t})$,
    $y(t) = \frac{1}{9}(e^{2t} - e^{-t} + 6te^{-t})$

11. $x' = -x - y - (1 + t^3)e^{-t}$, $x(0) = 0$,
    $y' = -x - y - (t - 3t^2)e^{-t}$, $y(0) = 1$;

$x(t) = e^{-t}(\sin t - t)$, $y(t) = e^{-t}(\cos t + t^3)$

12. $x'' + x = \sin t$, $x(0) = 0$;
    $x(t) = \frac{1}{2}(\sin t - t \cos t)$

13. Suppose that a crossbow bolt is shot straight upward with initial velocity 288 ft/s. If its deceleration due to air resistance is $(0.04)v$, then its height $x(t)$ satisfies the initial value problem

$$x'' = -32 - (0.04)x';   x(0) = 0,   x'(0) = 288.$$

Find the maximum height that the bolt attains and the time required for it to reach this height.

14. Repeat Problem 13, but assume instead that the deceleration of the bolt due to air resistance is $(0.0002)v^2$.

15. Suppose that a projectile is fired straight upward with initial velocity v_0 from the surface of the earth. If air resistance is not a factor, then its height $x(t)$ at time t satisfies the initial value problem

$$\frac{d^2x}{dt^2} = -\frac{gR^2}{(x + R)^2};   x(0) = 0,   x'(0) = v_0.$$

Use the values $g = 32.15$ ft/s$^2 \approx 0.006089$ mi/s^2 for the gravitational acceleration of the earth at its surface and $R = 3960$ mi as the radius of the earth. If $v_0 = 1$ mi/s, find the maximum height attained by the projectile and its time of ascent to this height.

Problems 16 through 18 deal with the batted baseball of Example 4, having initial velocity 160 ft/s and air resistance coefficient $c = 0.0025$.

16. Find the *range*—the horizontal distance the ball travels before it hits the ground—and its total time of flight with initial inclination angles 40°, 45°, and 50°.

17. Find (to the nearest degree) the initial inclination that maximizes the range. If there were no air resistance it would be exactly 45°, but your answer should be less than 45°.

18. Find (to the nearest half degree) the initial inclination angle greater than 45° for which the range is 300 ft.

19. Find the initial velocity of a baseball hit by Babe Ruth (with $c = 0.0025$ and initial inclination 40°) if it hit the bleachers at a point 50 ft high and 500 horizontal feet from home plate.

20. Consider the crossbow bolt of Problem 14, fired with the same initial velocity of 288 ft/s and with the air resistance deceleration $(0.0002)v^2$ directed opposite its direction of motion. Suppose that this bolt is fired from ground level at an initial angle of 45°. Find how high vertically and how far horizontally it goes, and how long it remains in the air.

21. Suppose that an artillery projectile is fired from ground level with initial velocity 3000 ft/s and initial inclination angle 40°. Assume that its air resistance deceleration is $(0.0001)v^2$. (a) What is the range of the projectile and what is its total time of flight? What is its speed at impact with the ground? (b) What is the maximum altitude of the projectile, and when is that altitude attained? (c) You will find that the projectile is still losing speed at the apex of its trajectory. What is the *minimum* speed that it attains during its descent?

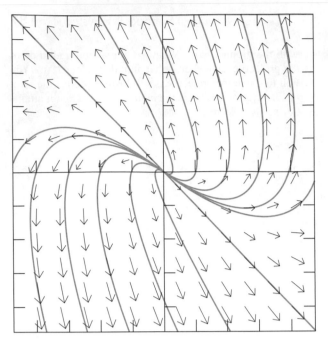

CHAPTER 5

Linear Systems of Differential Equations

5.1 MATRICES AND LINEAR SYSTEMS

Although the simple elimination techniques of Section 4.2 suffice for the solution of small linear systems containing only two or three equations with constant coefficients, the general properties of linear systems—as well as solution methods suitable for larger systems—are most easily and concisely described using the language and notation of vectors and matrices. For ready reference and review, this section begins with a complete and self-contained account of the matrix notation and terminology that is needed. Special techniques of linear algebra—specifically, those associated with eigenvalues and eigenvectors—are introduced as needed in subsequent sections of this chapter.

Review of Matrix Notation and Terminology

An $m \times n$ **matrix A** is a rectangular array of mn numbers (or **elements**) arranged in m (horizontal) **rows** and n (vertical) **columns**:

$$\mathbf{A} = \begin{bmatrix} a_{11} & a_{12} & a_{13} & \cdots & a_{1j} & \cdots & a_{1n} \\ a_{21} & a_{22} & a_{23} & \cdots & a_{2j} & \cdots & a_{2n} \\ a_{31} & a_{32} & a_{33} & \cdots & a_{3j} & \cdots & a_{3n} \\ \vdots & \vdots & \vdots & & \vdots & & \vdots \\ a_{i1} & a_{i2} & a_{i3} & \cdots & a_{ij} & \cdots & a_{in} \\ \vdots & \vdots & \vdots & & \vdots & & \vdots \\ a_{m1} & a_{m2} & a_{m3} & \cdots & a_{mj} & \cdots & a_{mn} \end{bmatrix}. \tag{1}$$

We will ordinarily denote matrices by **boldface** capital letters. Sometimes we use the abbreviation $\mathbf{A} = \begin{bmatrix} a_{ij} \end{bmatrix}$ for the matrix with the element a_{ij} in the ith row and jth column, as in Eq. (1). We denote the **zero matrix,** each entry of which is zero, by

$$\mathbf{0} = \begin{bmatrix} 0 & 0 & \cdots & 0 \\ 0 & 0 & \cdots & 0 \\ \vdots & \vdots & & \vdots \\ 0 & 0 & \cdots & 0 \end{bmatrix}. \tag{2}$$

Actually for each pair of positive integers m and n there is an $m \times n$ zero matrix, but the single symbol $\mathbf{0}$ will suffice for all these zero matrices.

Two $m \times n$ matrices $\mathbf{A} = \begin{bmatrix} a_{ij} \end{bmatrix}$ and $\mathbf{B} = \begin{bmatrix} b_{ij} \end{bmatrix}$ are said to be **equal** if corresponding elements are equal; that is, if $a_{ij} = b_{ij}$ for $1 \leq i \leq m$ and $1 \leq j \leq n$. We **add** $\mathbf{A}$ and $\mathbf{B}$ by adding corresponding entries:

$$\mathbf{A} + \mathbf{B} = \begin{bmatrix} a_{ij} \end{bmatrix} + \begin{bmatrix} b_{ij} \end{bmatrix} = \begin{bmatrix} a_{ij} + b_{ij} \end{bmatrix}. \tag{3}$$

Thus the element in row i and column j of $\mathbf{C} = \mathbf{A} + \mathbf{B}$ is $c_{ij} = a_{ij} + b_{ij}$. To multiply the matrix $\mathbf{A}$ by the number c, we simply multiply each of its elements by c:

$$c\mathbf{A} = \mathbf{A}c = [ca_{ij}]. \tag{4}$$

EXAMPLE 1 If

$$\mathbf{A} = \begin{bmatrix} 2 & -3 \\ 4 & 7 \end{bmatrix}, \quad \mathbf{B} = \begin{bmatrix} -13 & 10 \\ 7 & -5 \end{bmatrix}, \quad \text{and} \quad \mathbf{C} = \begin{bmatrix} 3 & 0 \\ 5 & -7 \end{bmatrix},$$

then

$$\mathbf{A} + \mathbf{B} = \begin{bmatrix} 2 & -3 \\ 4 & 7 \end{bmatrix} + \begin{bmatrix} -13 & 10 \\ 7 & -5 \end{bmatrix} = \begin{bmatrix} -11 & 7 \\ 11 & 2 \end{bmatrix}$$

and

$$6\mathbf{C} = 6 \cdot \begin{bmatrix} 3 & 0 \\ 5 & -7 \end{bmatrix} = \begin{bmatrix} 18 & 0 \\ 30 & -42 \end{bmatrix}. \qquad \blacksquare$$

We denote $(-1)\mathbf{A}$ by $-\mathbf{A}$ and define **subtraction** of matrices as follows:

$$\mathbf{A} - \mathbf{B} = \mathbf{A} + (-\mathbf{B}). \tag{5}$$

The matrix operations just defined have the following properties, each of which is analogous to a familiar algebraic property of the real number system:

$$\mathbf{A} + \mathbf{0} = \mathbf{0} + \mathbf{A} = \mathbf{A}, \qquad \mathbf{A} - \mathbf{A} = \mathbf{0}; \tag{6}$$

$$\mathbf{A} + \mathbf{B} = \mathbf{B} + \mathbf{A} \qquad \text{(commutativity)}; \tag{7}$$

$$\mathbf{A} + (\mathbf{B} + \mathbf{C}) = (\mathbf{A} + \mathbf{B}) + \mathbf{C} \qquad \text{(associativity)}; \tag{8}$$

$$c(\mathbf{A} + \mathbf{B}) = c\mathbf{A} + c\mathbf{B},$$
$$\qquad\qquad\qquad\qquad\qquad\qquad \text{(distributivity)} \tag{9}$$
$$(c + d)\mathbf{A} = c\mathbf{A} + d\mathbf{A}.$$

Each of these properties is readily verified by elementwise application of a corresponding property of the real numbers. For example, $a_{ij} + b_{ij} = b_{ij} + a_{ij}$ for all i and j because addition of real numbers is commutative. Consequently,

$$\mathbf{A} + \mathbf{B} = \begin{bmatrix} a_{ij} + b_{ij} \end{bmatrix} = \begin{bmatrix} b_{ij} + a_{ij} \end{bmatrix} = \mathbf{B} + \mathbf{A}.$$

The **transpose** $\mathbf{A}^T$ of the $m \times n$ matrix $\mathbf{A} = [a_{ij}]$ is the $n \times m$ (note!) matrix whose jth column is the jth row of $\mathbf{A}$ (and consequently, whose ith row is the ith column of $\mathbf{A}$). Thus $\mathbf{A}^T = \begin{bmatrix} a_{ji} \end{bmatrix}$, although this is not notationally perfect; you must remember that $\mathbf{A}^T$ will not have the same shape as $\mathbf{A}$ unless $\mathbf{A}$ is a **square** matrix—that is, unless $m = n$.

An $m \times 1$ matrix—one having only a single column—is called a **column vector**, or simply a **vector.** We often denote column vectors by **boldface** lowercase letters, as in

$$\mathbf{b} = \begin{bmatrix} 3 \\ -7 \\ 0 \end{bmatrix} \quad \text{or} \quad \mathbf{x} = \begin{bmatrix} x_1 \\ x_2 \\ \vdots \\ x_m \end{bmatrix}.$$

Similarly, a **row vector** is a $1 \times n$ matrix—one having only a single row, such as $\mathbf{c} = \begin{bmatrix} 5 & 17 & 0 & -3 \end{bmatrix}$. For aesthetic and typographical reasons, we will frequently write a column vector as the transpose of a row vector; for example, the two preceding column vectors may be written in the forms

$$\mathbf{b} = \begin{bmatrix} 3 & -7 & 0 \end{bmatrix}^T \quad \text{and} \quad \mathbf{x} = \begin{bmatrix} x_1 & x_2 & \cdots & x_m \end{bmatrix}^T.$$

Sometimes it is convenient to describe an $m \times n$ matrix in terms of either its m row vectors or its n column vectors. Thus if we write

$$\mathbf{A} = \begin{bmatrix} \mathbf{a}_1 \\ \mathbf{a}_2 \\ \vdots \\ \mathbf{a}_m \end{bmatrix} \quad \text{and} \quad \mathbf{B} = \begin{bmatrix} \mathbf{b}_1 & \mathbf{b}_2 & \cdots & \mathbf{b}_n \end{bmatrix},$$

it is understood that $\mathbf{a}_1, \mathbf{a}_2, \ldots,$ and $\mathbf{a}_m$ are the *row* vectors of the matrix $\mathbf{A}$ and that $\mathbf{b}_1, \mathbf{b}_2, \ldots,$ and $\mathbf{b}_n$ are the *column* vectors of the matrix $\mathbf{B}$.

Matrix Multiplication

The properties listed in Eqs. (6) through (9) are quite natural and expected. The first surprises in the realm of matrix arithmetic come with multiplication. We define first the **scalar product** of a row vector $\mathbf{a}$ and a column vector $\mathbf{b}$, each having the same number p of elements. If

$$\mathbf{a} = \begin{bmatrix} a_1 & a_2 & \cdots & a_p \end{bmatrix} \quad \text{and} \quad \mathbf{b} = \begin{bmatrix} b_1 & b_2 & \cdots & b_p \end{bmatrix}^T,$$

then $\mathbf{a} \cdot \mathbf{b}$ is defined as follows:

$$\mathbf{a} \cdot \mathbf{b} = \sum_{k=1}^{p} a_k b_k = a_1 b_1 + a_2 b_2 + \cdots + a_p b_p, \tag{10}$$

exactly as in the scalar or *dot* product of two vectors—a familiar topic from elementary calculus.

The product $\mathbf{AB}$ of two matrices is defined only if the number of columns of $\mathbf{A}$ is equal to the number of rows of $\mathbf{B}$. If $\mathbf{A}$ is an $m \times p$ matrix and $\mathbf{B}$ is a $p \times n$ matrix, then their product $\mathbf{AB}$ is the $m \times n$ matrix $\mathbf{C} = \begin{bmatrix} c_{ij} \end{bmatrix}$, where c_{ij} is the scalar product of the ith row vector $\mathbf{a}_i$ of $\mathbf{A}$ and the jth column vector $\mathbf{b}_j$ of $\mathbf{B}$. Thus

$$\mathbf{AB} = \begin{bmatrix} \mathbf{a}_i \cdot \mathbf{b}_j \end{bmatrix}. \tag{11}$$

In terms of the individual entries of $\mathbf{A} = \begin{bmatrix} a_{ij} \end{bmatrix}$ and $\mathbf{B} = \begin{bmatrix} b_{ij} \end{bmatrix}$, Eq. (11) can be recast in the form

$$c_{ij} = \sum_{k=1}^{p} a_{ik} b_{kj}. \tag{12}$$

For purposes of hand computation, the definition in Eqs. (11) and (12) is easy to remember by visualizing the picture

$$\mathbf{a}_i \longrightarrow \begin{bmatrix} a_{11} & a_{12} & \cdots & a_{1p} \\ a_{21} & a_{22} & \cdots & a_{2p} \\ \vdots & \vdots & & \vdots \\ a_{i1} & a_{i2} & \cdots & a_{ip} \\ \vdots & \vdots & & \vdots \\ a_{m1} & a_{m2} & \cdots & a_{mp} \end{bmatrix} \begin{bmatrix} b_{11} & b_{12} & \cdots & b_{1j} & \cdots & b_{1n} \\ b_{21} & b_{22} & \cdots & b_{2j} & \cdots & b_{2n} \\ \vdots & \vdots & & \vdots & & \vdots \\ & & & & & \\ b_{p1} & b_{p2} & \cdots & b_{pj} & \cdots & b_{pn} \end{bmatrix},$$

$$\underset{\mathbf{b}_j}{\uparrow}$$

which shows that one forms the dot product of the row vector $\mathbf{a}_i$ with the column vector $\mathbf{b}_j$ to obtain the element c_{ij} in the ith row and the jth column of $\mathbf{AB}$. It may help to think of "pouring the rows of $\mathbf{A}$ down the columns of $\mathbf{B}$." This also reminds us that the number of columns of $\mathbf{A}$ must be equal to the number of rows of $\mathbf{B}$.

EXAMPLE 2   Check your understanding of the definition of matrix multiplication by verifying that if

$$\mathbf{A} = \begin{bmatrix} 2 & -3 \\ -1 & 5 \end{bmatrix} \quad \text{and} \quad \mathbf{B} = \begin{bmatrix} 13 & 9 \\ 4 & 0 \end{bmatrix},$$

then

$$\mathbf{AB} = \begin{bmatrix} 2 & -3 \\ -1 & 5 \end{bmatrix} \begin{bmatrix} 13 & 9 \\ 4 & 0 \end{bmatrix} = \begin{bmatrix} 14 & 18 \\ 7 & -9 \end{bmatrix}.$$

Similarly, verify that

$$\begin{bmatrix} 2 & -3 & 1 \\ 4 & 5 & -2 \\ 6 & -7 & 0 \end{bmatrix} \begin{bmatrix} x \\ y \\ z \end{bmatrix} = \begin{bmatrix} 2x - 3y + z \\ 4x + 5y - 2z \\ 6x - 7y \end{bmatrix}$$

and that

$$\begin{bmatrix} 1 & 2 \\ 3 & 4 \\ 5 & 6 \\ 7 & 8 \end{bmatrix} \begin{bmatrix} 2 & 1 & 3 \\ -1 & 3 & -2 \end{bmatrix} = \begin{bmatrix} 0 & 7 & -1 \\ 2 & 15 & 1 \\ 4 & 23 & 3 \\ 6 & 31 & 5 \end{bmatrix}.$$

∎

It can be shown by direct (though lengthy) computation based on its definition that matrix multiplication is associative and is also distributive with respect to matrix addition; that is,

$$\mathbf{A}(\mathbf{BC}) = (\mathbf{AB})\mathbf{C} \tag{13}$$

and

$$\mathbf{A}(\mathbf{B} + \mathbf{C}) = \mathbf{AB} + \mathbf{AC}, \tag{14}$$

provided that the matrices are of such sizes that the indicated multiplications and additions are possible.

But matrix multiplication is not commutative. That is, if $\mathbf{A}$ and $\mathbf{B}$ are both $n \times n$ matrices (so that both the products $\mathbf{AB}$ and $\mathbf{BA}$ are defined and have the same dimensions—$n \times n$), then, in general,

$$\mathbf{AB} \neq \mathbf{BA}. \tag{15}$$

Moreover, it can happen that

$$\mathbf{AB} = \mathbf{0} \quad \text{even though} \quad \mathbf{A} \neq \mathbf{0} \quad \text{and} \quad \mathbf{B} \neq \mathbf{0}. \tag{16}$$

Examples illustrating the phenomena in (15) and (16) may be found in the problems, although you can easily construct your own examples using 2×2 matrices with small integral elements.

Inverse Matrices

A square $n \times n$ matrix is said to have **order** n. The **identity** matrix of order n is the square matrix

$$\mathbf{I} = \begin{bmatrix} 1 & 0 & 0 & 0 & \cdots & 0 \\ 0 & 1 & 0 & 0 & \cdots & 0 \\ 0 & 0 & 1 & 0 & \cdots & 0 \\ 0 & 0 & 0 & 1 & \cdots & 0 \\ \vdots & \vdots & \vdots & \vdots & & \vdots \\ 0 & 0 & 0 & 0 & \cdots & 1 \end{bmatrix} \tag{17}$$

for which each entry on the **principal diagonal** is 1 and all off-diagonal entries are zero. It is quite easy to verify that

$$\mathbf{AI} = \mathbf{A} = \mathbf{IA} \tag{18}$$

for every square matrix **A** of the same order as **I**.

If **A** is a square matrix, then an **inverse** of **A** is a square matrix **B** of the same order as **A** such that *both*

$$\mathbf{AB} = \mathbf{I} \quad \text{and} \quad \mathbf{BA} = \mathbf{I}.$$

It is not difficult to show that if the matrix **A** has an inverse, then this inverse is unique. Consequently, we may speak of *the* inverse of **A**, and we will denote it by $\mathbf{A}^{-1}$. Thus

$$\mathbf{AA}^{-1} = \mathbf{I} = \mathbf{A}^{-1}\mathbf{A}, \tag{19}$$

given the existence of $\mathbf{A}^{-1}$. It is clear that some square matrices do not have inverses—consider any square zero matrix. It is also easy to show that if $\mathbf{A}^{-1}$ exists, then $(\mathbf{A}^{-1})^{-1}$ exists and $(\mathbf{A}^{-1})^{-1} = \mathbf{A}$.

In linear algebra it is proved that $\mathbf{A}^{-1}$ exists if and only the determinant $\det(\mathbf{A})$ of the square matrix **A** is nonzero. If so, the matrix **A** is said to be **nonsingular;** if $\det(\mathbf{A}) = 0$, then **A** is called a **singular** matrix.

Determinants

We assume that the student has computed 2×2 and 3×3 determinants in earlier courses. If $\mathbf{A} = \left[a_{ij} \right]$ is a 2×2 matrix, then its **determinant** $\det(\mathbf{A}) = |\mathbf{A}|$ is defined as

$$|\mathbf{A}| = \begin{vmatrix} a_{11} & a_{12} \\ a_{21} & a_{22} \end{vmatrix} = a_{11}a_{22} - a_{12}a_{21}.$$

Determinants of higher order may be defined by induction, as follows. If $\mathbf{A} = \left[a_{ij} \right]$ is an $n \times n$ matrix, let $\mathbf{A}_{ij}$ denote the $(n-1) \times (n-1)$ matrix obtained from **A** by deleting its ith row and its jth column. The *expansion* of the determinant $|\mathbf{A}|$ along its ith row is given by

$$|\mathbf{A}| = \sum_{j=1}^{n} (-1)^{i+j} a_{ij} |\mathbf{A}_{ij}| \qquad (i \text{ fixed}), \tag{20a}$$

and its expansion along its jth column is given by

$$|\mathbf{A}| = \sum_{i=1}^{n} (-1)^{i+j} a_{ij} |\mathbf{A}_{ij}| \qquad (j \text{ fixed}). \tag{20b}$$

It is shown in linear algebra that whichever row we use in Eq. (20a) and whichever column we use in Eq. (20b), the results are the same in all $2n$ cases. Hence $|\mathbf{A}|$ is well defined by these formulas.

EXAMPLE 3   If

$$\mathbf{A} = \begin{bmatrix} 3 & 1 & -2 \\ 4 & 2 & 1 \\ -2 & 3 & 5 \end{bmatrix},$$

then the expansion of $|\mathbf{A}|$ along its second row is

$$|\mathbf{A}| = -4 \cdot \begin{vmatrix} 1 & -2 \\ 3 & 5 \end{vmatrix} + 2 \cdot \begin{vmatrix} 3 & -2 \\ -2 & 5 \end{vmatrix} - 1 \cdot \begin{vmatrix} 3 & 1 \\ -2 & 3 \end{vmatrix}$$

$$= -4 \cdot 11 + 2 \cdot 11 - 1 \cdot 11 = -33.$$

And the expansion of $|\mathbf{A}|$ along its third column is

$$|\mathbf{A}| = -2 \cdot \begin{vmatrix} 4 & 2 \\ -2 & 3 \end{vmatrix} - 1 \cdot \begin{vmatrix} 3 & 1 \\ -2 & 3 \end{vmatrix} + 5 \cdot \begin{vmatrix} 3 & 1 \\ 4 & 2 \end{vmatrix}$$

$$= -2 \cdot 16 - 1 \cdot 11 + 5 \cdot 2 = -33. \qquad \blacksquare$$

Calculators and computers are convenient for the calculation of higher-dimensional determinants and inverse matrices, but determinants and inverses of 2×2 matrices are easy to compute by hand. For instance, if the 2×2 matrix

$$\mathbf{A} = \begin{bmatrix} a & b \\ c & d \end{bmatrix}$$

has nonzero determinant $|\mathbf{A}| = ad - bc \neq 0$, then its inverse matrix is

$$\mathbf{A}^{-1} = \frac{1}{|\mathbf{A}|} \begin{bmatrix} d & -b \\ -c & a \end{bmatrix}. \qquad (21)$$

Note that the matrix on the right-hand side of Eq. (21) is obtained from $\mathbf{A}$ by interchanging the diagonal elements and changing the signs of the off-diagonal elements.

EXAMPLE 4 If

$$\mathbf{A} = \begin{bmatrix} 6 & 8 \\ 5 & 7 \end{bmatrix},$$

then $|\mathbf{A}| = 6 \cdot 7 - 5 \cdot 8 = 2$. Hence Eq. (21) gives

$$\mathbf{A}^{-1} = \frac{1}{2} \begin{bmatrix} 7 & -8 \\ -5 & 6 \end{bmatrix} = \begin{bmatrix} \frac{7}{2} & -4 \\ -\frac{5}{2} & 3 \end{bmatrix}.$$

You should pause to verify that

$$\mathbf{A}^{-1}\mathbf{A} = \begin{bmatrix} \frac{7}{2} & -4 \\ -\frac{5}{2} & 3 \end{bmatrix} \begin{bmatrix} 6 & 8 \\ 5 & 7 \end{bmatrix} = \begin{bmatrix} 1 & 0 \\ 0 & 1 \end{bmatrix}. \qquad \blacksquare$$

Matrix-Valued Functions

A **matrix-valued function,** or simply **matrix function,** is a matrix such as

$$\mathbf{x}(t) = \begin{bmatrix} x_1(t) \\ x_2(t) \\ \vdots \\ x_n(t) \end{bmatrix} \tag{22a}$$

or

$$\mathbf{A}(t) = \begin{bmatrix} a_{11}(t) & a_{12}(t) & \cdots & a_{1n}(t) \\ a_{21}(t) & a_{22}(t) & \cdots & a_{2n}(t) \\ \vdots & \vdots & & \vdots \\ a_{m1}(t) & a_{m2}(t) & \cdots & a_{mn}(t) \end{bmatrix}, \tag{22b}$$

in which each entry is a function of t. We say that the matrix function $\mathbf{A}(t)$ is **continuous** (or **differentiable**) at a point (or on an interval) if each of its elements has the same property. The **derivative** of a differentiable matrix function is defined by elementwise differentiation; that is,

$$\mathbf{A}'(t) = \frac{d\mathbf{A}}{dt} = \left[\frac{da_{ij}}{dt} \right]. \tag{23}$$

EXAMPLE 5   If

$$\mathbf{x}(t) = \begin{bmatrix} t \\ t^2 \\ e^{-t} \end{bmatrix} \quad \text{and} \quad \mathbf{A}(t) = \begin{bmatrix} \sin t & 1 \\ t & \cos t \end{bmatrix},$$

then

$$\frac{d\mathbf{x}}{dt} = \begin{bmatrix} 1 \\ 2t \\ -e^{-t} \end{bmatrix} \quad \text{and} \quad \mathbf{A}'(t) = \begin{bmatrix} \cos t & 0 \\ 1 & -\sin t \end{bmatrix}. \quad \blacksquare$$

The differentiation rules

$$\frac{d}{dt}(\mathbf{A} + \mathbf{B}) = \frac{d\mathbf{A}}{dt} + \frac{d\mathbf{B}}{dt} \tag{24}$$

and

$$\frac{d}{dt}(\mathbf{A}\mathbf{B}) = \mathbf{A}\frac{d\mathbf{B}}{dt} + \frac{d\mathbf{A}}{dt}\mathbf{B} \tag{25}$$

follow readily by elementwise application of the analogous differentiation rules of elementary calculus for real-valued functions. If c is a (constant) real number and $\mathbf{C}$ is a constant matrix, then

$$\frac{d}{dt}(c\mathbf{A}) = c\frac{d\mathbf{A}}{dt}, \quad \frac{d}{dt}(\mathbf{C}\mathbf{A}) = \mathbf{C}\frac{dA}{dt}, \quad \text{and} \quad \frac{d}{dt}(\mathbf{A}\mathbf{C}) = \frac{dA}{dt}\mathbf{C}. \tag{26}$$

Because of the noncommutativity of matrix multiplication, it is important not to reverse the order of the factors in Eqs. (25) and (26).

First-Order Linear Systems

The notation and terminology of matrices and vectors may seem rather elaborate when first encountered, but it is readily assimilated with practice. Our main use for matrix notation will be the simplification of computations with systems of differential equations, especially those computations that would be burdensome in scalar notation.

We discuss here the general system of n first-order linear equations

$$
\begin{aligned}
x_1' &= p_{11}(t)x_1 + p_{12}(t)x_2 + \cdots + p_{1n}(t)x_n + f_1(t), \\
x_2' &= p_{21}(t)x_1 + p_{22}(t)x_2 + \cdots + p_{2n}(t)x_n + f_2(t), \\
x_3' &= p_{31}(t)x_1 + p_{32}(t)x_2 + \cdots + p_{3n}(t)x_n + f_3(t), \qquad (27) \\
&\;\;\vdots \\
x_n' &= p_{n1}(t)x_1 + p_{n2}(t)x_2 + \cdots + p_{nn}(t)x_n + f_n(t).
\end{aligned}
$$

If we introduce the *coefficient matrix*

$$
\mathbf{P}(t) = \left[\, p_{ij}(t) \,\right]
$$

and the column vectors

$$
\mathbf{x} = \left[\, x_i \,\right] \quad \text{and} \quad \mathbf{f}(t) = \left[\, f_i(t) \,\right],
$$

then the system in (27) takes the form of a single matrix equation

$$
\frac{d\mathbf{x}}{dt} = \mathbf{P}(t)\mathbf{x} + \mathbf{f}(t). \qquad (28)
$$

We will see that the general theory of the linear system in (27) closely parallels that of a single nth-order equation. The matrix notation used in Eq. (28) not only emphasizes this analogy, but also saves a great deal of space.

A **solution** of Eq. (28) on the open interval I is a column vector function $\mathbf{x}(t) = \left[\, x_i(t) \,\right]$ such that the component functions of $\mathbf{x}$ satisfy the system in (27) identically on I. If the functions $p_{ij}(t)$ and $f_i(t)$ are all continuous on I, then Theorem 1 of Section 4.1 guarantees the existence on I of a unique solution $\mathbf{x}(t)$ satisfying preassigned initial conditions $\mathbf{x}(a) = \mathbf{b}$.

EXAMPLE 6   The first-order system

$$
\begin{aligned}
x_1' &= 4x_1 - 3x_2, \\
x_2' &= 6x_1 - 7x_2
\end{aligned}
$$

can be written as the single matrix equation

$$
\frac{d\mathbf{x}}{dt} = \begin{bmatrix} 4 & -3 \\ 6 & -7 \end{bmatrix} \mathbf{x} = \mathbf{P}\mathbf{x}.
$$

To verify that the vector functions

$$
\mathbf{x}_1(t) = \begin{bmatrix} 3e^{2t} \\ 2e^{2t} \end{bmatrix} \quad \text{and} \quad \mathbf{x}_2(t) = \begin{bmatrix} e^{-5t} \\ 3e^{-5t} \end{bmatrix}
$$

are both solutions of the matrix differential equation with coefficient matrix $\mathbf{P}$, we need only calculate

$$
\mathbf{P}\mathbf{x}_1 = \begin{bmatrix} 4 & -3 \\ 6 & -7 \end{bmatrix}\begin{bmatrix} 3e^{2t} \\ 2e^{2t} \end{bmatrix} = \begin{bmatrix} 6e^{2t} \\ 4e^{2t} \end{bmatrix} = \mathbf{x}_1'
$$

and

$$
\mathbf{P}\mathbf{x}_2 = \begin{bmatrix} 4 & -3 \\ 6 & -7 \end{bmatrix}\begin{bmatrix} e^{-5t} \\ 3e^{-5t} \end{bmatrix} = \begin{bmatrix} -5e^{-5t} \\ -15e^{-5t} \end{bmatrix} = \mathbf{x}_2'. \qquad ∎
$$

To investigate the general nature of the solutions of Eq. (28), we consider first the **associated homogeneous equation**

$$\frac{d\mathbf{x}}{dt} = \mathbf{P}(t)\mathbf{x}, \tag{29}$$

which has the form shown in Eq. (28), but with $\mathbf{f}(t) \equiv \mathbf{0}$. We expect it to have n solutions $\mathbf{x}_1, \mathbf{x}_2, \ldots, \mathbf{x}_n$ that are independent in some appropriate sense, and such that every solution of Eq. (29) is a linear combination of these n particular solutions. Given n solutions $\mathbf{x}_1, \mathbf{x}_2, \ldots, \mathbf{x}_n$ of Eq. (29), let us write

$$\mathbf{x}_j(t) = \begin{bmatrix} x_{1j}(t) \\ \vdots \\ x_{ij}(t) \\ \vdots \\ x_{nj}(t) \end{bmatrix}. \tag{30}$$

Thus $x_{ij}(t)$ denotes the ith component of the vector $\mathbf{x}_j(t)$, so the second subscript refers to the vector function $\mathbf{x}_j(t)$, whereas the first subscript refers to a component of this function. Theorem 1 is analogous to Theorem 1 of Section 3.2.

THEOREM 1: Principle of Superposition

Let $\mathbf{x}_1, \mathbf{x}_2, \ldots, \mathbf{x}_n$ be n solutions of the homogeneous linear equation in (29) on the open interval I. If $c_1, c_2, \ldots, c_n$ are constants, then the linear combination

$$\mathbf{x}(t) = c_1\mathbf{x}_1(t) + c_2\mathbf{x}_2(t) + \cdots + c_n\mathbf{x}_n(t) \tag{31}$$

is also a solution of Eq. (29) on I.

Proof: We know that $\mathbf{x}_i' = \mathbf{P}(t)\mathbf{x}_i$ for each i ($1 \leqq i \leqq n$), so it follows immediately that

$$\begin{aligned} \mathbf{x}' &= c_1\mathbf{x}_1' + c_2\mathbf{x}_2' + \cdots + c_n\mathbf{x}_n' \\ &= c_1\mathbf{P}(t)\mathbf{x}_1 + c_2\mathbf{P}(t)\mathbf{x}_2 + \cdots + c_n\mathbf{P}(t)\mathbf{x}_n \\ &= \mathbf{P}(t)(c_1\mathbf{x}_1 + c_2\mathbf{x}_2 + \cdots + c_n\mathbf{x}_n). \end{aligned}$$

That is, $\mathbf{x}' = \mathbf{P}(t)\mathbf{x}$, as desired. The remarkable simplicity of this proof demonstrates clearly one advantage of matrix notation. ∎

EXAMPLE 6
CONTINUED

If $\mathbf{x}_1$ and $\mathbf{x}_2$ are the two solutions of

$$\frac{d\mathbf{x}}{dt} = \begin{bmatrix} 4 & -3 \\ 6 & -7 \end{bmatrix} \mathbf{x}$$

discussed in Example 6, then the linear combination

$$\mathbf{x}(t) = c_1\mathbf{x}_1(t) + c_2\mathbf{x}_2(t) = c_1 \begin{bmatrix} 3e^{2t} \\ 2e^{2t} \end{bmatrix} + c_2 \begin{bmatrix} e^{-5t} \\ 3e^{-5t} \end{bmatrix}$$

is also a solution. In scalar form with $\mathbf{x} = [x_1 \quad x_2]^T$, this gives the solution

$$\begin{aligned} x_1(t) &= 3c_1e^{2t} + c_2e^{-5t}, \\ x_2(t) &= 2c_1e^{2t} + 3c_2e^{-5t}, \end{aligned}$$

which is equivalent to the general solution we found by the method of elimination in Example 2 of Section 4.2. ∎

Independence and General Solutions

Linear independence is defined in the same way for vector-valued functions as for real-valued functions (Section 3.2). The vector-valued functions $\mathbf{x}_1$, $\mathbf{x}_2$, ..., $\mathbf{x}_n$ are **linearly dependent** on the interval I provided that there exist constants $c_1, c_2, \ldots,$ c_n *not all zero* such that

$$c_1\mathbf{x}_1(t) + c_2\mathbf{x}_2(t) + \cdots + c_n\mathbf{x}_n(t) = \mathbf{0} \tag{32}$$

for all t in I. Otherwise, they are **linearly independent.** Equivalently, they are linearly independent provided that no one of them is a linear combination of the others. For instance, the two solutions $\mathbf{x}_1$ and $\mathbf{x}_2$ of Example 6 are linearly independent because, clearly, neither is a scalar multiple of the other.

Just as in the case of a single nth-order equation, there is a Wronskian determinant that tells us whether or not n given solutions of the homogeneous equation in (29) are linearly dependent. If $\mathbf{x}_1$, $\mathbf{x}_2$, ..., $\mathbf{x}_n$ are such solutions, then their **Wronskian** is the $n \times n$ determinant

$$W = \begin{bmatrix} x_{11}(t) & x_{12}(t) & \cdots & x_{1n}(t) \\ x_{21}(t) & x_{22}(t) & \cdots & x_{2n}(t) \\ \vdots & \vdots & & \vdots \\ x_{n1}(t) & x_{n2}(t) & \cdots & x_{nn}(t) \end{bmatrix}, \tag{33}$$

using the notation in (30) for the components of the solutions. We may write either $W(t)$ or $W(\mathbf{x}_1, \mathbf{x}_2, \ldots, \mathbf{x}_n)$. Note that W is the determinant of the matrix that has as its *column* vectors the solutions $\mathbf{x}_1, \mathbf{x}_2, \ldots, \mathbf{x}_n$. Theorem 2 is analogous to Theorem 3 of Section 3.2. Moreover, its proof is essentially the same, with the definition of $W(\mathbf{x}_1, \mathbf{x}_2, \ldots, \mathbf{x}_n)$ in Eq. (33) substituted for the definition of the Wronskian of n solutions of a single nth-order equation (see Problems 42 through 44).

THEOREM 2: Wronskians of Solutions

Suppose that $\mathbf{x}_1$, $\mathbf{x}_2$, ..., $\mathbf{x}_n$ are n solutions of the homogeneous linear equation $\mathbf{x}' = \mathbf{P}(t)\mathbf{x}$ on an open interval I. Suppose also that $\mathbf{P}(t)$ is continuous on I. Let

$$W = W(\mathbf{x}_1, \mathbf{x}_2, \ldots, \mathbf{x}_n).$$

Then:

- If $\mathbf{x}_1, \mathbf{x}_2, \ldots, \mathbf{x}_n$ are linearly dependent on I, then $W = 0$ at every point of I.
- If $\mathbf{x}_1, \mathbf{x}_2, \ldots, \mathbf{x}_n$ are linearly independent on I, then $W \neq 0$ at each point of I.

Thus there are only two possibilities for solutions of homogeneous systems: Either $W = 0$ at *every* point of I, or $W = 0$ at *no* point of I. ∎

EXAMPLE 7   It is readily verified (as in Example 6) that

$$\mathbf{x}_1(t) = \begin{bmatrix} 2e^t \\ 2e^t \\ e^t \end{bmatrix}, \quad \mathbf{x}_2(t) = \begin{bmatrix} 2e^{3t} \\ 0 \\ -e^{3t} \end{bmatrix}, \quad \text{and} \quad \mathbf{x}_3(t) = \begin{bmatrix} 2e^{5t} \\ -2e^{5t} \\ e^{5t} \end{bmatrix}$$

are solutions of the equation

$$\frac{d\mathbf{x}}{dt} = \begin{bmatrix} 3 & -2 & 0 \\ -1 & 3 & -2 \\ 0 & -1 & 3 \end{bmatrix} \mathbf{x}. \tag{34}$$

The Wronskian of these solutions is

$$W = \begin{vmatrix} 2e^t & 2e^{3t} & 2e^{5t} \\ 2e^t & 0 & -2e^{5t} \\ e^t & -e^{3t} & e^{5t} \end{vmatrix} = e^{9t} \begin{vmatrix} 2 & 2 & 2 \\ 2 & 0 & -2 \\ 1 & -1 & 1 \end{vmatrix} = -16e^{9t},$$

which is never zero. Hence Theorem 2 implies that the solutions $\mathbf{x}_1$, $\mathbf{x}_2$, and $\mathbf{x}_3$ are linearly independent (on any open interval). ∎

Theorem 3 is analogous to Theorem 4 of Section 3.2. It says that the **general solution** of the *homogeneous* $n \times n$ system $\mathbf{x}' = \mathbf{P}(t)\mathbf{x}$ is a linear combination

$$\mathbf{x} = c_1\mathbf{x}_1 + c_2\mathbf{x}_2 + \cdots + c_n\mathbf{x}_n \tag{35}$$

of any n given linearly independent solutions $\mathbf{x}_1, \mathbf{x}_2, \ldots, \mathbf{x}_n$.

THEOREM 3: General Solutions of Homogeneous Systems

Let $\mathbf{x}_1, \mathbf{x}_2, \ldots, \mathbf{x}_n$ be n linearly independent solutions of the homogeneous linear equation $\mathbf{x}' = \mathbf{P}(t)\mathbf{x}$ on an open interval I where $\mathbf{P}(t)$ is continuous. If $\mathbf{x}(t)$ is any solution whatsoever of the equation $\mathbf{x}' = \mathbf{P}(t)\mathbf{x}$ on I, then there exist numbers c_1, $c_2, \ldots, c_n$ such that

$$\mathbf{x}(t) = c_1\mathbf{x}_1(t) + c_2\mathbf{x}_2(t) + \cdots + c_n\mathbf{x}_n(t) \tag{35}$$

for all t in I.

Proof: Let a be a fixed point of I. We show first that there exist numbers c_1, $c_2, \ldots, c_n$ such that the solution

$$\mathbf{y}(t) = c_1\mathbf{x}_1(t) + c_2\mathbf{x}_2(t) + \cdots + c_n\mathbf{x}_n(t) \tag{36}$$

has the same initial values at $t = a$ as does the given solution $\mathbf{x}(t)$; that is, such that

$$c_1\mathbf{x}_1(a) + c_2\mathbf{x}_2(a) + \cdots + c_n\mathbf{x}_n(a) = \mathbf{x}(a). \tag{37}$$

Let $\mathbf{X}(t)$ be the $n \times n$ matrix with column vectors $\mathbf{x}_1, \mathbf{x}_2, \ldots, \mathbf{x}_n$, and let $\mathbf{c}$ be the column vector with components $c_1, c_2, \ldots, c_n$. Then Eq. (37) may be written in the form

$$\mathbf{X}(a)\mathbf{c} = \mathbf{x}(a). \tag{38}$$

The Wronskian determinant $W(a) = |\mathbf{X}(a)|$ is nonzero because the solutions $\mathbf{x}_1$, $\mathbf{x}_2, \ldots, \mathbf{x}_n$ are linearly independent. Hence the matrix $\mathbf{X}(a)$ has an inverse matrix $\mathbf{X}(a)^{-1}$. Therefore the vector $\mathbf{c} = \mathbf{X}(a)^{-1}\mathbf{x}(a)$ satisfies Eq. (38), as desired.

Finally, note that the given solution $\mathbf{x}(t)$ and the solution $\mathbf{y}(t)$ of Eq. (36)—with the values of c_i determined by the equation $\mathbf{c} = \mathbf{X}(a)^{-1}\mathbf{x}(a)$—have the same initial values (at $t = a$). It follows from the existence-uniqueness theorem of Section 4.1 that $\mathbf{x}(t) = \mathbf{y}(t)$ for all t in I. This establishes Eq. (35). ∎

Remark: Every $n \times n$ system $\mathbf{x}' = \mathbf{P}(t)\mathbf{x}$ with continuous coefficient matrix does have a set of n linearly independent solutions $\mathbf{x}_1, \mathbf{x}_2, \ldots, \mathbf{x}_n$ as in the hypotheses of Theorem 3. It suffices to choose for $\mathbf{x}_j(t)$ the unique solution such that

$$\mathbf{x}_j(a) = \begin{bmatrix} 0 \\ 0 \\ 0 \\ \vdots \\ 0 \\ 1 \\ 0 \\ \vdots \\ 0 \end{bmatrix} \quad \leftarrow \text{position } j$$

—that is, the column vector with all elements zero except for a 1 in row j. (In other words, $\mathbf{x}_j(a)$ is merely the jth column of the identity matrix.) Then

$$W(\mathbf{x}_1, \mathbf{x}_2, \ldots, \mathbf{x}_n)\big|_{t=a} = |\mathbf{I}| \neq 0,$$

so the solutions $\mathbf{x}_1, \mathbf{x}_2, \ldots, \mathbf{x}_n$ are linearly independent by Theorem 2. How actually to find these solutions explicitly is another matter—one that we address in Section 5.2 (for the case of constant coefficient matrices). ∎

Initial Value Problems and Elementary Row Operations

The general solution in Eq. (35) of the homogeneous linear system $\mathbf{x}' = \mathbf{P}(t)\mathbf{x}$ can be written in the form

$$\mathbf{x}(t) = \mathbf{X}(t)\mathbf{c}, \tag{39}$$

where

$$\mathbf{X}(t) = \begin{bmatrix} \mathbf{x}_1(t) & \mathbf{x}_2(t) & \cdots & \mathbf{x}_n(t) \end{bmatrix} \tag{40}$$

is the $n \times n$ matrix whose *column vectors* are the linearly independent solutions $\mathbf{x}_1$, $\mathbf{x}_2, \ldots, \mathbf{x}_n$, and $\mathbf{c} = \begin{bmatrix} c_1 & c_2 & \cdots & c_n \end{bmatrix}^T$ is the vector of coefficients in the linear combination

$$\mathbf{x}(t) = c_1\mathbf{x}_1(t) + c_2\mathbf{x}_2(t) + \cdots + c_n\mathbf{x}_n(t). \tag{35}$$

Suppose now that we wish to solve the *initial value problem*

➤ $$\frac{d\mathbf{x}}{dt} = \mathbf{P}\mathbf{x}, \quad \mathbf{x}(a) = \mathbf{b}, \tag{41}$$

where the initial vector $\mathbf{b} = \begin{bmatrix} b_1 & b_2 & \cdots & b_n \end{bmatrix}^T$ is given. Then, according to Eq. (39), it suffices to solve the system

$$\mathbf{X}(a)\mathbf{c} = \mathbf{b} \tag{42}$$

to find the coefficients $c_1, c_2, \ldots, c_n$ in Eq. (35).

We therefore review briefly the elementary technique of *row reduction* to solve an $n \times n$ *algebraic* linear system

$$\begin{aligned}
a_{11}x_1 + a_{12}x_2 + \cdots + a_{1n}x_n &= b_1, \\
a_{21}x_1 + a_{22}x_2 + \cdots + a_{2n}x_n &= b_2, \\
&\vdots \\
a_{n1}x_1 + a_{n2}x_2 + \cdots + a_{nn}x_n &= b_n
\end{aligned} \tag{43}$$

with nonsingular coefficient matrix $\mathbf{A} = [a_{ij}]$, constant vector $\mathbf{b} = [b_i]$, and unknowns $x_1, x_2, \ldots, x_n$. The basic idea is to transform the system in (43) into the simpler *upper triangular form*

$$\begin{aligned}
\overline{a}_{11}x_1 + \overline{a}_{12}x_2 + \cdots + \overline{a}_{1n}x_n &= \overline{b}_1, \\
\overline{a}_{22}x_2 + \cdots + \overline{a}_{2n}x_n &= \overline{b}_2, \\
&\vdots \\
\overline{a}_{nn}x_n &= \overline{b}_n
\end{aligned} \tag{44}$$

in which only the unknowns $x_j, x_{j+1}, \ldots, x_n$ appear explicitly in the jth equation $(j = 1, 2, \ldots, n)$. The transformed system is then easily solved by the process of *back substitution.* First the last equation in (44) is solved for x_n, then the next-to-last is solved for x_{n-1}, and so forth, until the first equation is finally solved for x_1.

The transformation of the system in (43) to upper triangular form is most easily described in terms of elementary row operations on the *augmented coefficient matrix*

$$
\begin{bmatrix} \mathbf{A} & \vdots & \mathbf{b} \end{bmatrix} =
\begin{bmatrix}
a_{11} & a_{12} & \cdots & a_{1n} & b_1 \\
a_{21} & a_{22} & \cdots & a_{2n} & b_2 \\
\vdots & \vdots & & \vdots & \vdots \\
a_{n1} & a_{n2} & \cdots & a_{nn} & b_n
\end{bmatrix}
\tag{45}
$$

that is obtained by adjoining the vector $\mathbf{b}$ to the matrix $\mathbf{A}$ as an additional column. The admissible **elementary row operations** are of the following three types:

1. Multiply any (single) row of the matrix by a nonzero constant.
2. Interchange any two rows of the matrix.
3. Subtract a constant multiple of one row from any other row.

The goal is to use a sequence of such operations (one by one, in turn) to transform $\begin{bmatrix} \mathbf{A} & \vdots & \mathbf{b} \end{bmatrix}$ into an upper triangular matrix, one that has only zeros beneath its principal diagonal. This upper triangular augmented coefficient matrix then corresponds to an upper triangular system as in (44). The process of transforming $\begin{bmatrix} \mathbf{A} & \vdots & \mathbf{b} \end{bmatrix}$ is carried out one column at a time, from left to right, as in the next example.

EXAMPLE 8   Use the solution vectors given in Example 7 to solve the initial value problem

$$
\frac{d\mathbf{x}}{dt} =
\begin{bmatrix}
3 & -2 & 0 \\
-1 & 3 & -2 \\
0 & -1 & 3
\end{bmatrix} \mathbf{x}, \quad
\mathbf{x}(0) =
\begin{bmatrix} 0 \\ 2 \\ 6 \end{bmatrix}.
\tag{46}
$$

Solution   It follows from Theorem 3 that the linear combination

$$
\mathbf{x}(t) = c_1 \mathbf{x}_1(t) + c_2 \mathbf{x}(t) + c_3 \mathbf{x}_3(t)
$$

$$
= c_1 \begin{bmatrix} 2e^t \\ 2e^t \\ e^t \end{bmatrix}
+ c_2 \begin{bmatrix} 2e^{3t} \\ 0 \\ -e^{3t} \end{bmatrix}
+ c_3 \begin{bmatrix} 2e^{5t} \\ -2e^{5t} \\ e^{5t} \end{bmatrix}
$$

is a general solution of the 3×3 linear system in (46). In scalar form, this gives the general solution

$$
\begin{aligned}
x_1(t) &= 2c_1 e^t + 2c_2 e^{3t} + 2c_3 e^{5t}, \\
x_2(t) &= 2c_1 e^t \qquad\quad - 2c_3 e^{5t}, \\
x_3(t) &= c_1 e^t - c_2 e^{3t} + c_3 e^{5t}.
\end{aligned}
$$

We seek the particular solution satisfying the initial conditions

$$
x_1(0) = 0, \quad x_2(0) = 2, \quad x_3(0) = 6.
$$

When we substitute these values in the three scalar equations above, we get the algebraic linear system

$$
\begin{aligned}
2c_1 + 2c_2 + 2c_3 &= 0, \\
2c_2 \qquad\; - 2c_3 &= 2, \\
c_1 - c_2 + c_3 &= 6
\end{aligned}
$$

with augmented coefficient matrix

$$
\begin{bmatrix}
2 & 2 & 2 & 0 \\
2 & 0 & -2 & 2 \\
1 & -1 & 1 & 6
\end{bmatrix}.
$$

Multiplication of each of the first two rows by $\frac{1}{2}$ gives

$$\left[\begin{array}{ccc|c} 1 & 1 & 1 & 0 \\ 1 & 0 & -1 & 1 \\ 1 & -1 & 1 & 6 \end{array}\right],$$

then subtraction of the first row both from the second row and from the third row gives the matrix

$$\left[\begin{array}{ccc|c} 1 & 1 & 1 & 0 \\ 0 & -1 & -2 & 1 \\ 0 & -2 & 0 & 6 \end{array}\right].$$

The first column of this matrix now has the desired form.

Now we multiply the second row by -1, then add twice the result to the third row. Thereby we get the upper triangular augmented coefficient matrix

$$\left[\begin{array}{ccc|c} 1 & 1 & 1 & 0 \\ 0 & 1 & 2 & -1 \\ 0 & 0 & 4 & 4 \end{array}\right]$$

that corresponds to the transformed system

$$\begin{aligned} c_1 + c_2 + c_3 &= 0, \\ c_2 + 2c_3 &= -1, \\ 4c_3 &= 4. \end{aligned}$$

We finally solve in turn for $c_3 = 1$, $c_2 = -3$, and $c_1 = 2$. Thus the desired particular solution is given by

$$\mathbf{x}(t) = 2\mathbf{x}_1(t) - 3\mathbf{x}_2(t) + \mathbf{x}_3(t) = \left[\begin{array}{c} 4e^t - 6e^{3t} + 2e^{5t} \\ 4e^t \quad\quad - 2e^{5t} \\ 2e^t + 3e^{3t} + e^{5t} \end{array}\right]. \quad\blacksquare$$

Nonhomogeneous Solutions

We finally turn our attention to a *nonhomogeneous* linear system of the form

$$\frac{d\mathbf{x}}{dt} = \mathbf{P}(t)\mathbf{x} + \mathbf{f}(t). \tag{47}$$

The following theorem is analogous to Theorem 5 of Section 3.2 and is proved in precisely the same way, substituting the preceding theorems in this section for the analogous theorems of Section 3.2. In brief, Theorem 4 means that the general solution of Eq. (47) has the form

$$\mathbf{x}(t) = \mathbf{x}_c(t) + \mathbf{x}_p(t), \tag{48}$$

where $\mathbf{x}_p(t)$ is a single particular solution of Eq. (47) and the **complementary function** $\mathbf{x}_c(t)$ is a general solution of the associated homogeneous equation $\mathbf{x}' = \mathbf{P}(t)\mathbf{x}$.

THEOREM 4: Solutions of Nonhomogeneous Systems

Let $\mathbf{x}_p$ be a particular solution of the nonhomogeneous linear equation in (47) on an open interval I on which the functions $\mathbf{P}(t)$ and $\mathbf{f}(t)$ are continuous. Let $\mathbf{x}_1, \mathbf{x}_2, \ldots,$ $\mathbf{x}_n$ be linearly independent solutions of the associated homogeneous equation on I.

If $\mathbf{x}(t)$ is any solution whatsoever of Eq. (47) on I, then there exist numbers $c_1, c_2, \ldots, c_n$ such that

$$\mathbf{x}(t) = c_1\mathbf{x}_1(t) + c_2\mathbf{x}_2(t) + \cdots + c_n\mathbf{x}_n(t) + \mathbf{x}_p(t) \qquad (49)$$

for all t in I.   ∎

Thus finding a general solution of a homogeneous linear system involves two separate steps:

1. Finding the general solution $\mathbf{x}_c(t)$ of the associated homogeneous system;
2. Finding a single particular solution $\mathbf{x}_p(t)$ of the nonhomogeneous system.

The sum $\mathbf{x}(t) = \mathbf{x}_c(t) + \mathbf{x}_p(t)$ will then be a general solution of the nonhomogeneous system.

EXAMPLE 9   The nonhomogeneous linear system

$$\begin{aligned}
x_1' &= 3x_1 - 2x_2 && - 9t + 13\,, \\
x_2' &= -x_1 + 3x_2 - 2x_3 + 7t - 15, \\
x_3' &= - x_2 + 3x_3 - 6t + 7
\end{aligned}$$

is of the form in (47) with

$$\mathbf{P}(t) = \begin{bmatrix} 3 & -2 & 0 \\ -1 & 3 & -2 \\ 0 & -1 & 3 \end{bmatrix}, \quad \mathbf{f}(t) = \begin{bmatrix} -9t + 13 \\ 7t - 15 \\ -6t + 7 \end{bmatrix}.$$

In Example 7 we saw that a general solution of the associated homogeneous linear system

$$\frac{d\mathbf{x}}{dt} = \begin{bmatrix} 3 & -2 & 0 \\ -1 & 3 & -2 \\ 0 & -1 & 3 \end{bmatrix} \mathbf{x}$$

is given by

$$\mathbf{x}_c(t) = \begin{bmatrix} 2c_1e^t + 2c_2e^{3t} + 2c_3e^{5t} \\ 2c_1e^t \phantom{+ 2c_2e^{3t}} - 2c_3e^{5t} \\ c_1e^t - c_2e^{3t} + c_2e^{5t} \end{bmatrix},$$

and we can verify by substitution that the function

$$\mathbf{x}_p(t) = \begin{bmatrix} 3t \\ 5 \\ 2t \end{bmatrix}$$

(found using a computer algebra system) is a particular solution of the original nonhomogeneous system. Consequently, Theorem 4 implies that a general solution of the nonhomogeneous system is given by

$$\mathbf{x}(t) = \mathbf{x}_c(t) + \mathbf{x}_p(t);$$

that is, by

$$\begin{aligned}
x_1(t) &= 2c_1e^t + 2c_2e^{3t} + 2c_3e^{5t} + 3t, \\
x_2(t) &= 2c_1e^t \phantom{+ 2c_2e^{3t}} - 2c_3e^{5t} + 5, \\
x_3(t) &= c_1e^t - c_2e^{3t} + c_3e^{5t} + 2t.
\end{aligned}$$ ∎

5.1 *Problems*

1. Let

$$\mathbf{A} = \begin{bmatrix} 2 & -3 \\ 4 & 7 \end{bmatrix} \quad \text{and} \quad \mathbf{B} = \begin{bmatrix} 3 & -4 \\ 4 & 1 \end{bmatrix}.$$

Find (a) $2\mathbf{A} + 3\mathbf{B}$; (b) $3\mathbf{A} - 2\mathbf{B}$; (c) $\mathbf{AB}$; (d) $\mathbf{BA}$.

2. Verify that (a) $\mathbf{A}(\mathbf{BC}) = (\mathbf{AB})\mathbf{C}$ and that (b) $\mathbf{A}(\mathbf{B}+\mathbf{C}) = \mathbf{AB} + \mathbf{AC}$, where $\mathbf{A}$ and $\mathbf{B}$ are the matrices given in Problem 1 and

$$\mathbf{C} = \begin{bmatrix} 0 & 2 \\ 3 & -1 \end{bmatrix}.$$

3. Find $\mathbf{AB}$ and $\mathbf{BA}$ given

$$\mathbf{A} = \begin{bmatrix} 2 & 0 & -1 \\ 3 & -4 & 5 \end{bmatrix} \quad \text{and} \quad \mathbf{B} = \begin{bmatrix} 1 & 3 \\ -7 & 0 \\ 3 & -2 \end{bmatrix}.$$

4. Let $\mathbf{A}$ and $\mathbf{B}$ be the matrices given in Problem 3 and let

$$\mathbf{x} = \begin{bmatrix} 2t \\ e^{-t} \end{bmatrix} \quad \text{and} \quad \mathbf{y} = \begin{bmatrix} t^2 \\ \sin t \\ \cos t \end{bmatrix}.$$

Find $\mathbf{Ay}$ and $\mathbf{Bx}$. Are the products $\mathbf{Ax}$ and $\mathbf{By}$ defined? Explain your answer.

5. Let

$$\mathbf{A} = \begin{bmatrix} 3 & 2 & -1 \\ 0 & 4 & 3 \\ -5 & 2 & 7 \end{bmatrix} \quad \text{and} \quad \mathbf{B} = \begin{bmatrix} 0 & -3 & 2 \\ 1 & 4 & -3 \\ 2 & 5 & -1 \end{bmatrix}.$$

Find (a) $7\mathbf{A} + 4\mathbf{B}$; (b) $3\mathbf{A} - 5\mathbf{B}$; (c) $\mathbf{AB}$; (d) $\mathbf{BA}$; (e) $\mathbf{A} - t\mathbf{I}$.

6. Let

$$\mathbf{A}_1 = \begin{bmatrix} 2 & 1 \\ -3 & 2 \end{bmatrix}, \quad \mathbf{A}_2 = \begin{bmatrix} 1 & 3 \\ -1 & -2 \end{bmatrix},$$

$$\mathbf{B} = \begin{bmatrix} 2 & 4 \\ 1 & 2 \end{bmatrix}.$$

(a) Show that $\mathbf{A}_1\mathbf{B} = \mathbf{A}_2\mathbf{B}$ and note that $\mathbf{A}_1 \neq \mathbf{A}_2$. Thus the cancellation law does not hold for matrices; that is, if $\mathbf{A}_1\mathbf{B} = \mathbf{A}_2\mathbf{B}$ and $\mathbf{B} \neq \mathbf{0}$, it does not follow that $\mathbf{A}_1 = \mathbf{A}_2$. (b) Let $\mathbf{A} = \mathbf{A}_1 - \mathbf{A}_2$ and show that $\mathbf{AB} = \mathbf{0}$. Thus the product of two nonzero matrices may be the zero matrix.

7. Compute the determinants of the matrices $\mathbf{A}$ and $\mathbf{B}$ in Problem 6. Are your results consistent with the theorem to the effect that

$$\det(\mathbf{AB}) = \det(\mathbf{A}) \cdot \det(\mathbf{B})$$

for any two square matrices $\mathbf{A}$ and $\mathbf{B}$ of the same order?

8. Suppose that $\mathbf{A}$ and $\mathbf{B}$ are the matrices of Problem 5. Verify that $\det(\mathbf{AB}) = \det(\mathbf{BA})$.

In Problems 9 and 10, verify the product law for differentiation, $(\mathbf{AB})' = \mathbf{A}'\mathbf{B} + \mathbf{AB}'$.

9. $\mathbf{A}(t) = \begin{bmatrix} t & 2t-1 \\ t^3 & \dfrac{1}{t} \end{bmatrix}$ and $\mathbf{B}(t) = \begin{bmatrix} 1-t & 1+t \\ 3t^2 & 4t^3 \end{bmatrix}.$

10. $\mathbf{A}(t) = \begin{bmatrix} e^t & t & t^2 \\ -t & 0 & 2 \\ 8t & -1 & t^3 \end{bmatrix}$ and $\mathbf{B}(t) = \begin{bmatrix} 3 \\ 2e^{-t} \\ 3t \end{bmatrix}.$

In Problems 11 through 20, write the given system in the form $\mathbf{x}' = \mathbf{P}(t)\mathbf{x} + \mathbf{f}(t)$.

11. $x' = -3y,\ y' = 3x$

12. $x' = 3x - 2y,\ y' = 2x + y$

13. $x' = 2x + 4y + 3e^t,\ y' = 5x - y - t^2$

14. $x' = tx - e^t y + \cos t,\ y' = e^{-t}x + t^2 y - \sin t$

15. $x' = y + z,\ y' = z + x,\ z' = x + y$

16. $x' = 2x - 3y,\ y' = x + y + 2z,\ z' = 5y - 7z$

17. $x' = 3x - 4y + z + t,\ y' = x - 3z - t^2,\ z' = 6y - 7z + t^3$

18. $x' = tx - y + e^t z,\ y' = 2x + t^2 y - z,\ z' = e^{-t}x + 3ty + t^3 z$

19. $x_1' = x_2,\ x_2' = 2x_3,\ x_3' = 3x_4,\ x_4' = 4x_1$

20. $x_1' = x_2 + x_3 + 1,\ x_2' = x_3 + x_4 + t,$
$x_3' = x_1 + x_4 + t^2,\ x_4' = x_1 + x_2 + t^3$

In Problems 21 through 30, first verify that the given vectors are solutions of the given system. Then use the Wronskian to show that they are linearly independent. Finally, write the general solution of the system.

21. $\mathbf{x}' = \begin{bmatrix} 4 & 2 \\ -3 & -1 \end{bmatrix}\mathbf{x};\ \mathbf{x}_1 = \begin{bmatrix} 2e^t \\ -3e^t \end{bmatrix},\ \mathbf{x}_2 = \begin{bmatrix} e^{2t} \\ -e^{2t} \end{bmatrix}$

22. $\mathbf{x}' = \begin{bmatrix} -3 & 2 \\ -3 & 4 \end{bmatrix}\mathbf{x};\ \mathbf{x}_1 = \begin{bmatrix} e^{3t} \\ 3e^{3t} \end{bmatrix},\ \mathbf{x}_2 = \begin{bmatrix} 2e^{-2t} \\ e^{-2t} \end{bmatrix}$

23. $\mathbf{x}' = \begin{bmatrix} 3 & -1 \\ 5 & -3 \end{bmatrix}\mathbf{x};\ \mathbf{x}_1 = e^{2t}\begin{bmatrix} 1 \\ 1 \end{bmatrix},\ \mathbf{x}_2 = e^{-2t}\begin{bmatrix} 1 \\ 5 \end{bmatrix}$

24. $\mathbf{x}' = \begin{bmatrix} 4 & 1 \\ -2 & 1 \end{bmatrix}\mathbf{x};\ \mathbf{x}_1 = e^{3t}\begin{bmatrix} 1 \\ -1 \end{bmatrix},\ \mathbf{x}_2 = e^{2t}\begin{bmatrix} 1 \\ -2 \end{bmatrix}$

25. $\mathbf{x}' = \begin{bmatrix} 4 & -3 \\ 6 & -7 \end{bmatrix}\mathbf{x};\ \mathbf{x}_1 = \begin{bmatrix} 3e^{2t} \\ 2e^{2t} \end{bmatrix},\ \mathbf{x}_2 = \begin{bmatrix} e^{-5t} \\ 3e^{-5t} \end{bmatrix}$

26. $\mathbf{x}' = \begin{bmatrix} 3 & -2 & 0 \\ -1 & 3 & -2 \\ 0 & -1 & 3 \end{bmatrix}\mathbf{x};\ \mathbf{x}_1 = e^t\begin{bmatrix} 2 \\ 2 \\ 1 \end{bmatrix},$

$\mathbf{x}_2 = e^{3t}\begin{bmatrix} -2 \\ 0 \\ 1 \end{bmatrix},\ \mathbf{x}_3 = e^{5t}\begin{bmatrix} 2 \\ -2 \\ 1 \end{bmatrix}$

27. $\mathbf{x}' = \begin{bmatrix} 0 & 1 & 1 \\ 1 & 0 & 1 \\ 1 & 1 & 0 \end{bmatrix}\mathbf{x};\ \mathbf{x}_1 = e^{2t}\begin{bmatrix} 1 \\ 1 \\ 1 \end{bmatrix},$

$\mathbf{x}_2 = e^{-t}\begin{bmatrix} 1 \\ 0 \\ -1 \end{bmatrix},\ \mathbf{x}_3 = e^{-t}\begin{bmatrix} 0 \\ 1 \\ -1 \end{bmatrix}$

28. $\mathbf{x}' = \begin{bmatrix} 1 & 2 & 1 \\ 6 & -1 & 0 \\ -1 & -2 & -1 \end{bmatrix}\mathbf{x};\ \mathbf{x}_1 = \begin{bmatrix} 1 \\ 6 \\ -13 \end{bmatrix},$

$\mathbf{x}_2 = e^{3t}\begin{bmatrix} 2 \\ 3 \\ -2 \end{bmatrix},\ \mathbf{x}_3 = e^{-4t}\begin{bmatrix} -1 \\ 2 \\ 1 \end{bmatrix}$

29. $\mathbf{x}' = \begin{bmatrix} -8 & -11 & -2 \\ 6 & 9 & 2 \\ -6 & -6 & 1 \end{bmatrix} \mathbf{x}; \ \mathbf{x}_1 = e^{-2t} \begin{bmatrix} 3 \\ -2 \\ 2 \end{bmatrix}$,

$$\mathbf{x}_2 = e^t \begin{bmatrix} 1 \\ -1 \\ 1 \end{bmatrix}, \ \mathbf{x}_3 = e^{3t} \begin{bmatrix} 1 \\ -1 \\ 0 \end{bmatrix}$$

30. $\mathbf{x}' = \begin{bmatrix} 1 & -4 & 0 & -2 \\ 0 & 1 & 0 & 0 \\ 6 & -12 & -1 & -6 \\ 0 & -4 & 0 & -1 \end{bmatrix} \mathbf{x}; \ \mathbf{x}_1 = e^{-t} \begin{bmatrix} 1 \\ 0 \\ 0 \\ 1 \end{bmatrix}$,

$$\mathbf{x}_2 = e^{-t} \begin{bmatrix} 0 \\ 0 \\ 1 \\ 0 \end{bmatrix}, \ \mathbf{x}_3 = e^t \begin{bmatrix} 0 \\ 1 \\ 0 \\ -2 \end{bmatrix}, \ \mathbf{x}_4 = e^t \begin{bmatrix} 1 \\ 0 \\ 3 \\ 0 \end{bmatrix}$$

In Problems 31 through 40, find a particular solution of the indicated linear system that satisfies the given initial conditions.

31. The system of Problem 22: $x_1(0) = 0$, $x_2(0) = 5$

32. The system of Problem 23: $x_1(0) = 5$, $x_2(0) = -3$

33. The system of Problem 24: $x_1(0) = 11$, $x_2(0) = -7$

34. The system of Problem 25: $x_1(0) = 8$, $x_2(0) = 0$

35. The system of Problem 26: $x_1(0) = 0$, $x_2(0) = 0$, $x_3(0) = 4$

36. The system of Problem 27: $x_1(0) = 10$, $x_2(0) = 12$, $x_3(0) = -1$

37. The system of Problem 29: $x_1(0) = 1$, $x_2(0) = 2$, $x_3(0) = 3$

38. The system of Problem 29: $x_1(0) = 5$, $x_2(0) = -7$, $x_3(0) = 11$

39. The system of Problem 30: $x_1(0) = x_2(0) = x_3(0) = x_4(0) = 1$

40. The system of Problem 30: $x_1(0) = 1$, $x_2(0) = 3$, $x_3(0) = 4$, $x_4(0) = 7$

41. (a) Show that the vector functions

$$\mathbf{x}_1(t) = \begin{bmatrix} t \\ t^2 \end{bmatrix} \quad \text{and} \quad \mathbf{x}_2 = \begin{bmatrix} t^2 \\ t^3 \end{bmatrix}$$

are linearly independent on the real line. (b) Why does it follow from Theorem 2 that there is *no* continuous matrix $\mathbf{P}(t)$ such that $\mathbf{x}_1$ and $\mathbf{x}_2$ are both solutions of $\mathbf{x}' = \mathbf{P}(t)\mathbf{x}$?

42. Suppose that one of the vector functions

$$\mathbf{x}_1(t) = \begin{bmatrix} x_{11}(t) \\ x_{21}(t) \end{bmatrix} \quad \text{and} \quad \mathbf{x}_2(t) = \begin{bmatrix} x_{12}(t) \\ x_{22}(t) \end{bmatrix}$$

is a constant multiple of the other on the open interval I. Show that their Wronskian $W(t) = |[x_{ij}(t)]|$ must vanish identically on I. This proves part (a) of Theorem 2 in the case $n = 2$.

43. Suppose that the vectors $\mathbf{x}_1(t)$ and $\mathbf{x}_2(t)$ of Problem 42 are solutions of the equation $\mathbf{x}' = \mathbf{P}(t)\mathbf{x}$, where the 2×2 matrix $\mathbf{P}(t)$ is continuous on the open interval I. Show that if there exists a point a of I at which their Wronskian $W(a)$ is zero, then there exist numbers c_1 and c_2 not both zero such that $c_1\mathbf{x}_1(a) + c_2\mathbf{x}_2(a) = \mathbf{0}$. Then conclude from the uniqueness of solutions of the equation $\mathbf{x}' = \mathbf{P}(t)\mathbf{x}$ that

$$c_1\mathbf{x}_1(t) + c_2\mathbf{x}_2(t) = \mathbf{0}$$

for all t in I; that is, that $\mathbf{x}_1$ and $\mathbf{x}_2$ are linearly dependent. This proves part (b) of Theorem 2 in the case $n = 2$.

44. Generalize Problems 42 and 43 to prove Theorem 2 for n an arbitrary positive integer.

45. Let $\mathbf{x}_1(t), \mathbf{x}_2(t), \ldots, \mathbf{x}_n(t)$ be vector functions whose ith components (for some fixed i) $x_{i1}(t), x_{i2}(t), \ldots, x_{in}(t)$ are linearly independent real-valued functions. Conclude that the vector functions are themselves linearly independent.

5.2 THE EIGENVALUE METHOD FOR HOMOGENEOUS SYSTEMS

We now introduce a powerful alternative to the method of elimination for constructing the general solution of a *homogeneous* first-order linear system with *constant* coefficients,

$$\begin{aligned} x_1' &= a_{11}x_1 + a_{12}x_2 + \cdots + a_{1n}x_n, \\ x_2' &= a_{21}x_1 + a_{22}x_2 + \cdots + a_{2n}x_n, \\ &\vdots \\ x_n' &= a_{n1}x_1 + a_{n2}x_2 + \cdots + a_{nn}x_n. \end{aligned} \tag{1}$$

By Theorem 3 of Section 5.1, we know that it suffices to find n linearly independent solution vectors $\mathbf{x}_1, \mathbf{x}_2, \ldots, \mathbf{x}_n$; the linear combination

$$\mathbf{x}(t) = c_1\mathbf{x}_1 + c_2\mathbf{x}_2 + \cdots + c_n\mathbf{x}_n \tag{2}$$

with arbitrary coefficients will then be a general solution of the system in (1).

To search for the n needed linearly independent solution vectors, we proceed by analogy with the characteristic root method for solving a single homogeneous equation with constant coefficients (Section 3.3). It is reasonable to anticipate solution vectors of the form

$$\mathbf{x}(t) = \begin{bmatrix} x_1 \\ x_2 \\ x_3 \\ \vdots \\ x_n \end{bmatrix} = \begin{bmatrix} v_1 e^{\lambda t} \\ v_2 e^{\lambda t} \\ v_3 e^{\lambda t} \\ \vdots \\ v_n e^{\lambda t} \end{bmatrix} = \begin{bmatrix} v_1 \\ v_2 \\ v_3 \\ \vdots \\ v_n \end{bmatrix} e^{\lambda t} = \mathbf{v} e^{\lambda t} \qquad (3)$$

where $\lambda, v_1, v_2, v_3, \ldots, v_n$ are appropriate scalar constants. For if we substitute

$$x_i = v_i e^{\lambda t}, \qquad x_i' = \lambda v_i e^{\lambda t}$$

$(i = 1, 2, \ldots, n)$ in (1), then the factor $e^{\lambda t}$ will cancel throughout. This will leave us with n linear equations which—for appropriate values of λ—we can hope to solve for values of the coefficients $v_1, v_2, \ldots, v_n$ in Eq. (3) so that $\mathbf{x}(t) = \mathbf{v} e^{\lambda t}$ is, indeed, a solution of the system in (1).

To investigate this possibility, it is more efficient to write the system in (1) in the matrix form

$$\mathbf{x}' = \mathbf{A}\mathbf{x} \qquad (4)$$

where $\mathbf{A} = \begin{bmatrix} a_{ij} \end{bmatrix}$. When we substitute the trial solution $\mathbf{x} = \mathbf{v} e^{\lambda t}$ with derivative $\mathbf{x}' = \lambda \mathbf{v} e^{\lambda t}$ in Eq. (4), the result is

$$\lambda \mathbf{v} e^{\lambda t} = \mathbf{A} \mathbf{v} e^{\lambda t}.$$

We cancel the nonzero scalar factor $e^{\lambda t}$ to get

$$\mathbf{A}\mathbf{v} = \lambda \mathbf{v}. \qquad (5)$$

This means that $\mathbf{x} = \mathbf{v} e^{\lambda t}$ will be a nontrivial solution of Eq. (4) provided that $\mathbf{v}$ is a *nonzero* vector and λ is a constant such that Eq. (5) holds; that is, the *matrix product* $\mathbf{A}\mathbf{v}$ *is a scalar multiple of the vector* $\mathbf{v}$. The question now is this: How do we find $\mathbf{v}$ and λ?

To answer this question, we rewrite Eq. (5) in the form

$$(\mathbf{A} - \lambda \mathbf{I})\mathbf{v} = \mathbf{0}. \qquad (6)$$

Given λ, this is a system of n nonhomogeneous linear equations in the unknowns $v_1, v_2, \ldots, v_n$. By a standard theorem of linear algebra, it has a nontrivial solution if and only if the determinant of its coefficient matrix vanishes; that is, if and only if

$$|\mathbf{A} - \lambda \mathbf{I}| = \det(\mathbf{A} - \lambda \mathbf{I}) = 0. \qquad (7)$$

In its simplest formulation, the **eigenvalue method** for solving the system $\mathbf{x}' = \mathbf{A}\mathbf{x}$ consists of finding λ so that Eq. (7) holds and next solving Eq. (6) with this value of λ to obtain $v_1, v_2, \ldots, v_n$. Then $\mathbf{x} = \mathbf{v} e^{\lambda t}$ will be a solution vector. The name of the method comes from the following definition.

DEFINITION: Eigenvalues and Eigenvectors

The number λ (either zero or nonzero) is called an **eigenvalue** of the $n \times n$ matrix $\mathbf{A}$ provided that

$$|\mathbf{A} - \lambda \mathbf{I}| = 0. \qquad (7)$$

An **eigenvector** associated with the eigenvalue λ is a *nonzero* vector $\mathbf{v}$ such that $\mathbf{A}\mathbf{v} = \lambda\mathbf{v}$, so that

$$(\mathbf{A} - \lambda\mathbf{I})\mathbf{v} = \mathbf{0}. \tag{6}$$

■

Note that if $\mathbf{v}$ is an eigenvector associated with the eigenvalue λ, then so is any nonzero constant scalar multiple $c\mathbf{v}$ of $\mathbf{v}$—this follows upon multiplication of each side in Eq. (6) by $c \neq 0$.

The prefix *eigen* is a German word with the approximate translation *characteristic* in this context; the terms *characteristic value* and *characteristic vector* are in common use. For this reason, the equation

$$|\mathbf{A} - \lambda\mathbf{I}| = \begin{vmatrix} a_{11} - \lambda & a_{12} & \cdots & a_{1n} \\ a_{21} & a_{22} - \lambda & \cdots & a_{2n} \\ \vdots & \vdots & & \vdots \\ a_{n1} & a_{n2} & \cdots & a_{nn} - \lambda \end{vmatrix} = 0 \tag{8}$$

is called the **characteristic equation** of the matrix $\mathbf{A}$; its roots are the eigenvalues of $\mathbf{A}$. Upon expanding the determinant in (8), we evidently get an nth-degree polynomial of the form

$$(-1)^n\lambda^n + b_{n-1}\lambda^{n-1} + \cdots + b_1\lambda + b_0 = 0. \tag{9}$$

By the fundamental theorem of algebra, this equation has n roots—possibly some are complex, possibly some are repeated—and thus an $n \times n$ matrix has n eigenvalues (counting repetitions, if any). Although we assume that the elements of $\mathbf{A}$ are real numbers, we allow the possibility of complex eigenvalues and complex-valued eigenvectors.

Our discussion of Eqs. (4) through (7) provides a proof of the following theorem, which is the basis for the eigenvalue method of solving a first-order linear system with constant coefficients.

THEOREM: Eigenvalue Solutions of $\mathbf{x}' = \mathbf{A}\mathbf{x}$

Let λ be an eigenvalue of the [constant] coefficient matrix $\mathbf{A}$ of the first-order linear system

$$\frac{d\mathbf{x}}{dt} = \mathbf{A}\mathbf{x}.$$

If $\mathbf{v}$ is an eigenvector associated with λ, then

$$\mathbf{x}(t) = \mathbf{v}e^{\lambda t}$$

is a nontrivial solution of the system.   ■

In outline, the eigenvalue method for solving the $n \times n$ system $\mathbf{x}' = \mathbf{A}\mathbf{x}$ proceeds as follows.

1. We first solve the characteristic equation in (8) for the eigenvalues $\lambda_1, \lambda_2, \ldots,$ λ_n of the matrix $\mathbf{A}$.
2. Next we attempt to find n *linearly independent* eigenvectors $\mathbf{v}_1, \mathbf{v}_2, \ldots, \mathbf{v}_n$ associated with these eigenvalues.

3. Step 2 is not always possible, but when it is, we get n linearly independent solutions

$$\mathbf{x}_1(t) = \mathbf{v}_1 e^{\lambda_1 t}, \quad \mathbf{x}_2(t) = \mathbf{v}_2 e^{\lambda_2 t}, \quad \ldots, \quad \mathbf{x}_n(t) = \mathbf{v}_n e^{\lambda_n t}. \tag{10}$$

In this case the general solution of $\mathbf{x}' = \mathbf{A}\mathbf{x}$ is a linear combination

$$\mathbf{x}(t) = c_1 \mathbf{x}_1(t) + c_2 \mathbf{x}_2(t) + \cdots + c_n \mathbf{x}_n(t)$$

of these n solutions.

We will discuss separately the generic cases of distinct real eigenvalues and complex eigenvalues.

Distinct Real Eigenvalues

If the eigenvalues $\lambda_1, \lambda_2, \ldots, \lambda_n$ are real and distinct, then we substitute each of them in turn in Eq. (6) and solve for the associated eigenvectors $\mathbf{v}_1, \mathbf{v}_2, \ldots, \mathbf{v}_n$. In this case it can be proved that the particular solution vectors given in (10) are always linearly independent. (For instance, see Section 6.2 of Edwards and Penney, *Elementary Linear Algebra* (Englewood Cliffs, N.J.: Prentice Hall, 1988).) In any particular example such linear independence can always be verified by using the Wronskian determinant of Section 5.1. The following example illustrates the procedure.

EXAMPLE 1   Find a general solution of the system

$$\begin{aligned} x_1' &= 4x_1 + 2x_2, \\ x_2' &= 3x_1 - x_2. \end{aligned} \tag{11}$$

Solution   The matrix form of the system in (11) is

$$\mathbf{x}' = \begin{bmatrix} 4 & 2 \\ 3 & -1 \end{bmatrix} \mathbf{x}. \tag{12}$$

The characteristic equation of the coefficient matrix is

$$\begin{vmatrix} 4 - \lambda & 2 \\ 3 & -1 - \lambda \end{vmatrix} = (4 - \lambda)(-1 - \lambda) - 6$$

$$= \lambda^2 - 3\lambda - 10 = (\lambda + 2)(\lambda - 5) = 0,$$

so we have the distinct real eigenvalues $\lambda_1 = -2$ and $\lambda_2 = 5$.

For the coefficient matrix $\mathbf{A}$ in Eq. (12) the eigenvector equation $(\mathbf{A} - \lambda \mathbf{I})\mathbf{v} = \mathbf{0}$ takes the form

$$\begin{bmatrix} 4 - \lambda & 2 \\ 3 & -1 - \lambda \end{bmatrix} \begin{bmatrix} a \\ b \end{bmatrix} = \begin{bmatrix} 0 \\ 0 \end{bmatrix} \tag{13}$$

for the associated eigenvector $\mathbf{v} = \begin{bmatrix} a & b \end{bmatrix}^T$.

CASE 1: $\lambda_1 = -2$. Substitution of the first eigenvalue $\lambda_1 = -2$ in Eq. (13) yields the system

$$\begin{bmatrix} 6 & 2 \\ 3 & 1 \end{bmatrix} \begin{bmatrix} a \\ b \end{bmatrix} = \begin{bmatrix} 0 \\ 0 \end{bmatrix};$$

that is, the two scalar equations

$$\begin{aligned} 6a + 2b &= 0, \\ 3a + b &= 0. \end{aligned} \tag{14}$$

In contrast with the nonsingular (algebraic) linear systems whose solutions we discussed in Section 5.1, the homogeneous linear system in (14) is *singular*—the two scalar equations obviously are equivalent (each being a multiple of the other). Therefore Eq. (14) has infinitely many nonzero solutions—we can choose a arbitrary (but nonzero) and then solve for b.

Substitution of an eigenvalue λ in the eigenvector equation $(\mathbf{A} - \lambda\mathbf{I})\mathbf{v} = \mathbf{0}$ always yields a singular homogeneous linear system, and among its infinity of solutions we generally seek a "simple" solution with small integer values (if possible). Looking at the second equation in (14), the choice $a = 1$ yields $b = -3$, and thus

$$\mathbf{v}_1 = \begin{bmatrix} 1 \\ -3 \end{bmatrix}$$

is an eigenvector associated with $\lambda_1 = -2$ (as is any nonzero constant multiple of $\mathbf{v}_1$).

Remark: If instead of the "simplest" choice $a = 1$, $b = -3$, we had made another choice $a = c$, $b = -3c$, we would have obtained the eigenvector

$$\mathbf{v}_1 = \begin{bmatrix} c \\ -3c \end{bmatrix} = c \begin{bmatrix} 1 \\ -3 \end{bmatrix}.$$

Because this is a constant multiple of our previous result, any choice we make leads to [a constant multiple of] the same solution

$$\mathbf{x}_1(t) = \begin{bmatrix} 1 \\ -3 \end{bmatrix} e^{-2t}.$$

CASE 2: $\lambda_2 = 5$. Substitution of the second eigenvalue $\lambda = 5$ in (13) yields the pair

$$\begin{aligned} -a + 2b &= 0, \\ 3a - 6b &= 0 \end{aligned} \tag{15}$$

of equivalent scalar equations. With $b = 1$ in the first equation we get $a = 2$, so

$$\mathbf{v}_2 = \begin{bmatrix} 2 \\ 1 \end{bmatrix}$$

is an eigenvector associated with $\lambda_2 = 5$. A different choice $a = 2c$, $b = c$ would merely give a [constant] multiple of $\mathbf{v}_2$.

These two eigenvalues and associated eigenvectors yield the two solutions

$$\mathbf{x}_1(t) = \begin{bmatrix} 1 \\ -3 \end{bmatrix} e^{-2t} \quad \text{and} \quad \mathbf{x}_2(t) = \begin{bmatrix} 2 \\ 1 \end{bmatrix} e^{5t}.$$

They are linearly independent because their Wronskian

$$\begin{vmatrix} e^{-2t} & 2e^{5t} \\ -3e^{-2t} & e^{5t} \end{vmatrix} = 7e^{3t}$$

is nonzero. Hence a general solution of the system in (11) is

$$\mathbf{x}(t) = c_1 \mathbf{x}_1(t) + c_2 \mathbf{x}_2(t) = c_1 \begin{bmatrix} 1 \\ -3 \end{bmatrix} e^{-2t} + c_2 \begin{bmatrix} 2 \\ 1 \end{bmatrix} e^{5t};$$

in scalar form,

$$\begin{aligned} x_1(t) &= c_1 e^{-2t} + 2c_2 e^{5t}, \\ x_2(t) &= -3c_1 e^{-2t} + c_2 e^{5t}. \end{aligned}$$

Fig. 5.2.1 shows some typical solution curves of the system in (11). We see two families of hyperbolas sharing the same pair of asymptotes: the line $x_1 = 2x_2$ obtained from the general solution with $c_1 = 0$ and the line $x_2 = -3x_1$ obtained with $c_2 = 0$. Given initial values $x_1(0) = b_1$, $x_2(0) = b_2$, it is apparent from the figure that:

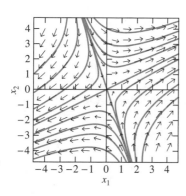

FIGURE 5.2.1. Direction field and solution curves for the linear system $x_1' = 4x_1 + 2x_2$, $x_2' = 3x_1 - x_2$ of Example 1.

- If (b_1, b_2) lies to the right of the line $x_2 = -3x_1$, then $x_1(t)$ and $x_2(t)$ both tend to $+\infty$ as $t \to +\infty$;
- If (b_1, b_2) lies to the left of the line $x_2 = -3x_1$, then $x_1(t)$ and $x_2(t)$ both tend to $-\infty$ as $t \to +\infty$. ∎

Remark: As in Example 1, it is convenient when discussing a linear system $\mathbf{x}' = \mathbf{Ax}$ to use vectors $\mathbf{x}_1, \mathbf{x}_2, \ldots, \mathbf{x}_n$ to denote different vector-valued solutions of the system, whereas the *scalars* $x_1, x_2, \ldots, x_n$ denote the components of a single vector-valued solution $\mathbf{x}$. ∎

Compartmental Analysis

Frequently a complex process or system can be broken down into simpler subsystems or "compartments" that can be analyzed separately. The whole system can then be modeled by describing the interactions between the various compartments. Thus a chemical plant may consist of a succession of separate stages (or even physical compartments) in which various reactants and products combine or are mixed. It may happen that a single differential equation describes each compartment of the system, and then the whole physical system is modeled by a system of differential equations.

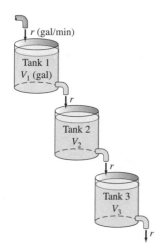

FIGURE 5.2.2. The three brine tanks of Example 2.

As a simple example of a three-stage system, Fig. 5.2.2 shows three brine tanks containing V_1, V_2, and V_3 gallons of brine, respectively. Fresh water flows into tank 1, while mixed brine flows from tank 1 into tank 2, from tank 2 into tank 3, and out of tank 3. Let $x_i(t)$ denote the amount (in pounds) of salt in tank i at time t for $i = 1, 2$, and 3. If each flow rate is r gallons per minute, then a simple accounting of salt concentrations, as in Example 2 of Section 4.1, yields the first-order system

$$\begin{aligned} x_1' &= -kx_1, \\ x_2' &= k_1 x_1 - k_2 x_2, \\ x_3' &= k_2 x_2 - k_3 x_3, \end{aligned} \tag{16}$$

where

$$k_i = \frac{r}{V_i}, \quad i = 1, 2, 3. \tag{17}$$

EXAMPLE 2   If $V_1 = 20$, $V_2 = 40$, $V_3 = 50$, $r = 10$ (gal/min), and the initial amounts of salt in the three brine tanks, in pounds, are

$$x_1(0) = 15, \quad x_2(0) = x_3(0) = 0,$$

find the amount of salt in each tank at time $t \geq 0$.

Solution   Substituting the given numerical values in (16) and (17), we get the initial value problem

$$\mathbf{x}'(t) = \begin{bmatrix} -0.5 & 0.0 & 0.0 \\ 0.5 & -0.25 & 0.0 \\ 0.0 & 0.25 & -0.2 \end{bmatrix} \mathbf{x}, \quad \mathbf{x}(0) = \begin{bmatrix} 15 \\ 0 \\ 0 \end{bmatrix} \tag{18}$$

for the vector $\mathbf{x}(t) = \begin{bmatrix} x_1(t) & x_2(t) & x_3(t) \end{bmatrix}^T$. The simple form of the matrix

$$\mathbf{A} - \lambda \mathbf{I} = \begin{bmatrix} -0.5 - \lambda & 0.0 & 0.0 \\ 0.5 & -0.25 - \lambda & 0.0 \\ 0.0 & 0.25 & -0.2 - \lambda \end{bmatrix} \tag{19}$$

leads readily to the characteristic equation

$$|\mathbf{A} - \lambda \mathbf{I}| = (-0.5 - \lambda)(-0.25 - \lambda)(-0.2 - \lambda) = 0.$$

Thus the coefficient matrix $\mathbf{A}$ in (18) has the distinct eigenvalues $\lambda_1 = -0.5$, $\lambda_2 = -0.25$, and $\lambda_3 = -0.2$.

CASE 1: $\lambda_1 = -0.5$.   Substituting $\lambda = -0.5$ in (19), we get the equation

$$\begin{bmatrix} \mathbf{A} + (0.5) \cdot \mathbf{I} \end{bmatrix} \mathbf{v} = \begin{bmatrix} 0.0 & 0.0 & 0.0 \\ 0.5 & 0.25 & 0.0 \\ 0.0 & 0.25 & 0.3 \end{bmatrix} \begin{bmatrix} a \\ b \\ c \end{bmatrix} = \begin{bmatrix} 0 \\ 0 \\ 0 \end{bmatrix}$$

for the associated eigenvector $\mathbf{v} = \begin{bmatrix} a & b & c \end{bmatrix}^T$. The last two rows, after division by 0.25 and 0.05, respectively, yield the scalar equations

$$\begin{aligned} 2a + b \quad\;\; &= 0, \\ 5b + 6c &= 0. \end{aligned}$$

The second equation is satisfied by $b = -6$ and $c = 5$, and then the first equation gives $a = 3$. Thus the eigenvector

$$\mathbf{v}_1 = \begin{bmatrix} 3 & -6 & 5 \end{bmatrix}^T$$

is associated with the eigenvalue $\lambda_1 = -0.5$.

CASE 2: $\lambda_2 = -0.25$.   Substituting $\lambda = -0.25$ in (19), we get the equation

$$\begin{bmatrix} \mathbf{A} + (0.25) \cdot \mathbf{I} \end{bmatrix} \mathbf{v} = \begin{bmatrix} -0.25 & 0 & 0 \\ 0.5 & 0 & 0 \\ 0 & 0.25 & 0.05 \end{bmatrix} \begin{bmatrix} a \\ b \\ c \end{bmatrix} = \begin{bmatrix} 0 \\ 0 \\ 0 \end{bmatrix}$$

for the associated eigenvector $\mathbf{v} = \begin{bmatrix} a & b & c \end{bmatrix}^T$. Each of the first two rows implies that $a = 0$, and division of the third row by 0.05 gives the equation

$$5b + c = 0,$$

which is satisfied by $b = 1$, $c = -5$. Thus the eigenvector

$$\mathbf{v}_2 = \begin{bmatrix} 0 & 1 & -5 \end{bmatrix}^T$$

is associated with the eigenvalue $\lambda_2 = -0.25$.

CASE 3: $\lambda_3 = -0.2$. Substituting $\lambda = -0.2$ in (19), we get the equation

$$\left[\,\mathbf{A} + (0.2) \cdot \mathbf{I}\,\right]\mathbf{v} = \begin{bmatrix} -0.3 & 0.0 & 0.0 \\ 0.5 & -0.05 & 0.0 \\ 0.0 & 0.25 & 0.0 \end{bmatrix} \begin{bmatrix} a \\ b \\ c \end{bmatrix} = \begin{bmatrix} 0 \\ 0 \\ 0 \end{bmatrix}$$

for the eigenvector $\mathbf{v}$. The first and third rows imply that $a = 0$, and $b = 0$, respectively, but the all-zero third column leaves c arbitrary (but nonzero). Thus

$$\mathbf{v}_3 = \begin{bmatrix} 0 & 0 & 1 \end{bmatrix}^T$$

is an eigenvector associated with $\lambda_3 = -0.2$.

The general solution

$$\mathbf{x}(t) = c_1 \mathbf{v}_1 e^{\lambda_1 t} + c_2 \mathbf{v}_2 e^{\lambda_2 t} + c_3 \mathbf{v}_3 e^{\lambda_3 t}$$

therefore takes the form

$$\mathbf{x}(t) = c_1 \begin{bmatrix} 3 \\ -6 \\ 5 \end{bmatrix} e^{(-0.5)t} + c_2 \begin{bmatrix} 0 \\ 1 \\ -5 \end{bmatrix} e^{(-0.25)t} + c_3 \begin{bmatrix} 0 \\ 0 \\ 1 \end{bmatrix} e^{(-0.2)t}.$$

The resulting scalar equations are

$$\begin{aligned} x_1(t) &= 3c_1 e^{(-0.5)t}, \\ x_2(t) &= -6c_1 e^{(-0.5)t} + c_2 e^{(-0.25)t}, \\ x_3(t) &= 5c_1 e^{(-0.5)t} - 5c_2 e^{(-0.25)t} + c_3 e^{(-0.2)t}. \end{aligned}$$

When we impose the initial conditions $x_1(0) = 15$, $x_2(0) = x_3(0) = 0$, we get the equations

$$\begin{aligned} 3c_1 &&&= 15, \\ -6c_1 &+ c_2 &&= 0, \\ 5c_1 &- 5c_2 &+ c_3 &= 0 \end{aligned}$$

that are readily solved (in turn) for $c_1 = 5$, $c_2 = 30$, and $c_3 = 125$. Thus, finally, the amounts of salt at time t in the three brine tanks are given by

$$\begin{aligned} x_1(t) &= 15 e^{(-0.5)t}, \\ x_2(t) &= -30 e^{(-0.5)t} + 30 e^{(-0.25)t}, \\ x_3(t) &= 25 e^{(-0.5)t} - 150 e^{(-0.25)t} + 125 e^{(-0.2)t}. \end{aligned}$$

Figure 5.2.3 shows the graphs of $x_1(t)$, $x_2(t)$, and $x_3(t)$. As one would expect, tank 1 is rapidly "flushed" by the incoming fresh water, and $x_1(t) \to 0$ as $t \to +\infty$. The amounts $x_2(t)$ and $x_3(t)$ of salt in tanks 2 and 3 peak in turn and then approach zero as the whole three-tank system is purged of salt as $t \to +\infty$. ∎

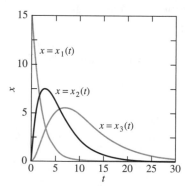

FIGURE 5.2.3. The salt content functions of Example 2.

Complex Eigenvalues

Even if some of the eigenvalues are complex, so long as they are distinct the method described previously still yields n linearly independent solutions. The only complication is that the eigenvectors associated with complex eigenvalues are ordinarily complex-valued, so we will have complex-valued solutions.

To obtain real-valued solutions, we note that—because we are assuming that the matrix $\mathbf{A}$ has only real entries—the coefficients in the characteristic equation in (8) will all be real. Consequently any complex eigenvalues must appear in complex conjugate pairs. Suppose then that $\lambda = p + qi$ and $\bar{\lambda} = p - qi$ are such a pair of eigenvalues. If $\mathbf{v}$ is an eigenvector associated with λ, so that

$$(\mathbf{A} - \lambda \mathbf{I})\mathbf{v} = \mathbf{0},$$

then taking complex conjugates in this equation yields

$$(\mathbf{A} - \bar{\lambda} \mathbf{I})\bar{\mathbf{v}} = \mathbf{0}.$$

Thus the conjugate $\bar{\mathbf{v}}$ of $\mathbf{v}$ is an eigenvector associated with $\bar{\lambda}$. Of course the conjugate of a vector is defined componentwise; if

$$\mathbf{v} = \begin{bmatrix} a_1 + b_1 i \\ a_2 + b_2 i \\ \vdots \\ a_n + b_n i \end{bmatrix} = \begin{bmatrix} a_1 \\ a_2 \\ \vdots \\ a_n \end{bmatrix} + \begin{bmatrix} b_1 \\ b_2 \\ \vdots \\ b_n \end{bmatrix} i = \mathbf{a} + \mathbf{b}i, \tag{20}$$

then $\bar{\mathbf{v}} = \mathbf{a} - \mathbf{b}i$. The complex-valued solution associated with λ and $\mathbf{v}$ is then

$$\mathbf{x}(t) = \mathbf{v}e^{\lambda t} = \mathbf{v}e^{(p+qi)t} = (\mathbf{a} + \mathbf{b}i)e^{pt}(\cos qt + i \sin qt);$$

that is,

$$\mathbf{x}(t) = e^{pt}(\mathbf{a}\cos qt - \mathbf{b}\sin qt) + ie^{pt}(\mathbf{b}\cos qt + \mathbf{a}\sin qt). \tag{21}$$

Because the real and imaginary parts of a complex-valued solution are also solutions, we thus get the two *real-valued* solutions

$$\begin{aligned} \mathbf{x}_1(t) &= \operatorname{Re}(\mathbf{x}(t)) = e^{pt}(\mathbf{a}\cos qt - \mathbf{b}\sin qt), \\ \mathbf{x}_2(t) &= \operatorname{Im}(\mathbf{x}(t)) = e^{pt}(\mathbf{b}\cos qt + \mathbf{a}\sin qt) \end{aligned} \tag{22}$$

associated with the complex conjugate eigenvalues $p \pm qi$. It is easy to check that the same two real-valued solutions result from taking real and imaginary parts of $\bar{\mathbf{v}}e^{\bar{\lambda}t}$. Rather than memorizing the formulas in (22), it is preferable in a specific example to proceed as follows:

- First find explicitly a single complex-valued solution $\mathbf{x}(t)$ associated with the complex eigenvalue λ;
- Then find the real and imaginary parts $\mathbf{x}_1(t)$ and $\mathbf{x}_2(t)$ to get two independent real-valued solutions corresponding to the two complex conjugate eigenvalues λ and $\bar{\lambda}$.

EXAMPLE 3 Find a general solution of the system

$$\begin{aligned} \frac{dx_1}{dt} &= 4x_1 - 3x_2, \\ \frac{dx_2}{dt} &= 3x_1 + 4x_2. \end{aligned} \tag{23}$$

Solution The coefficient matrix

$$\mathbf{A} = \begin{bmatrix} 4 & -3 \\ 3 & 4 \end{bmatrix}$$

has characteristic equation

$$|\mathbf{A} - \lambda \mathbf{I}| = \begin{vmatrix} 4 - \lambda & -3 \\ 3 & 4 - \lambda \end{vmatrix} = (4 - \lambda)^2 + 9 = 0,$$

and hence has the complex conjugate eigenvalues $\lambda = 4 - 3i$ and $\bar{\lambda} = 4 + 3i$.

Substituting $\lambda = 4 - 3i$ in the eigenvector equation $(\mathbf{A} - \lambda\mathbf{I})\mathbf{v} = \mathbf{0}$, we get the equation

$$[\mathbf{A} - (4 - 3i) \cdot \mathbf{I}]\mathbf{v} = \begin{bmatrix} 3i & -3 \\ 3 & 3i \end{bmatrix}\begin{bmatrix} a \\ b \end{bmatrix} = \begin{bmatrix} 0 \\ 0 \end{bmatrix}$$

for an associated eigenvalue $\mathbf{v} = \begin{bmatrix} a & b \end{bmatrix}^T$. Division of each row by 3 yields the two scalar equations

$$ia - b = 0,$$
$$a + ib = 0,$$

each of which is satisfied by $a = 1$ and $b = i$. Thus $\mathbf{v} = \begin{bmatrix} 1 & i \end{bmatrix}^T$ is a complex eigenvector associated with the complex eigenvalue $\lambda = 4 - 3i$.

The corresponding complex-valued solution $\mathbf{x}(t) = \mathbf{v}e^{\lambda t}$ of $\mathbf{x}' = \mathbf{A}\mathbf{x}$ is then

$$\mathbf{x}(t) = \begin{bmatrix} 1 \\ i \end{bmatrix} e^{(4-3i)t} = \begin{bmatrix} 1 \\ i \end{bmatrix} e^{4t}(\cos 3t - i \sin 3t) = e^{4t}\begin{bmatrix} \cos 3t - i \sin 3t \\ i \cos 3t + \sin 3t \end{bmatrix}.$$

The real and imaginary parts of $\mathbf{x}(t)$ are the real-valued solutions

$$\mathbf{x}_1(t) = e^{4t}\begin{bmatrix} \cos 3t \\ \sin 3t \end{bmatrix} \quad \text{and} \quad \mathbf{x}_2(t) = e^{4t}\begin{bmatrix} -\sin 3t \\ \cos 3t \end{bmatrix}.$$

A real-valued general solution of $\mathbf{x}' = \mathbf{A}\mathbf{x}$ is then given by

$$\mathbf{x}(t) = c_1\mathbf{x}_1(t) + c_2\mathbf{x}_2(t) = e^{4t}\begin{bmatrix} c_1 \cos 3t - c_2 \sin 3t \\ c_1 \sin 3t + c_2 \cos 3t \end{bmatrix}.$$

Finally, a general solution of the system in (23) in scalar form is

$$x_1(t) = e^{4t}(c_1 \cos 3t - c_2 \sin 3t),$$
$$x_2(t) = e^{4t}(c_1 \sin 3t + c_2 \cos 3t).$$

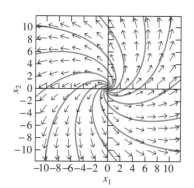

FIGURE 5.2.4. Direction field and solution curves for the linear system $x_1' = 4x_1 - 3x_2$, $x_2' = 3x_1 + 4x_2$ of Example 3.

Figure 5.2.4 shows some typical solution curves of the system in (23). Each appears to spiral counterclockwise as it emanates from the origin in the x_1x_2-plane. Actually, because of the factor e^{4t} in the general solution, we see that:

- Along each solution curve, the point $(x_1(t), x_2(t))$ approaches the origin as $t \to -\infty$, whereas
- The absolute values of $x_1(t)$ and $x_2(t)$ both increase without bound as $t \to +\infty$. ∎

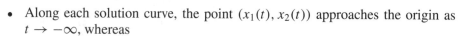

Figure 5.2.5 shows a "closed" system of three brine tanks with volumes V_1, V_2, and V_3. The difference between this system and the "open" system of Fig. 5.2.2 is that now the inflow to tank 1 is the outflow from tank 3. With the same notation as in Example 2, the appropriate modification of Eq. (16) is

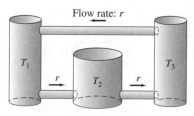

FIGURE 5.2.5. The three brine tanks of Example 4.

$$\frac{dx_1}{dt} = -k_1 x_1 \qquad\qquad + k_3 x_3,$$
$$\frac{dx_2}{dt} = \quad k_1 x_1 - k_2 x_2, \tag{24}$$
$$\frac{dx_3}{dt} = \qquad\qquad k_2 x_2 - k_3 x_3,$$

where $k_i = r/V_i$ as in (17).

EXAMPLE 4   Find the amounts $x_1(t)$, $x_2(t)$, and $x_3(t)$ of salt at time t in the three brine tanks of Fig. 5.2.5 if $V_1 = 50$ gal, $V_2 = 25$ gal, $V_3 = 50$ gal, and $r = 10$ gal/min.

Solution   With the given numerical values, (24) takes the form

$$\frac{d\mathbf{x}}{dt} = \begin{bmatrix} -0.2 & 0 & 0.2 \\ 0.2 & -0.4 & 0 \\ 0 & 0.4 & -0.2 \end{bmatrix} \mathbf{x} \tag{25}$$

with $\mathbf{x} = \begin{bmatrix} x_1 & x_2 & x_3 \end{bmatrix}^T$ as usual. When we expand the determinant of the matrix

$$\mathbf{A} - \lambda \cdot \mathbf{I} = \begin{bmatrix} -0.2 - \lambda & 0.0 & 0.2 \\ 0.2 & -0.4 - \lambda & 0.0 \\ 0.0 & 0.4 & -0.2 - \lambda \end{bmatrix} \tag{26}$$

along its first row, we find that the characteristic equation of $\mathbf{A}$ is

$$(-0.2 - \lambda)(-0.4 - \lambda)(-0.2 - \lambda) + (0.2)(0.2)(0.4)$$
$$= -\lambda^3 - (0.8) \cdot \lambda^2 - (0.2) \cdot \lambda$$
$$= -\lambda \left[(\lambda + 0.4)^2 + (0.2)^2 \right] = 0.$$

Thus $\mathbf{A}$ has the zero eigenvalue $\lambda_0 = 0$ and the complex conjugate eigenvalues λ, $\bar{\lambda} = -0.4 \pm (0.2)i$.

CASE 1: $\lambda_0 = 0$.   Substitution of $\lambda = 0$ in Eq. (26) gives the eigenvector equation

$$(\mathbf{A} - 0 \cdot \mathbf{I})\mathbf{v} = \begin{bmatrix} -0.2 & 0.0 & 0.2 \\ 0.2 & -0.4 & 0.0 \\ 0.0 & 0.4 & -0.2 \end{bmatrix} \begin{bmatrix} a \\ b \\ c \end{bmatrix} = \begin{bmatrix} 0 \\ 0 \\ 0 \end{bmatrix} \tag{26}$$

for $\mathbf{v} = \begin{bmatrix} a & b & c \end{bmatrix}^T$. The first row gives $a = c$ and the second row gives $a = 2b$, so $\mathbf{v}_0 = \begin{bmatrix} 2 & 1 & 2 \end{bmatrix}^T$ is an eigenvector associated with the eigenvalue $\lambda_0 = 0$. The corresponding solution $\mathbf{x}_0(t) = \mathbf{v}_0 e^{\lambda_0 t}$ of Eq. (25) is the constant solution

$$\mathbf{x}_0(t) = \begin{bmatrix} 2 \\ 1 \\ 2 \end{bmatrix}. \tag{27}$$

CASE 2: $\lambda = -0.4 - (0.2)i$.   Substitution of $\lambda = -0.4 - (0.2)i$ in Eq. (26) gives the eigenvector equation

$$[\mathbf{A} - (-0.4 - (0.2)i)\mathbf{I}]\,\mathbf{v} = \begin{bmatrix} 0.2 + (0.2)i & 0.0 & 0.2 \\ 0.2 & (0.2)i & 0.0 \\ 0.0 & 0.4 & 0.2 + (0.2)i \end{bmatrix} \begin{bmatrix} a \\ b \\ c \end{bmatrix}$$

$$= \begin{bmatrix} 0 \\ 0 \\ 0 \end{bmatrix}.$$

The second equation $(0.2)a + (0.2)ib$ is satisfied by $a = 1$ and $b = i$. Then the first equation

$$[0.2 + (0.2)i]a + (0.2)c = 0$$

gives $c = -1 - i$. Thus $\mathbf{v} = \begin{bmatrix} 1 & i & (-1 - i) \end{bmatrix}^T$ is a complex eigenvector associated with the complex eigenvalue $\lambda = -0.4 - (0.2)i$.

The corresponding complex-valued solution $\mathbf{x}(t) = \mathbf{v}e^{\lambda t}$ of (25) is

$$\mathbf{x}(t) = \begin{bmatrix} 1 & i & -1 - i \end{bmatrix}^T e^{(-0.4 - 0.2i)t}$$

$$= \begin{bmatrix} 1 & i & -1 - i \end{bmatrix}^T e^{(-0.4)t} (\cos 0.2t - i \sin 0.2t)$$

$$= e^{(-0.4)t} \begin{bmatrix} \cos 0.2t - i \sin 0.2t \\ \sin 0.2t + i \cos 0.2t \\ -\cos 0.2t - \sin 0.2t - i \cos 0.2t + i \sin 0.2t \end{bmatrix}.$$

The real and imaginary parts of $\mathbf{x}(t)$ are the real-valued solutions

$$\mathbf{x}_1(t) = e^{(-0.4)t} \begin{bmatrix} \cos 0.2t \\ \sin 0.2t \\ -\cos 0.2t - \sin 0.2t \end{bmatrix},$$

$$\mathbf{x}_2(t) = e^{(-0.4)t} \begin{bmatrix} -\sin 0.2t \\ \cos 0.2t \\ -\cos 0.2t + \sin 0.2t \end{bmatrix}. \tag{28}$$

The general solution

$$\mathbf{x}(t) = c_0 \mathbf{x}_0(t) + c_1 \mathbf{x}_1(t) + c_2 \mathbf{x}_2(t)$$

has scalar components

$$\begin{aligned} x_1(t) &= 2c_0 + e^{(-0.4)t}(c_1 \cos 0.2t - c_2 \sin 0.2t), \\ x_2(t) &= c_0 + e^{(-0.4)t}(c_1 \sin 0.2t + c_2 \cos 0.2t), \\ x_3(t) &= 2c_0 + e^{(-0.4)t}[(-c_1 - c_2) \cos 0.2t + (-c_1 + c_2) \sin 0.2t] \end{aligned} \tag{29}$$

giving the amounts of salt in the three tanks at time t.
Observe that

$$x_1(t) + x_2(t) + x_3(t) \equiv 5c_0. \tag{30}$$

Of course the total amount of salt in the closed system is constant; the constant c_0 in (30) is one-fifth the total amount of salt. Because of the factors of $e^{(-0.4)t}$ in (29), we see that

$$\lim_{t \to \infty} x_1(t) = 2c_0, \quad \lim_{t \to \infty} x_2(t) = c_0, \quad \text{and} \quad \lim_{t \to \infty} x_3(t) = 2c_0.$$

Thus as $t \to +\infty$ the salt in the system approaches a *steady-state* distribution with 40% of the salt in each of the two 50-gallon tanks and 20% in the 25-gallon tank. So whatever the initial distribution of salt among the three tanks, the limiting distribution is one of uniform concentration throughout the system. Figure 5.2.6 shows the graphs of the three solution functions with $c_0 = 10$, $c_1 = 30$, and $c_2 = -10$, in which case

$$x_1(0) = 50 \quad \text{and} \quad x_2(0) = x_3(0) = 0. \qquad \blacksquare$$

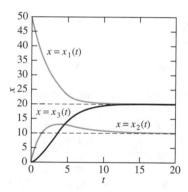

FIGURE 5.2.6. The salt content functions of Example 4.

5.2 *Problems*

In Problems 1 through 16, apply the eigenvalue method of this section to find a general solution of the given system. If initial values are given, find also the corresponding particular solution.

1. $x_1' = x_1 + 2x_2, \; x_2' = 2x_1 + x_2$
2. $x_1' = 2x_1 + 3x_2, \; x_2' = 2x_1 + x_2$
3. $x_1' = 3x_1 + 4x_2, \; x_2' = 3x_1 + 2x_2; \; x_1(0) = x_2(0) = 1$
4. $x_1' = 4x_1 + x_2, \; x_2' = 6x_1 - x_2$
5. $x_1' = 6x_1 - 7x_2, \; x_2' = x_1 - 2x_2$
6. $x_1' = 9x_1 + 5x_2, \; x_2' = -6x_1 - 2x_2; \; x_1(0) = 1, \; x_2(0) = 0$
7. $x_1' = -3x_1 + 4x_2, \; x_2' = 6x_1 - 5x_2$
8. $x_1' = x_1 - 5x_2, \; x_2' = x_1 - x_2$
9. $x_1' = 2x_1 - 5x_2, \; x_2' = 4x_1 - 2x_2; \; x_1(0) = 2, \; x_2(0) = 3$

10. $x_1' = -3x_1 - 2x_2, \; x_2' = 9x_1 + 3x_2$
11. $x_1' = x_1 - 2x_2, \; x_2' = 2x_1 + x_2; \; x_1(0) = 0, \; x_2(0) = 4$
12. $x_1' = x_1 - 5x_2, \; x_2' = x_1 + 3x_2$
13. $x_1' = 5x_1 - 9x_2, \; x_2' = 2x_1 - x_2$
14. $x_1' = 3x_1 - 4x_2, \; x_2' = 4x_1 + 3x_2$
15. $x_1' = 7x_1 - 5x_2, \; x_2' = 4x_1 + 3x_2$
16. $x_1' = -50x_1 + 20x_2, \; x_2' = 100x_1 - 60x_2$

In Problems 17 through 25, the eigenvalues of the coefficient matrix can be found by inspection and factoring. Apply the eigenvalue method to find a general solution of each system.

17. $x_1' = 4x_1 + x_2 + 4x_3,\ x_2' = x_1 + 7x_2 + x_3,$
  $x_3' = 4x_1 + x_2 + 4x_3$

18. $x_1' = x_1 + 2x_2 + 2x_3,\ x_2' = 2x_1 + 7x_2 + x_3,$

19. $x_1' = 4x_1 + x_2 + x_3,\ x_2' = x_1 + 4x_2 + x_3,\ x_3' = x_1 + x_2 + 4x_3$

20. $x_1' = 5x_1 + x_2 + 3x_3,\ x_2' = x_1 + 7x_2 + x_3,$
  $x_3' = 3x_1 + x_2 + 5x_3$

21. $x_1' = 5x_1 - 6x_3,\ x_2' = 2x_1 - x_2 - 2x_3,\ x_3' = 4x_1 - 2x_2 - 4x_3$

22. $x_1' = 3x_1 + 2x_2 + 2x_3,\ x_2' = -5x_1 - 4x_2 - 2x_3,$
  $x_3' = 5x_1 + 5x_2 + 3x_3$

23. $x_1' = 3x_1 + x_2 + x_3,\ x_2' = -5x_1 - 3x_2 - x_3,$
  $x_3' = 5x_1 + 5x_2 + 3x_3$

24. $x_1' = 2x_1 + x_2 - x_3,\ x_2' = -4x_1 - 3x_2 - x_3,$
  $x_3' = 4x_1 + 4x_2 + 2x_3$

25. $x_1' = 5x_1 + 5x_2 + 2x_3,\ x_2' = -6x_1 - 6x_2 - 5x_3,$
  $x_3' = 6x_1 + 6x_2 + 5x_3$

26. Find the particular solution of the system

$$\frac{dx_1}{dt} = 3x_1 \qquad\quad + x_3,$$

$$\frac{dx_2}{dt} = 9x_1 - x_2 + 2x_3,$$

$$\frac{dx_3}{dt} = -9x_1 + 4x_2 - x_3$$

that satisfies the initial conditions $x_1(0) = 0$, $x_2(0) = 0$, $x_3(0) = 17$.

The amounts $x_1(t)$ and $x_2(t)$ of salt in the two brine tanks of Fig. 5.2.7 satisfy the differential equations

$$\frac{dx_1}{dt} = -k_1x_1, \qquad \frac{dx_2}{dt} = k_1x_1 - k_2x_2,$$

where $k_i = r/V_i$ for $i = 1, 2$. In Problems 27 and 28 the volumes V_1 and V_2 are given. First solve for $x_1(t)$ and $x_2(t)$, assuming that $r = 10$ (gal/min), $x_1(0) = 15$ (gal), and $x_2(0) = 0$. Then find the maximum amount of salt ever in tank 2.

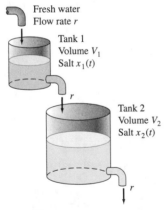

FIGURE 5.2.7. The two brine tanks of Problems 27 and 28.

27. $V_1 = 50$ (gal), $V_2 = 25$ (gal)

28. $V_1 = 25$ (gal), $V_2 = 40$ (gal)

The amounts $x_1(t)$ and $x_2(t)$ of salt in the two brine tanks of Fig. 5.2.8 satisfy the differential equations

$$\frac{dx_1}{dt} = -k_1x_1 + k_2x_2, \qquad \frac{dx_2}{dt} = k_1x_1 - k_2x_2,$$

where $k_i = r/V_i$ as usual. In Problems 29 and 30, solve for $x_1(t)$ and $x_2(t)$, assuming that $r = 10$ (gal/min), $x_1(0) = 15$ (gal), and $x_2(0) = 0$.

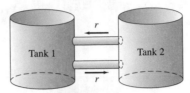

FIGURE 5.2.8. The two brine tanks of Problems 29 and 30.

29. $V_1 = 50$ (gal), $V_2 = 25$ (gal)

30. $V_1 = 25$ (gal), $V_2 = 40$ (gal)

Problems 31 through 34 deal with the open three-tank system of Fig. 5.2.2. Fresh water flows into tank 1; mixed brine flows from tank 1 into tank 2, from tank 2 into tank 3, and out of tank 3; all at the given flow rate r gallons per minute. The initial amounts $x_1(0) = x_0$ (lb), $x_2(0) = 0$, and $x_3(0) = 0$ of salt in the three tanks are given, as are their volumes V_1, V_2, and V_3 (in gallons). First solve for the amounts of salt in the three tanks at time t, then determine the maximal amount of salt that tank 3 ever contains.

31. $r = 30, x_0 = 27, V_1 = 30, V_2 = 15, V_3 = 10$

32. $r = 60, x_0 = 45, V_1 = 20, V_2 = 30, V_3 = 60$

33. $r = 60, x_0 = 45, V_1 = 15, V_2 = 10, V_3 = 30$

34. $r = 60, x_0 = 40, V_1 = 20, V_2 = 12, V_3 = 60$

Problems 35 through 37 deal with the closed three-tank system of Fig. 5.2.5, which is described by the equations in (24). Mixed brine flows from tank 1 into tank 2, from tank 2 into tank 3, and from tank 3 into tank 1, all at the given flow rate r gallons per minute. The initial amounts $x_1(0) = x_0$ (pounds), $x_2(0) = 0$, and $x_3(0) = 0$ of salt in the three tanks are given, as are their volumes V_1, V_2, and V_3 (in gallons). First solve for the amounts of salt in the three tanks at time t, then determine the limiting amount (as $t \to +\infty$) of salt in each tank.

35. $r = 120, x_0 = 33, V_1 = 20, V_2 = 6, V_3 = 40$

36. $r = 10, x_0 = 18, V_1 = 20, V_2 = 50, V_3 = 20$

37. $r = 60, x_0 = 55, V_1 = 60, V_2 = 20, V_3 = 30$

For each matrix **A** given in Problems 38 through 40, the zeros in the matrix make its characteristic polynomial easy to calculate. Find the general solution of $\mathbf{x}' = \mathbf{A}\mathbf{x}$.

38. $\mathbf{A} = \begin{bmatrix} 1 & 0 & 0 & 0 \\ 2 & 2 & 0 & 0 \\ 0 & 3 & 3 & 0 \\ 0 & 0 & 4 & 4 \end{bmatrix}$

39. $\mathbf{A} = \begin{bmatrix} -2 & 0 & 0 & 9 \\ 4 & 2 & 0 & -10 \\ 0 & 0 & -1 & 8 \\ 0 & 0 & 0 & 1 \end{bmatrix}$

40. $\mathbf{A} = \begin{bmatrix} 2 & 0 & 0 & 0 \\ -21 & -5 & -27 & -9 \\ 0 & 0 & 5 & 0 \\ 0 & 0 & -21 & -2 \end{bmatrix}$

41. The coefficient matrix **A** of the 4×4 system

$$x_1' = 4x_1 + x_2 + x_3 + 7x_4,$$
$$x_2' = x_1 + 4x_2 + 10x_3 + x_4,$$
$$x_3' = x_1 + 10x_2 + 4x_3 + x_4,$$
$$x_4' = 7x_1 + x_2 + x_3 + 4x_4$$

has eigenvalues $\lambda_1 = -3$, $\lambda_2 = -6$, $\lambda_3 = 10$, and $\lambda_4 = 15$. Find the particular solution of this system that satisfies the initial conditions

$$x_1(0) = 3, \quad x_2(0) = x_3(0) = 1, \quad x_4(0) = 3.$$

5.3 SECOND-ORDER SYSTEMS AND MECHANICAL APPLICATIONS*

In this section we apply the matrix methods of Sections 5.1 and 5.2 to investigate the oscillations of typical mass-and-spring systems having two or more degrees of freedom. Our examples are chosen to illustrate phenomena that are generally characteristic of complex mechanical systems.

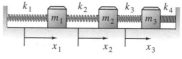

FIGURE 5.3.1. Three spring-coupled masses.

Figure 5.3.1 shows three masses connected to each other and to two walls by the four indicated springs. We assume that the masses slide without friction and that each spring obeys Hooke's law—its extension or compression x and force F of reaction are related by the formula $F = -kx$. If the rightward displacements x_1, x_2, and x_3 of the three masses (from their respective equilibrium positions) are all positive, then:

- The first spring is stretched the distance x_1;
- The second spring is stretched the distance $x_2 - x_1$;
- The third spring is stretched the distance $x_3 - x_2$;
- The fourth spring is compressed the distance x_3.

Therefore, application of Newton's law $F = ma$ to the three masses (as in Example 1 of Section 4.1) yields their equations of motion:

$$m_1 x_1'' = -k_1 x_1 + k_2(x_2 - x_1),$$
$$m_2 x_2'' = -k_2(x_2 - x_1) + k_3(x_3 - x_2), \tag{1}$$
$$m_3 x_3'' = -k_3(x_3 - x_2) - k_4 x_3.$$

In terms of the **displacement vector** $\mathbf{x} = \begin{bmatrix} x_1 & x_2 & x_3 \end{bmatrix}^T$, the **mass matrix**

$$\mathbf{M} = \begin{bmatrix} m_1 & 0 & 0 \\ 0 & m_2 & 0 \\ 0 & 0 & m_3 \end{bmatrix} \tag{2}$$

and the **stiffness matrix**

$$\mathbf{K} = \begin{bmatrix} -(k_1 + k_2) & k_2 & 0 \\ k_2 & -(k_2 + k_3) & k_3 \\ 0 & k_3 & -(k_3 + k_4) \end{bmatrix}, \tag{3}$$

the system in (1) takes the matrix form

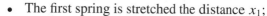

$$\mathbf{Mx}'' = \mathbf{Kx}. \tag{4}$$

FIGURE 5.3.2. A system of n spring-coupled masses.

The notation in Eqs. (1) through (4) generalizes in a natural way to the system of n spring-coupled masses shown in Fig. 5.3.2. We need only write

---

*This optional section may be omitted without loss of continuity. It provides a sample of the more technical applications of eigenvalues to physics and engineering problems.

$$\mathbf{M} = \begin{bmatrix} m_1 & 0 & \cdots & 0 \\ 0 & m_2 & \cdot & 0 \\ \vdots & \vdots & & \vdots \\ 0 & 0 & \cdots & m_n \end{bmatrix} \tag{5}$$

and

$$\mathbf{K} = \begin{bmatrix} -(k_1 + k_2) & k_2 & 0 & \cdots & 0 \\ k_2 & -(k_2 + k_3) & k_3 & \cdots & 0 \\ 0 & k_3 & -(k_3 + k_4) & \cdots & 0 \\ 0 & 0 & k_4 & \cdots & 0 \\ \vdots & \vdots & & & \vdots \\ 0 & 0 & \cdots & -(k_{n-1} + k_n) & k_n \\ 0 & 0 & \cdots & k_n & -(k_n + k_{n+1}) \end{bmatrix} \tag{6}$$

for the mass and stiffness matrices in Eq. (4).

The diagonal matrix $\mathbf{M}$ is obviously nonsingular; to get its inverse $\mathbf{M}^{-1}$ we need only replace each diagonal element with its reciprocal. Hence multiplication of each side in Eq. (4) by $\mathbf{M}^{-1}$ yields the homogeneous **second-order system**

$$\mathbf{x}'' = \mathbf{Ax}, \tag{7}$$

where $\mathbf{A} = \mathbf{M}^{-1}\mathbf{K}$. There is a wide variety of *frictionless* mechanical systems for which a displacement or position vector $\mathbf{x}$, a nonsingular mass matrix $\mathbf{M}$, and a stiffness matrix $\mathbf{K}$ satisfying Eq. (4) can be defined.

To seek a solution of Eq. (7), we substitute (as in Section 5.2 for a first-order system) a trial solution of the form

$$\mathbf{x}(t) = \mathbf{v}e^{\alpha t}, \tag{8}$$

where $\mathbf{v}$ is a constant vector. Then $\mathbf{x}'' = \alpha^2 \mathbf{v}e^{\alpha t}$, so substitution of Eq. (8) in (7) gives

$$\alpha^2 \mathbf{v}e^{\alpha t} = \mathbf{A}\mathbf{v}e^{\alpha t},$$

which implies that

$$\mathbf{Av} = \alpha^2 \mathbf{v}. \tag{9}$$

Therefore $\mathbf{x}(t) = \mathbf{v}e^{\alpha t}$ is a solution of $\mathbf{x}'' = \mathbf{Ax}$ if and only if $\alpha^2 = \lambda$, an eigenvalue of the matrix $\mathbf{A}$, and $\mathbf{v}$ is an associated eigenvector.

If $\mathbf{x}'' = \mathbf{Ax}$ models a mechanical system, then it is typical that the eigenvalues of $\mathbf{A}$ are *negative* real numbers. If

$$\alpha^2 = \lambda = -\omega^2 < 0,$$

then $\alpha = \pm \omega i$. In this case the solution given by Eq. (8) is

$$\mathbf{x}(t) = \mathbf{v}e^{i\omega t} = \mathbf{v}(\cos \omega t + i \sin \omega t).$$

The real and imaginary parts

$$\mathbf{x}_1(t) = \mathbf{v} \cos \omega t \quad \text{and} \quad \mathbf{x}_2(t) = \mathbf{v} \sin \omega t \tag{10}$$

of $\mathbf{x}(t)$ are then linearly independent *real-valued* solutions of the system. This analysis leads to the following theorem.

> **THEOREM 1:** Second-Order Homogeneous Linear Systems

If the $n \times n$ matrix $\mathbf{A}$ has distinct negative eigenvalues $-\omega_1^2, -\omega_2^2, \ldots, -\omega_n^2$ with associated [real] eigenvectors $\mathbf{v}_1, \mathbf{v}_2, \ldots, \mathbf{v}_n$, then a general solution of

$$\mathbf{x}'' = \mathbf{A}\mathbf{x}$$

is given by

$$\mathbf{x}(t) = \sum_{i=1}^{n} (a_i \cos \omega_i t + b_i \sin \omega_i t) \mathbf{v}_i \tag{11}$$

with a_i and b_i arbitrary constants. In the special case of a nonrepeated zero eigenvalue λ_0 with associated eigenvector $\mathbf{v}_0$,

$$\mathbf{x}_0(t) = (a_0 + b_0 t) \mathbf{v}_0 \tag{12}$$

is the corresponding part of the general solution.   ■

Remark: The nonzero vector $\mathbf{v}_0$ is an eigenvector corresponding to $\lambda_0 = 0$ provided that $\mathbf{A}\mathbf{v}_0 = \mathbf{0}$. If $\mathbf{x}(t) = (a_0 + b_0 t)\mathbf{v}_0$, then

$$\mathbf{x}'' = 0 \cdot \mathbf{v}_0 = (a_0 + b_0 t) \cdot \mathbf{0} = (a_0 + b_0 t) \cdot (\mathbf{A}\mathbf{v}_0) = \mathbf{A}\mathbf{x},$$

thus verifying the form in Eq. (12).   ■

EXAMPLE 1   Consider the mass-and-spring system with $n = 2$ shown in Fig. 5.3.3. Because there is no third spring connected to a right-hand wall, we set $k_3 = 0$. If $m_1 = 2$, $m_2 = 1$, $k_1 = 100$, and $k_2 = 50$, then the equation $\mathbf{M}\mathbf{x}'' = \mathbf{K}\mathbf{x}$ is

$$\begin{bmatrix} 2 & 0 \\ 0 & 1 \end{bmatrix} \mathbf{x}'' = \begin{bmatrix} -150 & 50 \\ 50 & -50 \end{bmatrix} \mathbf{x}, \tag{13}$$

which reduces to $\mathbf{x}'' = \mathbf{A}\mathbf{x}$ with

$$\mathbf{A} = \begin{bmatrix} -75 & 25 \\ 50 & -50 \end{bmatrix}.$$

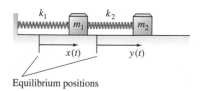

Equilibrium positions

FIGURE 5.3.3. The mass-and-spring system of Example 1.

The characteristic equation of $\mathbf{A}$ is

$$(-75 - \lambda)(-50 - \lambda) - 50 \cdot 25 = \lambda^2 + 125\lambda + 2500$$
$$= (\lambda + 25)(\lambda + 100) = 0,$$

so $\mathbf{A}$ has the negative eigenvalues $\lambda_1 = -25$ and $\lambda_2 = -100$. By Theorem 1, the system in (13) therefore has solutions with [circular] frequencies $\omega_1 = 5$ and $\omega_2 = 10$.

CASE 1: $\lambda_1 = -25$.   The eigenvector equation $(\mathbf{A} - \lambda \mathbf{I})\mathbf{v} = \mathbf{0}$ is

$$\begin{bmatrix} -50 & 25 \\ 50 & -25 \end{bmatrix} \begin{bmatrix} a \\ b \end{bmatrix} = \begin{bmatrix} 0 \\ 0 \end{bmatrix},$$

so an eigenvector associated with $\lambda_1 = -25$ is $\mathbf{v}_1 = \begin{bmatrix} 1 & 2 \end{bmatrix}^T$.

CASE 2: $\lambda_2 = -100$.   The eigenvector equation $(\mathbf{A} - \lambda \mathbf{I})\mathbf{v} = \mathbf{0}$ is

$$\begin{bmatrix} 25 & 25 \\ 50 & 50 \end{bmatrix} \begin{bmatrix} a \\ b \end{bmatrix} = \begin{bmatrix} 0 \\ 0 \end{bmatrix},$$

so an eigenvector associated with $\lambda_2 = -100$ is $\mathbf{v}_2 = \begin{bmatrix} 1 & -1 \end{bmatrix}^T$.

By Eq. (11) it follows that a general solution of the system in (13) is given by

$$\mathbf{x}(t) = (a_1 \cos 5t + b_1 \sin 5t)\mathbf{v}_1 + (a_2 \cos 10t + b_2 \sin 10t)\mathbf{v}_2. \tag{14}$$

As in the discussion of Example 3 of Section 4.2, the two terms on the right in Eq. (14) represent **free oscillations** of the mass-and-spring system. They describe the physical system's two **natural modes of oscillation** at its two [circular] **natural frequencies** $\omega_1 = 5$ and $\omega_2 = 10$. The natural mode

$$\mathbf{x}_1(t) = (a_1 \cos 5t + b_1 \sin 5t)\mathbf{v}_1 = c_1 \cos(5t - \alpha_1) \begin{bmatrix} 1 \\ 2 \end{bmatrix}$$

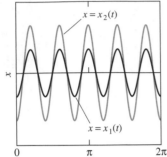

(with $c_1 = \sqrt{a_1^2 + b_1^2}$, $\cos\alpha_1 = a_1/c_1$, and $\sin\alpha_1 = b_1/c_1$) has the scalar component equations

$$\begin{aligned} x_1(t) &= c_1 \cos(5t - \alpha_1), \\ x_2(t) &= 2c_1 \cos(5t - \alpha_1), \end{aligned} \tag{15}$$

FIGURE 5.3.4. Oscillations in the same direction with frequency $\omega_1 = 5$; the amplitude of motion of mass 2 is twice that of mass 1.

and therefore describes a free oscillation in which the two masses move in synchrony in the same direction and with the same frequency $\omega_1 = 5$, but with the amplitude of motion of m_2 twice that of m_1 (see Fig. 5.3.4). The natural mode

$$\mathbf{x}_2(t) = (a_2 \cos 10t + b_2 \sin 10t)\mathbf{v}_2 = c_2 \cos(10t - \alpha_2) \begin{bmatrix} 1 \\ -1 \end{bmatrix}$$

has the scalar component equations

$$\begin{aligned} x_1(t) &= c_2 \cos(10t - \alpha_2), \\ x_2(t) &= -c_2 \cos(10t - \alpha_2), \end{aligned} \tag{16}$$

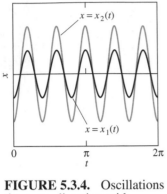

FIGURE 5.3.5. Oscillations in opposite directions with frequency $\omega_2 = 10$; the amplitude of motion of the two masses are the same.

and therefore describes a free oscillation in which the two masses move in synchrony in opposite directions with the same frequency $\omega_2 = 10$ and with equal amplitudes of oscillation (see Fig. 5.3.5).   ∎

EXAMPLE 2   Figure 5.3.6 shows three railway cars connected by buffer springs that react when compressed, but disengage instead of stretching. With $n = 3$, $k_1 = k_3 = k$, and $k_2 = k_4 = 0$ in Eqs. (2) through (4), we get the system

FIGURE 5.3.6.   The three railway cars of Example 2.

$$\begin{bmatrix} m_1 & 0 & 0 \\ 0 & m_2 & 0 \\ 0 & 0 & m_3 \end{bmatrix} \mathbf{x}'' = \begin{bmatrix} -k & k & 0 \\ k & -2k & k \\ 0 & k & -k \end{bmatrix} \mathbf{x}, \tag{17}$$

which is equivalent to

$$\mathbf{x}'' = \begin{bmatrix} -c_1 & c_1 & 0 \\ c_2 & -2c_2 & c_2 \\ 0 & c_3 & -c_3 \end{bmatrix} \mathbf{x} \tag{18}$$

with

$$c_i = \frac{k}{m_i} \quad (i = 1, 2, 3). \tag{19}$$

If we assume further that $m_1 = m_3$, so that $c_1 = c_3$, then a brief computation gives

$$-\lambda(\lambda + c_1)(\lambda + c_1 + 2c_2) = 0 \qquad (20)$$

for the characteristic equation of the coefficient matrix $\mathbf{A}$ in Eq. (18). Hence the matrix $\mathbf{A}$ has eigenvalues

$$\lambda_1 = 0, \quad \lambda_2 = -c_1, \quad \lambda_3 = -c_1 - 2c_2 \qquad (21\text{a})$$

corresponding to the natural frequencies

$$\omega_1 = 0, \quad \omega_2 = \sqrt{c_1}, \quad \omega_3 = \sqrt{c_1 + 2c_2} \qquad (21\text{b})$$

of the physical system.

For a numerical example, suppose that the first and third railway cars weigh 12 tons each, that the middle car weighs 8 tons, and that the spring constant is $k = 1.5$ tons/ft; i.e., $k = 3000$ lb/ft. Then, using fps units with mass measured in slugs (a weight of 32 pounds has a mass of 1 slug), we have

$$m_1 = m_3 = 750, \quad m_2 = 500,$$

and

$$c_1 = \frac{3000}{750} = 4, \quad c_2 = \frac{3000}{500} = 6.$$

Hence the coefficient matrix $\mathbf{A}$ is

$$\mathbf{A} = \begin{bmatrix} -4 & 4 & 0 \\ 6 & -12 & 6 \\ 0 & 4 & -4 \end{bmatrix}, \qquad (22)$$

and the eigenvalue-frequency pairs given by (21a) and (21b) are $\lambda_1 = 0$, $\omega_1 = 0$; $\lambda_2 = -4$, $\omega_2 = 2$; and $\lambda_3 = -16$, $\omega_3 = 4$.

CASE 1: $\lambda_1 = 0$, $\omega_1 = 0$.   The eigenvector equation $(\mathbf{A} - \lambda\mathbf{I})\mathbf{v} = \mathbf{0}$ is

$$\mathbf{Av} = \begin{bmatrix} -4 & 4 & 0 \\ 6 & -12 & 6 \\ 0 & 4 & -4 \end{bmatrix} \begin{bmatrix} a \\ b \\ c \end{bmatrix} = \begin{bmatrix} 0 \\ 0 \\ 0 \end{bmatrix},$$

so it is clear that $\mathbf{v}_1 = \begin{bmatrix} 1 & 1 & 1 \end{bmatrix}^T$ is an eigenvector associated with $\lambda_1 = 0$. According to Theorem 1, the corresponding part of a general solution of $\mathbf{x}'' = \mathbf{Ax}$ is

$$\mathbf{x}_1(t) = (a_1 + b_1 t)\mathbf{v}_1.$$

CASE 2: $\lambda_2 = -4$, $\omega_2 = 2$.   The eigenvector equation $(\mathbf{A} - \lambda\mathbf{I})\mathbf{v} = \mathbf{0}$ is

$$(\mathbf{A} + 4\mathbf{I})\mathbf{v} = \begin{bmatrix} 0 & 4 & 0 \\ 6 & -8 & 6 \\ 0 & 4 & 0 \end{bmatrix} \begin{bmatrix} a \\ b \\ c \end{bmatrix} = \begin{bmatrix} 0 \\ 0 \\ 0 \end{bmatrix}$$

so it is clear that $\mathbf{v}_2 = \begin{bmatrix} 1 & 0 & -1 \end{bmatrix}^T$ is an eigenvector associated with $\lambda_2 = -4$. According to Theorem 1, the corresponding part of a general solution of $\mathbf{x}'' = \mathbf{Ax}$ is

$$\mathbf{x}_2(t) = (a_2 \cos 2t + b_2 \sin 2t)\mathbf{v}_2.$$

CASE 3: $\lambda_3 = -16$, $\omega_3 = 4$. The eigenvector equation $(\mathbf{A} - \lambda \mathbf{I})\mathbf{v} = \mathbf{0}$ is

$$(\mathbf{A} + 16\mathbf{I})\mathbf{v} = \begin{bmatrix} 12 & 4 & 0 \\ 6 & 4 & 6 \\ 0 & 4 & 12 \end{bmatrix} \begin{bmatrix} a \\ b \\ c \end{bmatrix} = \begin{bmatrix} 0 \\ 0 \\ 0 \end{bmatrix},$$

so it is clear that $\mathbf{v}_3 = \begin{bmatrix} 1 & -3 & 1 \end{bmatrix}^T$ is an eigenvector associated with $\lambda_3 = -16$. According to Theorem 1, the corresponding part of a general solution of $\mathbf{x}'' = \mathbf{A}\mathbf{x}$ is

$$\mathbf{x}_3(t) = (a_3 \cos 4t + b_3 \sin 4t)\mathbf{v}_3.$$

The general solution $\mathbf{x} = \mathbf{x}_1 + \mathbf{x}_2 + \mathbf{x}_3$ of $\mathbf{x}'' = \mathbf{A}\mathbf{x}$ is therefore given by

$$\mathbf{x}(t) = a_1 \begin{bmatrix} 1 \\ 1 \\ 1 \end{bmatrix} + b_1 t \begin{bmatrix} 1 \\ 1 \\ 1 \end{bmatrix} + a_2 \begin{bmatrix} 1 \\ 0 \\ -1 \end{bmatrix} \cos 2t$$

$$+ b_2 \begin{bmatrix} 1 \\ 0 \\ -1 \end{bmatrix} \sin 2t + a_3 \begin{bmatrix} 1 \\ -3 \\ 1 \end{bmatrix} \cos 4t + b_3 \begin{bmatrix} 1 \\ -3 \\ 1 \end{bmatrix} \sin 4t. \quad (23)$$

To determine a particular solution, let us suppose that the leftmost car is moving to the right with velocity v_0 and at time $t = 0$ strikes the other two cars, which are together but at rest. The corresponding initial conditions are

$$x_1(0) = x_2(0) = x_3(0) = 0, \quad (24a)$$
$$x_1'(0) = v_0, \quad x_2'(0) = x_3'(0) = 0. \quad (24b)$$

Then substitution of (24a) in (23) gives the scalar equations

$$\begin{aligned} a_1 + a_2 + a_3 &= 0, \\ a_1 \qquad - 3a_3 &= 0, \\ a_1 - a_2 + a_3 &= 0, \end{aligned}$$

which readily yield $a_1 = a_2 = a_3 = 0$. Hence the position functions of the three cars are

$$\begin{aligned} x_1(t) &= b_1 t + b_2 \sin 2t + b_3 \sin 4t, \\ x_2(t) &= b_1 t \qquad\qquad - 3b_3 \sin 4t, \\ x_3(t) &= b_1 t - b_2 \sin 2t + b_3 \sin 4t, \end{aligned} \quad (25)$$

and their velocity functions are

$$\begin{aligned} x_1'(t) &= b_1 + 2b_2 \cos 2t + 4b_3 \cos 4t, \\ x_2'(t) &= b_1 \qquad\qquad - 12b_3 \cos 4t, \\ x_3'(t) &= b_1 - 2b_2 \cos 2t + 4b_3 \cos 4t. \end{aligned} \quad (26)$$

Substitution of (24b) in (26) gives the equations

$$\begin{aligned} b_1 + 2b_2 + 4b_3 &= v_0, \\ b_1 \qquad - 12b_3 &= 0, \\ b_1 - 2b_2 + 4b_3 &= 0 \end{aligned}$$

that readily yield $b_1 = \frac{3}{8} v_0$, $b_2 = \frac{1}{4} v_0$, and $b_3 = \frac{1}{32} v_0$. Finally, the position functions in (25) are

$$x_1(t) = \tfrac{1}{32} v_0 (12t + 8 \sin 2t + \sin 4t),$$

$$x_2(t) = \tfrac{1}{32} v_0 (12t \qquad\qquad - 3 \sin 4t), \quad (27)$$

$$x_3(t) = \tfrac{1}{32} v_0 (12t - 8 \sin 2t + \sin 4t).$$

But these equations hold only so long as the two buffer springs remain compressed; that is, while both

$$x_2 - x_1 < 0 \quad \text{and} \quad x_3 - x_2 < 0.$$

To discover what this implies about t, we compute

$$x_2(t) - x_1(t) = \tfrac{1}{32} v_0(-8 \sin 2t - 4 \sin 4t)$$

$$= -\tfrac{1}{32} v_0(8 \sin 2t + 8 \sin 2t \cos 2t)$$

$$= -\tfrac{1}{4} v_0(\sin 2t)(1 + \cos 2t)$$

and, similarly,

$$x_3(t) - x_2(t) = -\tfrac{1}{4} v_0(\sin 2t)(1 - \cos 2t).$$

It follows that $x_2 - x_1 < 0$ and $x_3 - x_2 < 0$ until $t = \pi/2 \approx 1.57$ (seconds), at which time the equations in (26) and (27) give the values

$$x_1\left(\frac{\pi}{2}\right) = x_2\left(\frac{\pi}{2}\right) = x_3\left(\frac{\pi}{2}\right) = \frac{3\pi v_0}{16},$$

$$x_1'\left(\frac{\pi}{2}\right) = x_2'\left(\frac{\pi}{2}\right) = 0, \quad x_3'\left(\frac{\pi}{2}\right) = v_0.$$

We conclude that the three railway cars remain engaged and moving to the right until disengagement occurs at time $t = \pi/2$. Thereafter, cars 1 and 2 remain at rest (!), while car 3 continues to the right with speed v_0. If, for instance, $v_0 = 48$ feet per second (about 33 miles per hour), then the three cars travel a distance of $9\pi \approx 28.27$ (ft) during their 1.57 seconds of engagement, and

$$x_1(t) = x_2(t) = 9\pi, \quad x_3(t) = 48t - 15\pi \tag{27'}$$

for $t > \pi/2$. Figure 5.3.7 illustrates the "before" and "after" situations, and Fig. 5.3.8 shows the graphs of the functions $x_1(t)$, $x_2(t)$, and $x_3(t)$ in Eqs. (27) and (27'). ■

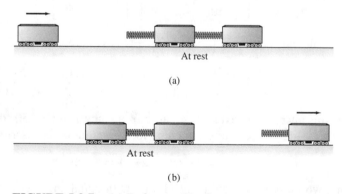

FIGURE 5.3.7. (a) Before; (b) after.

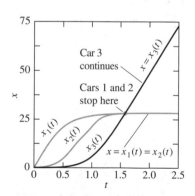

FIGURE 5.3.8. Position functions of the three railway cars of Example 2.

Forced Oscillations and Resonance

Suppose now that the ith mass of the mass-and-spring system in Fig. 5.3.2 is subject to an external force F_i ($i = 1, 2, \ldots, n$) in addition to the forces exerted by the springs attached to it. Then the homogeneous equation $\mathbf{Mx''} = \mathbf{Kx}$ is replaced with the nonhomogeneous equation

$$\mathbf{Mx''} = \mathbf{Kx} + \mathbf{F} \tag{28}$$

where $\mathbf{F} = \begin{bmatrix} F_1 & F_2 & \dots & F_n \end{bmatrix}^T$ is the **external force vector** for the system. Multiplication by $\mathbf{M}^{-1}$ yields

$$\mathbf{x}'' = \mathbf{Ax} + \mathbf{f} \qquad (29)$$

where $\mathbf{f}$ is the external force vector *per unit mass*. We are especially interested in the case of a *periodic external force*

$$\mathbf{f}(t) = \mathbf{F}_0 \cos \omega t \qquad (30)$$

(where $\mathbf{F}_0$ is a constant vector). We then anticipate a periodic particular solution

$$\mathbf{x}_p(t) = \mathbf{c} \cos \omega t \qquad (31)$$

with the known external frequency ω and with a coefficient vector $\mathbf{c}$ yet to be determined. Because $\mathbf{x}_p'' = -\omega^2 \mathbf{c} \cos \omega t$, substitution of (30) and (31) in (29), followed by cancellation of the common factor $\cos \omega t$, gives the linear system

$$(\mathbf{A} + \omega^2 \mathbf{I})\mathbf{c} = -\mathbf{F}_0 \qquad (32)$$

to be solved for $\mathbf{c}$.

Observe that the matrix $\mathbf{A} + \omega^2 \mathbf{I}$ is nonsingular—in which case Eq. (32) can be solved for $\mathbf{c}$—unless $-\omega^2 = \lambda$, an eigenvalue of $\mathbf{A}$. Thus a periodic particular solution of the form in Eq. (31) exists provided that the external forcing frequency does **not** equal one of the natural frequencies $\omega_1, \omega_2, \dots, \omega_n$ of the system. The case in which ω **is** a natural frequency corresponds to the phenomenon of **resonance** discussed in Section 3.6.

EXAMPLE 3   Suppose that the second mass in Example 1 is subjected to the external periodic force $50 \cos \omega t$. Then with $m_1 = 2$, $m_2 = 1$, $k_1 = 100$, $k_2 = 50$, and $F_0 = 50$ in Fig. 5.3.9, Eq. (29) takes the form

$$\mathbf{x}'' = \begin{bmatrix} -75 & 25 \\ 50 & -50 \end{bmatrix} \mathbf{x} + \begin{bmatrix} 0 \\ 50 \end{bmatrix} \cos \omega t, \qquad (33)$$

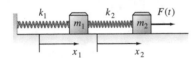

k_1 k_2 $F(t)$
m_1 m_2
x_1 x_2

FIGURE 5.3.9. The forced mass-and-spring system of Example 3.

and the substitution $\mathbf{x} = \mathbf{c} \cos \omega t$ leads to the equation

$$\begin{bmatrix} \omega^2 - 75 & 25 \\ 50 & \omega^2 - 50 \end{bmatrix} \mathbf{c} = \begin{bmatrix} 0 \\ -50 \end{bmatrix} \qquad (34)$$

for the coefficient vector $\mathbf{c} = \begin{bmatrix} -c_1 & c_2 \end{bmatrix}^T$. This system is readily solved for

$$c_1 = \frac{1250}{(\omega^2 - 25)(\omega^2 - 100)}, \quad c_2 = \frac{50(\omega^2 - 75)}{(\omega^2 - 25)(\omega^2 - 100)}. \qquad (35)$$

For instance, if the external squared frequency is $\omega^2 = 50$, then (35) yields $c_1 = 1$, $c_2 = -1$. The resulting forced periodic oscillation is described by

$$x_1(t) = \cos \omega t, \quad x_2(t) = -\cos \omega t.$$

Thus the two masses oscillate in synchrony with equal amplitudes but in opposite directions.

If the external squared frequency is $\omega^2 = 125$, then (35) yields $c_1 = \frac{1}{2}$, $c_2 = 1$. The resulting forced periodic oscillation is described by

$$x_1(t) = \tfrac{1}{2} \cos \omega t, \quad x_2(t) = \cos \omega t,$$

and now the two masses oscillate in synchrony in the same direction, but with the amplitude of motion of m_2 twice that of m_1.

It is evident from the denominators in (35) that c_1 and c_2 approach $+\infty$ as ω approaches either of the two natural frequencies $\omega_1 = 5$ and $\omega_2 = 10$ (found in Example 1). Figure 5.3.10 shows a plot of the amplitude $\sqrt{c_1^2 + c_2^2}$ of the forced periodic solution $\mathbf{x}(t) = \mathbf{c} \cos \omega t$ as a function of the forced frequency ω. The peaks at $\omega_2 = 5$ and $\omega_2 = 10$ exhibit visually the phenomenon of resonance. ∎

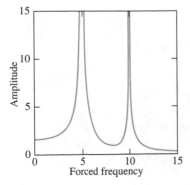

FIGURE 5.3.10. Frequency-amplitude plot for Example 3.

It follows from Theorem 4 of Section 5.1 that a particular solution of the forced system

$$\mathbf{x}'' = \mathbf{A}\mathbf{x} + \mathbf{F}_0 \cos \omega t \qquad (36)$$

will be of the form

➤ $$\mathbf{x}(t) = \mathbf{x}_c(t) + \mathbf{x}_p(t), \qquad (37)$$

where $\mathbf{x}_p(t)$ is a particular solution of the nonhomogeneous system and $\mathbf{x}_c(t)$ is a solution of the corresponding homogeneous system. It is typical for the effects of frictional resistance in mechanical systems to damp out the complementary function solution $\mathbf{x}_c(t)$, so that

$$\mathbf{x}_c(t) \to \mathbf{0} \quad \text{as} \quad t \to +\infty. \qquad (38)$$

Hence $\mathbf{x}_c(t)$ is a **transient solution** that depends only on the initial conditions; it dies out with time, leaving the **steady periodic solution** $\mathbf{x}_p(t)$ resulting from the external driving force:

$$\mathbf{x}(t) \to \mathbf{x}_p(t) \quad \text{as} \quad t \to +\infty. \qquad (39)$$

As a practical matter, every physical system includes frictional resistance (however small) that damps out transient solutions in this manner.

5.3 _Problems_

Problems 1 through 7 deal with the mass-and-spring system shown in Fig. 5.3.11 with stiffness matrix

$$\mathbf{K} = \begin{bmatrix} -(k_1 + k_2) & k_2 \\ k_2 & -(k_2 + k_3) \end{bmatrix}$$

and with the given fps values for the masses and spring constants. Find the two natural frequencies of the system and describe its two natural modes of oscillation.

1. $m_1 = m_2 = 1$; $k_1 = 0, k_2 = 2, k_3 = 0$ (no walls)

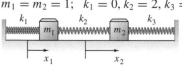

FIGURE 5.3.11. The mass-and-spring system for Problems 1 through 6.

2. $m_1 = m_2 = 1$; $k_1 = 1, k_2 = 4, k_3 = 1$

3. $m_1 = 1, m_2 = 2$; $k_1 = 1, k_2 = k_3 = 2$

4. $m_1 = m_2 = 1$; $k_1 = 1, k_2 = 2, k_3 = 1$

5. $m_1 = m_2 = 1$; $k_1 = 2, k_2 = 1, k_3 = 2$

6. $m_1 = 1, m_2 = 2$; $k_1 = 2, k_2 = k_3 = 4$

7. $m_1 = m_2 = 1$; $k_1 = 4, k_2 = 6, k_3 = 4$

In Problems 8 and 9 the indicated mass-and-spring system is set in motion from rest $(x_1'(0) = x_2'(0) = 0)$ in its equilibrium position $(x_1(0) = x_2(0) = 0)$ with the given external forces $F_1(t)$ and $F_2(t)$ acting on the masses m_1 and m_2, respectively. Find the resulting motion of the system and describe it as a superposition of oscillations at three different frequencies.

8. The mass-and-spring system of Problem 2, with $F_1(t) = 96 \cos 5t$, $F_2(t) \equiv 0$

9. The mass-and-spring system of Problem 3, with $F_1(t) \equiv 0$, $F_2(t) = 120 \cos 3t$

10. The mass-and-spring system of Problem 7, with $F_1(t) = 30 \cos t$, $F_2(t) = 60 \cos t$

11. Consider a mass-and-spring system containing two masses $m_1 = 1$ and $m_2 = 1$ whose displacement functions $x(t)$ and $y(t)$ satisfy the differential equations

$$x'' = -40x + 8y,$$
$$y'' = 12x - 60y.$$

(a) Describe the two fundamental modes of free oscillation of the system. (b) Assume that the two masses start in motion with the initial conditions

$$x(0) = 19, \quad x'(0) = 1$$

and

$$y(0) = 3, \quad y'(0) = 6$$

and are acted on by the same force, $F_1(t) = F_2(t) = -195 \cos 7t$. Describe the resulting motion as a superposition of oscillations at three different frequencies.

In Problems 12 and 13, find the natural frequencies of the three-mass system of Fig. 5.3.1, using the given masses and spring constants. For each natural frequency ω, give the ratio $a_1:a_2:a_3$ of amplitudes for a corresponding natural mode $x_1 = a_1 \cos \omega t, x_2 = a_2 \cos \omega t, x_3 = a_3 \cos \omega t$.

12. $m_1 = m_2 = m_3 = 1$; $k_1 = k_2 = k_3 = k_4 = 1$

13. $m_1 = m_2 = m_3 = 1$; $k_1 = k_2 = k_3 = k_4 = 2$
(*Hint:* One eigenvalue is $\lambda = -4$.)

14. In the system of Fig. 5.3.12, assume that $m_1 = 1$ (slug), $k_1 = 50$ (lb/ft), $k_2 = 10$ (lb/ft), $F_0 = 5$ (lb), and $\omega = 10$ (rad/s). Then find m_2 so that in the resulting steady periodic oscillations, the mass m_1 will remain at rest(!). Thus the effect of the second mass-and-spring pair will be to neutralize the effect of the force on the first mass. This is an example of a *dynamic damper*. It has an electrical analogy that some cable companies use to prevent your reception of certain cable channels.

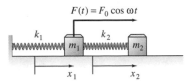

FIGURE 5.3.12.   The
mechanical system
of Problem 14.

15. Suppose that $m_1 = 2$, $m_2 = \frac{1}{2}$, $k_1 = 75$, $k_2 = 25$, $F_0 = 100$, and $\omega = 10$ (all in fps units) in the forced mass-and-spring system of Fig. 5.3.9. Find the solution of the system $\mathbf{Mx}'' = \mathbf{Kx} + \mathbf{F}$ that satisfies the initial conditions $\mathbf{x}(0) = \mathbf{x}'(0) = \mathbf{0}$.

16. Figure 5.3.13 shows two railway cars with a buffer spring. We want to investigate the transfer of momentum that occurs after car 1 with initial velocity v_0 impacts car 2 at rest. The analogue of Eq. (18) in the text is

$$\mathbf{x}'' = \begin{bmatrix} -c_1 & c_1 \\ c_2 & -c_2 \end{bmatrix} \mathbf{x}$$

with $c_i = k/m_i$ for $i = 1, 2$. Show that the eigenvalues of the coefficient matrix $\mathbf{A}$ are $\lambda_1 = 0$ and $\lambda_2 = -c_1 - c_2$, with associated eigenvectors $\mathbf{v}_1 = \begin{bmatrix} 1 & 1 \end{bmatrix}^T$ and $\mathbf{v}_2 = \begin{bmatrix} c_1 & -c_2 \end{bmatrix}^T$.

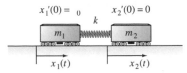

FIGURE 5.3.13.   The two
railway cars of Problems 16
through 19.

17. If the two cars of Problem 16 both weigh 16 tons (so that $m_1 = m_2 = 1000$ (slugs)) and $k = 1$ ton/ft (that is, 2000 lb/ft), show that the cars separate after $\pi/2$ seconds, and that $x_1'(t) = 0$ and $x_2'(t) = v_0$ thereafter. Thus the original momentum of car 1 is completely transferred to car 2.

18. If cars 1 and 2 weigh 8 and 16 tons, respectively, and $k = 3000$ lb/ft, show that the two cars separate after $\pi/3$ seconds, and that

$$x_1'(t) = -\tfrac{1}{3}v_0 \quad \text{and} \quad x_2'(t) = +\tfrac{2}{3}v_0$$

thereafter. Thus the two cars rebound in opposite directions.

19. If cars 1 and 2 weigh 24 and 8 tons, respectively, and $k = 1500$ lb/ft, show that the cars separate after $\pi/2$ seconds, and that

$$x_1'(t) = +\tfrac{1}{2}v_0 \quad \text{and} \quad x_2'(t) = +\tfrac{3}{2}v_0$$

thereafter. Thus both cars continue in the original direction of motion, but with different velocities.

20. In the three-railway-car system of Fig. 5.3.6, suppose that cars 1 and 3 each weigh 32 tons, that car 2 weighs 8 tons, and that each spring constant is 4 tons/ft. If $x_1'(0) = v_0$ and $x_2'(0) = x_3'(0) = 0$, show that the two springs are compressed until $t = \pi/2$ and that

$$x_1'(t) = -\tfrac{1}{9}v_0 \quad \text{and} \quad x_2'(t) = x_3'(t) = +\tfrac{8}{9}v_0$$

thereafter. Thus car 1 rebounds, but cars 2 and 3 continue with the same velocity.

The Two-Axle Automobile

In Example 4 of Section 3.6 we investigated the vertical oscillations of a one-axle car—actually a unicycle. Now we can analyze a more realistic model: a car with two axles and with separate front and rear suspension systems. Figure 5.3.14 represents the suspension system of such a car. We assume that the car body acts as would a solid bar of mass m and length $L = L_1 + L_2$. It has moment of inertia I about its center of mass C, which is at distance L_1 from the front of the car. The car has front and back suspension springs with Hooke's constants k_1 and k_2, respectively. When the car is in motion, let $x(t)$ denote the vertical displacement of the center of mass of the car from equilibrium; let $\theta(t)$ denote its angular displacement (in radians) from the horizontal. Then Newton's laws of motion for linear and angular acceleration can be used to derive the equations

$$mx'' = -(k_1 + k_2)x + (k_1 L_1 - k_2 L_2)\theta,$$
$$I\theta'' = (k_1 L_1 - k_2 L_2)x - (k_1 L_1^2 + k_2 L_2^2)\theta. \qquad (40)$$

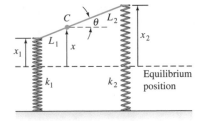

FIGURE 5.3.14.   Model of the
two-axle automobile.

21. Suppose that $m = 75$ slugs (the car weighs 2400 lb), $L_1 = 7$ ft, $L_2 = 3$ ft (it's a rear-engine car), $k_1 = k_2 = 2000$ lb/ft, and $I = 1000$ ft·lb·s². Then the equations in (40) take the form

$$75x'' + 4000x - \quad 8000\theta = 0,$$

$$1000\theta'' - 8000x + 116{,}000\theta = 0.$$

(a) Find the two natural frequencies ω_1 and ω_2 of the car.
(b) Now suppose that the car is driven at a speed of v feet per second along a washboard surface shaped like a sine curve with a wavelength of 40 ft. The result is a periodic force on the car with frequency $\omega = 2\pi v/40 = \pi v/20$. Resonance occurs when with $\omega = \omega_1$ or $\omega = \omega_2$. Find the corresponding two critical speeds of the car (in feet per second and in miles per hour).

22. Suppose that $k_1 = k_2 = k$ and $L_1 = L_2 = \frac{1}{2}L$ in Fig. 5.3.14 (the symmetric situation). Then show that every free oscillation is a combination of a vertical oscillation with frequency

$$\omega_1 = \sqrt{2k/m}$$

and an angular oscillation with frequency

$$\omega_2 = \sqrt{kL^2/(2I)}.$$

In Problems 23 through 25, the system of Fig. 5.3.14 is taken as a model for an undamped car with the given parameters in fps units. (a) Find the two natural frequencies of oscillation (in hertz). (b) Assume that this car is driven along a sinusoidal washboard surface with a wavelength of 40 ft. Find the two critical speeds.

23. $m = 100$, $I = 800$, $L_1 = L_2 = 5$, $k_1 = k_2 = 2000$
24. $m = 100$, $I = 1000$, $L_1 = 6$, $L_2 = 4$, $k_1 = k_2 = 2000$
25. $m = 100$, $I = 800$, $L_1 = L_2 = 5$, $k_1 = 1000$, $k_2 = 2000$

5.4 Lab 4: Solving Systems of ODEs Using Maple

In this tutorial you will learn a new technique for solving (systems of) differential equations numerically.

In the prelab you will see that the techniques that you learned in Lab 3 for solving a single differential equation apply equally well to **systems** of differential equations.

You need only read the prelab; there are no problems to hand in. (But you do have to read this if you want to finish in time.)

Some reminders from lab 3.

- end commands with a **;** or **:**
- always use ***** for multiplication
- use **:=** for assignment and **=** for equations
- use y(t) or y(x) not y in your equations
- use diff(y(t),t) not y**'**(t)

Solving Systems of Differential Equations Analytically

In what follows the Maple input is typed after the prompt **>** and the Maple output is **indented**.

The first 3 illustrative examples in the prelab refer to the system $x' = y$, $y' = -x - \dfrac{y(t)}{10}$. ($x'$ means $\dfrac{\partial}{\partial t}x$)

EXAMPLE 1 Write down the Maple commands to solve the **above system** of equations.

The syntax for solving a system of equations analytically is essentially the same as for solving a single equation.

> **dsolve({equations}, {unknown functions});**

Here is the answer to Example 1:

> **ex1a:=diff(x(t),t)=y(t);**
  ex1b:=diff(y(t),t)=-x(t)-y(t)/10;

$$ex1a := \frac{\partial}{\partial t}x(t) = y(t)$$

$$ex1b := \frac{\partial}{\partial t}y(t) = -x(t) - \frac{1}{10}y(t)$$

The first two commands give us a "pretty print" of the two equations; when we see that there are no typos we continue with

> **dsolve({ex1a, ex1b}, {x(t), y(t)});**

This command asks for the solution

$$\{x(t) = e^{(-1/20\,t)}\left(\_C1\sin\left(\frac{1}{20}\sqrt{399}\,t\right) + \_C2\cos\left(\frac{1}{20}\sqrt{399}\,t\right)\right),$$

$$y(t) = \frac{1}{20}e^{(-1/20\,t)}\left(-\_C1\sin\left(\frac{1}{20}\sqrt{399}\,t\right) + \_C1\cos\left(\frac{1}{20}\sqrt{399}\,t\right)\sqrt{399}\right.$$

$$\left. -\_C2\cos\left(\frac{1}{20}\sqrt{399}\,t\right) - \sin\left(\frac{1}{20}\sqrt{399}\,t\right)\_C2\sqrt{399}\right)\}$$

The answer has constants that are written a bit strangley; C1 sin .99t or even _C1 sin .99t seems clearer than sin .99t_C1 but Maple uses the third form. (.99 $\approx \frac{\sqrt{399}}{20}$)

EXAMPLE 2   Solve the above **system** of equations with initial conditions $x(0) = 1$, $y(0) = -3$ and evaluate the solution at $t = 2$.

     The syntax for solving a system of equations with initial conditions analytically is essentially the same as for solving a single equation.

> **dsolve({equations, initial conditions}, {unknown functions});**

Here is the answer to Example 2:

> **ans2:=dsolve({ex1a,ex1b,x(0)=1,y(0)=-3},{x(t),y(t)});**
> **eval(ans2,t=2);**

ans2 :=

$$\{y(t) = -\frac{1}{20}e^{(-1/20\,t)}\left(\frac{340}{399}\sqrt{399}\sin\left(\frac{1}{20}\sqrt{399}\,t\right) + 60\cos\left(\frac{1}{20}\sqrt{399}\,t\right)\right),$$

$$x(t) = e^{(-1/20\,t)}\left(-\frac{59}{399}\sqrt{399}\sin\left(\frac{1}{20}\sqrt{399}\,t\right) + \cos\left(\frac{1}{20}\sqrt{399}\,t\right)\right)\}$$

$$\{y(2) = -\frac{1}{20}e^{\left(\frac{-1}{10}\right)}\left(\frac{340}{399}\sqrt{399}\sin\left(\frac{1}{10}\sqrt{399}\right) + 60\cos\left(\frac{1}{10}\sqrt{399}\right)\right),$$

$$x(2) = e^{\left(\frac{-1}{10}\right)}\left(-\frac{59}{399}\sqrt{399}\sin\left(\frac{1}{10}\sqrt{399}\right) + \cos\left(\frac{1}{10}\sqrt{399}\right)\right)\}$$

The answer is exact but not easy to interpret so . . .

> **evalf(eval(ans2,t=2));**

This gives numerical values.

$$\{y(2) = .4224308642, x(2) = -2.807460825\}$$

EXAMPLE 3   For the solution to Example 2
(a) plot $x(t)$ for $0 \le t \le 30$
(b) plot $x(t)$ and $y(t)$ on the same graph for $0 \le t \le 30$
(c) plot $x(t)$ vs $y(t)$ for $0 \le t \le 30$.

     To do this example we must look at the answer to Example 2; it is a set of equations. To extract the functions $x(t)$, $y(t)$ from the pair we must select an equation and then take the right hand side (**rhs**) of the equations as follow:

> **ans2[1];**

This command selects the first of the two equations we got as an answer. This time it is the y equation; next time it might be the x equation.

$$y(t) = -\frac{1}{20}e^{(-1/20\,t)}\left(\frac{340}{399}\sqrt{399}\sin\left(\frac{1}{20}\sqrt{399}\,t\right) + 60\cos\left(\frac{1}{20}\sqrt{399}\,t\right)\right)$$

```
> Y:=rhs(ans2[1]); X:=rhs(ans2[2]);
```

These commands select and name the parts of the answer.

$$Y := -\frac{1}{20}e^{(-1/20\,t)}\left(\frac{340}{399}\sqrt{399}\,\sin\left(\frac{1}{20}\sqrt{399}\,t\right) + 60\cos\left(\frac{1}{20}\sqrt{399}\,t\right)\right)$$

$$X := e^{(-1/20\,t)}\left(-\frac{59}{399}\sqrt{399}\,\sin\left(\frac{1}{20}\sqrt{399}\,t\right) + \cos\left(\frac{1}{20}\sqrt{399}\,t\right)\right)$$

Now we can do the required plots. The answer to part (a) is

```
> plot(X,t = 0..30);
```

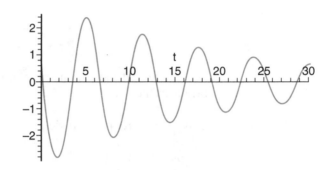

Legend

——— Curve 1

```
> plot( {X,Y}, t = 0..30);
```

This answers part (b). How can you know which curve is *x* and which is *y*?

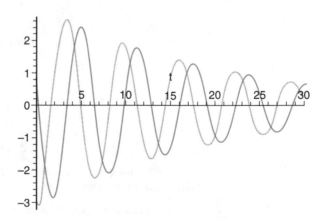

Legend

——— Curve 1

——— Curve 2

```
> plot([X,Y,t = 0..30]);
```

This is the answer to part (c). ($x(t)$ is plotted on the horizontal axis, $y(t)$ is plotted on the vertical axis.)

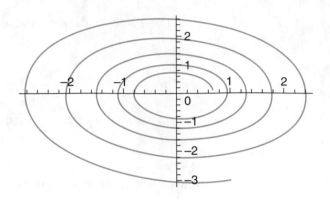

Legend

———————— Curve 1

Note that the parametric plot of Y vs X is spiraling into or away from the origin. Which is it?

EXAMPLE 4   Solve the **system** of equations $x' = y$, $y' = -x$ with initial conditions $x(0) = 1$, $y(0) = -3$. Then
(a) plot $x(t)$ for $0 \le t \le 30$
(b) plot $x(t)$ and $y(t)$ on the same graph for $0 \le t \le 30$
(c) plot $x(t)$ vs $y(t)$ for $0 \le t \le 30$.

Here is the answer to Example 4:

```
> ex4a:=diff(x(t),t)=y(t);ex4b:=diff(y(t),t)=-x(t);
  ans4:=dsolve({ex4a,ex4b,x(0)=1,y(0)=-3},{x(t),y(t)});
```

$$ex4a := \frac{\partial}{\partial t} x(t) = y(t)$$

$$ex4b := \frac{\partial}{\partial t} y(t) = -x(t)$$

$$ans4 : \{x(t) = -3\sin(t) + \cos(t), \, y(t) = -3\cos(t) - \sin(t)\}$$

To do the plots we can now select one of the equations and name it as above. Here is another method:

```
> X4:=subs(ans4,x(t)); Y4:=subs(ans4,y(t));
```

We *subs*titute the value of ans4 for $x(t)$ and call it X4.

$$X4 := -3\sin(t) + \cos(t)$$

$$Y4 := -3\cos(t) - \sin(t)$$

```
> plot(X4,t=0..30);plot({X4,Y4},t=0..30);
```

Here are the answers for parts (a) and (b).

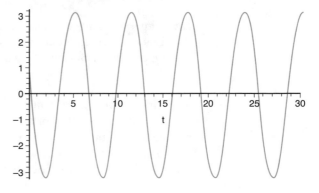

Legend

———— Curve 1

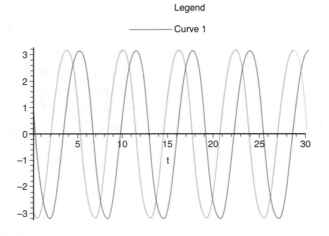

Legend

———— Curve 1

———— Curve 2

The solution seems to be periodic, that is, it repeats. Another way of saying that is that there is a number T (2π in this case) such that $x(t+T) = x(t)$ and $y(t+T) = y(t)$.

```
> plot([X4,Y4,t=0..20]);
```

Here is the answer to part (c). Note that the parametric plot of $x(t)$ vs $y(t)$ does not spiral, it repeats the same trajectory over and over.

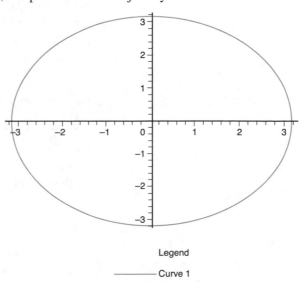

Legend

———— Curve 1

This is the end of the prelab.

Using Maple to Solve Systems of Differential Equations

There are 4 problems to do in this lab—some with several parts.
Enter and execute the examples to learn the techniques required.
Open Maple. Before you start typing clear out all previous definitions.

```
> restart;
```

This is a very important command; it erases Maple's memory.
Open a new Maple worksheet by selecting **New** in the **File** menu, Save the file
as **initials.mws**, that is, replace the ***.mws** by **fs.mws** if your name is Francis Smith.
Use **initials.mws** to record your answers (cut and paste) and then print it out at the
end of the lab. (Choose **Print** from the **File** menu on **initials.mws**.)
The techniques required for problem 1 were discussed in the prelab reading.

1. This problem refers to the following system of equations:

$$x' = -3x + 4y, \ y' = 5x - 7y + \cos(5t), \ x(0) = 0, \ y(0) = -1.$$

(a) Find the general solution to this **system** of equations.
(b) Solve the **system** of equations with initial conditions $x(0) = 1$, $y(0) = -3$
and evaluate the solution at $t = 2$.
(c) For the solution to part (b) create the following three plots: (i) plot $x(t)$
for $0 \leq t \leq 3$, (ii) plot $x(t)$ and $y(t)$ on the same graph for $0 \leq t \leq 20$
and (iii) plot $x(t)$ vs $y(t)$ for $0 \leq t \leq 20$.

Solving Systems of Differential Equations Numerically

Most systems of differential equations do not have explicit solutions in terms of
known functions; the best you can do is to find numerical solutions. The syntax for
solving systems of differential equations numerically is essentially the same as the
syntax for solving a single differential equation numerically so this part of the lab is
also a review of Lab 3.

2. (i) In each part of this problem find $x(1.2)$ and $y(1.2)$ to 2 decimal place
accuracy.

(ii) Plot $\dfrac{x}{1 + y^2}$ over the range $0 \leq t \leq 2$.

(iii) Plot $x(t)$ and $y(t)$ on the same graph over the range $0 \leq t \leq 2$.

(iv) Plot $y(t)$ vs $x(t)$ for $0 \leq t \leq 2$.
Hint: Copy the equations from problem 1 and modify them.

(a) $x' = -5x + 17y$, $y' = -2x^3 + 5y$, $x(0) = 1$, $y(0) = -3$.
The answer to (a) is given below; you must do part (b).

(b) $x' = x^2 - xy$, $y' = -y + x^3$, $x(0) = 1$, $y(0) = -1$.

Here is the answer to problem 2(a).

```
> eq2a1:=diff(x(t),t)=-5*x(t)+17*y(t);
  eq2a2:=diff(y(t),t)=-2*x(t)^3+5*y(t);
```

The answer is just a pretty print of the equations. There are no typos so
we ask for the solution.

$$eq2a1 := \frac{\partial}{\partial t} x(t) = -5x(t) + 17y(t)$$

$$eq2a2 := \frac{\partial}{\partial t} y(t) = -2x(t)^3 + 5y(t)$$

```
> ans2a:=dsolve({eq2a1,eq2a2,x(0)=1,y(0)=-3},
  [x(t),y(t)],numeric);
```

The syntax is

dsolve({equations, initial conditions}, {unknown functions},numeric);

The word **numeric** tells Maple to calculate *numerically* rather than analytically. The output is a procedure.

$$ans2a := \textbf{proc}(\textit{rkf45\_x}) \ldots \textbf{end proc}$$

> `ans2a(1.2);`

This evaluates the answer at $t = 1.2$.

$$[t = 1.2, x(t) = -2.27758745938612694,$$
$$y(t) = 2.44292020429415712]$$

> `with(plots):`   That is how packages are loaded.

Use a **colon** after the command rather than a **semicolon** or the screen will fill up with a list of all the new commands available in **plots**.

> `Warning, the name changecoords has been redefined`

(You can ignore the warning that appears.)

Now we can use the **odeplot** command as we did in lab 3.

> `odeplot(ans2a,[t,x(t)/(1+y(t)^2)], 0..2);`

This plots the function requested in part (ii).

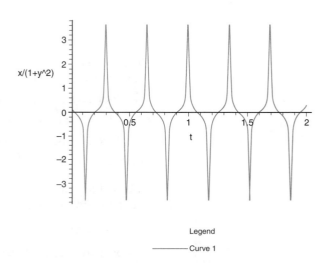

> `odeplot(ans2a,[[t,x(t)],[t,y(t)]],0..2);`

This command plots $x(t)$ and $y(t)$ on the same graph

Note that there are an extra pair of brackets [ ] when we have more than one curve on the same graph.

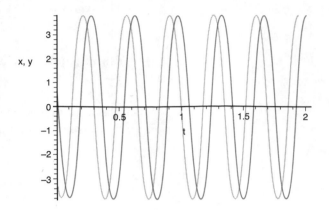

Legend

———— Curve 1

———— Curve 2

```
> odeplot(ans2a,[x(t),y(t)],0..2);
```

This command plots $y(t)$ vs $x(t)$

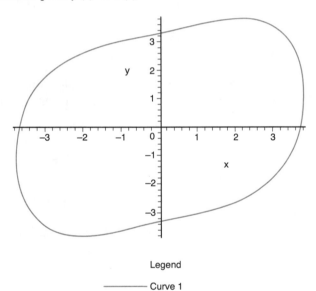

Legend

———— Curve 1

3. This problem refers to the system $x'' + xy^3 = 0$, $y' = x - y$ with initial conditions $x(0) = 1$, $y(0) = -2$, $x'(0) = 0$.

(a) Plot $x(t)$ and $y(t)$ on the same graph over the range $0 \le t \le 5$.

(b) Plot $x(t)$ and $y(t)$ on the same graph over the range $0 \le t \le 17$.

(c) Evaluate the solution to 2 decimal places at $t = 17$.

(d) Is the solution periodic?

We will now investigate the system $x' = -x - 4y^3$, $y' = 2x + y$. We enter our equations and look at the solution for various initial conditions.

```
> restart;   We erase Maple's memory and start fresh.
```

```
> ex1:=diff(x(t),t)=-(x(t)+4*y(t)^3);
  ex2:=diff(y(t),t)=2*x(t)+y(t);
```

$$ex1 := \frac{\partial}{\partial t} x(t) = -x(t) - 4y(t)^3$$

$$ex2 := \frac{\partial}{\partial t} y(t) = 2x(t) + y(t)$$

```
> ans:=dsolve({ex1,ex2,x(0)=1,y(0)=0},
  [x(t),y(t)],numeric);
```

$$ans := \mathbf{proc}(rkf45\_x) \ldots \mathbf{end\ proc}$$

```
> with(plots):
```
This is only necessary because we have restarted.

```
> odeplot(ans,[[t,x(t)],[t,y(t)]],0..10);
```

This plots x vs t and y vs t on the same graph. We can guess from the graph that the solution is *periodic*, that is, there is some number T so that $x(t+T) = x(t)$, $y(t+T) = y(t)$. To get a better estimate of T we note that $y(0) = 0$ and we zoom in on the second zero of y to get the value of T. Seems to be about 2.7 so we issue the command

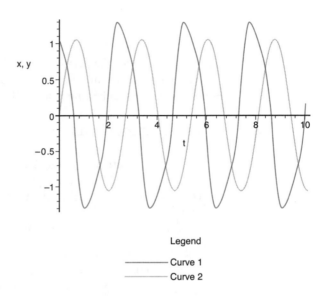

```
> odeplot(ans,[t,y(t)],2.6..2.8);
```
$T = 2.69$ approximately.

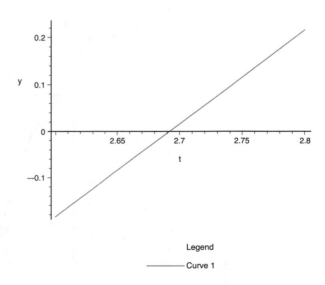

```
> odeplot(ans,[x(t),y(t)],0..30);
```

This parametric plot of y vs x shows that the solution is repeating itself.

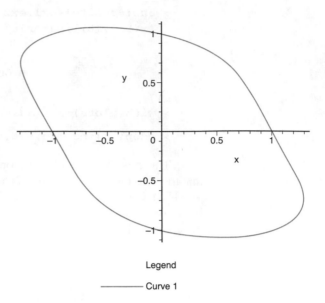

Legend

———— Curve 1

How does the period vary with the initial conditions? Since **odeplot** only lets us use one set of initial conditions at a time it is hard to say unless we run it many times and remember the results. Here is an alternative method.

The DEplot Command

There is an alternative to the **dsolve(... numeric)** and **odeplot** commands for solving systems of differential equations numerically called **DEplot**. The advantage of **DEplot** is that you can see the solutions for different initial conditions on the same plot.

First you must load the DEtools package.

```
> with(DEtools):
> DEplot({ex1,ex2},{x(t),y(t)},t=0..5,
    [[x(0)=0,y(0)=.1],[x(0)=0,y(0)=.2],
    [x(0)=0,y(0)=.3]],scene=[t,x],
    linecolor=[red,green,blue]);
```

There are several things to explain about this command. First of all the syntax is

DEplot({equations}, {names of variables}, range of t values, list of initial conditions (each one of which is a list), options);

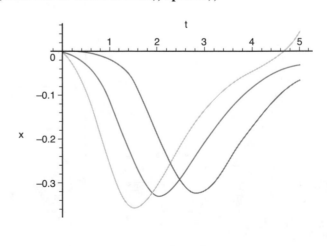

Legend

———— Curve 2

———— Curve 3

The range is given in the form t=1 .. 5 or t=-3 .. 7 or some such. Each initial condition has the form [x(to)=2, y(to)=6] if there are two dependent variables. In our case we had 3 sets of initial conditions and we told DEplot to color the first red, the second green and the third blue. That is what linecolor=[red, green, blue] means. The scene option tells DEplot we want a plot of $x(t)$ vs t for each initial condition. If we set scene=[x,y] then we get a parametric plot for each initial condition.

We did not go far enough to see what the periods are so we lengthen the t-range to t=0..20.

```
> DEplot({ex1,ex2},{x(t),y(t)},t=0..20,
  [[x(0)=0,y(0)=.1],[x(0)=0,y(0)=.2],
  [x(0)=0,y(0)=.3]],scene=[t,x],
  linecolor=[red,green,blue]);
```

The answer is very peculiar and NOT to be trusted. We reissue the command but insist that the step in the numerical integration process is less than .05 by adding the optional argument stepsize=.05.

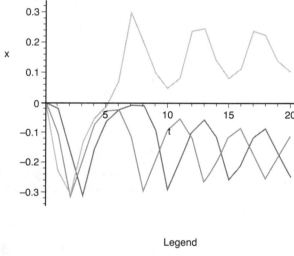

Legend

———— Curve 2
———— Curve 3

```
> DEplot({ex1,ex2},{x(t),y(t)},t=0..20,
  [[x(0)=0,y(0)=.1],[x(0)=0,y(0)=.2],
  [x(0)=0,y(0)=.3]],stepsize=.05,scene=[t,x],
  linecolor=[red,green,blue]);
```

Note that the results are quite different and much more believable.

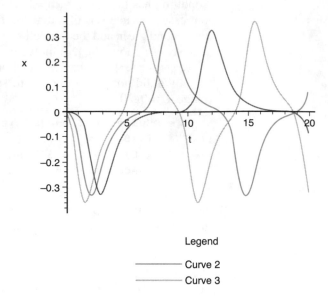

Legend

———— Curve 2

———— Curve 3

```
> DEplot({ex1,ex2},{x(t),y(t)},t=0..20,
  [[x(0)=0,y(0)=.1],[x(0)=0,y(0)=.2],
  [x(0)=0,y(0)=.3]],stepsize=.05,scene=[x,y],
  linecolor=[red,green,blue]);
```

We get a parametric plot of y vs x by setting scene=[x,y]. Note that the solutions do seem to be periodic. Note also that we automatically get a direction field because the system is autonomous.

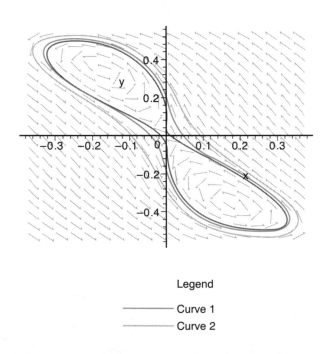

Legend

———— Curve 1

———— Curve 2

```
> DEplot({ex1,ex2},{x(t),y(t)},t=0..20,
  [[x(0)=0,y(0)=.1],[x(0)=0,y(0)=.2],
  [x(0)=0,y(0)=.3]],stepsize=.05,scene=[x,y],
  linecolor=[red,green,blue],thickness=1);
```

The plot above was a bit coarse so we included the option thickness=1. The choices are 1, 2, 3, or 4.

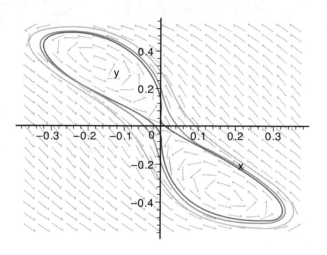

Legend

———— Curve 1

———— Curve 2

7. A mass m suspended from an undamped "hard" spring moves according to the system of equations $x' = v$, $mv' + kx(1 + sx^2) = 0$. Here x is displacement in meters and v is velocity in meters/sec. (A hard spring is a nonlinear spring; the "stiffness" increases with displacement.) The mass is 2 kilograms, the spring constant k is 3 N/m and we will assume that the nonlinearity is given by $s = 0.2$. The position at time $t = 0$ is 0 and the initial velocity is Vo m/sec. The kinetic energy of such a system is given by

$$KE = \frac{mv^2}{2}$$

and the potential energy stored in the spring is given by

$$PE = \frac{kx^2}{2} + \frac{sx^4}{4}.$$

(a) (Conservation of energy.) Show that KE + PE is constant for any choice of Vo. You can do that analytically or graphically for a few values of Vo.

(b) The solutions to the system are periodic and the period depends on Vo. How does the period vary as Vo increases from .01 to 10 say? You do not need to find formula for the period T(Vo); a qualitative answer is good enough.

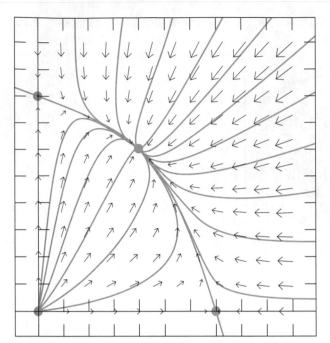

CHAPTER 6

Nonlinear Systems and Phenomena

6.1 STABILITY AND THE PHASE PLANE

A wide variety of natural phenomena are modeled by two-dimensional first-order systems of the form

$$\frac{dx}{dt} = F(x, y),$$
$$\frac{dy}{dt} = G(x, y)$$

(1)

in which the independent variable t does not appear explicitly. Such a system is called an **autonomous system.** The absence of t on the right-hand sides in (1) makes the system easier to analyze and its solutions easier to visualize. We assume that the functions F and G are continuously differentiable in some region R in the xy-plane, which is called the **phase plane** for the system in (1). Then, according to the existence and uniqueness theorems of the Appendix, given t_0 and any point (x_0, y_0) of R, there is a *unique* solution $x = x(t)$, $y = y(t)$ of (1) that is defined on some open interval (a, b) containing t_0 and satisfies the initial conditions

$$x(t_0) = x_0, \quad y(t_0) = y_0.$$

(2)

The equations $x = x(t)$, $y = y(t)$ then describe a parametrized solution curve in the phase plane. Any such solution curve is called a **trajectory** of the system in (1), and precisely one trajectory passes through each point of the region R (Problem 29). A **critical point** of the system in (1) is a point $(x_\star, y_\star)$ such that

$$F(x_\star, y_\star) = G(x_\star, y_\star) = 0.$$

(3)

If $(x_\star, y_\star)$ is a critical point of the system, then the constant-valued functions

$$x(t) \equiv x_\star, \quad y(t) \equiv y_\star$$

(4)

satisfy the equations in (1). Such a constant-valued solution is called an **equilibrium solution** of the system. Note that the trajectory of the equilibrium solution in (4) consists of the single point $(x_\star, y_\star)$.

In some practical situations these very simple solutions and trajectories are the ones of greatest interest. For example, suppose that the system $x' = F(x, y)$, $y' = G(x, y)$ models two populations $x(t)$ and $y(t)$ of animals that cohabit the same environment, and perhaps compete for the same food or prey on one another; $x(t)$

might denote the number of rabbits and $y(t)$ the number of squirrels present at time t. Then a critical point $(x_\star, y_\star)$ of the system specifies a *constant* population $x_\star$ of rabbits and a *constant* population $y_\star$ of squirrels that can coexist with one another in the environment. If (x_0, y_0) is *not* a critical point of the system, then it is *not* possible for constant populations of x_0 rabbits and y_0 squirrels to coexist; one or both must change with time.

EXAMPLE 1   Find the critical points of the system

$$\frac{dx}{dt} = 14x - 2x^2 - xy,$$

$$\frac{dy}{dt} = 16y - 2y^2 - xy. \tag{5}$$

Solution   When we look at the equations

$$14x - 2x^2 - xy = x(14 - 2x - y) = 0,$$
$$16y - 2y^2 - xy = y(16 - 2y - x) = 0$$

that a critical point (x, y) must satisfy, we see that either

$$x = 0 \quad \text{or} \quad 14 - 2x - y = 0, \tag{6a}$$

and either

$$y = 0 \quad \text{or} \quad 16 - 2y - x = 0. \tag{6b}$$

If $x = 0$ and $y \neq 0$, then the second equation in (6b) gives $y = 8$. If $y = 0$ and $x \neq 0$, then the second equation in (6a) gives $x = 7$. If both x and y are nonzero, then we solve the simultaneous equations

$$2x + y = 14, \quad x + 2y = 16$$

for $x = 4$, $y = 6$. Thus the system in (5) has the four critical points $(0, 0)$, $(0, 8)$, $(7, 0)$, and $(4, 6)$. If $x(t)$ and $y(t)$ denote the number of rabbits and the number of squirrels, respectively, and if both populations are *constant*, it follows that the equations in (5) allow only three nontrivial possibilities: either no rabbits and 8 squirrels, or 7 rabbits and no squirrels, or 4 rabbits and 6 squirrels. In particular, the critical point $(4, 6)$ describes the *only* possibility for the coexistence of constant nonzero populations of both species. ∎

Phase Portraits

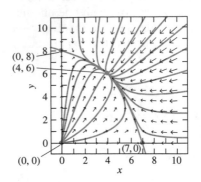

FIGURE 6.1.1. Direction field and phase portrait for the rabbit-squirrel system
$x' = 14x - 2x^2 - xy$,
$y' = 16y - 2y^2 - xy$ of
Example 1.

If the initial point (x_0, y_0) is not a critical point, then the corresponding trajectory is a curve in the xy-plane along which the point $(x(t), y(t))$ moves as t increases. It turns out that any trajectory not consisting of a single point is a nondegenerate curve with no self-intersections (Problem 30). We can exhibit qualitatively the behavior of solutions of the system in (1) by sketching its **phase portrait**—a phase plane picture of its critical points and typical nondegenerate trajectories. We may construct a **slope field** by drawing typical line segments having slope

$$\frac{dy}{dx} = \frac{y'}{x'} = \frac{G(x, y)}{F(x, y)},$$

or a **direction field** by drawing typical vectors pointing in the same direction at each point as the vector $(F(x, y), G(x, y))$. Such a vector field then indicates which direction along a trajectory to travel in order to "go with the flow" described by the system.

Figure 6.1.1 shows a direction field and phase portrait for the rabbit-squirrel system of Example 1. The direction field arrows indicate the direction of motion of the point $(x(t), y(t))$. We see that, given any positive initial numbers $x_0 \neq 4$ and $y_0 \neq 6$ of rabbits and squirrels, this point moves along a trajectory approaching the critical point $(4, 6)$ as t increases.

EXAMPLE 2   For the system

$$\begin{aligned} x' &= x - y, \\ y' &= 1 - x^2 \end{aligned} \tag{7}$$

we see from the first equation that $x = y$ and from the second that $x = \pm 1$ at each critical point. Thus this system has the two critical points $(-1, -1)$ and $(1, 1)$. The direction field in Fig. 6.1.2 suggests that trajectories somehow "circulate" counterclockwise around the critical point $(-1, -1)$, whereas it appears that some trajectories may approach, while others recede from, the critical point $(1, 1)$. These observations are corroborated by the phrase portrait in Fig. 6.1.3 for the system in (7). ∎

Critical Point Behavior

The behavior of the trajectories near an isolated critical point of an autonomous system is of particular interest. In the remainder of this section we illustrate with simple examples some of the most common possibilities.

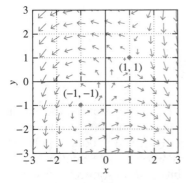

FIGURE 6.1.2. Direction field for the system in Eq. (7).

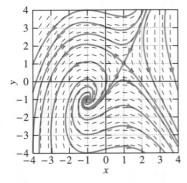

FIGURE 6.1.3. Phase portrait for the system in Eq. (7).

EXAMPLE 3 Consider the autonomous linear system

$$\frac{dx}{dt} = -x,$$

$$\frac{dy}{dt} = -ky \quad (k \text{ a nonzero constant}),$$

(8)

which has the origin $(0, 0)$ as its only critical point. The solution with initial point (x_0, y_0) is

$$x(t) = x_0 e^{-t}, \quad y(t) = y_0 e^{-kt}.$$

(9)

If $x_0 \neq 0$, we can write

$$y = y_0 e^{-kt} = \frac{y_0}{x_0^k}(x_0 e^{-t})^k = bx^k,$$

(10)

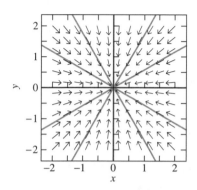

FIGURE 6.1.4. A proper node; the trajectories approach the origin, so it is a nodal sink.

where $b = y_0/x_0^k$. The nature of the critical point $(0, 0)$ depends on whether the nonzero parameter k is positive or negative.

CASE 1: $k > 0$. If k is positive then we see from (9) that the point $(x(t), y(t))$ approaches the origin along the curve $y = bx^k$ as $t \to +\infty$. The appearance of this curve depends on the magnitude of k:

- If $k = 1$, then $y = bx$ with $b = y_0/x_0$ is a straight line through the point (x_0, y_0). These straight-line trajectories are illustrated by the phase portrait in Fig. 6.1.4.
- If $k > 1$ and neither x_0 nor y_0 in Eq. (10) is zero, then the curve $y = bx^k$ is tangent to the x-axis at the origin. This case is illustrated by the phase portrait in Fig. 6.1.5, where $k = 2$ and the trajectories are parabolas. More precisely, the trajectories are the *semi*axes and the right and left *halves* of these parabolas.
- If $0 < k < 1$ and neither x_0 nor y_0 is zero, then the phase portrait is similar to Fig. 6.1.5, except that each curve $y = bx^k$ is tangent to the y-axis (rather than to the x-axis) at the origin.

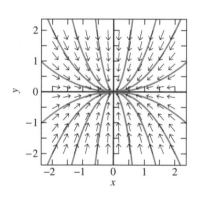

FIGURE 6.1.5. An improper node because all trajectories are tangent to a single line; they approach the origin, so it is a nodal sink.

The type of critical point illustrated in Figs. 6.1.4 and 6.1.5 is called a *node*. In general, the critical point $(x_\star, y_\star)$ of the autonomous system in (1) is called a **node** provided that:

- *Either* every trajectory approaches $(x_\star, y_\star)$ as $t \to +\infty$ *or* every trajectory recedes from $(x_\star, y_\star)$ as $t \to +\infty$, *and*
- Every trajectory is tangent at $(x_\star, y_\star)$ to some straight line through the critical point.

A node is said to be **proper** provided that no two different pairs of "opposite" trajectories are tangent to the same straight line through the critical point. This is the situation in Fig. 6.1.4 (in which the trajectories *are* straight lines, not merely tangent to straight lines). A proper node might be called a "star point." In Fig. 6.1.5 all trajectories except for a single opposite pair are tangent to a single straight line through the critical point. This type of node is said to be **improper.**

A node is also called a **sink** if all trajectories approach the critical point, a **source** if all trajectories recede (or emanate) from it. Thus the origin in Fig. 6.1.4 is a *proper nodal sink*, whereas in Fig. 6.1.5 it is an *improper nodal sink*. If the direction field arrows in each figure were reversed, then the origin would be a *nodal source* in each figure.

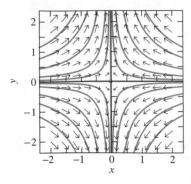

FIGURE 6.1.6. A saddle point with trajectories resembling the contour curves of a saddle point on a surface.

CASE 2: $k < 0$. If k is negative, then the trajectories resemble those for the case $k = -1$, which is illustrated in Fig. 6.1.6. If neither x_0 nor y_0 is zero, then the corresponding trajectory in Fig. 6.1.6 is one branch of the rectangular hyperbola $xy = b$, and $|y(t)| \to +\infty$ as $t \to +\infty$. If either x_0 or y_0 *is* zero, then the trajectory is a semiaxis of the hyperbola. The point $(x(t), y(t))$ approaches the origin along the x-axis, but recedes from it along the y-axis, as $t \to +\infty$. Thus there are two trajectories that approach the critical point $(0, 0)$, but all others are unbounded as $t \to +\infty$. This type of critical point, illustrated in Fig. 6.1.6, is called a **saddle point.**

Stability

A critical point $(x_\star, y_\star)$ of the autonomous system in (1) is said to be *stable* provided that if the initial point (x_0, y_0) is sufficiently close to $(x_\star, y_\star)$, then $(x(t), y(t))$ remains close to $(x_\star, y_\star)$ for all $t > 0$. In vector notation, with $\mathbf{x}(t) = (x(t), y(t))$, the distance between the initial point $\mathbf{x}_0 = (x_0, y_0)$ and the critical point $\mathbf{x}_\star = (x_\star, y_\star)$ is

$$|\mathbf{x}_0 - \mathbf{x}_\star| = \sqrt{(x_0 - x_\star)^2 + (y_0 - y_\star)^2}.$$

Thus the critical point $\mathbf{x}_\star$ is **stable** provided that, for each $\epsilon > 0$, there exists $\delta > 0$ such that

$$|\mathbf{x}_0 - \mathbf{x}_\star| < \delta \quad \text{implies that} \quad |\mathbf{x}(t) - \mathbf{x}_\star| < \epsilon \tag{11}$$

for all $t > 0$. Note that the condition in (11) certainly holds if $\mathbf{x}(t) \to \mathbf{x}_\star$ as $t \to +\infty$, as in the case of a nodal sink. Thus the nodal sinks illustrated in Figs. 6.1.4 and 6.1.5 can also be described as *stable nodes*.

The critical point $(x_\star, y_\star)$ is called **unstable** if it is not stable. The saddle point at $(0, 0)$ in Fig. 6.1.6 is an unstable critical point because the point $(x(t), y(t))$ goes to infinity as $t \to +\infty$, and hence the condition in (11) is not satisfied.

EXAMPLE 3 CONTINUED

If the signs on the right-hand side in (8) are changed to obtain the system

$$\frac{dx}{dt} = x,$$

$$\frac{dy}{dt} = ky \quad (k \text{ a nonzero constant}), \tag{12}$$

then the solution is $x(t) = x_0 e^t$, $y(t) = y_0 e^{kt}$. Then with $k = 1$ and $k = 2$, the trajectories are the same as those shown in Figs. 6.1.4 and 6.1.5, respectively, but with the arrows reversed, so that the point $(x(t), y(t))$ goes to infinity as $t \to \infty$. The result in each case is a nodal source—that is, an *unstable node*—at $(0, 0)$. ∎

If $(x_\star, y_\star)$ is a critical point, then the equilibrium solution $x(t) \equiv x_\star$, $y(t) \equiv y_\star$ is called **stable** or **unstable** depending on the nature of the critical point. In applications the stability of an equilibrium solution is often a crucial matter. For instance, suppose in Example 1 that $x(t)$ and $y(t)$ denote the rabbit and squirrel populations, respectively, *in hundreds*. We will see in Section 6.3 that the critical point $(4, 6)$ in Fig. 6.1.1 is stable. It follows that if we begin with *close to* 400 rabbits and 600 squirrels—rather than exactly these equilibrium values—then for all future time there will remain close to 400 rabbits and close to 600 squirrels. Thus the practical consequence of stability is that slight changes (perhaps due to random births and deaths) in the equilibrium populations will not so upset the equilibrium as to result in large deviations from the equilibrium solutions.

It is possible for trajectories to remain near a stable critical point without approaching it, as Example 4 shows.

EXAMPLE 4   Consider a mass m that oscillates without damping on a spring with Hooke's constant k, so that its position function $x(t)$ satisfies the differential equation $x'' + \omega^2 x = 0$ (where $\omega^2 = k/m$). If we introduce the velocity $y = dx/dt$ of the mass, we get the system

$$\frac{dx}{dt} = y,$$

$$\frac{dy}{dt} = -\omega^2 x \tag{13}$$

with general solution

$$x(t) = \quad A \cos \omega t + \quad B \sin \omega t, \tag{14a}$$
$$y(t) = -A\omega \sin \omega t + B\omega \cos \omega t. \tag{14b}$$

With $C = \sqrt{A^2 + B^2}$, $A = C \cos \alpha$, and $B = C \sin \alpha$, we can rewrite the solution in (14) in the form

$$x(t) = \quad C \cos(\omega t - \alpha), \tag{15a}$$
$$y(t) = -\omega C \sin(\omega t - \alpha), \tag{15b}$$

so it becomes clear that each trajectory other than the critical point $(0, 0)$ is an ellipse with equation of the form

$$\frac{x^2}{C^2} + \frac{y^2}{\omega^2 C^2} = 1. \tag{16}$$

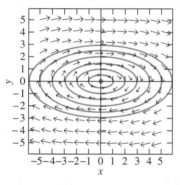

As illustrated by the phase portrait in Fig. 6.1.7 (where $\omega = \frac{1}{2}$), each point (x_0, y_0) other than the origin in the xy-plane lies on exactly one of these ellipses, and each solution $(x(t), y(t))$ traverses the ellipse through its initial point (x_0, y_0) in the clockwise direction with *period* $P = 2\pi/\omega$. (It is clear from (15) that $x(t + P) = x(t)$ and $y(t + P) = y(t)$ for all t.) Thus each nontrivial solution of the system in (13) is periodic and its trajectory is a simple closed curve enclosing the critical point at the origin. ■

FIGURE 6.1.7. Direction field and elliptical trajectories for the system $x' = y$, $y' = -\frac{1}{4}x$. The origin is a stable center.

Figure 6.1.8 shows a typical elliptical trajectory in Example 4, with its minor semiaxis denoted by δ and its major semiaxis by ϵ. We see that if the initial point (x_0, y_0) lies within distance δ of the origin—so that its elliptical trajectory lies inside the one shown—then the point $(x(t), y(t))$ always remains within distance ϵ of the origin. Hence the origin $(0, 0)$ is a stable critical point of the system $x' = y$, $y' = -\omega^2 x$. Unlike the situation illustrated in Figs. 6.1.4 and 6.1.5, however, no single trajectory approaches the point $(0, 0)$. A stable critical point surrounded by simple closed trajectories representing periodic solutions is called a **(stable) center.**

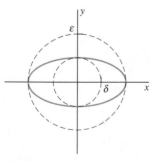

FIGURE 6.1.8. If the initial point (x_0, y_0) lies within distance δ of the origin, then the point $(x(t), y(t))$ stays within distance ϵ of the origin.

Asymptotic Stability

The critical point $(x_\star, y_\star)$ is called **asymptotically stable** if it is stable and, moreover, every trajectory that begins sufficiently close to $(x_\star, y_\star)$ also approaches $(x_\star, y_\star)$ as $t \to +\infty$. That is, there exists $\delta > 0$ such that

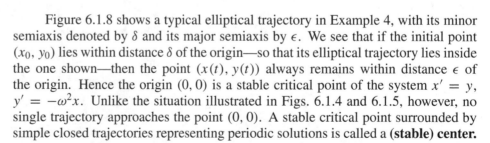

$$|\mathbf{x} - \mathbf{x}_\star| < \delta \quad \text{implies that} \quad \lim_{t \to \infty} \mathbf{x}(t) = \mathbf{x}_\star, \tag{17}$$

where $\mathbf{x}_0 = (x_0, y_0)$, $\mathbf{x}_\star = (x_\star, y_\star)$, and $\mathbf{x}(t) = (x(t), y(t))$ is a solution with $\mathbf{x}(0) = \mathbf{x}_0$.

Remark: The stable nodes shown in Figs. 6.1.4 and 6.1.5 are asymptotically stable because every trajectory approaches the critical point $(0, 0)$ as $t \to +\infty$. The center $(0, 0)$ shown in Fig. 6.1.7 is stable but not asymptotically stable, because however small an elliptical trajectory we consider, a point moving around this ellipse does not approach the origin. Thus asymptotic stability is a stronger condition than mere stability. ∎

Now suppose that $x(t)$ and $y(t)$ denote coexisting populations for which $(x_\star, y_\star)$ is an asymptotically stable critical point. Then if the initial populations x_0 and y_0 are sufficiently close to $x_\star$ and $y_\star$, respectively, it follows that both

$$\lim_{t\to\infty} x(t) = x_\star \quad \text{and} \quad \lim_{t\to\infty} y(t) = y_\star. \tag{18}$$

That is, $x(t)$ and $y(t)$ actually approach the equilibrium populations $x_\star$ and $y_\star$ as $t \to +\infty$, rather than merely remaining close to those values.

For a mechanical system as in Example 4, a critical point represents an *equilibrium state* of the system—if the velocity $y = x'$ and the acceleration $y' = x''$ vanish simultaneously, then the mass remains at rest with no net force acting on it. Stability of a critical point concerns the question whether, when the mass is displaced slightly from its equilibrium, it

1. Moves back toward the equilibrium point as $t \to +\infty$,
2. Merely remains near the equilibrium point without approaching it, or
3. Moves farther away from equilibrium.

In Case 1 the critical [equilibrium] point is asymptotically stable; in Case 2 it is stable but not asymptotically so; in Case 3 it is an unstable critical point. A marble balanced on the top of a soccer ball is an example of an unstable critical point. A mass on a spring with damping illustrates the case of asymptotic stability of a mechanical system. The mass-and-spring without damping in Example 4 is an example of a system that is stable but not asymptotically stable.

EXAMPLE 5 Suppose that $m = 1$ and $k = 2$ for the mass and spring of Example 4 and that the mass is attached also to a dashpot with damping constant $c = 2$. Then its displacement function $x(t)$ satisfies the second-order equation

$$x''(t) + 2x'(t) + 2x(t) = 0. \tag{19}$$

With $y = x'$ we obtain the equivalent first-order system

$$\frac{dx}{dt} = y,$$
$$\frac{dy}{dt} = -2x - 2y \tag{20}$$

with critical point $(0,0)$. The characteristic equation $r^2 + 2r + 2 = 0$ of Eq. (19) has roots $-1 + i$ and $-1 - i$, so the general solution of the system in (20) is given by

$$x(t) = e^{-t}(A\cos t + B\sin t) = Ce^{-t}\cos(t - \alpha), \tag{21a}$$
$$y(t) = e^{-t}[(B - A)\cos t - (A + B)\sin t]$$
$$= -C\sqrt{2}e^{-t}\sin\left(t - \alpha + \tfrac{1}{4}\pi\right), \tag{21b}$$

where $C = \sqrt{A^2 + B^2}$ and $\alpha = \tan^{-1}(B/A)$. We see that $x(t)$ and $y(t)$ oscillate between positive and negative values and that both approach zero as $t \to +\infty$. Thus a typical trajectory spirals inward toward the origin, as illustrated by the spiral in Fig. 6.1.9. ∎

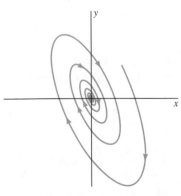

FIGURE 6.1.9. A stable spiral point and one nearby trajectory.

It is clear from (21) that the point $(x(t), y(t))$ approaches the origin as $t \to +\infty$, so it follows that $(0, 0)$ is an asymptotically stable critical point for the system $x' = y$, $y' = -2x - 2y$ of Example 5. Such an asymptotically stable critical point—around which the trajectories spiral as they approach it—is called a **stable spiral point** (or a **spiral sink**). In the case of a mass-spring-dashpot system, a spiral sink is the manifestation in the phase plane of the damped oscillations that occur because of resistance.

If the arrows in Fig. 6.1.9 were reversed, we would see a trajectory spiraling *outward* from the origin. An unstable critical point—around which the trajectories spiral as they emanate and recede from it—is called an **unstable spiral point** (or a **spiral source**). Example 6 shows that it also is possible for a trajectory to spiral into a **closed trajectory**—a simple closed solution curve that represents a periodic solution (like the elliptical trajectories in Fig. 6.1.7).

EXAMPLE 6   Consider the system

$$\frac{dx}{dt} = -ky + x(1 - x^2 - y^2),$$

$$\frac{dy}{dt} = kx + y(1 - x^2 - y^2). \tag{22}$$

In Problem 21 we ask you to show that $(0, 0)$ is its only critical point. This system can be solved explicitly by introducing polar coordinates $x = r\cos\theta$, $y = r\sin\theta$, as follows. First note that

$$\frac{d\theta}{dt} = \frac{d}{dt}\left(\arctan\frac{y}{x}\right) = \frac{xy' - x'y}{x^2 + y^2}.$$

Then substitute the expressions given in (22) for x' and y' to obtain

$$\frac{d\theta}{dt} = \frac{k(x^2 + y^2)}{x^2 + y^2} = k.$$

It follows that

$$\theta(t) = kt + \theta_0, \qquad \text{where } \theta_0 = \theta(0). \tag{23}$$

Then differentiation of $r^2 = x^2 + y^2$ yields

$$2r\frac{dr}{dt} = 2x\frac{dx}{dt} + 2y\frac{dy}{dt}$$

$$= 2(x^2 + y^2)(1 - x^2 - y^2) = 2r^2(1 - r^2),$$

so $r = r(t)$ satisfies the differential equation

$$\frac{dr}{dt} = r(1 - r^2). \tag{24}$$

In Problem 22 we ask you to derive the solution

$$r(t) = \frac{r_0}{\sqrt{r_0^2 + (1 - r_0^2)e^{-2t}}}, \tag{25}$$

where $r_0 = r(0)$. Thus the typical solution of Eq. (22) may be expressed in the form

$$x(t) = r(t)\cos(kt + \theta_0),$$
$$y(t) = r(t)\sin(kt + \theta_0). \tag{26}$$

If $r_0 = 1$, then Eq. (25) gives $r(t) \equiv 1$ (the unit circle). Otherwise, if $r_0 > 0$, then Eq. (25) implies that $r(t) \to 1$ as $t \to +\infty$. Hence the trajectory defined in (26) spirals in toward the unit circle if $r_0 > 1$ and spirals out toward this closed trajectory if $0 < r_0 < 1$. Figure 6.1.10 shows a trajectory spiraling outward from the origin and four trajectories spiraling inward, all approaching the closed trajectory $r(t) \equiv 1$. ∎

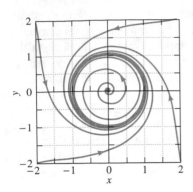

FIGURE 6.1.10. Spiral trajectories of the system in Eq. (22) with $k = 5$.

Under rather general hypotheses it can be shown that there are four possibilities for a nondegenerate trajectory of the autonomous system

$$\frac{dx}{dt} = F(x, y), \quad \frac{dy}{dt} = G(x, y).$$

The four possibilities are these:

1. $(x(t), y(t))$ approaches a critical point as $t \to +\infty$.
2. $(x(t), y(t))$ is unbounded with increasing t.
3. $(x(t), y(t))$ is a periodic solution with a closed trajectory.
4. $(x(t), y(t))$ spirals toward a closed trajectory as $t \to +\infty$.

As a consequence, the qualitative nature of the phase plane picture of the trajectories of an autonomous system is determined largely by the locations of its critical points and by the behavior of its trajectories near its critical points. We will see in Section 6.2 that, subject to mild restrictions on the functions F and G, each isolated critical point of the system $x' = F(x, y)$, $y' = G(x, y)$ resembles qualitatively one of the examples of this section—it is either a node (proper or improper), a saddle point, a center, or a spiral point.

6.1 Problems

In Problems 1 through 8, find the critical point or points of the given autonomous system, and thereby match each system with its phase portrait among Figs. 6.1.11 through 6.1.18.

1. $\dfrac{dx}{dt} = 2x - y, \quad \dfrac{dy}{dt} = x - 3y$

2. $\dfrac{dx}{dt} = x - y, \quad \dfrac{dy}{dt} = x + 3y - 4$

3. $\dfrac{dx}{dt} = x - 2y + 3, \quad \dfrac{dy}{dt} = x - y + 2$

4. $\dfrac{dx}{dt} = 2x - 2y - 4, \quad \dfrac{dy}{dt} = x + 4y + 3$

5. $\dfrac{dx}{dt} = 1 - y^2, \quad \dfrac{dy}{dt} = x + 2y$

6. $\dfrac{dx}{dt} = 2 - 4x - 15y, \quad \dfrac{dy}{dt} = 4 - x^2$

7. $\dfrac{dx}{dt} = x - 2y, \quad \dfrac{dy}{dt} = 4x - x^3$

8. $\dfrac{dx}{dt} = x - y - x^2 + xy, \quad \dfrac{dy}{dt} = -y - x^2$

In Problems 9 through 12, find all equilibrium solutions (of the form $x(t) \equiv x_0$, a constant) of the given second-order differential equation.

9. $x'' + 4x - x^3 = 0$

10. $x'' + 2x' + x + 4x^3 = 0$

11. $x'' + 3x' + 4\sin x = 0$

12. $x'' + (x^2 - 1)x' + x = 0$

Solve each of the linear systems in Problems 13 through 20 to determine whether the critical point $(0, 0)$ is stable, asymptotically stable, or unstable. Sketch typical trajectories and indicate the direction of motion with increasing t. Identify each critical point as a node, a saddle point, a center, or a spiral point.

13. $\dfrac{dx}{dt} = -2x, \quad \dfrac{dy}{dt} = -2y$

14. $\dfrac{dx}{dt} = 2x, \quad \dfrac{dy}{dt} = -2y$

15. $\dfrac{dx}{dt} = -2x, \quad \dfrac{dy}{dt} = -y$

16. $\dfrac{dx}{dt} = x, \quad \dfrac{dy}{dt} = 3y$

17. $\dfrac{dx}{dt} = y, \quad \dfrac{dy}{dt} = -x$

18. $\dfrac{dx}{dt} = -y, \quad \dfrac{dy}{dt} = 4x$

19. $\dfrac{dx}{dt} = 2y, \quad \dfrac{dy}{dt} = -2x$

20. $\dfrac{dx}{dt} = y, \quad \dfrac{dy}{dt} = -5x - 4y$

21. Verify that $(0, 0)$ is the only critical point of the system in Example 6.

22. Separate variables in Eq. (24) to derive the solution in (25).

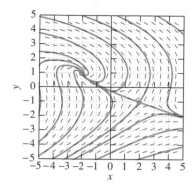

FIGURE 6.1.11. Spiral point $(-2, 1)$ and saddle point $(2, -1)$.

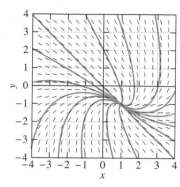

FIGURE 6.1.12. Spiral point $(1, -1)$.

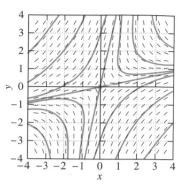

FIGURE 6.1.13. Saddle point $(0, 0)$.

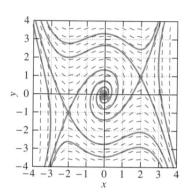

FIGURE 6.1.14. Spiral point $(0, 0)$; saddle points $(-2, -1)$ and $(2, 1)$.

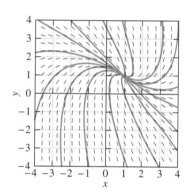

FIGURE 6.1.15. Node $(1, 1)$.

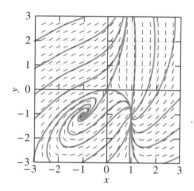

FIGURE 6.1.16. Spiral point $(-1, -1)$, saddle point $(0, 0)$, and node $(1, -1)$.

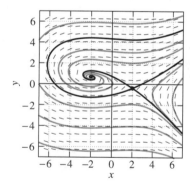

FIGURE 6.1.17. Spiral point $\left(-2, \frac{2}{3}\right)$ and saddle point $\left(2, -\frac{2}{5}\right)$.

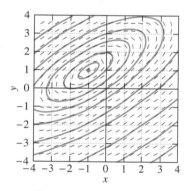

FIGURE 6.1.18. Stable center $(-1, 1)$.

In Problems 23 through 26, a system $dx/dt = F(x, y)$, $dy/dt = G(x, y)$ is given. Solve the equation

$$\frac{dy}{dx} = \frac{G(x, y)}{F(x, y)}$$

to find the trajectories of the given system.

23. $\dfrac{dx}{dt} = y, \quad \dfrac{dy}{dt} = -x$

24. $\dfrac{dx}{dt} = y(1 + x^2 + y^2), \quad \dfrac{dy}{dt} = x(1 + x^2 + y^2)$

25. $\dfrac{dx}{dt} = 4y(1 + x^2 + y^2), \quad \dfrac{dy}{dt} = -x(1 + x^2 + y^2)$

26. $\dfrac{dx}{dt} = y^3 e^{x+y}, \quad \dfrac{dy}{dt} = -x^3 e^{x+y}$

27. Let $(x(t), y(t))$ be a nontrivial solution of the nonautonomous system

$$\frac{dx}{dt} = y, \quad \frac{dy}{dt} = tx.$$

Suppose that $\phi(t) = x(t + \gamma)$ and $\psi(t) = y(t + \gamma)$, where $\gamma \neq 0$. Show that $(\phi(t), \psi(t))$ is *not* a solution of the system.

Problems 28 through 30 deal with the system

$$\frac{dx}{dt} = F(x, y), \quad \frac{dy}{dt} = G(x, y)$$

in a region where the functions F and G are continuously differentiable, so for each number a and point (x_0, y_0), there is a unique solution with $x(a) = x_0$ and $y(a) = y_0$.

28. Suppose that $(x(t), y(t))$ is a solution of the autonomous system and that $\gamma \neq 0$. Define $\phi(t) = x(t + \gamma)$ and $\psi(t) = y(t + \gamma)$. Then show (in contrast with the situation in Problem 27) that $(\phi(t), \psi(t))$ is also a solution of the system. Thus autonomous systems have the simple but important property that a "t-translate" of a solution is again a solution.

29. Let $(x_1(t), y_1(t))$ and $(x_2(t), y_2(t))$ be two solutions having trajectories that meet at the point (x_0, y_0); thus $x_1(a) = x_2(b) = x_0$ and $y_1(a) = y_2(b) = y_0$ for some values a and b of t. Define

$$x_3(t) = x_2(t + \gamma) \quad \text{and} \quad y_3(t) = y_2(t + \gamma)$$

where $\gamma = b - a$, so $(x_2(t), y_2(t))$ and $(x_3(t), y_3(t))$ have the same trajectory. Apply the uniqueness theorem to show that $(x_1(t), y_1(t))$ and $(x_3(t), y_3(t))$ are identical solutions. Hence the original two trajectories are identical. Thus no two different trajectories of an autonomous system can intersect.

30. Suppose that the solution $(x_1(t), y_1(t))$ is defined for all t and that its trajectory has an apparent self-intersection:

$$x_1(a) = x_1(a + P) = x_0, \quad y_1(a) = y_1(a + P) = y_0$$

for some $P > 0$. Introduce the solution

$$x_2(t) = x_1(t + P), \quad y_2(t) = y_1(t + P)$$

and then apply the uniqueness theorem to show that

$$x_1(t + P) = x_1(t) \quad \text{and} \quad y_1(t) = y_1(t + P)$$

for *all* t. Thus the solution $(x_1(t), y_1(t))$ is periodic with period P and has a closed trajectory. Consequently a solution of an autonomous system either is periodic with a closed trajectory, or else its trajectory never passes through the same point twice.

6.2 LINEAR AND ALMOST LINEAR SYSTEMS

We now discuss the behavior of solutions of the autonomous system

$$\frac{dx}{dt} = F(x, y), \qquad \frac{dy}{dt} = G(x, y) \tag{1}$$

near an isolated critical point (x_0, y_0) at which $F(x_0, y_0) = G(x_0, y_0) = 0$. A critical point is called **isolated** if some neighborhood of it contains no other critical point. We assume throughout that the functions F and G are continuously differentiable in a neighborhood of (x_0, y_0).

We can assume without loss of generality that $x_0 = y_0 = 0$. Otherwise, we make the substitutions $u = x - x_0$, $v = y - y_0$. Then $dx/dt = du/dt$ and $dy/dt = dv/dt$, so (1) is equivalent to the system

$$\frac{du}{dt} = F(u + x_0, v + y_0) = F_1(u, v),$$

$$\frac{dv}{dt} = G(u + x_0, v + y_0) = G_1(u, v) \tag{2}$$

that has $(0, 0)$ as an isolated critical point.

EXAMPLE 1   The system

$$\frac{dx}{dt} = 3x - x^2 - xy = x(3 - x - y),$$

$$\frac{dy}{dt} = y + y^2 - 3xy = y(1 - 3x + y) \tag{3}$$

has $(1, 2)$ as one of its critical points. We substitute $u = x - 1$, $v = y - 2$; that is, $x = u + 1$, $y = v + 2$. Then

$$3 - x - y = 3 - (u + 1) - (v + 2) = -u - v$$

and

$$1 - 3x + y = 1 - 3(u + 1) + (v + 2) = -3u + v,$$

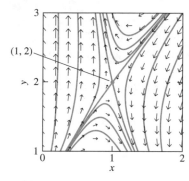

FIGURE 6.2.1. The saddle point $(1, 2)$ for the system $x' = 3x - x^2 - xy,$ $y' = y + y^2 - 3xy$ of Example 1.

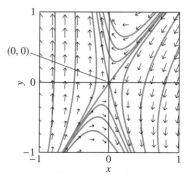

FIGURE 6.2.2. The saddle point $(0, 0)$ for the equivalent system $u' = -u - v - u^2 - uv,$ $v' = -6u + 2v + v^2 - 3uv.$

so the system in (3) takes the form

$$\frac{du}{dt} = (u + 1)(-u - v) = -u - v - u^2 - uv,$$

$$\frac{dv}{dt} = (v + 2)(-3u + v) = -6u + 2v + v^2 - 3uv \tag{4}$$

and has $(0, 0)$ as a critical point. If we can determine the trajectories of the system in (4) near $(0, 0)$, then their translations under the rigid motion that carries $(0, 0)$ to $(1, 2)$ will be the trajectories near $(1, 2)$ of the original system in (3). This equivalence is illustrated by Fig. 6.2.1 (which shows computer-plotted trajectories of the system in (3) near the critical point $(1, 2)$ in the xy-plane) and Fig. 6.2.2 (which shows computer-plotted trajectories of the system in (4) near the critical point $(0, 0)$ in the uv-plane). ∎

We therefore assume hereafter that $(0, 0)$ is an *isolated* critical point of the autonomous system in (1). It then follows from Taylor's formula for functions of two variables that (1) can be written in the form

$$\frac{dx}{dt} = ax + by + f(x, y),$$

$$\frac{dy}{dt} = cx + dy + g(x, y), \tag{5}$$

where $a = F_x(0, 0)$, $b = F_y(0, 0)$, $c = G_x(0, 0)$, and $d = G_y(0, 0)$, and the functions $f(x, y)$ and $g(x, y)$ have the property that

$$\lim_{(x,y)\to(0,0)} \frac{f(x, y)}{\sqrt{x^2 + y^2}} = \lim_{(x,y)\to(0,0)} \frac{g(x, y)}{\sqrt{x^2 + y^2}} = 0. \tag{6}$$

That is, when (x, y) is near $(0, 0)$, the quantities $f(x, y)$ and $g(x, y)$ are small in comparison with $r = (x^2 + y^2)^{1/2}$, which itself is small. Thus, when (x, y) is near $(0, 0)$, the nonlinear system in (5) is in some sense "near" the **linearized** system

$$\frac{dx}{dt} = ax + by,$$

$$\frac{dy}{dt} = cx + dy. \tag{7}$$

Under the assumption that $(0, 0)$ is also an isolated critical point of this linear system, the autonomous system in (5) is therefore called **almost linear** provided that f and g satisfy the conditions in (6). It turns out that in most (but not all) cases, the trajectories near $(0, 0)$ of the almost linear system in (5) strongly resemble—qualitatively—those of its "linearization" in (7). Consequently, the first step toward understanding general autonomous systems is to characterize the critical points of linear systems.

Critical Points of Linear Systems

We can use the eigenvalue-eigenvector method of Section 5.2 to solve the linear system

$$\begin{bmatrix} x' \\ y' \end{bmatrix} = \begin{bmatrix} a & b \\ c & d \end{bmatrix} \begin{bmatrix} x \\ y \end{bmatrix} \tag{8}$$

in (7) with coefficient matrix $\mathbf{A}$. Recall that the eigenvalues λ_1 and λ_2 of $\mathbf{A}$ are the solutions of the characteristic equation

$$\det(\mathbf{A} - \lambda\mathbf{I}) = \begin{vmatrix} a - \lambda & b \\ c & d - \lambda \end{vmatrix} = 0. \tag{9}$$

We assume that $(0, 0)$ is an *isolated* critical point of the system in (8), so it follows that the coefficient determinant $ad - bc$ of the system $ax + by = 0$, $cx + dy = 0$ is *nonzero*. This implies that $\lambda = 0$ is *not* a solution of (8), and hence that both eigenvalues of the matrix **A** are nonzero.

The nature of the isolated critical point $(0, 0)$ then depends on whether the two nonzero eigenvalues λ_1 and λ_2 of **A** are

- real and unequal with the same sign;
- real and unequal with opposite signs;
- real and equal;
- complex conjugates with nonzero real part; or
- pure imaginary numbers.

These five cases are discussed separately. In each case the critical point $(0, 0)$ resembles one of those we saw in the examples of Section 6.1—a node (proper or improper), a saddle point, a spiral point, or a center.

UNEQUAL REAL EIGENVALUES WITH THE SAME SIGN: In this case the matrix **A** has linearly independent eigenvectors $\mathbf{v}_1$ and $\mathbf{v}_2$ and the general solution $\mathbf{x}(t) = \begin{bmatrix} x(t) & y(t) \end{bmatrix}^T$ of (8) takes the form

$$\mathbf{x}(t) = c_1\mathbf{v}_1 e^{\lambda_1 t} + c_2\mathbf{v}_2 e^{\lambda_2 t}. \tag{10}$$

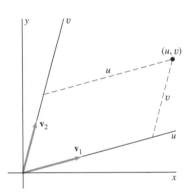

FIGURE 6.2.3. The oblique uv-coordinate system determined by the eigenvectors $\mathbf{v}_1$ and $\mathbf{v}_2$.

This solution is most simply described in the oblique uv-coordinate system indicated in Fig. 6.2.3, in which the u- and v-axes are determined by the eigenvectors $\mathbf{v}_1$ and $\mathbf{v}_2$. Then the uv-coordinate functions $u(t)$ and $v(t)$ of the moving point $\mathbf{x}(t)$ are simply its distances from the origin measured in the directions parallel to the vectors $\mathbf{v}_1$ and $\mathbf{v}_2$, so it follows from Eq. (10) that a trajectory of the system is described by

$$u(t) = u_0 e^{\lambda_1 t}, \quad v(t) = v_0 e^{\lambda_2 t} \tag{11}$$

where $u_0 = u(0)$ and $v_0 = v(0)$. If $v_0 = 0$ then this trajectory lies on the u-axis, whereas if $u_0 = 0$ then it lies on the v-axis. Otherwise—if u_0 and v_0 are both nonzero—the parametric curve in (11) takes the explicit form $v = Cu^k$ where $k = \lambda_2/\lambda_1 > 0$. These solution curves are tangent at $(0, 0)$ to the u-axis if $k > 1$, to the v-axis if $0 < k < 1$. Thus we have in this case an **improper node** as in Example 3 of Section 6.1. If λ_1 and λ_2 are both positive, then we see from (10) and (11) that these solution curves "depart from the origin" as t increases, so $(0, 0)$ is a **nodal source.** But if λ_1 and λ_2 are both negative, then these solution curves approach the origin as t increases, so $(0, 0)$ is a **nodal sink.**

EXAMPLE 2   (a) The matrix

$$\mathbf{A} = \tfrac{1}{8} \begin{bmatrix} 7 & 3 \\ -3 & 17 \end{bmatrix}$$

has eigenvalues $\lambda_1 = 1$ and $\lambda_2 = 2$ with associated eigenvectors $\mathbf{v}_1 = \begin{bmatrix} 3 & 1 \end{bmatrix}^T$ and $\mathbf{v}_2 = \begin{bmatrix} 1 & 3 \end{bmatrix}^T$. Figure 6.2.4 shows a direction field and typical trajectories of the corresponding linear system $\mathbf{x}' = \mathbf{Ax}$. Note that the two eigenvectors point in the directions of the linear trajectories. As is typical of an improper node, all other trajectories are tangent to one of the oblique axes through the origin. In this example the two unequal real eigenvalues are both positive, so the critical point $(0, 0)$ is an improper nodal source.

(b) The matrix

$$\mathbf{B} = -\mathbf{A} = \tfrac{1}{8} \begin{bmatrix} -7 & -3 \\ 3 & -17 \end{bmatrix}$$

has eigenvalues $\lambda_1 = -1$ and $\lambda_2 = -2$ with the same associated eigenvectors $\mathbf{v}_1 = \begin{bmatrix} 3 & 1 \end{bmatrix}^T$ and $\mathbf{v}_2 = \begin{bmatrix} 1 & 3 \end{bmatrix}^T$. The new linear system $\mathbf{x}' = \mathbf{Bx}$ has the same direction field and trajectories as in Fig. 6.2.4 except with the direction field arrows now all reversed, so $(0, 0)$ is now an improper nodal sink.   ◼

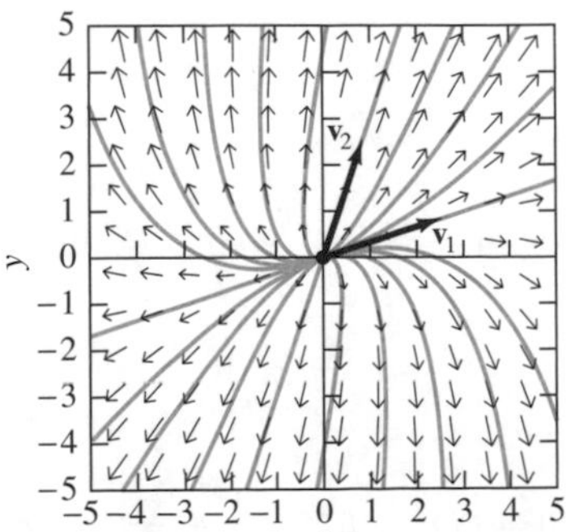

FIGURE 6.2.4. The improper nodal source of Example 2.

UNEQUAL REAL EIGENVALUES WITH OPPOSITE SIGNS: Here the situation is the same as in the previous case, except that $\lambda_2 < 0 < \lambda_1$ in (11). The trajectories with $u_0 = 0$ or $v_0 = 0$ lie on the u- and v-axes through the critical point $(0, 0)$. Those with u_0 and v_0 both nonzero are curves of the explicit form $v = Cu^k$ where $k = \lambda_2/\lambda_1 < 0$. As in the case $k < 0$ of Example 3 in Section 6.1, the nonlinear trajectories resemble hyperbolas, and the critical point $(0, 0)$ is therefore an unstable **saddle point.**

EXAMPLE 3   The matrix

$$\mathbf{A} = \tfrac{1}{4} \begin{bmatrix} 5 & -3 \\ 3 & -5 \end{bmatrix}$$

has eigenvalues $\lambda_1 = 1$ and $\lambda_2 = -1$ with associated eigenvectors $\mathbf{v}_1 = \begin{bmatrix} 3 & 1 \end{bmatrix}^T$ and $\mathbf{v}_2 = \begin{bmatrix} 1 & 3 \end{bmatrix}^T$. Figure 6.2.5 shows a direction field and typical trajectories of the corresponding linear system $\mathbf{x}' = \mathbf{A}\mathbf{x}$. Note that the two eigenvectors again point in the directions of the linear trajectories. Here $k = -1$ and the nonlinear trajectories are hyperbolas in the oblique uv-coordinate system, so we have the saddle point indicated in the figure. Note that the two eigenvectors point in the directions of the asymptotes to these hyperbolas.   ■

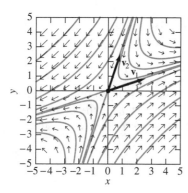

FIGURE 6.2.5. The saddle point of Example 3.

EQUAL REAL ROOTS: In this case, with $\lambda = \lambda_1 = \lambda_2 \neq 0$, the character of the critical point $(0, 0)$ depends on whether or not the coefficient matrix $\mathbf{A}$ has two linearly independent eigenvectors $\mathbf{v}_1$ and $\mathbf{v}_2$. If so, then we have oblique uv-coordinates as in Fig. 6.2.3, and the trajectories are described by

$$u(t) = u_0 e^{\lambda t}, \quad v(t) = v_0 e^{\lambda t} \tag{12}$$

as in (11). But now $k = \lambda_2/\lambda_1 = 1$, so the trajectories with $u_0 \neq 0$ are all of the form $v = Cu$ and hence lie on straight lines through the origin. Therefore $(0, 0)$ is a **proper node** (or **star**) as illustrated in Fig. 6.1.4, and is a source if $\lambda > 0$, a sink if $\lambda < 0$.

If the multiple eigenvalue $\lambda \neq 0$ has only a single associated eigenvector $\mathbf{v}_1$, then (as we saw in Section 5.4) there nevertheless exists a generalized eigenvector $\mathbf{v}_2$ such that $(\mathbf{A} - \lambda\mathbf{I})\mathbf{v}_2 = \mathbf{v}_1$, and the linear system $\mathbf{x}' = \mathbf{A}\mathbf{x}$ has the two linearly independent solutions

$$\mathbf{x}_1(t) = \mathbf{v}_1 e^{\lambda t} \quad \text{and} \quad \mathbf{x}_2(t) = (\mathbf{v}_1 t + \mathbf{v}_2)e^{\lambda t}. \tag{13}$$

We can still use the two vectors $\mathbf{v}_1$ and $\mathbf{v}_2$ to introduce oblique uv-coordinates as in Fig. 6.2.3. Then it follows from (13) that the coordinate functions $u(t)$ and $v(t)$ of the moving point $\mathbf{x}(t)$ on a trajectory are given by

$$u(t) = (u_0 + v_0 t)e^{\lambda t}, \quad v(t) = v_0 e^{\lambda t} \tag{14}$$

where $u_0 = u(0)$ and $v_0 = v(0)$. If $v_0 = 0$ then this trajectory lies on the u-axis. Otherwise we have a nonlinear trajectory with

$$\frac{dv}{du} = \frac{dv/dt}{du/dt} = \frac{\lambda v_0 e^{\lambda t}}{v_0 e^{\lambda t} + \lambda(u_0 + v_0 t)e^{\lambda t}} = \frac{\lambda v_0}{v_0 + \lambda(u_0 + v_0 t)}.$$

We see that $dv/du \to 0$ as $t \to \pm\infty$, so it follows that each trajectory is tangent to the u-axis. Therefore $(0, 0)$ is an **improper node.** If $\lambda < 0$ then we see from (14) that this node is a sink, but it is a source if $\lambda > 0$.

EXAMPLE 4   The matrix

$$\mathbf{A} = \tfrac{1}{8} \begin{bmatrix} -11 & 9 \\ -1 & -5 \end{bmatrix}$$

has the multiple eigenvalue $\lambda = -1$ with the single associated eigenvector $\mathbf{v}_1 = \begin{bmatrix} 3 & 1 \end{bmatrix}^T$. It happens that $\mathbf{v}_2 = \begin{bmatrix} 1 & 3 \end{bmatrix}^T$ is a generalized eigenvector based on

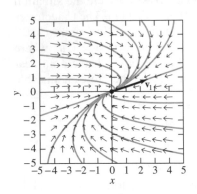

FIGURE 6.2.6. The improper nodal sink of Example 4.

$\mathbf{v}_1$, but only the actual eigenvector shows up in a phase portrait for the linear system $\mathbf{x}' = \mathbf{Ax}$. As indicated in Fig. 6.2.6, the eigenvector $\mathbf{v}_1$ determines the u-axis through the improper nodal sink $(0, 0)$, this axis being tangent to each of the nonlinear trajectories. ■

COMPLEX CONJUGATE EIGENVALUES: Suppose that the matrix $\mathbf{A}$ has eigenvalues $\lambda = p + qi$ and $\overline{\lambda} = p - qi$ (with p and q both nonzero) having associated complex conjugate eigenvectors $\mathbf{v} = \mathbf{a} + \mathbf{b}i$ and $\overline{\mathbf{v}} = \mathbf{a} - \mathbf{b}i$. Then we saw in Section 5.2—see Eq. (22) there—that the linear system $\mathbf{x}' = \mathbf{Ax}$ has the two independent real-valued solutions

$$\mathbf{x}_1(t) = e^{pt}(\mathbf{a}\cos qt - \mathbf{b}\sin qt) \quad \text{and} \quad \mathbf{x}_2(t) = e^{pt}(\mathbf{b}\cos qt + \mathbf{a}\sin qt). \quad (15)$$

Thus the components $x(t)$ and $y(t)$ of any solution $\mathbf{x}(t) = c_1\mathbf{x}_1(t) + c_2\mathbf{x}_2(t)$ oscillate between positive and negative values as t increases, so the critical point $(0, 0)$ is a **spiral point** as in Example 5 of Section 6.1. If the real part p of the eigenvalues is negative, then it is clear from (15) that $\mathbf{x}(t) \to \mathbf{0}$ as $t \to +\infty$, so the origin is a spiral sink. But if p is positive then the critical point is a spiral source.

EXAMPLE 5   The matrix

$$\mathbf{A} = \tfrac{1}{4}\begin{bmatrix} -10 & 15 \\ -15 & 8 \end{bmatrix}$$

has the complex conjugate eigenvalues $\lambda = -\tfrac{1}{4} \pm 3i$ with negative real part, so $(0, 0)$ is a spiral sink. Figure 6.2.7 shows a direction field and a typical spiral trajectory approaching the origin as $t \to +\infty$. ■

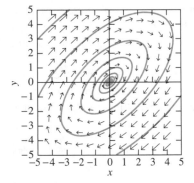

FIGURE 6.2.7. The spiral sink of Example 5.

PURE IMAGINARY EIGENVALUES: If the matrix $\mathbf{A}$ has conjugate imaginary eigenvalues $\lambda = qi$ and $\overline{\lambda} = -qi$ with associated complex conjugate eigenvectors $\mathbf{v} = \mathbf{a} + \mathbf{b}i$ and $\overline{\mathbf{v}} = \mathbf{a} - \mathbf{b}i$, then (15) with $p = 0$ gives the independent solutions

$$\mathbf{x}_1(t) = \mathbf{a}\cos qt - \mathbf{b}\sin qt \quad \text{and} \quad \mathbf{x}_2(t) = \mathbf{b}\cos qt + \mathbf{a}\sin qt \quad (16)$$

of the linear system $\mathbf{x}' = \mathbf{Ax}$. Just as in Example 4 of Section 6.1, it follows that any solution $\mathbf{x}(t) = c_1\mathbf{x}_1(t) + c_2\mathbf{x}_2(t)$ describes an ellipse centered at the origin in the xy-plane. Hence $(0, 0)$ is a **stable center** in this case.

EXAMPLE 6   The matrix

$$\mathbf{A} = \tfrac{1}{4}\begin{bmatrix} -9 & 15 \\ -15 & 9 \end{bmatrix}$$

has the pure imaginary conjugate eigenvalues $\lambda = \pm 3i$, and therefore $(0, 0)$ is a stable center. Figure 6.2.8 shows a direction field and typical elliptical trajectories enclosing the critical point. ■

For the two-dimensional linear system $\mathbf{x}' = \mathbf{Ax}$ with $\det \mathbf{A} \neq 0$, the table in Fig. 6.2.9 lists the type of critical point at $(0, 0)$ found in the five cases discussed here, according to the nature of the eigenvalues λ_1 and λ_2 of the coefficient matrix $\mathbf{A}$. Our discussion of the various cases shows that the stability of the critical point $(0, 0)$ is determined by the *signs* of the real parts of these eigenvalues, as summarized in Theorem 1. Note that if λ_1 and λ_2 are real, then they are themselves their real parts.

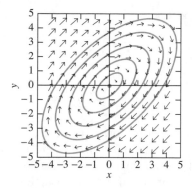

FIGURE 6.2.8. The stable center of Example 6.

Eigenvalues of A	Type of Critical Point
Real, unequal, same sign	Improper node
Real, unequal, opposite sign	Saddle point
Real and equal	Proper or improper node
Complex conjugate	Spiral point
Pure imaginary	Center

FIGURE 6.2.9. Classification of the critical point $(0, 0)$ of the two-dimensional system $\mathbf{x}' = \mathbf{Ax}$.

THEOREM 1: Stability of Linear Systems

Let λ_1 and λ_2 be the eigenvalues of the coefficient matrix $\mathbf{A}$ of the two-dimensional linear system

$$\frac{dx}{dt} = ax + by,$$

$$\frac{dy}{dt} = cx + dy \tag{17}$$

with $ad - bc \neq 0$. Then the critical point $(0, 0)$ is:

1. Asymptotically stable if the real parts of λ_1 and λ_2 are both negative;
2. Stable but not asymptotically stable if the real parts of λ_1 and λ_2 are both zero (so that $\lambda_1, \lambda_2 = \pm qi$);
3. Unstable if either λ_1 or λ_2 has a positive real part. ∎

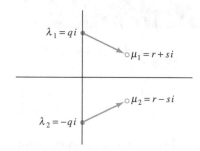

FIGURE 6.2.10. The effects of perturbation of pure imaginary roots.

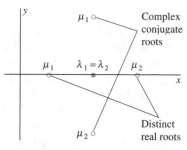

FIGURE 6.2.11. The effects of perturbation of real equal roots.

It is worthwhile to consider the effect of small perturbations in the coefficients a, b, c, and d of the linear system in (17), which result in small perturbations of the eigenvalues λ_1 and λ_2. If these perturbations are sufficiently small, then positive real parts (of λ_1 and λ_2) remain positive and negative real parts remain negative. Hence an asymptotically stable critical point remains asymptotically stable and an unstable critical point remains unstable. Part 2 of Theorem 1 is therefore the only case in which arbitrarily small perturbations can affect the stability of the critical point $(0, 0)$. In this case pure imaginary roots $\lambda_1, \lambda_2 = \pm qi$ of the characteristic equation can be changed to nearby complex roots $\mu_1, \mu_2 = r \pm si$, with r either positive or negative (see Fig. 6.2.10). Consequently, a small perturbation of the coefficients of the linear system in (7) can change a stable center to a spiral point that is either unstable or asymptotically stable.

There is one other exceptional case in which the type, though not the stability, of the critical point $(0, 0)$ can be altered by a small perturbation of its coefficients. This is the case with $\lambda_1 = \lambda_2$, equal roots that (under a small perturbation of the coefficients) can split into two roots μ_1 and μ_2, which are either complex conjugates or unequal real roots (see Fig. 6.2.11). In either case, the sign of the real parts of the roots is preserved, so the stability of the critical point is unaltered. Its nature may change, however; the table in Fig. 6.2.9 shows that a node with $\lambda_1 = \lambda_2$ can either remain a node (if μ_1 and μ_2 are real) or change to a spiral point (if μ_1 and μ_2 are complex conjugates).

Suppose that the linear system in (17) is used to model a physical situation. It is unlikely that the coefficients in (17) can be measured with total accuracy, so let the unknown precise linear model be

$$\frac{dx}{dt} = a^\star x + b^\star y,$$

$$\frac{dy}{dt} = c^\star x + d^\star y. \tag{17*}$$

If the coefficients in (17) are sufficiently close to those in (17*), it then follows from the discussion in the preceding paragraph that the origin $(0, 0)$ is an asymptotically stable critical point for (17) if it is an asymptotically stable critical point for (17*), and is an unstable critical point for (17) if it is an unstable critical point for (17*). Thus in this case the approximate model in (17) and the precise model in (17*) predict the same qualitative behavior (with respect to asymptotic stability versus instability).

Almost Linear Systems

We now return to the almost linear system

$$\frac{dx}{dt} = ax + by + f(x, y),$$

$$\frac{dy}{dt} = cx + dy + g(x, y) \tag{18}$$

having $(0, 0)$ as an isolated critical point with $ad - bc \neq 0$. Theorem 2, which we state without proof, essentially implies that—with regard to the type and stability of the critical point $(0, 0)$—the effect of the small nonlinear terms $f(x, y)$ and $g(x, y)$ is equivalent to the effect of a small perturbation in the coefficients of the associated *linear* system in (17).

THEOREM 2: Stability of Almost Linear Systems

Let λ_1 and λ_2 be the eigenvalues of the coefficient matrix of the linear system in (17) associated with the almost linear system in (18). Then:

1. If $\lambda_1 = \lambda_2$ are equal real eigenvalues, then the critical point $(0, 0)$ of (18) is either a node or a spiral point, and is asymptotically stable if $\lambda_1 = \lambda_2 < 0$, unstable if $\lambda_1 = \lambda_2 > 0$.

2. If λ_1 and λ_2 are pure imaginary, then $(0, 0)$ is either a center or a spiral point, and may be either asymptotically stable, stable, or unstable.

3. Otherwise—that is, unless λ_1 and λ_2 are either real equal or pure imaginary— the critical point $(0, 0)$ of the almost linear system in (18) is of the same type and stability as the critical point $(0, 0)$ of the associated linear system in (17).

Thus, if $\lambda_1 \neq \lambda_2$ and $\text{Re}(\lambda_1) \neq 0$, then the type and stability of the critical point of the almost linear system in (18) can be determined by analysis of its associated linear system in (17), and only in the case of pure imaginary eigenvalues is the stability of $(0, 0)$ not determined by the linear system. Except in the sensitive cases $\lambda_1 = \lambda_2$ and $\text{Re}(\lambda_i) = 0$, the trajectories near $(0, 0)$ will resemble qualitatively those of the associated linear system—they enter or leave the critical point in the same way, but may be "deformed" in a nonlinear manner. The table in Fig. 6.2.12 summarizes the situation.

An important consequence of the classification of cases in Theorem 2 is that a *critical point of an almost linear system is asymptotically stable if it is an asymptotically stable critical point of the linearization of the system.* Moreover, a critical point of the almost linear system is unstable if it is an unstable critical point of the

Eigenvalues λ_1, λ_2 for the Linearized System	Type of Critical Point of the Almost Linear System
$\lambda_1 < \lambda_2 < 0$	Stable improper node
$\lambda_1 = \lambda_2 < 0$	Stable node or spiral point
$\lambda_1 < 0 < \lambda_2$	Unstable saddle point
$\lambda_1 = \lambda_2 > 0$	Unstable node or spiral point
$\lambda_1 > \lambda_2 > 0$	Unstable improper node
$\lambda_1, \lambda_2 = a \pm bi \quad (a < 0)$	Stable spiral point
$\lambda_1, \lambda_2 = a \pm bi \quad (a > 0)$	Unstable spiral point
$\lambda_1, \lambda_2 = \pm bi$	Stable or unstable, center or spiral point

FIGURE 6.2.12. Classification of critical points of an almost linear system.

linearized system. If an almost linear system is used to model a physical situation, then—apart from the sensitive cases mentioned earlier—it follows that the qualitative behavior of the system near a critical point can be determined by examining its linearization.

EXAMPLE 7   Determine the type and stability of the critical point $(0, 0)$ of the almost linear system

$$\frac{dx}{dt} = 4x + 2y + 2x^2 - 3y^2,$$

$$\frac{dy}{dt} = 4x - 3y + 7xy. \tag{19}$$

Solution   The characteristic equation for the associated linear system (obtained simply by deleting the quadratic terms in (19)) is

$$(4 - \lambda)(-3 - \lambda) - 8 = (\lambda - 5)(\lambda + 4) = 0,$$

so the eigenvalues $\lambda_1 = 5$ and $\lambda_2 = -4$ are real, unequal, and have opposite signs. By our discussion of this case we know that $(0, 0)$ is an unstable saddle point of the linear system, and hence by Part 3 of Theorem 2, it is also an unstable saddle point of the almost linear system in (19). The trajectories of the linear system near $(0, 0)$ are shown in Fig. 6.2.13, and those of the nonlinear system in (19) are shown in Fig. 6.2.14. Figure 6.2.15 shows a phase portrait of the nonlinear system in (19) from a "wider view." In addition to the saddle point at $(0, 0)$, there are spiral points near the points $(0.279, 1.065)$ and $(0.933, -1.057)$, and a node near $(-2.354, -0.483)$. ■

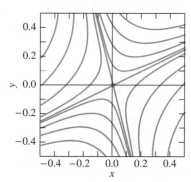

FIGURE 6.2.13. Trajectories of the linearized system of Example 7.

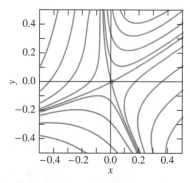

FIGURE 6.2.14. Trajectories of the original almost linear system of Example 7.

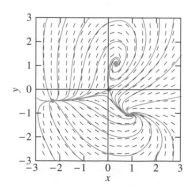

FIGURE 6.2.15. Phase portrait for the almost linear system in Eq. (19).

EXAMPLE 8   Determine the type and stability of the critical point $(4, 3)$ of the almost linear system

$$\frac{dx}{dt} = 33 - 10x - 3y + x^2,$$

$$\frac{dy}{dt} = -18 + 6x + 2y - xy. \tag{20}$$

Solution   The substitutions $u = x - 4$, $v = y - 3$ (that is, $x = u + 4$, $y = v + 3$) in (20) yield the almost linear system

$$\frac{du}{dt} = -2u - 3v + u^2,$$

$$\frac{dv}{dt} = 3u - 2v - uv \tag{21}$$

having $(0, 0)$ as the corresponding critical point. The associated linear system

$$\frac{du}{dt} = -2u - 3v,$$

$$\frac{dv}{dt} = 3u - 2v \tag{22}$$

has characteristic equation $(\lambda + 2)^2 + 9 = 0$, with complex conjugate roots $\lambda = -2 \pm 3i$. Hence $(0, 0)$ is an asymptotically stable spiral point of the linear system in (22), so Theorem 2 implies that $(4, 3)$ is an asymptotically stable spiral point of the original almost linear system in (20). Figure 6.2.16 shows a typical trajectory of the linear system in (22), and Fig. 6.2.17 shows how this spiral point fits into the phase portrait for the original almost linear system in (20). ∎

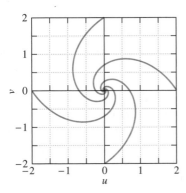

FIGURE 6.2.16.   Spiral trajectories of the linear system in Eq. (22).

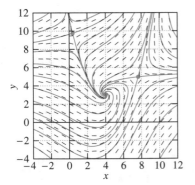

FIGURE 6.2.17.   Phase portrait for the almost linear system in Eq. (20).

6.2 *Problems*

In Problems 1 through 10, determine the type of the critical point $(0, 0)$ and whether it is asymptotically stable, stable, or unstable.

1. $\dfrac{dx}{dt} = -2x + y,$ $\dfrac{dy}{dt} = x - 2y$

2. $\dfrac{dx}{dt} = 4x - y,$ $\dfrac{dy}{dt} = 2x + y$

3. $\dfrac{dx}{dt} = x + 2y,$ $\dfrac{dy}{dt} = 2x + y$

4. $\dfrac{dx}{dt} = 3x + y,$ $\dfrac{dy}{dt} = 5x - y$

5. $\dfrac{dx}{dt} = x - 2y,$ $\dfrac{dy}{dt} = 2x - 3y$

6. $\dfrac{dx}{dt} = 5x - 3y,$ $\dfrac{dy}{dt} = 3x - y$

7. $\dfrac{dx}{dt} = 3x - 2y, \quad \dfrac{dy}{dt} = 4x - y$

8. $\dfrac{dx}{dt} = x - 3y, \quad \dfrac{dy}{dt} = 6x - 5y$

9. $\dfrac{dx}{dt} = 2x - 2y, \quad \dfrac{dy}{dt} = 4x - 2y$

10. $\dfrac{dx}{dt} = x - 2y, \quad \dfrac{dy}{dt} = 5x - y$

Each of the systems in Problems 11 through 18 has a single critical point (x_0, y_0). Classify it as to type and stability. Begin by making substitutions of the form $u = x - x_0$, $v = y - y_0$, as in Example 1.

11. $\dfrac{dx}{dt} = x - 2y, \quad \dfrac{dy}{dt} = 3x - 4y - 2$

12. $\dfrac{dx}{dt} = x - 2y - 8, \quad \dfrac{dy}{dt} = x + 4y + 10$

13. $\dfrac{dx}{dt} = 2x - y - 2, \quad \dfrac{dy}{dt} = 3x - 2y - 2$

14. $\dfrac{dx}{dt} = x + y - 7, \quad \dfrac{dy}{dt} = 3x - y - 5$

15. $\dfrac{dx}{dt} = x - y, \quad \dfrac{dy}{dt} = 5x - 3y - 2$

16. $\dfrac{dx}{dt} = x - 2y + 1, \quad \dfrac{dy}{dt} = x + 3y - 9$

17. $\dfrac{dx}{dt} = x - 5y - 5, \quad \dfrac{dy}{dt} = x - y - 3$

18. $\dfrac{dx}{dt} = 4x - 5y + 3, \quad \dfrac{dy}{dt} = 5x - 4y + 6$

In Problems 19 through 28, investigate the type and stability of the critical point $(0, 0)$ of the given almost linear system.

19. $\dfrac{dx}{dt} = x - 3y + 2xy, \quad \dfrac{dy}{dt} = 4x - 6y - xy$

20. $\dfrac{dx}{dt} = 6x - 5y + x^2, \quad \dfrac{dy}{dt} = 2x - y + y^2$

21. $\dfrac{dx}{dt} = x + 2y + x^2 + y^2, \quad \dfrac{dy}{dt} = 2x - 2y - 3xy$

22. $\dfrac{dx}{dt} = x + 4y - xy^2, \quad \dfrac{dy}{dt} = 2x - y + x^2y$

23. $\dfrac{dx}{dt} = 2x - 5y + x^3, \quad \dfrac{dy}{dt} = 4x - 6y + y^4$

24. $\dfrac{dx}{dt} = 5x - 3y + y(x^2 + y^2), \quad \dfrac{dy}{dt} = 5x + y(x^2 + y^2)$

25. $\dfrac{dx}{dt} = x - 2y + 3xy, \quad \dfrac{dy}{dt} = 2x - 3y - x^2 - y^2$

26. $\dfrac{dx}{dt} = 3x - 2y - x^2 - y^2, \quad \dfrac{dy}{dt} = 2x - y + 3xy$

27. $\dfrac{dx}{dt} = x - y + x^4 - y^2, \quad \dfrac{dy}{dt} = 2x - y + y^4 - x^2$

28. $\dfrac{dx}{dt} = 3x - y + x^3 + y^3, \quad \dfrac{dy}{dt} = 13x - 3y + 3xy$

In Problems 29 through 32, find all critical points of the given system and investigate the type and stability of each.

29. $\dfrac{dx}{dt} = x - y, \quad \dfrac{dy}{dt} = x^2 - y$

30. $\dfrac{dx}{dt} = y - 1, \quad \dfrac{dy}{dt} = x^2 - y$

31. $\dfrac{dx}{dt} = y^2 - 1, \quad \dfrac{dy}{dt} = x^3 - y$

32. $\dfrac{dx}{dt} = xy - 2, \quad \dfrac{dy}{dt} = x - 2y$

Bifurcations

The term *bifurcation* generally refers to something "splitting apart." With regard to differential equations or systems involving a parameter, it refers to abrupt changes in the character of the solutions as the parameter is changed continuously. Problems 33 through 36 illustrate sensitive cases in which small perturbations in the coefficients of a linear or almost linear system can change the type or stability (or both) of a critical point.

33. Consider the linear system

$$\frac{dx}{dt} = \epsilon x - y, \quad \frac{dy}{dt} = x + \epsilon y.$$

Show that the critical point $(0, 0)$ is (a) a stable spiral point if $\epsilon < 0$; (b) a center if $\epsilon = 0$; (c) an unstable spiral point if $\epsilon > 0$. Thus small perturbations of the system $x' = -y, y' = x$ can change both the type and stability of the critical point. Figures 6.2.18(a)–(e) illustrate the loss of stability that occurs at $\epsilon = 0$ as the parameter increases from $\epsilon < 0$ to $\epsilon > 0$.

34. Consider the linear system

$$\frac{dx}{dt} = -x + \epsilon y, \quad \frac{dy}{dt} = x - y.$$

Show that the critical point $(0, 0)$ is (a) a stable spiral point if $\epsilon < 0$; (b) a stable node if $0 \leq \epsilon < 1$. Thus small perturbations of the system $x' = -x, y' = x - y$ can change the type of the critical point $(0, 0)$ without changing its stability.

35. This problem deals with the almost linear system

$$\frac{dx}{dt} = y + hx(x^2 + y^2), \quad \frac{dy}{dt} = -x + hy(x^2 + y^2),$$

in illustration of the sensitive case of Theorem 2, in which the theorem provides no information about the stability of the critical point $(0, 0)$. (a) Show that $(0, 0)$ is a center of the linear system obtained by setting $h = 0$. (b) Suppose that $h \neq 0$. Let $r^2 = x^2 + y^2$, then apply the fact that

$$x\frac{dx}{dt} + y\frac{dy}{dt} = r\frac{dr}{dt}$$

to show that $dr/dt = hr^3$. (c) Suppose that $h = -1$. Integrate the differential equation in (b); then show that $r \to 0$ as $t \to +\infty$. Thus $(0, 0)$ is an asymptotically stable critical point of the almost linear system in this case. (d) Suppose that $h = +1$. Show that $r \to +\infty$ as t increases, so $(0, 0)$ is an unstable critical point in this case.

36. This problem presents the famous *Hopf bifurcation* for the almost linear system

$$\frac{dx}{dt} = \epsilon x + y - x(x^2 + y^2),$$

$$\frac{dy}{dt} = -x + \epsilon y - y(x^2 + y^2),$$

which has imaginary characteristic roots $\lambda = \pm i$ if $\epsilon = 0$. (a) Change to polar coordinates as in Example 6 of Section 6.1 to obtain the system $r' = r(\epsilon - r^2), \theta' = -1$.

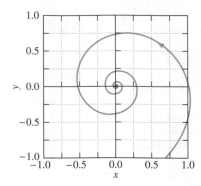

FIGURE 6.2.18(a). Stable spiral with $\epsilon = -0.2$.

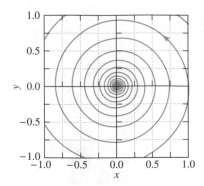

FIGURE 6.2.18(b). Stable spiral with $\epsilon = -0.05$.

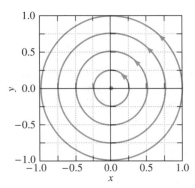

FIGURE 6.2.18(c). Stable center with $\epsilon = 0$.

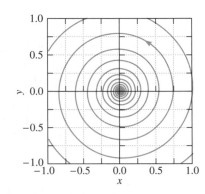

FIGURE 6.2.18(d). Unstable spiral with $\epsilon = 0.05$.

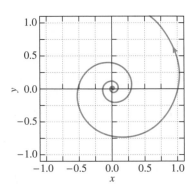

FIGURE 6.2.18(e). Unstable spiral with $\epsilon = 0.2$.

(b) Separate variables and integrate directly to show that if $\epsilon \leqq 0$ then $r(t) \to 0$ as $t \to +\infty$, so in this case the origin is a stable spiral point. (c) Show similarly that if $\epsilon > 0$ then $r(t) \to \sqrt{\epsilon}$ as $t \to +\infty$, so in this case the origin is an unstable spiral point. The circle $r(t) \equiv \sqrt{\epsilon}$ itself is a closed periodic solution or *limit cycle*. Thus a limit cycle of increasing size is spawned as the parameter ϵ increases through the critical value 0.

37. In the case of a two-dimensional system that is *not* almost linear, the trajectories near an isolated critical point can exhibit a considerably more complicated structure than those near the nodes, centers, saddle points, and spiral points discussed in this section. For example, consider the system

$$\frac{dx}{dt} = x(x^3 - 2y^3),$$
$$\frac{dy}{dt} = y(2x^3 - y^3)$$

(23)

having $(0, 0)$ as an isolated critical point. This system is not almost linear because $(0, 0)$ is not an *isolated* critical point of the trivial associated linear system $x' = 0$, $y' = 0$.

Solve the homogeneous first-order equation

$$\frac{dy}{dx} = \frac{y(2x^3 - y^3)}{x(x^3 - 2y^3)}$$

to show that the trajectories of the system in (23) are *folia of Descartes* of the form

$$x^3 + y^3 = 3cxy$$

where c is an arbitrary constant (Fig. 6.2.19).

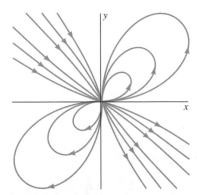

FIGURE 6.2.19. Trajectories of the system in Eq. (23).

6.3 ECOLOGICAL MODELS: PREDATORS AND COMPETITORS

Some of the most interesting and important applications of stability theory involve the interactions between two or more biological populations occupying the same environment. We consider first a **predator-prey** situation involving two species. One species—the **predators**—feeds on the other species—the **prey**—which in turn feeds on some third food item readily available in the environment. A standard example is a population of foxes and rabbits in a woodland; the foxes (predators) eat rabbits (the prey), while the rabbits eat certain vegetation in the woodland. Other examples are sharks (predators) and food fish (prey), bass (predators) and sunfish (prey), ladybugs (predators) and aphids (prey), and beetles (predators) and scale insects (prey).

The classical mathematical model of a predator-prey situation was developed in the 1920s by the Italian mathematician Vito Volterra (1860–1940) in order to analyze the cyclic variations observed in the shark and food fish populations in the Adriatic Sea. To construct such a model, we denote the number of prey at time t by $x(t)$, the number of predators by $y(t)$, and make the following simplifying assumptions.

1. In the absence of predators, the prey population would grow at a natural rate, with $dx/dt = ax, a > 0$.

2. In the absence of prey, the predator population would decline at a natural rate, with $dy/dt = -by, b > 0$.

3. When both predators and prey are present, there occurs, in combination with these natural rates of growth and decline, a decline in the prey population and a growth in the predator population, each at a rate proportional to the frequency of encounters between individuals of the two species. We assume further that the frequency of such encounters is proportional to the product xy, reasoning that doubling either population along should double the frequency of encounters, while doubling both populations ought to quadruple the frequency of encounters. Consequently, the consumption of prey by predators results in:

   - an interaction rate of decline $-pxy$ in the prey population x, and
   - an interaction rate of growth qxy in the predator population y.

When we combine the natural and interaction rates ax and $-pxy$ for the prey population x, as well as the natural and interaction rates $-by$ and qxy for the predator population y, we get the **predator-prey system**

$$\frac{dx}{dt} = ax - pxy = x(a - py),$$

$$\frac{dy}{dt} = -by + qxy = y(-b + qx),$$

(1)

with the constants $a, b, p,$ and q all positive. *Note:* You may see the predator and prey equations written in either order in (1). It is important to recognize that the predator equation has negative linear term and positive interaction term, whereas the prey equation has positive linear term and negative interaction term.

EXAMPLE 1   **The Critical Points**   The predator-prey system in (1) is an almost linear system with the two critical points $(0, 0)$ and $(b/q, a/p)$. Deletion of the xy-terms in (1) leaves the linear system $x' = ax, y' = -by$ with characteristic equation $(\lambda - a)(\lambda + b) = 0$. The corresponding eigenvalues are $\lambda_1 = a > 0$ and $\lambda_2 = -b < 0$. Thus the critical point $(0, 0)$ is a saddle point, both of the linearized system and (by Theorem 2 in Section 6.2) of the predator-prey system itself. But the corresponding equilibrium solution $x(t) \equiv 0, y(0) \equiv 0$ merely describes simultaneous extinction of both species.

The critical point $(b/q, a/p)$ is of greater interest, because $x(t) \equiv b/q$ and $y(t) \equiv a/p$ are the *nonzero* constant prey and predator populations (respectively) that can coexist in equilibrium. To investigate the stability of this equilibrium, we substitute $x = u + (b/q)$, $y = v + (a/p)$ in (1), and thereby obtain (Problem 1) the almost linear system

$$
\frac{du}{dt} = -\frac{bp}{q}v - puv,
$$

$$
\frac{dv}{dt} = \frac{aq}{p}u + quv, \tag{2}
$$

which has the critical point $(0, 0)$ corresponding to the critical point $(b/q, a/p)$ of the original system in (1). In Problem 1 we ask you to show that $(0, 0)$ is a stable center of the linear system obtained from (2) by deleting the uv-terms. Thus we have the indeterminate case of Theorem 2 in Section 6.2, in which case the critical point can (aside from a stable center) also be either a stable spiral sink or an unstable spiral source for the original system. Hence further investigation is required.

Division of the second equation in (1) by the first gives the separable first-order equation

$$
\frac{dy}{dx} = \frac{y(-b + qx)}{x(a - py)}. \tag{3}
$$

In Problem 2 we ask you to separate variables and derive the general solution

$$
a \ln y + b \ln x - qx - py = C, \tag{4}
$$

where C is a constant determined by the initial point (x_0, y_0). It turns out that the phase plane trajectories defined implicitly by Eq. (4) are simple closed curves (as illustrated in Fig. 6.3.1) that enclose the critical point $(b/q, a/p)$—which therefore actually is a stable center for the predator-prey system. It follows from Problem 30 of Section 6.1 that $x(t)$ and $y(t)$ are both periodic functions of t; this explains the periodic fluctuations that are observed empirically in predator-prey populations. ∎

EXAMPLE 2

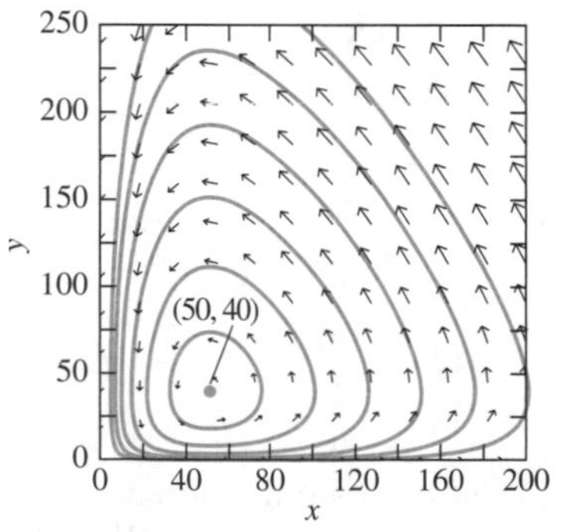

FIGURE 6.3.1. The predator-prey phase portrait of Example 2.

Oscillating Populations Figure 6.3.1 shows a computer-generated direction field and phase portrait for the predator-prey system

$$
\frac{dx}{dt} = (0.2)x - (0.005)xy = (0.005)x(40 - y),
$$

$$
\frac{dy}{dt} = -(0.5)y + (0.01)xy = (0.01)y(-50 + x), \tag{5}
$$

where $x(t)$ denotes the number of rabbits and $y(t)$ the number of foxes after t months. Evidently the critical point $(50, 40)$ is a stable center representing equilibrium populations of 50 rabbits and 40 foxes. Any other initial point lies on a closed trajectory enclosing this equilibrium point. The direction field indicates that the point $(x(t), y(t))$ traverses its trajectory in a counterclockwise direction, with the rabbit and fox populations oscillating periodically between their separate maximum and minimum values. A drawback is that the phase plane plot provides no indication as to the speed with which each trajectory is traversed.

This lost "sense of time" is recaptured by graphing the two individual population functions as functions of time t. In Fig. 6.3.2 we have graphed approximate solution functions $x(t)$ and $y(t)$ calculated using the Runge-Kutta method of Section 4.3 with initial values $x(0) = 70$ and $y(0) = 40$. We see that the rabbit population oscillates between the extreme values $x_{max} \approx 72$ and $x_{min} \approx 33$, while the fox population oscillates (out of phase) between the extreme values $y_{max} \approx 70$ and $y_{min} \approx 20$. A careful measurement indicates that the period P of oscillation of each population is slightly over 20 months. One could "zoom in" on the maximum/minimum points on each graph in order to refine these estimates of the period and the maximum and minimum rabbit and fox populations.

Any positive initial conditions $x_0 = x(0)$ and $y_0 = y(0)$ yield a similar picture, with the rabbit and fox populations both surviving in coexistence with each other. ■

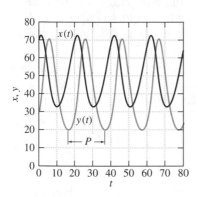

FIGURE 6.3.2. Periodic oscillations of the predator and prey populations in Example 2.

Competing Species

Now we consider two species (of animals, plants, or bacteria, for instance) with populations $x(t)$ and $y(t)$ at time t and which compete with each other for the food available in their common environment. This is in marked contrast to the case in which one species preys on the other. To construct a mathematical model that is as realistic as possible, let us assume that in the absence of either species, the other would have a bounded [logistic] population like those considered in Section 2.1. In the absence of any interaction or competition between the two species, their populations $x(t)$ and $y(t)$ would then satisfy the differential equations

$$\frac{dx}{dt} = a_1 x - b_1 x^2,$$

$$\frac{dy}{dt} = a_2 y - b_2 y^2, \tag{6}$$

each of the form of Eq. (2) of Section 2.1. But in addition, we assume that competition has the effect of a rate of decline in each population that is proportional to their product xy. We insert such terms with *negative* proportionality constants $-c_1$ and $-c_2$ in the equations in (6) to obtain the **competition system**

$$\frac{dx}{dt} = a_1 x - b_1 x^2 - c_1 xy = x(a_1 - b_1 x - c_1 y),$$

$$\frac{dy}{dt} = a_2 y - b_2 y^2 - c_2 xy = y(a_2 - b_2 y - c_2 x), \tag{7}$$

where the coefficients a_1, a_2, b_1, b_2, c_1, and c_2 are all positive.

The almost linear system in (7) has four critical points. Upon setting the right-hand sides of the two equations equal to zero, we see that if $x = 0$, then either $y = 0$ or $y = a_2/b_2$, whereas if $y = 0$, then either $x = 0$ or $x = a_1/b_1$. This gives the three critical points $(0, 0)$, $(0, a_2/b_2)$, and $(a_1/b_1, 0)$. The fourth critical point is obtained from the simultaneous solution of the equations

$$b_1 x + c_1 y = a_1, \quad b_2 x + c_2 y = a_2. \tag{8}$$

We assume that, as in most interesting applications, these equations have a single solution and that the corresponding critical point lies in the first quadrant of the xy-plane. This point (x_E, y_E) is then the fourth critical point of the system in (7), and it represents the possibility of coexistence of the two species, with constant nonzero equilibrium populations $x(t) \equiv x_E$ and $y(t) \equiv y_E$.

We are interested in the stability of the critical point (x_E, y_E). This turns out to depend on whether

$$c_1 c_2 < b_1 b_2 \quad \text{or} \quad c_1 c_2 > b_1 b_2. \tag{9}$$

Each inequality in (9) has a natural interpretation. Examining the equations in (6), we see that the coefficients b_1 and b_2 represent the inhibiting effect of each population on its own growth (possibly due to limitations of food or space). On the other hand, c_1 and c_2 represent the effect of competition between the two populations. Thus $b_1 b_2$ is a measure of *inhibition* while $c_1 c_2$ is a measure of *competition*. A general analysis of the system in (7) shows the following:

1. If $c_1c_2 < b_1b_2$, so that competition is small in comparison with inhibition, then (x_E, y_E) is an asymptotically stable critical point that is approached by each solution as $t \to +\infty$. Thus the two species can and do coexist in this case.

2. If $c_1c_2 > b_1b_2$, so that competition is large in comparison with inhibition, then (x_E, y_E) is an unstable critical point, and either $x(t)$ or $y(t)$ approaches zero as $t \to +\infty$. Thus the two species cannot coexist in this case; one survives and the other becomes extinct.

Rather than carrying out this general analysis, we present two examples that illustrate these two possibilities.

EXAMPLE 3 **Survival of a Single Species** Suppose that the populations $x(t)$ and $y(t)$ satisfy the equations

$$\frac{dx}{dt} = 14x - \tfrac{1}{2}x^2 - xy,$$

$$\frac{dy}{dt} = 16y - \tfrac{1}{2}y^2 - xy,$$

(10)

in which $a_1 = 14$, $a_2 = 16$, $b_1 = b_2 = \tfrac{1}{2}$, and $c_1 = c_2 = 1$. Then $c_1c_2 = 1 > \tfrac{1}{4} = b_1b_2$, so we should expect survival of a single species as predicted in Case 2 above. We find readily that the four critical points are $(0, 0)$, $(0, 32)$, $(28, 0)$, and $(12, 8)$. We shall investigate them individually.

THE CRITICAL POINT $(0, 0)$: We linearize the system in (10) simply by dropping the quadratic terms. The coefficient matrix of the resulting linear system

$$\begin{bmatrix} x' \\ y' \end{bmatrix} = \begin{bmatrix} 14 & 0 \\ 0 & 16 \end{bmatrix} \begin{bmatrix} x \\ y \end{bmatrix}$$

(11)

has eigenvalues

$$\lambda_1 = 14 \quad \text{with eigenvector} \quad \mathbf{v}_1 = \begin{bmatrix} 1 & 0 \end{bmatrix}^T$$

and

$$\lambda_2 = 16 \quad \text{with eigenvector} \quad \mathbf{v}_2 = \begin{bmatrix} 0 & 1 \end{bmatrix}^T.$$

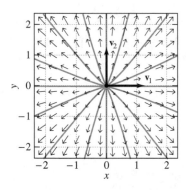

FIGURE 6.3.3. Phase plane portrait for the linear system in Eq. (11) corresponding to the critical point $(0, 0)$.

Both eigenvalues are positive, so it follows that $(0, 0)$ is a nodal source for the linearized system, and hence—by Theorem 2 in Section 6.2—is also an unstable nodal source for the original system in (10). Figure 6.3.3 shows a phase portrait for the linearized system near $(0, 0)$.

THE CRITICAL POINT $(0, 32)$: Substitution of $x = u$, $y = v + 32$ in (10) yields the almost linear system

$$\frac{du}{dt} = -18u - \tfrac{1}{2}u^2 - uv,$$

$$\frac{dv}{dt} = -32u - 16v - \tfrac{1}{2}v^2 - uv,$$

(12)

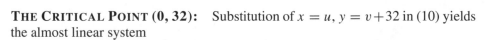

with critical point $(0, 0)$. The coefficient matrix of the corresponding linear system

$$\begin{bmatrix} u' \\ v' \end{bmatrix} = \begin{bmatrix} -18 & 0 \\ -32 & -16 \end{bmatrix} \begin{bmatrix} u \\ v \end{bmatrix}$$

(13)

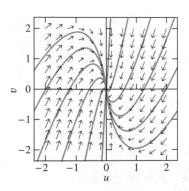

FIGURE 6.3.4. Phase plane portrait for the linear system in Eq. (13) corresponding to the critical point $(0, 32)$.

has eigenvalues $\lambda_1 = -18$ with eigenvector $\mathbf{v}_1 = \begin{bmatrix} 1 & 16 \end{bmatrix}^T$ and $\lambda_2 = -32$ with eigenvector $\mathbf{v}_2 = \begin{bmatrix} 0 & 1 \end{bmatrix}^T$. Because both eigenvalues are negative, it follows that $(0, 0)$ is a nodal sink for the linearized system, and hence—by Theorem 2 in Section 6.2—that $(0, 32)$ is also a stable nodal sink for the original system in (10). Figure 6.3.4 shows a phase portrait for the linearized system near $(0, 0)$.

THE CRITICAL POINT (28, 0):   Substitution of $x = u + 28$ and $y = v$ in (10) yields the almost linear system

$$\frac{du}{dt} = -14u - 28v - \tfrac{1}{2}u^2 - uv,$$

$$\frac{dv}{dt} = -12v - \tfrac{1}{2}v^2 - uv,$$

(14)

with critical point $(0, 0)$. The corresponding linear system

$$\begin{bmatrix} u' \\ v' \end{bmatrix} = \begin{bmatrix} -14 & -28 \\ 0 & -12 \end{bmatrix} \begin{bmatrix} u \\ v \end{bmatrix}$$

(15)

has eigenvalues $\lambda_1 = -14$ with eigenvector $\mathbf{v}_1 = \begin{bmatrix} 1 & 0 \end{bmatrix}^T$ and $\lambda_2 = -12$ with eigenvector $\mathbf{v}_2 = \begin{bmatrix} -14 & 1 \end{bmatrix}^T$. Because both eigenvalues are negative, it follows that $(0, 0)$ is a nodal sink for the linearized system, and hence—by Theorem 2 in Section 6.2—that $(28, 0)$ is also a stable nodal sink for the original nonlinear system in (10). Figure 6.3.5 shows a phase portrait for the linearized system near $(0, 0)$.

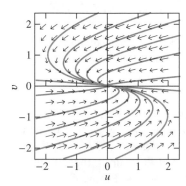

FIGURE 6.3.5. Phase plane portrait for the linear system in Eq. (15) corresponding to the critical point $(28, 0)$.

THE CRITICAL POINT (12, 8):   Substitution of $x = u + 12$ and $y = v + 8$ in (10) yields the almost linear system

$$\frac{du}{dt} = -6u - 12v - \tfrac{1}{2}u^2 - uv,$$

$$\frac{dv}{dt} = -8u - 4v - \tfrac{1}{2}v^2 - uv,$$

(16)

with critical point $(0, 0)$. The coefficient matrix of the corresponding linear system

$$\begin{bmatrix} u' \\ v' \end{bmatrix} = \begin{bmatrix} -6 & -12 \\ -8 & -4 \end{bmatrix} \begin{bmatrix} u \\ v \end{bmatrix}$$

(17)

has eigenvalues

$$\lambda_1 = -5 - \sqrt{97} < 0 \quad \text{with eigenvector} \quad \mathbf{v}_1 = \begin{bmatrix} \tfrac{1}{8}\left(1 + \sqrt{97}\right) & 1 \end{bmatrix}^T$$

and

$$\lambda_2 = -5 + \sqrt{97} > 0 \quad \text{with eigenvector} \quad \mathbf{v}_2 = \begin{bmatrix} \tfrac{1}{8}\left(1 - \sqrt{97}\right) & 1 \end{bmatrix}^T.$$

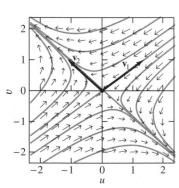

FIGURE 6.3.6. Phase plane portrait for the linear system in Eq. (17) corresponding to the critical point $(12, 8)$.

Because the two eigenvalues have opposite signs, it follows that $(0, 0)$ is a saddle point for the linearized system and hence—by Theorem 2 in Section 6.2—that $(12, 8)$ is also an unstable saddle point for the original system in (10). Figure 6.3.6 shows a phase portrait for the linearized system near $(0, 0)$.

Now that our local analysis of each of the four critical points is complete, it remains to assemble the information found into a coherent global picture. If we accept the facts that:

- Near each critical point, the trajectories for the original system in (10) resemble qualitatively the linearized trajectories shown in Figs. 6.3.3–6.3.6, and

- As $t \to +\infty$ each trajectory either approaches a critical point or diverges toward infinity,

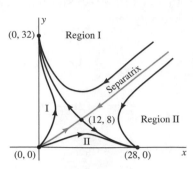

FIGURE 6.3.7. Rough sketch consistent with the analysis in Example 3.

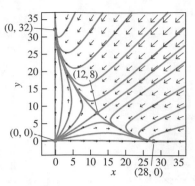

FIGURE 6.3.8. Phase plane portrait for the system in Example 3.

then it would appear that the phase plane portrait for the original system must resemble the rough sketch shown in Fig. 6.3.7. This sketch shows a few typical freehand trajectories connecting a nodal source at $(0, 0)$, nodal sinks at $(0, 32)$ and $(28, 0)$, and a saddle point at $(12, 8)$, with indicated directions of flow along these trajectories consistent with the known character of these critical points. Figure 6.3.8 shows a more precise computer-generated phase portrait and direction field for the nonlinear system in (10).

The two trajectories that approach the saddle point $(12, 8)$, together with that saddle point, form a **separatrix** that separates regions I and II in Figure 6.3.8. It plays a crucial role in determining the long-term behavior of the two populations. If the initial point (x_0, y_0) lies precisely on the separatrix, then $(x(t), y(t))$ approaches $(12, 8)$ as $t \to +\infty$. Of course, random events make it extremely unlikely that $(x(t), y(t))$ will remain on the separatrix. If not, peaceful coexistence of the two species is impossible. If (x_0, y_0) lies in Region I above the separatrix, then $(x(t), y(t))$ approaches $(0, 32)$ as $t \to +\infty$, so the population $x(t)$ decreases to zero. Alternatively, if (x_0, y_0) lies in Region II below the separatrix, then $(x(t), y(t))$ approaches $(28, 0)$ as $t \to +\infty$, so the population $y(t)$ dies out. In short, whichever population has the initial competitive advantage survives, while the other faces extinction. ∎

EXAMPLE 4 **Peaceful Coexistence of Two Species** Suppose that the populations $x(t)$ and $y(t)$ satisfy the competition system

$$\frac{dx}{dt} = 14x - 2x^2 - xy,$$

$$\frac{dy}{dt} = 16y - 2y^2 - xy,$$

(18)

for which $a_1 = 14$, $a_2 = 16$, $b_1 = b_2 = 2$, and $c_1 = c_2 = 1$. Then $c_1 c_2 = 1 < 4 = b_1 b_2$, so now the effect of inhibition is greater than that of competition. We find readily that the four critical points are $(0, 0)$, $(0, 8)$, $(7, 0)$, and $(4, 6)$. We proceed as in Example 3.

THE CRITICAL POINT (0,0): When we drop the quadratic terms in (18), we get the same linear system that we obtained earlier in (11). Thus its coefficient matrix has the two positive eigenvalues $\lambda_1 = 14$ and $\lambda_2 = 16$, and its phase portrait is the same as that shown in Fig. 6.3.3. Therefore $(0, 0)$ is an unstable nodal source for the original system in (18).

THE CRITICAL POINT (0,8): Substitution of $x = u$ and $y = v + 8$ in (18) yields the almost linear system

$$\frac{du}{dt} = 6u - 2u^2 - uv,$$

$$\frac{dv}{dt} = -8u - 16v - 2v^2 - uv \tag{19}$$

with critical point $(0, 0)$. The coefficient matrix of the corresponding linear system

$$\begin{bmatrix} u' \\ v' \end{bmatrix} = \begin{bmatrix} 6 & 0 \\ -8 & -16 \end{bmatrix} \begin{bmatrix} u \\ v \end{bmatrix} \tag{20}$$

has the positive eigenvalue $\lambda_1 = 6$ with eigenvector $\mathbf{v}_1 = \begin{bmatrix} 11 & -4 \end{bmatrix}^T$ and the negative eigenvalue $\lambda_2 = -16$ with eigenvector $\mathbf{v}_2 = \begin{bmatrix} 0 & 1 \end{bmatrix}^T$. It follows that $(0, 0)$ is a saddle point for the linearized system, and hence that $(0, 8)$ is an unstable saddle point for the original system in (18). Figure 6.3.9 shows a phase portrait for the linearized system near $(0, 0)$.

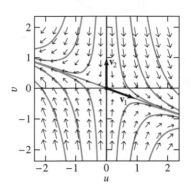

FIGURE 6.3.9. Phase plane portrait for the linear system in Eq. (20) corresponding to the critical point $(0, 8)$.

THE CRITICAL POINT (7, 0): Substitution of $x = u + 7$ and $y = v$ in (18) yields the almost linear system

$$\frac{du}{dt} = -14u - 7v - 2u^2 - uv,$$

$$\frac{dv}{dt} = 9v - 2v^2 - uv \tag{21}$$

with critical point $(0, 0)$. The coefficient matrix of the corresponding linear system

$$\begin{bmatrix} u' \\ v' \end{bmatrix} = \begin{bmatrix} -14 & -7 \\ 0 & 9 \end{bmatrix} \begin{bmatrix} u \\ v \end{bmatrix} \tag{22}$$

has the negative eigenvalue $\lambda_1 = -14$ with eigenvector $\mathbf{v}_1 = \begin{bmatrix} 1 & 0 \end{bmatrix}^T$ and the positive eigenvalue $\lambda_2 = 9$ with eigenvector $\mathbf{v}_2 = \begin{bmatrix} -7 & 23 \end{bmatrix}^T$. It follows that $(0, 0)$ is a saddle point for the linearized system, and hence that $(7, 0)$ is an unstable saddle point for the original system in (18). Figure 6.3.10 shows a phase portrait for the linearized system near $(0, 0)$.

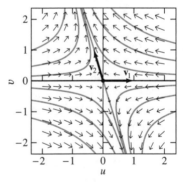

FIGURE 6.3.10. Phase plane portrait for the linear system in Eq. (22) corresponding to the critical point $(7, 0)$.

THE CRITICAL POINT (4,6): Substitution of $x = u + 4$ and $y = v + 6$ in (18) yields the almost linear system

$$\frac{du}{dt} = -8u - 4v - 2u^2 - uv,$$

$$\frac{dv}{dt} = -6u - 12v - 2v^2 - uv \tag{23}$$

with critical point $(0, 0)$. The coefficient matrix of the corresponding linear system

$$\begin{bmatrix} u' \\ v' \end{bmatrix} = \begin{bmatrix} -8 & -4 \\ -6 & -12 \end{bmatrix} \begin{bmatrix} u \\ v \end{bmatrix} \tag{24}$$

has the two negative eigenvalues

$$\lambda_1 = 2(-5 - \sqrt{7}) \quad \text{with eigenvector} \quad \mathbf{v}_1 = \begin{bmatrix} \frac{1}{3}(-1 + \sqrt{7}) & 1 \end{bmatrix}^T$$

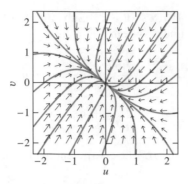

FIGURE 6.3.11. Phase plane portrait for the linear system in Eq. (24) corresponding to the critical point $(4, 6)$.

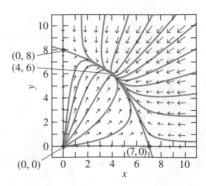

FIGURE 6.3.12. Direction field and phase portrait for the competition system
$$x' = 14x - 2x^2 - xy,$$
$$y' = 16y - 2y^2 - xy \text{ of Example 4.}$$

and

$$\lambda_2 = 2(-5 + \sqrt{7}) \quad \text{with eigenvector} \quad \mathbf{v}_2 = \left[\tfrac{1}{3}(-1 - \sqrt{7}) \quad 1 \right]^T.$$

It follows that $(0, 0)$ is a nodal sink for the linearized system, and hence that $(4, 6)$ is a stable nodal sink for the original system in (18). Figure 6.3.11 shows a phase portrait for the linearized system near $(0, 0)$.

Figure 6.3.12 assembles all this local information into a global phase plane portrait for the original system in (18). The notable feature of this system is that—for *any* positive initial population values x_0 and y_0—the point $(x(t), y(t))$ approaches the single critical point $(4, 6)$ as $t \to +\infty$. It follows that the two species both survive in stable (peaceful) existence. ■

Examples 3 and 4 illustrate the power of elementary critical point analysis. But remember that ecological systems in nature are seldom so simple as in these examples. Frequently they involve more than two species, and the growth rates of these populations and the interactions among them often are more complicated than those discussed in this section. Consequently, the mathematical modeling of ecological systems remains an active area of current research.

6.3 _Problems_

Problems 1 and 2 deal with the predator-prey system

$$\frac{dx}{dt} = ax - pxy, \quad \frac{dy}{dt} = -by + qxy. \tag{1}$$

1. Substitute $x = u + (b/q)$ and $y = v + (a/p)$ in (1) to linearize the predator-prey system near the critical point $(b/q, a/p)$. Show that the origin is a stable center of the resulting linear system.

2. Separate variables in (1) to derive the general solution

$$a \ln y + b \ln x - qx - py = C.$$

If an implicit function plotter is available, choose fixed positive values of a, b, p, and q, then plot contour curves through selected initial points near the critical point $(b/q, a/p)$.

3. Let $x(t)$ be a harmful insect population (aphids?) that under natural conditions is held somewhat in check by a benign predator insect population $y(t)$ (ladybugs?). Assume that $x(t)$ and $y(t)$ satisfy the predator-prey equations in (1), so that the stable equilibrium populations are $x_E = b/q$ and $y_E = a/p$. Now suppose that an insecticide is employed that kills (per unit time) the same fraction $f < a$ of each species of insect. Show that the harmful population x_E is increased, while the benign population y_E is decreased, so the use of the insecticide is counterproductive. This is an instance in which mathematical analysis reveals undesirable consequences of a well-intentioned interference with nature.

Problems 4 through 7 deal with the competition system

$$\frac{dx}{dt} = 60x - 4x^2 - 3xy,$$
$$\frac{dy}{dt} = 42y - 2y^2 - 3xy, \tag{2}$$

in which $c_1c_2 = 9 > 8 = b_1b_2$, so the effect of competition should exceed that of inhibition. Problems 4 through 7 imply that the four critical points $(0, 0)$, $(0, 21)$, $(15, 0)$, and $(6, 12)$ of the system in (2) resemble those shown in Fig. 6.3.8—a nodal source at the origin, a nodal sink on each coordinate axis, and a saddle point interior to the first quadrant.

4. Show that the coefficient matrix of the linearization $x' = 60x$, $y' = 42y$ of (2) at $(0, 0)$ has positive eigenvalues $\lambda_1 = 60$ and $\lambda_2 = 42$. Hence $(0, 0)$ is a nodal source for (2).

5. Show that the linearization of (2) at $(0, 21)$ is $u' = -3u$, $v' = -63u - 42v$. Then show that the coefficient matrix of this linear system has negative eigenvalues $\lambda_1 = -3$ and $\lambda_2 = -42$. Hence $(0, 21)$ is a nodal sink for the system in (2).

6. Show that the linearization of (2) at $(15, 0)$ is $u' = -60u - 45v$, $v' = -3v$. Then show that the coefficient matrix of this linear system has negative eigenvalues $\lambda_1 = -60$ and $\lambda_2 = -3$. Hence $(15, 0)$ is a nodal sink for the system in (2).

7. Show that the linearization of (2) at $(6, 12)$ is $u' = -24u - 18v$, $v' = -36u - 24v$. Then show that the coefficient matrix of this linear system has eigenvalues $\lambda_1 = -24 - 18\sqrt{2} < 0$ and $\lambda_2 = -24 + 18\sqrt{2} > 0$. Hence $(6, 12)$ is a saddle point for the system in (2).

Problems 8 through 10 deal with the competition system

$$\frac{dx}{dt} = 60x - 3x^2 - 4xy,$$
$$\frac{dy}{dt} = 42y - 3y^2 - 2xy, \tag{3}$$

in which $c_1c_2 = 8 < 9 = b_1b_2$, so the effect of inhibition should exceed that of competition. The linearization of the system in (3) at $(0, 0)$ is the same as that of (2). This observation and Problems 8 through 10 imply that the four critical points $(0, 0)$, $(0, 14)$, $(20, 0)$, and $(12, 6)$ of (3) resemble those shown in Fig. 6.3.12—a nodal source at the origin, a saddle point on each coordinate axis, and a nodal sink interior to the first quadrant.

8. Show that the linearization of (3) at $(0, 14)$ is $u' = 4u$, $v' = -28u - 42v$. Then show that the coefficient matrix of this linear system has the positive eigenvalue $\lambda_1 = 4$ and the negative eigenvalue $\lambda_2 = -42$. Hence $(0, 14)$ is a saddle point for the system in (3).

9. Show that the linearization of (3) at $(20, 0)$ is $u' = -60u - 80v$, $v' = 2v$. Then show that the coefficient matrix of this linear system has the negative eigenvalue $\lambda_1 = -60$ and the positive eigenvalue $\lambda_2 = 2$. Hence $(20, 0)$ is a saddle point for the system in (3).

10. Show that the linearization of (3) at $(12, 6)$ is $u' = -36u - 48v$, $v' = -12u - 18v$. Then show that the coefficient matrix of this linear system has eigenvalues $\lambda_1 = -27 + 3\sqrt{73}$ and $\lambda_2 = -27 - 3\sqrt{73}$, both of which are negative. Hence $(12, 6)$ is a nodal sink for the system in (3).

Problems 11 through 13 deal with the predator-prey system

$$\frac{dx}{dt} = 5x - x^2 - xy,$$
$$\frac{dy}{dt} = -2y + xy, \tag{4}$$

in which the prey population $x(t)$ is logistic but the predator population $y(t)$ would (in the absence of any prey) decline naturally. Problems 11 through 13 imply that the three critical points $(0, 0)$, $(5, 0)$, and $(2, 3)$ of the system in (4) are as shown in Fig. 6.3.13—with saddle points at the origin and on the positive x-axis, and with a spiral sink interior to the first quadrant.

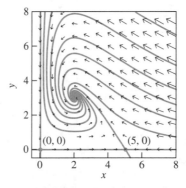

FIGURE 6.3.13. Direction field and phase portrait for the predator-prey system of Problems 11 through 13.

11. Show that the coefficient matrix of the linearization $x' = 5x$, $y' = -2y$ of (4) at $(0, 0)$ has the positive eigenvalue $\lambda_1 = 5$ and the negative eigenvalue $\lambda_2 = -2$. Hence $(0, 0)$ is a saddle point of the system in (4).

12. Show that the linearization of (4) at $(5, 0)$ is $u' = -5u - 5v$, $v' = 3v$. Then show that the coefficient matrix of this linear system has the negative eigenvalue $\lambda_1 = -5$ and the positive eigenvalue $\lambda_2 = 3$. Hence $(5, 0)$ is a saddle point for the system in (4).

13. Show that the linearization of (4) at $(2, 3)$ is $u' = -2u - 2v$, $v' = 3u$. Then show that the coefficient matrix of this linear system has the complex conjugate eigenvalues λ_1, $\lambda_2 = -1 \pm i\sqrt{5}$ with negative real part. Hence $(2, 3)$ is a spiral sink for the system in (4).

Problems 14 through 17 deal with the predator-prey system

$$\frac{dx}{dt} = x^2 - 2x - xy,$$
$$\frac{dy}{dt} = y^2 - 4y + xy. \tag{5}$$

Here each population—the prey population $x(t)$ and the predator population $y(t)$—is an unsophisticated population (like the alligators of Section 2.1) for which the only alternatives (in the absence of the other population) are doomsday and extinction. Problems 14 through 17 imply that the four critical points $(0, 0)$, $(0, 4)$, $(2, 0)$, and $(3, 1)$ of the system in (5) are as shown in Fig. 6.3.14—a nodal sink at the origin, a saddle point on each coordinate axis, and a spiral source interior to the first quadrant. This is a two-dimensional version of "doomsday versus extinction." If the initial point (x_0, y_0) lies in Region I, then both populations increase without bound (until dooms-day), whereas if it lies in Region II then both populations de-crease to zero (and thus both become extinct).

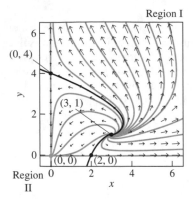

FIGURE 6.3.14. Direction field and phase portrait for the predator-prey system of Problems 14 through 17.

14. Show that the coefficient matrix of the linearization $x' = -2x$, $y' = -4y$ of the system in (5) at $(0, 0)$ has the neg-ative eigenvalues $\lambda_1 = -2$ and $\lambda_2 = -4$. Hence $(0, 0)$ is a nodal sink for (5).

15. Show that the linearization of (5) at $(0, 4)$ is $u' = -6u$, $v' = 4u + 4v$. Then show that the coefficient matrix of this linear system has the negative eigenvalue $\lambda_1 = -6$ and the positive eigenvalue $\lambda_2 = 4$. Hence $(0, 4)$ is a sad-dle point for the system in (5).

16. Show that the linearization of (5) at $(2, 0)$ is $u' = 2u - 2v$, $v' = -2v$. Then show that the coefficient matrix of this linear system has the positive eigenvalue $\lambda_1 = 2$ and the negative eigenvalue $\lambda_2 = -2$. Hence $(2, 0)$ is a saddle point for the system in (5).

17. Show that the linearization of (5) at $(3, 1)$ is $u' = 3u - 3v$, $v' = u + v$. Then show that the coefficient matrix of this linear system has complex conjugate eigenvalues λ_1, $\lambda_2 = 2 \pm i\sqrt{2}$ with positive real part. Hence $(3, 1)$ is a spiral source for (5).

Problems 18 through 25 deal with the predator-prey sys-tem

$$\frac{dx}{dt} = 2x - xy + \epsilon x(5 - x),$$

$$\frac{dy}{dt} = -5y + xy, \tag{6}$$

for which a bifurcation occurs at the value $\epsilon = 0$ of the param-eter ϵ. Problems 18 and 19 deal with the case $\epsilon = 0$, in which case the system in (6) takes the form

$$\frac{dx}{dt} = 2x - xy, \quad \frac{dy}{dt} = -5x + xy, \tag{7}$$

and these problems suggest that the two critical points $(0, 0)$ and $(5, 2)$ of the system in (7) are as shown in Fig. 6.3.15—a saddle point at the origin and a center at $(5, 2)$.

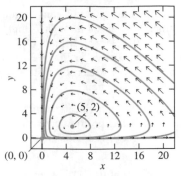

FIGURE 6.3.15. The case $\epsilon = 0$ (Problems 18 and 19).

18. Show that the coefficient matrix of the linearization $x' = 2x$, $y' = -5y$ of (7) at $(0, 0)$ has the positive eigenvalue $\lambda_1 = 2$ and the negative eigenvalue $\lambda_2 = -5$. Hence $(0, 0)$ is a saddle point for the system in (7).

19. Show that the linearization of the system in (7) at $(5, 2)$ is $u' = -5v$, $v' = 2u$. Then show that the coefficient matrix of this linear system has conjugate imaginary eigenvalues λ_1, $\lambda_2 = \pm i\sqrt{10}$. Hence $(0, 0)$ is a stable center for the linear system. Although this is the indeterminate case of Theorem 2 in Section 6.2, Fig. 6.3.15 suggests that $(5, 2)$ also is a stable center for (7).

Problems 20 through 22 deal with the case $\epsilon = -1$, for which the system in (6) becomes

$$\frac{dx}{dt} = -3x + x^2 - xy, \quad \frac{dy}{dt} = -5y + xy, \tag{8}$$

and imply that the three critical points $(0, 0)$, $(3, 0)$, and $(5, 2)$ of (8) are as shown in Fig. 6.3.16—with a nodal sink at the ori-gin, a saddle point on the positive x-axis, and a spiral source at $(5, 2)$.

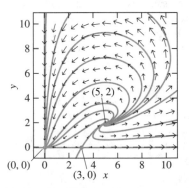

FIGURE 6.3.16. The case $\epsilon = -1$ (Problems 20 through 22).

20. Show that the coefficient matrix of the linearization $x' = -3x$, $y' = -5y$ of the system in (8) at $(0, 0)$ has the neg-ative eigenvalues $\lambda_1 = -3$ and $\lambda_2 = -5$. Hence $(0, 0)$ is a nodal sink for (8).

21. Show that the linearization of the system in (8) at $(3, 0)$ is $u' = 3u - 3v$, $v' = -2v$. Then show that the coefficient matrix of this linear system has the positive eigenvalue $\lambda_1 = 3$ and the negative eigenvalue $\lambda_2 = -2$. Hence $(3, 0)$ is a saddle point for (8).

22. Show that the linearization of (8) at (5, 2) is $u' = 5u - 5v$, $v' = 2u$. Then show that the coefficient matrix of this linear system has complex conjugate eigenvalues $\lambda_1, \lambda_2 = \frac{1}{2}\left(5 \pm i\sqrt{15}\right)$ with positive real part. Hence (5, 2) is a spiral source for the system in (8).

Problems 23 through 25 deal with the case $\epsilon = 1$, so that the system in (6) takes the form

$$\frac{dx}{dt} = 7x - x^2 - xy, \qquad \frac{dy}{dt} = -5y + xy, \qquad (9)$$

and these problems imply that the three critical points (0, 0), (7, 0), and (5, 2) of the system in (9) are as shown in Fig. 6.3.17—with saddle points at the origin and on the positive x-axis and with a spiral sink at (5, 2).

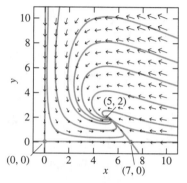

FIGURE 6.3.17. The case $\epsilon = +1$ (Problems 23 through 25).

23. Show that the coefficient matrix of the linearization $x' = 7x$, $y' = -5y$ of (9) at (0, 0) has the positive eigenvalue $\lambda_1 = 7$ and the negative eigenvalue $\lambda_2 = -5$. Hence (0, 0) is a saddle point for the system in (9).

24. Show that the linearization of (9) at (7, 0) is $u' = -7u - 7v$, $v' = 2v$. Then show that the coefficient matrix of this linear system has the negative eigenvalue $\lambda_1 = -7$ and the positive eigenvalue $\lambda_2 = 2$. Hence (7, 0) is a saddle point for the system in (9).

25. Show that the linearization of (9) at (5, 2) is $u' = -5u - 5v$, $v' = 2u$. Then show that the coefficient matrix of this linear system has the complex conjugate eigenvalues λ_1, $\lambda_2 = \frac{1}{2}\left(-5 \pm i\sqrt{15}\right)$ with negative real part. Hence (5, 2) is a spiral sink for the system in (9).

6.4 NONLINEAR MECHANICAL SYSTEMS

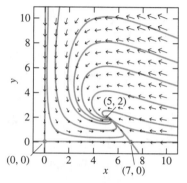

FIGURE 6.4.1. The mass on a spring.

Now we apply the qualitative methods of Sections 6.1 and 6.2 to the analysis of simple mechanical systems like the mass-on-a-spring system shown in Fig. 6.4.1. Let m denote the mass in a suitable system of units and let $x(t)$ denote the displacement of the mass at time t from its equilibrium position (in which the spring is unstretched). Previously we have always assumed that the force $F(x)$ exerted by the spring on the mass is a *linear* function of x: $F(x) = -kx$ (Hooke's law). In reality, however, every spring in nature actually is nonlinear (even if only slightly so). Moreover, springs in some automobile suspension systems deliberately are designed to be nonlinear. Here, then, we are interested specifically in the effects of nonlinearity.

So now we allow the force function $F(x)$ to be nonlinear. Because $F(0) = 0$ at the equilibrium position $x = 0$, we may assume that F has a power series expansion of the form

$$\blacktriangleright \qquad F(x) = -kx + \alpha x^2 + \beta x^3 + \cdots. \qquad (1)$$

We take $k > 0$ so that the reaction of the spring is directed opposite to the displacement when x is sufficiently small. If we assume also that the reaction of the spring is symmetric with respect to positive and negative displacements by the same distance, then $F(-x) = -F(x)$, so F is an *odd* function. In this case it follows that the coefficient of x^n in Eq. (1) is zero if n is even, so the first nonlinear term is the one involving x^3.

For a simple mathematical model of a nonlinear spring we therefore take

$$\blacktriangleright \qquad F(x) = -kx + \beta x^3, \qquad (2)$$

ignoring all terms in Eq. (1) of degree greater than 3. The equation of motion of the mass m is then

$$\blacktriangleright \qquad mx'' = -kx + \beta x^3. \qquad (3)$$

The Position-Velocity Phase Plane

If we introduce the *velocity*

$$y(t) = x'(t) \tag{4}$$

of the mass with *position* $x(t)$, then we get from Eq. (3) the equivalent first-order system

$$\frac{dx}{dt} = y,$$

$$m\frac{dy}{dt} = -kx + \beta x^3. \tag{5}$$

A phase plane trajectory of this system is a position-velocity plot that illustrates the motion of the mass on the spring. We can solve explicitly for the trajectories of this system by writing

$$\frac{dy}{dx} = \frac{dy/dt}{dx/dt} = \frac{-kx + \beta x^3}{my},$$

whence

$$my\,dy + (kx - \beta x^3)\,dx = 0.$$

Integration then yields

$$\tfrac{1}{2}my^2 + \tfrac{1}{2}kx^2 - \tfrac{1}{4}\beta x^4 = E \tag{6}$$

for the equation of a typical trajectory. We write E for the arbitrary constant of integration because $KE = \tfrac{1}{2}my^2$ is the kinetic energy of the mass with velocity y, and it is natural to define

$$PE = \tfrac{1}{2}kx^2 - \tfrac{1}{4}\beta x^4 \tag{7}$$

as the potential energy of the spring. Then Eq. (6) takes the form $KE + PE = E$, and thus expresses conservation of energy for the *undamped* motion of a mass on a spring.

The behavior of the mass depends on the sign of the nonlinear term in Eq. (2). The spring is called

- *hard* if $\beta < 0$,
- *soft* if $\beta > 0$.

We consider the two cases separately.

HARD SPRING OSCILLATIONS: If $\beta < 0$ then the second equation in (5) takes the form $my' = -x\left(|\beta|x^2 + k\right)$, so it follows that the only critical point of the system is the origin $(0, 0)$. Each trajectory

$$\tfrac{1}{2}my^2 + \tfrac{1}{2}kx^2 + \tfrac{1}{4}|\beta|x^4 = E > 0 \tag{8}$$

is an oval closed curve like those shown in Fig. 6.4.2, and thus $(0, 0)$ is a stable center. As the point $(x(t), y(t))$ traverses a trajectory in the clockwise direction, the position $x(t)$ and velocity $y(t)$ of the mass oscillate alternately as illustrated in Fig. 6.4.3. The mass is moving to the right (with x increasing) when $y > 0$, to the left when $y < 0$. Thus the behavior of a mass on a nonlinear hard spring resembles qualitatively that of a mass on a linear spring with $\beta = 0$ (as in Example 4 of Section 6.1). But one difference between the linear and nonlinear situations is that, whereas the period $T = 2\pi\sqrt{m/k}$ of oscillation of a mass on a linear spring is independent of the initial conditions, the period of a mass on a nonlinear spring depends on its initial position $x(0)$ and initial velocity $y(0)$ (Problems 17 through 22).

SOFT SPRING OSCILLATIONS: If $\beta > 0$ then the second equation in (5) takes the form $my' = x\left(\beta x^2 - k\right)$, so it follows that the system has the two critical points $\left(\pm\sqrt{k/\beta}, 0\right)$ in addition to the critical point $(0, 0)$. These three critical points yield the only solutions for which the mass can remain at rest. The following example illustrates the greater range of possible behaviors of a mass on a soft spring.

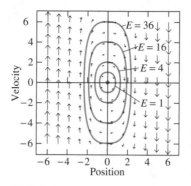

FIGURE 6.4.2. Position-velocity phase plane portrait for the hard mass-and-spring system with $m = k = 2$ and $\beta = -4 < 0$.

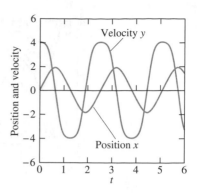

FIGURE 6.4.3. Position and velocity solution curves for the hard mass-and-spring system with $m = k = 2$ and $\beta = -4 < 0$.

EXAMPLE 1   If $m = 1$, $k = 4$, and $\beta = 1$, then the equation of motion of the mass is

$$\frac{d^2x}{dt^2} + 4x - x^3 = 0, \tag{9}$$

and Eq. (6) gives the trajectories in the form

$$\tfrac{1}{2}y^2 + 2x^2 - \tfrac{1}{4}x^4 = E. \tag{10}$$

After solving for

$$y = \pm\sqrt{2E - 4x^2 + \tfrac{1}{2}x^2}, \tag{10'}$$

we could select a fixed value of the constant energy E and plot manually a trajectory like one of those shown in the computer-generated position-velocity phase plane portrait in Fig. 6.4.4.

The different types of phase plane trajectories correspond to different values of the energy E. If we substitute $x = \pm\sqrt{k/\beta}$ and $y = 0$ into (6), we get the energy value $E = k^2/(4\beta) = 4$ (because $k = 4$ and $\beta = 1$) that corresponds to the trajectories that intersect the x-axis at the nontrivial critical points $(-2, 0)$ and $(2, 0)$. These emphasized trajectories are called **separatrices** because they separate phase plane regions of different behavior.

The nature of the motion of the mass is determined by which type of trajectory its initial conditions determine. The simple closed trajectories encircling $(0, 0)$ in the region bounded by the separatrices correspond to energies in the range $0 < E < 4$. These closed trajectories represent *periodic* oscillations of the mass back and forth around the equilibrium point $x = 0$.

The unbounded trajectories lying in the regions above and below the separatrices correspond to values of E greater than 4. These represent motions in which the mass approaches $x = 0$ with sufficient energy that it continues on through the equilibrium point, never to return again (as indicated in Fig. 6.4.5).

The unbounded trajectories opening to the right and left correspond to negative values of E. These represent motions in which the mass initially is headed toward the equilibrium point $x = 0$, but with insufficient energy to reach it. At some point the mass reverses direction and heads back whence it came.

In Fig. 6.4.4 it appears that the critical point $(0, 0)$ is a stable center, whereas the other two critical points are unstable saddle points. With the indicated parameter values, the nonlinear system in (5) is

$$\frac{dx}{dt} = y, \qquad \frac{dy}{dt} = -4x + x^3. \tag{11}$$

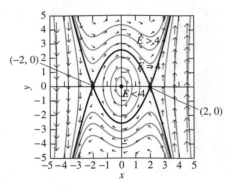

FIGURE 6.4.4. Position-velocity phase plane portrait for the soft mass-and-spring system with $m = 1$, $k = 4$, and $\beta = 1 > 0$. The separatrices are emphasized.

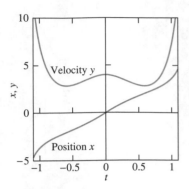

FIGURE 6.4.5. Position and velocity solution curves for the soft mass-and-spring system with $m = 1$, $k = 4$, $\beta = 1 > 0$, and energy $E = 8$—sufficiently great that the mass approaches the origin from the left and continues on indefinitely to the right.

Its linearization $x' = y$, $y' = -4x$ at $(0, 0)$ has the coefficient matrix

$$\mathbf{A} = \begin{bmatrix} 0 & 1 \\ -4 & 0 \end{bmatrix}$$

with characteristic equation $\lambda^2 + 4 = 0$ and conjugate imaginary eigenvalues $\lambda = \pm 2i$—consistent with a stable center at $(0, 0)$.

At $(2, 0)$ the substitutions $x = u + 2$, $y = v$ in (11) yield the almost linear system

$$\frac{du}{dt} = v, \quad \frac{dv}{dt} = 8u + 6u^2 + u^3.$$

Its linearization $u' = v$, $v' = 8u$ has the coefficient matrix

$$\mathbf{A} = \begin{bmatrix} 0 & 1 \\ 8 & 0 \end{bmatrix}$$

with characteristic equation $\lambda^2 - 8 = 0$ and real eigenvalues $\lambda = \pm\sqrt{8}$ of opposite sign—corresponding to a saddle point at the critical point $(2, 0)$ in the xy-plane. The situation at the third critical point $(-2, 0)$ is essentially the same.   ∎

Damped Nonlinear Vibrations

Suppose now that the mass on a spring is connected also to a dashpot that provides a force of resistance proportional to the velocity $y = dx/dt$ of the mass. If the spring is still assumed nonlinear as in Eq. (2), then the equation of motion of the mass is

➤ $$mx'' = -cx' - kx + \beta x^3, \tag{12}$$

where $c > 0$ is the resistance constant. If $\beta > 0$, then the equivalent first-order system

$$\frac{dx}{dt} = y, \quad m\frac{dy}{dt} = -kx - cy + \beta x^3 \tag{13}$$

has critical points $(0, 0)$ and $\left(\pm\sqrt{k/\beta}, 0\right)$, but now the critical point at the origin is the most interesting one. The linearization $x' = y$, $y' = (-kx - cy)/m$ at $(0, 0)$ has coefficient matrix

$$\mathbf{A} = \begin{bmatrix} 0 & 1 \\ -k/m & -c/m \end{bmatrix}$$

with characteristic equation $m\lambda^2 + c\lambda + k = 0$ and eigenvalues

$$\lambda = \frac{-c \pm \sqrt{c^2 - 4km}}{2m}.$$

It follows that the critical point $(0, 0)$ of the system in (13) is

- a nodal sink if the resistance is so great that $c^2 \geq 4km$ (so the eigenvalues are both negative), but is
- a spiral sink if $c^2 < 4km$ (so the eigenvalues are complex conjugates with negative real parts).

The following example illustrates the latter case.

EXAMPLE 2 Suppose that $m = 1$, $k = 5$, $\beta = \frac{5}{4}$, and $c = 2$. Then the nonlinear system in (13) is

$$\frac{dx}{dt} = y, \quad \frac{dy}{dt} = -5x - 2y + \frac{5}{4}x^3. \tag{14}$$

In this example no explicit solution for the phase plane trajectories is available, so we proceed to investigate the critical points $(0, 0)$, $(2, 0)$, and $(-2, 0)$.

At $(0, 0)$ the coefficient matrix of the linearized system

$$\frac{dx}{dt} = y, \quad \frac{dy}{dt} = -5x - 2y$$

has characteristic equation $\lambda^2 + 2\lambda + 5 = 0$ with roots $\lambda = -1 \pm 2i$. Hence $(0, 0)$ is a stable spiral sink of the system in (14), and the linearized position function of the mass is of the form

$$x(t) = e^{-t}(A \cos 2t + B \sin 2t),$$

an exponentially damped oscillation around $x = 0$.

At $(2, 0)$ the substitutions $u = x - 2$, $v = y$ in (14) yield the system

$$\frac{du}{dt} = v, \quad \frac{dv}{dt} = 10u - 2v + \frac{15}{2}u^2 + \frac{5}{4}u^3$$

with corresponding critical point $(0, 0)$. The coefficient matrix of the linearized system

$$\frac{du}{dy} = v, \quad \frac{dv}{dt} = 10u - 2v$$

has characteristic equation $\lambda^2 + 2\lambda - 10 = 0$ with roots $\lambda_1 = -1 - \sqrt{11} < 0$ and $\lambda_2 = -1 + \sqrt{11} > 0$. It follows that $(2, 0)$ is an unstable saddle point of the original system in (14). A similar analysis shows that $(-2, 0)$ is also an unstable saddle point.

The position-velocity phase plane portrait in Fig. 6.4.6 shows trajectories of (14) and the spiral sink at $(0, 0)$, as well as the unstable saddle points at $(-2, 0)$ and $(2, 0)$. The emphasized separatrices divide the phase plane into regions of different behavior. The behavior of the mass depends on the region in which its initial point (x_0, y_0) is located. If this initial point lies in:

- Region I between the separatrices, then the trajectory spirals into the origin as $t \to +\infty$, and hence the periodic oscillations of the undamped case (Fig. 6.4.4) are now replaced with damped oscillations around the stable equilibrium position $x = 0$;
- Region II, then the mass passes through $x = 0$ moving from left to right (x increasing);

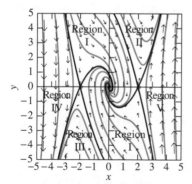

FIGURE 6.4.6. Position-velocity phase plane portrait for the soft mass-and-spring system with $m = 1$, $k = 5$, $\beta = \frac{5}{4}$, and resistance constant $c = 2$. The separatrices are emphasized.

- Region III, then the mass passes through $x = 0$ moving from right to left (x decreasing);
- Region IV, then the mass approaches (but does not reach) the unstable equilibrium position $x = -2$ from the left, but stops and then returns to the left;
- Region V, then the mass approaches (but does not reach) the unstable equilibrium position $x = 2$ from the right, but stops and then returns to the right.

If the initial point (x_0, y_0) lies precisely on one of the separatrices, then the corresponding trajectory either approaches the stable spiral point or recedes to infinity from a saddle point as $t \to +\infty$. ∎

The Nonlinear Pendulum

In Section 3.4 we derived the equation

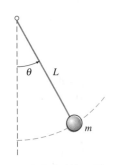

FIGURE 6.4.7. The simple pendulum.

$$\frac{d^2\theta}{dt^2} + \frac{g}{L}\sin\theta = 0 \tag{15}$$

for the undamped oscillations of the simple pendulum shown in Fig. 6.4.7. There we used the approximation $\sin\theta \approx \theta$ for θ near zero to replace Eq. (15) with the linear model

$$\frac{d^2\theta}{dt^2} + \omega^2\theta = 0 \tag{16}$$

where $\omega^2 = g/L$. The general solution

$$\theta(t) = A\cos\omega t + B\sin\omega t \tag{17}$$

of Eq. (16) describes oscillations around the equilibrium position $\theta = 0$ with circular frequency ω and amplitude $C = (A^2 + B^2)^{1/2}$.

The linear model does not adequately describe the possible motions of the pendulum for large values of θ. For instance, the equilibrium solution $\theta(t) \equiv \pi$ of Eq. (15), with the pendulum standing straight up, does not satisfy the linear equation in (16). Nor does Eq. (17) include the situation in which the pendulum "goes over the top" repeatedly, so that $\theta(t)$ is a steadily increasing rather than an oscillatory function of t. To investigate these phenomena we must analyze the nonlinear equation $\theta'' + \omega^2\sin\theta = 0$ rather than merely its linearization $\theta'' + \omega^2\theta = 0$. We also want to include the possibility of resistance proportional to velocity, so we consider the general *nonlinear pendulum equation*

$$\frac{d^2\theta}{dt^2} + c\frac{d\theta}{dt} + \omega^2\sin\theta = 0. \tag{18}$$

We examine first the undamped case, in which $c = 0$. With $x(t) = \theta(t)$ and $y(t) = \theta'(t)$ the equivalent first-order system is

$$\frac{dx}{dt} = y, \quad \frac{dy}{dt} = -\omega^2\sin x. \tag{19}$$

We see that this system is almost linear by writing it in the form

$$\frac{dx}{dt} = y,$$

$$\frac{dy}{dt} = -\omega^2 x + g(x), \tag{20}$$

where

$$g(x) = -\omega^2(\sin x - x) = \omega^2\left(\frac{x^3}{3!} - \frac{x^5}{5!} + \cdots\right)$$

has only higher-degree terms.

The critical points of the system in (19) are the points $(n\pi, 0)$ with n an integer. The nature of the critical point $(n\pi, 0)$ depends on whether n is even or odd.

EVEN CASE: If $n = 2m$ is even then $\sin(u + 2m\pi) = \sin u$, so the substitutions $x = u + 2m\pi$, $y = v$ in (19) yield the almost linear system

$$\frac{du}{dt} = v, \quad \frac{dv}{dt} = -\omega^2 \sin u \tag{21}$$

having $(0, 0)$ as the corresponding critical point. Just as in (20), the linearization of (21) is the system

$$\frac{du}{dt} = v, \quad \frac{dv}{dt} = -\omega^2 u$$

for which $(0, 0)$ is the familiar stable center enclosed by elliptical trajectories (as in Example 4 of Section 6.1). Although this is the delicate case in which Theorem 2 of Section 6.2 does not settle the matter, we will see presently that $(2m\pi, 0)$ is also a stable center for the original nonlinear pendulum system in (19).

ODD CASE: If $n = 2m + 1$ is odd, then $\sin(u + (2m + 1)\pi) = -\sin u$, so the substitutions $x = u + (2m + 1)\pi$, $y = v$ in (19) yield the system

$$\frac{du}{dt} = v, \quad \frac{dv}{dt} = +\omega^2 \sin u \tag{22}$$

having $(0, 0)$ as the corresponding critical point. The linearization

$$\frac{du}{dt} = v, \quad \frac{dv}{dt} = +\omega^2 u \tag{23}$$

of (22) has the coefficient matrix

$$\mathbf{A} = \begin{bmatrix} 0 & 1 \\ \omega^2 & 0 \end{bmatrix}$$

with characteristic equation $\lambda^2 - \omega^2 = 0$ and real eigenvalues $\lambda = \pm\omega$ of opposite sign. Thus $(0, 0)$ is an unstable saddle point of the linear system in (23), so it follows from Theorem 2 of Section 6.2 that $((2m + 1)\pi, 0)$ is a similar saddle point for the original almost linear system in (19).

THE TRAJECTORIES: We can see how these "even centers" and "odd saddle points" fit together by solving the system in (19) explicitly for the phase plane trajectories. If we write

$$\frac{dy}{dx} = \frac{dy/dt}{dx/dt} = -\frac{\omega^2 \sin x}{y}$$

and separate the variables,

$$y \, dy + \omega^2 \sin x \, dx = 0,$$

then integration from $x = 0$ to $x = x$ yields

$$\tfrac{1}{2}y^2 + \omega^2(1 - \cos x) = E. \tag{24}$$

We write E for the arbitrary constant of integration because, if physical units are so chosen that $m = L = 1$, then the first term on the left is the kinetic energy and the second term the potential energy of the mass on the end of the pendulum. Then E is the total mechanical energy; Eq. (24) thus expresses conservation of mechanical energy for the undamped pendulum.

If we solve Eq. (24) for y and use a half-angle identity, we get the equation

$$y = \pm\sqrt{2E - 4\omega^2 \sin^2 \tfrac{1}{2}x} \tag{25}$$

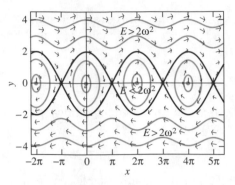

FIGURE 6.4.8. Position-velocity phase plane portrait for the undamped pendulum system $x' = y$, $y' = -\sin x$. The separatrices are emphasized.

that defines the phase plane trajectories. Note that the radicand in (25) remains positive if $E > 2\omega^2$. Figure 6.4.8 shows (along with a direction field) the results of plotting these trajectories for various values of the energy E.

The emphasized separatrices in Fig. 6.4.8 correspond to the critical value $E = 2\omega^2$ of the energy; they enter and leave the unstable critical points $(n\pi, 0)$ with n an odd integer. Following the arrows along a separatrix, the pendulum theoretically approaches a balanced vertical position $\theta = x = (2m+1)\pi$ with just enough energy to reach it but not enough to "go over the top." The instability of this equilibrium position indicates that this behavior may never be observed in practice!

The simple closed trajectories encircling the stable critical points—all of which correspond to the downward position $\theta = 2m\pi$ of the pendulum—represent periodic oscillations of the pendulum back and forth around the stable equilibrium position $\theta = 0$. These correspond to energies $E < 2\omega^2$ that are insufficient for the pendulum to ascend to the vertical upward position.

The unbounded trajectories with $E > 2\omega^2$ represent whirling motions of the pendulum in which it goes over the top repeatedly—in a clockwise direction if $y(t)$ remains positive, in a counterclockwise direction if $y(t)$ is negative.

Undamped Period of Oscillation

If the pendulum is released from rest with initial conditions

$$x(0) = \theta(0) = \alpha, \quad y(0) = \theta'(0) = 0, \tag{26}$$

then Eq. (24) with $t = 0$ reduces to

$$\omega^2(1 - \cos\alpha) = E. \tag{27}$$

Hence $E < 2\omega^2$ if $0 < \alpha < \pi$, so a periodic oscillation of the pendulum ensues. To determine the *period* of this oscillation, we subtract Eq. (27) from Eq. (24) and write the result (with $x = \theta$ and $y = d\theta/dt$) in the form

$$\tfrac{1}{2}\left(\frac{d\theta}{dt}\right)^2 = \omega^2(\cos\theta - \cos\alpha). \tag{28}$$

The period T of time required for one complete oscillation is four times the amount of time required for θ to decrease from $\theta = \alpha$ to $\theta = 0$, one-fourth of an oscillation. Hence we solve Eq. (28) for $dt/d\theta$ and integrate to get

$$T = \frac{4}{\omega\sqrt{2}} \int_0^\alpha \frac{d\theta}{\sqrt{\cos\theta - \cos\alpha}}. \tag{29}$$

To attempt to evaluate this integral we first use the identity $\cos\theta = 1 - 2\sin^2(\theta/2)$ and get

$$T = \frac{2}{\omega}\int_0^\alpha \frac{d\theta}{\sqrt{k^2 - \sin^2(\theta/2)}},$$

where

$$k = \sin\frac{\alpha}{2}.$$

Next, the substitution $u = (1/k)\sin(\theta/2)$ yields

$$T = \frac{4}{\omega}\int_0^1 \frac{du}{\sqrt{(1 - u^2)(1 - k^2 u^2)}}.$$

Finally, the substitution $u = \sin\phi$ gives

$$T = \frac{4}{\omega}\int_0^{\pi/2} \frac{d\phi}{\sqrt{1 - k^2\sin^2\phi}}. \tag{30}$$

The integral in (30) is the *elliptic integral of the first kind* that is often denoted by $F(k, \pi/2)$. It can be evaluated numerically as follows. First we use the binomial series

$$\frac{1}{\sqrt{1-x}} = 1 + \sum_{n=1}^\infty \frac{1 \cdot 3 \cdots (2n-1)}{2 \cdot 4 \cdots (2n)}x^n \tag{31}$$

with $x = k^2\sin^2\phi < 1$ to expand the integrand in (30). Then we integrate termwise using the tabulated integral formula

$$\int_0^{\pi/2}\sin^{2n}\phi\, d\phi = \frac{\pi}{2}\cdot\frac{1 \cdot 3 \cdots (2n-1)}{2 \cdot 4 \cdots (2n)}. \tag{32}$$

The final result is the formula

$$T = \frac{2\pi}{\omega}\left[1 + \sum_{n=1}^\infty\left(\frac{1 \cdot 3 \cdots (2n-1)}{2 \cdot 4 \cdots (2n)}\right)^2 k^{2n}\right]$$

$$= T_0\left[1 + \left(\frac{1}{2}\right)^2 k^2 + \left(\frac{1 \cdot 3}{2 \cdot 4}\right)^2 k^4 + \left(\frac{1 \cdot 3 \cdot 5}{2 \cdot 4 \cdot 6}\right)^2 k^6 + \cdots\right] \tag{33}$$

for the period T of the nonlinear pendulum released from rest with initial angle $\theta(0) = \alpha$, in terms of the linearized period $T_0 = 2\pi/\omega$ and $k = \sin(\alpha/2)$.

The infinite series within the second pair of brackets in Eq. (33) gives the factor T/T_0 by which the nonlinear period T is longer than the linearized period. The table in Fig. 6.4.9, obtained by summing this series numerically, shows how T/T_0 increases as α is increased. Thus T is 0.19% greater than T_0 if $\alpha = 10°$, whereas T is 18.03% greater than T_0 if $\alpha = 90°$. But even a 0.19% discrepancy is significant—the calculation

$$(0.0019) \times 3600\frac{\text{seconds}}{\text{hour}} \times 24\frac{\text{hours}}{\text{day}} \times 7\frac{\text{days}}{\text{week}} \approx 1149 \text{ (seconds/week)}$$

shows that the linearized model is quite inadequate for a pendulum clock; a discrepancy of 19 min 9 s after only one week is unacceptable.

α	T/T_0
10°	1.0019
20°	1.0077
30°	1.0174
40°	1.0313
50°	1.0498
60°	1.0732
70°	1.1021
80°	1.1375
90°	1.1803

FIGURE 6.4.9. Dependence of the period T of a nonlinear pendulum on its initial angle α.

Damped Pendulum Oscillations

Finally, we discuss briefly the *damped* nonlinear pendulum. The almost linear first-order system equivalent to Eq. (19) is

$$\frac{dx}{dt} = y,$$

$$\frac{dy}{dt} = -\omega^2 \sin x - cy,$$

(34)

and again the critical points are of the form $(n\pi, 0)$ where n is an integer. In Problems 9 through 11 we ask you to verify that

- If n is odd, then $(n\pi, 0)$ is an unstable saddle point of (34), just as in the undamped case; but
- If n is even and $c^2 > 4\omega^2$, then $(n\pi, 0)$ is a nodal sink; whereas
- If n is even and $c^2 < 4\omega^2$, then $(n\pi, 0)$ is a spiral sink.

Figure 6.4.10 shows the phase plane trajectories for the more interesting underdamped case, $c^2 < 4\omega^2$. Other than the physically unattainable separatrix trajectories that enter unstable saddle points, every trajectory eventually is "trapped" by one of the stable spiral points $(n\pi, 0)$ with n an even integer. What this means is that even if the pendulum starts with enough energy to go over the top, after a certain (finite) number of revolutions it has lost enough energy that thereafter it undergoes damped oscillations around its stable (lower) equilibrium position.

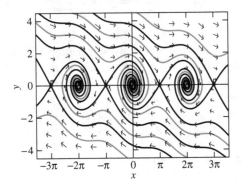

FIGURE 6.4.10. Position-velocity phase plane portrait for the damped pendulum system $x' = y$, $y' = -\sin x - (0.25)y$. The separatrices are emphasized.

6.4 Problems

In Problems 1 through 4, show that the given system is almost linear with $(0, 0)$ as a critical point, and classify this critical point as to type and stability.

1. $\dfrac{dx}{dt} = 1 - e^x + 2y, \quad \dfrac{dy}{dt} = -x - 4\sin y$

2. $\dfrac{dx}{dt} = 2\sin x + \sin y, \quad \dfrac{dy}{dt} = \sin x + 2\sin y$ (Fig. 6.4.11)

3. $\dfrac{dx}{dt} = e^x + 2y - 1, \quad \dfrac{dy}{dt} = 8x + e^y - 1$

4. $\dfrac{dx}{dt} = \sin x \cos y - 2y, \quad \dfrac{dy}{dt} = 4x - 3\cos x \sin y$

Find and classify each of the critical points of the almost linear systems in Problems 5 through 8.

5. $\dfrac{dx}{dt} = -x + \sin y, \quad \dfrac{dy}{dt} = 2x$

6. $\dfrac{dx}{dt} = y, \quad \dfrac{dy}{dt} = \sin \pi x - y$

7. $\dfrac{dx}{dt} = 1 + e^{x-y}, \quad \dfrac{dy}{dt} = 2\sin x$

8. $\dfrac{dx}{dt} = 3\sin x + y, \quad \dfrac{dy}{dt} = \sin x + 2y$

Problems 9 through 11 deal with the damped pendulum system $x' = y$, $y' = -\omega^2 \sin x - cy$.

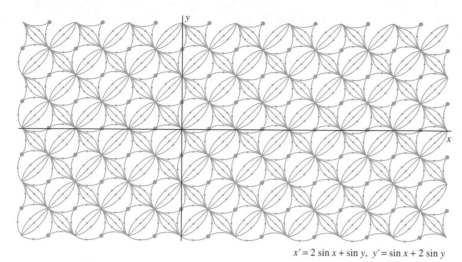

$x' = 2 \sin x + \sin y, \quad y' = \sin x + 2 \sin y$

FIGURE 6.4.11. Trajectories of the system in Problem 2.

9. Show that if n is an odd integer, then the critical point $(n\pi, 0)$ is a saddle point for the damped pendulum system.

10. Show that if n is an even integer and $c^2 > 4\omega^2$, then the critical point $(n\pi, 0)$ is a nodal sink for the damped pendulum system.

11. Show that if n is an even integer and $c^2 < 4\omega^2$, then the critical point $(n\pi, 0)$ is a spiral sink for the damped pendulum system.

In each of Problems 12 through 16, a second-order equation of the form $x'' + f(x, x') = 0$, corresponding to a certain mass-and-spring system, is given. Find and classify the critical points of the equivalent first-order system.

12. $x'' + 20x - 5x^3 = 0$: Verify that the critical points resemble those shown in Fig. 6.4.4.

13. $x'' + 2x' + 20x - 5x^3 = 0$: Verify that the critical points

resemble those shown in Fig. 6.4.6.

14. $x'' - 8x + 2x^3 = 0$: Here the linear part of the force is repulsive rather than attractive (as for an ordinary spring). Verify that the critical points resemble those shown in Fig. 6.4.12. Thus there are two stable equilibrium points and three types of periodic oscillations.

15. $x'' + 4x - x^2 = 0$: Here the force function is nonsymmetric. Verify that the critical points resemble those shown in Fig. 6.4.13.

16. $x'' + 4x - 5x^3 + x^5 = 0$: The idea here is that terms through the fifth degree in an odd force function have been retained. Verify that the critical points resemble those shown in Fig. 6.4.14.

Problems 17 through 22 outline an investigation of the period T of oscillation of a mass on a nonlinear spring with

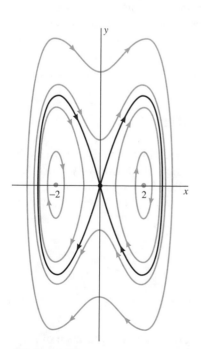

FIGURE 6.4.12. The phase portrait for Problem 14.

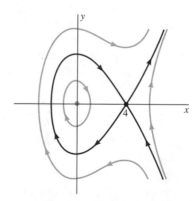

FIGURE 6.4.13. The phase portrait for Problem 15.

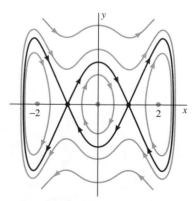

FIGURE 6.4.14. The phase portrait for Problem 16.

equation of motion

$$\frac{d^2x}{dt^2} + \phi(x) = 0. \tag{35}$$

If $\phi(x) = kx$ with $k > 0$, then the spring actually is linear with period $T_0 = 2\pi/\sqrt{k}$.

17. Integrate once (as in Eq. (6)) to derive the energy equation

$$\tfrac{1}{2}y^2 + V(x) = E \tag{36}$$

where $y = dx/dt$ and

$$V(x) = \int_0^x \phi(u)\,du. \tag{37}$$

18. If the mass is released from rest with initial conditions $x(0) = x_0$, $y(0) = 0$ and periodic oscillations ensue, conclude from Eq. (36) that $E = V(x_0)$ and that the time T required for one complete oscillation is

$$T = \frac{4}{\sqrt{2}} \int_0^{x_0} \frac{du}{\sqrt{V(x_0) - V(u)}}. \tag{38}$$

19. If $\phi(x) = kx - \beta x^3$ as in the text, deduce from Eqs. (37) and (38) that

$$T = 4\sqrt{2} \int_0^{x_0} \frac{dx}{\sqrt{(x_0^2 - u^2)(2k - \beta x_0^2 - \beta u^2)}}. \tag{39}$$

20. Substitute $u = x_0 \cos\phi$ in (39) to show that

$$T = \frac{2T_0}{\pi\sqrt{1 - \epsilon}} \int_0^{\pi/2} \frac{d\phi}{\sqrt{1 - \mu \sin^2\phi}}, \tag{40}$$

where $T_0 = 2\pi/\sqrt{k}$ is the linear period,

$$\epsilon = \frac{\beta}{k}x_0^2, \quad \text{and} \quad \mu = -\frac{1}{2} \cdot \frac{\epsilon}{1 - \epsilon}. \tag{41}$$

21. Finally, use the binomial series in (31) and the integral formula in (32) to evaluate the elliptic integral in (40) and thereby show that the period T of oscillation is given by

$$T = \frac{T_0}{\sqrt{1 - \epsilon}}\left(1 + \frac{1}{4}\mu + \frac{9}{64}\mu^2 + \frac{25}{256}\mu^3 + \cdots\right). \tag{42}$$

22. If $\epsilon = \beta x_0^2/k$ is sufficiently small that ϵ^2 is negligible, deduce from Eqs. (41) and (42) that

$$T \approx T_0\left(1 + \frac{3}{8}\epsilon\right) = T_0\left(1 + \frac{3\beta}{8k}x_0^2\right). \tag{43}$$

It follows that:

- If $\beta > 0$, so the spring is *soft*, then $T > T_0$, and increasing x_0 increases T, so the larger ovals in Fig. 6.4.4 correspond to smaller frequencies.
- If $\beta < 0$, so the spring is *hard*, then $T < T_0$, and increasing x_0 decreases T, so the larger ovals in Fig. 6.4.2 correspond to larger frequencies.

6.4 Lab 5: Nonlinear Systems

Goals

In this lab you will use the **pplane6** program to study two nonlinear systems by direct numerical simulation. The first model, from population biology, displays interesting nonlinear oscillations (so-called **limit cycles**). The second is a system whose solutions depend on a parameter. Neither of these systems is described by exactly solvable systems of differential equations. Although much may be learned from strictly theoretical analyses, we must ultimately rely on computational methods to extract their quantitative predictions.

Application 1: Predator-Prey Species Interactions

In class we considered a model of predator-prey species interactions known as the Lotka-Volterra model (referred to in Section 6.3 as the predator-prey system). If x describes the size of a population of rabbits and y describes a population of foxes (which like to eat said rabbits) then the Lotka-Volterra model of their interactions says that there are positive constants a, b, c, d so that

$$\frac{dx}{dt} = x(a - by) \tag{1}$$

$$\frac{dy}{dt} = y(-c + dx) \tag{2}$$

That is, the exponential growth rate of rabbits is decreased by the presence of foxes and the exponential death rate of foxes is decreased by the presence of rabbits. This model predicts some unlikely behavior. In the absence of foxes ($y = 0$), equation

(1) becomes $\frac{dx}{dt} = ax$. In other words, without any foxes the rabbits will always grow exponentially without bound. And even if the predator population is small, they will always eat the prey at a rate proportional to their product. In other words, 10 foxes surrounded by 100,000 rabbits would each have to eat ten times more than 10 foxes surrounded by 10,000 rabbits. If the rabbit population could be held at a fixed level $x_0 > c/d$, equation (2) becomes $\frac{dy}{dt} = Cy$ where $C = -c + dx_0 > 0$. In other words, if the rabbit population is maintained at a given level, above some threshold, the fox population will always grow exponentially without bound. None of these predictions are ecologically reasonable. The following model addresses these problems.

For positive values of r, the two populations are modelled by:

$$\frac{dx}{dt} = x(1-x) - \frac{xy}{x + \frac{1}{5}} \tag{3}$$

$$\frac{dy}{dt} = ry\left(1 - \frac{y}{x}\right). \tag{4}$$

In the absence of predators, the prey satisfies the logistic equation with equilibrium population $x = 1$. In the presence of predators, prey is consumed at a rate $\frac{xy}{x + \frac{1}{5}}$. That is, if $x \gg \frac{1}{5}$, then the predators consume prey at a rate proportional to the predator population. Only if $x \ll \frac{1}{5}$ do the predators consume prey at a rate proportional to xy as in the Lotka-Volterra model. And for a fixed prey population, the predator population satisfies logistic growth with equilibrium population x. The parameter r is the inverse relaxation time for the predator population, i.e., $\frac{1}{r}$ is proportional to the time it takes the predator population to equilibrate. (Note: We have already scaled the variables and chosen some parameter values in equations (3) and (4). The general version of the model would have many more parameters.)

Application 2: Bifurcation

When one tries to understand the behavior of a nonlinear system one of the first things one looks at is the set of equilibrium solutions. The number and type of equilibrium solutions may well depend on some parameter(s) of the system: the mass of a component, the stiffness of a spring, the length of a lever, the resistance of an electronic component, etc. In this section of the lab you will observe in a very simple case how the structure of the equilibrium points of a system of equations changes as a parameter varies. Such a qualitative change is called a bifurcation and the associated parameter value is called a bifurcation point. The system in question is:

$$\frac{dx}{dt} = ax - y \tag{5}$$

$$\frac{dy}{dt} = x + ay + x^2 \tag{6}$$

In this system a is the parameter.

Prelab Assignment

Before arriving in lab, answer the following questions. Your answers should be neatly presented and handed in at the beginning of lab.

1. Find the fixed points (critical points) of the Predator-Prey system, equations (3) and (4). Calculate the numerical value of the coexistence point corresponding to positive values of x and y.

2. Find the curve in the phase plane where the trajectories of (3) and (4) are vertical (the x-nullcline) and the curve in the phase plane where the trajectories are horizontal (the y-nullcline). Use the information from Prelab Problem 1 along with these curves to sketch possible phase portraits.

3. The system exhibits very different behavior depending on whether $r > r_c$ or $r < r_c$, where $r_c = .053576 \ldots$. In one regime, the coexistence point is stable and all solutions are attracted to it. In the other region, the coexistence point is unstable and population levels starting near the point spiral outward. Which do you think happens for which values of r? That is, do you think that a large or a small value of r ought to correspond to the stable coexistence or to the oscillatory behavior? (Either provide a coherent logical argument or do a stability analysis of the coexistence fixed point to justify your prediction.)

4. Find the equilibrium points for the second system; that is, for equations (5) and (6).

Phase Portraits

To study the evolution of the fox and rabbit populations over time, you will want to generate a phase portrait plotting x against y. The following describes how you are to use **pplane6** to generate these phase portraits:

    After you log on and open Matlab, type **pplane6**. As happened with the **dfield6** program you used in Lab 1 a dialog box will open with lots of little boxes all filled in; ignore them and click on the **Proceed** button. You will see a graph with a direction field corresponding to a system of equations. Put the cursor on any point and click. You have just chosen initial conditions for the system. Now you know what the solution to the system of ODEs with your choice of initial conditions looks like.

    Plot a few solutions (your graph should suggest an insect) and then go to the **Graph** menu and select **y vs t**. Your cursor will become cross hairs; center the cross hairs on a solution curve and click. You will see a plot of—surprise—y vs t. You can change your mind and click on **x vs t** or both or **3D**, etc.

    If your graph is getting too cluttered go to the **Edit** menu and select **Erase all solutions**.

    Finally, go to the **Solutions** menu and choose **Find an equilibrium point**; your cursor will again become a cross hair and if you position the cross hairs near an equilibrium point and click you will get a red dot at the equilibrium point and some info in a dialog box. You can repeat the command and find another equilibrium point for this system.

    When you use **pplane6** to do this lab you will, of course, change the system in the **pplane6** dialog box to the system you want to study. In the first case, the predator-prey system, there is a parameter r in the system. You can enter the equations with the r in them and then, underneath the equations box, enter r=0.5 or whatever in the parameters or expressions box. (A parameter is a constant of the problem that changes from one problem to the next.)

    Some important points: when you set up your equation you also enter the minimum and maximum values for x and y as you did with **dfield6** but it is often more convenient to **zoom in** or **zoom out**. You will find those commands under the **Edit** menu. In addition you should have the solver evolve the solution *forward* in time. This can be done by changing the solution direction in the **options** menu for the **pplane6 Display** window. (Looking at the solution only in the forward direction tells you whether solutions are moving towards or away from an equilibrium point.) Now you have the tools to do the lab.

Lab Problems

1. Use **pplane6** to solve equations (3) and (4) and print phase portraits. Start from various initial conditions, and use $r = .07$, .05 and .03. **Zoom in** on important features.

2. Check your prediction from Prelab Problem 3. What, if anything, surprised you about the behavior of the system?

3. What is different about the oscillatory state here compared to that of the Lotka-Volterra predator-prey model? Discuss. (Hint: Consider the dependence of the steady state oscillation amplitude on the initial condition. How many different closed orbits do you see for each value of r?)

4. Classify the equilibrium points of the second system (equations (5) and (6)) when $a = -0.5$, $a = 0$ and $a = 0.5$.

5. Provide a sketch or printout of the behavior of solutions near the equilibrium points in each of the three cases.

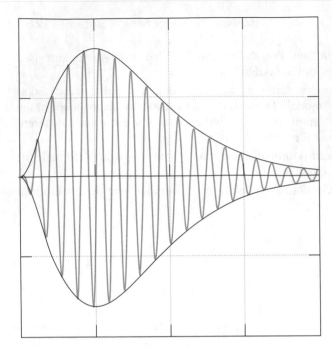

CHAPTER 7

Laplace Transform Methods

7.1 LAPLACE TRANSFORMS AND INVERSE TRANSFORMS

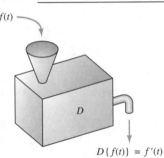

$D\{f(t)\} = f'(t)$

$\mathcal{L}\{f(t)\} = F(s)$

FIGURE 7.1.1. Transformation of a function: $\mathcal{L}$ in analogy with D.

In Chapter 3 we saw that linear differential equations with constant coefficients have numerous applications and can be solved systematically. There are common situations, however, in which the alternative methods of this chapter are preferable. For example, recall the differential equations

$$mx'' + cx' + kx = F(t) \quad \text{and} \quad LI'' + RI' + \frac{1}{C}I = E'(t)$$

corresponding to a mass-spring-dashpot system and a series RLC circuit, respectively. It often happens in practice that the forcing term, $F(t)$ or $E'(t)$, has discontinuities—for example, when the voltage supplied to an electrical circuit is turned off and on periodically. In this case the methods of Chapter 3 can be quite awkward, and the Laplace transform method is more convenient.

The differentiation operator D can be viewed as a transformation which, when applied to the function $f(t)$, yields the new function $D\{f(t)\} = f'(t)$. The Laplace transformation $\mathcal{L}$ involves the operation of integration and yields the new function $\mathcal{L}\{f(t)\} = F(s)$ of a new independent variable s. The situation is diagrammed in Fig. 7.1.1. After learning in this section how to compute the Laplace transform $F(s)$ of a function $f(t)$, we will see in Section 7.2 that the Laplace transform converts a *differential* equation in the unknown function $f(t)$ into an *algebraic* equation in $F(s)$. Because algebraic equations are generally easier to solve than differential equations, this is one method that simplifies the problem of finding the solution $f(t)$.

DEFINITION: The Laplace Transform

Given a function $f(t)$ defined for all $t \geq 0$, the *Laplace transform* of f is the function F defined as follows:

$$F(s) = \mathcal{L}\{f(t)\} = \int_0^\infty e^{-st} f(t)\, dt \qquad (1)$$

for all values of s for which the improper integral converges.

Recall that an **improper integral** over an infinite interval is defined as a limit of integrals over bounded intervals; that is,

$$\int_a^\infty g(t)\, dt = \lim_{b \to \infty} \int_a^b g(t)\, dt. \tag{2}$$

If the limit in (2) exists, then we say that the improper integral **converges;** otherwise, it **diverges** or fails to exist. Note that the integrand of the improper integral in (1) contains the parameter s in addition to the variable of integration t. Therefore, when the integral in (1) converges, it converges not merely to a number, but to a *function* F of s. As in the following examples, it is typical for the improper integral in the definition of $\mathcal{L}\{f(t)\}$ to converge for some values of s and diverge for others.

EXAMPLE 1 With $f(t) \equiv 1$ for $t \geq 0$, the definition of the Laplace transform in (1) gives

$$\mathcal{L}\{1\} = \int_0^\infty e^{-st}\, dt = \left[-\frac{1}{s} e^{-st} \right]_0^\infty = \lim_{b \to \infty} \left[-\frac{1}{s} e^{-bs} + \frac{1}{s} \right],$$

and therefore

$$\mathcal{L}\{1\} = \frac{1}{s} \quad \text{for} \quad s > 0. \tag{3}$$

As in (3), it's good practice to specify the domain of the Laplace transform—in problems as well as in examples. Also, in this computation we have used the common abbreviation

$$\left[g(t) \right]_a^\infty = \lim_{b \to \infty} \left[g(t) \right]_a^b. \tag{4}$$

∎

Remark: The limit we computed in Example 1 would not exist if $s < 0$, for then $(1/s)e^{-bs}$ would become unbounded as $b \to +\infty$. Hence $\mathcal{L}\{1\}$ is defined only for $s > 0$. This is typical of Laplace transforms; the domain of a transform is normally of the form $s > a$ for some number a. ∎

EXAMPLE 2 With $f(t) = e^{at}$ for $t \geq 0$, we obtain

$$\mathcal{L}\{e^{at}\} = \int_0^\infty e^{-st} e^{at}\, dt = \int_0^\infty e^{-(s-a)t}\, dt = \left[-\frac{e^{-(s-a)t}}{s-a} \right]_{t=0}^\infty.$$

If $s - a > 0$, then $e^{-(s-a)t} \to 0$ as $t \to +\infty$, so it follows that

➤
$$\mathcal{L}\{e^{at}\} = \frac{1}{s-a} \quad \text{for} \quad s > a. \tag{5}$$

Note here that the improper integral giving $\mathcal{L}\{e^{at}\}$ diverges if $s \leq a$. It is worth noting also that the formula in (5) holds if a is a complex number. For then, with $a = \alpha + i\beta$,

$$e^{-(s-a)t} = e^{i\beta t} e^{-(s-\alpha)t} \to 0$$

as $t \to +\infty$, provided that $s > \alpha = \mathrm{Re}(a)$; recall that $e^{i\beta t} = \cos \beta t + i \sin \beta t$. ∎

The Laplace transform $\mathcal{L}\{t^a\}$ of a power function is most conveniently expressed in terms of the **gamma function** $\Gamma(x)$, which is defined for $x > 0$ by the formula

➤
$$\Gamma(x) = \int_0^\infty e^{-t} t^{x-1}\, dt. \tag{6}$$

For an elementary discussion of $\Gamma(x)$, see the subsection on the gamma function in Section 8.5, where it is shown that

$$\Gamma(1) = 1 \tag{7}$$

and that

$$\Gamma(x + 1) = x\Gamma(x) \tag{8}$$

for $x > 0$. It then follows that if n is a positive integer, then

$$
\begin{aligned}
\Gamma(n + 1) &= n\Gamma(n) \\
&= n \cdot (n - 1)\Gamma(n - 1) \\
&= n \cdot (n - 1) \cdot (n - 2)\Gamma(n - 2) \\
&\ \ \vdots \\
&= n(n - 1)(n - 2) \cdots 2 \cdot \Gamma(2) \\
&= n(n - 1)(n - 2) \cdots 2 \cdot 1 \cdot \Gamma(1);
\end{aligned}
$$

thus

➤ $$\Gamma(n + 1) = n! \tag{9}$$

if n is a positive integer. Therefore the function $\Gamma(x + 1)$, which is defined and continuous for all $x > -1$, agrees with the factorial function for $x = n$, a positive integer.

EXAMPLE 3 Suppose that $f(t) = t^a$ where a is real and $a > -1$. Then

$$\mathcal{L}\{t^a\} = \int_0^\infty e^{-st} t^a \, dt.$$

If we substitute $u = st$, $t = u/s$, and $dt = du/s$ in this integral, we get

$$\mathcal{L}\{t^a\} = \frac{1}{s^{a+1}} \int_0^\infty e^{-u} u^a \, du = \frac{\Gamma(a + 1)}{s^{a+1}} \tag{10}$$

for all $s > 0$ (so that $u = st > 0$). Because $\Gamma(n + 1) = n!$ if n is a nonnegative integer, we see that

➤ $$\mathcal{L}\{t^n\} = \frac{n!}{s^{n+1}} \quad \text{for} \quad s > 0. \tag{11}$$

For instance,

$$\mathcal{L}\{t\} = \frac{1}{s^2}, \quad \mathcal{L}\{t^2\} = \frac{2}{s^3}, \quad \text{and} \quad \mathcal{L}\{t^3\} = \frac{6}{s^4}.$$

As in Problems 1 and 2, these formulas can be derived immediately from the definition, without the use of the gamma function. ∎

Linearity of Transforms

It is not necessary for us to proceed much further in the computation of Laplace transforms directly from the definition. Once we know the Laplace transforms of several functions, we can combine them to obtain transforms of other functions. The reason is that the Laplace transformation is a *linear* operation.

THEOREM 1: Linearity of the Laplace Transform

If a and b are constants, then

$$\mathcal{L}\{af(t) + bg(t)\} = a\mathcal{L}\{f(t)\} + b\mathcal{L}\{g(t)\} \tag{12}$$

for all s such that the Laplace transforms of the functions f and g both exist. ■

The proof of Theorem 1 follows immediately from the linearity of the operations of taking limits and of integration:

$$\mathcal{L}\{af(t) + bg(t)\} = \int_0^\infty e^{-st}[af(t) + bg(t)]\,dt$$

$$= \lim_{c \to \infty} \int_0^c e^{-st}[af(t) + bg(t)]\,dt$$

$$= a\left(\lim_{c \to \infty} \int_0^c e^{-st}f(t)\,dt\right) + b\left(\lim_{c \to \infty} \int_0^c e^{-st}g(t)\,dt\right)$$

$$= a\mathcal{L}\{f(t)\} + b\mathcal{L}\{g(t)\}.$$

EXAMPLE 4 The computation of $\mathcal{L}\{t^{n/2}\}$ is based on the known special value

$$\Gamma\left(\frac{1}{2}\right) = \sqrt{\pi} \tag{13}$$

of the gamma function. For instance, it follows that

$$\Gamma\left(\frac{5}{2}\right) = \frac{3}{2}\Gamma\left(\frac{3}{2}\right) = \frac{3}{2} \cdot \frac{1}{2}\Gamma\left(\frac{1}{2}\right) = \frac{3}{4}\sqrt{\pi},$$

using the formula $\Gamma(x + 1) = x\Gamma(x)$ in (9), first with $x = \frac{3}{2}$ and then with $x = \frac{1}{2}$. Now the formulas in (10) through (12) yield

$$\mathcal{L}\{3t^2 + 4t^{3/2}\} = 3 \cdot \frac{2!}{s^3} + \frac{4\Gamma\left(\frac{5}{2}\right)}{s^{5/2}} = \frac{6}{s^3} + 3\sqrt{\frac{\pi}{s^5}}.$$

EXAMPLE 5 Recall that $\cosh kt = (e^{kt} + e^{-kt})/2$. If $k > 0$, then Theorem 1 and Example 2 together give

$$\mathcal{L}\{\cosh kt\} = \frac{1}{2}\mathcal{L}\{e^{kt}\} + \frac{1}{2}\mathcal{L}\{e^{-kt}\} = \frac{1}{2}\left(\frac{1}{s-k} + \frac{1}{s+k}\right);$$

that is,

$$\mathcal{L}\{\cosh kt\} = \frac{s}{s^2 - k^2} \quad \text{for } s > k > 0. \tag{14}$$

Similarly,

$$\mathcal{L}\{\sinh kt\} = \frac{k}{s^2 - k^2} \quad \text{for } s > k > 0. \tag{15}$$

Because $\cos kt = (e^{ikt} + e^{-ikt})/2$, the formula in (5) (with $a = ik$) yields

$$\mathcal{L}\{\cos kt\} = \frac{1}{2}\left(\frac{1}{s-ik} + \frac{1}{s+ik}\right) = \frac{1}{2} \cdot \frac{2s}{s^2 - (ik)^2},$$

and thus

$$\mathcal{L}\{\cos kt\} = \frac{s}{s^2 + k^2} \quad \text{for } s > 0. \tag{16}$$

(The domain follows from $s > \text{Re}(ik) = 0$.) Similarly,

$$\mathcal{L}\{\sin kt\} = \frac{k}{s^2 + k^2} \quad \text{for } s > 0. \tag{17}$$

EXAMPLE 6   Applying linearity, the formula in (16), and a familiar trigonometric identity, we get

$$\mathcal{L}\{3e^{2t} + 2\sin^2 3t\} = \mathcal{L}\{3e^{2t} + 1 - \cos 6t\}$$

$$= \frac{3}{s-2} + \frac{1}{s} - \frac{s}{s^2 + 36}$$

$$= \frac{3s^3 + 144s - 72}{s(s-2)(s^2 + 36)} \quad \text{for } s > 0. \qquad \blacksquare$$

Inverse Transforms

According to Theorem 3 of this section, no two different functions that are both continuous for all $t \geq 0$ can have the same Laplace transform. Thus if $F(s)$ is the transform of some continuous function $f(t)$, then $f(t)$ is uniquely determined. This observation allows us to make the following definition: If $F(s) = \mathcal{L}\{f(t)\}$, then we call $f(t)$ the **inverse Laplace transform** of $F(s)$ and write

$$\blacktriangleright \qquad\qquad f(t) = \mathcal{L}^{-1}\{F(s)\}. \tag{18}$$

EXAMPLE 7 $\mathcal{L}^{-1}\left\{\dfrac{1}{s^3}\right\} = \dfrac{1}{2}t^2, \quad \mathcal{L}^{-1}\left\{\dfrac{1}{s+2}\right\} = e^{-2t}, \quad \mathcal{L}^{-1}\left\{\dfrac{2}{s^2+9}\right\} = \dfrac{2}{3}\sin 3t,$

and so on. $\blacksquare$

NOTATION: FUNCTIONS AND THEIR TRANSFORMS.   Throughout this chapter we denote functions of t by lowercase letters. The transform of a function will always be denoted by that same letter capitalized. Thus $F(s)$ is the Laplace transform of $f(t)$ and $x(t)$ is the inverse Laplace transform of $X(s)$.

A table of Laplace transforms serves a purpose similar to that of a table of integrals. The table in Fig. 7.1.2 lists the transforms derived in this section; many additional transforms can be derived from these few, using various general properties of the Laplace transformation (which we will discuss in subsequent sections).

Piecewise Continuous Functions

As we remarked at the beginning of this section, we need to be able to handle certain types of discontinuous functions. The function $f(t)$ is said to be **piecewise continuous** on the bounded interval $a \leq t \leq b$ provided that $[a, b]$ can be subdivided into finitely many abutting subintervals in such a way that:

1. f is continuous in the interior of each of these subintervals; and

$f(t)$	$F(s)$	
1	$\dfrac{1}{s}$	$(s > 0)$
t	$\dfrac{1}{s^2}$	$(s > 0)$
$t^n \ (n \geqq 0)$	$\dfrac{n!}{s^{n+1}}$	$(s > 0)$
$t^a \ (a > -1)$	$\dfrac{\Gamma(a+1)}{s^{a+1}}$	$(s > 0)$
e^{at}	$\dfrac{1}{s-a}$	$(s > 0)$
$\cos kt$	$\dfrac{s}{s^2+k^2}$	$(s > 0)$
$\sin kt$	$\dfrac{k}{s^2+k^2}$	$(s > 0)$
$\cosh kt$	$\dfrac{s}{s^2-k^2}$	$(s > |k|)$
$\sinh kt$	$\dfrac{k}{s^2-k^2}$	$(s > |k|)$
$u(t-a)$	$\dfrac{e^{-as}}{s}$	$(s > 0)$

FIGURE 7.1.2. A short table of Laplace transforms.

2. $f(t)$ has a finite limit as t approaches each endpoint of each subinterval from its interior.

We say that f is piecewise continuous for $t \geqq 0$ if it is piecewise continuous on every bounded subinterval of $[0, +\infty)$. Thus a piecewise continuous function has only simple discontinuities (if any) and only at isolated points. At such points the value of the function experiences a finite jump, as indicated in Fig. 7.1.3. The **jump in $f(t)$ at the point** c is defined to be $f(c+) - f(c-)$, where

$$f(c+) = \lim_{\epsilon \to 0^+} f(c + \epsilon) \quad \text{and} \quad f(c-) = \lim_{\epsilon \to 0^+} f(c - \epsilon).$$

Perhaps the simplest piecewise continuous (but discontinuous) function is the unit step function, whose graph appears in Fig. 7.1.4. It is defined as follows:

$$u(t) = \begin{cases} 0 & \text{for } t < 0, \\ 1 & \text{for } t \geqq 0. \end{cases} \tag{19}$$

Because $u(t) = 1$ for $t \geqq 0$ and because the Laplace transform involves only the values of a function for $t \geqq 0$, we see immediately that

$$\mathcal{L}\{u(t)\} = \frac{1}{s} \quad (s > 0). \tag{20}$$

The graph of the unit step function $u_a(t) = u(t - a)$ appears in Fig. 7.1.5. Its jump occurs at $t = a$ rather than at $t = 0$; equivalently,

$$u_a(t) = u(t-a) = \begin{cases} 0 & \text{for } t < a, \\ 1 & \text{for } t \geqq a. \end{cases} \tag{21}$$

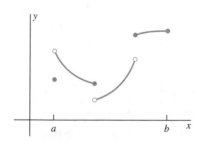

FIGURE 7.1.3. The graph of a piecewise continuous function; the solid dots indicate values of the function at discontinuities.

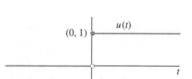

FIGURE 7.1.4. The graph of the unit step function.

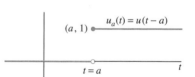

FIGURE 7.1.5. The unit step function $u_a(t)$ has a jump at $t = a$.

EXAMPLE 8 Find $\mathcal{L}\{u_a(t)\}$ if $a > 0$.

Solution We begin with the definition of the Laplace transform. We obtain

$$\mathcal{L}\{u_a(t)\} = \int_0^\infty e^{-st} u_a(t)\, dt = \int_a^\infty e^{-st}\, dt = \lim_{b \to \infty} \left[-\frac{e^{-st}}{s} \right]_{t=a}^{b};$$

consequently,

$$\mathcal{L}\{u_a(t)\} = \frac{e^{-as}}{s} \quad (s > 0,\ a > 0). \tag{22}$$

General Properties of Transforms

It is a familiar fact from calculus that the integral

$$\int_a^b g(t)\, dt$$

exists if g is piecewise continuous on the bounded interval $[a, b]$. Hence if f is piecewise continuous for $t \geq 0$, it follows that the integral

$$\int_0^b e^{-st} f(t)\, dt$$

exists for all $b < +\infty$. But in order for $F(s)$—the limit of this last integral as $b \to +\infty$—to exist, we need some condition to limit the rate of growth of $f(t)$ as $t \to +\infty$. The function f is said to be **of exponential order** as $t \to +\infty$ if there exist nonnegative constants M, c, and T such that

$$|f(t)| \leq Me^{ct} \quad \text{for } t \geq T. \tag{23}$$

Thus a function is of exponential order provided that it grows no more rapidly (as $t \to +\infty$) than a constant multiple of some exponential function with a linear exponent. The particular values of M, c, and T are not so important. What is important is that some such values exist so that the condition in (23) is satisfied.

Every polynomial $p(t)$ is of exponential order, with $m = c = 1$ in (23); this follows from the fact that $p(t)/e^t \to 0$ as $t \to +\infty$. The function $g(t) = e^{t^2}$ is an example of one that is *not* of exponential order—because

$$\lim_{t \to \infty} \frac{e^{t^2}}{e^{ct}} = \lim_{t \to \infty} e^{t^2 - ct} = +\infty,$$

the condition in (23) cannot hold for any [finite] value of M. The condition in (23) merely says that $f(t)/e^{ct}$ is *bounded* for t sufficiently large. In particular, any bounded function—such as $\cos kt$ or $\sin kt$—is of exponential order.

THEOREM 2: Existence of Laplace Transforms

If the function f is piecewise continuous for $t \geq 0$ and is of exponential order as $t \to +\infty$, then its Laplace transform $F(s) = \mathcal{L}\{f(t)\}$ exists. More precisely, if f is piecewise continuous and satisfies the condition in (23), then $F(s)$ exists for all $s > c$.

Proof: First we note that we can take $T = 0$ in (23). For by piecewise continuity, $|f(t)|$ is bounded on $[0, T]$. Increasing M in (23) if necessary, we can therefore assume that $|f(t)| \leq M$ if $0 \leq t \leq T$. Because $e^{ct} \geq 1$ for $t \geq 0$, it then follows that $|f(t)| \leq Me^{ct}$ for all $t \geq 0$.

By a standard theorem on convergence of improper integrals—the fact that absolute convergence implies convergence—it suffices for us to prove that the integral

$$\int_0^\infty |e^{-st} f(t)|\, dt$$

exists for $s > c$. To do this, it suffices in turn to show that the value of the integral

$$\int_0^b |e^{-st} f(t)|\, dt$$

remains bounded as $b \to +\infty$. But the fact that $|f(t)| \leq Me^{ct}$ for all $t \geq 0$ implies that

$$\int_0^b |e^{-st} f(t)| \, dt \leq \int_0^b |e^{-st} Me^{ct}| \, dt = M \int_0^b e^{-(s-c)t} \, dt$$

$$\leq M \int_0^\infty e^{-(s-c)t} \, dt = \frac{M}{s-c}$$

if $s > c$. This proves Theorem 2. ∎

We have shown, moreover, that

$$|F(s)| \leq \int_0^\infty |e^{-st} f(t)| \, dt \leq \frac{M}{s-c} \tag{24}$$

if $s > c$. When we take limits as $s \to +\infty$, we get the following result.

COROLLARY: $F(s)$ for s Large

If $f(t)$ satisfies the hypotheses of Theorem 2, then

$$\lim_{s \to \infty} F(s) = 0. \tag{25}$$

∎

The condition in (25) severely limits the functions that can be Laplace transforms. For instance, the function $G(s) = s/(s+1)$ cannot be the Laplace transform of any "reasonable" function because its limit as $s \to +\infty$ is 1, not 0. More generally, a rational function—a quotient of two polynomials—can be (and is, as we shall see) a Laplace transform only if the degree of its numerator is less than that of its denominator.

On the other hand, the hypotheses of Theorem 2 are sufficient, but not necessary, conditions for existence of the Laplace transform of $f(t)$. For example, the function $f(t) = 1/\sqrt{t}$ fails to be piecewise continuous (at $t = 0$), but nevertheless (Example 3 with $a = -\frac{1}{2} > -1$) its Laplace transform

$$\mathcal{L}\{t^{-1/2}\} = \frac{\Gamma\left(\frac{1}{2}\right)}{s^{1/2}} = \sqrt{\frac{\pi}{s}}$$

both exists and violates the condition in (24), which would imply that $sF(s)$ remains bounded as $s \to +\infty$.

The remainder of this chapter is devoted largely to techniques for solving a differential equation by first finding the Laplace transform of its solution. It is then vital for us to know that this uniquely determines the solution of the differential equation; that is, that the function of s we have found has only one inverse Laplace transform that could be the desired solution. The following theorem is proved in Chapter 6 of Churchill's *Operational Mathematics,* 3rd ed. (New York: McGraw-Hill, 1972).

THEOREM 3: Uniqueness of Inverse Laplace Transforms

Suppose that the functions $f(t)$ and $g(t)$ satisfy the hypotheses of Theorem 2, so that their Laplace transforms $F(s)$ and $G(s)$ both exist. If $F(s) = G(s)$ for all $s > c$ (for some c), then $f(t) = g(t)$ wherever on $[0, +\infty)$ both f and g are continuous. ∎

Thus two piecewise continuous functions of exponential order with the same Laplace transform can differ only at their isolated points of discontinuity. This is of no importance in most practical applications, so we may regard inverse Laplace transforms as being essentially unique. In particular, two solutions of a differential equation must both be continuous, and hence must be the same solution if they have the same Laplace transform.

Historical Remark: Laplace transforms have an interesting history. The integral in the definition of the Laplace transform probably appeared first in the work of Euler. It is customary in mathematics to name a technique or theorem for the next person after Euler to discover it (else there will be several hundred different examples of "Euler's theorem"). In this case, the next person was the French mathematician Pierre Simon de Laplace (1749–1827), who employed such integrals in his work on probability theory. The so-called operational techniques for solving differential equations, which are based on Laplace transforms, were not exploited by Laplace. Indeed, they were discovered and popularized by practicing engineers—notably the English electrical engineer Oliver Heaviside (1850–1925). These techniques were successfully and widely applied before they had been rigorously justified, and around the beginning of the twentieth century their validity was the subject of considerable controversy.

7.1 *Problems*

Apply the definition in (1) to find directly the Laplace transforms of the functions described (by formula or graph) in Problems 1 through 10.

1. $f(t) = t$

2. $f(t) = t^2$

3. $f(t) = e^{3t+1}$

4. $f(t) = \cos t$

5. $f(t) = \sinh t$

6. $f(t) = \sin^2 t$

7.

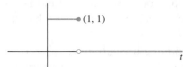

FIGURE 7.1.6.

8.

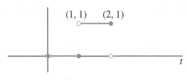

FIGURE 7.1.7.

9.

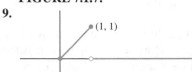

FIGURE 7.1.8.

10.

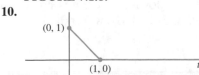

FIGURE 7.1.9.

Use the transforms in Fig. 7.1.2 to find the Laplace transforms of the functions in Problems 11 through 22. A preliminary integration by parts may be necessary.

11. $f(t) = \sqrt{t} + 3t$

12. $f(t) = 3t^{5/2} - 4t^3$

13. $f(t) = t - 2e^{3t}$

14. $f(t) = t^{3/2} - e^{-10t}$

15. $f(t) = 1 + \cosh 5t$

16. $f(t) = \sin 2t + \cos 2t$

17. $f(t) = \cos^2 2t$

18. $f(t) = \sin 3t \cos 3t$

19. $f(t) = (1 + t)^3$

20. $f(t) = te^t$

21. $f(t) = t \cos 2t$

22. $f(t) = \sinh^2 3t$

Use the transforms in Fig. 7.1.2 to find the inverse Laplace transforms of the functions in Problems 23 through 32.

23. $F(s) = \dfrac{3}{s^4}$

24. $F(s) = s^{-3/2}$

25. $F(s) = \dfrac{1}{s} - \dfrac{2}{s^{5/2}}$

26. $F(s) = \dfrac{1}{s+5}$

27. $F(s) = \dfrac{3}{s-4}$

28. $F(s) = \dfrac{3s+1}{s^2+4}$

29. $F(s) = \dfrac{5-3s}{s^2+9}$

30. $F(s) = \dfrac{9+s}{4-s^2}$

31. $F(s) = \dfrac{10s-3}{25-s^2}$

32. $F(s) = 2s^{-1}e^{-3s}$

33. Derive the transform of $f(t) = \sin kt$ by the method used in the text to derive the formula in (16).

34. Derive the transform of $f(t) = \sinh kt$ by the method used in the text to derive the formula in (14).

35. Use the tabulated integral

$$\int e^{ax} \cos bx \, dx = \frac{e^{ax}}{a^2+b^2}(a \cos bx + b \sin bx) + C$$

to obtain $\mathcal{L}\{\cos kt\}$ directly from the definition of the Laplace transform.

36. Show that the function $f(t) = \sin(e^{t^2})$ is of exponential order as $t \to +\infty$ but that its derivative is not.

37. Let $f(t) = 1$ for $0 \leq t \leq a$, $f(t) = 0$ for $t > a$ (where $a > 0$). Express f in terms of unit step functions to show that $\mathcal{L}\{f(t)\} = (1 - e^{-as})/s$.

38. Let $f(t) = 1$ if $a \le t \le b$, $f(t) = 0$ if either $t < a$ or $t > b$ (where $0 < a < b$). Express f in terms of unit step functions to show that

$$\mathcal{L}\{f(t)\} = s^{-1}(e^{-as} - e^{-bs}).$$

39. The unit staircase function is defined as follows:

$$f(t) = n \quad \text{if} \quad n - 1 < t \le n, \quad n = 1, 2, 3, \ldots .$$

(a) Sketch the graph of f to see why its name is appropriate.   (b) Show that

$$f(t) = \sum_{n=0}^{\infty} u(t - n)$$

for all $t > 0$.   (c) Assume that the Laplace transform of the infinite series in part (b) can be taken termwise (it can). Apply the geometric series to obtain the result

$$\mathcal{L}\{f(t)\} = \frac{1}{s(1 - e^{-s})}.$$

40. (a) The graph of the function f is shown in Fig. 7.1.10. Show that f can be written in the form

$$f(t) = \sum_{n=0}^{\infty} (-1)^n u(t - n).$$

(b) Use the method of Problem 39 to show that

$$\mathcal{L}\{f(t)\} = \frac{1}{s(1 + e^{-s})}.$$

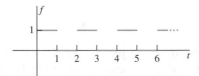

FIGURE 7.1.10.   The graph of the function of Problem 40.

41. The graph of the square wave function $g(t)$ is shown in Fig. 7.1.11. Express g in terms of the function f of Problem 40 and hence deduce that

$$\mathcal{L}\{g(t)\} = \frac{1 - e^{-s}}{s(1 + e^{-s})} = \frac{1}{s} \tanh \frac{s}{2}.$$

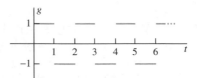

FIGURE 7.1.11.   The graph of the function of Problem 41.

42. Consider the function $f(t) \equiv 0$.   (a) Compute $f'(t) = D_t\{f(t)\}$ and sketch its graph.   (b) Now modify f to obtain the new function

$$g(t) = \begin{cases} 1 & \text{if } 0 \le t \le 1, \\ 0 & \text{otherwise.} \end{cases}$$

Compute $g'(t) = D_t\{g(t)\}$ and sketch its graph. Note that g is obtained from f by modifying f *only* on the interval $[0, 1]$. Where do the functions $f'(t)$ and $g'(t)$ agree?

43. Consider the function $f(t) \equiv 0$.   (a) Compute $F(s) = \mathcal{L}\{f(t)\}$ and sketch its graph.   (b) Now modify f to obtain the new function

$$g(t) = \begin{cases} 1 & \text{if } 0 \le t \le 1, \\ 0 & \text{otherwise.} \end{cases}$$

Compute $G(s) = \mathcal{L}\{g(t)\}$ and sketch its graph. Note that g is obtain from f by modifying f *only* on the interval $[0, 1]$. Where do the functions $F(s)$ and $G(s)$ agree?   (c) Comment on the difference between the operators D_t and $\mathcal{L}$ illustrated by Problems 42 and 43.

7.2 TRANSFORMATION OF INITIAL VALUE PROBLEMS

We now discuss the application of Laplace transforms to solve a linear differential equation with constant coefficients, such as

$$ax''(t) + bx'(t) + cx(t) = f(t), \tag{1}$$

with given initial conditions $x(0) = x_0$ and $x'(0) = x_0'$. By the linearity of the Laplace transformation, we can transform Eq. (1) by separately taking the Laplace transform of each term in the equation. The transformed equation is

$$a\mathcal{L}\{x''(t)\} + b\mathcal{L}\{x'(t)\} + c\mathcal{L}\{x(t)\} = \mathcal{L}\{f(t)\}; \tag{2}$$

it involves the transforms of the derivatives x' and x'' of the unknown function $x(t)$. The key to the method is Theorem 1, which tells us how to express the transform of the *derivative* of a function in terms of the transform of the function itself.

> **THEOREM 1:   Transforms of Derivatives**

Suppose that the function $f(t)$ is continuous and piecewise smooth for $t \ge 0$ and is of exponential order as $t \to +\infty$, so that there exist nonnegative constants M, c,

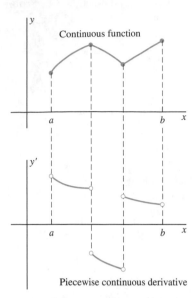

FIGURE 7.2.1. The discontinuities of f' correspond to "corners" on the graph of f.

and T such that

$$|f(t)| \leqq Me^{ct} \quad \text{for } t \geqq T. \tag{3}$$

Then $\mathcal{L}\{f'(t)\}$ exists for $s > c$, and

$$\mathcal{L}\{f'(t)\} = s\mathcal{L}\{f(t)\} - f(0) = sF(s) - f(0). \tag{4}$$

∎

The function f is called **piecewise smooth** on the bounded interval $[a, b]$ if it is piecewise continuous on $[a, b]$ and differentiable except at finitely many points, with $f'(t)$ being piecewise continuous on $[a, b]$. We may assign arbitrary values to $f(t)$ at the isolated points at which f is not differentiable. We say that f is piecewise smooth for $t \geqq 0$ if it is piecewise smooth on every bounded subinterval of $[0, +\infty)$. Figure 7.2.1 indicates how "corners" on the graph of f correspond to discontinuities in its derivative f'.

The main idea of the proof of Theorem 1 is exhibited best by the case in which $f'(t)$ is continuous (not merely piecewise continuous) for $t \geqq 0$. Then, beginning with the definition of $\mathcal{L}\{f'(t)\}$ and integrating by parts, we get

$$\mathcal{L}\{f'(t)\} = \int_0^\infty e^{-st} f'(t)\, dt = \left[e^{-st} f(t) \right]_{t=0}^\infty + s \int_0^\infty e^{-st} f(t)\, dt.$$

Because of (3), the integrated term $e^{-st} f(t)$ approaches zero (when $s > c$) as $t \to +\infty$, and its value at the lower limit $t = 0$ contributes $-f(0)$ to the evaluation of the preceding expression. The integral that remains is simply $\mathcal{L}\{f(t)\}$; by Theorem 2 of Section 7.1, the integral converges when $s > c$. Then $\mathcal{L}\{f'(t)\}$ exists when $s > c$, and its value is that given in Eq. (4). We will defer the case in which $f'(t)$ has isolated discontinuities to the end of this section.

Solution of Initial Value Problems

In order to transform Eq. (1), we need the transform of the second derivative as well. If we assume that $g(t) = f'(t)$ satisfies the hypotheses of Theorem 1, then that theorem implies that

$$\begin{aligned}
\mathcal{L}\{f''(t)\} = \mathcal{L}\{g'(t)\} &= s\mathcal{L}\{g(t)\} - g(0) \\
&= s\mathcal{L}\{f'(t)\} - f'(0) \\
&= s\,[s\mathcal{L}\{f(t)\} - f(0)] - f'(0),
\end{aligned}$$

and thus

$$\mathcal{L}\{f''(t)\} = s^2 F(s) - sf(0) - f'(0). \tag{5}$$

A repetition of this calculation gives

$$\mathcal{L}\{f'''(t)\} = s\mathcal{L}\{f''(t)\} - f''(0) = s^3 F(s) - s^2 f(0) - sf'(0) - f''(0). \tag{6}$$

After finitely many such steps we obtain the following extension of Theorem 1.

COROLLARY: Transforms of Higher Derivatives

Suppose that the functions $f, f', f'', \ldots, f^{(n-1)}$ are continuous and piecewise smooth for $t \geqq 0$, and that each of these functions satisfies the conditions in (3) with the same values of M and c. Then $\mathcal{L}\{f^{(n)}(t)\}$ exists when $s > c$, and

$$\begin{aligned}
\mathcal{L}\{f^{(n)}(t)\} &= s^n \mathcal{L}\{f(t)\} - s^{n-1} f(0) - s^{n-2} f'(0) - \cdots - f^{(n-1)}(0) \\
&= s^n F(s) - s^{n-1} f(0) - \cdots - sf^{(n-2)}(0) - f^{(n-1)}(0). \tag{7}
\end{aligned}$$

∎

EXAMPLE 1   Solve the initial value problem

$$x'' - x' - 6x = 0; \quad x(0) = 2, \quad x'(0) = -1.$$

Solution   With the given initial values, Eqs. (4) and (5) yield

$$\mathcal{L}\{x'(t)\} = s\mathcal{L}\{x(t)\} - x(0) = sX(s) - 2$$

and

$$\mathcal{L}\{x''(t)\} = s^2\mathcal{L}\{x(t)\} - sx(0) - x'(0) = s^2X(s) - 2s + 1,$$

where (according to our convention about notation) $X(s)$ denotes the Laplace transform of the (unknown) function $x(t)$. Hence the transformed equation is

$$[s^2X(s) - 2s + 1] - [sX(s) - 2] - 6[X(s)] = 0,$$

which we quickly simplify to

$$(s^2 - s - 6)X(s) - 2s + 3 = 0.$$

Thus

$$X(s) = \frac{2s - 3}{s^2 - s - 6} = \frac{2s - 3}{(s - 3)(s + 2)}.$$

By the method of partial fractions (of integral calculus), there exist constants A and B such that

$$\frac{2s - 3}{(s - 3)(s + 2)} = \frac{A}{s - 3} + \frac{B}{s + 2},$$

and multiplication of both sides of this equation by $(s - 3)(s + 2)$ yields the identity

$$2s - 3 = A(s + 2) + B(s - 3).$$

If we substitute $s = 3$, we find that $A = \frac{3}{5}$; substitution of $s = -2$ shows that $B = \frac{7}{5}$. Hence

$$X(s) = \mathcal{L}\{x(t)\} = \frac{\frac{3}{5}}{s - 3} + \frac{\frac{7}{5}}{s + 2}.$$

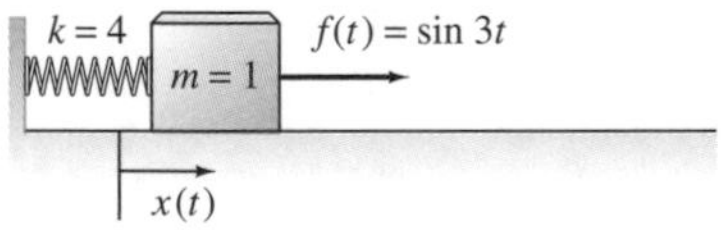

Because $\mathcal{L}^{-1}\{1/(s - a)\} = e^{at}$, it follows that

$$x(t) = \tfrac{3}{5}e^{3t} + \tfrac{7}{5}e^{-2t}$$

is the solution of the original initial value problem. Note that we did not first find the general solution of the differential equation. The Laplace transform method directly yields the desired particular solution, automatically taking into account—via Theorem 1 and its corollary—the given initial conditions.   ∎

$k = 4$ $f(t) = \sin 3t$ $m = 1$ $x(t)$

FIGURE 7.2.2. A mass-and-spring system satisfying the initial value problem in Example 2. The mass is initially at rest in its equilibrium position.

EXAMPLE 2   Solve the initial value problem

$$x'' + 4x = \sin 3t; \quad x(0) = x'(0) = 0.$$

Such a problem arises in the motion of a mass-and-spring system with external force, as shown in Fig. 7.2.2.

Solution   Because both initial values are zero, Eq. (5) yields $\mathcal{L}\{x''(t)\} = s^2X(s)$. We read the transform of $\sin 3t$ from the table in Fig. 7.1.2 (Section 7.1) and thereby get the transformed equation

$$s^2X(s) + 4X(s) = \frac{3}{x^2 + 9}.$$

Therefore

$$X(s) = \frac{3}{(s^2 + 4)(s^2 + 9)}.$$

The method of partial fractions calls for

$$\frac{3}{(s^2+4)(s^2+9)} = \frac{As+B}{s^2+4} + \frac{Cs+D}{s^2+9}.$$

The fact that there are no terms of odd degree on the left-hand side suggests that we set $A = C = 0$, because nonzero values for A or C would lead to terms of odd degree—but no such terms are present in the numerator on the left. So we replace A and C with zero, then multiply both sides by $(s^2+4)(s^2+9)$. The result is the identity

$$3 = B(s^2+9) + D(s^2+4) = (B+D)s^2 + (9B+4D).$$

When we equate coefficients of like powers of s we get the linear equations

$$B + D = 0,$$
$$9B + 4D = 3,$$

which are readily solved for $B = \frac{3}{5}$ and $D = -\frac{3}{5}$. Hence

$$X(s) = \mathcal{L}\{x(t)\} = \frac{3}{10} \cdot \frac{2}{s^2+4} - \frac{1}{5} \cdot \frac{3}{s^2+9}.$$

Because $\mathcal{L}\{\sin 2t\} = 2/(s^2+4)$ and $\mathcal{L}\{\sin 3t\} = 3/(s^2+9)$, it follows that

$$x(t) = \tfrac{3}{10} \sin 2t - \tfrac{1}{5} \sin 3t.$$

Note that the Laplace transform method again gives the solution directly, without the necessity of first finding the complementary function and a particular solution of the original nonhomogeneous differential equation. Thus nonhomogeneous equations are solved in exactly the same manner as are homogeneous equations. ■

Linear Systems

Laplace transforms are used frequently in engineering problems to solve linear systems in which the coefficients are all constants. When initial conditions are specified, the Laplace transform reduces such a linear system of differential equations to a linear system of algebraic equations in which the unknowns are the transforms of the solution functions. As Example 3 illustrates, the technique for a system is essentially the same as for a single linear differential equation with constant coefficients.

EXAMPLE 3   Solve the system

$$\begin{aligned} 2x'' &= -6x + 2y, \\ y'' &= 2x - 2y + 40\sin 3t, \end{aligned} \tag{8}$$

subject to the initial conditions

$$x(0) = x'(0) = y(0) = y'(0) = 0. \tag{9}$$

Thus the force $f(t) = 40\sin 3t$ is suddenly applied to the second mass of Fig. 7.2.3 at the time $t = 0$ when the system is at rest in its equilibrium position.

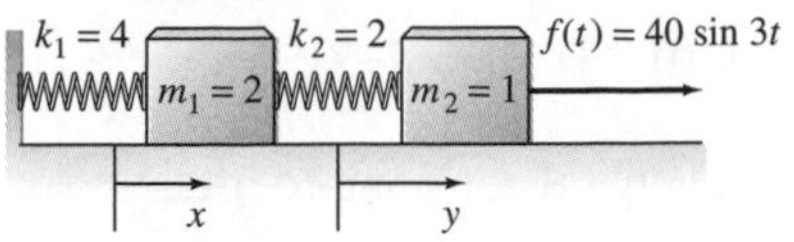

FIGURE 7.2.3. A mass-and-spring system satisfying the initial value problem in Example 3. Both masses are initially at rest in their equilibrium positions.

Solution We write $X(s) = \mathcal{L}\{x(t)\}$ and $Y(s) = \mathcal{L}\{y(t)\}$. Then the initial conditions in (9) imply that

$$\mathcal{L}\{x''(t)\} = s^2 X(s) \quad \text{and} \quad \mathcal{L}\{y''(t)\} = s^2 Y(s).$$

Because $\mathcal{L}\{\sin 3t\} = 3/(s^2 + 9)$, the transforms of the equations in (8) are the equations

$$2s^2 X(s) = -6X(s) + 2Y(s),$$

$$s^2 Y(s) = 2X(s) - 2Y(s) + \frac{120}{s^2 + 9}.$$

Thus the transformed system is

$$(s^2 + 3)X(s) \qquad - Y(s) = 0,$$

$$-2X(s) + (s^2 + 2)Y(s) = \frac{120}{s^2 + 9}. \tag{10}$$

The determinant of this pair of linear equations in $X(s)$ and $Y(s)$ is

$$\begin{vmatrix} s^2 + 3 & -1 \\ -2 & s^2 + 2 \end{vmatrix} = (s^2 + 3)(s^2 + 2) - 2 = (s^2 + 1)(s^2 + 4),$$

and we readily solve—using Cramer's rule, for instance—the system in (10) for

$$X(s) = \frac{120}{(s^2 + 1)(s^2 + 4)(s^2 + 9)} = \frac{5}{s^2 + 1} - \frac{8}{s^2 + 4} + \frac{3}{s^2 + 9} \tag{11a}$$

and

$$Y(s) = \frac{120(s^2 + 3)}{(s^2 + 1)(s^2 + 4)(s^2 + 9)} = \frac{10}{s^2 + 1} + \frac{8}{s^2 + 4} - \frac{18}{s^2 + 9}. \tag{11b}$$

The partial fraction decompositions in Eqs. (11a) and (11b) are readily found using the method of Example 2. For instance, noting that the denominator factors are linear in s^2, we can write

$$\frac{120}{(s^2 + 1)(s^2 + 4)(s^2 + 9)} = \frac{A}{s^2 + 1} + \frac{B}{s^2 + 4} + \frac{C}{s^2 + 9},$$

and it follows that

$$120 = A(s^2 + 4)(s^2 + 9) + B(s^2 + 1)(s^2 + 9) + C(s^2 + 1)(s^2 + 4). \tag{12}$$

Substitution of $s^2 = -1$ (that is, $s = i$, a zero of the factor $s^2 + 1$) in Eq. (12) gives $120 = A \cdot 3 \cdot 8$, so $A = 5$. Similarly, substitution of $s^2 = -4$ in Eq. (12) yields $B = -8$, and substitution of $s^2 = -9$ yields $C = 3$. Thus we obtain the partial fraction decomposition shown in Eq. (11a).

At any rate, the inverse Laplace transforms of the expressions in Eqs. (11a) and (11b) give the solution

$$x(t) = 5 \sin t - 4 \sin 2t + \sin 3t,$$
$$y(t) = 10 \sin t + 4 \sin 2t - 6 \sin 3t. \qquad \blacksquare$$

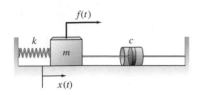

FIGURE 7.2.4. A mass-spring-dashpot system with external force $f(t)$.

The Transform Perspective

Let us regard the general constant-coefficient second-order equation as the equation of motion

$$mx'' + cx' + kx = f(t)$$

of the familiar mass-spring-dashpot system (Fig. 7.2.4). Then the transformed equation is

$$m\left[s^2 X(s) - sx(0) - x'(0)\right] + c\left[sX(s) - x(0)\right] + kX(s) = F(s). \tag{13}$$

Note that Eq. (13) is an *algebraic* equation—indeed, a linear equation—in the "unknown" $X(s)$. This is the source of the power of the Laplace transform method:

> Linear **differential** equations are transformed
> into readily solved **algebraic** equations.

If we solve Eq. (13) for $X(s)$, we get

$$X(s) = \frac{F(s)}{Z(s)} + \frac{I(s)}{Z(s)} \tag{14}$$

where

$$Z(s) = ms^2 + cs + k \quad \text{and} \quad I(s) = mx(0)s + mx'(0) + cx(0).$$

Note that $Z(s)$ depends only on the physical system itself. Thus Eq. (14) presents $X(s) = \mathcal{L}\{x(t)\}$ as the sum of a term depending only on the external force and one depending only on the initial conditions. In the case of an underdamped system, these two terms are the transforms

$$\mathcal{L}\{x_{\text{sp}}(t)\} = \frac{F(s)}{Z(s)} \quad \text{and} \quad \mathcal{L}\{x_{\text{tr}}(t)\} = \frac{I(s)}{Z(s)}$$

of the steady periodic solution and the transient solution, respectively. The only potential difficulty in finding these solutions is in finding the inverse Laplace transform of the right-hand side in Eq. (14). Much of the remainder of this chapter is devoted to finding Laplace transforms and inverse transforms. In particular, we seek those methods that are sufficiently powerful to enable us to solve problems that—unlike those in Examples 1 and 2—cannot be solved readily by the methods of Chapter 3.

Additional Transform Techniques

EXAMPLE 4   Show that

$$\mathcal{L}\{te^{at}\} = \frac{1}{(s-a)^2}.$$

Solution   If $f(t) = te^{at}$, then $f(0) = 0$ and $f'(t) = e^{at} + ate^{at}$. Hence Theorem 1 gives

$$\mathcal{L}\{e^{at} + ate^{at}\} = \mathcal{L}\{f'(t)\} = s\mathcal{L}\{f(t)\} = s\mathcal{L}\{te^{at}\}.$$

It follows from the linearity of the transform that

$$\mathcal{L}\{e^{at}\} + a\mathcal{L}\{te^{at}\} = s\mathcal{L}\{te^{at}\}.$$

Hence

$$\mathcal{L}\{te^{at}\} = \frac{\mathcal{L}\{e^{at}\}}{s-a} = \frac{1}{(s-a)^2} \tag{15}$$

because $\mathcal{L}\{e^{at}\} = 1/(s-a)$.   ∎

EXAMPLE 5 Find $\mathcal{L}\{t \sin kt\}$.

Solution Let $f(t) = t \sin kt$. Then $f(0) = 0$ and

$$f'(t) = \sin kt + kt \cos kt.$$

The derivative involves the new function $t \cos kt$, so we note that $f'(0) = 0$ and differentiate again. The result is

$$f''(t) = 2k \cos kt - k^2 t \sin kt.$$

But $\mathcal{L}\{f''(t)\} = s^2 \mathcal{L}\{f(t)\}$ by the formula in (5) for the transform of the second derivative, and $\mathcal{L}\{\cos kt\} = s/(s^2 + k^2)$, so we have

$$\frac{2ks}{s^2 + k^2} - k^2 \mathcal{L}\{t \sin kt\} = s^2 \mathcal{L}\{t \sin kt\}.$$

Finally, we solve this equation for

$$\mathcal{L}\{t \sin kt\} = \frac{2ks}{(s^2 + k^2)^2}. \tag{16}$$

This procedure is considerably more pleasant than the alternative of evaluating the integral

$$\mathcal{L}\{t \sin kt\} = \int_0^\infty t e^{-st} \sin kt \, dt. \qquad \blacksquare$$

Examples 4 and 5 exploit the fact that if $f(0) = 0$, then differentiation of f corresponds to multiplication of its transform by s. It is reasonable to expect the inverse operation of integration (antidifferentiation) to correspond to division of the transform by s.

THEOREM 2: Transforms of Integrals

If $f(t)$ is a piecewise continuous function for $t \geq 0$ and satisfies the condition of exponential order $|f(t)| \leq M e^{ct}$ for $t \geq T$, then

$$\mathcal{L}\left\{\int_0^t f(\tau) \, d\tau\right\} = \frac{1}{s} \mathcal{L}\{f(t)\} = \frac{F(s)}{s} \tag{17}$$

for $s > c$. Equivalently,

$$\mathcal{L}^{-1}\left\{\frac{F(s)}{s}\right\} = \int_0^t f(\tau) \, d\tau. \tag{18}$$

Proof: Because f is piecewise continuous, the fundamental theorem of calculus implies that

$$g(t) = \int_0^t f(\tau) \, d\tau$$

is continuous and that $g'(t) = f(t)$ where f is continuous; thus g is continuous and piecewise smooth for $t \geq 0$. Furthermore,

$$|g(t)| \leq \int_0^t |f(\tau)| \, d\tau \leq M \int_0^t e^{c\tau} \, d\tau = \frac{M}{c}(e^{ct} - 1) < \frac{M}{c} e^{ct},$$

so $g(t)$ is of exponential order as $t \to +\infty$. Hence we can apply Theorem 1 to g; this gives

$$\mathcal{L}\{f(t)\} = \mathcal{L}\{g'(t)\} = s\mathcal{L}\{g(t)\} - g(0).$$

Now $g(0) = 0$, so division by s yields

$$\mathcal{L}\left\{\int_0^t f(\tau)\, d\tau\right\} = \mathcal{L}\{g(t)\} = \frac{\mathcal{L}\{f(t)\}}{s},$$

which completes the proof. ∎

EXAMPLE 6 Find the inverse Laplace transform of

$$G(s) = \frac{1}{s^2(s-a)}.$$

Solution In effect, Eq. (18) means that we can delete a factor of s from the denominator, find the inverse transform of the resulting simpler expression, and finally integrate from 0 to t (to "correct" for the missing factor s). Thus

$$\mathcal{L}^{-1}\left\{\frac{1}{s(s-a)}\right\} = \int_0^t \mathcal{L}^{-1}\left\{\frac{1}{s-a}\right\} d\tau = \int_0^t e^{a\tau}\, d\tau = \frac{1}{a}(e^{at} - 1).$$

We now repeat the technique to obtain

$$\mathcal{L}^{-1}\left\{\frac{1}{s^2(s-a)}\right\} = \int_0^t \mathcal{L}^{-1}\left\{\frac{1}{s(s-a)}\right\} d\tau = \int_0^t \frac{1}{a}(e^{a\tau} - 1)\, d\tau$$

$$= \left[\frac{1}{a}\left(\frac{1}{a}e^{a\tau} - \tau\right)\right]_0^t = \frac{1}{a^2}(e^{at} - at - 1).$$

This technique is often a more convenient way than the method of partial fractions for finding an inverse transform of a fraction of the form $P(s)/[s^n Q(s)]$. ∎

Proof of Theorem 1: We conclude this section with the proof of Theorem 1 in the general case in which f' is merely piecewise continuous. We need to prove that the limit

$$\lim_{b \to \infty} \int_0^b e^{-st} f'(t)\, dt$$

exists and also need to find its value. With b fixed, let $t_1, t_2, \ldots, t_{k-1}$ be the points interior to the interval $[0, b]$ at which f' is discontinuous. Let $t_0 = 0$ and $t_k = b$. Then we can integrate by parts on each interval (t_{n-1}, t_n) where f' is continuous. This yields

$$\int_0^b e^{-st} f'(t)\, dt = \sum_{n=1}^k \int_{t_{n-1}}^{t_n} e^{-st} f'(t)\, dt$$

$$= \sum_{n=1}^k \left(\left[e^{-st} f(t)\right]_{t_{n-1}}^{t_n} + s\int_{t_{n-1}}^{t_n} e^{-st} f(t)\, dt\right)$$

$$= -f(0) - \sum_{n=1}^{k-1} e^{-st_n} j_f(t_n) + e^{-sb} f(b) + s\int_0^b e^{-st} f(t)\, dt,$$

$$(19)$$

where

$$j_f(t_n) = f(t_n+) - f(t_n-) \tag{20}$$

is the jump in $f(t)$ at $t = t_n$. But because f is continuous, each jump is zero: $j_f(t_n) = 0$ for all n. Moreover, if $b > c$, then $e^{-sb} f(b) \to 0$ as $b \to +\infty$. Therefore when we take the limit in (16) as $b \to +\infty$, we get the desired result:

$$\mathcal{L}\{f'(t)\} = s\mathcal{L}\{f(t)\} - f(0).$$ ∎

Extension of Theorem 1

Suppose that the original function $f(t)$ is itself only piecewise continuous (instead of continuous), with its (finite jump) discontinuities located at the points t_1, t_2, $t_3, \ldots$ Assuming that $\mathcal{L}\{f'(t)\}$ exists, when we take the limit in (19) as $b \to +\infty$, we get

$$\mathcal{L}\{f'(t)\} = sF(s) - f(0) - \sum_{n=1}^{\infty} e^{-st_n} j_f(t_n). \qquad (21)$$

EXAMPLE 7   Let $f(t) = 1 + [\![t]\!]$ be the unit staircase function; its graph is shown in Fig. 7.2.5. Then $f(0) = 1$, $f'(0) \equiv 0$, and $j_f(n) = 1$ for each integer $n = 1, 2, 3, \ldots$ Hence Eq. (21) yields

$$0 = sF(s) - 1 - \sum_{n=1}^{\infty} e^{-ns},$$

so the Laplace transform of $f(t)$ is

$$F(s) = \frac{1}{s} \sum_{n=1}^{\infty} e^{-ns} = \frac{1}{s(1 - e^{-s})}.$$

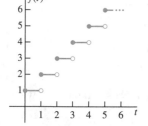

FIGURE 7.2.5. The graph of the unit staircase function of Example 7.

In the last step we used the formula for the sum of a geometric series,

$$\sum_{n=1}^{\infty} x^n = \frac{1}{1 - x},$$

with $x = e^{-s} < 1$. ∎

7.2 *Problems*

Use Laplace transforms to solve the initial value problems in Problems 1 through 16.

1. $x'' + 4x = 0$; $x(0) = 5$, $x'(0) = 0$

2. $x'' + 9x = 0$; $x(0) = 3$, $x'(0) = 4$

3. $x'' - x' - 2x = 0$; $x(0) = 0$, $x'(0) = 2$

4. $x'' + 8x' + 15x = 0$; $x(0) = 2$, $x'(0) = -3$

5. $x'' + x = \sin 2t$; $x(0) = 0 = x'(0)$

6. $x'' + 4x = \cos t$; $x(0) = 0 = x'(0)$

7. $x'' + x = \cos 3t$; $x(0) = 1$, $x'(0) = 0$

8. $x'' + 9x = 1$; $x(0) = 0 = x'(0)$

9. $x'' + 4x' + 3x = 1$; $x(0) = 0 = x'(0)$

10. $x'' + 3x' + 2x = t$; $x(0) = 0$, $x'(0) = 2$

11. $x' = 2x + y$, $y' = 6x + 3y$; $x(0) = 1$, $y(0) = -2$

12. $x' = x + 2y$, $y' = x + e^{-t}$; $x(0) = y(0) = 0$

13. $x' + 2y' + x = 0$, $x' - y' + y = 0$; $x(0) = 0$, $y(0) = 1$

14. $x'' + 2x + 4y = 0$, $y'' + x + 2y = 0$; $x(0) = y(0) = 0$, $x'(0) = y'(0) = -1$

15. $x'' + x' + y' + 2x - y = 0$, $y'' + x' + y' + 4x - 2y = 0$; $x(0) = y(0) = 1$, $x'(0) = y'(0) = 0$

16. $x' = x + z$, $y' = x + y$, $z' = -2x - z$; $x(0) = 1$, $y(0) = 0$, $z(0) = 0$

Apply Theorem 2 to find the inverse Laplace transforms of the functions in Problems 17 through 24.

17. $F(s) = \dfrac{1}{s(s - 3)}$

18. $F(s) = \dfrac{3}{s(s + 5)}$

19. $F(s) = \dfrac{1}{s(s^2 + 4)}$

20. $F(s) = \dfrac{2s + 1}{s(s^2 + 9)}$

21. $F(s) = \dfrac{1}{s^2(s^2 + 1)}$

22. $F(s) = \dfrac{1}{s(s^2 - 9)}$

23. $F(s) = \dfrac{1}{s^2(s^2 - 1)}$

24. $F(s) = \dfrac{1}{s(s + 1)(s + 2)}$

25. Apply Theorem 1 to derive $\mathcal{L}\{\sin kt\}$ from the formula for $\mathcal{L}\{\cos kt\}$.

26. Apply Theorem 1 to derive $\mathcal{L}\{\cosh kt\}$ from the formula for $\mathcal{L}\{\sinh kt\}$.

27. (a) Apply Theorem 1 to show that

$$\mathcal{L}\{t^n e^{at}\} = \frac{n}{s-a}\mathcal{L}\{t^{n-1}e^{at}\}.$$

(b) Deduce that $\mathcal{L}\{t^n e^{at}\} = n!/(s-a)^{n+1}$ for $n = 1, 2, 3, \dots$.

Apply Theorem 1 as in Example 5 to derive the Laplace transforms in Problems 28 through 30.

28. $\mathcal{L}\{t\cos kt\} = \dfrac{s^2 - k^2}{(s^2 + k^2)^2}$

29. $\mathcal{L}\{t\sinh kt\} = \dfrac{2ks}{(s^2 - k^2)^2}$

30. $\mathcal{L}\{t\cosh kt\} = \dfrac{s^2 + k^2}{(s^2 - k^2)^2}$

31. Apply the results in Example 5 and Problem 28 to show that

$$\mathcal{L}^{-1}\left\{\frac{1}{(s^2 + k^2)^2}\right\} = \frac{1}{2k^3}(\sin kt - kt\cos kt).$$

Apply the extension of Theorem 1 in Eq. (21) to derive the Laplace transforms given in Problems 32 through 37.

32. $\mathcal{L}\{u(t-a)\} = s^{-1}e^{-as}$ for $a > 0$.

33. If $f(t) = 1$ on the interval $[a, b]$ (where $0 < a < b$) and $f(t) = 0$ otherwise, then

$$\mathcal{L}\{f(t)\} = \frac{e^{-as} - e^{-bs}}{s}.$$

34. If $f(t) = (-1)^{[\![t]\!]}$ is the square wave function whose graph is shown in Fig. 7.2.6, then

$$\mathcal{L}\{f(t)\} = \frac{1}{s}\tanh\frac{s}{2}.$$

(*Suggestion*: Use the geometric series.)

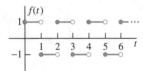

FIGURE 7.2.6. The graph of the square wave function of Problem 34.

35. If $f(t)$ is the unit on-off function whose graph is shown in Fig. 7.2.7, then

$$\mathcal{L}\{f(t)\} = \frac{1}{s(1 + e^{-s})}.$$

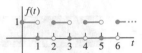

FIGURE 7.2.7. The graph of the off-on function of Problem 35.

36. If $g(t)$ is the triangular wave function whose graph is shown in Fig. 7.2.8, then

$$\mathcal{L}\{g(t)\} = \frac{1}{s^2}\tanh\frac{s}{2}.$$

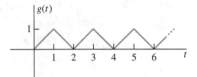

FIGURE 7.2.8. The graph of the triangular wave function of Problem 36.

37. If $f(t)$ is the sawtooth function whose graph is shown in Fig. 7.2.9, then

$$\mathcal{L}\{f(t)\} = \frac{1}{s^2} - \frac{e^{-s}}{s(1 - e^{-s})}.$$

(*Suggestion*: Note that $f'(t) \equiv 1$ where it is defined.)

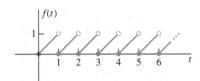

FIGURE 7.2.9. The graph of the sawtooth function of Problem 37.

7.3 TRANSLATION AND PARTIAL FRACTIONS

As illustrated by Examples 1 and 2 of Section 7.2, the solution of a linear differential equation with constant coefficients can often be reduced to the matter of finding the inverse Laplace transform of a rational function of the form

$$R(s) = \frac{P(s)}{Q(s)} \tag{1}$$

where the degree of $P(s)$ is less than that of $Q(s)$. The technique for finding $\mathcal{L}^{-1}\{R(s)\}$ is based on the same method of partial fractions that we use in elementary calculus to integrate rational functions. The following two rules describe the **partial fraction decomposition** of $R(s)$, in terms of the factorization of the denominator $Q(s)$ into linear factors and irreducible quadratic factors corresponding to the real and complex zeros, respectively, of $Q(s)$.

> **RULE 1: Linear Factor Partial Fractions**

The part of the partial fraction decomposition of $R(s)$ corresponding to the linear factor $s - a$ of multiplicity n is a sum of n partial fractions, having the form

$$\frac{A_1}{s - a} + \frac{A_2}{(s - a)^2} + \cdots + \frac{A_n}{(s - a)^n}, \tag{2}$$

where $A_1, A_2, \ldots,$ and A_n are constants. ■

> **RULE 2: Quadratic Factor Partial Fractions**

The part of the partial fraction decomposition corresponding to the irreducible quadratic factor $(s - a)^2 + b^2$ of multiplicity n is a sum of n partial fractions, having the form

$$\frac{A_1 s + B_1}{(s - a)^2 + b^2} + \frac{A_2 s + B_2}{[(s - a)^2 + b^2]^2} + \cdots + \frac{A_n s + B_n}{[(s - a)^2 + b^2]^n}, \tag{3}$$

where $A_1, A_2, \ldots, A_n, B_1, B_2, \ldots,$ and B_n are constants. ■

Finding $\mathcal{L}^{-1}\{R(s)\}$ involves two steps. First we must find the partial fraction decomposition of $R(s)$, and then we must find the inverse Laplace transform of each of the individual partial fractions of the types that appear in (2) and (3). The latter step is based on the following elementary property of Laplace transforms.

> **THEOREM 1: Translation on the s-Axis**

If $F(s) = \mathcal{L}\{f(t)\}$ exists for $s > c$, then $\mathcal{L}\{e^{at} f(t)\}$ exists for $s > a + c$, and

$$\mathcal{L}\{e^{at} f(t)\} = F(s - a). \tag{4}$$

Equivalently,

$$\mathcal{L}^{-1}\{F(s - a)\} = e^{at} f(t). \tag{5}$$

Thus the translation $s \to s - a$ in the transform corresponds to multiplication of the original function of t by e^{at}.

Proof: If we simply replace s with $s - a$ in the definition of $F(s) = \mathcal{L}\{f(t)\}$, we obtain

$$F(s - a) = \int_0^\infty e^{-(s-a)t} f(t)\, dt = \int_0^\infty e^{-st} \left[e^{at} f(t) \right] dt = \mathcal{L}\{e^{at} f(t)\}.$$

This is Eq. (4), and it is clear that Eq. (5) is the same. ■

If we apply the translation theorem to the formulas for the Laplace transforms of t^n, $\cos kt$, and $\sin kt$ that we already know—multiplying each of these functions by e^{at} and replacing s with $s - a$ in the transforms—we get the following additions to the table in Fig. 7.1.2.

$$\text{If} \quad f(t) = e^{at} t^n, \qquad \text{then} \quad F(s) = \frac{n!}{(s - a)^{n+1}}, \qquad s > a; \tag{6}$$

$$\text{If} \quad f(t) = e^{at} \cos kt, \quad \text{then} \quad F(s) = \frac{s - a}{(s - a)^2 + k^2}, \quad s > a; \tag{7}$$

$$\text{If} \quad f(t) = e^{at} \sin kt, \quad \text{then} \quad F(s) = \frac{k}{(s - a)^2 + k^2}, \quad s > a. \tag{8}$$

For ready reference, all the Laplace transforms derived in this chapter are listed in the table of transforms that appears in the endpapers.

EXAMPLE 1 Consider a mass-and-spring system with $m = \frac{1}{2}$, $k = 17$, and $c = 3$ in mks units (Fig. 7.3.1). As usual, let $x(t)$ denote the displacement of the mass m from its equilibrium position. If the mass is set in motion with $x(0) = 3$ and $x'(0) = 1$, find $x(t)$ for the resulting damped free oscillations.

Solution The differential equation is $\frac{1}{2}x'' + 3x' + 17x = 0$, so we need to solve the initial value problem

$$x'' + 6x' + 34x = 0; \quad x(0) = 3, \quad x'(0) = 1.$$

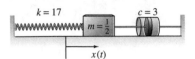

FIGURE 7.3.1. The mass-spring-dashpot system of Example 1.

We take the Laplace transform of each term of the differential equation. Because [obviously] $\mathcal{L}\{0\} \equiv 0$, we get the equation

$$\left[s^2 X(s) - 3s - 1\right] + 6\left[s X(s) - 3\right] + 34 X(s) = 0,$$

which we solve for

$$X(s) = \frac{3s + 19}{s^2 + 6s + 34} = 3 \cdot \frac{s+3}{(s+3)^2 + 25} + 2 \cdot \frac{5}{(s+3)^2 + 25}.$$

Applying the formulas in (7) and (8) with $a = -3$ and $k = 5$, we now see that

$$x(t) = e^{-3t}\left(3\cos 5t + 2\sin 5t\right).$$ ∎

Example 2 illustrates a useful technique for finding the partial fraction coefficients in the case of nonrepeated linear factors.

EXAMPLE 2 Find the inverse Laplace transform of

$$R(s) = \frac{s^2 + 1}{s^3 - 2s^2 - 8s}.$$

Solution Note that the denominator of $R(s)$ factors as $Q(s) = s(s+2)(s-4)$. Hence

$$\frac{s^2 + 1}{s^3 - 2s^2 - 8s} = \frac{A}{s} + \frac{B}{s+2} + \frac{C}{s-4}.$$

Multiplication of each term of this equation by $Q(s)$ yields

$$s^2 + 1 = A(s+2)(s-4) + Bs(s-4) + Cs(s+2).$$

When we successively substitute the three zeros $s = 0$, $s = -2$, and $s = 4$ of the denominator $Q(s)$ in this equation, we get the results

$$-8A = 1, \quad 12B = 5, \quad \text{and} \quad 24C = 17.$$

Thus $A = -\frac{1}{8}$, $B = \frac{5}{12}$, and $C = \frac{17}{24}$, so

$$\frac{s^2 + 1}{s^3 - 2s^2 - 8s} = -\frac{\frac{1}{8}}{s} + \frac{\frac{5}{12}}{s+2} + \frac{\frac{17}{24}}{s-4},$$

and therefore

$$\mathcal{L}^{-1}\left\{\frac{s^2 + 1}{s^3 - 2s^2 - 8s}\right\} = -\frac{1}{8} + \frac{5}{12}e^{-2t} + \frac{17}{24}e^{4t}.$$ ∎

Example 3 illustrates a differentiation technique for finding the partial fraction coefficients in the case of repeated linear factors.

EXAMPLE 3   Solve the initial value problem

$$y'' + 4y' + 4y = t^2; \quad y(0) = y'(0) = 0.$$

Solution   The transformed equation is

$$s^2 Y(s) + 4s Y(s) + 4Y(s) = \frac{2}{s^3}.$$

Thus

$$Y(s) = \frac{2}{s^3(s+2)^2} = \frac{A}{s^3} + \frac{B}{s^2} + \frac{C}{s} + \frac{D}{(s+2)^2} + \frac{E}{s+2}. \tag{9}$$

To find A, B, and C, we multiply both sides by s^3 to obtain

$$\frac{2}{(s+2)^2} = A + Bs + Cs^2 + s^3 F(s), \tag{10}$$

where $F(s) = D(s+2)^{-2} + E(s+2)^{-1}$ is the sum of the two partial fractions corresponding to $(s+2)^2$. Substitution of $s = 0$ in Eq. (10) yields $A = \frac{1}{2}$. To find B and C, we differentiate Eq. (10) twice to obtain

$$\frac{-4}{(s+2)^3} = B + 2Cs + 3s^2 F(s) + s^3 F'(s) \tag{11}$$

and

$$\frac{12}{(s+2)^4} = 2C + 6s F(s) + 6s^2 F'(s) + s^3 F''(s). \tag{12}$$

Now substitution of $s = 0$ in Eq. (11) yields $B = -\frac{1}{2}$, and substitution of $s = 0$ in Eq. (12) yields $C = \frac{3}{8}$.

To find D and E, we multiply each side in Eq. (9) by $(s+2)^2$ to get

$$\frac{2}{s^3} = D + E(s+2) + (s+2)^2 G(s), \tag{13}$$

where $G(s) = As^{-3} + Bs^{-2} + Cs^{-1}$, and then differentiate to obtain

$$-\frac{6}{s^4} = E + 2(s+2)G(s) + (s+2)^2 G'(s). \tag{14}$$

Substitution of $s = -2$ in Eqs. (13) and (14) now yields $D = -\frac{1}{4}$ and $E = -\frac{3}{8}$. Thus

$$Y(s) = \frac{\frac{1}{2}}{s^3} - \frac{\frac{1}{2}}{s^2} + \frac{\frac{3}{8}}{s} - \frac{\frac{1}{4}}{(s+2)^2} - \frac{\frac{3}{8}}{s+2},$$

so the solution of the given initial value problem is

$$y(t) = \tfrac{1}{4}t^2 - \tfrac{1}{2}t + \tfrac{3}{8} - \tfrac{1}{4}te^{-2t} - \tfrac{3}{8}e^{-2t}. \qquad \blacksquare$$

Examples 4, 5, and 6 illustrate techniques for dealing with quadratic factors in partial fraction decompositions.

EXAMPLE 4   Consider the mass-spring-dashpot system as in Example 1, but with initial conditions $x(0) = x'(0) = 0$ and with the imposed external force $F(t) = 15 \sin 2t$. Find the resulting transient motion and steady periodic motion of the mass.

Solution The initial value problem we need to solve is

$$x'' + 6x' + 34x = 30 \sin 2t; \quad x(0) = x'(0) = 0.$$

The transformed equation is

$$s^2 X(s) + 6s X(s) + 34 X(s) = \frac{60}{s^2 + 4}.$$

Hence

$$X(s) = \frac{60}{(s^2 + 4)[(s + 3)^2 + 25]} = \frac{As + B}{s^2 + 4} + \frac{Cs + D}{(s + 3)^2 + 25}.$$

When we multiply both sides by the common denominator, we get

$$60 = (As + B)[(s + 3)^2 + 25] + (Cs + D)(s^2 + 4). \tag{15}$$

To find A and B, we substitute the zero $s = 2i$ of the quadratic factor $s^2 + 4$ in Eq. (15); the result is

$$60 = (2i A + B)[(2i + 3)^2 + 25],$$

which we simplify to

$$60 = (-24A + 30B) + (60A + 12B)i.$$

We now equate real parts and imaginary parts on each side of this equation to obtain the two linear equations

$$-24A + 30B = 60 \quad \text{and} \quad 60A + 12B = 0,$$

which are readily solved for $A = -\frac{10}{29}$ and $B = \frac{50}{29}$.

To find C and D, we substitute the zero $s = -3 + 5i$ of the quadratic factor $(s + 3)^2 + 25$ in Eq. (15) and get

$$60 = [C(-3 + 5i) + D][(-3 + 5i)^2 + 4],$$

which we simplify to

$$60 = (186C - 12D) + (30C - 30D)i.$$

Again we equate real parts and imaginary parts; this yields the two linear equations

$$186C - 12D = 60 \quad \text{and} \quad 30C - 30D = 0,$$

and we readily find their solution to be $C = D = \frac{10}{29}$.

With these values of the coefficients A, B, C, and D, our partial decomposition of $X(s)$ is

$$X(s) = \frac{1}{29}\left(\frac{-10s + 50}{s^2 + 4} + \frac{10s + 10}{(s + 3)^2 + 25}\right)$$

$$= \frac{1}{29}\left(\frac{-10s + 25 \cdot 2}{s^2 + 4} + \frac{10(s + 3) - 4 \cdot 5}{(s + 3)^2 + 25}\right).$$

After we compute the inverse Laplace transforms, we get the position function

$$x(t) = \frac{5}{29}(-2\cos 2t + 5\sin 2t) + \frac{2}{29}e^{-3t}(5\cos 5t - 2\sin 5t).$$

The terms of circular frequency 2 constitute the steady periodic forced oscillation of the mass, whereas the exponentially damped terms of circular frequency 5 constitute its transient motion, which disappears very rapidly (see Fig. 7.3.2). Note that the transient motion is nonzero even though both initial conditions are zero. ∎

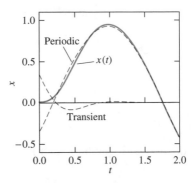

FIGURE 7.3.2. The periodic forced oscillations and transient exponentially damped motions in Example 4.

Resonance and Repeated Quadratic Factors

The following two inverse Laplace transforms are useful in inverting partial fractions that correspond to the case of repeated quadratic factors:

$$\mathcal{L}^{-1}\left\{\frac{s}{(s^2+k^2)^2}\right\} = \frac{1}{2k}t\sin kt, \tag{16}$$

$$\mathcal{L}^{-1}\left\{\frac{1}{(s^2+k^2)^2}\right\} = \frac{1}{2k^3}(\sin kt - kt\cos kt). \tag{17}$$

These follow from Example 5 and Problem 31 of Section 7.2, respectively. Because of the presence in Eqs. (16) and (17) of the terms $t\sin kt$ and $t\cos kt$, a repeated quadratic factor ordinarily signals the phenomenon of resonance in an undamped mechanical or electrical system.

EXAMPLE 5   Use Laplace transforms to solve the initial value problem

$$x'' + \omega_0^2 x = F_0\sin\omega t; \quad x(0) = 0 = x'(0)$$

that determines the undamped forced oscillations of a mass on a spring.

Solution   When we transform the differential equation, we get the equation

$$s^2 X(s) + \omega_0^2 X(s) = \frac{F_0\omega}{s^2+\omega^2}, \quad \text{so} \quad X(s) = \frac{F_0\omega}{(s^2+\omega^2)(s^2+\omega_0^2)}.$$

If $\omega \neq \omega_0$, we find without difficulty that

$$X(s) = \frac{F_0\omega}{\omega^2-\omega_0^2}\left(\frac{1}{s^2+\omega_0^2} - \frac{1}{s^2+\omega^2}\right),$$

so it follows that

$$x(t) = \frac{F_0\omega}{\omega^2-\omega_0^2}\left(\frac{1}{\omega_0}\sin\omega_0 t - \frac{1}{\omega}\sin\omega t\right).$$

But if $\omega = \omega_0$, we have

$$X(s) = \frac{F_0\omega_0}{(s^2+\omega_0^2)^2},$$

so Eq. (17) yields the resonance solution

$$x(t) = \frac{F_0}{2\omega_0^2}(\sin\omega_0 t - \omega_0 t\cos\omega_0 t). \tag{18}$$

∎

Remark: The solution curve defined in Eq. (18) bounces back and forth (see Fig. 7.3.3) between the "envelope curves" $x = \pm C(t)$ that are obtained by writing (18) in the form

$$x(t) = A(t)\cos\omega_0 t + B(t)\sin\omega_0 t$$

and then defining the usual "amplitude" $C = \sqrt{A^2+B^2}$. In this case we find that

$$C(t) = \frac{F_0}{2\omega_0^2}\sqrt{\omega_0^2 t^2 + 1}.$$

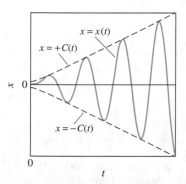

FIGURE 7.3.3. The resonance solution and its envelope curves.

This technique for constructing envelope curves of resonance solutions is illustrated further in the project material for this section.

∎

EXAMPLE 6   Solve the initial value problem

$$y^{(4)} + 2y'' + y = 4te^t; \quad y(0) = y'(0) = y''(0) = y^{(3)}(0) = 0.$$

Solution   First we observe that

$$\mathcal{L}\{y''(t)\} = s^2 Y(s), \quad \mathcal{L}\{y^{(4)}(t)\} = s^4 Y(s), \quad \text{and} \quad \mathcal{L}\{te^t\} = \frac{1}{(s-1)^2}.$$

Hence the transformed equation is

$$(s^4 + 2s^2 + 1)Y(s) = \frac{4}{(s-1)^2}.$$

Thus our problem is to find the inverse transform of

$$Y(s) = \frac{4}{(s-1)^2(s^2+1)^2}$$

$$= \frac{A}{(s-1)^2} + \frac{B}{s-1} + \frac{Cs+D}{(s^2+1)^2} + \frac{Es+F}{s^2+1}. \tag{19}$$

If we multiply by the common denominator $(s-1)^2(s^2+1)^2$, we get the equation

$$A(s^2+1)^2 + B(s-1)(s^2+1)^2 + Cs(s-1)^2$$
$$+ D(s-1)^2 + Es(s-1)^2(s^2+1) + F(s-1)^2(s^2+1) = 4. \tag{20}$$

Upon substituting $s = 1$ we find that $A = 1$.

Equation (20) is an identity that holds for all values of s. To find the values of the remaining coefficients, we substitute in succession the values $s = 0$, $s = -1$, $s = 2$, $s = -2$, and $s = 3$ in Eq. (20). This yields the system

$$\begin{aligned}
-B \quad\quad + D \quad\quad + F &= 3, \\
-8B - 4C + 4D - 8E + 8F &= 0, \\
25B + 2C + D + 10E + 5F &= -21, \\
-75B - 18C + 9D - 90E + 45F &= -21, \\
200B + 12C + 4D + 120E + 40F &= -96
\end{aligned} \tag{21}$$

of five linear equations in B, C, D, E, and F. With the aid of a calculator programmed to solve linear systems, we find that $B = -2$, $C = 2$, $D = 0$, $E = 2$, and $F = 1$.

We now substitute in Eq. (18) the coefficients we have found, and thus obtain

$$Y(s) = \frac{1}{(s-1)^2} - \frac{2}{s-1} + \frac{2s}{(s^2+1)^2} + \frac{2s+1}{s^2+1}.$$

Recalling Eq. (16), the translation property, and the familiar transforms of $\cos t$ and $\sin t$, we see finally that the solution of the given initial value problem is

$$y(t) = (t-2)e^t + (t+1)\sin t + 2\cos t. \quad \blacksquare$$

7.3 *Problems*

Apply the translation theorem to find the Laplace transforms of the functions in Problems 1 through 4.

1. $f(t) = t^4 e^{\pi t}$

2. $f(t) = t^{3/2} e^{-4t}$

3. $f(t) = e^{-2t} \sin 3\pi t$

4. $f(t) = e^{-t/2} \cos 2 \left(t - \frac{1}{8}\pi \right)$

Apply the translation theorem to find the inverse Laplace transforms of the functions in Problems 5 through 10.

5. $F(s) = \dfrac{3}{2s-4}$

6. $F(s) = \dfrac{s-1}{(s+1)^3}$

7. $F(s) = \dfrac{1}{s^2 + 4s + 4}$

8. $F(s) = \dfrac{s + 2}{s^2 + 4s + 5}$

9. $F(s) = \dfrac{3s + 5}{s^2 - 6s + 25}$

10. $F(s) = \dfrac{2s - 3}{9s^2 - 12s + 20}$

Use partial fractions to find the inverse Laplace transforms of the functions in Problems 11 through 22.

11. $F(s) = \dfrac{1}{s^2 - 4}$

12. $F(s) = \dfrac{5s - 6}{s^2 - 3s}$

13. $F(s) = \dfrac{5 - 2s}{s^2 + 7s + 10}$

14. $F(s) = \dfrac{5s - 4}{s^3 - s^2 - 2s}$

15. $F(s) = \dfrac{1}{s^3 - 5s^2}$

16. $F(s) = \dfrac{1}{(s^2 + s - 6)^2}$

17. $F(s) = \dfrac{1}{s^4 - 16}$

18. $F(s) = \dfrac{s^3}{(s - 4)^4}$

19. $F(s) = \dfrac{s^2 - 2s}{s^4 + 5s^2 + 4}$

20. $F(s) = \dfrac{1}{s^4 - 8s^2 + 16}$

21. $F(s) = \dfrac{s^2 + 3}{(s^2 + 2s + 2)^2}$

22. $F(s) = \dfrac{2s^3 - s^2}{(4s^2 - 4s + 5)^2}$

Use the factorization

$$s^4 + 4a^4 = (s^2 - 2as + 2a^2)(s^2 + 2as + 2a^2)$$

to derive the inverse Laplace transforms listed in Problems 23 through 26.

23. $\mathcal{L}^{-1}\left\{\dfrac{s^3}{s^4 + 4a^4}\right\} = \cosh at \cos at$

24. $\mathcal{L}^{-1}\left\{\dfrac{s}{s^4 + 4a^4}\right\} = \dfrac{1}{2a^2} \sinh at \sin at$

25. $\mathcal{L}^{-1}\left\{\dfrac{s^2}{s^4 + 4a^4}\right\} = \dfrac{1}{2a}(\cosh at \sin at + \sinh at \cos at)$

26. $\mathcal{L}^{-1}\left\{\dfrac{1}{s^4 + 4a^4}\right\} = \dfrac{1}{4a^3}(\cosh at \sin at - \sinh at \cos at)$

Use Laplace transforms to solve the initial value problems in Problems 27 through 38.

27. $x'' + 6x' + 25x = 0;\ x(0) = 2,\ x'(0) = 3$

28. $x'' - 6x' + 8x = 2;\ x(0) = x'(0) = 0$

29. $x'' - 4x = 3t;\ x(0) = x'(0) = 0$

30. $x'' + 4x' + 8x = e^{-t};\ x(0) = x'(0) = 0$

31. $x^{(3)} + x'' - 6x' = 0;\ x(0) = 0,\ x'(0) = x''(0) = 1$

32. $x^{(4)} - x = 0;\ x(0) = 1,\ x'(0) = x''(0) = x^{(3)}(0) = 0$

33. $x^{(4)} + x = 0;\ x(0) = x'(0) = x''(0) = 0,\ x^{(3)}(0) = 1$

34. $x^{(4)} + 13x'' + 36x = 0;\ x(0) = x''(0) = 0,\ x'(0) = 2,$ $x^{(3)}(0) = -13$

35. $x^{(4)} + 8x'' + 16x = 0;\ x(0) = x'(0) = x''(0) = 0,$ $x^{(3)}(0) = 1$

36. $x^{(4)} + 2x'' + x = e^{2t};\ x(0) = x'(0) = x''(0) = x^{(3)}(0) = 0$

37. $x'' + 4x' + 13x = te^{-t};\ x(0) = 0,\ x'(0) = 2$

38. $x'' + 6x' + 18x = \cos 2t;\ x(0) = 1,\ x'(0) = -1$

Problems 39 and 40 illustrate two types of resonance in a mass-spring-dashpot system with given external force $f(t)$ and with the initial conditions $x(0) = x'(0) = 0$.

39. Suppose that $m = 1$, $k = 9$, $c = 0$, and $f(t) = 6\cos 3t$. Use the inverse transform given in Eq. (16) to derive the solution $x(t) = t \sin 3t$.

40. Suppose that $m = 1$, $k = 9.04$, $c = 0.4$, and $f(t) = 6e^{-t/5}\sin 3t$. Derive the solution

$$x(t) = te^{-t/5}\sin 3t.$$

Show that the maximum value of the amplitude function $A(t) = te^{-t/5}$ is $A(5) = 5/e$. Thus (as indicated in Fig. 7.3.4) the oscillations of the mass increase in amplitude during the first 5 s before being damped out as $t \to +\infty$.

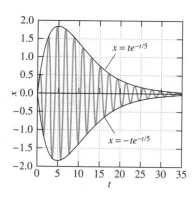

FIGURE 7.3.4. The graph of the amplitude function in Problem 40.

7.4 DERIVATIVES, INTEGRALS, AND PRODUCTS OF TRANSFORMS

The Laplace transform of the (initially unknown) solution of a differential equation is sometimes recognizable as the product of the transforms of two *known* functions. For example, when we transform the initial value problem

$$x'' + x = \cos t;\qquad x(0) = x'(0) = 0,$$

we get

$$X(s) = \dfrac{s}{(s^2 + 1)^2} = \dfrac{s}{s^2 + 1} \cdot \dfrac{1}{s^2 + 1} = \mathcal{L}\{\cos t\} \cdot \mathcal{L}\{\sin t\}.$$

This strongly suggests that there ought to be a way of combining the two functions $\sin t$ and $\cos t$ to obtain a function $x(t)$ whose transform is the *product* of *their* transforms. But obviously $x(t)$ is *not* simply the product of $\cos t$ and $\sin t$, because

$$\mathcal{L}\{\cos t \sin t\} = \mathcal{L}\left\{\tfrac{1}{2}\sin 2t\right\} = \frac{1}{s^2+4} \neq \frac{s}{(s^2+1)^2}.$$

Thus $\mathcal{L}\{\cos t \sin t\} \neq \mathcal{L}\{\cos t\} \cdot \mathcal{L}\{\sin t\}$.

Theorem 1 of this section will tell us that the function

$$h(t) = \int_0^t f(\tau)g(t-\tau)\,d\tau \tag{1}$$

has the desired property that

$$\mathcal{L}\{h(t)\} = H(s) = F(s) \cdot G(s). \tag{2}$$

The new function of t defined as the integral in (1) depends only on f and g and is called the *convolution* of f and g. It is denoted by $f * g$, the idea being that it is a new type of product of f and g, so tailored that its transform is the product of the transforms of f and g.

DEFINITION: The Convolution of Two Functions

The **convolution** $f * g$ of the piecewise continuous functions f and g is defined for $t \geq 0$ as follows:

➤
$$(f * g)(t) = \int_0^t f(\tau)g(t-\tau)\,d\tau. \tag{3}$$

∎

We will also write $f(t) * g(t)$ when convenient. In terms of the convolution product, Theorem 1 of this section says that

➤
$$\mathcal{L}\{f * g\} = \mathcal{L}\{f\} \cdot \mathcal{L}\{g\}.$$

If we make the substitution $u = t - \tau$ in the integral in (3), we see that

$$f(t) * g(t) = \int_0^t f(\tau)g(t-\tau)\,d\tau = \int_t^0 f(t-u)g(u)(-du)$$

$$= \int_0^t g(u)f(t-u)\,du = g(t) * f(t).$$

Thus the convolution is *commutative*: $f * g = g * f$.

EXAMPLE 1   The convolution of $\cos t$ and $\sin t$ is

$$(\cos t) * (\sin t) = \int_0^t \cos \tau \sin(t-\tau)\,d\tau.$$

We apply the trigonometric identity

$$\cos A \sin B = \tfrac{1}{2}[\sin(A+B) - \sin(A-B)]$$

to obtain

$$(\cos t) * (\sin t) = \int_0^t \tfrac{1}{2}[\sin t - \sin(2\tau - t)]\,d\tau$$

$$= \tfrac{1}{2}\left[\tau \sin t + \tfrac{1}{2}\cos(2\tau - t)\right]_{\tau=0}^t;$$

that is,

$$(\cos t) * (\sin t) = \tfrac{1}{2} t \sin t.$$

And we recall from Example 5 of Section 7.2 that the Laplace transform of $\tfrac{1}{2} t \sin t$ is indeed $s/(s^2 + 1)^2$. ∎

Theorem 1 is proved at the end of this section.

THEOREM 1: The Convolution Property

Suppose that $f(t)$ and $g(t)$ are piecewise continuous for $t \geq 0$ and that $|f(t)|$ and $|g(t)|$ are bounded by Me^{ct} as $t \to +\infty$. Then the Laplace transform of the convolution $f(t) * g(t)$ exists for $s > c$; moreover,

$$\mathcal{L}\{f(t) * g(t)\} = \mathcal{L}\{f(t)\} \cdot \mathcal{L}\{g(t)\} \tag{4}$$

and

$$\mathcal{L}^{-1}\{F(s) \cdot G(s)\} = f(t) * g(t). \tag{5}$$

∎

Thus we can find the inverse transform of the product $F(s) \cdot G(s)$, provided that we can evaluate the integral

$$\mathcal{L}^{-1}\{F(s) \cdot G(s)\} = \int_0^t f(\tau)g(t - \tau) \, d\tau. \tag{5'}$$

Example 2 illustrates the fact that convolution often provides a convenient alternative to the use of partial fractions for finding inverse transforms.

EXAMPLE 2 With $f(t) = \sin 2t$ and $g(t) = e^t$, convolution yields

$$\mathcal{L}^{-1}\left\{ \frac{2}{(s-1)(s^2+4)} \right\} = (\sin 2t) * e^t = \int_0^t e^{t-\tau} \sin 2\tau \, d\tau$$

$$= e^t \int_0^t e^{-\tau} \sin 2\tau \, d\tau = e^t \left[\frac{e^{-\tau}}{5}(-\sin 2\tau - 2\cos 2\tau) \right]_0^t,$$

so

$$\mathcal{L}^{-1}\left\{ \frac{2}{(s-1)(s^2+4)} \right\} = \frac{2}{5}e^t - \frac{1}{5}\sin 2t - \frac{2}{5}\cos 2t. \quad ∎$$

Differentiation of Transforms

According to Theorem 1 of Section 7.2, if $f(0) = 0$ then differentiation of $f(t)$ corresponds to multiplication of its transform by s. Theorem 2, proved at the end of this section, tells us that differentiation of the transform $F(s)$ corresponds to multiplication of the original function $f(t)$ by $-t$.

THEOREM 2: Differentiation of Transforms

If $f(t)$ is piecewise continuous for $t \geq 0$ and $|f(t)| \leq Me^{ct}$ as $t \to +\infty$, then

$$\mathcal{L}\{-tf(t)\} = F'(s) \tag{6}$$

for $s > c$. Equivalently,

$$f(t) = \mathcal{L}^{-1}\{F(s)\} = -\frac{1}{t}\mathcal{L}^{-1}\{F'(s)\}. \tag{7}$$

Repeated application of Eq. (6) gives

$$\mathcal{L}\{t^n f(t)\} = (-1)^n F^{(n)}(s) \tag{8}$$

for $n = 1, 2, 3, \ldots$. ∎

EXAMPLE 3   Find $\mathcal{L}\{t^2 \sin kt\}$.

Solution   Equation (8) gives

$$\mathcal{L}\{t^2 \sin kt\} = (-1)^2 \frac{d^2}{ds^2}\left(\frac{k}{s^2 + k^2}\right)$$

$$= \frac{d}{ds}\left[\frac{-2ks}{(s^2 + k^2)^2}\right] = \frac{6ks^2 - 2k^3}{(s^2 + k^2)^3}. \tag{9}$$

∎

The form of the differentiation property in Eq. (7) is often helpful in finding an inverse transform when the *derivative* of the transform is easier to work with than the transform itself.

EXAMPLE 4   Find $\mathcal{L}\{\tan^{-1}(1/s)\}$.

Solution   The derivative of $\tan^{-1}(1/s)$ is a simple rational function, so we apply Eq. (7):

$$\mathcal{L}^{-1}\left\{\tan^{-1}\frac{1}{s}\right\} = -\frac{1}{t}\mathcal{L}^{-1}\left\{\frac{d}{ds}\tan^{-1}\frac{1}{s}\right\} = -\frac{1}{t}\mathcal{L}^{-1}\left\{\frac{-1/s^2}{1 + (1/s)^2}\right\}$$

$$= -\frac{1}{t}\mathcal{L}^{-1}\left\{\frac{-1}{s^2 + 1}\right\} = -\frac{1}{t}(-\sin t).$$

Therefore

$$\mathcal{L}^{-1}\left\{\tan^{-1}\frac{1}{s}\right\} = \frac{\sin t}{t}. \qquad\blacksquare$$

Equation (8) can be applied to transform a linear differential equation having polynomial, rather than constant, coefficients. The result will be a differential equation involving the transform; whether this procedure leads to success depends, of course, on whether we can solve the new equation more readily than the old one.

EXAMPLE 5   Let $x(t)$ be the solution of Bessel's equation of order zero,

$$tx'' + x' + tx = 0,$$

such that $x(0) = 1$ and $x'(0) = 0$. This solution of Bessel's equation is customarily denoted by $J_0(t)$. Because

$$\mathcal{L}\{x'(t)\} = sX(s) - 1 \quad \text{and} \quad \mathcal{L}\{x''(t)\} = s^2X(s) - s,$$

and because x and x'' are each multiplied by t, application of Eq. (7) yields the transformed equation

$$-\frac{d}{ds}\left[s^2X(s) - s\right] + [sX(s) - 1] - \frac{d}{ds}[X(s)] = 0.$$

The result of differentiation and simplification is the differential equation

$$(s^2 + 1)X'(s) + sX(s) = 0.$$

This equation is separable—

$$\frac{X'(s)}{X(s)} = -\frac{s}{s^2 + 1};$$

its general solution is

$$X(s) = \frac{C}{\sqrt{s^2 + 1}}.$$

In Problem 39 we outline the argument that $C = 1$. Because $X(s) = \mathcal{L}\{J_0(t)\}$, it follows that

$$\mathcal{L}\{J_0(t)\} = \frac{1}{\sqrt{s^2 + 1}}. \tag{10}$$

∎

Integration of Transforms

Differentiation of $F(s)$ corresponds to multiplication of $f(t)$ by t (together with a change of sign). It is therefore natural to expect that integration of $F(s)$ will correspond to division of $f(t)$ by t. Theorem 3, proved at the end of this section, confirms this, provided that the resulting quotient $f(t)/t$ remains well behaved as $t \to 0$ from the right; that is, provided that

$$\lim_{t \to 0^+} \frac{f(t)}{t} \quad \text{exists and is finite.} \tag{11}$$

THEOREM 3: Integration of Transforms

Suppose that $f(t)$ is piecewise continuous for $t \geq 0$, that $f(t)$ satisfies the condition in (11), and that $|f(t)| \leq Me^{ct}$ as $t \to +\infty$. Then

$$\mathcal{L}\left\{\frac{f(t)}{t}\right\} = \int_s^\infty F(\sigma)\,d\sigma \tag{12}$$

for $s > c$. Equivalently,

$$f(t) = \mathcal{L}^{-1}\{F(s)\} = t\mathcal{L}^{-1}\left\{\int_s^\infty F(\sigma)\,d\sigma\right\}. \tag{13}$$

∎

EXAMPLE 6   Find $\mathcal{L}\{(\sinh t)/t\}$.

Solution   We first verify that the condition in (11) holds:

$$\lim_{t \to 0} \frac{\sinh t}{t} = \lim_{t \to 0} \frac{e^t - e^{-t}}{2t} = \lim_{t \to 0} \frac{e^t + e^{-t}}{2} = 1,$$

with the aid of l'Hôpital's rule. Then Eq. (12), with $f(t) = \sinh t$, yields

$$\mathcal{L}\left\{\frac{\sinh t}{t}\right\} = \int_s^\infty \mathcal{L}\{\sinh t\}\,d\sigma = \int_s^\infty \frac{d\sigma}{\sigma^2 - 1}$$

$$= \frac{1}{2}\int_s^\infty \left(\frac{1}{\sigma - 1} - \frac{1}{\sigma + 1}\right)d\sigma = \frac{1}{2}\left[\ln\frac{\sigma - 1}{\sigma + 1}\right]_s^\infty.$$

Therefore,

$$\mathcal{L}\left\{\frac{\sinh t}{t}\right\} = \frac{1}{2}\ln\frac{s+1}{s-1},$$

because $\ln 1 = 0$. ∎

The form of the integration property in Eq. (13) is often helpful in finding an inverse transform when the indefinite *integral* of the transform is easier to handle than the transform itself.

EXAMPLE 7   Find $\mathcal{L}^{-1}\{2s/(s^2-1)^2\}$.

Solution   We could use partial fractions, but it is much simpler to apply Eq. (13). This gives

$$\mathcal{L}^{-1}\left\{\frac{2s}{(s^2-1)^2}\right\} = t\,\mathcal{L}^{-1}\left\{\int_s^\infty \frac{2\sigma}{(\sigma^2-1)^2}\,d\sigma\right\}$$

$$= t\,\mathcal{L}^{-1}\left\{\left[\frac{-1}{\sigma^2-1}\right]_s^\infty\right\} = t\,\mathcal{L}^{-1}\left\{\frac{1}{s^2-1}\right\},$$

and therefore

$$\mathcal{L}^{-1}\left\{\frac{2s}{(s^2-1)^2}\right\} = t\sinh t. ∎$$

*Proofs of Theorems

Proof of Theorem 1: The transforms $F(s)$ and $G(s)$ exist when $s > c$ by Theorem 2 of Section 7.1. The definition of the Laplace transform gives

$$G(s) = \int_0^\infty e^{-su}g(u)\,du = \int_{-\tau}^\infty e^{-s(t-\tau)}g(t-\tau)\,dt \quad (u = t-\tau),$$

and therefore

$$G(s) = e^{s\tau}\int_0^\infty e^{-st}g(t-\tau)\,dt,$$

because we may *define* $f(t)$ and $g(t)$ to be zero for $t < 0$. Then

$$F(s)G(s) = G(s)\int_0^\infty e^{-s\tau}f(\tau)\,d\tau = \int_0^\infty e^{-s\tau}f(\tau)G(s)\,d\tau$$

$$= \int_0^\infty e^{-s\tau}f(\tau)\left(e^{s\tau}\int_0^\infty e^{-st}g(t-\tau)\,dt\right)d\tau$$

$$= \int_0^\infty \left(\int_0^\infty e^{-st}f(\tau)g(t-\tau)\,dt\right)d\tau.$$

Now our hypotheses on f and g imply that the order of integration may be reversed. (The proof of this requires a discussion of uniform convergence of improper integrals, and can be found in Chapter 2 of Churchill's *Operational Mathematics*, 3rd ed. (New York: McGraw-Hill, 1972).) Hence

$$F(s)G(s) = \int_0^\infty \left(\int_0^\infty e^{-st}f(\tau)g(t-\tau)\,d\tau\right)dt$$

$$= \int_0^\infty e^{-st}\left(\int_0^t f(\tau)g(t-\tau)\,d\tau\right)dt$$

$$= \int_0^\infty e^{-st}[f(t) * g(t)]\,dt,$$

and therefore,

$$F(s)G(s) = \mathcal{L}\{f(t) * g(t)\}.$$

We replace the upper limit of the inner integral with t because $g(t-\tau) = 0$ whenever $\tau > t$. This completes the proof of Theorem 1.

Proof of Theorem 2: Because

$$F(s) = \int_0^\infty e^{-st} f(t)\,dt,$$

differentiation under the integral sign yields

$$F(s) = \frac{d}{ds} \int_0^\infty e^{-st} f(t)\,dt$$

$$= \int_0^\infty \frac{d}{ds}\left[e^{-st} f(t)\right]\,dt = \int_0^\infty e^{-st}\left[-tf(t)\right]\,dt;$$

thus

$$F'(s) = \mathcal{L}\{-tf(t)\},$$

which is Eq. (6). We obtain Eq. (7) by applying $\mathcal{L}^{-1}$ and then dividing by $-t$. The validity of differentiation under the integral sign depends on uniform convergence of the resulting integral; this is discussed in Chapter 2 of the book by Churchill just mentioned.

Proof of Theorem 3: By definition,

$$F(\sigma) = \int_0^\infty e^{-\sigma t} f(t)\,dt.$$

So integration of $F(\sigma)$ from s to $+\infty$ gives

$$\int_s^\infty F(\sigma)\,d\sigma = \int_s^\infty \left(\int_0^\infty e^{-\sigma t} f(t)\,dt\right)d\sigma.$$

Under the hypotheses of the theorem, the order of integration may be reversed (see Churchill's book again); it follows that

$$\int_s^\infty F(\sigma)\,d\sigma = \int_0^\infty \left(\int_s^\infty e^{-\sigma t} f(t)\,d\sigma\right)dt$$

$$= \int_0^\infty \left[\frac{e^{-\sigma t}}{-t}\right]_{\sigma=s}^\infty f(t)\,dt$$

$$= \int_0^\infty e^{-st}\frac{f(t)}{t}\,dt = \mathcal{L}\left\{\frac{f(t)}{t}\right\}.$$

This verifies Eq. (12), and Eq. (13) follows upon first applying $\mathcal{L}^{-1}$ and then multiplying by t.

7.4 Problems

Find the convolution $f(t) * g(t)$ in Problems 1 through 6.

1. $f(t) = t, g(t) \equiv 1$

2. $f(t) = t, g(t) = e^{at}$

3. $f(t) = g(t) = \sin t$

4. $f(t) = t^2, g(t) = \cos t$

5. $f(t) = g(t) = e^{at}$

6. $f(t) = e^{at}, g(t) = e^{bt}$ $(a \neq b)$

Apply the convolution theorem to find the inverse Laplace transforms of the functions in Problems 7 through 14.

7. $F(s) = \dfrac{1}{s(s-3)}$

8. $F(s) = \dfrac{1}{s(s^2+4)}$

9. $F(s) = \dfrac{1}{(s^2+9)^2}$

10. $F(s) = \dfrac{1}{s^2(s^2+k^2)}$

11. $F(s) = \dfrac{s^2}{(s^2+4)^2}$

12. $F(s) = \dfrac{1}{s(s^2+4s+5)}$

13. $F(s) = \dfrac{s}{(s-3)(s^2+1)}$

14. $F(s) = \dfrac{s}{s^4+5s^2+4}$

In Problems 15 through 22, apply either Theorem 2 or Theorem 3 to find the Laplace transform of $f(t)$.

15. $f(t) = t \sin 3t$

16. $f(t) = t^2 \cos 2t$

17. $f(t) = te^{2t} \cos 3t$

18. $f(t) = te^{-t} \sin^2 t$

19. $f(t) = \dfrac{\sin t}{t}$

20. $f(t) = \dfrac{1 - \cos 2t}{t}$

21. $f(t) = \dfrac{e^{3t} - 1}{t}$

22. $f(t) = \dfrac{e^t - e^{-t}}{t}$

Find the inverse transforms of the functions in Problems 23 through 28.

23. $F(s) = \ln \dfrac{s-2}{s+2}$

24. $F(s) = \ln \dfrac{s^2+1}{s^2+4}$

25. $F(s) = \ln \dfrac{s^2+1}{(s+2)(s-3)}$

26. $F(s) = \tan^{-1} \dfrac{3}{s+2}$

27. $F(s) = \ln\left(1 + \dfrac{1}{s^2}\right)$

28. $F(s) = \dfrac{s}{(s^2+1)^3}$

In Problems 29 through 34, transform the given differential equation to find a nontrivial solution such that $x(0) = 0$.

29. $tx'' + (t-2)x' + x = 0$

30. $tx'' + (3t-1)x' + 3x = 0$

31. $tx'' - (4t+1)x' + 2(2t+1)x = 0$

32. $tx'' + 2(t-1)x' - 2x = 0$

33. $tx'' - 2x' + tx = 0$

34. $tx'' + (4t-2)x' + (13t-4)x = 0$

35. Apply the convolution theorem to show that

$$\mathcal{L}^{-1}\left\{\dfrac{1}{(s-1)\sqrt{s}}\right\} = \dfrac{2e^t}{\sqrt{\pi}} \int_0^{\sqrt{t}} e^{-u^2}\, du = e^t \operatorname{erf}\sqrt{t}.$$

(*Suggestion*: Substitute $u = \sqrt{t}$.)

In Problems 36 through 38, apply the convolution theorem to derive the indicated solution $x(t)$ of the given differential equation with initial conditions $x(0) = x'(0) = 0$.

36. $x'' + 4x = f(t)$; $x(t) = \dfrac{1}{2}\displaystyle\int_0^t f(t-\tau)\sin 2\tau\, d\tau$

37. $x'' + 2x' + x = f(t)$; $x(t) = \displaystyle\int_0^t \tau e^{-\tau} f(t-\tau)\, d\tau$

38. $x'' + 4x' + 13x = f(t)$;

$$x(t) = \dfrac{1}{3}\int_0^t f(t-\tau)e^{-2\tau}\sin 3\tau\, d\tau$$

Termwise Inverse Transformation of Series

In Chapter 2 of Churchill's *Operational Mathematics*, the following theorem is proved. Suppose that $f(t)$ is continuous for $t \geq 0$, that $f(t)$ is of exponential order as $t \to +\infty$, and that

$$F(s) = \sum_{n=0}^{\infty} \dfrac{a_n}{s^{n+k+1}}$$

where $0 \leq k < 1$ and the series converges absolutely for $s > c$. Then

$$f(t) = \sum_{n=0}^{\infty} \dfrac{a_n t^{n+k}}{\Gamma(n+k+1)}.$$

Apply this result in Problems 39 through 41.

39. In Example 5 it was shown that

$$\mathcal{L}\{J_0(t)\} = \dfrac{C}{\sqrt{s^2+1}} = \dfrac{C}{s}\left(1 + \dfrac{1}{s^2}\right)^{-1/2}.$$

Expand with the aid of the binomial series and then compute the inverse transformation term by term to obtain

$$J_0(t) = C\sum_{n=0}^{\infty} \dfrac{(-1)^n t^{2n}}{2^{2n}(n!)^2}.$$

Finally, note that $J_0(0) = 1$ implies that $C = 1$.

40. Expand the function $F(s) = s^{-1/2}e^{-1/s}$ in powers of s^{-1} to show that

$$\mathcal{L}^{-1}\left\{\dfrac{1}{\sqrt{s}}e^{-1/s}\right\} = \dfrac{1}{\sqrt{\pi t}}\cos 2\sqrt{t}.$$

41. Show that

$$\mathcal{L}^{-1}\left\{\dfrac{1}{s}e^{-1/s}\right\} = J_0\left(2\sqrt{t}\right).$$

7.5 PERIODIC AND PIECEWISE CONTINUOUS INPUT FUNCTIONS

Mathematical models of mechanical or electrical systems often involve functions with discontinuities corresponding to external forces that are turned abruptly on or off. One such simple off-on function is the **unit step function** at $t = a$; its formula is

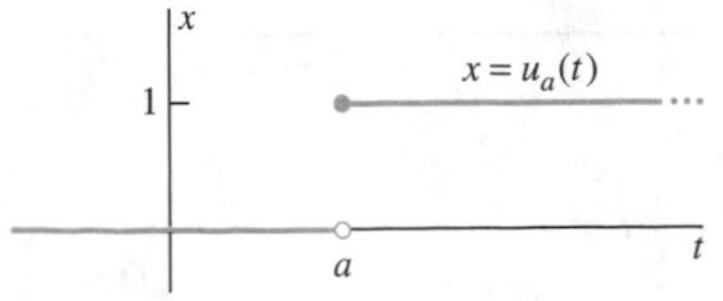

$$u_a(t) = u(t-a) = \begin{cases} 0 & \text{if } t < a, \\ 1 & \text{if } t \geq a, \end{cases} \tag{1}$$

FIGURE 7.5.1. The graph of the unit step function at $t = a$.

and its graph appears in Fig. 7.5.1.

In Example 8 of Section 7.1 we saw that if $a \geq 0$, then

$$\mathcal{L}\{u(t - a)\} = \frac{e^{-as}}{s}. \tag{2}$$

Because $\mathcal{L}\{u(t)\} = 1/s$, Eq. (2) implies that multiplication of the transform of $u(t)$ by e^{-as} corresponds to the translation $t \to t - a$ in the original independent variable. Theorem 1 tells us that this fact, when properly interpreted, is a general property of the Laplace transformation.

THEOREM 1: Translation on the t-Axis

If $\mathcal{L}\{f(t)\}$ exists for $s > c$, then

$$\mathcal{L}\{u(t - a)f(t - a)\} = e^{-as}F(s) \tag{3a}$$

and

$$\mathcal{L}^{-1}\{e^{-as}F(s)\} = u(t - a)f(t - a) \tag{3b}$$

for $s > c + a$. ∎

Note that

$$u(t - a)f(t - a) = \begin{cases} 0 & \text{if } t < a, \\ f(t - a) & \text{if } t \geq a. \end{cases} \tag{4}$$

Thus Theorem 1 implies that $\mathcal{L}^{-1}\{e^{-as}F(s)\}$ is the function whose graph for $t \geq a$ is the translation a units to the right of the graph of $f(t)$. Note that the part of the graph of $f(t)$ to the left of $t = 0$ is cut off and not translated (Fig. 7.5.2).

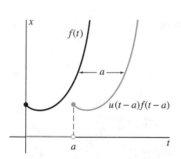

FIGURE 7.5.2. Translation of $f(t)$ a units to the right.

Proof of Theorem 1: From the definition of $\mathcal{L}\{f(t)\}$, we get

$$e^{-as}F(s) = e^{-as}\int_0^\infty e^{-s\tau}f(\tau)\,d\tau = \int_0^\infty e^{-s(\tau+a)}f(\tau)\,d\tau.$$

The substitution $t = \tau + a$ then yields

$$e^{-as}F(s) = \int_a^\infty e^{-st}f(t - a)\,dt.$$

From Eq. (4) we see that this is the same as

$$e^{-as}F(s) = \int_0^\infty e^{-st}u(t - a)f(t - a)\,dt = \mathcal{L}\{u(t - a)f(t - a)\},$$

because $u(t - a)f(t - a) = 0$ for $t < a$. This completes the proof of Theorem 1. ∎

EXAMPLE 1 With $f(t) = \frac{1}{2}t^2$, Theorem 1 gives

$$\mathcal{L}^{-1}\left\{\frac{e^{-as}}{s^3}\right\} = u(t - a)\frac{1}{2}(t - a)^2 = \begin{cases} 0 & \text{if } t < a, \\ \frac{1}{2}(t - a)^2 & \text{if } t \geq a \end{cases} \quad \text{(Fig. 7.5.3)}.$$

EXAMPLE 2 Find $\mathcal{L}\{g(t)\}$ if

$$g(t) = \begin{cases} 0 & \text{if } t < 3, \\ t^2 & \text{if } t \geq 3 \end{cases} \quad \text{(Fig. 7.5.4)}.$$

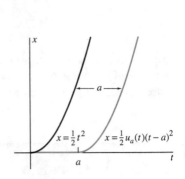

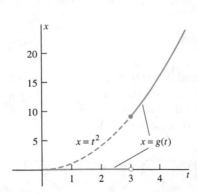

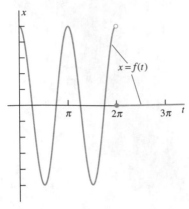

FIGURE 7.5.3. The graph of the inverse transform of Example 1.

FIGURE 7.5.4. The graph of the function $g(t)$ of Example 2.

FIGURE 7.5.5. The function $f(t)$ of Examples 3 and 4

Solution   Before applying Theorem 1, we must first write $g(t)$ in the form $u(t-3)f(t-3)$. The function $f(t)$ whose translation 3 units to the right agrees (for $t \geq 3$) with $g(t) = t^2$ is $f(t) = (t+3)^2$ because $f(t-3) = t^2$. But then

$$F(s) = \mathcal{L}\{t^2 + 6t + 9\} = \frac{2}{s^3} + \frac{6}{s^2} + \frac{9}{s},$$

so now Theorem 1 yields

$$\mathcal{L}\{g(t)\} = \mathcal{L}\{u(t-3)f(t-3)\} = e^{-3s}F(s) = e^{-3s}\left(\frac{2}{s^3} + \frac{6}{s^2} + \frac{9}{s}\right). \quad \blacksquare$$

EXAMPLE 3   Find $\mathcal{L}\{f(t)\}$ if

$$f(t) = \begin{cases} \cos 2t & \text{if } 0 \leq t < 2\pi, \\ 0 & \text{if } t \geq 2\pi \end{cases} \qquad \text{(Fig. 7.5.5).}$$

Solution   We note first that

$$f(t) = [1 - u(t-2\pi)]\cos 2t = \cos 2t - u(t-2\pi)\cos 2(t-2\pi)$$

because of the periodicity of the cosine function. Hence Theorem 1 gives

$$\mathcal{L}\{f(t)\} = \mathcal{L}\{\cos 2t\} - e^{-2\pi s}\mathcal{L}\{\cos 2t\} = \frac{s(1 - e^{-2\pi s})}{s^2 + 4}. \quad \blacksquare$$

EXAMPLE 4   A mass that weighs 32 lb (mass $m = 1$ slug) is attached to the free end of a long light spring that is stretched 1 ft by a force of 4 lb ($k = 4$ lb/ft). The mass is initially at rest in its equilibrium position. Beginning at time $t = 0$ (seconds), an external force $F(t) = \cos 2t$ is applied to the mass, but at time $t = 2\pi$ this force is turned off (abruptly discontinued) and the mass is allowed to continue its motion unimpeded. Find the resulting position function $x(t)$ of the mass.

Solution   We need to solve the initial value problem

$$x'' + 4x = f(t); \quad x(0) = x'(0) = 0,$$

where $f(t)$ is the function of Example 3. The transformed equation is

$$(s^2 + 4)X(s) = F(s) = \frac{s(1 - e^{-2\pi s})}{s^2 + 4},$$

so

$$X(s) = \frac{s}{(x^2 + 4)^2} - e^{-2\pi s} \frac{s}{(s^2 + 4)^2}.$$

Because

$$\mathcal{L}^{-1} \left\{ \frac{2s}{(s^2 + 4)^2} \right\} = \tfrac{1}{4} t \sin 2t$$

by Eq. (16) of Section 7.3, it follows from Theorem 1 that

$$x(t) = \tfrac{1}{4} t \sin 2t - u(t - 2\pi) \cdot \tfrac{1}{4}(t - 2\pi) \sin 2(t - 2\pi)$$

$$= \tfrac{1}{4} [t - u(t - 2\pi) \cdot (t - 2\pi)] \sin 2t.$$

If we separate the cases $t < 2\pi$ and $t \geq 2\pi$, we find that the position function may be written in the form

$$x(t) = \begin{cases} \tfrac{1}{4} t \sin 2t & \text{if } t < 2\pi, \\ \tfrac{1}{2}\pi \sin 2t & \text{if } t \geq 2\pi. \end{cases}$$

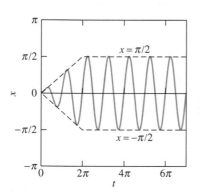

FIGURE 7.5.6. The graph of the function $x(t)$ of Example 4.

As indicated by the graph of $x(t)$ shown in Fig. 7.5.6, the mass oscillates with circular frequency $\omega = 2$ and with linearly increasing amplitude until the force is removed at time $t = 2\pi$. Thereafter, the mass continues to oscillate with the same frequency but with constant amplitude $\pi/2$. The force $F(t) = \cos 2t$ would produce pure resonance if continued indefinitely, but we see that its effect ceases immediately at the moment it is turned off. ∎

If we were to attack Example 4 with the methods of Chapter 3, we would need to solve one problem for the interval $0 \leq t < 2\pi$ and then solve a new problem with different initial conditions for the interval $t \geq 2\pi$. In such a situation the Laplace transform method enjoys the distinct advantage of not requiring the solution of different problems on different intervals.

EXAMPLE 5   Consider the RLC circuit shown in Fig. 7.5.7, with $R = 110\,\Omega$, $L = 1\,\text{H}$, $C = 0.001$ F, and a battery supplying $E_0 = 90\,\text{V}$. Initially there is no current in the circuit and no charge on the capacitor. At time $t = 0$ the switch is closed and left closed for 1 second. At time $t = 1$ it is opened and left open thereafter. Find the resulting current in the circuit.

Solution   We recall from Section 3.7 the basic series circuit equation

$$L\frac{di}{dt} + Ri + \frac{1}{C}q = e(t); \tag{5}$$

we use lowercase letters for current, charge, and voltage and reserve uppercase letters for their transforms. With the given circuit elements, Eq. (5) is

$$\frac{di}{dt} + 110i + 1000q = e(t), \tag{6}$$

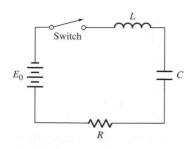

FIGURE 7.5.7. The series RLC circuit of Example 5.

where $e(t) = 90[1 - u(t - 1)]$, corresponding to the opening and closing of the switch.

In Section 3.7 our strategy was to differentiate both sides of Eq. (5), then apply the relation

$$i = \frac{dq}{dt} \tag{7}$$

to obtain the second-order equation

$$L\frac{d^2i}{dt^2} + R\frac{di}{dt} + \frac{1}{C}i = e'(t).$$

Here we do not use that method, because $e'(t) = 0$ except at $t = 1$, whereas the jump from $e(t) = 90$ when $t < 1$ to $e(t) = 0$ when $t > 1$ would seem to require that $e'(1) = -\infty$. Thus $e'(t)$ appears to have an infinite discontinuity at $t = 1$. This phenomenon will be discussed in Section 7.6. For now, we will simply note that it is an odd situation and circumvent it rather than attempt to deal with it here.

To avoid the possible problem at $t = 1$, we observe that the initial value $q(0) = 0$ and Eq. (7) yield, upon integration,

$$q(t) = \int_0^t i(\tau)\,d\tau. \tag{8}$$

We substitute Eq. (8) in Eq. (5) to obtain

$$L\frac{di}{dt} + Ri + \frac{1}{C}\int_0^t i(\tau)\,d\tau = e(t). \tag{9}$$

This is the **integrodifferential equation** of a series RLC circuit; it involves both the integral and the derivative of the unknown function $i(t)$. The Laplace transform method works well with such an equation.

In the present example, Eq. (9) is

$$\frac{di}{dt} + 110i + 1000\int_0^t i(\tau)\,d\tau = 90\,[1 - u(t-1)]. \tag{10}$$

Because

$$\mathcal{L}\left\{ \int_0^t i(\tau)\,d\tau \right\} = \frac{I(s)}{s}$$

by Theorem 2 of Section 7.2 on transforms of integrals, the transformed equation is

$$sI(s) + 110I(s) + 1000\frac{I(s)}{s} = \frac{90}{s}(1 - e^{-s}).$$

We solve this equation for $I(s)$ to obtain

$$I(s) = \frac{90(1 - e^{-s})}{s^2 + 110s + 1000}.$$

But

$$\frac{90}{s^2 + 110s + 1000} = \frac{1}{s+10} - \frac{1}{s+100},$$

so we have

$$I(s) = \frac{1}{s+10} - \frac{1}{s+100} - e^{-s}\left(\frac{1}{s+10} - \frac{1}{s+100} \right).$$

We now apply Theorem 1 with $f(t) = e^{-10t} - e^{-100t}$; thus the inverse transform is

$$i(t) = e^{-10t} - e^{-100t} - u(t-1)\left[e^{-10(t-1)} - e^{-100(t-1)} \right].$$

After we separate the cases $t < 1$ and $t \geq 1$, we find that the current in the circuit is given by

$$i(t) = \begin{cases} e^{-10t} - e^{-100t} & \text{if } t < 1, \\ e^{-10t} - e^{-10(t-1)} - e^{-100t} + e^{-100(t-1)} & \text{if } t \geq 1. \end{cases}$$

The portion $e^{-10t} - e^{-100t}$ of the solution would describe the current if the switch were left closed for all t rather than being open for $t \geq 1$.   ■

Transforms of Periodic Functions

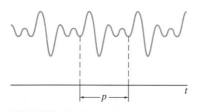

FIGURE 7.5.8. The graph of a function with period p.

Periodic forcing functions in practical mechanical or electrical systems often are more complicated than pure sines or cosines. The nonconstant function $f(t)$ defined for $t \geq 0$ is said to be **periodic** if there is a number $p > 0$ such that

$$f(t + p) = f(t) \tag{11}$$

for all $t \geq 0$. The least positive value of p (if any) for which Eq. (11) holds is called the **period** of f. Such a function is shown in Fig. 7.5.8. Theorem 2 simplifies the computation of the Laplace transform of a periodic function.

THEOREM 2: Transforms of Periodic Functions

Let $f(t)$ be periodic with period p and piecewise continuous for $t \geq 0$. Then the transform $F(s) = \mathcal{L}\{f(t)\}$ exists for $s > 0$ and is given by

$$F(s) = \frac{1}{1 - e^{-ps}} \int_0^p e^{-st} f(t) \, dt. \tag{12}$$

Proof: The definition of the Laplace transform gives

$$F(s) = \int_0^\infty e^{-st} f(t) \, dt = \sum_{n=0}^\infty \int_{np}^{(n+1)p} e^{-st} f(t) \, dt.$$

The substitution $t = \tau + np$ in the nth integral following the summation sign yields

$$\int_{np}^{(n+1)p} e^{-st} f(t) \, dt = \int_0^p e^{-s(\tau+np)} f(\tau + np) \, d\tau = e^{-nps} \int_0^p e^{-s\tau} f(\tau) \, d\tau$$

because $f(\tau + np) = f(\tau)$ by periodicity. Thus

$$F(s) = \sum_{n=0}^\infty \left(e^{-nps} \int_0^p e^{-s\tau} f(\tau) \, d\tau \right)$$

$$= \left(1 + e^{-ps} + e^{-2ps} + \cdots \right) \int_0^p e^{-s\tau} f(\tau) \, d\tau.$$

Consequently,

$$F(s) = \frac{1}{1 - e^{-ps}} \int_0^p e^{-s\tau} f(\tau) \, d\tau.$$

We use the geometric series

$$\frac{1}{1 - x} = 1 + x + x^2 + x^3 + \cdots,$$

with $x = e^{-ps} < 1$ (for $s > 0$) to sum the series in the final step. Thus we have derived Eq. (12). ∎

The principal advantage of Theorem 2 is that it enables us to find the Laplace transform of a periodic function without the necessity of an explicit evaluation of an improper integral.

EXAMPLE 6   Figure 7.5.9 shows the graph of the square wave function $f(t) = (-1)^{[\![at]\!]}$ of period $p = 2a$; $[\![x]\!]$ denotes the greatest integer not exceeding x. By Theorem 2 the Laplace transform of $f(t)$ is

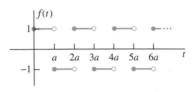

FIGURE 7.5.9. The graph of the square wave function of Example 6.

$$F(s) = \frac{1}{1 - e^{-2as}} \int_0^{2a} e^{-st} f(t)\, dt$$

$$= \frac{1}{1 - e^{-2as}} \left(\int_0^a e^{-st}\, dt + \int_a^{2a} (-1)e^{-st}\, dt \right)$$

$$= \frac{1}{1 - e^{-2as}} \left(\left[-\frac{1}{s} e^{-st} \right]_0^a - \left[-\frac{1}{s} e^{-st} \right]_a^{2a} \right)$$

$$= \frac{(1 - e^{-as})^2}{s(1 - e^{-2as})} = \frac{1 - e^{-as}}{s(1 + e^{-as})}.$$

Therefore,

$$F(s) = \frac{1 - e^{-as}}{s(1 + e^{-as})} \tag{13a}$$

$$= \frac{e^{as/2} - e^{-as/2}}{s(e^{as/2} + e^{-as/2})} = \frac{1}{s} \tanh \frac{as}{2}. \tag{13b}$$

∎

EXAMPLE 7   Figure 7.5.10 shows the graph of a triangular wave function $g(t)$ of period $p = 2a$. Because the derivative $g'(t)$ is the square wave function of Example 6, it follows from the formula in (13b) and Theorem 2 of Section 7.2 that the transform of this triangular wave function is

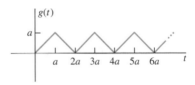

FIGURE 7.5.10. The graph of the triangular wave function of Example 7.

$$G(s) = \frac{F(s)}{s} = \frac{1}{s^2} \tanh \frac{as}{2}. \tag{14}$$

∎

EXAMPLE 8   Consider a mass-spring-dashpot system with $m = 1$, $c = 4$, and $k = 20$ in appropriate units. Suppose that the system is initially at rest at equilibrium ($x(0) = x'(0) = 0$) and that the mass is acted on beginning at time $t = 0$ by the external force $f(t)$ whose graph is shown in Fig. 7.5.11: the square wave with amplitude 20 and period 2π. Find the position function $f(t)$.

Solution   The initial value problem is

$$x'' + 4x' + 20x = f(t); \quad x(0) = x'(0) = 0.$$

The transformed equation is

$$s^2 X(s) + 4s X(s) + 20 X(s) = F(s). \tag{15}$$

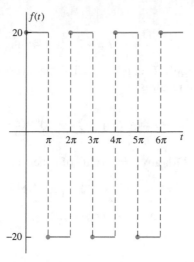

FIGURE 7.5.11. The graph of the external force function of Example 8.

From Example 6 with $a = \pi$ we see that the transform of $f(t)$ is

$$F(s) = \frac{20}{s} \cdot \frac{1 - e^{-\pi s}}{1 + e^{-\pi s}}$$

$$= \frac{20}{s} \left(1 - e^{-\pi s}\right)\left(1 - e^{-\pi s} + e^{-2\pi s} - e^{-3\pi s} + \cdots\right)$$

$$= \frac{20}{s} \left(1 - 2e^{-\pi s} + 2e^{-2\pi s} - 2e^{-3\pi s} + \cdots\right),$$

so that

$$F(s) = \frac{20}{s} + \frac{40}{s} \sum_{n=1}^{\infty} (-1)^n e^{-n\pi s}. \tag{16}$$

Substitution of Eq. (16) in Eq. (15) yields

$$X(s) = \frac{F(s)}{s^2 + 4s + 20}$$

$$= \frac{20}{s[(s+2)^2 + 16]} + 2 \sum_{n=1}^{\infty} (-1)^n \frac{20 e^{-n\pi s}}{s[(s+2)^2 + 16]}. \tag{17}$$

From the transform in Eq. (8) of Section 7.3, we get

$$\mathcal{L}^{-1} \left\{ \frac{20}{(s+2)^2 + 16} \right\} = 5 e^{-2t} \sin 4t,$$

so by Theorem 2 of Section 7.2 we have

$$g(t) = \mathcal{L}^{-1} \left\{ \frac{20}{s[(s+2)^2 + 16]} \right\} = \int_0^t 5 e^{-2\tau} \sin 4\tau \, d\tau.$$

Using a tabulated formula for $\int e^{at} \sin bt \, dt$, we get

$$g(t) = 1 - e^{-2t} \left(\cos 4t + \tfrac{1}{2} \sin 4t \right) = 1 - h(t), \tag{18}$$

where

$$h(t) = e^{-2t} \left(\cos 4t + \tfrac{1}{2} \sin 4t \right). \tag{19}$$

Now we apply Theorem 1 to find the inverse transform of the right-hand term in Eq. (17). The result is

$$x(t) = g(t) + 2 \sum_{n=1}^{\infty} (-1)^n u(t - n\pi) g(t - n\pi), \tag{20}$$

and we note that for any fixed value of t the sum in Eq. (20) is finite. Moreover,

$$g(t - n\pi) = 1 - e^{-2(t-n\pi)} \left[\cos 4(t - n\pi) + \tfrac{1}{2} \sin 4(t - n\pi) \right]$$

$$= 1 - e^{2n\pi} e^{-2t} \left(\cos 4t + \tfrac{1}{2} \sin 4t \right).$$

Therefore,

$$g(t - n\pi) = 1 - e^{2n\pi} h(t). \tag{21}$$

Hence if $0 < t < \pi$, then

$$x(t) = 1 - h(t).$$

If $\pi < t < 2\pi$, then

$$x(t) = [1 - h(t)] - 2\left[1 - e^{2\pi} h(t)\right] = -1 + h(t) - 2h(t)\left[1 - e^{2\pi}\right].$$

If $2\pi < t < 3\pi$, then

$$x(t) = [1 - h(t)] - 2\left[1 - e^{2\pi} h(t)\right] + 2\left[1 - e^{4\pi} h(t)\right]$$

$$= 1 + h(t) - 2h(t)\left[1 - e^{2\pi} + e^{4\pi}\right].$$

The general expression for $n\pi < t < (n+1)\pi$ is

$$x(t) = h(t) + (-1)^n - 2h(t)\left[1 - e^{2\pi} + \cdots + (-1)^n e^{2n\pi}\right]$$

$$= h(t) + (-1)^n - 2h(t) \frac{1 + (-1)^n e^{2(n+1)\pi}}{1 + e^{2\pi}}, \tag{22}$$

which we obtained with the aid of the familiar formula for the sum of a finite geometric progression. A rearrangement of Eq. (22) finally gives, with the aid of Eq. (19),

$$x(t) = \frac{e^{2\pi} - 1}{e^{2\pi} + 1} e^{-2t} \left(\cos 4t + \tfrac{1}{2} \sin 4t \right) + (-1)^n$$

$$- \frac{2 \cdot (-1)^n e^{2\pi}}{e^{2\pi} + 1} e^{-2(t-n\pi)} \left(\cos 4t + \tfrac{1}{2} \sin 4t \right) \tag{23}$$

for $n\pi < t < (n+1)\pi$. The first term in Eq. (23) is the transient solution

$$x_{\mathrm{tr}}(t) \approx (0.9963) e^{-2t} \left(\cos 4t + \tfrac{1}{2} \sin 4t \right) \approx (1.1139) e^{-2t} \cos(4t - 0.4636). \tag{24}$$

The last two terms in Eq. (23) give the steady periodic solution x_{sp}. To investigate it, we write $\tau = t - n\pi$ for t in the interval $n\pi < t < (n+1)\pi$. Then

$$x_{\mathrm{sp}}(t) = (-1)^n \left[1 - \frac{2 e^{2\pi}}{e^{2\pi} + 1} e^{-2\tau} \left(\cos 4\tau + \tfrac{1}{2} \sin 4\tau \right) \right] \tag{25}$$

$$\approx (-1)^n \left[1 - (2.2319) e^{-2\tau} \cos(4\tau - 0.4636) \right].$$

Figure 7.5.12 shows the graph of $x_{\mathrm{sp}}(t)$. Its most interesting feature is the appearance of periodically damped oscillations with a frequency *four times* that of the imposed force $f(t)$. In Chapter 9 (Fourier Series) we will see why a periodic external force sometimes excites oscillations at a higher frequency than the imposed frequency. ∎

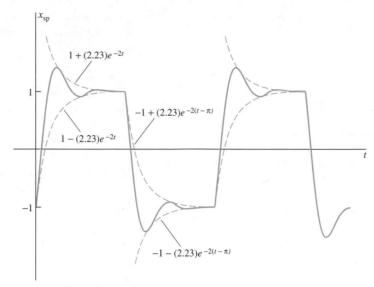

FIGURE 7.5.12. The graph of the steady periodic solution for Example 8; note the "periodically damped" oscillations with frequency four times that of the imposed force.

7.5 *Problems*

Find the inverse Laplace transform $f(t)$ of each function given in Problems 1 through 10. Then sketch the graph of f.

1. $F(s) = \dfrac{e^{-3s}}{s^2}$

2. $F(s) = \dfrac{e^{-s} - e^{-3s}}{s^2}$

3. $F(s) = \dfrac{e^{-s}}{s+2}$

4. $F(s) = \dfrac{e^{-s} - e^{2-2s}}{s-1}$

5. $F(s) = \dfrac{e^{-\pi s}}{s^2+1}$

6. $F(s) = \dfrac{se^{-s}}{s^2+\pi^2}$

7. $F(s) = \dfrac{1 - e^{-2\pi s}}{s^2+1}$

8. $F(s) = \dfrac{s(1 - e^{-2s})}{s^2+\pi^2}$

9. $F(s) = \dfrac{s(1 + e^{-3s})}{s^2+\pi^2}$

10. $F(s) = \dfrac{2s(e^{-\pi s} - e^{-2\pi s})}{s^2+4}$

Find the Laplace transforms of the functions given in Problems 11 through 22.

11. $f(t) = 2$ if $0 \leqq t < 3$; $f(t) = 0$ if $t \geqq 3$

12. $f(t) = 1$ if $1 \leqq t \leqq 4$; $f(t) = 0$ if $t < 1$ or if $t > 4$

13. $f(t) = \sin t$ if $0 \leqq t \leqq 2\pi$; $f(t) = 0$ if $t > 2\pi$

14. $f(t) = \cos \pi t$ if $0 \leqq t \leqq 2$; $f(t) = 0$ if $t > 2$

15. $f(t) = \sin t$ if $0 \leqq t \leqq 3\pi$; $f(t) = 0$ if $t > 3\pi$

16. $f(t) = \sin 2t$ if $\pi \leqq t \leqq 2\pi$; $f(t) = 0$ if $t < \pi$ or if $t > 2\pi$

17. $f(t) = \sin \pi t$ if $2 \leqq t \leqq 3$; $f(t) = 0$ if $t < 2$ or if $t > 3$

18. $f(t) = \cos \frac{1}{2}\pi t$ if $3 \leqq t \leqq 5$; $f(t) = 0$ if $t < 3$ or if $t > 5$

19. $f(t) = 0$ if $t < 1$; $f(t) = t$ if $t \geqq 1$

20. $f(t) = t$ if $t \leqq 1$; $f(t) = 1$ if $t > 1$

21. $f(t) = t$ if $t \leqq 1$; $f(t) = 2 - t$ if $1 \leqq t \leqq 2$; $f(t) = 0$ if $t > 2$

22. $f(t) = t^3$ if $1 \leqq t \leqq 2$; $f(t) = 0$ if $t < 1$ or if $t > 2$

23. Apply Theorem 2 with $p = 1$ to verify that $\mathcal{L}\{1\} = 1/s$.

24. Apply Theorem 2 to verify that $\mathcal{L}\{\cos kt\} = s/(s^2 + k^2)$.

25. Apply Theorem 2 to show that the Laplace transform of the square wave function of Fig. 7.5.13 is

$$\mathcal{L}\{f(t)\} = \frac{1}{s(1 + e^{-as})}.$$

FIGURE 7.5.13. The graph of the square wave function of Problem 25.

26. Apply Theorem 2 to show that the Laplace transform of the sawtooth function $f(t)$ of Fig. 7.5.14 is

$$F(s) = \frac{1}{as^2} - \frac{e^{-as}}{s(1 - e^{-as})}.$$

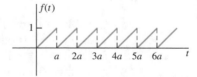

FIGURE 7.5.14. The graph of the sawtooth function of Problem 26.

27. Let $g(t)$ be the staircase function of Fig. 7.5.15. Show that $g(t) = (t/a) - f(t)$, where f is the sawtooth function of Fig. 7.5.14, and hence deduce that

$$\mathcal{L}\{g(t)\} = \frac{e^{-as}}{s(1 - e^{-as})}.$$

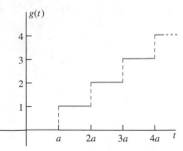

FIGURE 7.5.15. The graph of the staircase function of Problem 27.

28. Suppose that $f(t)$ is a periodic function of period $2a$ with $f(t) = t$ if $0 \leq t < a$ and $f(t) = 0$ if $a \leq t < 2a$. Find $\mathcal{L}\{f(t)\}$.

29. Suppose that $f(t)$ is the half-wave rectification of $\sin kt$, shown in Fig. 7.5.16. Show that

$$\mathcal{L}\{f(t)\} = \frac{k}{(s^2 + k^2)(1 - e^{-\pi s/k})}.$$

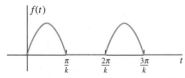

FIGURE 7.5.16. The half-wave rectification of $\sin kt$.

30. Let $g(t) = u(t - \pi/k) f(t - \pi/k)$, where $f(t)$ is the function of Problem 29 and $k > 0$. Note that $h(t) = f(t) + g(t)$ is the full-wave rectification of $\sin kt$ shown in Fig. 7.5.17. Hence deduce from Problem 29 that

$$\mathcal{L}\{h(t)\} = \frac{k}{s^2 + k^2} \coth \frac{\pi s}{2k}.$$

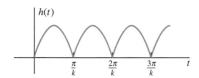

FIGURE 7.5.17. The full-wave rectification of $\sin kt$.

In Problems 31 through 35, the values of mass m, spring constant k, dashpot resistance c, and force $f(t)$ are given for a mass-spring-dashpot system with external forcing function. Solve the initial value problem

$$mx'' + cx' + kx = f(t); \quad x(0) = x'(0) = 0$$

with the given data.

31. $m = 1, k = 4, c = 0; f(t) = 1$ if $0 \leq t < \pi$, $f(t) = 0$ if $t \geq \pi$

32. $m = 1, k = 4, c = 5; f(t) = 1$ if $0 \leq t < 2$, $f(t) = 0$ if $t \geq 2$

33. $m = 1, k = 9, c = 0; f(t) = \sin t$ if $0 \leq t \leq 2\pi$, $f(t) = 0$ if $t > 2\pi$

34. $m = 1, k = 1, c = 0; f(t) = t$ if $0 \leq t < 1$, $f(t) = 0$ if $t \geq 1$

35. $m = 1, k = 4, c = 4; f(t) = t$ if $0 \leq t \leq 2$, $f(t) = 0$ if $t > 2$

In Problems 36 through 40, the values of the elements of an RLC circuit are given. Solve the initial value problem

$$L\frac{di}{dt} + Ri + \frac{1}{C}\int_0^t i(\tau)\, d\tau = e(t); \quad i(0) = 0$$

with the given impressed voltage $e(t)$.

36. $L = 0, R = 100, C = 10^{-3}; e(t) = 100$ if $0 \leq t < 1$; $e(t) = 0$ if $t \geq 1$

37. $L = 1, R = 0, C = 10^{-4}; e(t) = 100$ if $0 \leq t < 2\pi$; $e(t) = 0$ if $t \geq 2\pi$

38. $L = 1, R = 0, C = 10^{-4}; e(t) = 100\sin 10t$ if $0 \leq t < \pi; e(t) = 0$ if $t \geq \pi$

39. $L = 1, R = 150, C = 2 \times 10^{-4}; e(t) = 100t$ if $0 \leq t < 1$; $e(t) = 0$ if $t \geq 1$

40. $L = 1, R = 100, C = 4 \times 10^{-4}; e(t) = 50t$ if $0 \leq t < 1$; $e(t) = 0$ if $t \geq 1$

In Problems 41 and 42, a mass-spring-dashpot system with external force $f(t)$ is described. Under the assumption that $x(0) = x'(0) = 0$, use the method of Example 8 to find the transient and steady periodic motions of the mass.

41. $m = 1, k = 4, c = 0; f(t)$ is a square wave function with amplitude 4 and period 2π.

42. $m = 1, k = 10, c = 2; f(t)$ is a square wave function with amplitude 10 and period 2π.

7.6 IMPULSES AND DELTA FUNCTIONS

Consider a force $f(t)$ that acts only during a very short time interval $a \leq t \leq b$, with $f(t) = 0$ outside this interval. A typical example would be the *impulsive force* of a bat striking a ball—the impact is almost instantaneous. A quick surge of voltage (resulting from a lightning bolt, for instance) is an analogous electrical phenomenon. In such a situation it often happens that the principal effect of the force depends only on the value of the integral

$$p = \int_a^b f(t)\, dt \tag{1}$$

and does not depend otherwise on precisely how $f(t)$ varies with time t. The number p in Eq. (1) is called the **impulse** of the force $f(t)$ over the interval $[a, b]$.

In the case of a force $f(t)$ that acts on a particle of mass m in linear motion, integration of Newton's law

$$f(t) = mv'(t) = \frac{d}{dt}[mv(t)]$$

yields

$$p = \int_a^b \frac{d}{dt}[mv(t)]\,dt = mv(b) - mv(a). \tag{2}$$

Thus the impulse of the force is equal to the change in momentum of the particle. So if change in momentum is the only effect with which we are concerned, we need know only the impulse of the force; we need know neither the precise function $f(t)$ nor even the precise time interval during which it acts. This is fortunate, because in a situation such as that of a batted ball, we are unlikely to have such detailed information about the impulsive force that acts on the ball.

Our strategy for handling such a situation is to set up a reasonable mathematical model in which the unknown force $f(t)$ is replaced with a simple and explicit force that has the same impulse. Suppose for simplicity that $f(t)$ has impulse 1 and acts during some brief time interval beginning at time $t = a \geq 0$. Then we can select a fixed number $\epsilon > 0$ that approximates the length of this time interval and replace $f(t)$ with the specific function

$$d_{a,\epsilon}(t) = \begin{cases} \dfrac{1}{\epsilon} & \text{if } a \leq t < a + \epsilon, \\[2mm] 0 & \text{otherwise.} \end{cases} \tag{3}$$

This is a function of t, with a and ϵ being parameters that specify the time interval $[a, a + \epsilon]$. If $b \geq a + \epsilon$, then we see (Fig. 7.6.1) that the impulse of $d_{a,\epsilon}$ over $[a, b]$ is

$$p = \int_a^b d_{a,\epsilon}(t)\,dt = \int_a^{a+\epsilon} \frac{1}{\epsilon}\,dt = 1.$$

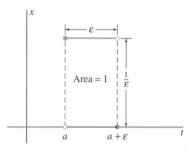

FIGURE 7.6.1. The graph of the impulse function $d_{a,\epsilon}(t)$.

Thus $d_{a,\epsilon}$ has a *unit* impulse, whatever the number ϵ may be. Essentially the same computation gives

$$\int_0^\infty d_{a,\epsilon}(t)\,dt = 1. \tag{4}$$

Because the precise time interval during which the force acts seems unimportant, it is tempting to think of an *instantaneous impulse* that occurs precisely at the instant $t = a$. We might try to model such an instantaneous unit impulse by taking the limit as $\epsilon \to 0$, thereby defining

$$\delta_a(t) = \lim_{\epsilon \to 0} d_{a,\epsilon}(t), \tag{5}$$

where $a \geq 0$. If we could also take the limit under the integral sign in Eq. (4), then it would follow that

$$\int_0^\infty \delta_a(t)\,dt = 1. \tag{6}$$

But the limit in Eq. (5) gives

$$\delta_a(t) = \begin{cases} +\infty & \text{if } t = a, \\ 0 & \text{if } t \neq a. \end{cases} \tag{7}$$

Obviously, no function can satisfy both (6) and (7)—if a function is zero except at a single point, then its integral is not 1 but zero. Nevertheless, the symbol $\delta_a(t)$ is very useful. However interpreted, it is called the **Dirac delta function** at a after the British theoretical physicist P. A. M. Dirac (1902–1984), who in the early 1930s introduced a "function" allegedly enjoying the properties in Eqs. (6) and (7).

Delta Functions as Operators

The following computation motivates the meaning that we will attach here to the symbol $\delta_a(t)$. If $g(t)$ is continuous function, then the mean value theorem for integrals implies that

$$\int_a^{a+\epsilon} g(t)\,dt = \epsilon g\left(\bar{t}\right)$$

for some point $\bar{t}$ in $[a, a + \epsilon]$. It follows that

$$\lim_{\epsilon \to 0} \int_0^\infty g(t) d_{a,\epsilon}(t)\,dt = \lim_{\epsilon \to 0} \int_a^{a+\epsilon} g(t) \cdot \frac{1}{\epsilon}\,dt = \lim_{\epsilon \to 0} g\left(\bar{t}\right) = g(a) \qquad (8)$$

by continuity of g at $t = a$. If $\delta_a(t)$ *were* a function in the strict sense of the definition, and if we could interchange the limit and the integral in Eq. (8), we therefore could conclude that

$$\int_0^\infty g(t)\delta_a(t)\,dt = g(a). \qquad (9)$$

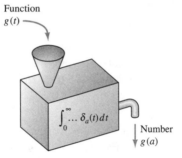

Function
$g(t)$

$\int_0^\infty \cdots \delta_a(t)\,dt$

Number
$g(a)$

FIGURE 7.6.2. A diagram illustrating how the delta function "sifts out" the value $g(a)$.

We take Eq. (9) as the *definition* (!) of the symbol $\delta_a(t)$. Although we call it the delta function, it is not a genuine function; instead, it specifies the *operation*

$$\int_0^\infty \cdots \delta_a(t)\,dt$$

which—when applied to a continuous function $g(t)$—sifts out or selects the value $g(a)$ of this function at the point $a \geq 0$. This idea is shown schematically in Fig. 7.6.2. Note that we will use the symbol $\delta_a(t)$ only in the context of integrals such as that in Eq. (9), or when it will appear subsequently in such an integral.

For instance, if we take $g(t) = e^{-st}$ in Eq. (9), the result is

$$\int_0^\infty e^{-st}\delta_a(t)\,dt = e^{-as}. \qquad (10)$$

We therefore *define* the Laplace transform of the delta function to be

$$\mathcal{L}\{\delta_a(t)\} = e^{-as} \quad (a \geq 0). \qquad (11)$$

If we write

$$\delta(t) = \delta_0(t) \quad \text{and} \quad \delta(t - a) = \delta_a(t), \qquad (12)$$

then (11) with $a = 0$ gives

$$\mathcal{L}\{\delta(t)\} = 1. \qquad (13)$$

Note that if $\delta(t)$ were an actual function, then Eq. (13) would contradict the corollary to Theorem 2 of Section 7.1. There is no problem here; $\delta(t)$ is not a function, and Eq. (13) is our *definition* of $\mathcal{L}\{\delta(t)\}$.

Delta Function Inputs

Now, finally, suppose that we are given a mechanical system whose response $x(t)$ to the external force $f(t)$ is determined by the differential equation

$$Ax'' + Bx' + Cx = f(t). \tag{14}$$

To investigate the response of this system to a unit impulse at the instant $t = a$, it seems reasonable to replace $f(t)$ with $\delta_a(t)$ and begin with the equation

$$Ax'' + Bx' + Cx = \delta_a(t). \tag{15}$$

But what is meant by the solution of such an equation? We will call $x(t)$ a solution of Eq. (15) provided that

$$x(t) = \lim_{\epsilon \to 0} x_\epsilon(t), \tag{16}$$

where $x_\epsilon(t)$ is a solution of

$$Ax'' + Bx' + Cx = d_{a,\epsilon}(t). \tag{17}$$

Because

$$d_{a,\epsilon}(t) = \frac{1}{\epsilon} \left[u_a(t) - u_{a+\epsilon}(t) \right] \tag{18}$$

is an ordinary function, Eq. (17) makes sense. For simplicity suppose the initial conditions to be $x(0) = x'(0) = 0$. When we transform Eq. (17), writing $X_\epsilon = \mathcal{L}\{x_\epsilon\}$, we get the equation

$$(As^2 + Bs + C)X_\epsilon(s) = \frac{1}{\epsilon} \left(\frac{e^{-as}}{s} - \frac{e^{-(a+\epsilon)s}}{s} \right) = \left(e^{-as} \right) \frac{1 - e^{-s\epsilon}}{s\epsilon}.$$

If we take the limit in the last equation as $\epsilon \to 0$, and note that

$$\lim_{\epsilon \to 0} \frac{1 - e^{-s\epsilon}}{s\epsilon} = 1$$

by l'Hôpital's rule, we get the equation

$$(As^2 + Bs + C)X(s) = e^{-as}, \tag{19}$$

if

$$X(s) = \lim_{\epsilon \to 0} X_\epsilon(x).$$

Note that this is precisely the same result that we would obtain if we transformed Eq. (15) directly, using the fact that $\mathcal{L}\{\delta_a(t)\} = e^{-as}$.

   On this basis it is reasonable to solve a differential equation involving a delta function by employing the Laplace transform method exactly as if $\delta_a(t)$ were an ordinary function. It is important to verify that the solution so obtained agrees with the one defined in Eq. (16), but this depends on a highly technical analysis of the limiting procedures involved; we consider it beyond the scope of the present discussion. The formal method is valid in all the examples of this section and will produce correct results in the subsequent problem set.

EXAMPLE 1   A mass $m = 1$ is attached to a spring with constant $k = 4$; there is no dashpot. The mass is released from rest with $x(0) = 3$. At the instant $t = 2\pi$ the mass is struck with a hammer, providing an impulse $p = 8$. Determine the motion of the mass.

Solution We need to solve the initial value problem

$$x'' + 4x = 8\delta_{2\pi}(t); \quad x(0) = 3, \quad x'(0) = 0.$$

We apply the Laplace transform to get

$$s^2 X(s) - 3s + 4X(s) = 8e^{-2\pi s},$$

so

$$X(s) = \frac{3s}{s^2 + 4} + \frac{8e^{-2\pi s}}{s^2 + 4}.$$

Recalling the transforms of sine and cosine, as well as the theorem on translations on the t-axis (Theorem 1 of Section 7.5), we see that the inverse transform is

$$x(t) = 3\cos 2t + 4u(t - 2\pi)\sin 2(t - 2\pi)$$
$$= 3\cos 2t + 4u_{2\pi}(t)\sin 2t.$$

Because $3\cos 2t + 4\sin 2t = 5\cos(2t - \alpha)$ with $\alpha = \tan^{-1}(4/3) \approx 0.9273$, separation of the cases $t < 2\pi$ and $t \geqq 2\pi$ gives

$$x(t) \approx \begin{cases} 3\cos 2t & \text{if } t \leqq 2\pi, \\ 5\cos(2t - 0.9273) & \text{if } t \geqq 2\pi. \end{cases}$$

The resulting motion is shown in Fig. 7.6.3. Note that the impulse at $t = 2\pi$ results in a visible discontinuity in the velocity at $t = 2\pi$, as it instantaneously increases the amplitude of the oscillations of the mass from 3 to 5. ∎

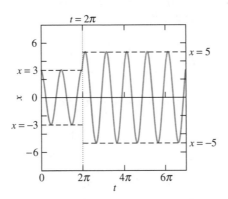

FIGURE 7.6.3. The motion of the mass of Example 1.

Delta Functions and Step Functions

It is useful to regard the delta function $\delta_a(t)$ as the derivative of the unit step function $u_a(t)$. To see why this is reasonable, consider the continuous approximation $u_{a,\epsilon}(t)$ to $u_a(t)$ shown in Fig. 7.6.4. We readily verify that

$$\frac{d}{dt}u_{a,\epsilon}(t) = d_{a,\epsilon}(t).$$

Because

$$u_a(t) = \lim_{\epsilon \to 0} u_{a,\epsilon}(t) \quad \text{and} \quad \delta_a(t) = \lim_{\epsilon \to 0} d_{a,\epsilon}(t),$$

an interchange of limits and derivatives yields

$$\frac{d}{dt}u_a(t) = \lim_{\epsilon \to 0} \frac{d}{dt}u_{a,\epsilon}(t) = \lim_{\epsilon \to 0} d_{a,\epsilon}(t),$$

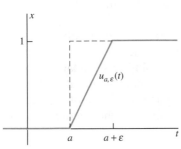

FIGURE 7.6.4. Approximation of $u_a(t)$ by $u_{a,\epsilon}(t)$.

and therefore

$$\frac{d}{dt}u_a(t) = \delta_a(t) = \delta(t - a). \tag{20}$$

We may regard this as the *formal definition* of the derivative of the unit step function, although $u_a(t)$ is not differentiable in the ordinary sense at $t = a$.

EXAMPLE 2   We return to the RLC circuit of Example 5 of Section 7.5, with $R = 110\ \Omega$, $L = 1$ H, $C = 0.001$ F, and a battery supplying $e_0 = 90$ V. Suppose that the circuit is initially passive—no current and no charge. At time $t = 0$ the switch is closed and at time $t = 1$ it is opened and left open. Find the resulting current $i(t)$ in the circuit.

Solution   In Section 7.5 we circumvented the discontinuity in the voltage by employing the integrodifferential form of the circuit equation. Now that delta functions are available, we may begin with the ordinary circuit equation

$$Li'' + Ri' + \frac{1}{C}i = e'(t).$$

In this example we have

$$e(t) = 90 - 90u(t - 1) = 90 - 90u_1(t),$$

so $e'(t) = -90\delta(t-1)$ by Eq. (20). Hence we want to solve the initial value problem

$$i'' + 110i' + 1000i = -90\delta(t - 1); \quad i(0) = 0, \quad i'(0) = 90. \tag{21}$$

The fact that $i'(0) = 90$ comes from substitution of $t = 0$ in the equation

$$Li'(t) + Ri(t) + \frac{1}{C}q(t) = e(t)$$

with the numerical values $i(0) = q(0) = 0$ and $e(0) = 90$.

When we transform the problem in (21), we get the equation

$$s^2I(s) - 90 + 110sI(s) + 1000I(s) = -90e^{-s}.$$

Hence

$$I(s) = \frac{90(1 - e^{-s})}{s^2 + 110s + 1000}.$$

This is precisely the same transform $I(s)$ we found in Example 5 of Section 7.5, so inversion of $I(s)$ yields the same solution $i(t)$ recorded there.   ■

EXAMPLE 3   Consider a mass on a spring with $m = k = 1$ and $x(0) = x'(0) = 0$. At each of the instants $t = 0, \pi, 2\pi, 3\pi, \ldots, n\pi, \ldots$, the mass is struck a hammer blow with a unit impulse. Determine the resulting motion.

Solution   We need to solve the initial value problem

$$x'' + x = \sum_{n=0}^{\infty} \delta_{n\pi}(t); \quad x(0) = 0 = x'(0).$$

Because $\mathcal{L}\{\delta_{n\pi}(t)\} = e^{-n\pi s}$, the transformed equation is

$$s^2X(s) + X(s) = \sum_{n=0}^{\infty} e^{-n\pi s},$$

so

$$X(s) = \sum_{n=0}^{\infty} \frac{e^{-n\pi s}}{s^2 + 1}.$$

We compute the inverse Laplace transform term by term; the result is

$$x(t) = \sum_{n=0}^{\infty} u(t - n\pi) \sin(t - n\pi).$$

Because $\sin(t - n\pi) = (-1)^n \sin t$ and $u(t - n\pi) = 0$ for $t < n\pi$, we see that if $n\pi < t < (n+1)\pi$, then

$$x(t) = \sin t - \sin t + \sin t - \cdots + (-1)^n \sin t;$$

that is,

$$x(t) = \begin{cases} \sin t & \text{if } n \text{ is even,} \\ 0 & \text{if } n \text{ is odd.} \end{cases}$$

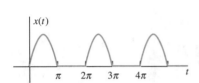

FIGURE 7.6.5. The half-wave rectification of $\sin t$.

Hence $x(t)$ is the half-wave rectification of $\sin t$ shown in Fig. 7.6.5. The physical explanation is that the first hammer blow (at time $t = 0$) starts the mass moving to the right; just as it returns to the origin, the second hammer blow stops it dead; it remains motionless until the third hammer blow starts it moving again, and so on. Of course, if the hammer blows are not perfectly synchronized then the motion of the mass will be quite different. ∎

Systems Analysis and Duhamel's Principle

Consider a physical system in which the *output* or *response* $x(t)$ to the *input* function $f(t)$ is described by the differential equation

$$ax'' + bx' + cx = f(t), \tag{22}$$

where the constant coefficients a, b, and c are determined by the physical parameters of the system and are independent of $f(t)$. The mass-spring-dashpot system and the series RLC circuit are familiar examples of this general situation.

For simplicity we assume that the system is initially passive: $x(0) = x'(0) = 0$. Then the transform of Eq. (22) is

$$as^2 X(s) + bs X(s) + c X(s) = F(s),$$

so

$$X(s) = \frac{F(s)}{as^2 + bs + c} = W(s)F(s). \tag{23}$$

The function

$$W(s) = \frac{1}{as^2 + bs + c} \tag{24}$$

is called the **transfer function** of the system. Thus the transform of the response to the input $f(t)$ is the product of $W(s)$ and the transform $F(s)$.

The function

$$w(t) = \mathcal{L}^{-1}\{W(s)\} \tag{25}$$

is called the **weight function** of the system. From Eq. (24) we see by convolution that

$$x(t) = \int_0^t w(\tau)f(t - \tau)\,d\tau. \tag{26}$$

This formula is **Duhamel's principle** for the system. What is important is that the weight function $w(t)$ is determined completely by the parameters of the system. Once $w(t)$ has been determined, the integral in (26) gives the response of the system to an arbitrary input function $f(t)$.

EXAMPLE 4 Consider a mass-spring-dashpot system (initially passive) that responds to the external force $f(t)$ in accord with the equation $x'' + 6x' + 10x = f(t)$. Then

$$W(s) = \frac{1}{s^2 + 6s + 10} = \frac{1}{(s+3)^2 + 1},$$

so the weight function is $w(t) = e^{-3t} \sin t$. Then Duhamel's principle implies that the response $x(t)$ to the force $f(t)$ is

$$x(t) = \int_0^t e^{-3\tau} (\sin \tau) f(t - \tau) \, d\tau. \qquad \blacksquare$$

Note that

$$W(s) = \frac{1}{as^2 + bs + c} = \frac{\mathcal{L}\{\delta(t)\}}{as^2 + bs + c}.$$

Consequently, it follows from Eq. (23) that the weight function is simply the response of the system to the delta function input $\delta(t)$. For this reason $w(t)$ is sometimes called the **unit impulse response**. A response that is usually easier to measure in practice is the response $h(t)$ to the unit step function $u(t)$; $h(t)$ is the **unit step response**. Because $\mathcal{L}\{u(t)\} = 1/s$, we see from Eq. (23) that the transform of $h(t)$ is

$$H(s) = \frac{W(s)}{s}.$$

It follows from the formula for transforms of integrals that

$$h(t) = \int_0^t w(\tau) \, d\tau, \quad \text{so that} \quad w(t) = h'(t). \qquad (27)$$

Thus the weight function, or unit impulse response, is the derivative of the unit step response. Substitution of (27) in Duhamel's principle gives

$$x(t) = \int_0^t h'(t) f(t - \tau) \, d\tau \qquad (28)$$

for the response of the system to the input $f(t)$.

APPLICATIONS: To describe a typical application of Eq. (28), suppose that we are given a complex series circuit containing many inductors, resistors, and capacitors. Assume that its circuit equation is a linear equation of the form in (22), but with i in place of x. What if the coefficients a, b, and c are unknown, perhaps only because they are too difficult to compute? We would still want to know the current $i(t)$ corresponding to any input $f(t) = e'(t)$. We connect the circuit to a linearly increasing voltage $e(t) = t$, so that $f(t) = e'(t) = 1 = u(t)$, and measure the response $h(t)$ with an ammeter. We then compute the derivative $h'(t)$, either numerically or graphically. Then according to Eq. (28), the output current $i(t)$ corresponding to the input voltage $e(t)$ will be given by

$$i(t) = \int_0^t h'(\tau) e'(t - \tau) \, d\tau$$

(using the fact that $f(t) = e'(t)$).

HISTORICAL REMARK: In conclusion, we remark that around 1950, after engineers and physicists had been using delta functions widely and fruitfully for about 20 years without rigorous justification, the French mathematician Laurent Schwartz developed a rigorous mathematical theory of *generalized functions* that supplied the missing logical foundation for delta function techniques. Every piecewise continuous ordinary function is a generalized function, but the delta function is an example of a generalized function that is not an ordinary function.

7.6 *Problems*

Solve the initial value problems in Problems 1 through 8.

1. $x'' + 4x = \delta(t)$; $x(0) = x'(0) = 0$

2. $x'' + 4x = \delta(t) + \delta(t - \pi)$; $x(0) = x'(0) = 0$

3. $x'' + 4x' + 4x = 1 + \delta(t - 2)$; $x(0) = x'(0) = 0$

4. $x'' + 2x' + x = t + \delta(t)$; $x(0) = 0$, $x'(0) = 1$

5. $x'' + 2x' + 2x = 2\delta(t - \pi)$; $x(0) = x'(0) = 0$

6. $x'' + 9x = \delta(t - 3\pi) + \cos 3t$; $x(0) = x'(0) = 0$

7. $x'' + 4x' + 5x = \delta(t - \pi) + \delta(t - 2\pi)$; $x(0) = 0$, $x'(0) = 2$

8. $x'' + 2x' + x = \delta(t) - \delta(t - 2)$; $x(0) = x'(0) = 2$

Apply Duhamel's principle to write an integral formula for the solution of each initial value problem in Problems 9 through 12.

9. $x'' + 4x = f(t)$; $x(0) = x'(0) = 0$

10. $x'' + 6x' + 9x = f(t)$; $x(0) = x'(0) = 0$

11. $x'' + 6x' + 8x = f(t)$; $x(0) = x'(0) = 0$

12. $x'' + 4x' + 8x = f(t)$; $x(0) = x'(0) = 0$

13. This problem deals with a mass m, initially at rest at the origin, that receives an impulse p at time $t = 0$. (a) Find the solution $x_\epsilon(t)$ of the problem

$$mx'' = pd_{0,\epsilon}(t); \quad x(0) = x'(0) = 0.$$

(b) Show that $\lim_{\epsilon \to 0} x_\epsilon(t)$ agrees with the solution of the problem

$$mx'' = p\delta(t); \quad x(0) = x'(0) = 0.$$

(c) Show that $mv = p$ for $t > 0$ ($v = dx/dt$).

14. Verify that $u'(t - a) = \delta(t - a)$ by solving the problem

$$x' = \delta(t - a); \quad x(0) = 0$$

to obtain $x(t) = u(t - a)$.

15. This problem deals with a mass m on a spring (with constant k) that receives an impulse $p_0 = mv_0$ at time $t = 0$. Show that the initial value problems

$$mx'' + kx = 0; \quad x(0) = 0, \quad x'(0) = v_0$$

and

$$mx'' + kx = p_0\delta(t); \quad x(0) = 0, \quad x'(0) = 0$$

have the same solution. Thus the effect of $p_0\delta(t)$ is, indeed, to impart to the particle an initial momentum p_0.

16. This is a generalization of Problem 15. Show that the problems

$$ax'' + bx' + cx = f(t); \quad x(0) = 0, \quad x'(0) = v_0$$

and

$$ax'' + bx' + cx = f(t) + av_0\delta(t); \quad x(0) = x'(0) = 0$$

have the same solution for $t > 0$. Thus the effect of the term $av_0\delta(t)$ is to supply the initial condition $x'(0) = v_0$.

17. Consider an initially passive RC circuit (no inductance) with a battery supplying e_0 volts. (a) If the switch to the battery is closed at time $t = a$ and opened at time $t = b > a$ (and left open thereafter), show that the current in the circuit satisfies the initial value problem

$$Ri' + \frac{1}{C}i = e_0\delta(t - a) - e_0\delta(t - b); \quad i(0) = 0.$$

(b) Solve this problem if $R = 100\ \Omega$, $C = 10^{-4}$ F, $e_0 = 100$ V, $a = 1$ (s), and $b = 2$ (s). Show that $i(t) > 0$ if $1 < t < 2$ and that $i(t) < 0$ if $t > 2$.

18. Consider an initially passive LC circuit (no resistance) with a battery supplying e_0 volts. (a) If the switch is closed at time $t = 0$ and opened at time $t = a > 0$, show that the current in the circuit satisfies the initial value problem

$$Li'' + \frac{1}{C}i = e_0\delta(t) - e_0\delta(t - a);$$

$$i(0) = i'(0) = 0.$$

(b) If $L = 1$ H, $C = 10^{-2}$ F, $e_0 = 10$ V, and $a = \pi$ (s), show that

$$i(t) = \begin{cases} \sin 10t & \text{if } t < \pi, \\ 0 & \text{if } t > \pi. \end{cases}$$

Thus the current oscillates through five cycles and then stops abruptly when the switch is opened.

19. Consider the LC circuit of Problem 18(b), except suppose that the switch is alternately closed and opened at times $t = 0, \pi/10, 2\pi/10, \ldots$. (a) Show that $i(t)$ satisfies the initial value problem

$$i'' + 100i = 10\sum_{n=0}^{\infty}(-1)^n\delta\left(t - \frac{n\pi}{10}\right); \quad i(0) = i'(0) = 0.$$

(b) Solve this initial value problem to show that

$$i(t) = (n + 1)\sin 10t \quad \text{if } \frac{n\pi}{10} < t < \frac{(n + 1)\pi}{10}.$$

Thus a resonance phenomenon occurs (see Fig. 7.6.6).

20. Repeat Problem 19, except suppose that the switch is alternately closed and opened at times $t = 0, \pi/5, 2\pi/5, \ldots, n\pi/5, \ldots$. Now show that if

$$\frac{n\pi}{5} < t < \frac{(n + 1)\pi}{5},$$

then

$$i(t) = \begin{cases} \sin 10t & \text{if } n \text{ is even}; \\ 0 & \text{if } n \text{ is odd}. \end{cases}$$

Thus the current in alternate cycles of length $\pi/5$ first executes a sine oscillation during one cycle, then is dormant during the next cycle, and so on (see Fig. 7.6.7).

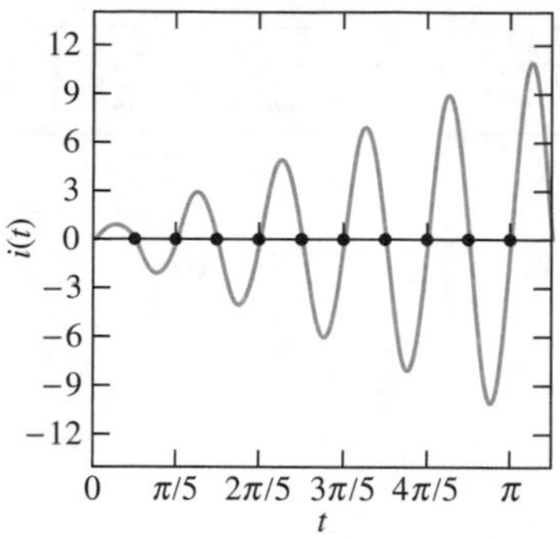

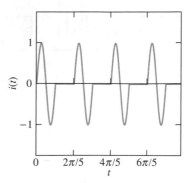

FIGURE 7.6.6. The current function of Problem 19.

FIGURE 7.6.7. The current function of Problem 20.

21. Consider an RLC circuit in series with a battery, with $L = 1$ H, $R = 60$ Ω, $C = 10^{-3}$ F, and $e_0 = 10$ V. (a) Suppose that the switch is alternately closed and opened at times $t = 0, \pi/10, 2\pi/10, \ldots$. Show that $i(t)$ satisfies the initial value problem

$$i'' + 60i' + 1000i = 10 \sum_{n=0}^{\infty} (-1)^n \delta\left(t - \frac{n\pi}{10}\right);$$

$$i(0) = i'(0) = 0.$$

(b) Solve this problem to show that if

$$\frac{n\pi}{10} < t < \frac{(n+1)\pi}{10},$$

then

$$i(t) = \frac{e^{3n\pi+3\pi} - 1}{e^{3\pi} - 1} e^{-30t} \sin 10t.$$

22. Consider a mass $m = 1$ on a spring with constant $k = 1$, initially at rest, but struck with a hammer at each of the instants $t = 0, 2\pi, 4\pi, \ldots$. Suppose that each hammer blow imparts an impulse of $+1$. Show that the position function $x(t)$ of the mass satisfies the initial value problem

$$x'' + x = \sum_{n=0}^{\infty} \delta(t - 2n\pi); \quad x(0) = x'(0) = 0.$$

Solve this problem to show that if $2n\pi < t < 2(n+1)\pi$, then $x(t) = (n+1)\sin t$. Thus resonance occurs because the mass is struck each time it passes through the origin moving to the right—in contrast with Example 3, in which the mass was struck each time it returned to the origin.

REFERENCES FOR FURTHER STUDY

The literature of the theory and applications of differential equations is vast. The following list includes a selection of books that might be useful to readers who wish to pursue further the topics introduced in this book.

1. ABRAMOWITZ, M. and I. A. STEGUN, *Handbook of Mathematical Functions*. New York: Dover, 1965. The comprehensive collection of tables to which frequent reference is made in the text.

2. BIRKHOFF, G. and G.-C. ROTA, *Ordinary Differential Equations* (2nd ed.). New York: John Wiley, 1969. An intermediate-level text that includes more complete treatment of existence and uniqueness theorems, Sturm-Liouville problems, and eigenfunction expansions.

3. BRAUN, M., *Differential Equations and Their Applications* (3rd ed.). New York: Springer-Verlag, 1983. An introductory text at a slightly higher level than this book; it includes several interesting "case study" applications.

4. CHURCHILL, R. V., *Operational Mathematics* (3rd ed.). New York: McGraw-Hill, 1972. The standard reference for theory and applications of Laplace transforms, starting at about the same level as Chapter 7 of this book.

5. CHURCHILL, R. V. and J. W. BROWN, *Fourier Series and Boundary Value Problems* (3rd ed.). New York: McGraw-Hill, 1978. At about the same level as Chapters 9 and 10 of this book.

6. CODDINGTON, E. A., *An Introduction to Ordinary Differential Equations*. Englewood Cliffs, N.J.: Prentice Hall, 1961. An intermediate-level introduction; Chapters 3 and 4 include proofs of the theorems on power series and Frobenius series solutions stated in Chapter 8 of this book.

7. CODDINGTON, E. A. and N. LEVINSON, *Theory of Ordinary Differential Equations*. New York: McGraw-Hill, 1955. An advanced theoretical text; Chapter 5 discusses solutions near an irregular singular point.

8. DORMAND, J. R., *Numerical Methods for Differential Equations*. Boca Raton: CRC Press, 1996. More complete coverage of modern computational methods for approximate solution of differential equations.

9. HABERMAN, R., *Elementary Applied Partial Differential Equations* (3rd ed.). Upper Saddle River, N.J.: Prentice Hall, 1998. A next step beyond Chapters 9 and 10 of this book, but still quite accessible.

10. HUBBARD, J. H. and B. H. WEST, *Differential Equations: A Dynamical Systems Approach*. New York: Springer-Verlag, 1992 (part I) and 1995 (Higher-Dimensional Systems). Detailed treatment of qualitative phenomena, with a balanced combination of computational and theoretical viewpoints.

11. INCE, E. L., *Ordinary Differential Equations*. New York: Dover, 1956. First published in 1926, this is the classic older reference work on the subject.

12. LEBEDEV, N. N., *Special Functions and Their Applications*. New York: Dover, 1972. A comprehensive account of Bessel functions and the other special functions of mathematical physics.

13. LEBEDEV, N. N., I. P. SKALSKAYA, and Y. S. UFLYAND, *Worked Problems in Applied Mathematics*. New York: Dover, 1979. A large collection of applied examples and problems similar to those discussed in Chapter 10 of this book.

14. MCLACHLAN, N. W., *Bessel Functions for Engineers* (2nd ed.). London: Oxford University Press, 1955. Includes numerous physical applications of Bessel functions.

15. McLachlan, N. W., *Ordinary Non-Linear Differential Equations in Engineering and Physical Sciences*. London: Oxford University Press, 1956. A concrete introduction to the effects of nonlinearity in physical systems.

16. Polking, J. C. and D. Arnold, *Ordinary Differential Equations Using MATLAB* (2nd ed.). Upper Saddle River, N.J.: Prentice Hall, 1999. A manual for using MATLAB in an elementary differential equations course; based on the MATLAB programs `dfield` and `pplane` that are used and referenced in this text.

17. Press, W. H., B. P. Flannery, S. A. Teukolsky, and W. T. Vetterling, *Numerical Recipes: The Art of Scientific Computing*. Cambridge: Cambridge University Press, 1986. Chapter 15 discusses modern techniques for the numerical solution of differential equations. This edition include FORTRAN programs; Pascal and C editions have also been published.

18. Rainville, E., *Intermediate Differential Equations* (2nd ed.). New York: Macmillan, 1964. Chapters 3 and 4 include proofs of the theorems on power series and Frobenius series solutions stated in Chapter 8 of this book.

19. Sagan, H., *Boundary and Eigenvalue Problems in Mathematical Physics*. New York: John Wiley, 1961. Discusses the classical boundary value problems and the variational approach to Sturm-Liouville problems, eigenvalues, and eigenfunctions.

20. Simmons, G. F., *Differential Equations*. New York: McGraw-Hill, 1972. An introductory text with interesting historical notes and fascinating applications and with the most eloquent preface in any mathematics book currently in print.

21. Tolstov, G. P., *Fourier Series*. New York: Dover, 1976. An introductory text including detailed discussion of both convergence and applications of Fourier series.

22. Thompson, J. M. T. and H. B. Stewart, *Nonlinear Dynamics and Chaos*. New York: John Wiley, 1986. Includes more detailed discussions of the forced Duffing, Lorenz, and Rossler systems (among others that exhibit nonlinear chaos phenomena).

23. Weinberger, H. F., *A First Course in Partial Differential Equations*. New York: Blaisdell, 1965. Includes separation of variables, Sturm-Liouville methods, and applications of Laplace transform methods to partial differential equations.

24. Weinstock, R., *Calculus of Variations*. New York: Dover, 1974. Includes variational derivations of the partial differential equations of vibrating strings, membranes, rods, and bars.

APPENDIX A
Existence and
Uniqueness of Solutions

In Chapter 1 we saw that an initial value problem of the form

$$\frac{dy}{dx} = f(x, y), \quad y(a) = b \tag{1}$$

can fail (on a given interval containing the point $x = a$) to have a unique solution. For instance, in Example 4 of Section 1.3, we saw that the initial value problem

$$x^2 \frac{dy}{dx} + y^2 = 0, \quad y(0) = b \tag{2}$$

has no solutions at all unless $b = 0$, in which case there are infinitely many solutions. According to Problem 31 of Section 1.3, the initial value problem

$$\frac{dy}{dx} = -\sqrt{1 - y^2}, \quad y(0) = 1 \tag{3}$$

has the two distinct solutions $y_1(x) \equiv 1$ and $y_2(x) = \cos x$ on the interval $0 \leqq x \leqq \pi$. In this appendix we investigate conditions on the function $f(x, y)$ that suffice to guarantee that the initial value problem in (1) has one and only one solution, and then proceed to establish appropriate versions of the existence-uniqueness theorems that were stated without proof in Sections 1.3, 3.1, 3.2, and 4.1.

A.1 EXISTENCE OF SOLUTIONS

The approach we employ is the **method of successive approximations**, which was developed by the French mathematician Emile Picard (1856–1941). This method is based on the fact that the function $y(x)$ satisfies the initial value problem in (1) on the open interval I containing $x = a$ if and only if it satisfies the integral equation

$$y(x) = b + \int_a^x f(t, y(t)) \, dt \tag{4}$$

for all x in I. In particular, if $y(x)$ satisfies Eq. (4), then clearly $y(a) = b$, and differentiation of both sides in (4)—using the fundamental theorem of calculus—yields the differential equation $y'(x) = f(x, y(x))$.

To attempt to solve Eq. (4), we begin with the initial function

$$y_0(x) \equiv b, \tag{5}$$

and then define iteratively a sequence $y_1, y_2, y_3, \ldots$ of functions that we hope will converge to the solution. Specifically, we let

$$y_1(x) = b + \int_a^x f(t, y_0(t)) \, dt \quad \text{and} \quad y_2(x) = b + \int_a^x f(t, y_1(t)) \, dt. \tag{6}$$

In general, y_{n+1} is obtained by substitution of y_n for y in the right-hand side in Eq. (4):

$$y_{n+1}(x) = b + \int_a^x f(t, y_n(t)) \, dt. \tag{7}$$

Suppose we know that each of these functions $\{y_n(x)\}_0^\infty$ is defined on some open interval (the same for each n) containing $x = a$, and that the limit

$$y(x) = \lim_{n \to \infty} y_n(x) \tag{8}$$

exists at each point of this interval. Then it will follow that

$$y(x) = \lim_{n \to \infty} y_{n+1}(x) = \lim_{n \to \infty} \left[b + \int_a^x f(t, y_n(t)) \, dt \right]$$

$$= b + \lim_{n \to \infty} \int_a^x f(t, y_n(t)) \, dt \tag{9}$$

$$= b + \int_a^x f\left(t, \lim_{n \to \infty} y_n(t)\right) dt \tag{10}$$

and hence that

$$y(x) = b + \int_a^x f(t, y(t)) \, dt,$$

provided that we can validate the interchange of limit operations involved in passing from (9) to (10). It is therefore reasonable to expect that, under favorable conditions, the sequence $\{y_n(x)\}$ defined iteratively in Eqs. (5) and (7) will converge to a solution $y(x)$ of the integral equation in (4), and hence to a solution of the original initial value problem in (1).

EXAMPLE 1   To apply the method of successive approximations to the initial value problem

$$\frac{dy}{dx} = y, \quad y(0) = 1, \tag{11}$$

we write Eqs. (5) and (7), thereby obtaining

$$y_0(x) \equiv 1, \quad y_{n+1}(x) = 1 + \int_0^x y_n(t) \, dt. \tag{12}$$

The iteration formula in (12) yields

$$y_1(x) = 1 + \int_0^x 1 \, dt = 1 + x,$$

$$y_2(x) = 1 + \int_0^x (1 + t) \, dt = 1 + x + \tfrac{1}{2}x^2,$$

$$y_3(x) = 1 + \int_0^x \left(1 + t + \tfrac{1}{2}t^2\right) dt = 1 + x + \tfrac{1}{2}x^2 + \tfrac{1}{6}x^3,$$

and

$$y_4(x) = 1 + \int_0^x \left(1 + t + \tfrac{1}{2}t^2 + \tfrac{1}{6}t^3\right) dt$$

$$= 1 + x + \tfrac{1}{2}x^2 + \tfrac{1}{6}x^3 + \tfrac{1}{24}x^4.$$

It is clear that we are generating the sequence of partial sums of a power series solution; indeed, we immediately recognize the series as that of $y(x) = e^x$. There is no difficulty in demonstrating that the exponential function is indeed the solution of the initial value problem in (11); moreover, a diligent student can verify (using a proof by induction on n) that $y_n(x)$, obtained in the aforementioned manner, is indeed the nth partial sum for the Taylor series with center zero for $y(x) = e^x$. ∎

EXAMPLE 2   To apply the method of successive approximations to the initial value problem

$$\frac{dy}{dx} = 4xy, \qquad y(0) = 3, \tag{13}$$

we write Eqs. (5) and (7) as in Example 1. Now we obtain

$$y_0(x) \equiv 3, \quad y_{n+1}(x) = 3 + \int_0^x 4t\, y_n(t)\, dt. \tag{14}$$

The iteration formula in (14) yields

$$y_1(x) = 3 + \int_0^x (4t)(3)\, dt = 3 + 6x^2,$$

$$y_2(x) = 3 + \int_0^x (4t)(3 + 6t^2)\, dt = 3 + 6x^2 + 6x^4,$$

$$y_3(x) = 3 + \int_0^x (4t)(3 + 6t^2 + 6t^4)\, dt = 3 + 6x^2 + 6x^4 + 4x^6,$$

and

$$y_4(x) = 3 + \int_0^x (4t)(3 + 6t^2 + 6t^4 + 4t^6)\, dt$$

$$= 3 + 6x^2 + 6x^4 + 4x^6 + 2x^8.$$

It is again clear that we are generating partial sums of a power series solution. It is not quite so obvious what function has such a power series representation, but the initial value problem in (13) is readily solved by separation of variables:

$$y(x) = 3 \exp\left(2x^2\right) = 3 \sum_{n=0}^{\infty} \frac{(2x^2)^n}{n!}$$

$$= 3 + 6x^2 + 6x^4 + 4x^6 + 2x^8 + \tfrac{4}{5}x^{10} + \cdots. \qquad \blacksquare$$

In some cases it may be necessary to compute a much large number of terms, either in order to identify the solution or to use a partial sum of its series with large subscript to approximate the solution accurately for x near its initial value. Fortunately, computer algebra systems such as *Maple* and *Mathematica* can perform the symbolic integrations (as opposed to numerical integrations) of the sort in Examples 1 and 2. If necessary, you could generate the first hundred terms in Example 2 in a matter of minutes.

In general, of course, we apply Picard's method because we cannot find a solution by elementary methods. Suppose that we have produced a large number of terms of what we believe to be the correct power series expansion of the solution. We *must* have conditions under which the sequence $\{y_n(x)\}$ provided by the method of successive approximations is guaranteed in advance to converge to a solution. It is just as convenient to discuss the initial value problem

$$\frac{d\mathbf{x}}{dt} = \mathbf{f}(\mathbf{x}, t), \quad \mathbf{x}(a) = \mathbf{b} \tag{15}$$

for a system of m first-order equations, where

$$\mathbf{x} = \begin{bmatrix} x_1 \\ x_2 \\ x_3 \\ \vdots \\ x_m \end{bmatrix}, \quad \mathbf{f} = \begin{bmatrix} f_1 \\ f_2 \\ f_3 \\ \vdots \\ f_m \end{bmatrix}, \quad \text{and} \quad \mathbf{b} = \begin{bmatrix} b_1 \\ b_2 \\ b_3 \\ \vdots \\ b_m \end{bmatrix}.$$

It turns out that with the aid of this vector notation (which we introduced in Section 5.1), most results concerning a single [scalar] equation $x' = f(x, t)$ can be generalized readily to analogous results for a system of m first-order equations, as abbreviated in (15). Consequently, the effort of using vector notation is amply justified by the generality it provides.

The method of successive approximations for the system in (15) calls for us to compute the sequence $\{\mathbf{x}_n(t)\}_0^\infty$ of vector-valued functions of t,

$$\mathbf{x}_n(t) = \begin{bmatrix} x_{1n}(t) \\ x_{2n}(t) \\ x_{3n}(t) \\ \vdots \\ x_{mn}(t) \end{bmatrix},$$

defined iteratively by

$$\mathbf{x}_0(a) \equiv \mathbf{b}, \quad \mathbf{x}_{n+1}(t) = \mathbf{b} + \int_a^t \mathbf{f}(\mathbf{x}_n(s), s)\, ds. \tag{16}$$

Recall that vector-valued functions are integrated componentwise.

EXAMPLE 3   Consider the m-dimensional initial value problem

$$\frac{d\mathbf{x}}{dt} = \mathbf{A}\mathbf{x}, \quad \mathbf{x}(0) = \mathbf{b} \tag{17}$$

for a homogeneous linear system with $m \times m$ constant coefficient matrix $\mathbf{A}$. The equations in (16) take the form

$$\mathbf{x}_0(t) = \mathbf{b}, \quad \mathbf{x}_{n+1} = \mathbf{b} + \int_0^x \mathbf{A}\mathbf{x}_n(s)\, ds. \tag{18}$$

Thus

$$\mathbf{x}_1(t) = \mathbf{b} + \int_0^t \mathbf{A}\mathbf{b}\, ds = \mathbf{b} + \mathbf{A}\mathbf{b}t = (\mathbf{I} + \mathbf{A}t)\mathbf{b};$$

$$\mathbf{x}_2(t) = \mathbf{b} + \int_0^t \mathbf{A}(\mathbf{b} + \mathbf{A}\mathbf{b}s)\, ds = \mathbf{b} + \mathbf{A}\mathbf{b}t + \tfrac{1}{2}\mathbf{A}^2\mathbf{b}t^2 = (\mathbf{I} + \mathbf{A}t + \tfrac{1}{2}\mathbf{A}^2t^2)\mathbf{b}$$

and

$$\mathbf{x}_3(t) = \mathbf{b} + \int_0^t \mathbf{A}(\mathbf{b} + \mathbf{A}\mathbf{b}s + \tfrac{1}{2}\mathbf{A}^2\mathbf{b}s^2)\, ds = (\mathbf{I} + \mathbf{A}t + \tfrac{1}{2}\mathbf{A}^2t^2 + \tfrac{1}{6}\mathbf{A}^3t^3)\mathbf{b}.$$

We have therefore obtained the first several partial sums of the exponential series solution

$$\mathbf{x}(t) = e^{\mathbf{A}t}\mathbf{b} = \left(\sum_{n=0}^\infty \frac{(\mathbf{A}t)^n}{n!}\right)\mathbf{b} \tag{19}$$

of (17), which was derived earlier in Section 5.5. ∎

The key to establishing convergence in the method of successive approximations is an appropriate condition on the rate at which $\mathbf{f}(\mathbf{x}, t)$ changes when $\mathbf{x}$ varies but t is held fixed. If R is a region in $(m + 1)$-dimensional $(\mathbf{x}, t)$-space, then the function $\mathbf{f}(\mathbf{x}, t)$ is said to be **Lipschitz continuous** on R if there exists a constant $k > 0$ such that

$$|\mathbf{f}(\mathbf{x}_1, t) - \mathbf{f}(\mathbf{x}_2, t)| \leq k|\mathbf{x}_1 - \mathbf{x}_2| \tag{20}$$

if $(\mathbf{x}_1, t)$ and $(\mathbf{x}_2, t)$ are points of R. Recall that the **norm** of an m-dimensional point or vector $\mathbf{x}$ is defined to be

$$|\mathbf{x}| = \sqrt{x_1^2 + x_2^2 + x_3^2 + \cdots + x_m^2}. \tag{21}$$

Then $|\mathbf{x}_1 - \mathbf{x}_2|$ is simply the Euclidean distance between the points $\mathbf{x}_1$ and $\mathbf{x}_2$.

EXAMPLE 4 Let $f(x, t) = x^2 \exp\left(-t^2\right) \sin t$ and let R be the strip $0 \leq x \leq 2$ in the xy-plane. If (x_1, t) and (x_2, t) are both points of R, then

$$|f(x_1, t) - f(x_2, t)| = |\exp\left(-t^2\right) \sin t| \cdot |x_1 + x_2| \cdot |x_1 - x_2| \leq 4|x_1 - x_2|,$$

because $\left|\exp\left(-t^2\right) \sin t\right| \leq 1$ for all t and $|x_1 + x_2| \leq 4$ if x_1 and x_2 are both in the interval $[0, 2]$. Thus f satisfies the Lipschitz condition in (20) with $k = 4$ and is therefore Lipschitz continuous in the strip R.   ∎

EXAMPLE 5 Let $f(x, t) = t\sqrt{x}$ on the rectangle R consisting of the points (x, t) in the xt-plane for which $0 \leq x \leq 1$ and $0 \leq t \leq 1$. Then, taking $x_1 = x$, $x_2 = 0$, and $t = 1$, we find that

$$|f(x, 1) - f(0, 1)| = \sqrt{x} = \frac{1}{\sqrt{x}}|x - 0|.$$

Because $x^{-1/2} \to +\infty$ as $x \to 0^+$, we see that the Lipschitz condition in (20) cannot be satisfied by any (finite) constant $k > 0$. Thus the function f, though obviously continuous on R, is *not* Lipschitz continuous on R.   ∎

Suppose, however, that the function $f(x, t)$ has a continuous partial derivative $f_x(x, t)$ on the closed rectangle R in the xt-plane, and denote by k the maximum value of $|f_x(x, t)|$ on R. Then the mean value theorem of differential calculus yields

$$|f(x_1, t) - f(x_2, t)| = |f_x(\overline{x}, t) \cdot (x_1 - x_2)|$$

for some $\overline{x}$ in (x_1, x_2), so it follows that

$$|f(x_1, t) - f(x_2, t)| \leq k|x_1 - x_2|$$

because $|f_x(\overline{x}, t)| \leq k$. Thus a continuously differentiable function $f(x, t)$ defined on a closed rectangle *is* Lipschitz continuous there. More generally, the multivariable mean value theorem of advanced calculus can be used similarly to prove that a *vector-valued function $\mathbf{f}(\mathbf{x}, t)$ with continuously differentiable component functions on a closed rectangular region R in $(\mathbf{x}, t)$-space is Lipschitz continuous on R.*

EXAMPLE 6 The function $f(x, t) = x^2$ is Lipschitz continuous on any closed [bounded] region in the xt-plane. But consider this function on the infinite strip R consisting of the points (x, t) for which $0 \leq t \leq 1$ and x is arbitrary. Then

$$|f(x_1, t) - f(x_2, t)| = |x_1^2 - x_2^2| = |x_1 + x_2| \cdot |x_1 - x_2|.$$

Because $|x_1 + x_2|$ can be made arbitrarily large, it follows that f is *not* Lipschitz continuous on the infinite strip R.   ∎

If I is an interval on the t-axis, then the set of all points $(\mathbf{x}, t)$ with t in I is an infinite strip or slab in $(m + 1)$-space (as indicated in Fig. A.1). Example 6 shows that Lipschitz continuity of $\mathbf{f}(\mathbf{x}, t)$ on such an infinite slab is a very strong condition. Nevertheless, the existence of a solution of the initial value problem

$$\frac{d\mathbf{x}}{dt} = \mathbf{f}(\mathbf{x}, t), \quad \mathbf{x}(a) = \mathbf{b} \tag{15}$$

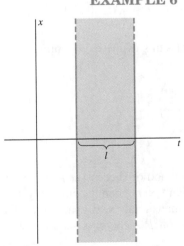

FIGURE A.1. An infinite slab in $(m + 1)$-space.

under the hypothesis of Lipschitz continuity of $\mathbf{f}$ in such a slab is of considerable importance.

> **THEOREM 1: Global Existence of Solutions**

Let $\mathbf{f}$ be a vector-valued function (with m components) of $m + 1$ real variables, and let I be a [bounded or unbounded] open interval containing $t = a$. If $\mathbf{f}(\mathbf{x}, t)$ is continuous and satisfies the Lipschitz condition in (20) for all t in I and for all $\mathbf{x}_1$ and $\mathbf{x}_2$, then the initial value problem in (15) has a solution on the [entire] interval I.

Proof: We want to show that the sequence $\{\mathbf{x}_n(t)\}_0^\infty$ of successive approximations determined iteratively by

$$\mathbf{x}_0(a) = \mathbf{b}, \quad \mathbf{x}_{n+1}(t) = \mathbf{b} + \int_0^t \mathbf{f}(\mathbf{x}_n(s), s)\, ds \tag{16}$$

converges to a solution $\mathbf{x}(t)$ of (15). We see that each of these functions in turn is continuous on I, as each is an [indefinite] integral of a continuous function.

We may assume that $a = 0$, because the transformation $t \to t + a$ converts (15) into an equivalent problem with initial point $t = 0$. Also, we will consider only the portion $t \geq 0$ of the interval I; the details for the case $t \leq 0$ are very similar.

The main part of the proof consists in showing that if $[0, T]$ is a closed (and bounded) interval contained in I, then the sequence $\{\mathbf{x}_n(t)\}$ converges *uniformly* on $[0, T]$ to a limit function $\mathbf{x}(t)$. This means that, given $\epsilon > 0$, there exists an integer N such that

$$|\mathbf{x}_n(t) - \mathbf{x}(t)| < \epsilon \tag{22}$$

for all $n \geq N$ and all t in $[0, T]$. For ordinary (perhaps nonuniform) convergence the integer N, for which (22) holds for all $n \geq N$, may depend on t, with no single value of N working for all t in I. Once this uniform convergence of the sequence $\{\mathbf{x}_n(t)\}$ has been established, the following conclusions will follow from standard theorems of advanced calculus (see pages 620–622 of A. E. Taylor and W. R. Mann, *Advanced Calculus*, 3rd ed. (New York: John Wiley, 1983)):

1. The limit function $\mathbf{x}(t)$ is continuous on $[0, T]$.
2. If N is so chosen that the inequality in (22) holds for $n \geq N$, then the Lipschitz continuity of $\mathbf{f}$ implies that

$$|\mathbf{f}(\mathbf{x}_n(t), t) - \mathbf{f}(\mathbf{x}(t), t)| \leq k|\mathbf{x}_n(t) - \mathbf{x}(t)| < k\epsilon$$

for all t in $[0, T]$ and $n \geq N$, so it follows that the sequence $\{\mathbf{f}(\mathbf{x}_n(t), t)\}_0^\infty$ converges uniformly to $\mathbf{f}(\mathbf{x}(t), t)$ on $[0, T]$.

3. But a uniformly convergent sequence or series can be integrated termwise, so it follows that, on taking limits in the iterative formula in (16),

$$\mathbf{x}(t) = \lim_{n \to \infty} \mathbf{x}_{n+1}(t) = \mathbf{b} + \lim_{n \to \infty} \int_0^t \mathbf{f}(\mathbf{x}_n(s), s)\, ds$$

$$= \mathbf{b} + \int_0^t \lim_{n \to \infty} \mathbf{f}(\mathbf{x}_n(s), s)\, ds;$$

thus

$$\mathbf{x}(t) = \mathbf{b} + \int_0^t \mathbf{f}(\mathbf{x}(s), s)\, ds. \tag{23}$$

4. Because the function $\mathbf{x}(t)$ is continuous on $[0, T]$, the integral equation in (23) (analogous to the one-dimensional case in (4)) implies that $\mathbf{x}'(t) = \mathbf{f}(\mathbf{x}(t), t)$ on $[0, T]$. But if this is true on every closed subinterval of the open interval I, then it is true on the entire interval I as well.

It therefore remains only to prove that the sequence $\{\mathbf{x}_n(t)\}_0^\infty$ converges uniformly on the closed interval $[0, T]$. Let M be the maximum value of $|\mathbf{f}(\mathbf{b}, t)|$ for t in $[0, T]$. Then

$$|\mathbf{x}_1(t) - \mathbf{x}_0(t)| = \left| \int_0^t \mathbf{f}(\mathbf{x}_0(s), s)\, ds \right| \leq \int_0^t |\mathbf{f}(\mathbf{b}, s)|\, ds \leq Mt. \tag{24}$$

Next,

$$|\mathbf{x}_2(t) - \mathbf{x}_1(t)| = \left| \int_0^t [\mathbf{f}(\mathbf{x}_1(s), s) - \mathbf{f}(\mathbf{x}_0(s), s)]\, ds \right| \leq k \int_0^t |\mathbf{x}_1(s) - \mathbf{x}_0(s)|\, ds,$$

and hence

$$|\mathbf{x}_2(t) - \mathbf{x}_1(t)| \leq k \int_0^t Ms\, ds = \tfrac{1}{2}kMt^2. \tag{25}$$

We now proceed by induction. Assume that

$$|\mathbf{x}_n(t) - \mathbf{x}_{n-1}(t)| \leq \frac{M}{k} \cdot \frac{(kt)^n}{n!}. \tag{26}$$

It then follows that

$$|\mathbf{x}_{n+1}(t) - \mathbf{x}_n(t)| = \left| \int_0^t \mathbf{f}(\mathbf{x}_n(s), s) - \mathbf{f}(\mathbf{x}_{n-1}(s), s)]\, ds \right|$$

$$\leq k \int_0^t |\mathbf{x}_n(s) - \mathbf{x}_{n-1}(s)|\, ds;$$

consequently,

$$|\mathbf{x}_{n+1}(t) - \mathbf{x}_n(t)| \leq k \int_0^t \frac{M}{k} \cdot \frac{(ks)^n}{n!}\, ds.$$

It follows upon evaluating this integral that

$$|\mathbf{x}_{n+1}(t) - \mathbf{x}_n(t)| \leq \frac{M}{k} \cdot \frac{(kt)^{n+1}}{(n+1)!}.$$

Thus (26) holds on $[0, T]$ for all $n \geq 1$.

Hence the terms of the infinite series

$$\mathbf{x}_0(t) + \sum_{n=1}^{\infty} \left[\mathbf{x}_n(t) - \mathbf{x}_{n-1}(t) \right] \tag{27}$$

are dominated (in magnitude on the interval $[0, T]$) by the terms of the convergent series

$$\sum_{n=1}^{\infty} \frac{M}{k} \cdot \frac{(kT)^{n+1}}{(n+1)!} = \frac{M}{k}(e^{kT} - 1), \tag{28}$$

which is a series of positive constants. It therefore follows (from the Weierstrass M-test on pages 618–619 of Taylor and Mann) that the series in (27) converges uniformly on $[0, T]$. But the sequence of partial sums of this series is simply our original sequence $\{\mathbf{x}_n(t)\}_0^\infty$ of successive approximations, so the proof of Theorem 1 is finally complete. ∎

A.2 LINEAR SYSTEMS

An important application of the global existence theorem just given is to the initial value problem

$$\frac{d\mathbf{x}}{dt} = \mathbf{A}(t)\mathbf{x} + \mathbf{g}(t), \quad \mathbf{x}(a) = \mathbf{b} \tag{29}$$

for a linear system, where the $m \times m$ matrix-valued function $\mathbf{A}(t)$ and the vector-valued function $\mathbf{g}(t)$ are continuous on a [bounded or unbounded] open interval I containing the point $t = a$. In order to apply Theorem 1 to the linear system in (29), we note first that the proof of Theorem 1 requires only that, for each closed and bounded subinterval J of I, there exists a Lipschitz constant k such that

$$|\mathbf{f}(\mathbf{x}_1, t) - \mathbf{f}(\mathbf{x}_2, t)| \leqq k|\mathbf{x}_1 - \mathbf{x}_2| \tag{20}$$

for all t in J (and all $\mathbf{x}_1$ and $\mathbf{x}_2$). Thus we do not need a single Lipschitz constant for the entire open interval I.

In (29) we have $\mathbf{f}(\mathbf{x}, t) = \mathbf{A}(t)\mathbf{x} + \mathbf{g}$, so

$$\mathbf{f}(\mathbf{x}_1, t) - \mathbf{f}(\mathbf{x}_2, t) = \mathbf{A}(t)(\mathbf{x}_1 - \mathbf{x}_2). \tag{30}$$

It therefore suffices to show that, if $\mathbf{A}(t)$ is continuous on the closed and bounded interval J, then there is a constant k such that

$$|\mathbf{A}(t)\mathbf{x}| \leqq k|\mathbf{x}| \tag{31}$$

for all t in J. But this follows from the fact (Problem 17) that

$$|\mathbf{A}\mathbf{x}| \leqq \|\mathbf{A}\| \cdot |\mathbf{x}|, \tag{32}$$

where the **norm** $\|\mathbf{A}\|$ of the matrix $\mathbf{A}$ is defined to be

$$\|\mathbf{A}\| = \left(\sum_{i,j=1}^{m} (a_{ij})^2 \right)^{1/2}. \tag{33}$$

Because $\mathbf{A}(t)$ is continuous on the closed and bounded interval J, the norm $\|\mathbf{A}\|$ is bounded on J, so Eq. (31) follows, as desired. Thus we have the following global existence theorem for the linear initial value problem in (29).

THEOREM 2:   Existence for Linear Systems

Let the $m \times m$ matrix-valued function $\mathbf{A}(t)$ and the vector-valued function $\mathbf{g}(t)$ be continuous on the [bounded or unbounded] open interval I containing the point $t = a$. Then the initial value problem

$$\frac{d\mathbf{x}}{dt} = \mathbf{A}(t)\mathbf{x} + \mathbf{g}(t), \quad \mathbf{x}(a) = \mathbf{b} \tag{29}$$

has a solution on the [entire] interval I.   ∎

As we saw in Section 4.1, the mth-order initial value problem

$$x^{(m)} + a_1(t)x^{(m-1)} + \cdots + a_{m-1}(t)x' + a_m(t)x = p(t),$$
$$x(a) = b_0, \quad x'(a) = b_1, \quad \ldots, \quad x^{(m-1)}(a) = b_{m-1} \tag{34}$$

is readily transformed into an equivalent $m \times m$ system of the form in (29). It therefore follows from Theorem 2 that if the functions $a_1(t), a_2(t), \ldots, a_m(t)$ and $p(t)$ in (34) are all continuous on the [bounded or unbounded] open interval I containing $t = a$, then the initial value problem in (34) has a solution on the [entire] interval I.

A.3   LOCAL EXISTENCE

In the case of a *nonlinear* initial value problem

$$\frac{d\mathbf{x}}{dt} = \mathbf{f}(\mathbf{x}, t), \quad \mathbf{x}(a) = \mathbf{b}, \tag{35}$$

the hypothesis in Theorem 1 that $\mathbf{f}$ satisfies a Lipschitz condition on a slab $(\mathbf{x}, t)$ (t in I, all $\mathbf{x}$) is unrealistic and rarely satisfied. This is illustrated by the following simple example.

EXAMPLE 1   Consider the initial value problem

$$\frac{dy}{dx} = x^2, \quad x(0) = b > 0. \tag{36}$$

As we saw in Example 6, the equation $x' = x^2$ does not satisfy a "strip Lipschitz condition." When we solve (36) by separation of variables, we get

$$x(t) = \frac{b}{1 - bt}. \tag{37}$$

Because the denominator vanishes for $t = 1/b$, Eq. (37) provides a solution of the initial value problem in (36) only for $t < 1/b$, despite the fact that the differential equation $x' = x^2$ "looks nice" on the entire real line—certainly the function appearing on the right-hand side of the equation is continuous everywhere. In particular, if b is large, then we have a solution only on a very small interval to the right of $t = 0$. ∎

Although Theorem 2 assures us that *linear* equations have global solutions, Example 7 shows that, in general, even a "nice" nonlinear differential equation can be expected to have a solution only on a small interval around the initial point $t = a$, and that the length of this interval of existence can depend on the initial value $\mathbf{x}(a) = \mathbf{b}$, as well as on the differential equation itself. The reason is·this: If $\mathbf{f}(\mathbf{x}, t)$ is continuously differentiable in a neighborhood of the point $(\mathbf{b}, a)$ in $(m + 1)$-dimensional space, then—as indicated in the discussion preceding Example 6—we can conclude that $\mathbf{f}(\mathbf{x}, t)$ satisfies a Lipschitz condition on some rectangular region R centered at $(\mathbf{b}, a)$, of the form

$$|t - a| < A, \quad |x_i - b_i| < B_i \tag{38}$$

$(i = 1, 2, \ldots, m)$. In the proof of Theorem 1, we need to apply the Lipschitz condition on the function $\mathbf{f}$ in analyzing the iterative formula

$$\mathbf{x}_{n+1}(t) = \mathbf{b} + \int_a^t \mathbf{f}(\mathbf{x}_n(s), s) \, ds. \tag{39}$$

The potential difficulty is that unless the values of t are suitably restricted, then the point $(\mathbf{x}_n(t), t)$ appearing in the integrand in (39) may not lie in the region R where $\mathbf{f}$ is known to satisfy a Lipschitz condition. On the other hand, it can be shown that—on a sufficiently small open interval J containing the point $t = a$—the graphs of the functions $\{\mathbf{x}_n(t)\}$ given iteratively by the formula in (39) remain within the region R, so the proof of convergence can then be carried out as in the proof of Theorem 1. A proof of the following *local* existence theorem can be found in Chapter 6 of G. Birkhoff and G.-C. Rota, *Ordinary Differential Equations*, 2nd ed. (New York: John Wiley, 1969).

THEOREM 3: Local Existence of Solutions

Let $\mathbf{f}$ be a vector-valued function (with m components) of the $m + 1$ real variables $x_1, x_2, \ldots, x_m$, and t. If the first-order partial derivatives of $\mathbf{f}$ all exist and are continuous in some neighborhood of the point $\mathbf{x} = \mathbf{b}$, $t = a$, then the initial value problem

$$\frac{d\mathbf{x}}{dt} = \mathbf{f}(\mathbf{x}, t), \quad \mathbf{x}(a) = \mathbf{b}, \tag{35}$$

has a solution on some open interval containing the point $t = a$. ∎

A.4 UNIQUENESS OF SOLUTIONS

It is possible to establish the existence of solutions of the initial value problem in (35) under the much weaker hypothesis that $\mathbf{f}(\mathbf{x}, t)$ is merely continuous; techniques other than those used in this section are required. By contrast, the Lipschitz condition that we used in proving Theorem 1 is the key to *uniqueness* of solutions. In particular, the solution provided by Theorem 3 is unique near the point $t = a$.

THEOREM 4: Uniqueness of Solutions

Suppose that on some region R in $(m+1)$-space, the function $\mathbf{f}$ in (35) is continuous and satisfies the Lipschitz condition

$$|\mathbf{f}(\mathbf{x}_1, t) - \mathbf{f}(\mathbf{x}_2, t)| \leq k \cdot |\mathbf{x}_1 - \mathbf{x}_2|. \tag{20}$$

If $\mathbf{x}_1(t)$ and $\mathbf{x}_2(t)$ are two solutions of the initial problem in (35) on some open interval I containing $x = a$, such that the solution curves $(\mathbf{x}_1(t), t)$ and $(\mathbf{x}_2(t), t)$ both lie in R for all t in I, then $\mathbf{x}_1(t) = \mathbf{x}_2(t)$ for all t in I. ∎

We will outline the proof of Theorem 4 for the one-dimensional case in which x is a real variable. A generalization of this proof to the multivariable case can be found in Chapter 6 of Birkhoff and Rota.

Let us consider the function

$$\phi(t) = [x_1(t) - x_2(t)]^2 \tag{40}$$

for which $\phi(a) = 0$, because $x_1(a) = x_2(a) = b$. We want to show that $\phi(t) \equiv 0$, so that $x_1(t) \equiv x_2(t)$. We will consider only the case $t \geq a$; the details are similar for the case $t \leq a$.

If we differentiate each side in Eq. (40), we find that

$$\begin{aligned}
|\phi'(t)| &= |2[x_1(t) - x_2(t)] \cdot [x_1'(t) - x_2'(t)]| \\
&= \left|2[x_1(t) - x_2(t)] \cdot [f(x_1(t), t) - f(x_2(t), t)]\right| \\
&\leq 2k|x_1(t) - x_2(t)|^2 = 2k\phi(t),
\end{aligned}$$

using the Lipschitz condition on f. Hence

$$\phi'(t) \leq 2k\phi(t). \tag{41}$$

Now let us temporarily ignore the fact that $\phi(a) = 0$ and compare $\phi(t)$ with the solution of the differential equation

$$\Phi'(t) = 2k\Phi(t) \tag{42}$$

such that $\Phi(a) = \phi(a)$; clearly

$$\Phi(t) = \Phi(a)e^{2k(t-a)}. \tag{43}$$

In comparing (41) with (42), it seems inevitable that

$$\phi(t) \leq \Phi(t) \qquad \text{for } t \geq a, \tag{44}$$

and this is easily proved (Problem 18). Hence

$$0 \leq [x_1(t) - x_2(t)]^2 \leq [x_1(a) - x_2(a)]^2 e^{2k(t-a)}.$$

On taking square roots, we get

$$0 \leq |x_1(t) - x_2(t)| \leq |x_1(a) - x_2(a)|e^{k(t-a)}. \tag{45}$$

But $x_1(a) - x_2(a) = 0$, so (45) implies that $x_1(t) \equiv x_2(t)$.

EXAMPLE 1   The initial value problem

$$\frac{dx}{dt} = 3x^{2/3}, \quad x(0) = 0 \tag{46}$$

has both the obvious solution $x_1(t) \equiv 0$ and the solution $x_2(t) = t^3$ that is readily found by separation of variables. Hence the function $f(x, t)$ must *fail* to satisfy a Lipschitz condition near $(0, 0)$. Indeed, the mean value theorem yields

$$|f(x, 0) - f(0, 0)| = |f_x(\overline{x}, 0)| \cdot |x - 0|$$

for some $\overline{x}$ between 0 and x. But $f_x(x, 0) = 2x^{-1/3}$ is unbounded as $x \to 0$, so no Lipschitz condition can be satisfied.   ∎

1.4 *Problems*

In Problems 1 through 8, apply the successive approximation formula to compute $y_n(x)$ for $n \leq 4$. Then write the exponential series for which these approximations are partial sums (perhaps with the first term or two missing; for example,

$$e^x - 1 = x + \tfrac{1}{2}x^2 + \tfrac{1}{6}x^3 + \tfrac{1}{24}x^4 + \cdots).$$

1. $\dfrac{dy}{dx} = y, \; y(0) = 3$

2. $\dfrac{dy}{dx} = -2y, \; y(0) = 4$

3. $\dfrac{dy}{dx} = -2xy, \; y(0) = 1$

4. $\dfrac{dy}{dx} = 3x^2y, \; y(0) = 2$

5. $\dfrac{dy}{dx} = 2y + 2, \; y(0) = 0$

6. $\dfrac{dy}{dx} = x + y, \; y(0) = 0$

7. $\dfrac{dy}{dx} = 2x(1 + y), \; y(0) = 0$

8. $\dfrac{dy}{dx} = 4x(y + 2x^2), \; y(0) = 0$

In Problems 9 through 12, compute the successive approximations $y_n(x)$ for $n \leq 3$; then compare them with the appropriate partial sums of the Taylor series of the exact solution.

9. $\dfrac{dy}{dx} = x + y, \; y(0) = 1$

10. $\dfrac{dy}{dx} = y + e^x, \; y(0) = 0$

11. $\dfrac{dy}{dx} = y^2, \; y(0) = 1$

12. $\dfrac{dy}{dx} = \tfrac{1}{2}y^3, \; y(0) = 1$

13. Apply the iterative formula in (16) to compute the first three successive approximations to the solution of the ini-

tial value problem

$$\frac{dx}{dt} = 2x - y, \quad x(0) = 1;$$

$$\frac{dy}{dt} = 3x - 2y, \quad y(0) = -1.$$

14. Apply the matrix exponential series in (19) to solve (in closed form) the initial value problem

$$\mathbf{x}'(t) = \begin{bmatrix} 1 & 1 \\ 0 & 1 \end{bmatrix} \mathbf{x}, \quad \mathbf{x}(0) = \begin{bmatrix} 1 \\ 1 \end{bmatrix}.$$

(*Suggestion*: Show first that

$$\begin{bmatrix} 1 & 1 \\ 0 & 1 \end{bmatrix}^n = \begin{bmatrix} 1 & n \\ 0 & 1 \end{bmatrix}$$

for each positive integer n.)

15. For the initial value problem $dy/dx = 1 + y^3$, $y(1) = 1$, show that the second Picard approximation is

$$y_2(x) = 1 + 2(x - 1) + 3(x - 1)^2 + 4(x - 1)^3 + 2(x - 1)^4.$$

Then compute $y_2(1.1)$ and $y_2(1.2)$. The fourth-order Runge-Kutta method with step size $h = 0.005$ yields $y(1.1) \approx 1.2391$ and $y(1.2) \approx 1.6269$.

16. For the initial value problem $dy/dx = x^2 + y^2$, $y(0) = 0$, show that the third Picard approximation is

$$y_3(x) = \frac{1}{3}x^3 + \frac{1}{63}x^7 + \frac{2}{2079}x^{11} + \frac{1}{59535}x^{15}.$$

Compute $y_3(1)$. The fourth-order Runge-Kutta method yields $y(1) \approx 0.350232$, both with step size $h = 0.05$ and with step size $h = 0.025$.

17. Prove as follows the inequality $|\mathbf{A}\mathbf{x}| \leq \|\mathbf{A}\| \cdot |\mathbf{x}|$, where $\mathbf{A}$ is an $m \times m$ matrix with row vectors $\mathbf{a}_1, \mathbf{a}_2, \ldots, \mathbf{a}_m$, and $\mathbf{x}$ is an m-dimensional vector. First note that the components of the vector $\mathbf{A}\mathbf{x}$ are $\mathbf{a}_1 \cdot \mathbf{x}, \mathbf{a}_2 \cdot \mathbf{x}, \ldots, \mathbf{a}_m \cdot \mathbf{x}$, so

$$|\mathbf{A}\mathbf{x}| = \left[\sum_{n=1}^{m} (\mathbf{a}_i \cdot \mathbf{x})^2 \right]^{1/2}.$$

Then use the Cauchy-Schwarz inequality $(\mathbf{a} \cdot \mathbf{x})^2 \leq |\mathbf{a}|^2 |\mathbf{x}|^2$ for the dot product.

18. Suppose that $\phi(t)$ is a differentiable function with

$$\phi'(t) \leqq k\phi(t) \qquad (k > 0)$$

for $t \geqq a$. Multiply both sides by e^{-kt}, then transpose to show that

$$\frac{d}{dt}\left[\phi(t)e^{-kt}\right] \leqq 0$$

for $t \geqq a$. Then apply the mean value theorem to conclude that

$$\phi(t) \leqq \phi(a)e^{k(t-a)}$$

for $t \geqq a$.

APPENDIX B

Matlab - A Short Introduction

In this course, the principal computational tool will be a software package called **Matlab**. Matlab (Matrix laboratory) is an interactive system designed for matrix computations: solving systems of linear equations, multiplying matrices, computing eigenvalues and eigenvectors, and much more. In this brief introduction, we will present some of the main features of Matlab, emphasizing some of the commands and functions that will be useful for this course. In a sense this introduction is a short version of the excellent manual: A Practical Introduction to Matlab, by Mark S. Gockenbach. We encourage the reader to experiment with the commands and to try out the examples while reading the material.

Matlab is available on the University of Michigan campus on the MACs in the Angel Hall fishbowl and on those of the CAEN system. To use Matlab MAC users can do the following: Click on **Sites Applications**. Click On **Matlabf** and follow the instructions. When the file is copied, open the hard drive and click on the file. After the file has been extracted (**sea** stands for Self Extracting Archive) and unstuffed, open the **Matlabf** folder on your hard-drive and click on the colorful **Matlab** icon. On the workstations of the Math department in East Hall, after you login, a window will appear with a unix prompt; type **matlab** (all lower case) and you will shortly be running Matlab. It is possible to change the size, shape and position of the window using the mouse. All the Matlab commands are to be entered in the Matlab window. A command is entered by typing it and then hitting the Return key.

B.1 VECTORS AND MATRICES; VARIABLES AND FUNCTIONS; HELP

When using Matlab, one of the most useful things to remember is that every variable is a matrix; that is, a box of numbers. The following commands show how to assign numbers, vectors, and matrices to variables:

```
>>  a=5

a =

      5

>>  v=[1;3;0]
```

$$v = \begin{bmatrix} 1 \\ 3 \\ 0 \end{bmatrix}$$

```
>> A = [1,2,3;4,5,6;7,8,9]
```

$$A = \begin{bmatrix} 1 & 2 & 3 \\ 4 & 5 & 6 \\ 7 & 8 & 9 \end{bmatrix}$$

Notice that the rows of a matrix are separated by semicolons, while the entries on any given row are separated by commas (or spaces). As mentioned above, each of these three variables is regarded as a matrix: the scalar **a** is a 1×1 matrix, the vector **v** is a 3×1 matrix, and **A** is a 3×3 matrix.

Indices of variables must be positive and integral. Thus, 'x(0)' and 'x(1.2)' are not allowed, nor is 'A(0,1)' permitted. The size of a matrix can be found using the function $\mathtt{size(A)}$, which returns the pair of numbers m, n when **A** is an $m \times n$ matrix. The length of the vector **v** is found by using the function $\mathtt{length(v)}$.

When entering a matrix, if you want to suppress displaying it, you need to end the line with a semicolon:

```
>> x=[1,2,6];
```

(If you create a list of 100 x-values for a plot, say x=0, x=0.1, x=0.2 etc there is no need to fill the screen with those values. Suppress them with a semicolon.)

Another useful thing to remember is that the complex unit i $(= \sqrt{-1})$ is represented by either one of the built-in variables `i` or `j`. The following examples demonstrate how complex numbers are displayed in Matlab. They also show that the square root function is a built-in feature:

```
>> sqrt(-1)

ans =

   0 + 1.0000i
```

The variable **ans** contains the result of the most recent computation which can then be used as an ordinary variable in subsequent computations:

```
>> 10000-4*2*3

ans =

   9976

>> sqrt(ans)

   99.8799

>> (-100+ans)/4

ans =

   -0.0300
```

A built-in variable that is often useful is π:

```
>> pi

ans =

   3.1416
```

Besides the square root function, other common functions are predefined. They include:

abs	absolute value
angle	phase angle of a complex number
sqrt	square root
real, imag	real part, imaginary part of complex numbers
conj	complex conjugation
round	rounds to the nearest integer
fix	rounds towards zero
floor	rounds towards $-\infty$
ceil	rounds towards ∞
sign	signum function
rem	remainder (needs two input variables)
sin, cos, tan	usual trigonometric functions
asin, atan	usual inverse trigonometric functions

Examples:

```
>> cos(1)^2+sin(1)^2

ans =

   1
```

```
>> exp(1)

ans =

    2.7183

>> log(ans)

ans =

    1
```

Matlab has a comprehensive online help system which includes a list of built-in special functions and routines, as well as a list of other commands on which help is available. To obtain the list just type **help**. To get help on a particular command, type **help** followed by the command.

For example

```
>> help pi
PI = 3.1415926535897....

    PI = 4*atan(1)=imag(log(-1))=3.1415916535897
```

Another command is **help help** which describes how to find help. To view a few demonstrations, click the **demo** option using the mouse.

B.2 GRAPHS

Among the many features of Matlab, as one probably expects, creating graphs is one of the most useful. Here, we will present how to deal with the usual situations, including plots of points in the Cartesian plane and graphs of the built-in functions.

Let us start examining the simplest examples. But first, we need a command for introducing vectors having entries running from a to b in steps of size s. If we type

```
>> t = 1:2:9
```

we get the vector $t = \begin{bmatrix} 1 & 3 & 5 & 7 & 9 \end{bmatrix}$.

When no size step is indicated, it is assumed to be 1:

```
>> t = 2:4
t = [2 3 4]
```

These types of commands are usually used in establishing the pairs (x, y) of points that will be connected in plane by straight lines. The same commands are encountered when one defines the domain of the function that needs to be graphed.

```
>> x = ( 1:5 );
>> y = ( 0:.1:.4);
>> plot (x,y)
```

A necessary remark is that the vectors **x** and **y** must have the same length. If one wants to exhibit only the points (without connecting them with straight lines) the last command needs to be replaced by **plot (x,y,'o')**.

Here are some examples for you to look at and play with.

Conventions:

>> is the matlab prompt. You must hit return after entering a command. Lines with % in front of them are ignored by Matlab; they are comments for use by human beings. You do NOT have to enter those lines into Matlab.

Examples:

```
>> x=0:.01:500;
```

% We make a list of *x*-values for our plots.

```
>> plot(x,sin(x)+sin(.9*x))
```

% You are seeing a phenomena called beats.

```
>> axis([28 31 -0.5 0.5])
```

% This restricts the graph to the portion with x-values between 28 and % 31 and y-values between −0.5 and 0.5.

```
>> axis([28 38 -0.5 0.5])
```

% This shows a different portion of the graph.

```
>> grid
```

% Obviously this adds a grid to the plot.

```
>> plot(x,sin(x/10)+sin(.09*x),'r',x,cos(x/5),'g')
```

% This generates two plots, one in red and another in green.

```
>> legend('sin(x/10)+sin(.09*x)','cos(x/5)')
```

% This adds legend to your graph so you know which function is which.

Colors are very nice for distinguishing curves on your monitor but if you want to print out a plot on a black and white printer you won't see the colors. Instead, you can use different symbols to mark the plots.

```
>> t=0:.1:2;
```

% We make up a small list of x-values.

```
plot(t,sin(t),'+',t,cos(t),'--')
```

% Now you can see the two plots and if you add a legend.

```
>> legend('sin t', 'cos t')
```

% You know which is which.

```
>> plot(sin(x),cos(3*x),'r.',cos(2*x),sin(4*x),
'b:',sin(3*x),cos(5*x+2),'g-')
>> title(' I like to play')
>> legend('double ellipse','Lissajous figure','third
curve')
```

End of examples.

Display and graphics:

xlabel('string'), ylabel('string') label the horizontal and vertical axes, respectively, in the current plot;

title('string') adds a title to the current plot;

axis([a b c d]) changes the window on the current graph to $a \leq x \leq b$, $c \leq y \leq d$;

grid adds a rectangular grid to the current plot;

hold on freezes the current plot so that the subsequent graph will be displayed with the current one;

hold off releases the current plot; the next plot will erase the current before displaying;

subplot puts multiple plots in one graphics window.

legend creates a box which distinguishes and identifies multiple plots.

num2str(N) returns the value of N as a string, helpful in titles of graphs.

Because the Matlab functions are 'vectorized', constructing the needed vectors to graph a built-in function is easy. If we apply a built-in function (for example, cosine) to a matrix the system will create a new matrix of the same size whose entries are now the function values of the entries of the original matrix.

```
>> x = ( 0:.2:2*pi );

y = cos(x);

>> plot( x,y )
```

The same 'vectorized' arithmetic operations provided by Matlab help us to create plots for functions such as $y = \frac{2x}{x+3}$.

```
>> x = ( -1:.1:1 );

>> y = 2.*x./(3+x) ;

>> plot(x,y)
```

The 'vectorized' operations (except for addition and subtraction) must be preceded by '.'. For example `2.*x.` multiplies each component of **x** by 2, and `x./z` divides each component of **x** by the corresponding component of **z**.

We end this section with a remark regarding the 'vectorized' operations just used above. If A is a square matrix then typing `A^2` gives us $A * A$, while `A.^2` means to square each entry of our matrix.

B.3   OPERATIONS ON MATRICES

Using Matlab we can perform standard arithmetic operations on matrices: addition, subtraction, and multiplication, as well as more advanced computations: finding row echelon form, finding eigenvalues and eigenvectors of a matrix and much more. We now present some of the operations that are often used in the Lab Projects of this class.

Standard operations

If A and B are matrices, then Matlab can compute the sum, difference and the multiplication of these two matrices (when these operations are well defined). To do this, it is enough to type **A+B**, **A-B**, and **A*B**, respectively.

Raising a matrix to a power

If A is a square ($n \times n$) matrix, then typing `A^2` yields the product $A * A$, which is the same as A^2. In general typing `A^m` gives A^m.

Determinant of a matrix

If A is a square matrix, then by typing

```
>> det(A)
```

we get its determinant.

As mentioned above, Matlab can be used to do more advanced operations on matrices. In solving systems of linear equations, computing both the row echelon form of a matrix and finding the eigenvalues and eigenvectors of the matrix are very important tools. Let's see how to do this using Matlab:

Eigenvalues and Eigenvectors

If one has a square $n \times n$ matrix A, then if one types

```
>> [r,s] = eig(A)
```

(the letters **r**, **s** are arbitrary choices) one gets a matrix $\mathbf{r} = \begin{bmatrix} v_1, v_2, \dots, v_n \end{bmatrix}$ and a diagonal matrix s. The entries of the diagonal matrix s represent the eigenvalues of the matrix A. The columns of the matrix r are the corresponding eigenvectors of the matrix A.

To be more precise, let us consider an example:

Let A be $\begin{bmatrix} 1 & 0 \\ 2 & 2 \end{bmatrix}$ and type

```
>> A = [1,0;2,2];
```

```
>> [r,s] = eig(A)
```

You will get $r = \begin{bmatrix} 0 & 0.4472 \\ 1 & -0.8944 \end{bmatrix}$ and $s = \begin{bmatrix} 2 & 0 \\ 0 & 1 \end{bmatrix}$.

Here, the vector $\begin{bmatrix} 0 \\ 1 \end{bmatrix}$ is an eigenvector for A with the corresponding eigenvalue 2. Similarly, the vector $\begin{bmatrix} 0.4472 \\ -0.8944 \end{bmatrix}$ is the eigenvector of A corresponding to the eigenvalue 1.

Row echelon form

If A is a matrix then typing

```
>> rref(A)
```

yields a row echelon of A. The particular row echelon form this gives is called the row reduced echelon form (row canonical form). This is a matrix for which all the pivots are 1 and all entries above the pivots are zero. Usually, a row echelon form is not unique. For example, the matrix

$$\begin{bmatrix} 1 & 1 & 1 \\ 0 & -1 & 2 \end{bmatrix}$$

is in row echelon form, but not in row reduced echelon form. However, this matrix is equivalent to

$$\begin{bmatrix} 1 & 0 & 3 \\ 0 & 1 & -2 \end{bmatrix}$$

which is in row reduced form.

B.4   MISCELLANEOUS COMMANDS

Creating matrices:

zeros(m,n) creates an $m \times n$ matrix of zeros;

ones(m,n) creates an $m \times n$ matrix of one;

eye(n) creates the $n \times n$ identity matrix;

diag(v) (assuming **v** is an n-vector) creates an $n \times n$ diagonal matrix with **v** on the diagonal.

To terminate a Matlab session, type **exit** or **quit**. The word **clear** wipes out Matlab work done in the session and brings you back to the beginning of the session.

ANSWERS TO SELECTED PROBLEMS

Chapter 1

Section 1.1

11. If $y = y_1 = x^{-2}$, then $y'(x) = -2x^{-3}$ and $y''(x) = 6x^{-4}$, so
$x^2y'' + 5xy' + 4y = x^2(6x^{-4}) + 5x(-2x^{-3}) + 4(x^{-2}) =$
$6x^{-2} - 10x^{-2} + 4x^{-2} = 0$. If $y = y_2 = x^{-2} \ln x$, then
$y'(x) = x^{-3} - 2x^{-3} \ln x$ and $y''(x) = -5x^{-4} + 6x^{-4} \ln x$, so
$x^2y'' + 5xy' + 4y =$
$x^2(-5x^{-4} + 6x^{-4} \ln x) + 5x(x^{-3} - 2x^{-3} \ln x) + 4(x^{-2} \ln x) = 0.$

13. $r = \frac{2}{3}$

14. $r = \pm\frac{1}{2}$

15. $r = -2, 1$

17. $C = 2$

18. $C = 3$

19. $C = 6$

20. $C = 11$

21. $C = 7$

22. $C = 1$

23. $C = -56$

24. $C = 17$

25. $C = \pi/4$

26. $C = -\pi$

27. $y' = x + y$

28. $y' = 2y/x$

29. $y' = x/(1 - y)$

31. $y' = (y - x)/(y + x)$

32. $dP/dt = k\sqrt{P}$

33. $dv/dt = kv^2$

35. $dN/dt = k(P - N)$

37. $y \equiv 1$ or $y = x$

39. $y = x^2$

41. $y = \frac{1}{2}e^x$

42. $y = \cos x$ or $y = \sin x$

43. (a) $C = 10.1$; (b) No such C, but the constant function $y(x) \equiv 0$ satisfies the conditions $y' = y^2$ and $y(0) = 0$.

Section 1.2

1. $y(x) = x^2 + x + 3$

3. $y(x) = \frac{1}{3}(2x^{3/2} - 16)$

5. $y(x) = 2\sqrt{x + 2} - 5$

7. $y(x) = 10 \tan^{-1} x$

9. $y(x) = \sin^{-1} x$

11. $x(t) = 25t^2 + 10t + 10$

13. $x(t) = \frac{1}{2}t^3 + 5t$

15. $x(t) = \frac{1}{3}(t + 3)^4 - 37t - 26$

17. $x(t) = \frac{1}{2}\left[(t + 1)^{-1} + t - 1\right]$

19. $v(t) = -(9.8)t + 49$, so the ball reaches its maximum height ($v = 0$) after $t = 5$ seconds. Its maximum height then is $y(5) = 122.5$ (m).

21. The car stops when $t \approx 2.78$ (s), so the distance traveled before stopping is approximately $x(2.78) \approx 38.58$ (m).

23. $y_0 \approx 178.57$ (m)

25. After 10 seconds the car has traveled 200 ft and is traveling at 70 ft/s.

27. $v_0 = 10\sqrt{30}$ (m/s), about 197.18 km/h

29. $20\sqrt{10} \approx 63.25$ (ft/s)

33. 25 (mi)

Section 1.3

1.

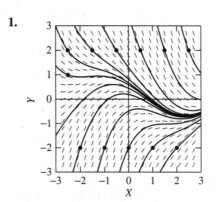

2.

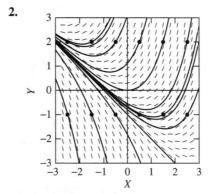

3.

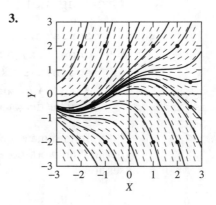

4.
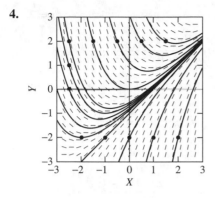

5.
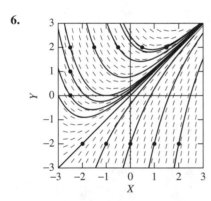

6.
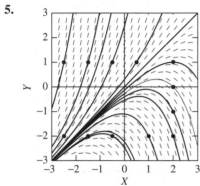

7.
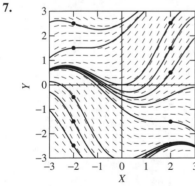

8.
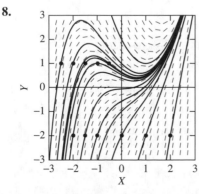

9.
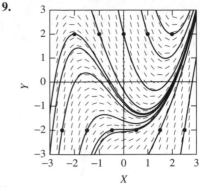

10.
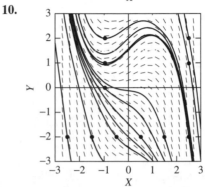

11. Each isocline is a vertical straight line.
13. Each isocline is a horizontal straight line.
15. Each isocline is a straight line through the origin.
17. Each isocline $xy = C$ is a rectangular hyperbola that opens along the line $y = x$ if $C > 0$, along the line $y = -x$ if $C < 0$.
19. Each isocline is a parabola symmetric around the y-axis.
21. A unique solution exists in some neighborhood of $x = 1$.
23. A unique solution exists in some neighborhood of $x = 0$.
25. Neither existence nor uniqueness is guaranteed in any neighborhood of $x = 2$.
27. A unique solution exists in some neighborhood of $x = 0$.
29. A unique solution exists in some neighborhood of $x = 0$.
31. $\partial y / \partial x$ is not continuous when $y = 1$, so the theorem does not guarantee uniqueness.

Section 1.4

1. $y(x) = C \exp(-x^2)$
3. $y(x) = C \exp(-\cos x)$
5. $y(x) = \sin\left(C + \sqrt{x}\right)$
7. $y(x) = (2x^{4/3} + C)^{3/2}$
9. $y(x) = C(1 + x)/(1 - x)$
11. $y(x) = (C - x^2)^{-1/2}$
13. $\ln(y^4 + 1) = C + 4 \sin x$
15. $1/(3y^3) - 2/y = 1/x + \ln|x| + C$
17. $\ln|1 + y| = x + \frac{1}{2}x^2 + C$
19. $y(x) = 2 \exp(e^x)$
21. $y^2 = 1 + \sqrt{x^2 - 16}$
23. $\ln(2y - 1) = 2(x - 1)$
25. $\ln y = x^2 - 1 + \ln x$
27. $y = \ln|3e^{2x} - 2|$
29. About 51840 persons
31. About 14735 years
33. $21103.48
35. 2585 mg
37. About 4.86×10^9 years ago
39. After a total of about 63 min have elapsed
41. (a) 0.495 m; (b $(8.32 \times 10^{-7})I_0$; (c) 3.29 m
43. (a) $dA/dt = rA + Q$; (b) $Q = 0.70482$, so you make deposits at the rate of $704.82 per year.
45. After about 66 min 40 s
47. After about 46 days
49. 972 s
50. At time $t = 2048/1562 \approx 1.31$ (in hours)
52. 1:20 P.M.
53. (a) $y(t) = (8 - 7t)^{2/3}$; (b) at 1:08:34 P.M.;
   (c) $r = \frac{1}{60}\sqrt{\frac{7}{12}} \approx 0.15$ (in.)
55. Approximately 14 min 29 s
56. The tank is empty about 14 seconds after 2:00 P.M.
57. (a) 1:53:34 P.M.; (b) $r \approx 0.04442$ ft ≈ 0.53 in.
58. $r = \frac{1}{720}\sqrt{3}$ ft, about $\frac{1}{35}$ in.
59. At approximately 10:29 A.M.

Section 1.5

1. $y(x) = 2(1 - e^{-x})$
2. $\rho(x) = e^{-2x}$
3. $y(x) = e^{-3x}(x^2 + C)$
4. $\rho(x) = \exp(-x^2)$
5. $y(x) = x + 4x^{-2}$
6. $\rho(x) = x^5$
7. $y(x) = 5x^{1/2} + Cx^{-1/2}$
8. $\rho(x) = x^{1/3}$
9. $y(x) = x(7 + \ln x)$
10. $\rho(x) = x^{-3/2}$
11. $y(x) \equiv 0$
12. $\rho(x) = x^3$
13. $y(x) = (e^x + e^{-x})/2$
14. $\rho(x) = x^{-3}$
15. $y(x) = [1 - 5\exp(-x^2)]/2$
16. $\rho(x) = \exp(\sin x)$
17. $y(x) = (1 + \sin x)/(1 + x)$
18. $\rho(x) = x^{-2}$
19. $y(x) = \frac{1}{2}\sin x + C\csc x$
20. $\rho(x) = \exp\left(-x - \frac{1}{2}x^2\right)$
21. $y(x) = x^3 \sin x$
22. $\rho(x) = \exp(-x^2)$
23. $y(x) = x^3(2 + Ce^{-2x})$
24. $\rho(x) = (x^2 + 4)^{3/2}$
25. $y(x) = \left[\exp\left(-\frac{3}{2}x^2\right)\right]\left[3(x^2 + 1)^{3/2} - 2\right]$
26. $\rho(y) = y^4$
27. $x(y) = e^y\left(C + \frac{1}{2}y^2\right)$
28. $\rho(y) = (1 + y^2)^{-1}$
29. $y(x) = \left[\exp(x^2)\right]\left[C + \frac{1}{2}\sqrt{\pi}\,\text{erf}(x)\right]$
33. After about 7 min 41 s
34. About 22.2 days
35. About 5.5452 years
37. 393.75 lb
39. (b) $y_{max} = 100e^{-1} \approx 36.79$ (gal)
41. (b) Approximately $1,308,283
43. $-50.0529, -28.0265, -6.0000, 16.0265, 38.0529$
44. $3.99982, 4.00005, 4.00027, 4.00050, 4.00073$

Chapter 2

Section 2.1

1. $x(t) = \dfrac{40}{8 - 3e^{-15t}}$
2. $x(t) = \dfrac{10}{2 + 3e^{15t}}$
3. $x(t) = \dfrac{77}{11 - 4e^{-28t}}$
4. $x(t) = \dfrac{221}{17 - 4e^{91t}}$
5. 484
6. 20 weeks
7. (b) $P(t) = \left(\frac{1}{2}t + 10\right)^2$
8. $P(t) = \dfrac{240}{20 - t}$
9. $P(t) = \dfrac{180}{30 - t}$
10. $P(t) = \dfrac{P_0}{1 + kP_0 t}$
12. About 27.69 months
13. About 44.22 months
15. About 24.41 months
16. About 42.12 months
18. About 34.66 days
19. $\frac{5}{4}\ln 3$ (s)
20. About 9.24 days
21. (a) $M = 100$ and $k = 0.0002$; (b) In the year 2035
22. $50\ln\frac{9}{8}$ months
23. (a) $100\ln\frac{9}{5}$ months; (b) $100\ln 2$ months
26. $\alpha \approx 0.3915$; 2.15×10^6 cells
29. $k \approx 0.0000668717$, $M \approx 338.027$
30. $k \approx 0.000146679$, $M \approx 208.250$

Section 2.2

1. Unstable critical point: $x = 4$;
$$x(t) = 4 + (x_0 - 4)e^t$$
2. Stable critical point: $x = 3$;
$$x(t) = 3 + (x_0 - 3)e^{-t}$$
3. Stable critical point: $x = 0$; unstable critical point: $x = 4$;
$$x(t) = \frac{4x_0}{x_0 + (4 - x_0)e^{4t}}$$
4. Stable critical point: $x = 3$; unstable critical point: $x = 0$;
$$x(t) = \frac{3x_0}{x_0 + (3 - x_0)e^{-3t}}$$

5. Stable critical point: $x = -2$; unstable critical point: $x = 2$;
$$x(t) = \frac{2[x_0 + 2 + (x_0 - 2)e^{4t}]}{x_0 + 2 - (x_0 - 2)e^{4t}}$$
6. Stable critical point: $x = 3$; unstable critical point: $x = -3$;
$$x(t) = \frac{3[x_0 - 3 + (x_0 + 3)e^{6t}]}{3 - x_0 + (x_0 + 3)e^{6t}}$$
7. Semi-stable (see Problem 18) critical point: $x = 2$;
$$x(t) = \frac{(2t - 1)x_0 - 4t}{tx_0 - 2t + 1}$$
8. Semi-stable critical point: $x = 3$;
$$x(t) = \frac{(3t + 1)x_0 - 9t}{tx_0 - 3t + 1}$$
9. Stable critical point: $x = 1$; unstable critical point: $x = 4$;
$$x(t) = \frac{4(1 - x_0) + (x_0 - 4)e^{3t}}{1 - x_0 + (x_0 - 4)e^{3t}}$$
10. Stable critical point: $x = 5$; unstable critical point: $x = 2$;
$$x(t) = \frac{2(5 - x_0) + 5(x_0 - 2)e^{3t}}{5 - x_0 + (x_0 - 2)e^{3t}}$$
11. Unstable critical point: $x = 1$;
$$\frac{1}{(x(t) - 1)^2} = \frac{1}{(x_0 - 1)^2} - 2t$$
12. Stable critical point: $x = 2$;
$$\frac{1}{(2 - x(t))^2} = \frac{1}{(2 - x_0)^2} + 2t$$

Section 2.3

1. Approximately 31.5 s
3. $400/(\ln 2)$ ft
5. $400\ln 7$ ft
7. $x(t) = 100t - 1000(1 - e^{-t/10})$
8. (b) $x(t) = 1000\ln\cosh(t/10)$
9. 50 ft/s
10. About 5 min 47 s
11. Time of fall: about 12.5 s
12. Approximately 648 ft
19. Approximately 30.46 ft/s; exactly 40 ft/s
20. Approximately 277.26 ft
22. Approximately 20.67 ft/s; about 484.57 s
23. Approximately 259.304 s
24. (a) About 0.88 cm; (b) about 2.91 km
27. About 51.427 km
28. Approximately 11109 m/s

Section 2.4

Note: Most of the problems in this section call for a table of values. Space limitations prohibit reproduction of the complete tables in the book; we have chosen in most cases to give only data from the last line of the table. Your answers may differ slightly because of variations in hardware and software.

1. $y_{n+1} = y_n + h(-y_n)$; $y(x) = 2e^{-x}$. Results:

x	$h = 0.1$ y	$h = 0.05$ y	Actual y
0.0	2.0000	2.0000	2.0000
0.1	1.8000	1.8050	1.8097
0.2	1.6200	1.6290	1.6375
0.3	1.4580	1.4702	1.4816
0.4	1.3122	1.3268	1.3406
0.5	1.1810	1.1975	1.2131

2. $y_{n+1} = y_n + h(2y_n)$; $y(x) = \frac{1}{2}e^{2x}$. At $x = 0.5$ we should see $y = 1.2442$ ($h = 0.1$), 1.2969 ($h = 0.05$), and 1.3591 (true value).

Note: In the answers to Problem 3 through 24, we give first the x-value, then the y-values obtained with decreasing values of h, and finally the true value of y.

3. 0.5, 2.2210, 2.2578, 2.2974
4. 0.5, 0.6810, 0.6975, 0.7131
5. 0.5, 0.8895, 0.8711, 0.8513
6. 0.5, 1.6272, 1.5912, 1.5576
7. 0.5, 2.7373, 2.6930, 2.6475
8. 0.5, 0.4198, 0.4124, 0.4055
9. 0.5, 1.2785, 1.2828, 1.2874
10. 0.5, 1.2313, 1.2776, 1.3333
11. 1.0, −0.7048, −0.7115, −0.7183
12. 1.0, 2.9864, 2.9931, 3.0000
13. 2.0, 4.8890, 4.8940, 4.8990
14. 2.0, 3.2031, 3.2304, 3.2589
15. 3.0, 3.4422, 3.4433, 3.4444
16. 3.0, 8.8440, 8.8445, 8.8451
17. 1.0, 0.2925, 0.3379, 0.3477, 0.3497
18. 2.0, 1.6680, 1.6771, 1.6790, 1.6794
19. 2.0, 6.1831, 6.3653, 6.4022, 6.4096
20. 2.0, −1.3792, −1.2843, −1.2649, −1.2610
21. 2.0, 2.8508, 2.8681, 2.8716, 2.8723
22. 2.0, 6.9879, 7.2601, 7.3154, 7.3264
23. 1.0, 1.2262, 1.2300, 1.2306, 1.2307
24. 1.0, 0.9585, 0.9918, 0.9984, 0.9997
25.

x	$h = 0.15$ y	$h = 0.03$ y	$h = 0.006$ y
−1.0	1.0000	1.0000	1.0000
−0.7	1.0472	1.0512	1.0521
−0.4	1.1213	1.1358	1.1390
−0.1	1.2826	1.3612	1.3835
0.2	0.8900	1.4711	0.8210
0.5	0.7460	1.2808	0.7192

26.

x	$h = 0.1$ y	$h = 0.01$ y
1.8	2.8200	4.3308
1.9	3.9393	7.9425
2.0	5.8521	28.3926

27.

x	$h = 0.1$ y	$h = 0.01$ y
0.7	4.3460	6.4643
0.8	5.8670	11.8425
0.9	8.3349	39.5010

Section 2.5

1.

x	Improved Euler y	Actual y
0.1	1.8100	1.8097
0.2	1.6381	1.6375
0.3	1.4824	1.4816
0.4	1.3416	1.3406
0.5	1.2142	1.2131

Note: In Problems 2 through 10, we give the value of x, the corresponding improved Euler value of y, and the true value of y.

2. 0.5, 1.3514, 1.3191
3. 0.5, 2.2949, 2.2974
4. 0.5, 0.7142, 0.7131
5. 0.5, 0.8526, 0.8513
6. 0.5, 1.5575, 1.5576
7. 0.5, 2.6405, 2.6475
8. 0.5, 0.4053, 0.4055
9. 0.5, 1.2873, 1.2874
10. 0.5, 1.3309, 1.3333

In Problems 11 through 16 we give the final value of x, the corresponding values of y with $h = 0.01$ and with $h = 0.005$, and the true value of y.

11. 1.0, −0.71824, −0.71827, −0.71828
12. 1.0, 2.99995, 2.99999, 3.00000
13. 2.0, 4.89901, 4.89899, 4.89898
14. 2.0, 3.25847, 3.25878, 3.25889
15. 3.0, 3.44445, 3.44445, 3.44444
16. 3.0, 8.84511, 8.84509, 8.84509

In Problems 17 through 24 we give the final value of x and the corresponding values of y for $h = 0.1, 0.02, 0.004$, and 0.0008.

17. 1.0, 0.35183, 0.35030, 0.35023, 0.35023
18. 2.0, 1.68043, 1.67949, 1.67946, 1.67946
19. 2.0, 6.40834, 6.41134, 6.41147, 6.41147
20. 2.0, −1.26092, −1.26003, −1.25999, −1.25999
21. 2.0, 2.87204, 2.87245, 2.87247, 2.87247
22. 2.0, 7.31578, 7.32841, 7.32916, 7.32920
23. 1.0, 1.22967, 1.23069, 1.23073, 1.23073
24. 1.0, 1.00006, 1.00000, 1.00000, 1.00000
25. Impact speed approximately 43.22 m/s
26. Impact speed approximately 43.48 m/s

Section 2.6

1. $y(0.25) \approx 1.55762$; $y(0.25) = 1.55760$.
$y(0.5) \approx 1.21309$; $y(0.5) = 1.21306$.
Solution: $y = 2e^{-x}$

In Problems 2 through 10 we give the approximation to $y(0.5)$, its
true value, and the solution.

2. 1.35867, 1.35914; $y = \frac{1}{2}e^{2x}$
3. 2.29740, 2.29744; $y = 2e^x - 1$
4. 0.71309, 0.71306; $y = 2e^{-x} + x - 1$
5. 0.85130, 0.85128; $y = -e^x + x + 2$
6. 1.55759, 1.55760; $u = 2\exp\left(-x^2\right)$
7. 2.64745, 2.64749; $y = 3\exp\left(-x^3\right)$
8. 0.40547, 0.40547; $y = \ln(x + 1)$
9. 1.28743, 1.28743; $y = \tan\frac{1}{4}(x + \pi)$
10. 1.33337, 1.33333; $y = (1 - x^2)^{-1}$
11. *Solution:* $y(x) = 2 - e^x$.

x	$h = 0.2$ y	$h = 0.1$ y	**Exact** y
0.0	1.00000	1.00000	1.00000
0.2	0.77860	0.77860	0.77860
0.4	0.50818	0.50818	0.50818
0.6	0.17789	0.17788	0.17788
0.8	-0.22552	-0.22554	-0.22554
1.0	-0.71825	-0.71828	-0.71828

In Problems 12 through 16 we give the final value of x, the
corresponding Runge-Kutta approximations with $h = 0.2$ and with
$h = 0.1$, the exact value of y, and the solution.

12. 1.0, 2.99996, 3.00000, 3.00000;
$y = 1 + 2/(2 - x)$
13. 2.0, 4.89900, 4.89898, 4.89898;
$y = \sqrt{8 + x^4}$
14. 2.0, 3.25795, 3.25882, 3.25889;
$y = 1/(1 - \ln x)$
15. 3.0, 3.44445, 3.44444, 3.44444;
$y = x + 4x^{-2}$
16. 3.0, 8.84515, 8.84509, 8.84509;
$y = (x^6 - 37)^{1/3}$

In Problems 17 through 24 we give the final value of x and the
corresponding values of y with $h = 0.2, 0.1, 0.05,$ and 0.025.

17. 1.0, 0.350258, 0.350234, 0.350232, 0.350232
18. 2.0, 1.679513, 1.679461, 1.679459, 1.679459
19. 2.0, 6.411464, 6.411474, 6.411474, 6.411474
20. 2.0, -1.259990, -1.259992, -1.259993,
-1.259993
21. 2.0, 2.872467, 2.872468, 2.872468, 2.872468
22. 2.0, 7.326761, 7.328452, 7.328971, 7.329134
23. 1.0, 1.230735, 1.230731, 1.230731, 1.230731
24. 1.0, 1.000000, 1.000000, 1.000000, 1.000000
25. Time aloft: approximately 9.41 s
26. Time aloft: approximately 9.41 s

Chapter 3

Section 3.1

1. $y(x) = \frac{5}{2}e^x - \frac{5}{2}e^{-x}$
3. $y(x) = 3\cos 2x + 4\sin 2x$
5. $y(x) = 2e^x - e^{2x}$
7. $y(x) = 6 - 8e^{-x}$
9. $y(x) = 2e^{-x} + xe^{-x}$
11. $y(x) = 5e^x \sin x$
13. $y(x) = 5x - 2x^2$
15. $y(x) = 7x - 5x\ln x$
21. Linearly independent
23. Linearly independent

25. Linearly independent
29. There is no contradiction because if the given differential
equation is divided by x^2 to get the form in Eq. (8), then the
resulting coefficient functions $p(x) = -4/x$ and $q(x) = 6/x^2$
are not continuous at $x = 0$.
33. $y(x) = c_1 e^x + c_2 e^{2x}$
35. $y(x) = c_1 + c_2 e^{-5x}$
37. $y(x) = c_1 e^{-x/2} + c_2 e^x$
39. $y(x) = (c_1 + c_2 x)e^{-x/2}$
41. $y(x) = c_1 e^{-4x/3} + c^2 e^{-5x/2}$
43. $y'' + 10y' = 0$
45. $y'' + 20y' + 100y = 0$
47. $y'' = 0$
49. The high point is $\left(\ln\frac{7}{4}, \frac{16}{7}\right)$.

Section 3.3

1. $y(x) = c_1 e^{2x} + c_2 e^{-2x}$
3. $y(x) = c_1 e^{2x} + c_2 e^{-5x}$
5. $y(x) = c_1 e^{-3x} + c_2 xe^{-3x}$
7. $y(x) = c_1 e^{3x/2} + c_2 xe^{3x/2}$
9. $y(x) = e^{-4x}(c_1 \cos 3x + c_2 \sin 3x)$
11. $y(x) = c_1 + c_2 x + c_3 e^{4x} + c_4 xe^{4x}$
13. $y(x) = c_1 + c_2 e^{-2x/3} + c_3 xe^{-2x/3}$
15. $y(x) = c_1 e^{2x} + c_2 xe^{2x} + c_3 e^{-2x} + c_4 xe^{-2x}$
17. $y(x) = c_1 \cos\left(x/\sqrt{2}\right) + c_2 \sin\left(x/\sqrt{2}\right) + c_3 \cos\left(2x/\sqrt{3}\right) +$
$c_4 \sin\left(2x/\sqrt{3}\right)$
19. $y(x) = c_1 e^x + c_2 e^{-x} + c_3 xe^{-x}$
21. $y(x) = 5e^x + 2e^{3x}$
23. $y(x) = e^{3x}(3\cos 4x - 2\sin 4x)$
25. $y(x) = \frac{1}{4}(-13 + 6x + 9e^{-2x/3})$
27. $y(x) = c_1 e^x + c_2 e^{-2x} + c_3 xe^{-2x}$
29. $y(x) = c_1 e^{-3x} + e^{3x/2}\left[c_2 \cos\left(\frac{3}{2}x\sqrt{3}\right) + c_3 \sin\left(\frac{3}{2}x\sqrt{3}\right)\right]$
31. $y(x) = c_1 e^x + e^{-2x}(c_2 \cos 2x + c_3 \sin 2x)$
33. $y(x) = c_1 e^{3x} + e^{-3x}(c_2 \cos 3x + c_3 \sin 3x)$
35. $y(x) = c_1 e^{-x/2} + c_2 e^{-x/3} + c_3 \cos 2x + c_4 \sin 2x$
37. $y(x) = 11 + 5x + 3x^2 + 7e^x$
39. $y^{(3)} - 6y'' + 12y' - 8y = 0$
41. $y^{(4)} - 16y = 0$
45. $y(x) = c_1 e^{-ix} + c_2 e^{3ix}$
47. $y(x) = c_1 \exp\left(\left[1 + i\sqrt{3}\right]x\right) + c_2 \exp\left(-\left[1 + i\sqrt{3}\right]x\right)$
49. $y(x) = 2e^{2x} - 5e^{-x} + 3\cos x - 9\sin x$

Section 3.4

1. Frequency: 2 rad/s $(1/\pi$ Hz); period: π s
3. Amplitude: 2 m; frequency: 5 rad/s;
period: $2\pi/5$ s
7. About 10450 ft
11. About 3.8 in.
13. (a) $x(t) = 50(e^{-2t/5} - e^{-t/2})$; (b) 4.096 exactly
15. $x(t) = 4e^{-2t} - 2e^{-4t}$; overdamped
17. $x(t) = 5e^{-4t} + 10te^{-4t}$; critically damped
19. $x(t) \approx \frac{1}{3}\sqrt{313}e^{-5t/2}\cos(6t - 0.8254)$; underdamped
21. $x(t) = e^{-5t}(6\cos 10t + 8\sin 10t) \approx 10e^{-5t}\cos(10t - 0.9273)$;
underdamped
22. (b) The time-varying amplitude is $\frac{2}{3}\sqrt{3}$, the frequency is $4\sqrt{3}$
rad/s, and the phase angle is $\pi/6$.
23. (a) $k \approx 7018$ lb/ft; (b) After about 2.47 s
34. Damping constant: $c \approx 11.51$ lb/ft/s; spring constant:
$k \approx 189.68$ lb/ft

Section 3.5

1. $y_p(x) = \frac{1}{25}e^{3x}$

3. $y_p(x) = \frac{1}{39}(\cos 3x - 5\sin 3x)$

5. $y_p(x) = \frac{1}{26}(13 + 3\cos 2x - 2\sin 2x)$

7. $y_p(x) = -\frac{1}{6}(e^x - e^{-x}) = -\frac{1}{3}\sinh x$

9. $y_p(x) = -\frac{1}{3} + \frac{1}{16}(2x^2 - x)e^x$

11. $y_p(x) = \frac{1}{8}(3x^2 - 2x)$

13. $y_p(x) = \frac{1}{65}e^x(7\sin x - 4\cos x)$

15. $y_p(x) \equiv -17$

17. $y_p(x) = \frac{1}{4}(x^2 \sin x - x\cos x)$

19. $y_p(x) = \frac{1}{8}(10x^2 - 4x^3 + x^4)$

21. $y_p(x) = xe^x(A\cos x + B\sin x)$

23. $y_p(x) = Ax\cos 2x + Bx\sin 2x + Cx^2\cos 2x + Dx^2\sin 2x$

25. $y_p(x) = Axe^{-x} + Bx^2e^{-x} + Cxe^{-2x} + Dx^2e^{-2x}$

27. $y_p(x) = Ax\cos x + Bx\sin x + Cx\cos 2x + Dx\sin 2x$

29. $y_p(x) = Ax^3e^x + Bx^4e^x + Cxe^{2x} + Dxe^{-2x}$

31. $y(x) = \cos 2x + \frac{3}{4}\sin 2x + \frac{1}{2}x$

33. $y(x) = \cos 3x - \frac{2}{15}\sin 3x + \frac{1}{5}\sin 2x$

35. $y(x) = e^x(2\cos x - \frac{5}{2}\sin x) + \frac{1}{2}x + 1$

37. $y(x) = 4 - 4e^x + 3xe^x + x - \frac{1}{2}x^2e^x + \frac{1}{6}x^3e^x$

39. $y(x) = -3 + 3x - \frac{1}{2}x^2 + \frac{1}{6}x^3 + 4e^{-x} + xe^{-x}$

41. $y_p(x) = 255 - 450x + 30x^2 + 20x^3 + 10x^4 - 4x^5$

43. (b) $y(x) = c_1\cos 2x + c_2\sin 2x + \frac{1}{4}\cos x - \frac{1}{20}\cos 3x$

45. $y(x) = c_1\cos 3x + c_2\sin 3x + \frac{1}{24} - \frac{1}{10}\cos 2x - \frac{1}{56}\cos 4x$

47. $y_p(x) = \frac{2}{3}e^x$

49. $y_p(x) = x^2e^{2x}$

51. $y_p(x) = -\frac{1}{4}(\cos 2x \cos x - \sin 2x \sin x) + \frac{1}{20}(\cos 5x \cos 2x + \sin 5x \sin 2x) = -\frac{1}{5}\cos 3x$ (!)

53. $y_p(x) = \frac{2}{3}x\sin 3x + \frac{2}{9}(\cos 3x)\ln|\cos 3x|$

55. $y_p(x) = \frac{1}{8}(1 - x\sin 2x)$

59. $y_p(x) = \frac{1}{4}x^4$

61. $y_p(x) = \ln x$

Section 3.6

1. $x(t) = 2\cos 2t - 2\cos 3t$

3. $x(t) = \frac{1}{15}\sqrt{138,388}\cos(10t - \alpha) + \frac{1}{3}\cos(5t - \beta)$, where $\alpha = 2\pi - \tan^{-1}\left(\frac{1}{186}\right) \approx 6.2778$ and $\beta = \tan^{-1}\left(\frac{4}{3}\right) \approx 0.9273$

5. $x(t) = (x_0 - C)\cos\omega_0 t + C\cos\omega t$, where $C = F_0/(k - m\omega^2)$

7. $x_{sp}(t) = \frac{10}{13}\cos(3t - \alpha)$, where $\alpha = \pi - \tan^{-1}\left(\frac{12}{5}\right) \approx 1.9656$

9. $x_{sp}(t) = \left(3/\sqrt{40001}\right)\cos(10t - \alpha)$, where $\alpha = \pi + \tan^{-1}\left(\frac{199}{20}\right) \approx 4.6122$

11. $x_{sp}(t) = \frac{1}{4}\sqrt{10}\cos(3t - \alpha)$, where $\alpha = \pi - \tan^{-1}(3) \approx 1.8925$; $x_{tr}(t) = \frac{5}{4}\sqrt{2}e^{-2t}\cos(t - \beta)$, where $\beta = 2\pi - \tan^{-1}(7) \approx 4.8543$

13. $x_{sp}(t) = \left(3/\sqrt{9236}\right)\cos(10t - \alpha)$, where $\alpha = \pi - \tan^{-1}\left(\frac{10}{47}\right) \approx 2.9288$; $x_{tr}(t) = (10.9761)e^{-t}\cos\left(t\sqrt{5} - \beta\right)$, where $\beta \approx 0.4181$

15. There is no practical resonance frequency.

17. Practical resonance at $\omega = 3\sqrt{3}$

19. $\omega = \sqrt{384}$ rad/s (approximately 3.12 Hz)

21. $\omega_0 = \sqrt{(g/L) + (k/m)}$

23. (a) Natural frequency: $\sqrt{10}$ rad/s (approximately 0.50 Hz); (b) amplitude: approximately 10.625 in.

Chapter 4
Section 4.1

1. $x_1' = x_2,\ x_2' = -7x_1 - 3x_2 + t^2$

2. $x_1' = x_2,\ x_2' = x_3,\ x_3' = x_4,\ x_4' = -x_1 + 3x_2 - 6x_3 + \cos 3t$

3. $x_1' = x_2,\ t^2 x_2' = (1 - t^2)x_1 - tx_2$

5. $x_1' = x_2,\ x_2' = x_3,\ x_3' = x_2^2 + \cos x_1$

7. $x_1' = x_2,\ y_1' = y_2,\ x_2' = -kx_1 \cdot (x_1^2 + y_1^2)^{-3/2},$ $y_2' = -ky_1 \cdot (x_1^2 + y_1^2)^{-3/2}$

9. $x_1' = x_2,\ y_1' = y_2,\ z_1' = z_2,\ x_2' = 3x_1 - y_1 + 2z_1,$ $y_2' = x_1 + y_1 - 4z_1,\ z_2' = 5x_1 - y_1 - z_1$

11. $x(t) = A\cos t + B\sin t,\ y(t) = B\cos t - A\sin t$

12. $x(t) = Ae^t + Be^{-t},\ y(t) = Ae^t - Be^{-t}$

13. $x(t) = A\cos 2t + B\sin 2t,\ y(t) = -B\cos 2t + A\sin 2t;$ $x(t) = \cos 2t,\ y(t) = \sin 2t$

14. $x(t) = A\cos 10t + B\sin 10t,\ y(t) = B\cos 10t - A\sin 10t;$ $x(t) = 3\cos 10t + 4\sin 10t,\ y(t) = 4\cos 10t - 3\sin 10t$

15. $x(t) = A\cos 2t + B\sin 2t,\ y(t) = 4B\cos 2t - 4A\sin 2t$

16. $x(t) = A\cos 4t + B\sin 4t,\ y(t) = \frac{1}{2}B\cos 4t - \frac{1}{2}A\sin 4t$

17. $x(t) = Ae^{-3t} + Be^{2t},\ y(t) = -3Ae^{-3t} + 2Be^{2t};\ x(t) = e^{2t},$ $y(t) = 2e^{2t}$

18. $x(t) = Ae^{-2t} + Be^{-5t},\ y(t) = 2Ae^{-2t} + 5Be^{-5t};\ A = \frac{17}{3}$ and $B = -\frac{11}{3}$ in the particular solution.

19. $x(t) = -e^{-2t}\sin 3t,\ y(t) = e^{-2t}(3\cos 3t + 2\sin 3t)$

20. $x(t) = (A + B)e^{3t},\ y(t) = (3A + B + 3Bt)e^{3t}$

27. $2(I_1' - I_2') + 50I_1 = 100\sin 60t,\ 2(I_2' - I_1') + 25I_2 = 0$

28. $I_1' = -20(I_1 - I_2),\ I_2' = 40(I_1 - I_2)$

Section 4.2

1. $x(t) = a_1e^{-t} + a_2e^{2t},\ y(t) = a_2e^{2t}$

2. $x(t) = (c_1 + c_2t)e^{-t},\ y(t) = (c_1 - \frac{1}{2}c_2 + c_2t)e^{-t}$

3. $x(t) = \frac{4}{5}(e^{3t} - e^{-2t}),\ y(t) = \frac{2}{5}(6e^{3t} - e^{-2t})$

4. $x(t) = \frac{1}{2}(3e^{2t} - e^{-2t}),\ y(t) = \frac{1}{2}(3e^{2t} - 5e^{-2t})$

5. $x(t) = e^{-t}(a_1\cos 2t + a_2\sin 2t),$ $y(t) = -\frac{1}{2}e^{-t}[(a_1 + a_2)\cos 2t + (a_2 - a_1)\sin 2t]$

6. $x(t) = e^{-2t}(3\cos 3t + 9\sin 3t),\ y(t) = e^{-2t}(2\cos 3t - 4\sin 3t)$

7. $x(t) = a_1e^{2t} + a_2e^{3t} - \frac{1}{3}t + \frac{1}{18},\ y(t) = -2a_1e^{2t} - a_2e^{3t} - \frac{2}{3}t - \frac{5}{9}$

8. $x(t) = c_1e^t + c_2e^{3t} + e^{2t},\ y(t) = -c_1e^t + c_2e^{3t}$

9. $x(t) = 3a_1e^t + a_2e^{-t} - \frac{1}{5}(7\cos 2t + 4\sin 2t),$ $y(t) = a_1e^t + a_2e^{-t} - \frac{1}{5}(2\cos 2t + 4\sin 2t)$

10. $x(t) = e^t,\ y(t) = -e^t$

11. $x(t) = a_1\cos 3t + a_2\sin 3t - \frac{11}{20}e^t - \frac{1}{4}e^{-t},$ $y(t) = \frac{1}{3}[(a_1 - a_2)\cos 3t + (a_1 + a_2)\sin 3t] + \frac{1}{10}e^t$

12. $x(t) = c_1e^{2t} + c_2e^{-2t} + c_3e^{3t} + c_4e^{-3t},$ $y(t) = -c_1e^{2t} - c_2e^{-2t} + \frac{3}{2}c_3e^{3t} + \frac{3}{2}c_4e^{-3t}$

13. $x(t) = a_1\cos 2t + a_2\sin 2t + b_1\cos 3t + b_2\sin 3t,$ $y(t) = \frac{1}{2}(a_1\cos 2t + a_2\sin 2t) - 2(b_1\cos 3t + b_2\sin 3t)$

14. $x(t) = c_1\cos 2t + c_2\sin 2t + \frac{1}{3}\sin t,$ $y(t) = c_1\cos 2t + c_2\sin 2t + c_3\cos 2t\sqrt{2} + c_4\sin 2t\sqrt{2} + \frac{4}{21}\sin t$

15. $x(t) = a_1\cos t + a_2\sin t + b_1\cos 2t + b_2\sin 2t,$ $y(t) = a_2\cos t - a_1\sin t + b_2\cos 2t - b_1\sin 2t$

17. $x(t) = a_1\cos t + a_2\sin t + b_1e^{2t} + b_2e^{-2t},$ $y(t) = 3a_2\cos t - 3a_1\sin t + b_1e^{2t} - b_2e^{-2t}$

18. $x(t) = \frac{1}{6}(4c_1e^{3t} - 3c_2e^{-4t}),\ y(t) = c_1e^{3t} + c_2e^{-4t},$ $z(t) = \frac{1}{6}(-4c_1e^{3t} + 3c_2e^{-4t})$

19. $x(t) = a_1 + a_2e^{4t} + a_3e^{8t},\ y(t) = 2a_1 - 2a_3e^{8t},$ $z(t) = 2a_1 - 2a_2e^{4t} + 2a_3e^{8t}$

20. $x(t) = a_1e^{2t} + a_2e^{-t} + \frac{2}{3}te^{-t},\ y(t) = a_1e^{2t} + b_2e^{-t} - \frac{1}{3}te^{-t},$ $z(t) = a_1e^{2t} - (a_2 + b_2 + \frac{1}{3})e^{-t} - \frac{1}{3}te^{-t}$

23. Infinitely many solutions

24. No solution

25. Infinitely many solutions

26. Two arbitrary constants

27. No arbitrary constants

28. No solution

29. Four arbitrary constants

31. $I_1(t) = 2 + e^{-5t}\left[-2\cos\left(10t/\sqrt{6}\right) + 4\sqrt{6}\sin\left(10t/\sqrt{6}\right)\right],$ $I_2(t) = \left(20/\sqrt{6}\right)e^{-5t}\sin\left(10t/\sqrt{6}\right)$

32. $I_1(t) = \frac{1}{1321}(120e^{-25t/3} - 120\cos 60t + 1778\sin 60t)$,
$I_2(t) = \frac{1}{1321}(-240e^{-25t/3} + 240\cos 60t + 1728\sin 60t)$

33. $I_1(t) = \frac{2}{3}(2 + e^{-60t})$, $I_2(t) = \frac{4}{3}(1 - e^{-60t})$

37. (a) $x(t) = a_1\cos 5t + a_2\sin 5t + b_1\cos 5t\sqrt{3} + b_2\sin 5t\sqrt{3}$,
$y(t) = 2a_1\cos 5t + 2a_2\sin 5t - 2b_1\cos 5t\sqrt{3} - 2b_2\sin 5t\sqrt{3}$;
(b) In the natural mode with frequency $\omega_1 = 5$, the masses move in the same direction, whereas in the natural mode with frequency $\omega_2 = 5\sqrt{3}$ they move in opposite directions. In each case the amplitude of the motion of m_2 is twice that of m_1.

39. $x(t) = a_1\cos t + a_2\sin t + b_1\cos 2t + b_2\sin 2t$,
$y(t) = 2a_1\cos t + 2a_2\sin t - b_1\cos 2t - b_2\sin 2t$; in the natural mode with frequency $\omega_1 = 1$ the masses move in the same direction, with the amplitude of motion of the second mass twice that of the first. In the natural mode with frequency $\omega_2 = 2$ they move in opposite directions with the same amplitude of motion.

40. $x(t) = a_1\cos 5t + a_2\sin 5t + b_1\cos 10t + b_2\sin 10t$,
$y(t) = 2a_1\cos 5t + 2a_2\sin 5t - b_1\cos 10t - b_2\sin 10t$; in the natural mode with frequency $\omega_1 = 5$ the masses move in the same direction, with the amplitude of motion of the second mass twice that of the first. In the natural mode with frequency $\omega_2 = 10$ they move in opposite directions with the same amplitude of motion.

41. $x(t) = a_1\cos t + a_2\sin t + b_1\cos 3t + b_2\sin 3t$,
$y(t) = a_1\cos t + a_2\sin t - b_1\cos 3t - b_2\sin 3t$

42. In the natural mode with frequency $\omega_1 = 1$, the two masses move in the same direction with equal amplitudes of oscillation. In the natural mode with frequency $\omega_2 = 2$ the two masses move in opposite directions with the amplitude of motion of m_1 twice that of m_2.

43. $x(t) = a_1\cos t + a_2\sin t + b_1\cos t\sqrt{5} + b_2\sin t\sqrt{5}$,
$y(t) = a_1\cos t + a_2\sin t - b_1\cos t\sqrt{5} - b_2\sin t\sqrt{5}$

44. In the natural mode with frequency $\omega_1 = \sqrt{2}$, the two masses move in the same direction; in the natural mode with frequency $\omega_2 = 2$, they move in opposite directions. In each natural mode their amplitudes of oscillation are equal.

45. $x(t) = a_1\cos t\sqrt{2} + a_2\sin t\sqrt{2} + b_1\cos 2t\sqrt{2} + b_2\sin 2t\sqrt{2}$,
$y(t) = a_1\cos t\sqrt{2} + a_2\sin t\sqrt{2} - \frac{1}{2}b_1\cos 2t\sqrt{2} - \frac{1}{2}b_2\sin 2t\sqrt{2}$

46. $x(t) = a_1\cos 2t + a_2\sin 2t + b_1\cos 4t + b_2\sin 4t$,
$y(t) = a_1\cos 2t + a_2\sin 2t - b_1\cos 4t - b_2\sin 4t$; in the natural mode with frequency $\omega_1 = 2$ the masses move in the same direction with equal amplitudes of motion. In the natural mode with frequency $\omega_2 = 4$ they move in opposite directions with the same amplitude of motion.

Section 4.3

The format for the first eight answers is this: $(x(t), y(t))$ at $t = 0.2$ by the Euler method, by the improved Euler method, by the Runge-Kutta method, and finally the actual values.

1. (0.8800, 2.5000), (0.9600, 2.6000), (1.0027, 2.6401),
(1.0034, 2.6408)

2. (0.8100, −0.8100), (0.8200, −0.8200), (0.8187, −0.8187),
(0.8187, −0.8187)

3. (2.8100, 2.3100), (3.2200, 2.6200), (3.6481, 2.9407),
(3.6775, 2.9628)

4. (3.3100, −1.6200), (3.8200, −2.0400), (4.2274, −2.4060),
(4.2427, −2.4205)

5. (−0.5200, 2.9200), (−0.5400, 2.4400), (−0.5712, 2.4485),
(−0.5793, 2.4488)

6. (−1.7600, 4.6800), (−1.9200, 4.5600), (−1.9029, 4.4995),
(−1.9025, 4.4999)

7. (3.1200, 1.6800), (3.2400, 1.7600), (3.2816, 1.7899),
(3.2820, 1.7902)

8. (2.1600, −0.6300), (2.5200, −0.4600), (2.5320, −0.3867),
(2.5270, −0.3889)

9. At $t = 1$ we obtain $(x, y) = (3.99261, 6.21770)$ $(h = 0.1)$ and
(3.99234, 6.21768) $(h = 0.05)$; the actual value is
(3.99232, 6.21768).

10. At $t = 1$ we obtain $(x, y) = (1.31498, 1.02537)$ $(h = 0.1)$ and
(1.31501, 1.02538) $(h = 0.05)$; the actual value is
(1.31501, 1.02538).

11. At $t = 1$ we obtain $(x, y) = (-0.05832, 0.56664)$ $(h = 0.1)$ and
(−0.05832, 0.56665) $(h = 0.05)$; the actual value is
(−0.05832, 0.56665).

12. We solved $x' = y$, $y' = -x + \sin t$, $x(0) = y(0) = 0$. With
$h = 0.1$ and also with $h = 0.05$ we obtain the actual value
$x(1.0) \approx 0.15058$.

13. Runge-Kutta, $h = 0.1$: about 1050 ft in about 7.7 s

14. Runge-Kutta, $h = 0.1$: about 1044 ft in about 7.8 s

15. Runge-Kutta, $h = 1.0$: about 83.83 mi in about 168 s

16. At 40°: 5.0 s, 352.9 ft; at 45°: 5.4 s, 347.2 ft; at 50°: 5.8 s, 334.2 ft (all values approximate)

17. At 39.0° the range is about 352.7 ft. At 39.5° it is 352.8; at 40°, 352.9; at 40.5°, 352.6; at 41.0°, 352.1.

18. Just under 57.5°

19. Approximately 253 ft/s

20. Maximum height: about 1005 ft, attained in about 5.6 s; range: about 1880 ft; time aloft: about 11.6 s

21. Runge-Kutta with $h = 0.1$ yields these results:
(a) 21400 ft, 46 s, 518 ft/s; (b) 8970 ft, 17.5 s; (c) 368 ft/s (at $t \approx 23$).

Chapter 5

Section 5.1

1. (a) $\begin{bmatrix} 13 & -18 \\ 23 & 17 \end{bmatrix}$; (b) $\begin{bmatrix} 0 & -1 \\ 2 & 19 \end{bmatrix}$;

(c) $\begin{bmatrix} -9 & -11 \\ 47 & -9 \end{bmatrix}$; (d) $\begin{bmatrix} -10 & -37 \\ 14 & -8 \end{bmatrix}$

2. $(AB)C = A(BC) = \begin{bmatrix} -33 & -7 \\ -27 & 103 \end{bmatrix}$;

$A(B + C) = AB + AC = \begin{bmatrix} -18 & -4 \\ 68 & -8 \end{bmatrix}$

3. $AB = \begin{bmatrix} -1 & 8 \\ 46 & -1 \end{bmatrix}$; $BA = \begin{bmatrix} 11 & -12 & 14 \\ -14 & 0 & 7 \\ 0 & 8 & -13 \end{bmatrix}$

4. $Ay = \begin{bmatrix} 2t^2 - \cos t \\ 3t^2 - 4\sin t + 5\cos t \end{bmatrix}$, $Bx = \begin{bmatrix} 2t + 3e^{-t} \\ -14t \\ 6t - 2e^{-t} \end{bmatrix}$

5. (a) $\begin{bmatrix} 21 & 2 & 1 \\ 4 & 44 & 9 \\ -27 & 34 & 45 \end{bmatrix}$; (b) $\begin{bmatrix} 9 & 21 & -13 \\ -5 & -8 & 24 \\ -25 & -19 & 26 \end{bmatrix}$;

(c) $\begin{bmatrix} 0 & -6 & 1 \\ 10 & 31 & -15 \\ 16 & 58 & -23 \end{bmatrix}$; (d) $\begin{bmatrix} -10 & -8 & 5 \\ 18 & 12 & -10 \\ 11 & 22 & 6 \end{bmatrix}$;

(e) $\begin{bmatrix} 3 - t & 2 & -1 \\ 0 & 4 - t & 3 \\ -5 & 2 & 7 - t \end{bmatrix}$

7. $\det(A) = \det(B) = 0$ **8.** $\det(AB) = \det(BA) = 144$

9. $(AB)' = \begin{bmatrix} 1 - 8t + 18t^2 & 1 + 2t - 12t^2 + 32t^3 \\ 3 + 3t^2 - 4t^3 & 8t + 3t^2 + 4t^3 \end{bmatrix}$

11. $x = \begin{bmatrix} x \\ y \end{bmatrix}$, $P(t) = \begin{bmatrix} 0 & -3 \\ 3 & 0 \end{bmatrix}$, $f(t) = \begin{bmatrix} 0 \\ 0 \end{bmatrix}$

13. $x = \begin{bmatrix} x \\ y \end{bmatrix}$, $P(t) = \begin{bmatrix} 2 & 4 \\ 5 & -1 \end{bmatrix}$, $f(t) = \begin{bmatrix} 3e^t \\ -t^2 \end{bmatrix}$

15. $x = \begin{bmatrix} x \\ y \\ z \end{bmatrix}$, $P(t) = \begin{bmatrix} 0 & 1 & 1 \\ 1 & 0 & 1 \\ 1 & 1 & 0 \end{bmatrix}$, $f(t) = \begin{bmatrix} 0 \\ 0 \\ 0 \end{bmatrix}$

17. $x = \begin{bmatrix} x \\ y \\ z \end{bmatrix}$, $P(t) = \begin{bmatrix} 3 & -4 & 1 \\ 1 & 0 & -3 \\ 0 & 6 & -7 \end{bmatrix}$, $f(t) = \begin{bmatrix} t \\ t^2 \\ t^3 \end{bmatrix}$

19. $x = \begin{bmatrix} x_1 \\ x_2 \\ x_3 \\ x_4 \end{bmatrix}$, $P(t) = \begin{bmatrix} 0 & 1 & 0 & 0 \\ 0 & 0 & 2 & 0 \\ 0 & 0 & 0 & 3 \\ 4 & 0 & 0 & 0 \end{bmatrix}$, $f(t) = \begin{bmatrix} 0 \\ 0 \\ 0 \\ 0 \end{bmatrix}$

21. $W(t) = e^{3t}$; $x(t) = \begin{bmatrix} 2c_1e^t + c_2e^{2t} \\ -3c_1e^t - c_2e^{2t} \end{bmatrix}$

23. $W(t) \equiv 4$; $\mathbf{x}(t) = \begin{bmatrix} c_1 e^{2t} + c_2 e^{-2t} \\ 2c_1 e^{2t} + 3c_2 e^{-2t} \end{bmatrix}$

25. $W(t) = 7e^{-3t}$; $\mathbf{x}(t) = \begin{bmatrix} 3c_1 e^{2t} + c_2 e^{-5t} \\ 2c_1 e^{2t} + 3c_2 e^{-5t} \end{bmatrix}$

27. $W(t) = 3$; $\mathbf{x}(t) = \begin{bmatrix} c_1 e^{2t} + c_2 e^{-t} \\ c_1 e^{2t} + c_3 e^{-t} \\ c_1 e^{2t} - (c_2 + c_3)e^{-t} \end{bmatrix}$

29. $w(t) = e^{2t}$; $\mathbf{x}(t) = \begin{bmatrix} 3c_1 e^{-2t} + c_2 e^{t} + c_3 e^{3t} \\ -2c_1 e^{-2t} - c_2 e^{t} - c_3 e^{3t} \\ 2c_1 e^{-2t} + c_2 e^{t} \end{bmatrix}$

31. $\mathbf{x} = 2\mathbf{x}_1 - \mathbf{x}_2$ **33.** $\mathbf{x} = 3\mathbf{x}_1 + 4\mathbf{x}_2$

35. $\mathbf{x} = \mathbf{x}_1 + 2\mathbf{x}_2 + \mathbf{x}_3$ **37.** $\mathbf{x} = 3\mathbf{x}_1 - 3\mathbf{x}_2 - 5\mathbf{x}_3$

39. $\mathbf{x} = 3\mathbf{x}_1 + 7\mathbf{x}_2 + \mathbf{x}_3 - 2\mathbf{x}_4$ **40.** $\mathbf{x} = 13\mathbf{x}_1 + 41\mathbf{x}_2 + 3\mathbf{x}_3 - 12\mathbf{x}_4$

41. (a) $\mathbf{x}_2 = t\mathbf{x}_1$, so neither is a constant multiple of the other.
  (b) $W(\mathbf{x}_1, \mathbf{x}_2) \equiv 0$, whereas Theorem 2 implies that $W \neq 0$ if $\mathbf{x}_1$ and $\mathbf{x}_2$ were independent solutions of a system of the indicated form.

Section 5.2

1. Eigenvalues: $\lambda_1 = -1$, $\lambda_2 = 3$;
  eigenvectors: $\mathbf{v}_1 = \begin{bmatrix} 1 & -1 \end{bmatrix}^T$, $\mathbf{v}_2 = \begin{bmatrix} 1 & 1 \end{bmatrix}^T$;
  solution: $x_1 = c_1 e^{-t} + c_2 e^{3t}$, $x_2 = -c_1 e^{-t} + c_2 e^{3t}$

2. Eigenvalues: -1 and 4;
  solution: $x_1 = c_1 e^{-t} + 3c_2 e^{4t}$, $x_2 = -c_1 e^{-t} + 2c_2 e^{4t}$

3. $x_1 = \frac{1}{7}(-e^{-t} + 8e^{6t})$, $x_2 = \frac{1}{7}(e^{-t} + 6e^{6t})$

4. $x_1 = c_1 e^{-2t} + c_2 e^{5t}$, $x_2 = -6c_1 e^{-2t} + c_2 e^{5t}$

5. $x_1 = c_1 e^{-t} + 7c_2 e^{5t}$, $x_2 = c_1 e^{-t} + c_2 e^{5t}$

6. Eigenvalues: 3 and 4

7. $x_1 = c_1 e^{t} + 2c_2 e^{-9t}$, $x_2 = c_1 e^{t} - 3c_2 e^{-9t}$

9. Eigenvalue: $4i$;
  solution: $x_1 = 2\cos 4t - \frac{11}{4}\sin 4t$, $x_2 = 3\cos 4t + \frac{1}{2}\sin 4t$

11. $x_1 = -4e^{t}\sin 2t$, $x_2 = 4e^{t}\cos 2t$

13. $x_1 = 3e^{2t}(c_1 \cos 3t - c_2 \sin 3t)$,
  $x_2 = e^{2t}[(c_1 + c_2)\cos 3t + (c_1 - c_2)\sin 3t]$

14. Eigenvalue: $3 + 4i$

15. $x_1 = 5e^{5t}(c_1 \cos 4t - c_2 \sin 4t)$,
  $x_2 = e^{5t}[(2c_1 + 4c_2)\cos 4t + (4c_1 - 2c_2)\sin 4t]$

17. $x_1 = c_1 e^{9t} + c_2 e^{6t} + c_3$, $x_2 = c_1 e^{9t} - 2c_2 e^{6t}$,
  $x_3 = c_1 e^{9t} + c_2 e^{6t} - c_3$

19. $x_1 = c_1 e^{6t} + c_2 e^{3t} + c_3 e^{3t}$, $x_2 = c_1 e^{6t} - 2c_2 e^{3t}$,
  $x_3 = c_1 e^{6t} + c_2 e^{3t} - c_3 e^{3t}$

21. $x_1 = 6c_1 + 3c_2 e^{t} + 2c_3 e^{-t}$, $x_2 = 2c_1 + c_2 e^{t} + c_3 e^{-t}$,
  $x_3 = 5c_1 + 2c_2 e^{t} + 2c_3 e^{-t}$

23. $x_1 = c_1 e^{2t} + c_3 e^{3t}$, $x_2 = -c_1 e^{2t} + c_2 e^{-2t} - c_3 e^{3t}$,
  $x_3 = -c_2 e^{-2t} + c_3 e^{3t}$

25. Eigenvalues: $0, 2 \pm 3i$;
  solution: $x_1 = c_1 + e^{2t}[(-c_2 + c_3)\cos 3t + (c_2 + c_3)\sin 3t]$,
  $x_2 = -c_1 + 2e^{2t}(c_2 \cos 3t - c_3 \sin 3t)$,
  $x_3 = 2e^{2t}(-c_2 \cos 3t + c_3 \sin 3t)$

27. $x_1(t) = 15e^{-(0.2)t}$, $x_2(t) = 15(e^{-(0.2)t} - e^{-(0.4)t})$; the maximum of x_2 is 3.75 (lb)

29. $x_1(t) = 10 + 5e^{-(0.6)t}$, $x_2(t) = 5 - 5e^{-(0.6)t}$

31. $x_1(t) = 27e^{-t}$, $x_2(t) = 27e^{-t} - 27e^{-2t}$,
  $x_3(t) = 27e^{-t} - 54e^{-2t} + 27e^{-3t}$. The maximum amount of salt ever in tank 3 is $x_3(\ln 3) = 4$ lb.

33. $x_1(t) = 45e^{-4t}$, $x_2(t) = 90e^{-4t} - 90e^{-6t}$,
  $x_3(t) = -270e^{-4t} + 135e^{-6t} + 135e^{-2t}$. The maximum amount of salt ever in tank 2 is $x_3(\frac{1}{2}\ln 3) = 20$ lb.

35. $x_1(t) = 10 - \frac{1}{7}(55e^{-18t} - 216e^{-11t})$,
  $x_2(t) = 3 - \frac{1}{7}(165e^{-18t} - 144e^{-11t})$,
  $x_3(t) = 20 + \frac{1}{7}(220e^{-18t} - 360e^{-11t})$; the limiting amounts of salt in tanks 1, 2, and 3 are 10, 3, and 20 lb.

37. $x_1(t) = 30 + e^{-3t}\left[25\cos\left(t\sqrt{2}\right) + 10\sqrt{2}\sin\left(t\sqrt{2}\right)\right]$,
  $x_2(t) = 10 - e^{-3t}\left[10\cos\left(t\sqrt{2}\right) - \frac{25}{2}\sqrt{2}\sin\left(t\sqrt{2}\right)\right]$,
  $x_3(t) = 15 - e^{-3t}\left[15\cos\left(t\sqrt{2}\right) + \frac{45}{2}\sqrt{2}\sin\left(t\sqrt{2}\right)\right]$. The limiting amounts of salt in tanks 1, 2, and 3 are 30, 10, and 15 lb.

39. $x_1(t) = 3c_1 e^{t} + c_4 e^{-2t}$,
  $x_2(t) = -2c_1 e^{t} + c_3 e^{2t} - c_4 e^{-2t}$,
  $x_3(t) = 4c_1 e^{t} + c_2 e^{-t}$, $x_4(t) = c_1 e^{t}$

41. $x_1(t) = x_4(t) = 2e^{10t} + e^{15t}$,
  $x_2(t) = x_3(t) = -e^{10t} + 2e^{15t}$

Section 5.3

1. Natural frequencies: $\omega_1 = 0$, $\omega_2 = 2$ (rad/s). In the first degenerate natural mode, the two masses move by translation without oscillation. In the second natural mode, they oscillate in opposite directions with equal amplitudes.

2. Natural frequencies: $\omega_1 = 1$, $\omega_2 = 3$. In the first natural mode, the two masses move in the same direction with equal amplitudes of oscillation. In the second natural mode, they move in opposite directions with equal amplitudes.

3. Natural frequencies: $\omega_1 = 1$, $\omega_2 = 2$. In the natural mode with frequency $\omega_1 = 1$, the two masses move in the same direction with equal amplitudes of motion. In the natural mode with frequency $\omega_2 = 2$, the two masses move in opposite directions, with the amplitude of motion of m_1 twice that of m_2.

5. Natural frequencies: $\omega_1 = \sqrt{2}$, $\omega_2 = 2$. In each natural mode the two masses have equal amplitudes of oscillation. They move in the same direction at frequency ω_1, in opposite directions at frequency ω_2.

7. At the natural frequency $\omega_1 = 2$ the two masses move in the same direction with equal amplitudes of oscillation. At the natural frequency $\omega_2 = 2\sqrt{2}$ they move in opposite directions with equal amplitudes of oscillation.

9. We have a superposition of three oscillations, in which the two masses move: (a) In the same direction with frequency $\omega_1 = 1$ and with equal amplitudes; (b) In opposite directions with frequency $\omega_2 = 3$ and with the amplitude of motion of m_1 twice that of m_2; (c) In opposite directions with frequency $\omega_3 = 5$ and with the amplitude of motion of m_2 three times that of m_1.

11. (a) In mode 1 the two masses oscillate in the same direction with frequency $\omega_1 = 6$ and with the amplitude of motion of m_1 twice that of m_2. In mode 2 the two masses oscillate in opposite directions with frequency $\omega_2 = 8$ and with the amplitude of motion of m_2 twice that of m_1. (b) The expected oscillation with frequency $\omega_2 = 8$ is missing; there is a superposition of only two oscillations, in which the two masses move (first mode) in the same direction with frequency $\omega_1 = 6$ and with the amplitude of motion of m_1 twice that of m_2 and (second mode) in the same direction with frequency $\omega_3 = 7$ and with the amplitude of motion of m_1 $\frac{19}{7}$ times that of m_2.

12. $\omega_1 = \left(2 - \sqrt{2}\right)^{1/2}$ with amplitude ratios $1 : \sqrt{2} : 1$, $\omega_2 = \sqrt{2}$ with amplitude ratios $1 : 0 : -1$; $\omega_3 = \left(2 + \sqrt{2}\right)^{1/2}$ with amplitude ratios $1 : -\sqrt{2} : 1$

15. There is a superposition of two oscillations with the natural frequencies $\omega_1 = 5$ and $\omega_2 = 5\sqrt{3}$ and a forced oscillation with frequency $\omega = 10$. In both natural oscillations the amplitude of motion of m_2 is twice that of m_1, whereas in the forced oscillation the amplitude of motion of m_2 is four times that of m_1.

21. (a) $\omega_1 \approx 1.0293$ Hz; $\omega_2 \approx 1.7971$ Hz.
  (b) $v_1 \approx 28$ mi/h; $v_2 \approx 49$ mi/h

23. $\omega_1 = 2\sqrt{10}$, $v_1 \approx 40.26$ (ft/s (about 27 mi/h),
  $\omega_2 = 5\sqrt{5}$, $v_2 \approx 71.18$ ft/s (about 49 mi/h)

25. $\omega_1 \approx 5.0424$, $v_1 \approx 32.10$ ft/s (about 22 mi/h),
  $\omega_2 \approx 9.9158$, $v_2 \approx 63.13$ ft/s (about 43 mi/h)

Chapter 6

Section 6.1

1. 6.1.13	**2.** 6.1.15	**3.** 6.1.18	**4.** 6.1.12
5. 6.1.11	**6.** 6.1.17	**7.** 6.1.14	**8.** 6.1.16

9. $x(t) = 0, 2, -2$ **10.** $x(t) = 0$

11. $x(t) = n\pi$ where n is an integer.

12. $x(t) = 0$

13. The origin $(0, 0)$ is a stable proper node similar to the one shown in Fig. 6.1.4.

14. The origin is an unstable saddle point; reverse all arrows in Fig. 6.1.6 to see the trajectories.

15. The origin is a stable improper node similar to the one shown in Fig. 6.1.5, except that the trajectories consist of the x-axis and parabolas of the form $x = ky^2$.

16. The origin is an unstable proper node.

17. The origin is a stable center.

18. The origin is a stable center.

19. The origin is a stable center.

20. The origin is an asymptotically stable spiral point.

23. The origin and the circles $x^2 + y^2 = C > 0$

24. The origin and the hyperbolas $y^2 - x^2 = C$

25. The origin and the ellipses $x^2 + 4y^2 = C > 0$

26. The origin and the ovals of the form $x^4 + y^4 = C > 0$

Section 6.2

1. Asymptotically stable node

2. Unstable proper node

3. Unstable saddle point

4. Unstable saddle point

5. Asymptotically stable node

6. Unstable node

7. Unstable spiral point

8. Asymptotically stable spiral point

9. Stable, but not asymptotically stable, center

10. Stable, but not asymptotically stable, center

11. Asymptotically stable node: $(2, 1)$

12. Unstable improper node: $(2, -3)$

13. Unstable saddle point: $(2, 2)$

14. Unstable saddle point: $(3, 4)$

15. Asymptotically stable spiral point: $(1, 1)$

16. Unstable spiral point: $(3, 2)$

17. Stable center: $\left(\frac{5}{2}, -\frac{1}{2}\right)$

18. Stable, but not asymptotically stable, center: $(-2, -1)$

19. Asymptotically stable node

20. Unstable improper node

21. Unstable saddle point

22. Here, $(0, 0)$ is either a center or a spiral point, but its stability is not determined by Theorem 2.

23. Asymptotically stable spiral point

24. Unstable spiral point

25. Asymptotically stable node or spiral point

26. Either an unstable node or an unstable spiral point

27. The origin is either a center or a spiral point, but its stability is not determined by Theorem 2.

28. The origin is either a center or a spiral point, but its stability is not determined by Theorem 2.

29. The origin is an unstable saddle point. The point $(1, 1)$ is either a center or a spiral point, but its stability is indeterminate.

30. There is an unstable saddle point at $(1, 1)$ and an asymptotically stable spiral point at $(-1, 1)$.

31. There is an unstable saddle point at $(1, 1)$ and an asymptotically stable spiral point at $(-1, -1)$.

32. There is an unstable saddle point at $(2, 1)$ and an asymptotically stable spiral point at $(-2, -1)$.

37. Note that the differential equation is homogeneous.

Section 6.3

5. The characteristic equation is $\lambda^2 + 45\lambda + 126 = 0$.

7. The characteristic equation is $(-24 - \lambda)^2 - 2 \cdot (18)^2 = 0$.

9. The characteristic equation is $\lambda^2 + 58\lambda - 120 = 0$.

12. The characteristic equation is $\lambda^2 + 2\lambda - 15 = 0$.

13. The characteristic equation is $\lambda^2 + 2\lambda + 6 = 0$.

15. The characteristic equation is $\lambda^2 + 2\lambda - 24 = 0$.

17. The characteristic equation is $\lambda^2 - 4\lambda + 6 = 0$.

19. The characteristic equation is $\lambda^2 + 10 = 0$.

21. The characteristic equation is $\lambda^2 - \lambda - 6 = 0$.

24. The characteristic equation is $\lambda^2 + 5\lambda - 14 = 0$.

25. The characteristic equation is $\lambda^2 + 5\lambda + 10 = 0$.

Section 6.4

1. Eigenvalues: $-2, -3$; stable node

2. Eigenvalues: $1, 3$; unstable node

3. Eigenvalues: $-3, 5$; unstable saddle point

4. Eigenvalues: $-1 \pm 2i$; stable spiral point

5. Critical points: $(0, n\pi)$ where n is an integer; an unstable saddle point if n is even, a stable spiral point if n is odd

6. Critical points: $(n, 0)$ where n is an integer; an unstable saddle point if n is even, a stable spiral point if n is odd

7. Critical points: $(n\pi, n\pi)$ where n is an integer; an unstable saddle point if n is even, a stable spiral point if n is odd

8. Critical points: $(n\pi, 0)$ where n is an integer; an unstable node if n is even, an unstable saddle point if n is odd

9. If n is odd then $(n\pi, 0)$ is an unstable saddle point.

10. If n is odd then $(n\pi, 0)$ is a stable node.

11. $(n\pi, 0)$ is a stable spiral point.

12. Unstable saddle points at $(2, 0)$ and $(-2, 0)$, a stable center at $(0, 0)$

13. Unstable saddle points at $(2, 0)$ and $(-2, 0)$, a stable spiral point at $(0, 0)$

14. Stable centers at $(2, 0)$ and $(-2, 0)$, an unstable saddle point at $(0, 0)$

15. A stable center at $(0, 0)$ and an unstable saddle point at $(-4, 0)$

16. Stable centers at $(2, 0)$, $(0, 0)$, and $(-2, 0)$, unstable saddle points at $(1, 0)$ and $(-1, 0)$

Chapter 7

Section 7.1

1. $1/s^2$, $s > 0$	**2.** $2/s^3$, $s > 0$
3. $e/(s - 3)$, $s > 3$	**4.** $s/(s^2 + 1)$, $s > 0$
5. $1/(s^2 - 1)$, $s > 1$	**7.** $(1 - e^{-s})/s$, $s > 0$
8. $(e^{-s} - e^{-2s})/s$, $s > 0$	**9.** $(1 - e^{-s} - se^{-s})/s^2$, $s > 0$
11. $\frac{1}{2}\sqrt{\pi}s^{-3/2} + 3s^{-2}$, $s > 0$	**13.** $s^{-2} - 2(s - 3)^{-1}$, $s > 3$

15. $s^{-1} + s(s^2 - 25)^{-1}$, $s > 5$ **16.** $(s + 2)/(s^2 + 4)$, $s > 0$

17. $\cos^2 2t = \frac{1}{2}(1 + \cos 4t)$; $\frac{1}{2}\left[s^{-1} + s/(s^2 + 16)\right]$, $s > 0$

18. $3/(s^2 + 36)$, $s > 0$

19. $s^{-1} + 3s^{-2} + 6s^{-3} + 6s^{-4}$, $s > 0$

20. $1/(s - 1)^2$, $s > 1$	**21.** $(s^2 - 4)/(s^2 + 4)^2$, $s > 0$
22. $\frac{1}{2}\left[s/(s^2 - 36) - s^{-1}\right]$	**23.** $\frac{1}{2}t^3$
24. $2\sqrt{t/\pi}$	**25.** $1 - \frac{8}{3}t^{3/2}\pi^{-1/2}$
26. e^{-5t}	**27.** $3e^{4t}$
28. $3\cos 2t + \frac{1}{2}\sin 2t$	**29.** $\frac{5}{3}\sin 3t - 3\cos 3t$
30. $-\cosh 2t - \frac{9}{2}\sinh 2t$	**31.** $\frac{3}{5}\sinh 5t - 10\cosh 5t$

32. $2u(t - 3)$

37. $f(t) = 1 - u_a(t) = 1 - u(t - a)$

Section 7.2

1. $x(t) = 5\cos 2t$

2. $x(t) = 3\cos 3t + \frac{4}{3}\sin 3t$

3. $x(t) = \frac{2}{3}(e^{2t} - e^{-t})$

4. $x(t) = \frac{1}{2}(7e^{-3t} - 3e^{-5t})$

5. $x(t) = \frac{1}{3}(2\sin t - \sin 2t)$

6. $x(t) = \frac{1}{3}(\cos t - \cos 2t)$

7. $x(t) = \frac{1}{8}(9\cos t - \cos 3t)$

8. $x(t) = \frac{1}{9}(1 - \cos 3t)$

9. $x(t) = \frac{1}{6}(2 - 3e^{-t} + e^{-3t})$

10. $x(t) = \frac{1}{4}(2t - 3 + 12e^{-t} - 9e^{-2t})$

11. $x(t) = 1,\ y(t) = -2$

13. $x(t) = -\left(2/\sqrt{3}\right)\sinh\left(t/\sqrt{3}\right),$

$y(t) = \cosh\left(t/\sqrt{3}\right) + \left(1/\sqrt{3}\right)\sinh\left(t/\sqrt{3}\right)$

15. $x(t) = \frac{1}{3}\left(2 + e^{-3t/2}[\cos(rt/2) + r\sin(rt/2)]\right),$

$y(t) = \frac{1}{21}\left(28 - 9e^t + 2e^{-3t/2}[\cos(rt/2) + 4r\sin(rt/2)]\right)$ where

$r = \sqrt{3}$

16. $x(t) = \cos t + \sin t,\ y(t) = e^t - \cos t,\ z(t) = -2\sin t$

17. $f(t) = \frac{1}{3}(e^{3t} - 1)$

18. $f(t) = \frac{3}{5}(1 - e^{-5t})$

19. $f(t) = \frac{1}{4}(1 - \cos 2t) = \frac{1}{2}\sin^2 t$

20. $f(t) = \frac{1}{9}(6\sin 3t - \cos 3t + 1)$

21. $f(t) = t - \sin t$

22. $f(t) = \frac{1}{9}(-1 + \cosh 3t)$

23. $f(t) = -t + \sinh t$

24. $f(t) = \frac{1}{2}(e^{-2t} - 2e^{-t} + 1)$

Section 7.3

1. $24/(s - \pi)^5$

2. $\frac{3}{4}\sqrt{\pi}\,(s + 4)^{-5/2}$

3. $3\pi/[(s + 2)^2 + 9\pi^2]$

4. $\sqrt{2}\,(2s + 5)/(4s^2 + 4s + 17)$

5. $\frac{3}{2}e^{2t}$

6. $(t - t^2)e^{-t}$

7. te^{-2t}

8. $e^{-2t}\cos t$

9. $e^{3t}\left(3\cos 4t + \frac{7}{2}\sin 4t\right)$

10. $\frac{1}{36}e^{2t/3}\left(8\cos\frac{4}{3}t - 5\sin\frac{4}{3}t\right)$

11. $\frac{1}{2}\sinh 2t$

12. $2 + 3e^{3t}$

13. $3e^{-2t} - 5e^{-5t}$

14. $2 + e^{2t} - 3e^{-t}$

15. $\frac{1}{25}(e^{5t} - 1 - 5t)$

16. $\frac{1}{125}[e^{2t}(5t - 2) + e^{-3t}(5t + 2)]$

17. $\frac{1}{16}(\sinh 2t - \sin 2t)$

18. $e^{4t}\left(1 + 12t + 24t^2 + \frac{32}{3}t^3\right)$

19. $\frac{1}{3}(2\cos 2t + 2\sin 2t - 2\cos t - \sin t)$

20. $\frac{1}{32}[e^{2t}(2t - 1) + e^{-2t}(2t + 1)]$

21. $\frac{1}{2}e^{-t}(5\sin t - 3t\cos t - 2t\sin t)$

22. $\frac{1}{64}e^{t/2}[(4t + 8)\cos t + (4 - 3t)\sin t]$

27. $\frac{1}{4}e^{-3t}(8\cos 4t + 9\sin 4t)$

28. $\frac{1}{4}(1 - 2e^{2t} + e^{4t})$

29. $\frac{1}{8}(-6t + 3\sinh 2t)$

30. $\frac{1}{10}[2e^{-t} - e^{-2t}(2\cos 2t + \sin 2t)]$

31. $\frac{1}{15}(6e^{2t} - 5 - e^{-3t})$

32. $\frac{1}{2}(\cosh t + \cos t)$

33. $x(t) = r(\cosh rt\sin rt - \sinh rt\cos rt)$ where $r = 1/\sqrt{2}$

34. $\frac{1}{2}\sin 2t + \frac{1}{3}\sin 3t$

35. $\frac{1}{16}(\sin 2t - 2t\cos 2t)$

36. $\frac{1}{50}[2e^{2t} + (10t - 2)\cos t - (5t + 14)\sin t]$

37. $\frac{1}{50}[(5t - 1)e^{-t} + e^{-2t}(\cos 3t + 32\sin 3t)]$

38. $\frac{1}{510}e^{-3t}(489\cos 3t + 307\sin 3t) + \frac{1}{170}(7\cos 2t + 6\sin 2t)$

Section 7.4

1. $\frac{1}{2}t^2$

2. $(e^{at} - at - 1)/a^2$

3. $\frac{1}{2}(\sin t - t\cos t)$

4. $2(t - \sin t)$

5. te^{at}

6. $(e^{at} - e^{bt})/(a - b)$

7. $\frac{1}{3}(e^{3t} - 1)$

8. $\frac{1}{4}(1 - \cos 2t)$

9. $\frac{1}{54}(\sin 3t - 3t\cos 3t)$

10. $(kt - \sin kt)/k^3$

11. $\frac{1}{4}(\sin 2t + 2t\cos 2t)$

12. $\frac{1}{5}[1 - e^{-2t}(\cos t + 2\sin t)]$

13. $\frac{1}{10}(3e^{3t} - 3\cos t + \sin t)$

14. $\frac{1}{3}(\cos t - \cos 2t)$

15. $6s/(s^2 + 9)^2,\ s > 0$

16. $(2s^3 - 24s)/(s^2 + 4)^3,\ s > 0$

17. $(s^2 - 4s - 5)/(s^2 - 4s + 13)^2,\ s > 0$

18. $\dfrac{2(3s^2 + 6s + 7)}{(s + 1)^2(s^2 + 2s + 5)^2},\ s > 0$

19. $\frac{1}{2}\pi - \arctan s = \arctan(1/s),\ s > 0$

20. $\frac{1}{2}\ln(s^2 + 4) - \ln s,\ s > 0$

21. $\ln s - \ln(s - 3),\ s > 3$

22. $\ln(s + 1) - \ln(s - 1),\ s > 1$

23. $-(2\sinh 2t)/t$

24. $2(\cos 2t - \cos t)/t$

25. $e^{-2t} + e^{3t} - 2\cos t)/t$

26. $(e^{-2t}\sin 3t)/t$

27. $2(1 - 2\cos t)/t$

28. $\frac{1}{8}(t\sin t - t^2\cos t)$

29. $(s + 1)X'(s) + 4X(s) = 0;\ x(t) = Ct^3 e^{-t},\ C \neq 0$

30. $X(s) = A/(s + 3)^3;\ x(t) = Ct^2 e^{-3t},\ C \neq 0$

31. $(s - 2)X'(s) + 3X(s) = 0;\ x(t) = Ct^2 e^{2t},\ C \neq 0$

32. $(s^2 + 2s)X'(s) + (4s + 4)X(s) = 0;$
$x(t) = C(1 - t - e^{-2t} - te^{-2t}),\ C \neq 0$

33. $(s^2 + 1)X'(s) + 4sX(s) = 0;\ x(t) = C(\sin t - t\cos t),\ C \neq 0$

34. $x(t) = Ce^{-2t}(\sin 3t - 3t\cos 3t),\ C \neq 0$

Section 7.5

1. $f(t) = (t - 3)u_3(t)$

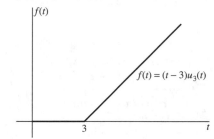

3. $f(t) = e^{-2(t-1)}u_1(t)$

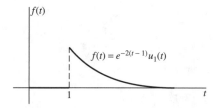

5. $f(t) = u_\pi(t)\sin(t - \pi) = -u_\pi(t)\sin t$

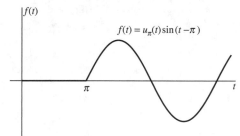

7. $f(t) = [1 - u_{2\pi}(t)]\sin t$

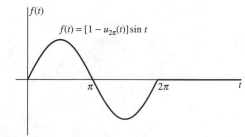

9. $f(t) = [1 - u_3(t)]\cos \pi t$

11. $f(t) = 2[1 - u_3(t)];\ F(s) = 2(1 - e^{-3s})/s$

12. $F(s) = 3(e^{-s} - e^{-4s})/s$

13. $F(s) = (1 - e^{-2\pi s})/(s^2 + 1)$

14. $F(s) = s(1 - e^{-2s})/(s^2 + \pi^2)$

15. $F(s) = (1 + e^{-3\pi s})/(s^2 + 1)$

16. $F(s) = 2(e^{-\pi s} - e^{-2\pi s})/(s^2 + 4)$

17. $F(s) = \pi(e^{-2s} + e^{-3s})/(s^2 + \pi^2)$

18. $F(s) = 2\pi(e^{-3s} + e^{-5s})/(4s^2 + \pi^2)$

19. $F(s) = e^{-s}(s^{-1} + s^{-2})$

20. $F(s) = (1 - e^{-s})/s^2$

21. $F(s) = (1 - 2e^{-s} + e^{-2s})/s^2$

28. $F(s) = (1 - e^{-as} - ase^{-as})/[s^2(1 - e^{-2as})]$

31. $x(t) = \frac{1}{2}[1 - u_\pi(t)]\sin^2 t$

32. $x(t) = g(t)$ if $t < 2$; $x(t) = g(t) - g(t-2)$ if $t \geqq 2$

33. $x(t) = \frac{1}{8}[1 - u_{2\pi}(t)]\left(\sin t - \frac{1}{3}\sin 3t\right)$

34. $x(t) = t - \sin t$ if $t < 1$,
$x(t) = -\sin t + \sin(t-1) + \cos(t-1)$ if $t > 1$

35. $x(t) = \frac{1}{4}\left(t - 1 + (t+1)e^{-2t} + u_2(t)\left[1 - t + (3t-5)e^{-2(t-2)}\right]\right)$

36. $i(t) = e^{-10t} - u_1(t)e^{-10(t-1)}$

37. $i(t) = [1 - u_{2\pi}(t)]\sin 100t$

38. $i(t) = g(t)$ if $t < \pi$, $i(t) = 0$ if $t > \pi$

39. $i(t) = \frac{1}{50}(1 - e^{-50t}) - \frac{1}{50}u_1(t)[1 + 98e^{-50(t-1)} - 99e^{-100(t-1)}]$

40. $i(t) = g(t) - u_1(t)g(t-1) - u_1(t)h(t-1)$

41. The complete solution $x(t) = 2|\sin t|\sin t$ is periodic, so the transient solution is zero.

42. $x(t) = g(t) + 2\sum(-1)^n u_{n\pi}(t)g(t - n\pi)$

Section 7.6

1. $x(t) = \frac{1}{2}\sin t$

2. $x(t) = \frac{1}{2}\sin 2t$ if $t < \pi$, $x(t) = \sin 2t$ if $t > \pi$

3. $x(t) = \frac{1}{4}(1 - e^{-2t}) - \frac{1}{2}te^{-2t} + u_2(t)(t-2)e^{-2(t-2)}$

4. $x(t) = t - 2 + 2e^{-t} + 3te^{-t}$

5. $x(t) = 0$ if $0 \leqq t < \pi$, $x(t) = -2e^{-(t-\pi)}\sin t$ if $t \geqq \pi$

6. $x(t) = -\frac{1}{3}u_{3\pi}(t)\sin 3t + \frac{1}{6}t\sin t$

7. $x(t) = \left[2 - e^{2\pi}u_\pi(t) + e^{4\pi}u_{2\pi}(t)\right]e^{-2t}\sin t$

8. $x(t) = (5t + 2)e^{-t} - u_2(t)(t-2)e^{-(t-2)}$

9. $x(t) = \int_0^t \frac{1}{2}(\sin 2\tau)f(t - \tau)\,d\tau$

10. $x(t) = \int_0^t \tau e^{-3\tau}f(t - \tau)\,d\tau$

11. $x(t) = \int_0^t (e^{-3\tau}\sinh\tau)f(t - \tau)\,d\tau$

12. $x(t) = \int_0^t (e^{-2\tau}\sin 2\tau)f(t - \tau)\,d\tau$

13. (a) $mx_\epsilon(t) = p[t^2 - u_\epsilon(t)(t - \epsilon)^2]/(2\epsilon)$;
(b) If $t > \epsilon$, then $mx_\epsilon(t) = p(2\epsilon t - \epsilon^2)/(2\epsilon)$, and hence $mx_\epsilon(t) \to pt$ as $\epsilon \to 0$;
(c) $mv = (mx)' = (pt)' = 0$.

15. The transform of each of the two given initial value problems is $(ms^2 + k)X(s) = mv_0 = p_0$.

17. (b) $i(t) = e^{-100(t-1)}u_1(t) - e^{-100(t-2)}u_2(t)$.
If $t > 2$, then $i(t) = -(e^{100} - 1)e^{100(1-t)} < 0$.

Appendix A

1. $y_0 = 3$, $y_1 = 3 + 3x$, $y_2 = 3 + 3x + \frac{3}{2}x^2$,
$y_3 = 3 + 3x + \frac{3}{2}x^2 + \frac{1}{2}x^3$,
$y_4 = 3 + 3x + \frac{3}{2}x^2 + \frac{1}{2}x^3 + \frac{1}{8}x^4$; $y(x) = 3e^x$

3. $y_0 = 1$, $y_1 = 1 - x^2$, $y_2 = 1 - x^2 + \frac{1}{2}x^4$,
$y_3 = 1 - x^2 + \frac{1}{2}x^4 - \frac{1}{6}x^6$,
$y_4 = 1 - x^2 + \frac{1}{2}x^4 - \frac{1}{6}x^6 + \frac{1}{24}x^8$; $y(x) = \exp(-x^2)$

5. $y_0 = 0$, $y_1 = 2x$, $y_2 = 2x + 2x^2$,
$y_3 = 2x + 2x^2 + \frac{4}{3}x^3$,
$y_4 = 2x + 2x^2 + \frac{4}{3}x^3 + \frac{2}{3}x^4$; $y(x) = e^{2x} - 1$

7. $y_0 = 0$, $y_1 = x^2$, $y_2 = x^2 + \frac{1}{2}x^4$, $y_3 = x^2 + \frac{1}{2}x^4 + \frac{1}{6}x^6$,
$y_4 = x^2 + \frac{1}{2}x^4 + \frac{1}{6}x^6 + \frac{1}{24}x^8$; $y(x) = \exp(x^2) - 1$

9. $y_0 = 1$, $y_1 = (1 + x) + \frac{1}{2}x^2$, $y_2 = (1 + x + x^2) + \frac{1}{6}x^3$,
$y_3 = \left(1 + x + x^2 + \frac{1}{3}x^3\right) + \frac{1}{24}x^4$;
$y(x) = 2e^x - 1 - x = 1 + x + x^2 + \frac{1}{3}x^3 + \cdots$

11. $y_0 = 1$, $y_1 = 1 + x$, $y_2 = (1 + x + x^2) + \frac{1}{3}x^3$,
$y_3 = (1 + x + x^2 + x^3) + \frac{2}{3}x^4 + \frac{1}{3}x^5 + \frac{1}{9}x^6 + \frac{1}{63}x^7$;
$y(x) = \dfrac{1}{1 - x} = 1 + x + x^2 + x^3 + x^4 + x^5 + \cdots$

12. $y_0 = 1$, $y_1 = 1 + \frac{1}{2}x$, $y_2 = 1 + \frac{1}{2}x + \frac{3}{8}x^3 + \frac{1}{8}x^3 + \frac{1}{64}x^4$,
$y_3 = 1 + \frac{1}{2}x + \frac{3}{8}x^2 + \frac{5}{16}x^3 + \frac{13}{64}x^4 + \cdots$; $y(x) = (1 - x)^{-1/2}$

13. $\begin{bmatrix} x_0 \\ y_0 \end{bmatrix} = \begin{bmatrix} 1 \\ -1 \end{bmatrix}$, $\begin{bmatrix} x_1 \\ y_1 \end{bmatrix} = \begin{bmatrix} 1 + 3t \\ -1 + 3t \end{bmatrix}$,

$\begin{bmatrix} x_2 \\ y_2 \end{bmatrix} = \begin{bmatrix} 1 + 3t + \frac{1}{2}t^2 \\ -1 + 5t - \frac{1}{2}t^2 \end{bmatrix}$,

$\begin{bmatrix} x_3 \\ y_3 \end{bmatrix} = \begin{bmatrix} 1 + 3t + \frac{1}{2}t^2 + \frac{1}{6}t^3 \\ -1 + 5t - \frac{1}{2}t^2 + \frac{3}{6}t^3 \end{bmatrix}$

14. $\mathbf{x}(t) = \begin{bmatrix} e^t + te^t \\ e^t \end{bmatrix}$

16. $y_3(1) \approx 0.350185$

Table of Laplace Transforms

This table summarizes the general properties of Laplace transforms and the Laplace transforms of particular functions derived in Chapter 7.

Function	Transform	Function	Transform
$f(t)$	$F(s)$	e^{at}	$\dfrac{1}{s-a}$
$af(t)+bg(t)$	$aF(s)+bG(s)$	$t^n e^{at}$	$\dfrac{n!}{(s-a)^{n+1}}$
$f'(t)$	$sF(s)-f(0)$	$\cos kt$	$\dfrac{s}{s^2+k^2}$
$f''(t)$	$s^2 F(s)-sf(0)-f'(0)$	$\sin kt$	$\dfrac{k}{s^2+k^2}$
$f^{(n)}(t)$	$s^n F(s)-s^{n-1}f(0)-\cdots-f^{(n-1)}(0)$	$\cosh kt$	$\dfrac{s}{s^2-k^2}$
$\displaystyle\int_0^t f(\tau)\,d\tau$	$\dfrac{F(s)}{s}$	$\sinh kt$	$\dfrac{k}{s^2-k^2}$
$e^{at}f(t)$	$F(s-a)$	$e^{at}\cos kt$	$\dfrac{s-a}{(s-a)^2+k^2}$
$u(t-a)f(t-a)$	$e^{-as}F(s)$	$e^{at}\sin kt$	$\dfrac{k}{(s-a)^2+k^2}$
$\displaystyle\int_0^t f(\tau)g(t-\tau)\,d\tau$	$F(s)G(s)$	$\dfrac{1}{2k^3}(\sin kt - kt\cos kt)$	$\dfrac{1}{(s^2+k^2)^2}$
$tf(t)$	$-F'(s)$	$\dfrac{t}{2k}\sin kt$	$\dfrac{s}{(s^2+k^2)^2}$
$t^n f(t)$	$(-1)^n F^{(n)}(s)$	$\dfrac{1}{2k}(\sin kt + kt\cos kt)$	$\dfrac{s^2}{(s^2+k^2)^2}$
$\dfrac{f(t)}{t}$	$\displaystyle\int_s^\infty F(\sigma)\,d\sigma$	$u(t-a)$	$\dfrac{e^{-as}}{s}$
$f(t),\quad$ period p	$\dfrac{1}{1-e^{-ps}}\displaystyle\int_0^p e^{-st}f(t)\,dt$	$\delta(t-a)$	e^{-as}
1	$\dfrac{1}{s}$	$(-1)^{[\![at]\!]}$ (square wave)	$\dfrac{1}{s}\tanh\dfrac{as}{2}$
t	$\dfrac{1}{s^2}$	$\left[\!\!\left[\dfrac{t}{a}\right]\!\!\right]$ (staircase)	$\dfrac{e^{-as}}{s(1-e^{-as})}$
t^n	$\dfrac{n!}{s^{n+1}}$		
$\dfrac{1}{\sqrt{\pi t}}$	$\dfrac{1}{\sqrt{s}}$		
t^a	$\dfrac{\Gamma(a+1)}{s^{a+1}}$		

Table of Integrals

ELEMENTARY FORMS

1. $\displaystyle\int u\,dv = uv - \int v\,du$

2. $\displaystyle\int u^n\,du = \frac{1}{n+1}u^{n+1} + C \quad \text{if } n \neq -1$

3. $\displaystyle\int \frac{du}{u} = \ln|u| + C$

4. $\displaystyle\int e^u\,du = e^u + C$

5. $\displaystyle\int a^u\,du = \frac{a^u}{\ln a} + C$

6. $\displaystyle\int \sin u\,du = -\cos u + C$

7. $\displaystyle\int \cos u\,du = \sin u + C$

8. $\displaystyle\int \sec^2 u\,du = \tan u + C$

9. $\displaystyle\int \csc^2 u\,du = -\cot u + C$

10. $\displaystyle\int \sec u\,\tan u\,du = \sec u + C$

11. $\displaystyle\int \csc u\,\cot u\,du = -\csc u + C$

12. $\displaystyle\int \tan u\,du = \ln|\sec u| + C$

13. $\displaystyle\int \cot u\,du = \ln|\sin u| + C$

14. $\displaystyle\int \sec u\,du = \ln|\sec u + \tan u| + C$

15. $\displaystyle\int \csc u\,du = \ln|\csc u - \cot u| + C$

16. $\displaystyle\int \frac{du}{\sqrt{a^2 - u^2}} = \sin^{-1}\frac{u}{a} + C$

17. $\displaystyle\int \frac{du}{a^2 + u^2} = \frac{1}{a}\tan^{-1}\frac{u}{a} + C$

18. $\displaystyle\int \frac{du}{a^2 - u^2} = \frac{1}{2a}\ln\left|\frac{u+a}{u-a}\right| + C$

TRIGONOMETRIC FORMS

19. $\displaystyle\int \sin^2 u\,du = \frac{1}{2}u - \frac{1}{4}\sin 2u + C$

20. $\displaystyle\int \cos^2 u\,du = \frac{1}{2}u + \frac{1}{4}\sin 2u + C$

21. $\displaystyle\int \tan^2 u\,du = \tan u - u + C$

22. $\displaystyle\int \cot^2 u\,du = -\cot u - u + C$

23. $\displaystyle\int \sin^3 u\,du = -\frac{1}{3}(2 + \sin^2 u)\cos u + C$

24. $\displaystyle\int \cos^3 u\,du = \frac{1}{3}(2 + \cos^2 u)\sin u + C$

25. $\displaystyle\int \tan^3 u\,du = \frac{1}{2}\tan^2 u + \ln|\cos u| + C$

26. $\displaystyle\int \cot^3 u\,du = -\frac{1}{2}\cot^2 u - \ln|\sin u| + C$

27. $\displaystyle\int \sec^3 u\,du = \frac{1}{2}\sec u\,\tan u + \frac{1}{2}\ln|\sec u + \tan u| + C$

28. $\displaystyle\int \csc^3 u\,du = -\frac{1}{2}\csc u\,\cot u + \frac{1}{2}\ln|\csc u - \cot u| + C$

29. $\displaystyle\int \sin au\,\sin bu\,du = \frac{\sin(a-b)u}{2(a-b)} - \frac{\sin(a+b)u}{2(a+b)} + C \quad \text{if } a^2 \neq b^2$

(Continued on Rear Endpaper)

30. $\int \cos au \, \cos bu \, du = \dfrac{\sin(a-b)u}{2(a-b)} + \dfrac{\sin(a+b)u}{2(a+b)} + C \quad$ if $a^2 \neq b^2$

31. $\int \sin au \, \cos bu \, du = -\dfrac{\cos(a-b)u}{2(a-b)} - \dfrac{\cos(a+b)u}{2(a+b)} + C \quad$ if $a^2 \neq b^2$

32. $\int \sin^n u \, du = -\dfrac{1}{n} \sin^{n-1} u \, \cos u + \dfrac{n-1}{n} \int \sin^{n-2} u \, du$

33. $\int \cos^n u \, du = \dfrac{1}{n} \cos^{n-1} u \, \sin u + \dfrac{n-1}{n} \int \cos^{n-2} u \, du$

34. $\int \tan^n u \, du = \dfrac{1}{n-1} \tan^{n-1} u - \int \tan^{n-2} u \, du \quad$ if $n \neq 1$

35. $\int \cot^n u \, du = -\dfrac{1}{n-1} \cot^{n-1} u - \int \cot^{n-2} u \, du \quad$ if $n \neq 1$

36. $\int \sec^n u \, du = \dfrac{1}{n-1} \sec^{n-2} u \, \tan u + \dfrac{n-2}{n-1} \int \sec^{n-2} u \, du \quad$ if $n \neq 1$

37. $\int \csc^n u \, du = -\dfrac{1}{n-1} \csc^{n-2} u \, \cot u + \dfrac{n-2}{n-1} \int \csc^{n-2} u \, du \quad$ if $n \neq 1$

38. $\int u \sin u \, du = \sin u - u \cos u + C$

39. $\int u \cos u \, du = \cos u + u \sin u + C$

40. $\int u^n \sin u \, du = -u^n \cos u + n \int u^{n-1} \cos u \, du$

41. $\int u^n \cos u \, du = u^n \sin u - n \int u^{n-1} \sin u \, du$

FORMS INVOLVING $\sqrt{u^2 \pm a^2}$

42. $\int \sqrt{u^2 \pm a^2} \, du = \dfrac{u}{2} \sqrt{u^2 \pm a^2} \pm \dfrac{a^2}{2} \ln \left| u + \sqrt{u^2 \pm a^2} \right| + C$

43. $\int \dfrac{du}{\sqrt{u^2 \pm a^2}} = \ln \left| u + \sqrt{u^2 \pm a^2} \right| + C$

FORMS INVOLVING $\sqrt{a^2 - u^2}$

44. $\int \sqrt{a^2 - u^2} \, du = \dfrac{u}{2} \sqrt{a^2 - u^2} + \dfrac{a^2}{2} \sin^{-1} \dfrac{u}{a} + C$

45. $\int \dfrac{\sqrt{a^2 - u^2}}{u} \, du = \sqrt{a^2 - u^2} - a \ln \left| \dfrac{a + \sqrt{a^2 - u^2}}{u} \right| + C$

Table of Integrals (cont.)

EXPONENTIAL AND LOGARITHMIC FORMS

46. $\int u e^u \, du = (u - 1)e^u + C$

47. $\int u^n e^u \, du = u^n e^u - n \int u^{n-1} e^u \, du$

48. $\int u^n \ln u \, du = \dfrac{u^{n+1}}{n+1} \ln u - \dfrac{u^{n+1}}{(n+1)^2} + C$

49. $\int e^{au} \sin bu \, du = \dfrac{e^{au}}{a^2 + b^2} (a \sin bu - b \cos bu) + C$

50. $\int e^{au} \cos bu \, du = \dfrac{e^{au}}{a^2 + b^2} (a \cos bu + b \sin bu) + C$

INVERSE TRIGONOMETRIC FORMS

51. $\int \sin^{-1} u \, du = u \sin^{-1} u + \sqrt{1 - u^2} + C$

52. $\int \tan^{-1} u \, du = u \tan^{-1} u - \dfrac{1}{2} \ln(1 + u^2) + C$

53. $\int \sec^{-1} u \, du = u \sec^{-1} u - \ln \left| u + \sqrt{u^2 - 1} \right| + C$

54. $\int u \sin^{-1} u \, du = \dfrac{1}{4}(2u^2 - 1) \sin^{-1} u + \dfrac{u}{4}\sqrt{1 - u^2} + C$

55. $u \tan^{-1} u \, du = \dfrac{1}{2}(u^2 + 1) \tan^{-1} u - \dfrac{u}{2} + C$

56. $\int u \sec^{-1} u \, du = \dfrac{u^2}{2} \sec^{-1} u - \dfrac{1}{2}\sqrt{u^2 - 1} + C$

57. $\int u^n \sin^{-1} u \, du = \dfrac{u^{n+1}}{n+1} \sin^{-1} u - \dfrac{1}{n+1} \int \dfrac{u^{n+1}}{\sqrt{1 - u^2}} \, du \quad \text{if } n \neq -1$

58. $\int u^n \tan^{-1} u \, du = \dfrac{u^{n+1}}{n+1} \tan^{-1} u - \dfrac{1}{n+1} \int \dfrac{u^{n+1}}{1 + u^2} \, du \quad \text{if } n \neq -1$

59. $\int u^n \sec^{-1} u \, du = \dfrac{u^{n+1}}{n+1} \sec^{-1} u - \dfrac{1}{n+1} \int \dfrac{u^{n+1}}{\sqrt{u^2 - 1}} \, du \quad \text{if } n \neq -1$

OTHER USEFUL FORMULAS

60. $\int_0^\infty u^n e^{-u} \, du = \Gamma(n + 1) = n! \quad (n \geq 0)$

61. $\int_0^\infty e^{-au^2} \, du = \dfrac{1}{2}\sqrt{\dfrac{\pi}{a}} \quad (a > 0)$

62. $\int_0^{\pi/2} \sin^n u \, du = \int_0^{\pi/2} \cos^n \, du = \begin{cases} \dfrac{1 \cdot 3 \cdot 5 \cdots (n-1)}{2 \cdot 4 \cdot 6 \cdots n} \cdot \dfrac{\pi}{2} & \text{if } n \text{ is an even integer and } n \geq 2 \\[2mm] \dfrac{2 \cdot 4 \cdot 6 \cdots (n-1)}{3 \cdot 5 \cdot 7 \cdots n} & \text{if } n \text{ is an odd integer and } n \geq 3 \end{cases}$